BY THE EDITORS OF CONSUMER GUIDE®

VEGETABLE & HERB GARDENING

Library of Congress Catalog Card Number: 86-60086

ISBN O-88176-296-2

Author, Parts 1, 2, and 3: Brian A. Williquette, County Extension Service Advisor, Horticulture and Urban Gardening Program Leader—Cooperative Extension Service, University of Illinois at Urbana-Champaign.

Revisions Consultant, Part 4: Drusilla McCorkle Banks.
Recipes Courtesy of Ball Corporation and University of Illinois Cooperative Extension Service.

Cover Design: Michael Johnson

Illustrations: Laura D'Argo and Nan Brooks

Contents

Part I: The Garden

Contents

Part 2: Vegetables and Herbs

Part 3: The Home Orchard

Part 4: The Kitchen

Contents

Part 5: References

Part I
The Garden

Growing vegetables, herbs, and fruits makes good sense—it's fun, it's a challenge, and it saves you money. Here's your complete guide to growing good things to eat in your garden, on your balcony or patio, or even in your apartment.

Planning Your Garden

Planning Your Garden

Any gardener will tell you that gardening is one of the most absorbing and rewarding occupations you can undertake. Any gardener will also tell you — probably loudly and at length — that gardening requires patience, resilience, hard work, and a lot of planning. Paperwork is probably the last thing you have in mind when you think about growing your own vegetables, herbs, and fruits. More likely you see yourself leaning contently on your spade as all sorts of lush, healthy plants shoot up in front of your eyes. The fact of the matter, though, is that gardening begins not with seeds and a spade but with paper and a pencil.

A successful garden begins with a well-organized plan of your garden space. Drawing a plan may not sound as exciting as getting outdoors and planting things. But if you don't spend the necessary time planning what to grow in your garden and when and where to plant it, you may spend the rest of the growing season correcting the mistakes you made because you didn't have a plan. It's a lot easier to erase a bed when it's a few lines on a piece of paper than when it's an expanse of soil and plants.

In the case of a vegetable garden, your plan should include not only the types and quantities of vegetables you're going to grow and how they'll be positioned in your garden, but also planting dates and approximate dates of harvest. Making a plan may seem like a lot of work to get done before you even start gardening, but careful planning will help you make the best use of your time and available space and will result in bigger, higher-quality crops.

This section discusses all the questions you need to take into account when you're planning your garden—the hows, whats, whys, whens, and wherefores. The specific cultural requirements of each vegetable, herb, and fruit tree or bush are given in detail in Parts 2 and 3. Much of the information applies to all types of gardens. Specific issues are discussed in the appropriate sections. The first type of garden we'll talk about is the vegetable garden.

PLANNING A VEGETABLE GARDEN

Many home gardeners concentrate primarily on growing vegetables, and the first step to planning a successful vegetable garden is to decide which vegetables to grow. This may sound fairly straightforward, but there are a lot of factors involved, and you need to answer some basic questions: What vegetables do you and your family like? Do you want to eat all your crop fresh, or store or preserve some of your harvest? Can you grow the vegetables you like successfully in your climate? How much time and energy can you put in your garden? The first factor to consider is personal preference.

What vegetables do you like to eat? The first decision to make in choosing what to grow in your vegetable garden is simple: What vegetables do you and your family like to eat? Perhaps you'd love to grow peas because you remember how wonderful they tasted fresh out of the garden in your childhood. Or maybe your family's crazy about spinach salad or broccoli casserole, or you're just plain tired of frozen vegetables.

What are you going to do with it? How do you plan to use your vegetables, and what are you going to do with the part of your crop that you don't eat as soon as it's harvested? Do you want to freeze, can, dry, store, or make preserves with some of your crop?

How much do you need? How you plan to use your vegetables directly affects how much of each vegetable you want to grow, and will influence your decision about the kind of vegetable you're going to plant — all carrots aren't alike, and there are hundreds of different tomato varieties.

Can you grow it? Not all vegetables grow satisfactorily in all climates. Some vegetables like it hot; some refuse to grow in hot weather. Some vegetables flourish when it's cold; others just shiver and die. Certain plants go from seed to harvest in a couple of months and will grow almost anywhere in the United States — green beans and some kinds of lettuce are among these obliging vegetables. Others are very picky and need a long stretch of warm or cool weather. You have to take the plant's needs into consideration before you can make a decision on whether or not it's a practical choice for your home garden.

Do you have room for it? There are plants that are rather like large pets — they're very endearing, but you just can't live with them because they're too big. You want to grow vegetables that will give you a reasonable amount of produce in the space that you have available. Some vegetables — especially some vining crops like pumpkins — need a great deal of room and give you only low yields, so they're not a practical choice in a small home garden. And if you're growing an indoor container garden, you'll do fine with cabbages in flowerpots, but there's simply no place you're going to put a healthy watermelon vine or a Jerusalem artichoke.

Is it worth the bother? Some vegetables require very little nurturing, and you can grow them with a minimum of toil. Others require special attention and need to be babied. Celery and cauliflower, for example, have to be blanched — blanching is a process that deprives the plant (or part of the plant) of sunlight in order to whiten it and improve its flavor, color, or texture. Before choosing a crop that's going to need special handling, be sure you really want to give it that much attention. Some crops, too, are bothered a lot by insects or plant diseases — corn is one of them. If you're not willing to deal with these problems as they occur, this type of crop is going to cause you more disappointment than satisfaction.

Are you trying to save money? Another factor to consider when you're deciding what to plant is the practical matter of economics — is the vegetable worth growing, or would it be cheaper to buy it? Some vegetables are readily available and inexpensive to buy, but would produce only low yields from a large space if you grew them in your garden. Corn, for instance, is inexpensive to buy when it's in season, but in your garden it needs a lot of growing space and often only gives you one harvestable ear from a whole plant. You may decide not to grow corn and settle instead for a crop like endive, which is expensive in the store but as easy as leaf lettuce to grow. Potatoes, too, are readily available and fairly inexpensive to buy, but they're space-hungry in the garden. You might like to plant an asparagus bed instead — it requires a little initial work, but gives you a gourmet crop for years afterwards.

The economy question, however, is not clear-cut. The fact remains that the vegetables you pick fresh from your own garden taste a whole lot better than the ones you buy in the store, so saving money may not be your prime purpose in growing them. You may be perfectly willing to give up half your garden (or all your balcony) in order to have a couple of ears of wonderful, milky, homegrown corn come harvesttime. You may consider the delicious flavor of fresh carrots a more important issue than the fact that store-bought ones are inexpensive. The only way you can get corn from the garden to the table in a matter of minutes is to grow your own, and the freshest possible carrots are the ones you pull out of the backyard at dinner time. These are judgments you make yourself, and they're just as important — if not more so — than whether or not a crop is easy to grow, economical in its use of space, or will save you money.

How much is enough — or too much?

Your initial decision about the vegetables you'd enjoy growing and eating — and that you think you can grow successfully in the conditions you have to deal with — is the first step to planning a well-thought-out, productive vegetable garden. But this is the point where you discover that you still have very little idea of how much of each vegetable to grow. You know you want to eat some of your crop and freeze, pickle, or preserve some. But how many seeds should you plant to enable you to achieve those ends? Again, advance planning can help you avoid getting swamped with squash or overrun by radishes — it's amazing how energetically your plants will prosper under your care and how large a plant a little seed will produce.

Planning for the yield you want

Some gardeners start off in an orderly manner by planting all their vegetables in rows of the same length, but space means something different to a carrot and a cauliflower. A 10-foot row of broccoli will give you a manageable amount of produce; a 10-foot row of parsley will provide enough for you and the entire neighborhood, but it isn't a big problem because you can freeze or dry parsley and use it all year around. A 10-foot row of radishes, however, can be a big mistake — no family can eat all those radishes, and they don't store well, so you could end up with a lot of wasted radishes. Cucumbers sprawl all over the place and need a lot of room; carrots are fairly picky about soil conditions, but they do stay where you put them. So you have to estimate how productive your plants are likely to be. The description of individual vegetables in Part 2 will help you estimate how many plants to grow.

Plan how to use your crop

Garden space, storage space for preserved vegetables, storage space for preserving equipment, family food preferences, your own preferences, your local climate, the energy costs, time involved in preserving, and the help available (if any), are all points you need to consider when you're deciding how much of a certain vegetable you want to grow. Before you plant large amounts of a vegetable, plan what you're going to do with the vegetables you can't eat at once. Check each vegetable's storage potential — detailed information on storing and preserving is given in Part 3 — and take into account whether or not you want to go to the trouble of storing or preserving what you don't eat immediately. Some people find canning, freezing, or drying their home crop a most pleasurable activity. Others don't have time or just don't like doing it. So counting your chickens before they're hatched is a vital part of your planning, and something to keep in mind even way back in the winter when you're spending a bleak December day studying your seed catalogs. Come summer, it will be too late.

Planning Your Garden

Do you want to freeze, can, dry, pickle, or store?

There's more than one way to preserve a crop. You can freeze, can, dry, or make preserves and pickles. You can construct a cold storage area or a root cellar in the basement. You can make a storage pit in the garden. Some vegetables are very obliging. For instance, extra green beans are no problem because you can freeze, can, dry, or pickle them. And some root vegetables are best stored in the ground for as long as possible — just go out and dig them up when you're ready to use them. If you have a big family and a lot of garden space, you may need to use several different methods to make the most of your crop. If you have only a small garden and a small family, perhaps freezing alone is all you need to consider. Read through the introductory sections on each method of preserving in Part 4, so you're aware of the space and equipment involved and the advantages and disadvantages of each method. Consider also the climate where you live and how much time you're able and willing to spend on preserving. At this point, as in your initial choice of which vegetables to grow, personal preferences are important. If your family hates turnips and only likes carrots raw, it's hardly going to be worthwhile to have a root cellar. If you're always on the run, it's pure fantasy to imagine yourself making preserves come fall. You may also want to investigate sharing the crop — and the work. If you live in a community of gardeners you may find it possible to get together on preserving projects, sharing crops, equipment, and labor.

CLIMATE: HOW WHERE YOU LIVE AFFECTS WHAT YOU GROW

Plants, like people, have definite ideas about where they like to live. Like people, they flourish in congenial conditions and become weak and dispirited if life is too difficult for them to cope with. Unlike people, however, plants can't take practical steps to improve their homesite — they can't up and move, and they can't protect themselves against adverse conditions. You, the gardener, are largely responsible for how well your plants do in the climatic conditions you offer them, and you'll save yourself a lot of frustration and disappointment if you have some understanding of how climate affects your garden and if you choose your crops according to your climate.

What gardeners mean by a "growing season"

Throughout this book you'll encounter references to the "growing season." The growing season is, essentially, the length of time your area can give plants the conditions they need to reach maturity and produce a crop. The growing season is measured in terms of the number of days between the last frost in spring and the first frost in fall. In general terms, these two dates mark the beginning and end of the time in which plants grow from seed to maturity. Some areas never have frost at all and use their dry season as their "winter." In these areas, however, it's still possible to use hypothetical "frost" dates. So the length of your growing season is (technically) totally dependent on your local climate. When you plant a vegetable depends on how well that vegetable handles extremes of temperature.

The dates on which a certain area can expect to have the last spring frost and the first fall frost are called the "average date of last frost" and the "average date of first frost," respectively. They are generally used as reference points for planning and planting vegetables, but they're not infallible. They do however, give you a fairly accurate guide as to which vegetables will do best in your area, and they are the reference points most generally used in this book. As with every other aspect of gardening you need to be a little bit flexible. The chart at the end of this chapter lists the average dates of first and last frosts in major cities throughout the United States. If you live within 10 miles of a city listed, you can take these dates as accurate; three or four days either way is just as acceptable, so don't feel you must do all your planting exactly on the one listed day. All these dates are average, and the weather can always spring surprises. If you live a long way from a listed city or are for any reason unsure when to plant, call your local Cooperative Extension Service or Weather Bureau for advice. The Cooperative Extension Service is a joint effort of the United States Department of Agriculture and the state land-grant colleges and universities. The service's local office is an invaluable resource for the gardener, and a list of offices throughout the country appears in Part 4.

Climatic or "hardiness" zones

The average date of last frost is not the only reference point used to determine when to plant a garden. At one time or other gardeners have made that date dependent on everything from "climatic zones" to the phases of the moon. Climatic zones are the small maps you find on the back of seed packages; they divide the United States into zones or areas with fairly similar climates. They're probably far more accurate references for planting than phases of the moon, but they're very general, and they don't tell the whole story. There are many incidental — sometimes almost accidental — conditions that can cause changes in climate within a climatic zone.

The climatic zone map in the seed catalog or on the back of a seed packet can give you a broad idea of how a vegetable (or vegetable variety, because carrots, tomatoes, and other popular vegetables don't by any means conform to a stereotype) will do in your area. Climatic zones, however, don't take into account the variations that occur within an area which, if you go by the book, has the same climatic conditions prevailing over many square miles. For instance, if the balcony of your downtown apartment faces south, you may be able to grow vegetables on it that would never survive in a north-facing garden of your apartment block. Lots of large buildings, a nearby body of water like a lake, or even heavy traffic can significantly alter the temperature (and pollution level) in a small garden. So, given all these imponderables, it's safer to judge how well a plant will grow by considering its own tolerance to certain conditions, rather than by a hard-and-fast map reference.

How "hardiness" affects your garden plan

The way a plant type reacts to climatic conditions —heat, cold, moisture, and so on—determines its "hardiness." It's another way of saying how tough it is, but the term hardiness is used specifically to indicate how well a plant tolerates cold. Before you study how climate affects your garden, it's as well to consider which hardiness categories certain vegetables fall into. The hardiness of each kind determines how that particular vegetable will fit into your growing season.

The vegetables that are grown in a home vegetable garden fall into one of four hardiness categories: *very hardy*, *hardy*, *tender*, and *very tender*. The date on which you can safely plant each vegetable in your garden depends on which hardiness category it falls into.

Very hardy vegetables can tolerate cold and frost and can be planted in the garden four to six weeks before the average date of last frost. They include asparagus, broccoli, Brussels sprouts, cabbage,

cauliflower, collards, Chinese cabbage, horseradish, Jerusalem artichokes, kale, kohlrabi, leeks, lettuce, onions, peas, rhubarb, rutabagas, and shallots; and the herbs chives, garlic, mint, tarragon and thyme.

Hardy vegetables can handle a certain amount of cold and frost and can be planted two to three weeks before the average date of last frost. They include beets, cardoon, carrots, celeriac, celery, chard, chicory, dandelion, endive, parsnips, Irish potatoes, radishes, salsify, turnips; and the herbs anise, borage, fennel, marjoram, oregano, parsley, rosemary, and savory.

Tender vegetables don't like cold weather and can be planted on the average date of last frost; you will need to protect them in some way if there's a late frost. These vegetables include most beans, cress, mustard, sorrel, corn, tomatoes; the perennial artichokes; and the herbs basil, caraway, chervil, coriander, dill, sage, and sesame.

Very tender vegetables will not survive any frost and must be planted after the soil has warmed up in the spring; they can be planted two to three weeks after the average date of last frost. These vegetables include lima beans, cucumbers, eggplant, muskmelons, okra, peanuts, peppers, pumpkins, winter and summer squash, and watermelons.

Gamblers can take a chance and plant earlier than these dates, but usually this gambling will not pay off. Even if you beat the odds and your plants are not frozen out, they will probably be inhibited by the cold soil, and they won't grow any faster than they would if you planted them at the proper time. The specific temperature requirements of herbs and fruits are discussed in the individual plant profiles.

THE CONDITIONS THAT ADD UP TO CLIMATE

The degree to which the successful growing of each vegetable type is dependent on hot and cold weather conditions indicates that temperature is the most important aspect of climate to consider when you're planning your vegetable garden. At this point it's helpful to take a good look at how temperature and other basic climatic conditions affect your garden. Rainfall and sunlight also play a most important part in how your garden grows, so let's take a look at these three elements and how they work with your plants.

Planning Your Garden

How temperature affects growth

Average day-to-day temperatures play an important part in how your vegetables and other plants grow. Temperatures, both high and low, affect growth, flowering, pollination, and the development of fruits. If the temperature is too high or too low, leafy crops may be forced to flower prematurely without producing the desired edible foliage. This early flowering is called "going to seed," and affects crops like cabbages and lettuce. If the night temperatures get too cool they may cause fruiting crops to drop their flowers—reducing yields considerably; peppers may react this way to cold weather. Generally, the ideal temperatures for vegetable plant growth are between 40° and 85°F. At warmer temperatures the plant's growth will increase, but this growth may not be sound structural growth. At lower temperatures the plant's growth will slow down or stop altogether.

Vegetables have different temperature preferences and tolerances and are usually classified as either cool-season crops or warm-season crops. Cool-season crops are those like cabbages, lettuce, and peas, which must have time to mature before the weather gets too warm; otherwise they will wilt, die, or go to seed prematurely. These vegetables can be started in warm weather only if there will be a long enough stretch of cool weather in the fall to allow the crop to mature before the first freeze. Warm-season crops are those vegetables that can't tolerate frost, like peppers, cucumbers, and melons. If the weather gets too cool they may not grow at all; if they do grow, yields will be reduced. Warm-season crops often have larger plants than cool-season crops and have larger, deeper root systems that enable them to go for relatively longer periods without being watered. Even though it is convenient to think of vegetables simply as either cool-season or warm-season crops, considerable differences can exist within each of these two groups.

The following lists offer a guide to cool- and warm-season crops. For specific planting dates for each type of vegetable, refer to the chart at the end of "Planting Your Garden."

Cool-season vegetables include: globe artichokes, asparagus, beets, broad beans, broccoli, Brussels sprouts, cabbage, carrots, cauliflower, celeriac, celery, chard, chicory, Chinese cabbage, collards, cress, dandelion, endive, cardoon, horseradish, Jerusalem artichokes, kale, kohlrabi, leeks, lentils, lettuce, onions, parsnips, sweet peas, white potatoes, radishes, rhubarb, rutabagas, salsify, shallots, sorrel, spinach, and turnips. Cool-season herbs include: anise, borage, chive, dill, oregano, parsley, peppermint, rosemary, sage, savory, spearmint, tarragon, and thyme.

Included among the warm-season vegetables are: dry beans, lima beans, mung beans, snap or green beans, chayote, chick peas, corn, cucumbers, eggplant, muskmelons, mustard, okra, black-eyed peas, peanuts, peppers, sweet potatoes, pumpkins, soybeans, New Zealand spinach, summer squash, winter squash, tomatoes, and watermelons. Warm-season herbs include: basil, caraway, chervil, coriander, marjoram, and sesame.

Rainfall: How plants use water

The amount and timing of the rainfall in your area also affects how your vegetables grow. Too much rain at one time can wash away seeds or young seedlings and damage or even kill mature plants. A constant rain when certain plants are flowering can reduce the pollination of the flowers and reduce yields. This can happen to tomatoes, peppers, beans, eggplant, melons, pumpkins, and both summer and winter squash. A constant rain can also tempt the honeybees to stay in their hives instead of pollinating the plants; again, yields will be affected.

Too little rain over a period of time can slow down plant growth and kill young seedlings or even mature plants. Limited moisture in the air can also inhibit pollination and reduce the yields of some vegetables. Too little rain can be more easily remedied than too much. If it rains too little, you can water the garden. If it rains too much, all you can do is pray.

Rainfall is probably the easiest climatic condition to improve. Farmers have worried and complained about the rainfall since the beginning of agriculture. If you've got thousands of acres of land and no control over the available water it can be very frustrating — if not a disaster. Since the home garden is usually small and fairly manageable in size, you can do something to regulate how much water it gets. If you don't get enough rain when you need it, you can simply water, and there are many different methods you can use. These are described in detail in "Caring for Your Garden." Too much rain can be more difficult to deal with, and here you need to take preventive measures. The better drained your soil is, the better it will be able to deal with too much water. When you select the site for your garden, avoid any area that is low-lying or poorly drained. If that's the only site that you have for the garden — and you're really serious about gardening — you can improve it by installing drainage tiles. This can be a costly and complicated process, so consider it only as a last resort.

Light: Your plants can't live without it

The third major climatic factor is light, and it's an important factor to consider when you plan your garden. Sunlight — or some type of light — provides energy that turns water and carbon dioxide into the sugar that plants use for food. Green plants use sugar to form new cells, to thicken existing cell walls, and to develop flowers and fruit. The more intense the light, the more effective it is. Light intensity, undiminished by obstructions, is greater in the summer than in the winter, and greater in areas where the days are sunny and bright than in areas where it's cloudy, hazy, or foggy. As a rule, the greater the light intensity the greater the plants' production of sugar — provided, of course, that it's not too hot or too cold and the plants get the right amount of water.

If a plant is going to produce flowers and fruit, it must have a store of energy beyond what it needs just to grow stems and leaves. If the light is limited, even a plant that looks green and healthy may never produce flowers or fruit. This can be a problem with vegetables like tomatoes, where you want to eat the fruit. With lettuce, where you're only interested in the leaves, it's not an issue. All the same, all vegetables need a certain amount of light in order to grow

properly, and without it all the watering, weeding, and wishing in the world will not make them flourish.

How day length affects your crops. Many plants, including tomatoes and many weeds, are not affected by day length — how long it stays light during the day. But for many others the length of the day plays a big part in regulating when they mature and flower. Some plants are long-day plants, which means they need 12 or more hours of sunlight daily in order to initiate flowering. Radishes and spinach are long-day plants, and this is the main reason they go to seed so fast in the middle of the summer when the day length is more than 12 hours. If you want to grow radishes or spinach in midsummer, you have to cover them with a light-proof box at about 4 p.m. every afternoon to fool them into thinking the day's over. Other plants are short-day plants and need less than 12 hours of light to initiate flowering; soybeans and corn are examples. Many varieties of short-day plants have been bred to resist the effects of long days, but most will still flower more quickly when the days are shorter.

How much sunlight is necessary? Vegetables grown for their fruits need a minimum of six to eight hours of direct light each day. Less light frequently means less than a full crop. It's very frustrating to try to grow tomatoes, peppers, or eggplants in the shade;

Your plants must have enough light, so plant where they won't be overshadowed by trees, shrubs, or buildings.

they'll often produce a good, green plant without giving you anything at all in the way of a vegetable. Crops that are grown for their roots and leaves, however, will give you satisfactory results in light shade.

Root crops, such as beets, carrots, radishes, and turnips, store up energy before they flower and do rather well in partial shade, especially if you don't compare them with the same crop grown in full sun. Plants like lettuce and spinach that are grown for their leaves are most tolerant of shade; in fact, where the sun is very hot and bright they may need some shade for protection. Only mushrooms and sprouts can be produced without any light at all.

Making the most of your garden light. If you have a choice of where to grow your vegetable garden, don't put it in the shade of buildings, trees, or shrubs. The accompanying illustration shows how to give plants enough light. Remember that as well as shading an area, trees and shrubs also have roots that may extend underground well beyond the overhead reach of their branches. These roots will compete with the vegetable plants for nutrients. Stay clear especially of walnut trees; they produce iodine, a growth retardant that will stunt or kill the vegetable plants in your garden. Go out and stand in your garden to see just how the light falls. Walk around and find where the light fails to penetrate. This knowledge will be very useful when you come to planting time.

Providing shade from too much sun. Most vegetables need full sun for best growth, but young or newly transplanted plants may need some protection from bright, direct sunlight. It's easier for

Extend your gardening season with a cold frame that uses solar heat to warm your plants.

you, as a gardener, to provide shade where there's too much sun than to brighten up a shady area. You can, for instance, plant large, sturdy plants like sunflowers or Jerusalem artichokes to provide a screen, and you can design your garden so that large plants and small ones each get the light they need. You can also shade young plants with boxes or screens when necessary. However, too little sun is far more serious a problem in a garden than too much.

How to make the most of your climate

Whatever the climate is like where you live, you are not entirely at the mercy of the elements. There are certain improvements you can make to enable you to grow some vegetables that would not normally do well in your area. Don't expect miracles — you can improve conditions, but you can't change the climate. No amount of watering can change a desert into a vegetable garden; however, if the average rainfall in your area is reasonable, a few hours of watering can improve it more than you'd think possible. Experiment with the microclimates in your neighborhood and your yard; it may be possible to increase your growing season and grow vegetables that need a longer growing season than your climate technically provides. Microclimates may also enable you to grow tender perennials that would not normally survive the winter in your area. The secret is to make the most of the conditions that exist in your garden. Experiment — plant a tender vegetable close to the south wall of your house; it may not get all the sun it needs, but protection from wind and cold may help it grow where it wouldn't grow at all in the open garden.

Another way to frustrate the natural temperature limitations of your local climate is by using transplants instead of seeds in spring. Transplants are young plants started from seed indoors or in a warm place and set out in the garden later; this gives you a head start on your growing season, but you can't do it with all vegetables. Growing transplants is discussed in detail in the chapter, "Planting Your Garden," along with ways of protecting plants against extremes of temperature.

Other weather conditions can also affect the yields of your vegetable crops. Dry, windy days and cool night temperatures (a 10°F drop from day temperatures) can cause fruiting crops — peppers, for instance — to drop their flowers before they're pollinated; this means you lose a lot of your crop. You can avoid it to some extent by putting up some type of windbreak to protect the crops from drying winds. It's comforting to remember that although you

can't make major changes in your climate, you can certainly do a lot to help your plants make the most of their environment.

Cold frames and hot frames: Extending your gardening season

If you have the space for it, a cold frame — a glass-enclosed growing area outside — can add an extra dimension to your garden. It's an ideal place to start hardy annuals and perennials or to put plants in the spring to harden them for the rigors of outdoor life. When you have started vegetables inside, especially the cold-tolerant ones, you can move them to a cold frame and give them the benefit of much more light in a protected place. And since a cold frame uses solar heat, it qualifies as an energy-saving device. The hardy herbs, radishes, lettuces, and other greens can be grown in a cold frame during a good part of the year, even in the North.

A cold frame, often called a "poor man's greenhouse," can be made from scrap lumber and old storm windows. It should not be too deep from front to back or you'll have trouble getting plants in and out. Cold frames capture solar heat, and if they slant to the south they can take advantage of the greatest amount of sun.

On the days when the sun is bright you may have to provide some shade to keep the plants from sunburning, or lift the cold frame windows to keep plants from steaming. If the sun is bright enough the temperature inside a cold frame can reach 85° to 95°F when the temperature outside is only 15°F. But on cold nights when the temperature drops below freezing, a cold frame will need some extra protection. An old quilt or blanket under a tarp is a good cover. If you have nothing else newspapers will do, although they are a bit harder to handle.

If a cold frame sounds like something you'd like to try, look around for some turn-of-the-century garden books. These provide excellent step-by-step instructions for building and using cold frames and offer suggestions on how to do all kinds of serious cold-frame growing.

Hot frames are a bit more challenging than cold frames, and the opportunities for frustration are multiplied. In hot frames, heat is provided either by rotting manure (the classic system) or by electricity (the modern way). Decomposing cow, horse, and mule manure do not work the same way, and the heat of decomposition depends on the age, the kinds, and amount of litter present. When you're using manure there are no thermostats or controls, except the gardener's know-how. Electricity is much easier but a lot more expensive than manure, and there is still work for the gardener to do.

If you have a basement window facing south with some space outside, you can incorporate it into your hot or cold frame. It will also provide a basic course in the management of a greenhouse — the next step in gardening addiction.

HOW TO GET YOUR GARDEN STARTED: PUTTING THE THEORIES TO WORK

Up to this point, most of your garden planning has been theoretical. You've given thought to the vegetables you want to grow, what you're going to do with them, and how much you need to grow. You've got an idea of how the climate in your area will influence your final choice of vegetables. You're beginning to understand your microclimate — how growing conditions in your own yard may differ from the general climate of your area. Now you're ready to start getting your plans on paper, but as soon as you open the seed catalog, confusion strikes again. You want to grow your own corn, tomatoes, lettuce, and carrots — but what kind?

How to choose the right vegetables

All these popular vegetables come in many varieties. The seed catalogs offer, for instance, a variety of tomatoes that is totally bewildering — big ones, little ones, cherry ones, green ones, canning ones. Some are disease-resistant, some aren't. Some are hybrids; what *is* a hybrid? Even the simple carrot isn't so simple after all — finger carrots, half-longs, standards — which to choose? And the names don't help because they all sound wonderful. Faced with the choice between a California Wonder and a Little Marvel, what can you do?

A number of factors will help you make the choice. Some of them you can control. You can choose the kinds you like personally — perhaps you prefer smaller tomatoes to the big, "beefsteak" kind, or tiny carrots taste better to you than the larger kind. If you're gardening in a small space you can select a bean variety that grows as a compact bush instead of on a trellis. You can choose a kind of green pepper that's an especially good shape for stuffing, or cucumbers to pickle rather than to eat.

Other factors are largely out of your control. Even if you'd like to grow pumpkins, you can't if there's no room for them in your small yard. And your garden soil may also dictate some selections. For instance, root vegetables need loose, well-worked soil if their roots are not to split and fork; so if you want to grow carrots in a heavy clay soil, you're going to do

better with the shorter or finger varieties. Once you start narrowing down the choices, the decisions become a lot more straightforward.

The most important factor, however, is your climate, and how long a crop will take to mature. Vegetables have very individual requirements, and they don't all take the same time to develop from seed to harvest. You need three vital pieces of information before you make a final choice: How will the plant handle hot and cold temperatures? When can you plant it? When can you harvest it?

Is the plant "hardy" or "tender"? Gardeners use the term "hardiness" to indicate how well a plant tolerates the cold. Plants range from very hardy, which means they can survive a hard frost, to very tender, which means the slightest frost will kill them. The date on which you can plant a certain vegetable depends on how hardy or tender it is.

Frost dates and planting dates. Because plants are so sensitive to temperature, when you can plant them is a question of when the weather's warm enough, and this is related to when an area has its last spell of freezing weather — even in frost-free climates gardeners talk about frost dates. The length of time between the last frost in spring and the first frost in fall is the gardener's growing season. According to how hardy or tender they are, spring crops are planted from six weeks *before* the last date on which the area can expect its final frost (the average date of last frost) to three or four weeks after that date — by which time the soil should be warm enough for even very tender plants.

Harvesting dates. How long it takes a plant to grow from seed to harvest is measured in terms of "days to maturity," and knowing how long each vegetable takes to mature is essential to your garden plan; it will have a significant effect on your choices of vegetable in each type — is it an early, midseason, or late-maturing vegetable? Each kind of vegetable has its "days to maturity" listed in the seed catalog, and you can figure exactly when you'll expect to harvest the crop. Detailed information on plant hardiness and how to figure planting and harvesting dates is given later in this chapter.

What vegetable varieties mean

It's worth taking time to consider why there are so many varieties of one vegetable. A variety is simply a botanical change or improvement in the original plant. These changes may be as obvious as a change in the color, size, or shape of the fruit — beefsteak tomatoes, for instance, are very large and less regularly shaped than other varieties. Other changes may be less obvious, like improved disease-resistance, improved uniformity of crop size, better flavor, or a more compact habit of growth. Some varieties have been specially bred to have better tolerance of extreme weather conditions in which they normally would not do well. Some lettuce varieties, for example, handle hot weather better than others. Details like this are well worth your attention; a wise choice of variety can mean the difference between success and failure.

Hybrids are bred for success. A variety may be a natural mutation that growers discovered and continued to propagate, or it may be the result of breeding two different pure lines to produce a "hybrid." A pure line is a plant that has been selected and bred for some desirable characteristic — like the size of the fruit or its ability to resist disease. When two different pure lines, each with a different desirable characteristic (perhaps one is disease-resistant and the other produces very uniform fruit), are bred together, the resulting hybrid inherits both those good characteristics. Hybrids are also genetic copies of each other and are entirely uniform. Given the same growing conditions, each hybrid plant will be the same size, mature at the same time, and generally produce the same results.

Finding the varieties suited to your area. Because there are so many varieties, it can be very difficult to choose the right one. Part 2 of this book describes the individual vegetables and their cultural requirements and lists some of the best and most widely used varieties. But in many cases the varieties listed represent only the tip of the iceberg. Where a large number of varieties are available (as with corn or tomatoes) or where success depends as much on growing conditions as on variety (as with onions), your best bet is to get in touch with your local Cooperative Extension

Service. The service's experts will be able to tell you exactly which varieties will do best in the growing conditions that exist in your part of the country. A complete list of Cooperative Extension Services is given at the end of this book, together with detailed information on how to get your gardening questions expertly answered by their qualified horticulturalists.

Guaranteed varieties: The All-America Selection. Another way to find the most reliable varieties for your area is through the All-America Selections. This is a nonprofit organization of seedsmen who develop and promote new varieties of vegetables and flowers. The organization awards gold, silver, or bronze medals to vegetable varieties that have been proven to produce reliable results in most areas of the United States. If a vegetable is listed in your seed catalog as an All-America Selection, you can be sure that if has been tested by growers all over the country and that it's a good bet for your own garden. The organization does not bestow its seal of approval lightly — only one or two vegetable varieties win a gold medal in any year.

Experiment with different varieties. Remember, too, that you don't always have to play by the rules. You can plant more than one variety of a vegetable and decide for yourself which one is best suited to your palate and your garden. You can also extend your harvest by planting varieties that mature at different times. Experimenting is a good part of the fun of growing a vegetable garden.

Dates: When to plant and when to harvest

Selecting the varieties you're going to grow gives you some hard information with which to work. You now know when to plant your vegetables. The hardiness chart in "Planting Your Garden" will tell you to which category — very hardy, hardy, tender, very tender — a vegetable belongs and when to plant it. Now is the time to decide whether to use seeds or transplants. Transplants are young plants started from seed indoors or in a warm place (like a hot frame) and planted in the garden when the weather's warm enough. By planting transplants you can often get a head start on your growing season and avoid some of the limitations placed on you by your area climate. Not all vegetables, however, take kindly to being transplanted. Full information about growing vegetables from transplants — including what to plant and when — is given in "Planting Your Garden."

It's important to plan your planting dates accurately. It's also important to know when your crop will be ready for harvest. The number of days it takes a plant to reach maturity varies according to type

Carrots come in many sizes

and to varieties within a type.

Each vegetable variety has its "days to maturity" listed in the seed catalog. Take a calendar, and see how the dates fall for the crops you're thinking of growing. For instance, "Jade Cross Hybrid" Brussels sprouts take 95 days to maturity. They're very hardy, so you can plant them six weeks before your last spring frost. If your area expects its last frost at the end of April, you can plant your Brussels sprouts in the garden in mid-March, and they'll mature in mid-June. They're a cool-season vegetable, so as **long** as the weather in your area won't be sizzling hot by mid-June, you should do well with them. In this way, work out all the dates on which you can expect to harvest your vegetables, and make a list of them. This will give you a chance to make changes if, despite all your planning, you've got too large a crop maturing at the same time. It will also give you some ideas about "pacing" your crop.

Pacing your harvest for best yield

Deciding when to plant involves more than avoiding killing frosts. It also means pacing your planting so you get maximum yields from limited space. You can harvest some crops gradually, enjoying them for a long period of time; others mature all at once. This takes careful planning. You have to have a good idea of how long it will take your vegetables to mature and how long the harvest will last. It will also take some self-control. The temptation to plant rows of everything at once is great.

Planting short rows. A simple way to pace your harvest is to plant only short rows or partial rows. Planting short rows is probably easier; you may feel more comfortable with a complete row, even if it is short. A 10-foot row looks short, but 10 feet of radishes ready to eat at once is more than most people can handle. Ten feet of parsley or garlic may be more than enough for the whole neighborhood. You can freeze parsley and dry the garlic, but what can you do with all those radishes? Unwanted excesses of crops can be avoided if you divide your seeds into groups before going out to plant. Put them in "budget" envelopes to be planted on definite dates later on in the season but before the early crops are harvested. For instance, plant lettuce every two weeks. This way you can have vegetables all season, rather than glut followed by famine.

Using several varieties. Another way to pace your harvest is to plant several varieties of the same vegetable that mature at different rates. For instance, on the average date of last frost plant three different tomato varieties: an early variety that will mature in about 60 to 70 days; a midseason variety that

will mature in about 75 to 80 days; and a late variety that will mature in about 80 to 90 days. By planting these three varieties on the same day you have spread your harvest over a 30- to 50-day period, instead of a 10- to 20-day period.

Succession planting. With careful planning you may also be able to save garden space and get two or more harvests from the same spot by succession planting. After early-maturing crops are harvested, you clear a portion of the garden and replant it with a new crop. Plant so that cool-season crops grow in the cooler part of the season, and warm-season crops can take advantage of warmer weather.

One example of succession planting is to start off with a fast-growing, cool-season crop that can be planted early — lettuce, spinach, and cabbage (cole) family vegetables are good examples. Replace these by warm-weather crops like New Zealand spinach, chard, corn, okra, and squash. Then in fall make another planting of cole crops, or put in root crops like turnips or beets.

In a small area, one simple plan is to start off with spinach, which is very hardy but hates hot weather, and replace it with heat-tolerant New Zealand spinach. Despite their different temperature requirements, the two can double for each other in taste, and you get spinach all season long.

You can also make double use of trellis space — a big plus in a small garden. Plant early peas, replace them with cucumbers, and after harvesting your cucumbers, plant peas again for a fall crop.

Companion planting. This is another way to double up on planting space. This you do by planting short-term crops between plants that will take a longer time to mature. The short-term crops are harvested by the time the longer-season crops need the extra room. A good example of this is to plant radishes between rows of tomatoes; by the time the tomatoes need the space, the radishes will be gone.

GETTING YOUR GARDEN ON PAPER

By this time you've put a lot of thought into your garden plan, and you've got some vital information and dates on paper — the names of the varieties you're going to plant and your planting and harvest dates. Now comes the real paperwork. The size of your garden depends on your interest in gardening and how much time you're going to be able to give to the garden. Some gardeners use every available inch of space; others use a small corner of their property — some, of course, don't have much choice, and this may be your case if you have a small garden to begin with or if you're gardening on a patio or balcony. The larger your garden, the more time and work it's going to need, so unless you're already hooked on gardening, it's probably better to start small and let your garden size increase as your interest in gardening and confidence in your ability develops.

Before you decide the exact dimensions, look at the list of the vegetables you've chosen and the amount you're going to grow of each one, and figure out if they're going to fit into the allotted space. You may see at once that you've overestimated what you can grow in the available space, so you'll have to do a little compromising between fantasy and reality. If your projected crops look as though they'll fit, you can now start drawing an actual plan.

Drawing a plot plan

This is the pencil-and-paper stage of planning, and if you use graph paper, you'll find it easier to work to scale. Don't be intimidated by all this talk about

Your vegetable garden in spring (5' × 10' plot)

Vegetable	Planting dates	No. of plants	Space between plants
Peas* (Sugar Snap)	April 1-10	30	2"
Lettuce (Great Lakes)	April 10-25	5	12"
Cabbage** (Early Jersey Wakefield)	May 1-25	5	12"
Mustard Greens (Southern Giant Curled)	April 15-May 15	10	6"
Peppers** (Bell Boy)	May 20-June 1	5	12"
Tomatoes** (Better Boy)	May 20-June 1	3	20"
Spring radishes	April 15-May 1	30	2"
Summer Squash (Gold Rush Zucchini)	May 20-June 1	3	20"

* Growing on trellis
** Grown from transplants

drawing and sketching. Your garden plan doesn't have to be a work of art — just a working document. Drawing to scale, however, is helpful. A commonly used scale is one inch on paper to eight feet of garden space — adapt the scale to whatever is easiest for you.

Draw up a simple plot plan giving your garden's measurements in all directions. Remember there's no law that says a garden has to be square or rectangular. Your vegetable garden can be round, triangular, curved, or any shape that fits your landscape and takes best advantage of the space you've got. When you've drawn the outline, sketch in all the nongrowing areas where you won't be able to plant — trees, shrubs, sidewalks, sheds, buildings, walls, and the garage. Indicate any areas that are particularly shady or poorly drained and, therefore, aren't suitable for fussy crops.

Planning for three stages. It's helpful to draw three plot plans: The first will show the garden at planting time in the spring; the second will show the garden in the summer; and the third will show the garden in

Your vegetable garden in summer (5' × 10' plot)

Vegetable	Planting dates	No. of plants	Space between plants
Cucumbers* (Market More)	June 15-20	10	6"
Carrots (Tendersweet)	June 15-20	30	2"
Beets (Early Wonder)	June 15-20	15	4"
Beans (Blue Lake)	June 10-15	15	4"
Peppers** (Bell Boy)	May 20-June 1	5	12"
Tomatoes** (Better Boy)	May 20-June 1	3	20"
Summer squash (Gold Rush Zucchini)	May 20-June 1	3	20"

* Growing on trellis
** Grown from transplants

the fall. These plans will reflect the changes that take place in your garden when you harvest early crops and replace them with new plantings. Make two copies of plans; keep one set inside where the plans will stay dry, clean, and legible. Use the other set in the garden — where it probably won't stay dry, clean, or legible for long. Plans have also been known to blow away in a spring breeze — a disaster if that's your only copy.

Putting the plants into the plan. Once you've outlined your plot and indicated all the nongrowing areas, get down to detail. Use the accompanying illustrations as a guide, and divide the plot among the vegetables you want to grow. The individual descriptions of vegetables in Part 2 give detailed information on the amount of space each vegetable needs for growth. For a quick check on spacing refer to the chart at the end of "Planting Your Garden." Don't try to economize on space — better a smaller number of healthy plants than a lot of starved ones.

Using your space efficiently. Take care in placing the vegetables. Place the taller plants on the north or

Your vegetable garden in fall (5' × 10' plot)

Vegetable	Planting dates	No. of plants	Space between plants
Cucumbers* (Market More)	June 15-20	10	6"
Carrots (Tendersweet)	June 15-20	30	2"
Mustard greens (Southern Giant Curled)	August 15-20	10	6"
Collards (Vates)	August 15-20	12	5"
Peppers** (Bell Boy)	May 20- June 1	5	12"
Tomatoes** (Better Boy)	May 15- June 12	3	20"
Summer squash (Gold Rush Zucchini)	May 20- June 1	3	20"

* Growing on trellis
** Grown from transplants

northeast side of the garden so that as they grow they won't shade the rest of the garden. In a large garden where you've got plenty of space, the most convenient way to lay out the vegetables is in rows and hills. Straight rows and hills are easier to water, weed, cultivate, mulch, and fertilize. If you are going to use a rototiller, make sure the rows are large enough to accommodate the machine.

In smaller gardens it's more space-efficient to plant in wide rows or in solid blocks four to five feet wide. You must always be able to reach the center of a wide row comfortably from either side and to get between the short rows in a block. You can also save space in a small garden by using vertical space — growing vining crops up a trellis, for example, rather than letting them spread all over the ground. Similarly, tomatoes can be staked or caged to contain their growth.

Adding dates and details. Finally, indicate whether you're planting from transplants or seeds, and add your planting dates for each vegetable; now your plan is complete, and you can see exactly what you'll be doing come spring. You'll also have compiled a good mental library of incidental knowledge about plants and how they grow and how your climate affects them; this knowledge is going to stand you in good stead throughout your growing season.

Recording the growth of your garden

If you're serious about gardening, you should keep records. Planning your records should be part of planning your garden. The better the planning, the more efficient use you'll be able to make of your time and the more time you will have for enjoying the pleasures of your garden — not just keeping up with the chores. Build your records the same way you build your garden; profit from past mistakes, and incorporate new ideas.

Start out with a ledger that has sewn-in pages. Don't write notes on slips of paper and expect to be able to find the one you want when you want it. Don't use a three-ring notebook, because if you can take a page out you will, and then you'll probably lose it. Your first entry in your record of your vegetable garden should be the plot you designed when you ordered the seeds. Mark this page with a paper clip so you can easily find it.

After the garden plot, you can keep a daily record of preparing the soil, planting, weeding, fertilizing, growing results (or lack of results); whether the harvest of each item was sufficient, too much, or not enough; and problems with weeds, bugs, or lack of rain. At the end of the growing season you'll have a complete record of what you did — and a record can be good for the morale.

Your record will list the plants that did well in your garden and those that didn't, and this information will give you the basics for planning next year's garden. Include in your ledger comments about the weather, varieties of plants that were productive or flopped, and notes about why you think some plants made it and others did not.

Small-space gardeners can grow cucumbers in a hanging basket.

The computerized garden plan

If all this planning thoroughly intimidates you, don't abandon the idea of gardening. It's the age of technology, and you can have your entire garden planned by a computer. The computer uses some basic information that you supply about your garden and develops a complete, easy-to-use plan that includes all the information the novice gardener needs to grow a vegetable garden. The only problem involved in having your garden planned by a computer is finding out who offers the service. At the moment only a few states' Cooperative Extension Services and a few seed companies provide computerized planning services, but they're rapidly becoming popular and more available. Ask your local Cooperative Extension Service if they offer computerized planning or can put you in touch with some organization that does. You may also find such services advertised in gardening magazines.

CONTAINER GARDENING

If you don't have a garden or even a balcony, you can still have a container vegetable garden. Don't underestimate the number of vegetables that can be grown successfully indoors. Near a bright window that is not too warm, leafy vegetables, such as lettuce, parsley, and chives, will do nicely. Fruiting plants are worth a try, but they take a lot more light at a higher intensity; unless the window is very bright, the plants may grow but not produce. Cherry tomatoes in hanging baskets will sometimes grow in very bright windows, and sometimes plants can be brought in from outdoors and grown on for several months. Herbs are rewarding indoor-garden plants, and they go a long way in adding your personal touch to everyday eating.

Plan a container garden the same way as a small garden plot, making the best possible use of your vertical space. Use a trellis for vining crops and stakes and cages for tomatoes or other semi-vining crops. If you're planting on a balcony, don't let any possible support go to waste. Position climbing plants where the railing provides a readymade trellis. There are also space-saving techniques unique to container gardens. You can use the vertical space of a container itself by planting in holes or pockets in the sides of the container. Growing some vining plants in hanging baskets will save space too, but be sure to place hanging baskets where they won't shade other plants. When you are growing a container garden, always select varieties that are suitable for container growing, and remember that containers dry out faster than a traditional garden, so you'll need to water more often. Plants growing in containers are also more affected by changes in temperature; you do have the advantage, though, of being able to move them to a more protected area or even inside on cool nights.

A point to remember about container gardening: The small volume of soil in a raised bed will warm up faster in spring than the soil in your open garden. This gives you a longer growing season, because you can start your cool-season crops earlier. You can also bring plants inside if the temperature takes an unexpected plunge — this mobility is an advantage you obviously lack in an open garden.

Essentially, planning a container garden is little different from planning an outdoor plot. The main difference may be in the varieties you choose—if you're planting in a confined space you're going to take a special interest in smaller varieties and plants with compact, contained growth habits. But basically, any plant that will grow in your garden will also grow on your balcony or patio. More information is given in the chapter on container and small-space gardening.

Gardening in a greenhouse: A refuge for plants and gardener

With a greenhouse you can garden all year around and experiment with all kinds of plants that you have little chance of growing out in the open garden. A greenhouse is also a nice, cozy, private place for the gardener whose gardening time is often interrupted by demands from other family members. If you're going to buy and install a greenhouse, it's worth getting a good one. Greenhouses vary vastly in size, price, and construction and many companies supply them; not all of them, however, are well-designed and well-put-together, so you need to do some homework. The following are reputable sources that can provide you with basic information to help you make a choice. Some of them will design a greenhouse to fit your available space and specifications.

Greenhouse suppliers:

Lord & Burnham
Irvington
New York, NY 10533

Planning Your Garden

Janco Greenhouses
J. A. Nearing Co., Inc.
9390 Davis Avenue
Lauren, MD 20180

Sunlan Greenhouses
412 8th Avenue
P.O. Box 1874
Smyrna, TN 37169

Everlight Aluminum Greenhouse, Inc.
14605 Lorain Avenue
Cleveland, OH 44111

GIVING YOUR CHILD A GARDEN

If you're a parent and you enjoy gardening, chances are you'd like to pass on some of that enjoyment to your children. A garden offers a child a multitude of learning experiences and teaches far more than basic biology. By growing a garden of his — or her — own, a child experiences delight and satisfaction when everything goes well, and frustration and disappointment when things go wrong. A child waiting to harvest his crop learns to be patient. By taking care of his plot he learns how much work is involved — and he'll be less casual about riding his bicycle over someone else's yard. By working with living plants a child learns respect for living things and becomes aware of what the word "ecology" really means. And he also learns that vegetables don't grow on supermarket shelves.

A child's garden is his own place

If a child's going to love his garden, it's got to be *his* garden. An odd corner of yours won't do. Give your child an area of his own, and make sure you both recognize the territorial boundaries. He'll need your help and encouragement, but be careful not to tread on his toes.

Children are naturally fascinated by the process of growth. It takes little effort to get a youngster involved in the biological wonders of how seeds germinate; how roots, leaves, and flowers develop; how insects pollinate the flowers; and how the seeds inside the fruit complete the life cycle. It's easier to teach a child to take care of living things by giving him a row of radishes than by getting him a live pet. A plant grows faster than a puppy, and you don't have to take it for walks.

Make it easy to succeed

You'll never get a child interested in gardening if you make it too hard for him. Set him up for success. Plan ahead yourself before you get together with the child to plan his garden. Prepare a list of vegetables that are sure-fire successes — like chard, beans, cucumbers, and squash. Try to make sure something's growing all the time, because April to August is a long time for a child to wait for results. Start off with vegetables that give quick results; leaf lettuce is obliging, and radishes (some produce in 20 to 30 days) are ideal for building up a young gardener's confidence that he can, indeed, grow things by himself. Include something large and dramatic — Jerusalem artichokes, for example, are striking plants; they produce attractive flowers and are extremely easy to grow.

Have your child grow plants that he likes to eat, which means spinach is probably out. Try peanuts instead — children are fascinated by the way peanuts grow. Or let him use up all his space on a watermelon if he wants to. Children often aren't much interested in root crops — apart from the satisfying rapid radish — because there's not much going on above ground. Asparagus is pretty, but no child is going to wait three years to harvest it, and he probably doesn't like it anyway. Corn has a lot of insect problems, so although it's a nice, big plant, it's not a suitable crop for a child. Cauliflower and broccoli are difficult to grow.

Caring for his garden helps a child learn what ecology really means.

Stay with the varieties that will reward the child. If he's got radishes, lettuce, cucumbers, chard, and a peanut plant, that's enough to start with. If he gets hooked on gardening he'll want to experiment next time.

Answer all his questions carefully

Help the child plant his garden, and explain why you're planting a certain crop on a certain date. Don't ever try to gamble by planting too early — it's the child's crop you're taking a chance with, not your own. As the young plants emerge, help the child recognize the difference between plants and weeds, and make sure he understands why it's necessary to remove the weeds; they'll starve out the plants. Show the child how to water plants thoroughly but without washing away the soil.

You'll probably need to explain the difference between "good" and "bad" insects, too. Tell him that aphids damage his plants, but that ladybugs eat aphids, so they're welcome in the garden. Let him pick caterpillars off the plants or set a saucer of stale beer in the soil to trap snails and slugs, but never let him handle pesticides. You want to answer all his questions and encourage the child to be as

independent as possible in caring for his garden, but the one area in which you can't let him be independent is chemical pest control.

Never let the child use pesticides or handle pesticide equipment. Explain what you're doing and why, but treat pesticides the way you would any other toxic product. Keep all pesticides and equipment out of the reach of children — preferably locked up — and tell the child that it's the one part of gardening that's strictly for adults.

Make gardening a delight — not a drag

Growing his or her own garden can teach a child a lot about patience — that's probably one reason you're encouraging it. But don't expect miracles. Patience doesn't come easily to children (or to many adults, for that matter), and a child who has to wait too long for results is going to lose interest in the whole project.

Another important point: Accept the fact that he's *not* going to be doing all the work. Some of it's going to fall into your own already crowded schedule. If you're going to get mad because you have to remind him to water his crop, you might as well find him some other spare-time activity and forget about the gardening. When did nagging ever get him to clean up his room, anyway, much less his vegetable patch? And be a bit flexible. Once in a while water the garden for your child so that he or she can go play or just watch a favorite program. The child can return the favor the next time you're pressed for time. And you're helping your child learn the meaning of give-and-take.

Make gardening a family affair

The child's not the only one who benefits from having a garden of his own. You'll get a lot of pleasure from working alongside him. Taking time to answer a curious child's questions gives you a new appreciation of the small wonders of nature. You probably haven't looked closely at a caterpillar since you were seven years old yourself. And don't you remember wondering if a plant would grow right before your eyes if you just sat there and watched it long enough?

Your child can get a lot of pleasure — and a lot of useful experience — from caring for a garden and watching it grow. You'll enjoy the feeling that you've shared part of your pleasure in gardening with him. And there's nothing more heartwarming than the sight of a child, beaming with pleasure, with his arms full of vegetables he's grown himself.

An armful of homegrown vegetables is something your child can be proud of.

First and last frost dates for major cities in the United States

State and city	Average date of last frost	Average date of first frost	Number of days in growing season
Alabama			
Birmingham	March 19	November 14	241
Mobile	February 17	December 12	298
Montgomery	February 27	December 3	279
Alaska			
Anchorage	May 18	September 13	118
Cordova	May 10	October 2	145
Fairbanks	May 24	August 29	97
Arizona			
Flagstaff	June 8	October 2	116
Phoenix	January 27	December 11	317
Winslow	April 28	October 21	176
Arkansas			
Fort Smith	March 23	November 9	231
Little Rock	March 16	November 15	244
California			
Bakersfield	February 14	November 28	287
Fresno	February 3	December 3	303
Sacramento	January 24	December 11	321
Colorado			
Denver	May 2	October 14	165
Pueblo	April 28	October 12	167
Connecticut			
Hartford	April 22	October 19	180
New Haven	April 15	October 25	193
District of Columbia			
Washington	April 10	October 28	200
Florida			
Jacksonville	February 6	December 16	313
Orlando	January 31	December 17	319
Tallahassee	February 26	December 3	280
Tampa	January 10	December 26	349
Georgia			
Atlanta	March 20	November 19	244
Macon	March 12	November 19	252
Savannah	February 21	December 9	291
Idaho			
Boise	April 29	October 16	171
Pocatello	May 8	September 30	155
Illinois			
Cairo	March 23	November 11	233
Chicago	April 19	October 28	192
Springfield	April 8	October 30	205
Urbana	April 22	October 20	151
Indiana			
Evansville	April 2	November 4	216
Fort Wayne	April 24	October 20	179
Indianapolis	April 17	October 27	193

Last frost 32°F.
First frost 32°F.
The growing season can be extended if the vegetables are protected, or if they are very hardy.

First and last frost dates for major cities in the United States (cont.)

State and city	Average date of last frost	Average date of first frost	Number of days in growing season
Iowa			
Des Moines	April 20	October 19	183
Dubuque	April 19	October 19	184
Kansas			
Concordia	April 16	October 24	191
Topeka	April 9	October 26	200
Wichita	April 5	November 1	210
Kentucky			
Lexington	April 13	October 28	198
Louisville	April 1	November 7	220
Louisiana			
Lake Charles	February 18	December 6	291
New Orleans	February 13	December 12	302
Shreveport	March 1	November 27	272
Maine			
Greenville	May 27	September 20	116
Presque Isle	May 31	September 18	110
Portland	April 29	October 15	169
Maryland			
Baltimore	March 28	November 17	234
Cumberland	May 1	October 10	163
Massachusetts			
Amherst	May 12	September 19	130
Boston	April 16	October 25	192
Nantucket	April 12	November 16	219
Michigan			
Detroit	April 25	October 23	181
Grand Rapids	April 25	October 27	185
Lansing	May 6	October 8	155
Minnesota			
Duluth	May 22	September 24	125
Minneapolis	April 30	October 13	166
Mississippi			
Jackson	March 10	November 13	248
Biloxi	February 22	November 28	279
Vicksburg	March 8	November 15	252
Missouri			
Columbia	April 9	October 24	198
Kansas City	April 5	October 31	210
St. Louis	April 2	November 8	220
Montana			
Billings	May 15	September 24	132
Glasgow	May 19	September 20	124
Havre	May 9	September 23	138
Nebraska			
Lincoln	April 20	October 17	180
Norfolk	May 4	October 3	152
Omaha	April 14	October 20	189

Last frost 32°F.
First frost 32°F.
The growing season can be extended if the vegetables are protected, or if they are very hardy.

First and last frost dates for major cities in the United States (cont.)

State and city	Average date of last frost	Average date of first frost	Number of days in growing season
Nevada			
Las Vegas	March 13	November 13	245
Reno	May 14	October 2	141
New Hampshire			
Concord	May 11	October 1	143
New Jersey			
New Brunswick	April 21	October 19	179
Trenton	April 8	November 5	211
New Mexico			
Albuquerque	April 16	October 29	196
Santa Fe	April 23	October 19	179
New York			
Binghamton	May 4	October 6	154
Buffalo	April 29	October 23	178
New York	April 7	November 12	219
North Carolina			
Charlotte	March 21	November 15	239
Raleigh	March 24	November 16	237
Wilmington	March 15	November 19	274
North Dakota			
Bismarck	May 11	September 24	136
Fargo	May 13	September 27	137
Williston	May 14	September 23	132
Ohio			
Cincinnati	April 15	October 25	192
Cleveland	April 21	November 2	195
Columbus	April 17	October 30	196
Dayton	April 20	October 21	184
Toledo	April 24	October 25	184
Oklahoma			
Oklahoma City	March 28	November 7	223
Tulsa	March 31	November 2	216
Oregon			
Medford	April 25	October 20	178
Portland	February 25	December 1	279
Salem	April 14	October 27	197
Pennsylvania			
Harrisburg	April 10	October 28	201
Philadelphia	March 30	November 17	232
Pittsburgh	April 20	October 23	187
Rhode Island			
Providence	April 13	October 27	197
South Carolina			
Charleston	February 19	December 10	294
Columbia	March 14	November 21	252
Greenville	March 23	November 17	239
South Dakota			
Huron	May 4	September 30	149
Rapid City	May 7	October 4	150
Sioux Falls	May 5	October 3	152

Last frost 32°F.
First frost 32°F.
The growing season can be extended if the vegetables are protected, or if they are very hardy.

Planning Your Garden

First and last frost dates for major cities in the United States (cont.)

State and city	Average date of last frost	Average date of first frost	Number of days in growing season
Tennessee			
Chattanooga	March 26	November 10	229
Knoxville	March 31	November 6	220
Memphis	March 20	November 12	237
Nashville	March 28	November 7	224
Texas			
Brownsville	February 15	December 10	298
Dallas	March 18	November 22	249
Houston	February 5	December 11	309
Plainview	April 10	November 6	211
Utah			
Blanding	May 18	October 14	148
Salt Lake City	April 12	November 1	202
Vermont			
Burlington	May 8	October 3	148
Saint Johnsbury	May 22	September 25	126
Virginia			
Norfolk	March 18	November 27	254
Richmond	April 2	November 8	220
Washington			
Seattle	February 23	December 1	281
Spokane	April 20	October 12	175
West Virginia			
Charleston	April 18	October 28	193
Parkersburg	April 16	October 21	189
Wisconsin			
Green Bay	May 6	October 13	161
La Crosse	May 1	October 8	161
Madison	April 26	October 19	177
Milwaukee	April 20	October 25	188
Wyoming			
Casper	May 18	September 25	130
Cheyenne	May 20	September 27	130
Sheridan	May 21	September 21	123

Last frost 32°F.
First frost 32°F.
The growing season can be extended if the vegetables are protected, or if they are very hardy.

This chart and tabulation were derived from the Freeze Date tabulation in Climatography of the United States No. 60 — Climates of the States; *and reprinted in* Gale Research's The Weather Almanac.

YOUR VEGETABLE RATING GUIDE

The following tailored rating guide incorporates your personal interests and the constraints of your geographic area to help you arrive at a rating for each vegetable you're interested in growing. If, as you fill out the chart, you find an item does not apply to your situation or the vegetable you're rating, go on to the next item. Bear in mind that this rating chart is set up for production in a single season. For some perennials you will have to accept the fact that there will be no crop the first year.

After you have rated a vegetable, parts I and II of the chart will generally remain the same from year to year. There may be a few changes: Your interest in gardening may increase, or you may have less time to work in your garden, or experience may prompt you to experiment with different varieties. But generally once you have figured out I and II for each vegetable, the points will remain fairly constant for you in your area. On the other hand, part V can change radically. Your tastes may change, those neighbors who love rutabagas may move away, or after you have grown Brussels sprouts and know how they do it, you may no longer want to bother with them. Your personal input, then, should be reevaluated every year since any change here can make a radical difference in the final analysis.

The analysis and final decision are yours, but generally if the vegetable rates 5 or over, you will have a successful experience. If it is 3 or 4, give it a try. If it is 1 or 2, why grow it, since you don't care for it that much?

Following the Rating Guide is your personal gardening calendar. Use it to plan your activities in the garden and to give you a useful at-a-glance check for what you've accomplished and what still needs to be done. Remember, gardening doesn't have to be restricted to your growing season—for the gardener, planning and hoping go on all year around.

Vegetable rating guide

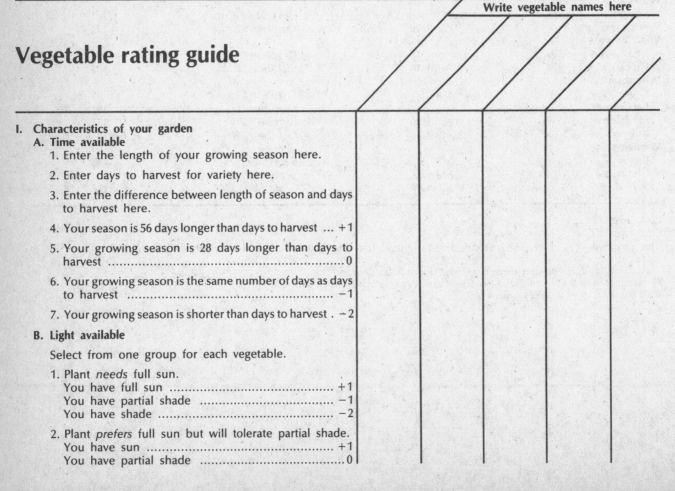

Write vegetable names here

I. Characteristics of your garden

A. Time available

1. Enter the length of your growing season here.

2. Enter days to harvest for variety here.

3. Enter the difference between length of season and days to harvest here.

4. Your season is 56 days longer than days to harvest ... +1

5. Your growing season is 28 days longer than days to harvest 0

6. Your growing season is the same number of days as days to harvest .... −1

7. Your growing season is shorter than days to harvest . −2

B. Light available

Select from one group for each vegetable.

1. Plant *needs* full sun.
   You have full sun .... +1
   You have partial shade .... −1
   You have shade .... −2

2. Plant *prefers* full sun but will tolerate partial shade.
   You have sun .... +1
   You have partial shade 0

Vegetable rating guide

3. Plant *prefers* partial shade.
You have partial shade .... +1
You have sun but are industrious enough to provide shade when it's needed .... +1
You have sun but are lazy or can't be around to provide shade .... −1

II. Characteristics of plant

A. Ease of growing

1. Plant grows by itself .... +1

2. Plant needs tying, staking, pruning, frequent picking or other special care.
If you enjoy doing it .... +1
If you don't enjoy doing it .... −1

3. Plant is vulnerable to many pests and diseases . −1

4. Plant is generally not bothered much by pests and diseases .... +1

5. Plant is sensitive to temperature and temperature sequences or daylength and daylength sequences.
Conditions occur naturally .... +1
You must modify conditions .... −1

B. Plant as potential pest

1. Plant stays where it's planted without spreading or dies at the end of the season .... +1

2. Plant spreads or seeds itself to the point of becoming a pest or is hard to move or dig up .... −1

C. Spread of harvest

1. Edible parts can be harvested over a period of time .. +1

2. Whole plant must be harvested all at once .... −1

III. Potential yield

Find the vegetable you are rating in one of the groups below and enter points accordingly. Remember, this is only the plant's potential; it may not grow at all in your area.

A. High potential yield

1. Jerusalem artichoke, basil, celeriac, chard, chive, collard, cress, cucumber, dill, fennel, garlic, horseradish, marjoram, okra, parsley, rosemary, sage, summer and winter squash, tarragon, thyme, tomato .... +5

2. Broad beans, dry beans, green or snap beans, beet, broccoli, cabbage, cardoon, Chinese cabbage, celery, chayote, kale, lettuce, mustard, New Zealand spinach, parsnip, radish, rhubarb, rutabaga, salsify, turnip .... +4

Vegetable rating guide

Write vegetable names here

B. Average to low potential yield

1. Asparagus, Brussels sprout, carrot, chicory, eggplant, endive, kohlrabi, leek, lima bean, onion, pepper, white potato .... +3

2. Cauliflower, muskmelon, sweet potato, pumpkin, watermelon .... +2

3. Globe artichoke, mung bean, corn, peanut, black-eyed pea, sweet pea, soybean, spinach .... +1

IV. Subtotal

Add plus points and subtract minus points. Divide the remaining points by two and enter the results here.

V. Personal preferences

Select only one point value.

A. Positive factors

1. You are curious about growing it .... +1

2. You like eating it and want to try growing it .... +2

3. You like it enough to go to a lot of trouble to grow it . +3

B. Negative factors

1. You are not particularly enthusiastic about either growing or eating it .... −1

2. No one in the family will eat it .... −2

3. No one in the neighborhood will eat it .... −3

VI. Analysis

Total your points for parts IV and V to find the rating for your vegetable as it could be grown in your area. If the rating is 5 or more, the vegetable is a good prospect. If the rating is 3 or 4, you might give it a try. If the rating is 2 or less, why bother?

Personal Gardening Calendar

Use this calendar to plan your gardening activities

	MARCH	APRIL	MAY	JUNE	JULY	AUGUST	SEPTEMBER	OCTOBER	NOVEMBER	DECEMBER	JANUARY	FEBRUARY
Start of growing season (average date of last spring frost)												
End of growing season (average date of first fall frost)												
Length of growing season												
Start hardy plants indoors (6-8 weeks before date to set out)												
Start tender plants indoors (6-8 weeks before date to set out)												
Plant very hardy plants and seeds outdoors (4-6 weeks before average date of last frost)												
Plant hardy plants and seeds outdoors (2-3 weeks before average date of last spring frost)												
Plant tender plants and seeds outdoors (on the average date of last frost)												
Plant very tender plants and seeds outdoors (2 weeks after average date of last frost)												
Clean up garden												
Plant next year's garden, order seeds												
Leave garden for vacation												

Your personal gardening calendar gives you a spot check on the important dates in your gardening season and lets you know how much you've already achieved and what is still left to do. Find the frost dates for your area and the length of your growing season from the chart earlier in this chapter. The hardiness chart at the end of "Planting Your Garden" will tell you which hardiness category your vegetables belong to and when to plant them.

Points to Remember When You Plan Your Garden

1. Plan what to grow, and how much. Your choice of what to grow, and how much of it you need to plant, depends on a number of factors. When you work out your garden plan on paper, ask yourself these questions:

   - What fruits and vegetables do you like to eat?
   - What do you plan to do with your harvest—or the part of it you don't eat at once?
   - Will the plants do well in the conditions your garden offers?
   - Do you have enough room for the plants or trees you like?
   - Will the plant require so much work—spraying, pruning, special handling—that it's really not worth the bother?
   - Do you hope growing it yourself will save you money?

2. Remember that where you live determines what you grow— to some extent at least. Make sure that the vegetables and fruits you want to cultivate will do well in your hardiness zone.

3. Even if your garden does not get as much sun as you would like, you can make the most of the sunlight you do get by planting in the right places. Check how much light the plants need *before* you set the seeds or transplants.

4. Even if you don't have a regular garden, you can still grow many vegetables and herbs and some fruits. Individual plant profiles later in this book tell you how to grow produce indoors, on a balcony or patio, in containers like hanging baskets or barrels, and in raised beds.

5. Consider building a cold frame that uses solar heat to warm your plants. You can get a head start on the growing season this way.

6. Some crops, especially vegetables, come in many varieties, some of which may be especially suited to your needs. Tomatoes, for instance, come in all sorts of shapes and sizes, among them huge beefsteak tomatoes which demand a lot of garden space, plum tomatoes for canning, or cherry tomatoes which will grow happily in a hanging basket. Put a little time into determining which varieties will be most rewarding.

7. If you have limited space, you can plan your garden so that you can use the space to give you successive crops. For instance, cool-weather vegetables like peas and lettuce can be replaced with tomatoes, peppers, beans, and other crops for a later harvest. Or plant your tomatoes and peppers alongside peas and lettuce which are already growing well. You'll harvest the peas and lettuce before the other plants grow big enough to need the space.

8. However eager you are to get out in the yard and dig, take time to plan your garden on paper. That way you won't waste space, time, or energy growing too much for your needs, or growing too much in too little space so that the crops are overcrowded and yield poorly.

9. If you have children in the family, make a small space in your garden (or in your container garden) that they can call their own. They will learn useful lessons about ecology; they'll have the pleasure of seeing plants grow and harvesting produce they've cared for themselves; and maybe they'll enjoy gardening enough to help *you* with some of your gardening chores.

10. Use the planting information in this book to help you determine frost dates, decide how to time planting for best results, and learn when and how to harvest.

Gardening Tools

Gardening Tools

There are a great many garden tools on the market. Some are necessary, some are helpful, and some are a complete waste of money. If you're a beginning gardener, approach all this equipment with caution—be sure that you're going to enjoy being a gardener before you spend a small fortune on tools. Remember, too, that one of your motives in being a gardener is to save money by growing your own vegetables; you'll have to grow a lot of lettuce to pay for a $300 rototiller.

When you decide which tools you need, buy the best you can find and take good care of them. As in so many other activities, it's a long-term economy move to buy good equipment right away—ask any serious cook. Good tools work better and last longer than the cheap kinds that fall to pieces the first time you need them to do any real work.

The first test of a tool is how it feels in your hands. Is it well-balanced? Can you lift it when it's full as well as when it's empty? Gardeners and gardening tools come in different sizes and weights; since you'll be working together, you and your equipment should be compatible.

In caring for your tools, there are three basic rules that are often stated and seldom followed:

1. Clean your tools before putting them away. It may be a bore, but it's even more boring to have to clean them before you can use them again.

2. Have a regular storage place for each tool. Visitors will be impressed by your orderliness, and you'll be able to tell at a glance if you've put everything away or if you've left some small item out in the rain to rust.

3. Use each tool the way it was meant to be used. For instance, a rake—even a good-quality rake—won't last long if you consistently use it to dig holes or turn soil. You've got a perfectly good spade for those tasks.

Follow these three simple rules and your tools will give you long, efficient, and economical service.

BASIC GARDENING TOOLS

The following are the basic tools of the gardener. You may not need them all. Consider the type and amount of gardening you do, and choose the implements that best suit your needs.

Shovel and spade. A shovel has a curved scoop and a handle with a handgrip. It's used for lifting, turning, and moving soil. A spade is a sturdy tool with a thick handle (and a handgrip) and a heavy blade that you press into the ground with your foot. The blade is usually flatter and sharper than the shovel's, and often squared off at the bottom. A spade is for hard digging work; it should be strong but light enough to handle comfortably. A nursery shovel or nursery spade is an excellent all-around tool in the vegetable garden.

Spading fork. A spading fork is also used for heavy digging, and its two to four prongs make it the best

Trowel

Spade

Shovel

Fork

tool for breaking up compacted soil, lifting root vegetables, and digging weeds. The handle is sturdy and has a handgrip; your foot presses the prongs into the ground. Forks with flexible prongs are called pitchforks; the ones with sturdier, rigid prongs are called spading forks.

Rake. A rake with a long handle and short sturdy metal prongs is used for leveling and grading soil, stirring up the soil surface, and removing lumps, rocks, and shallow-rooted weeds. It's an essential tool for the home gardener. You can also get rakes with longer, flexible fingers. This type is not as versatile as the first type, but it's good for gentle cultivating, cleaning-up chores like raking the leaves, and collecting trash from between plants.

Hoe. The hoe is a tool with a flat blade attached at right angles to a long handle. It's used for stirring or

mounding the soil and for making rows, and it's one of the gardener's most necessary tools. It's also used for cutting off weeds and cultivating.

Trowel. This is a short-handled implement with a pointed scoop-shaped blade. It can be used as a hand shovel or spade and is useful when transplanting young plants into the garden.

Hose. A garden hose is essential for carrying water to your garden. Hoses are usually made from rubber or vinyl; rubber is more expensive, but it's worth the initial extra cost because it's far more durable than vinyl and much easier to work with. Make sure your hose is long enough to reach comfortably to all parts of your garden. An effective hose should probably be no less than 50 feet long.

Hand cultivator

Rake

Rake

Hoe

Hand hoe

Gardening Tools

Sprayers. Sprayers are used for applying pesticides evenly to plants or other surfaces. Basically, there are three kinds to choose from. A hose-attachment jar sprayer has a container—usually a quart—with a screw-on lid and a nozzle that attaches to the end of your garden hose. It uses the pressure of the hose to spray the pesticide. This type of sprayer is fairly inexpensive; it does an efficient job, but can be messy. A hand-pump sprayer has a plastic or metal container and, as the name implies, the pesticide is applied manually by means of a pump. Hand-pump sprays come in capacities from one to five gallons, so you can choose the size that best meets your needs. They're neither expensive nor messy, and they do an efficient job. You can also get small electric-powered (rechargeable) sprayers. They're expensive, but they're convenient and easy to use. A power sprayer may be a good purchase if you have a good-sized garden, but it isn't really practical for a small home garden.

Dusters. These are used to apply dry powder or dust-type pesticides to plants or other surfaces. You can get a hand-crank or plunger type, and both are satisfactory. A hand-crank duster is usually more expensive but may do a slightly better job of applying the pesticide evenly.

Hand spreaders. You can use a hand spreader either to spread dry granule fertilizer or to sow seeds. It's a small box with a handle that you crank; a fan attached to the crank throws out the contents. It's effective for spreading an even layer of fertilizer or for planting a cover crop over a rough surface in fall. Don't try using an ordinary lawn fertilizer

spreader—it won't be effective in your vegetable garden.

Pocket knife. The pocket knife has any number of uses around the garden. It can be used to harvest fruits, separate clumps of plants, cut twine and string, and so on.

File. Even with the best care, the cutting edges of spades and hoes become blunt. You need a file to sharpen them when the edges start to get dull.

Thermometer. An outdoor thermometer can take a lot of the guesswork out of caring for plants that are sensitive to heat or cold. Especially useful is a thermometer that records maximum and minimum temperatures. A soil thermometer can help you answer questions about when to plant.

Basic supplies. There are any number of odds and ends that don't seem essential to your calling as a gardener until the moment you find you haven't got them. Some of these you'll buy; some of them are household discards that you recycle into equipment like seed flats and plant pots that you'd otherwise have to buy.

Among your purchases should be string and twine, stakes, plastic plant markers—small labels that you stick in the ground to remind you what you planted, and where—and waterproof marking pens. A calendar or diary helps you keep track of your gardening activities and estimate your time from planting to harvest for each crop. Although a good part of the pleasure of gardening is getting the soil on your hands, gardening gloves are useful for heavy work or in cold weather.

Find a place in your garden shed or garage for the kind of basic supplies you don't have to buy—the household rejects that you're going to use as gardening aids. Among them are coffee cans and gallon plastic milk containers that can be used with the bottoms removed to protect plants from bugs or from extremes of temperature. Brown grocery bags can also be used as weather shields. Wire coat hangers bent into shape and covered with plastic form homemade greenhouses. Broom handles and assorted sticks make splendid stakes for tomatoes. Practically any container can be used as a planter, and egg cartons make fine divided planters for seeds—unless the crop you're planting resents being transplanted and needs to be started in peat pots or some other type of plantable container.

EQUIPMENT FOR LARGE-SPACE GARDENING

As your interest in gardening develops, you'll probably want—if space allows—to enlarge your garden. As you do, you may want to consider investing in a few larger pieces of equipment. Here are

You'll need a file to sharpen the blades of your garden tools.

some items you might consider for use in your expanded—and more demanding—garden.

Rototiller. A rototiller is a machine, usually gas-powered, that uses multiple blades to turn the soil in preparation for planting or to cultivate between rows. You can get a rear-tyne or front-tyne tiller. Rear-tyne tillers are generally larger, more powerful, and easier to operate because they are self-propelled, but they cost more and are less convenient to move around. It makes sense to rent a rototiller the first year or two you have a large garden; don't invest in one until you're sure you'll use it.

Wheelbarrow. A wheelbarrow is essential when you have a large garden. It will save you a lot of time, energy, and backache. You can use it to transport soil, large quantities of plants—anything, in fact, that you'd rather not have to carry yourself.

Irrigation systems. When your garden gets too large to water by hand, you need an efficient alternative system. A sprinkler attached to the garden hose does a good job, but you have limited control over the direction of the water; your sprinkler may water areas (or people) that don't need watering. Also, a sprinkler leaves a lot of water on the foliage of the vegetable plants, and this is unsatisfactory because it can spread disease.

A drip or trickle irrigation system uses a permeable hose to direct water into the soil surrounding the plants. The hose may be all-over permeable or perforated at intervals—essentially, what you're using is a leaky hose. One type is manufactured from old rubber tires that are shredded up and put together again. A drip system attaches to a main line (your garden hose), and the permeable tubes are placed at the side of a row of plants or between rows so that they water the plants rather than the paths between the rows. Sometimes the tubes or hoses are covered by an inch or two of soil. Drip irrigation uses less water and provides a more even supply of moisture than other watering systems. A system like this tends to be expensive, but it does a good job of soaking the soil without drenching plant foliage, too.

Seed planter. A seed planter does just what the name suggests—it plants seeds, positioning them at precisely the correct spacing and depth for the variety. Apart from saving time when you're planting, you also save the time you'd otherwise spend thinning out overcrowded seedlings. Planters can be simple and cheap or complex and expensive. Some just space the seeds; some dig their own furrows, plant the seeds, and fill in the furrows afterwards.

A trickle irrigation system uses porous tubes to carry water directly to your plants.

Gardening Tools

Choose the planter best suited to your needs.

Planting row guide. A row guide is simply two stakes with a line marked at six-inch intervals stretched between them. It helps you mark straight rows and plant seeds or plants evenly and quickly. A row guide you make yourself works every bit as well as an expensive store-bought one. To make your own, just tie a good string line (as long as your garden at its longest point) between two stakes, and mark the line every six inches with colored markers. Come planting time, set up your guide and plant along it. The straight rows of plants you get when you use a guide are easier to weed, water, and harvest than random plantings.

Plant cages. Although these are commonly referred to as tomato cages, you can also use them to support vining crops like cucumbers and squashes. They're usually made of wire or covered wire and come in a variety of sizes. They contain the plant in a manageable space and keep it off the ground. Round cages are the most common, but you can now buy square ones that are a lot more convenient because they fold flat for storage. When you're buying cages, make sure that they're big enough and sturdy enough for the plant variety and that you can get your hand inside to harvest your crop.

TOOLS FOR CONTAINER GARDENING

If you're a container gardener, special tools—in many respects scaled-down versions of regular garden tools—are available for your use.

Hand cultivator. A hand cultivator helps you control weeds. One type has three prongs. The pickax kind has one single-pointed end and a double point on the other end. Choose whatever type you like best.

Hand hoe. This has a shorter handle and a smaller blade than a regular garden hoe.

Trowel. No container gardener should be without a trowel—it's even more useful here than in a full-size garden for filling containers, transplanting, dividing clumps of plants, and leveling soil.

Watering equipment. A watering wand makes it easier to reach the less accessible corners of your container garden. The wand is a hollow metal tube that attaches to the end of your hose, and it lets you water the back rows of your container garden without reaching over and possibly crushing the front rows. If you're an indoor gardener, you will also make good use of a small watering can, and a spray-mister to freshen foliage. Any household spray bottle makes a good mister, provided it is thoroughly washed out first.

Spadework: The Essential Soil

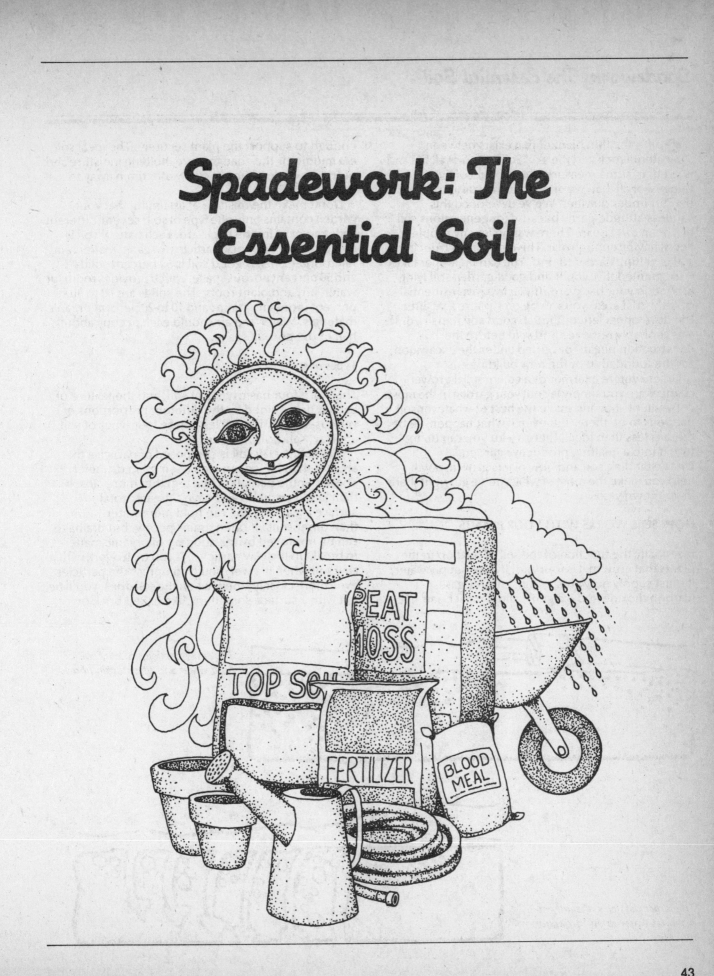

Spadework: The Essential Soil

Soil is the thin blanket that exists between sterile rock and the sky. Soil supports all life and is itself, in some measure, the product of living things. For all that, we often treat the soil like, literally, the dirt under our feet. We've developed this careless attitude partly because for generations soil has been dirt cheap. There was never any problem about having enough of it. This is no longer true; good soil is getting harder to find. You can no longer take it for granted that you'll find good garden soil lying around in your backyard. If you live in a residential or industrial area, you can be pretty sure that after the developers left, not much good soil remained. It was probably removed and sold before the construction began, or buried under the excavation for the foundation of the new buildings.

Unless you're a farmer or a commercial grower, chances are you simply lay out your garden in the most convenient spot and make the best of whatever soil happens to be there. But even if what happens to be there is less than ideal, there's a lot you can do to turn it into a healthy, productive garden. Understanding soil and how plants grow in it will help you make the most of what you've got right there in your own yard.

HOW SOIL WORKS WITH YOUR PLANTS

Essentially the function of the soil in relation to the plants that grow in it is fourfold: It must supply water; it must supply nutrients; it must supply gases (carbon dioxide and oxygen); and it must be firm enough to support the plant securely. The ideal soil is a middle-of-the-road mixture, holding moisture and nutrients while letting excess water drain away to make room for air.

Don't make the mistake of assuming that your garden contains only one type of soil; several different soils can exist in one backyard. Each natural soil is composed of fine rock particles, organic matter, and microorganisms. A good soil is 50 percent solids and 50 percent porous space, which provides room for water, air, and plant roots. The solids are 80 to 90 percent inorganic matter and 10 to 20 percent organic materials. Water and air should each occupy about half of the porous space.

Types of soil

There are four basic types of soil, and the texture of each is determined by the different proportions of various-sized soil particles. These four types of soil are clay, sand, silt, and loam.

Clay soil. A clay soil is composed of particles that are less than $\frac{1}{31750}$ of an inch ($\frac{1}{200}$ mm) in diameter. These minute particles pack together more closely than larger particles and have a greater total surface area. Clay soil can hold more water than other soils. It often drains poorly, but drainage can be improved by the addition of organic matter to break up the clay particles. If you try to work with a clay soil when it's wet, you'll compress the particles even more closely; then, when the soil dries, you'll be left with a surface something like baked brick or

The small particles of clay soil hold water and often drain poorly.

The larger particles of sandy soil often let water drain through too quickly.

concrete. Properly managed, however, clay soils can be the most productive of all.

Sandy soil. A sandy soil is made up mostly of particles that are over 1/3175 of an inch (1/20 mm) in diameter. They are much larger than clay particles and irregular in shape, so they don't pack as closely together as clay particles. Because they have less total surface area, these larger particles hold less water than smaller particles and are much more porous. Sandy soil drains like a sieve, but can be improved by the addition of organic matter, which helps retain moisture and nutrients.

Silt soil. In a silt soil the size of the particles is intermediate — between clay and sand. Depending on the size of its particles, a silt soil can act either like a clay soil or like a fine sandy soil. Silt consists of small, gritty particles that can pack down very hard, and it's not very fertile. Silt soil is often found on top of heavy clay, which slows or stops drainage.

Loam. Loam is a mixture of clay, silt, and sand particles. A good garden loam is something to cherish, particularly if it also contains a heavy supply of organic matter. All soil improvement is aimed at achieving a good loam — when you add organic matter or make other improvements to your clay or sandy soil, you're trying to provide the type of loam that lucky gardeners have without all that extra work.

A do-it-yourself test of soil texture

The best way to determine the approximate texture of the soil in your garden is by feeling it with your hands. Try this test: Take a small handful of moist garden soil, and hold some of the sample between your thumb and the first knuckle of your forefinger. Gradually squeeze the soil out with your thumb to form a ribbon. If you can easily form a ribbon that holds together for more than one inch, you have a very heavy clay soil. If a ribbon forms, but it holds together for only three-quarters of an inch to one inch, your soil is a silty clay loam. If the ribbon forms but breaks into pieces shorter than three-quarters of an inch, you have a silty soil. If a ribbon won't form at all, you have a sandy soil.

IMPROVING YOUR GARDEN SOIL

Unless you're one of the lucky people with a garden full of rich, productive loam, it's probable that you will want to improve your soil in the interests of harvesting a bigger and better crop of vegetables at the end of your growing season. When you're planning your soil-improvement program you have to take two issues into account: the texture of the soil and the nutrient content of the soil. You can improve both quite easily.

Improving soil texture

The physical texture of any soil can be improved by the addition of large amounts of organic matter. You can use materials like ground corncobs, sawdust, bark chips, straw, hay, peat moss, and cover crops; it's a great way to recycle a lot of garden wastes. You

A do-it-yourself test of soil texture—the longer the ribbon that forms when you squeeze the soil between your thumb and the knuckle of your forefinger, the more clay the soil contains.

can use grass clippings, provided the lawn has not been treated with a herbicide or weed killer; these substances will damage the plants you want to grow. Also avoid walnuts or walnut leaves. They contain iodine, which is a growth retardant. Making your own compost pile gives you excellent organic matter to enrich the soil and will be discussed later in this chapter.

The more organic matter you add, the more you can improve the texture of the soil. Blend the organic matter into the soil to a depth of 12 inches, making sure that it's evenly dispersed through the whole planting area. When organic matter is added to the soil, it will absorb some of the soil's nitrogen; to compensate for this, you should add two handfuls of a complete, well-balanced fertilizer (10-10-10) for each bushel of organic matter, working it thoroughly into the soil.

Improving nutrient content

The next step in your soil-improvement program is to have the soil tested to identify deficiencies — unless you correct those deficiencies, they can cause poor plant growth. In some states the Cooperative Extension Service will act as middleman and send your soil sample to the laboratory for you; in all states the extension service can give you information on firms in your area

Use a trowel to take a soil sample half an inch thick and eight inches down.

that do the tests. Either way, you will be charged a fee for the test.

The results of the soil test will give you the pH (acid-alkaline balance) of the soil and its content of three essential nutrients: nitrogen (N), which promotes leafy growth (although too much nitrogen will encourage too much foliage growth and slow down crop ripening); phosphorus (P), which is important for root growth and the production of flowers, fruits, and seeds; and potassium (K), which is necessary for the development of leaves and roots. The pH is measured on a scale of 1 (most acid or sour) to 14 (most alkaline or sweet), with 7 representing neutral. Most vegetables do best in soil that has a pH between 5.5 and 7.5, and most of them prefer soil to be on the acid side of neutral.

How to take a soil sample. Soil samples can be taken any time of the year, as long as the ground isn't frozen hard. Use a plastic bucket instead of metal, especially if the soil sample is to be used for testing micronutrients. You'll also need a digging tool, such as a spade or a trowel, and a clean container (a carefully washed-out one-pint milk carton or the container provided by the testing service). All equipment should be perfectly clean.

If there's any grass on the spot you're sampling, remove it. Then take a slice of soil half an inch thick and about eight inches deep straight down from a number of locations throughout your garden. If you're sampling a large area, 20 samples mixed together will do as fine a job as 40 or 100. If your garden is small, a minimum of five samples will be enough. Place all the samples in the plastic bucket, and then mix them thoroughly. If the soil is very wet, let it air-dry before mixing. Do *not* heat it in the oven or on a radiator; heat will kill the microorganisms and cause nitrogen and other elements to change form, making the test inaccurate. If there are a lot of lumps, crush them with a wooden spoon or a rolling pin on a wooden surface. After the soil is thoroughly mixed, fill your container and follow the laboratory's instructions for sending the sample.

Adjusting the pH balance. The results of your soil test will give you the pH balance of the soil. If you're lucky, the laboratory may say that the pH is just fine and you need make no adjustment. Or the laboratory may advise you to raise the pH by adding a recommended amount of lime or to lower the pH by adding a recommended amount of a sulfur product — ammonium sulfate is the one most commonly used. Don't use aluminum sulfate in your vegetable garden; the aluminum can be absorbed by the plant, making it toxic to you when you eat the vegetable. You can get lime and sulfur products from hardware stores and garden

STREET

Trees

Driveway

House

Garage

Compost
Pile

Mix soil samples from a number of locations in your garden for an accurate test of the pH balance and nutrient content of your soil.

centers; the laboratory report will tell you how much to use and how to apply it.

It's a good idea to have your soil tested every three to four years to make sure that the pH is in an acceptable range. If you've had a problem with the pH, it may be a good idea to test your soil even more often. This may seem like a lot of work, but good soil is essential to a good harvest, and your care and labor will pay off in higher yields and better-quality vegetables.

FERTILIZING: HOW TO DO IT (AND WHY)

Many inexperienced gardeners have the idea that since their vegetables have been doing fine so far without fertilizer, they'll do fine without it next year, too. But it's not quite that easy. Certainly, your plants may provide you with vegetables even if you

don't fertilize at all, but you won't be getting their best effort. Vegetable plants that are properly fertilized will be healthier and better able to resist disease and attacks from pests, thus giving you more — and higher-quality — produce.

Organic vs. synthetic fertilizers

There are two types of fertilizer: organic and inorganic. They're both means to the same end, but their composition and action differ in a number of ways. Some people make a sharp distinction between the two, and organic gardeners — as the name suggests — are strongly in favor of organic fertilizers and strongly opposed to the use of synthetics. This is more a matter of personal philosophy than of horticulture, because plants can't read the label on the package and can only absorb nutrients in an inorganic form. It makes no difference to a plant whether nutrients come from an organic or a synthetic source so long as the nutrients are available. All the same, the differences between the two types are worth your consideration.

Organic fertilizers. Organic fertilizers come from plants and animals. They are not water-soluble, and before the nutrients they contain can be made available to the plants, they have to be broken down over a period of time by microorganisms in the soil. This process requires temperatures over 40°F. So organic fertilizers do not offer instant solutions to nutrient deficiencies in the soil. Dried blood, kelp, bone meal, horn and hoof meal, and cottonseed meal are all organic fertilizers. It's not known how long any of them take to reach the stage where the nutrients they contain become available to the plant — some horticulturalists believe the process may take as long as 20 years — so there's no identifiable advantage to using one kind over another.

Manures are also organic fertilizers, but they are bulkier and contain lower percentages of nutrients than other natural fertilizers. However, they do offer an immediate advantage because they improve the texture of the soil by raising the level of organic matter.

The choice of either an organic or a synthetic fertilizer is a matter of personal conviction. The use of an organic type may support your own beliefs that the use of synthetic fertilizers is ecologically unacceptable. It's possible, however, that the organic material you use is not actually releasing nutrients fast enough to benefit your immediate crops.

Using an organic fertilizer

Because few organic fertilizers are what we have described as complete or well-balanced fertilizers, you will probably need to use a mixture of them in order to ensure a balanced nutrient content. Use the information in the table on this page to figure the composition of different organic materials to reach the balance you want. Each organic ingredient is packaged with directions for use. Take the amount of each ingredient indicated for your garden's size (find the square footage of your garden by multiplying its length by its width), and mix them together in a bucket. Apply this mixture in the spring before you plant, working it well into the soil, and repeat the treatment midway through your growing season.

Remember that when you use an organic fertilizer you don't know exactly when the nutrients will be available to the plants. With organic manure you'll have to use a lot, because

Organic fertilizers	Percentage of N-P-K
Blood	13-1.5-0
Fish scrap	9-7-0
Kelp	1-0.5-9
Bone meal, raw	4-22-0
Cottonseed meal	6-2.6-2
Hoof & bone meal, steamed	14-0-0
Cattle manure	0.5-0.3-0.5
Horse manure	0.6-0.3-0.5
Sheep manure	0.9-0.5-0.8
Chicken manure	0.9-0.5-0.8

manures are very low in nutrients. But the manures help greatly to improve the texture of the soil and are certainly worth their cost.

Using a synthetic fertilizer

When you fertilize with a synthetic fertilizer you know when and for approximately how long the nutrients will be available. If you've had your garden soil tested, and the testing laboratory has advised you how to raise the nutrient levels in the soil to acceptable levels, follow the laboratory's recommendations as closely as possible during the first growing season. Then it's a fairly straightforward matter to maintain the soil's fertility by following an annual plan.

FERTILIZING YOUR GARDEN: A TWO-STAGE PROGRAM

The first stage of your fertilizing program is an essential part of your spring preparation of your vegetable garden before planting. When you're digging over and clearing the area preparatory to planting your first vegetables, treat the soil with a complete, well-balanced (10-10-10) fertilizer at the rate of 10 pounds per 1,000 square feet or one pound per 100 square feet. Remember that a 12-12-12 or a 12-10-8 formula is close enough, as long as you make sure that the mix is well-balanced and the nitrogen content isn't over 20 percent. Follow the package directions carefully, and work the fertilizer evenly into the soil. Then, just before you plant, level off the surface or the seedbeds with the back of your rake.

This first fertilizing will see most of your vegetables comfortably through their initial period of growth, but by about halfway through your growing season they'll have used up a lot of the nutrients in the soil, and you'll need to replace these nutrients. This is the second stage of your fertilizing program. Use the

Phosphorus encourages root growth and fruiting.

Nitrogen is necessary for leafy growth.

Potassium promotes root growth and disease resistance.

A complete, well-balanced fertilizer provides nutrients to your plants.

same complete, well-balanced fertilizer at the same rate — 10 pounds per 1,000 square feet or one pound per 100 square feet — but apply it as a sidedressing to the plants. With a hoe, or similar tool, make trenches halfway between your rows of plants. The depth of the trenches will depend on what kinds of vegetables you're growing in the rows, because you have to take care not to disturb the roots of your plants. If there's no risk of disturbing the roots, make the trenches four to six inches deep. If the rows are close together, or if you're growing shallow-rooted crops or root vegetables that may be damaged by deep cultivation, keep the trenches only an inch or two in depth. Distribute the fertilizer in the trenches, and cover it with the soil you removed. The fertilizer will mingle with the earth and its nutrients will be drawn to the plants by the capillary moisture in the soil.

This two-part program of fertilizing will keep most of your crops well supplied with nutrients all through the growing season. Where a particular variety requires extra fertilizing or a different type of fertilizer, you'll find full information in our discussion of how to grow that vegetable.

THE COMPOST PILE: YOUR GARDEN'S RECYCLING CENTER

Composting is essentially a way of speeding up the natural process of decomposition by which organic materials are broken down and their components returned to the soil. It's a way of converting plant and other organic wastes into a loose, peatlike humus that provides nutrients to growing plants and increases the soil's ability to control water. The decaying process happens naturally, but slowly. The proximity, moisture, and air circulation of a compost pile encourage this process.

Composting also has another advantage over leaving organic wastes to decay naturally:

Layer organic materials to form a compost pile.

Organic matter has to take nitrogen from the soil in order to keep the decaying process going. Composting keeps the waste in one place where it's not depriving plants of nitrogen.

Composting can save money that you would otherwise spend on soil conditioners and fertilizers. It can save time, too, because it gives you a place to dispose of leaves and grass clippings.

How the composting process works

Compost forms as organic wastes are broken down by microorganisms in the soil. These microorganisms don't create nutrients; they just break down complex materials into simple ones that the plant can use. Most soil organisms are inactive when soil temperatures are below 40°F; they don't begin working in earnest until the temperature goes up to about 60°F, and most of them don't work well in a very acid element. Because they are extremely small, microorganisms work faster when not overwhelmed by large chunks of material.

There are two basic kinds of microorganisms: those that need air to work (aerobic) and those that don't (anaerobic). It's possible to compost in an airtight container, thanks to the microorganisms that don't need air. A tightly covered plastic trash can will convert an enormous amount of organic kitchen waste into compost in the course of a winter. The classic outdoor compost pile should be turned regularly with a pitchfork to provide air for the microorganisms that need it.

How to start a compost pile

If you have a fairly large garden, the best place to put your compost pile is at one end of the garden. The

A low wall of cinder blocks keeps the compost pile neat.

Small-space gardeners can compost in a plastic garbage bag.

pile can be square, rectangular or round; four to five feet across; and as long as the available space. You can use fencing or cinder blocks to keep the pile under control ·

If space is at a premium or if a compost pile doesn't fit in with your landscaping, start the heap behind some bushes or behind the garage. If the space available is extremely small, you can compost in a large heavy-duty plastic bag or plastic garbage can. You can also work the material directly into the soil.

To build a compost pile, start out with one to two feet of leaves, if you have them, or six to twelve inches of more compact material, such as grass clippings or sawdust. Over this put a layer of fertilizer (manure, blood, bone, cottonseed meal, or commercial fertilizer) and some finely ground limestone (most microorganisms like their environment sweet). Then add some soil to hold water and provide a starter colony of microorganisms. Water the compost carefully. Add a second layer of leaves or other garden waste and repeat the layers. If you have enough material or enough room, put on a third layer. The pile should be kept moist like a squeezed, but not sopping, sponge. As more material becomes available, make new layers, adding more fertilizer and lime each time. Turn the pile with a pitchfork about once a month.

You can use all garden waste on your compost pile except disease- and pest-laden materials, or those that have been treated with pesticides or weed-killers — for instance, grass clippings from an area that's been treated with a herbicide. Use nontreated grass clippings, leaves, weeds, and sod. You can also use kitchen leftovers like vegetable and fruit peels, vegetable tops, coffee grounds, tea leaves, and eggshells. The finer these materials are chopped and the deeper they're buried, the quicker they'll be converted and the less chance there is that they'll be dug up by inquisitive animals. You can also compost hay, straw, hulls, nutshells, and tree trimmings (not walnut). But unless they're shedded, these materials will take a long time to decompose.

There are a number of ways you can speed up the composting process. First, you can grind or shred all compost materials to give the microorganisms a head start. Second, make sure the pile doesn't dry out, and provide enough fertilizer to encourage rapid growth of the bacteria. Third, you can use a starter culture, either material from an established compost pile or a commercial starter culture.

Composting is a creative activity. There are almost as many different methods of composting as there are gardeners, and like a good stew, the proof is in the final product. And when other gardeners see your compost pile, they'll know you're taking good care of your garden and that you're not just a horticultural dabbler.

Compost and mulch — The difference is in the use

If you're an inexperienced gardener, you may be confused by the difference between composting and mulching — both processes use waste organic matter. The difference is in the use. Composted materials are dug back into the soil to enrich it and to enable the plants to use the nutrients that have been released by the decaying process. A mulch is a layer of material spread over the ground or around plants to provide protection from heat or cold, to retain soil moisture, or to maintain a certain soil temperature. Compost stays in the soil and eventually becomes part of it; a mulch is removed when the protection it provides is no longer needed.

HOW TO GARDEN WITH HOPELESS (OR NO) SOIL

You may be unlucky enough to have a garden full of hopeless soil—heavy clay, perhaps, or as sandy as a beach. Even if you're sure that no soil improvement program would help, you needn't give up hope of having a vegetable garden. It's not too difficult to

Any plant that will grow outdoors in your area will also grow in a raised bed or container garden.

Spadework: The Essential Soil

frustrate the natural state of the soil either by adding a layer of good soil on top of it, or by replacing the existing soil altogether. People who don't have garden space at all find that many vegetables do quite well in containers. And a raised bed, soil in a frame raised above ground level, is a sort of compromise between regular and container gardening. Raised-bed gardening will be discussed further in the section on container gardening.

Short on space? Try growing corn in an old washtub.

Planting Your Garden

Planting Your Garden

You've probably been looking forward to planting your garden all winter. And you've probably been thinking it's the easiest part, too. What can be so complicated about planting a garden? Nothing to it. Not so fast—there are a number of questions you have to consider before you start throwing seeds around.

For one thing, should you be planting seeds at all? Or should you be using transplants (young plants started from seed indoors)? If you're going to use transplants, should you grow them yourself or buy them from a nursery or garden store? And how should your crop be spaced—in rows, wide bands, or inverted hills? Like every other stage of growing a vegetable garden, planting poses a lot of questions; it's more complex than you may have figured.

SEEDS OR TRANSPLANTS: HOW TO DECIDE

The answers to the questions of what and where to plant depend on several factors: where you live, the kind of vegetables you decide to grow, and the amount of work you can reasonably handle. It's important to recognize your own limitations in terms of time, energy, and space. If you spend plenty of time at home, you may thoroughly enjoy nurturing your own transplants from seed. On the other hand, your home may not easily accommodate trays of young seedlings that need to be protected from cats, dogs, and curious children. And, if you're away a

lot or know you're only going to be able to garden on weekends, you may want to give yourself a break and buy your transplants when you're ready to put them in the ground. Giving due consideration to practical matters like these will ensure that gardening is a labor of love — not a sentence to hard labor.

Growing transplants: Pros and cons

Starting at square one and growing transplants from seeds can be a challenging and satisfying activity. It saves money, and it gives you a chance to experiment with varieties you can't buy locally as transplants. That's the good news. The bad news is that growing transplants yourself requires time, space, and attention. If you only want a few plants or you're just embarking on the gardening experience, you may do better to have someone do the preliminary work for you. Also, these little plants are going to be the foundation of your garden, so if you can't give them the environmental conditions they need for best early growth, it makes sense to let them start off with someone who can.

Transplants can be temperamental

When you're growing vegetables, the whole point of growing from transplants is to make the best use of your growing season. If a crop needs a long, cool growing season and you know that where you live the weather's going to be hot as Hades long before you can expect to harvest, you're going to have to use transplants. You have to consider, however, the flexibility of the plant variety. Some plants survive transplanting without any problem. Some hate it. Among vegetable plants that make the adjustment without much difficulty are broccoli, Brussels sprouts, cabbages, cauliflower, chard, lettuce, and tomatoes. Celery, eggplant, onions, and peppers are a little less tolerant and require some care in transplanting. Other vegetables, especially those with large seeds, resent transplanting and do much better when they're planted directly from seed after the soil warms up. Among these more temperamental crops are beans, corn, cucumbers, okra, peas, summer and winter squash, and watermelons. If you start any of these vegetables indoors, you'll have to use individual containers that can be planted along with them in order not to disturb their sensitive root systems.

Tomato seedlings can be started indoors for later transplanting.

Your three-stage planting plan

If you're planting a number of different vegetables, you will probably use all three of the systems we've mentioned. For instance, you may grow your own tomato and lettuce transplants from seed, direct-seed your peas and beans in the garden, and buy your young pepper plants from a garden center. In this case, your first task will probably be to start your transplants indoors, beginning eight weeks or more before your last date of average frost depending on the varieties you're growing. A couple of weeks later you can start direct-seeding—again timing your plantings according to the variety. Last, you can plant the transplants you purchased.

Good soil preparation is essential to all young plants. You'll be doing your soil preparation before direct-seeding, so the two procedures will be discussed together.

HOW TO GROW TRANSPLANTS AT HOME

It's counterproductive to start seeds too early; this holds true whether you're planting indoors or in the garden. Young plants that are started too early will get long and stringy, and they'll do poorly when they're planted outdoors. The average date of last frost for your area is your reference point for when to plant each vegetable in the garden, and the chart at the end of the chapter will give you this date. Set your indoor planting date six to eight weeks ahead of your outdoor planting date. Follow this rule for each vegetable, and with this schedule, your plants will be sturdy enough to face the outside world when it's time to introduce them to it.

Providing the right environment

The purpose of growing transplants from seed is to provide them with the correct environment for the important early growth period. This requires both care and common sense on your part. Cleanliness, temperature, moisture, and light all contribute to the healthy development of your plants. The following are supplies—or conditions—you'll need in order to grow transplants at home.

Planting medium. Young seedlings are subject to damping-off—a disease that can ruin your potential crop in infancy. Avoid disease problems by using a sterilized planting medium. Regular potting soil is too rich and will encourage the young plants to grow too quickly. Instead, buy a seed-starter medium from a reputable garden center.

Flats. These are low-sided plastic trays or containers used for planting seeds and are often subdivided into divisions for each half dozen or so plants. They're designed for use by nurseries and professional gardeners, and are usually sold wholesale. Make your own flats out of any shallow container that has sides a couple of inches high; an old cake pan is fine. Whatever container you use, be sure to punch a hole for drainage in the bottom.

Plantable containers. Some varieties of vegetables do not transplant well. They resent having their root systems disturbed and punish you by failing to thrive after transplanting. Among these varieties are corn, okra, beans, cucumbers, squashes, and watermelons. If you start these varieties indoors you must use containers that can be planted along with the seedling. There are several kinds.

Peat pots are simply compressed peat shaped into a plant pot, and they come in a number of shapes and sizes, so you can match them to the type of seedling you're growing. Jiffy pellets are also made of compressed peat, but you buy them as little flat discs a couple of inches across. When you add water they rise to two or three inches in height. Jiffy 7 pellets have a net wrapping holding the peat in place. This wrapping is supposed to disintegrate within a year after being planted out in the garden; in fact, the wrapping doesn't always disintegrate that fast. Jiffy 9 pellets do not have the wrapping. They disintegrate

Expanded peat pellets are planted along with the seedlings to avoid transplant shock.

faster in the soil, but crumble more easily with handling. You can buy trays to hold a dozen or more Jiffy pellets, or you can stand them side by side in a flat.

Labels and markers. It may seem like a bother to mark all your rows or containers, but it's worth it because it saves a lot of confusion. Cabbage family seedlings look much alike when young, as do hot and sweet peppers, or cherry and beefsteak tomatoes. The labels also tell you at a glance when you planted the seeds. This gives you a quick check on how they're developing. Buy plastic labels and waterproof marking pens from the garden center, or improvise with what you've got at home.

Lights. Light is essential to your seedlings, and it's not always possible to provide it naturally. Artificial light for plants must be provided by bulbs that don't put out a lot of heat — the light source must be close to the plants, and an ordinary light bulb will scorch them. Use cool-white fluorescent lights, or buy special plant lights, which are cool but put out a high level of the kind of light necessary for slow, steady growth.

Heating sources. According to variety, seedlings need to germinate at certain temperatures — 70° to 75° F is the approximate range, but the seed packet will tell you the precise temperature required. You can put your flats on a radiator or use a regular heating pad. You can also buy various types of pads and flats called germination pads, designed for use with germinating plants. The heat is supplied by a cable, which you plug into an electric outlet.

Starter fertilizer. When the time comes to transplant the seedlings into the garden, give them a boost with a starter fertilizer. These products are high in phosphorus, the nutrient that promotes root growth. Phosphorus is represented on the fertilizer package by the middle of three numbers; a 5-52-10 product is ideal, so buy one that matches those proportions as nearly as possible. A starter fertilizer is usually a concentrated liquid. You dilute it according to package directions and water the young transplanted seedlings with the solution.

Starting the transplants

You can grow transplants anywhere in your home that has a clear space where they won't be disturbed by the rest of the family or the family pets. A table in front of a sunny window is fine — preferably a south exposure, although a southeast or east window is also good. Don't set the containers right on the windowsill; set them back a little to mitigate the intensity of the light. If you can't provide natural light, use an artificial light source as recommended above. It takes some work to provide the right environment for your young plants, but if you do they'll reward you handsomely. You'll also have the satisfaction of knowing you started from scratch and did the whole job yourself. Here are the stages to follow when starting and raising your transplants:

Use the right container. Small numbers of seeds can be started in pots, flats (the low-sided plastic or wooden boxes that nurseries use), Styrofoam cups,

When you're starting transplants indoors, plant lights help provide the right environment for slow, steady growth.

or cut-off milk cartons. If you're starting plants that are fussy about transplanting, start them in individual containers from the beginning. Use Styrofoam cups, peat pots, or expanded peat pellets. Any container you use for starting seedlings should have drainage holes to keep the soil from getting soggy, and to allow watering from below once the seeds are planted.

Before using nonplantable containers, clean them thoroughly to reduce the chances of attack by pests and diseases. Scrub them well, then disinfect them by leaving them out for a couple of days in strong sunlight. Or wet or submerge the clean-scrubbed containers in a solution of three tablespoons bleach to one quart of water; leave the solution on for five minutes and then rinse the containers with clean water.

Use a sterile planting mix. Once your containers are thoroughly clean, fill them with a planting medium. Because the young sprouts are subject to damping-off — or being killed by disease — an artificial mix is the best choice for starting seeds. These mixes are light, easy to handle, and sterile. Some of them come pre-fertilized, so young plants can continue in them for quite some time.

Water well before seeding. Press the planting medium down firmly into the container and water it thoroughly. Let the excess water drain away before you add the seeds. To plant seeds in a flat or tray, mark rows and then distribute the seeds as evenly as possible along the rows. If you're using a separate container for each kind of seed, sprinkle two or three seeds on the surface.

Label as you go along. You'll save yourself a lot of work by labeling each row or container with the plant name and date as you work. Good labels can be made from the plastic trays that meat and produce are packed in; if you press hard enough, the pencil or marking pen won't fade. You can also use commercial plant labels and marking pens.

Regulate moisture, light, and heat. Unless the seed is very tiny, cover it lightly with sifted sphagnum moss. Mist it gently with water, and cover the container with a sheet of plastic wrap. Pull the wrap flat across the container, so that a "rain" of condensation falls evenly on the seed bed. Watch carefully that the system does not become too wet. If it looks too moist, punch a few more holes in the bottom of the container and lift the plastic up from time to time. Since most seeds germinate best at a temperature that is higher than their growing temperature, place the containers in a warm spot or use a heating pad as recommended above. Check the seed package for the specific temperature that each vegetable needs. Give the seedlings bright but not direct sunlight

until they are growing well. Seeds of different varieties germinate at different times. You can start several different kinds of seed together in one flat, but this is easier if they all germinate at about the same time.

Once the plants germinate, it will not be long before they have used up all the energy stored in their seeds and they will have to start growing on their own. This is an important stage in a plant's life, and what you do in these few critical days can make a big difference in the final product. It's vital that the seedlings do not dry out. Also, once they've gotten started, many will grow better if you decrease the temperature from germinating temperature and give them more light.

THINNING AND TRANSPLANTING

When you're growing seedlings in individual containers, you put two or three seeds in each. If all the seeds grow, you must thin out the extras, leaving the strongest seedling with the container to itself. Don't pull out the extras—you'll disturb the survivor's roots; pinch out the smaller plants at soil level. Seeds grown in flats are more difficult to space evenly, and you may need to transplant the seedlings into individual containers before planting them outdoors. Do this when they've

Transplanting to individual containers gives seedlings room to develop.

developed a couple of "true" leaves. The first leaves that appear are called cotyledons and are used only for food storage; they're slightly fleshy and usually a simple oval in shape. The true leaves appear next and are recognizable as characteristic of the variety. Don't wait before making this first transplanting; the seedlings do better and recover from the shock faster if they're transplanted when small.

Move the seedlings into individual containers or flats that you've prepared and filled as you did for seeding. Gently lift the fattest, healthiest-looking seedlings out of the seedbed. Lift them from underneath with a knife, spatula, or stick, and hold them by their leaves to avoid permanent damage to the stems. Make a hole in the new planting medium deep enough to accept the roots without crowding, and set the seedling's roots into the hole. Press the soil gently around the roots. Water newly planted seedlings carefully to get rid of air pockets and to ensure that the roots will not dry out; then label them.

Caring for the seedlings

At this state of their development young seedlings have very definite requirements. They need temperatures that are a little on the cool side. For most vegetables a nighttime low of 55°F and a daytime high of 70°F is about right—if it's cooler, disease problems may show up; if it's warmer, the plants will get tall and spindly. It's also important that the seedlings get plenty of light—at least six hours of bright light a day. If your indoor space can't provide enough natural light for your vegetable seedlings, use artificial light as recommended earlier. The best kind are plant growth lights; they emit high levels of blue light, which encourages good stocky vegetative growth. The lights should be close to the leaves of the plants—about six to eight inches is ideal. Keep the lights on for about 12 hours a day; an automatic timer is handy if you're not going to be around.

Preparing your transplants for the garden

Clearly you cannot take these pampered young seedlings straight from their protected indoor setting into the cold, cruel garden. They'd literally die of shock. You have to prepare them for the change in environment, a process known in horticultural terms as hardening-off. You can do this by taking the plants outside during the day and bringing them back in at night for at least two weeks—keep them in, though, if there's likely to be a frost. You can also put them outside in a protected place—a cold frame or a large box—and cover them with a rug or blanket at night. This treatment will ready them for their final place in the garden.

BUYING TRANSPLANTS FOR YOUR GARDEN

A lot of people find that buying transplants from a reputable nursery or garden center is the easiest way to start their vegetable garden, providing high-quality transplants and few problems. Growing your own transplants from seed is a challenge to your growing skills; it requires a lot of time and planning, and it can be messy. It's more expensive to buy transplants than to grow your own, and you have fewer varieties to choose from. But buying transplants is a lot less work, and if you buy wisely you can get high-quality plants.

Choose the vegetables you buy as transplants on the same principles that you'd use if you were going to grow your own from seed at home; base your decision on the length of your growing season and the flexibility of the plant variety. Plants that adjust without much difficulty to transplanting are broccoli, Brussels sprouts, cabbage, cauliflower, chard, lettuce, and tomatoes. Celery, eggplant, onions, and peppers are slightly less tolerant and require more careful handling. Plants that do not transplant easily are beans, corn, cucumbers, okra, peas, summer and winter squash, and watermelons. Don't buy these vegetables as transplants unless your growing season is too short to let you grow from seed. If you do buy them as transplants, make sure they're in individual containers that can be planted with them.

Choosing healthy transplants

Always buy your transplants from a reputable source—a good nursery or garden center, or through the mail from an established supplier. The supermarket is not the place to look for vegetable plants. If you buy from an established source you know that the plants have been grown with care, and you know who to go to with questions or problems.

If you're buying from a mail order seed company, the company will usually ship your plants at the right time for planting. If you're buying from a garden center or nursery, buy the transplants just before you plan to set them in the garden, and take time to choose healthy young plants that are free of pests or diseases. Before you go to the nursery or garden center, make a written list of disease-resistant varieties, and stick to it. Check plants carefully before you buy, remembering that they're fragile and not made for manhandling. Check stems and leaves for any signs of pest or disease problems. Just before

Boards can protect young plants from hot sun.

Break off the lip of a peat pot before transplanting.

you buy them, slip a seedling out of its container to make sure that the roots are white and healthy. And don't forget to find out if they've already been hardened-off.

If you buy your transplants and find you can't put them into your garden right away, leave them outside in a sunny area. If they're tender varieties, bring them inside at night before the temperature drops. Remember, too, that your transplants are in very small containers and will use up the available supply of moisture quickly. Check them often and water them as necessary.

MOVING YOUR TRANSPLANTS OUTDOORS

When you move your own transplants or bought plants into the vegetable garden depends on the variety and your average date of last frost. Refer to the chart at the end of this chapter to find out when you can transplant each type of vegetable. Arrange them on the prepared soil bed so that you can judge the correct spacing. The spacing chart at the end of this chapter gives you detailed information on how much space each variety needs. If the vegetable will need a support later — stakes for tomatoes, for instance, or trellises for beans — set the support at the time of planting. If you wait to stake or set up a support you risk damaging the plant's developing root system.

Dig a hole under each plant as you're ready to set it in the ground, then slip each plant gently out of its container—unless the seedling is in a plantable pot, in which case you plant the whole thing. If you're planting seedlings in peat pots, break off any part of the lip of the pot that might stick up out of the garden soil. If you leave the lip above the soil level it will act like a wick to dry out the soil inside the container, and this could kill the young plant. If the plant is in a clay or plastic container and doesn't pop out easily, slide a knife carefully around the inside of the container. Remember that bruising the stem can cause permanent damage to the young plant. If you have to handle the plant, hold it by the leaves, not the stem. Set each transplant in the soil, and tamp the soil around it firmly with your hands.

Don't plant transplants too deep; set them at the same depth they were in the container. If they are tall and leggy, make a small trench and set the plant at an angle so that some of the stem is also under the soil and the remainder stands straight — the illustration on the next page shows how. This will mean that only as much stem as the plant can support comfortably is left above the ground so that the plant won't get top heavy as it develops.

When you've planted each seedling and firmed the soil with your hands, give it a good send-off with an application of a starter fertilizer. Starter fertilizers are high in phosphorus (the middle number on the

Long-stemmed tomato seedlings can be planted deeper or on a slant so that they won't grow top heavy.

fertilizer package), which stimulates root growth; if the roots are growing strongly, the rest of the plant will also grow sturdy and healthy. An ideal fertilizer is a 5-52-10 product—52 percent phosphorus in relation to other nutrients. Buy one that matches this formula as closely as possible. Mix the fertilizer with water according to the package directions, and carefully

water each transplanted seedling with this solution. Then relax—for the time being, you've done your best for your young plants. Refer to the following section, in which direct-seeding is discussed, for information on how to protect the plants from unforeseen threats like extreme temperatures, pests, and the like. Whether vegetables are grown

Transplanting your seedlings: Set the seedling in a hole large enough to accept the roots without crowding; fill in and firm the soil; and water with a starter fertilizer solution.

from seed or transplants, they require the same care once they're in the garden. Follow the protective procedures indicated to keep your plants healthy until harvesttime.

PLANTING FROM SEEDS IN THE GARDEN

Direct-seeding straight into the garden is the easiest and least expensive way to grow vegetables. But you may not have the sort of climate that will let you direct-seed some vegetables; the seedlings may take longer to grow, making them a lot more susceptible to weather conditions than transplants grown indoors.

The vegetables to grow from seed are those that will mature within the span of your growing season and those that don't like to be transplanted. If your growing season will accommodate them, all these vegetables do well grown from seed in your garden: beans, beets, carrots, collards, corn, cucumbers, dandelions, kale, kohlrabi, lettuce, mustard, okra, peas, peanuts, pumpkins, rutabagas, soybeans, spinach, squash, turnips, and watermelons.

Preparing the soil for direct-seeding

Soil preparation is the key to successful planting. The first step is to dig up and turn over the soil to a depth of eight to 12 inches—hard work, but a good way to spend a crisp, early spring day. It's important that the soil is neither too wet nor too dry when you dig. Soil that's too wet will compact or form into large clumps that will be so hard when they dry out that nothing short of a sledgehammer will break them. If the soil is too dry, the topsoil will just blow away. Before you get into a good day's digging, pick up a handful of soil and squeeze it; if it forms into a ball that will hold together, yet crumbles easily, the soil is ready to work.

Adding organic matter. Organic matter enriches the soil and improves its ability to control moisture, so add organic matter in the spring to benefit the new season's crop. If you planted a green manure or cover crop in the fall to protect the topsoil, dig it all back into the soil now as organic matter. Do the same if you laid mulch over the soil instead of planting a cover crop; dig the mulch in as you turn the soil. You can also dig in compost that has been simmering nicely all winter.

Fertilizing. You should fertilize your vegetable garden twice a year. As part of your spring soil preparation, dig in a complete, well-balanced fertilizer (10-10-10 or a similar formulation) at the rate of one pound per 100 square feet or 10

pounds per 1,000 square feet. Work the fertilizer evenly into the soil. This application will keep your plants supplied with nutrients until about halfway through the growing season. Then you'll apply the same fertilizer at the same rate, but instead of spreading it over the whole area you'll side-dress by distributing the fertilizer in trenches between the rows of plants. (Some herbs need little or no fertilizing; fruit trees and bushes also have different fertilizer requirements. Specific information is given in the appropriate sections.)

Removing obstacles. When you're preparing the soil, remove all stones, rocks, and lumps, and all the assorted debris that has accumulated over the winter. This is especially important if you're planting root crops, because they'll fork and split if they have to contend with large obstacles; but all seeds do better in well-worked soil. Just before planting, rake the seedbeds smooth and level off the surface by drawing the back of your rake across the soil.

Spacing and sowing the seeds

Sowing seeds sounds like a straightforward procedure; but like most of your other gardening activities, there's a procedure to follow to ensure success. One of the easiest mistakes to make is to plant the seeds too deep—or to assume that all seeds are planted at the same depth.

How deep you plant seeds depends on their size; they need only enough soil to cover them and supply moisture for germination, and seeds that are buried too deep may not be able to struggle through the soil surface. The planting guide at the end of this chapter tells you exactly how deep to plant seeds of each vegetable variety. The rule of thumb is that seeds should be covered up to twice their diameter at their largest point. That means if a seed is half an inch in diameter, plant it an inch deep; if the seeds are so small you can hardly see them, just press them

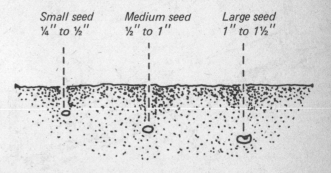

Small seed   *Medium seed*   *Large seed*
¼" to ½"   ½" to 1"   1" to 1½"

Don't bury the seeds; judge the planting depth by the size of the seed.

into the surface of the soil. After you've set seeds at the correct depth, firm the soil by tamping it with your hands or (gently) with your foot. This prevents the soil from drying out too fast; it also helps keep rain from washing away both the soil and the seeds.

Spacing seeds is critical, because if plants are forced to grow too close together they may produce a poor yield or no yield at all. If the seeds are large enough to handle, like beans and peas, it's fairly easy to space them correctly. With tiny seeds or seeds that come in clusters, such as chard, beet, and spinach, spacing can be tricky. Take time over it, however, because if you plant in a hurry now you'll spend tedious hours later on, crawling around on your hands and knees to thin out overcrowded plants. The planting guide at the end of the chapter details how much space each plant needs for best growth.

Choosing a planting pattern

There are three basic patterns you can use in laying out your vegetable garden: single file (rows), groups or bands (wide row plantings), or depressed circles or inverted hills. You can use one, two, or all three of these arrangements at one time for seeds or transplants. Your layout will depend on how much space you've got, which vegetables you're planting, and your own preferences.

Single row planting. This is the most commonly used arrangement. It's the least economical of the three in terms of space, but it's the easiest to maintain because you can cultivate comfortably between those tidy straight rows. Use a planting guide to make sure that your straight rows really will be straight. To make a planting guide, tie a heavy string tightly between two stakes placed at either end of your row. Then take a stick, or the handle of your rake or hoe, and draw a line in the soil under the string. If the rows are very long, stake the line at intervals along its length to keep it straight. For short rows you don't even need a planting guide. Simply make a depression in the soil with the handle of your rake or hoe, and plant your seeds in this depression.

Wide row planting. This type of planting, as the name implies, uses wide rows with two or three plants across instead of just one. The wide rows can be as long as you like, but take care not to make them so wide that they're unmanageable—you must be able to reach the center of the row comfortably from either side. A good width is 24 to 36 inches. Wide row planting is a space-efficient arrangement for most small-seeded vegetables.

To plant in wide rows, mark off the dimensions of the row, place a stake at each corner, and tie a heavy string around all four stakes. If the row is long, stake

Squash planted in an inverted hill are thinned to the three strongest seedlings.

For direct seeding, mark rows with the handle of your rake; or use a planting guide to keep the rows straight.

the string at intervals as you would for a single row. Then remove a layer of soil to the depth at which you want to plant the seeds. Sprinkle the seeds evenly over the wide row, spacing them as accurately as possible so that you won't have to do a lot of thinning later. Cover the seeds with the soil you removed earlier, and firm the soil. One point to remember with wide row plantings: The outer areas of the row will dry out more quickly than the middle, so the plants on the outside will need more watering.

Planting in inverted hills. An inverted hill is a shallow depression made by removing an inch of soil from a circle about a foot across and using the soil you've removed to form a rim round the circle. Plant cucumbers, melons, squash, and other vining plants in inverted hills; their roots stay in one place for easy cultivation and watering, but the vines have plenty of room to spread beyond the circle.

The inverted hill is a new and improved version of the old-fashioned hill or mound system of planting vining crops. The hill or mound system presented some problems, because the soil tended to dry out

Remove both ends of a two-pound coffee can to create a cold weather protector.

quickly, and a hard rain could wash away the mounded soil and expose the root systems of the plants. The inverted hill, on the other hand, catches and holds extra moisture, and during a heavy rain the outer rim of soil, instead of being washed away, falls in toward the plants and provides extra anchorage for shallow-rooted vegetables.

To plant an inverted hill, plant five or six seeds at the correct depth under the surface of the soil inside the circle. When the seedlings have developed two or three true leaves, thin them out, leaving the two or three strongest plants in place in each hill. Cut the weaker plants off at the soil surface—if you pull them out you may disturb the tender root systems of the remaining seedlings.

Caring for the seedlings

Unforeseen circumstances—like uncooperative weather—can frustrate even the most carefully calculated planning and planting programs, so take as few chances as possible. Keep a close and cautious eye on your young seedlings and do everything you

can to help them through the tough times.

Protect the young plants. Extreme weather conditions pose a threat to tender young plants. If hot sun threatens to dry the topsoil where the roots are developing, shade the plants with a board, a basket, or a layer of burlap. Provide this shade also on a bright, cloudless day—even if the temperature is not high—or on a windy day; wind can dry out the soil quickly. The plants need nighttime protection if there's any risk of frost; cover them with a light mulch of straw or hay, or with a double layer of burlap. Support burlap over stakes so that the weight won't crush the plants, and anchor it on either side of the rows by burying or staking the edges. If birds, rodents, or other pests are showing too much interest in your crop, keep them off with nets, fences, screens stapled to frames, or a scarecrow—whatever is appropriate to the kind of pest that's causing the trouble.

Frustrate the troublemakers. Some garden pests are particularly troublesome to transplants. Cutworms spend the day curled up just under the soil surface and come out at night to feed on the tender stems of the young plants. They often cut the stems off at the soil surface, killing the plant. Guard against cutworms by putting a collar around each seedling when it's transplanted. The collar should go down into the soil at least an inch, and should stand away from the plant 1½ to three inches all round. You can cut a circle of thin cardboard as a collar or use a Styrofoam cup with the bottom cut out.

Cucumber beetles also pose a threat to young plants. They don't do much direct damage, but they spread cucumber bacterial wilt, which can kill

Bottomless plastic jugs make good insulators against cold night temperatures.

Water generously; deep watering encourages healthy root growth in young plants.

vining crops like cucumbers, melons, squash, and watermelons. Keep an eye out for these pests and hand-pick or wash them off the plants quickly, or spray the plants with carbaryl before they can spread disease. Detailed information on pest control and disease prevention is given in ''Keeping Your Garden Healthy.''

Don't let your seedlings die of thirst. Adequate watering is essential to young plants in their early stages of growth. Be careful when you water your seedlings, because a forceful blast of water can damage them permanently or even wash them right out of the ground, but be generous. Water to a depth of six to eight inches to encourage deep rooting and stronger growth. If your area is likely to have heavy rains when you're waiting for the seeds to germinate, apply a very light mulch over the seedbed — this will also help to retain the moisture that's in the soil. Don't overdo the mulch or put it on so thickly that the germinating seeds can't push through it.

Give plants room to grow. Thinning is another essential task in the early stages of the seedlings' development. Refer to the planting guide at the end of this chapter for specific instructions on spacing each variety. Thin when the plants are young — when they have formed two true leaves. If you wait too long they may already have suffered from being overcrowded. Thinning is a job that a lot of gardeners do with some reluctance. It seems wasteful to throw out all the extra little seedlings, but if you don't do it you're condemning all your plants to overcrowding and a miserable existence fighting for food, light, and water. You're also defeating your own purpose, because overcrowded plants will give you a poor crop.

STARTING NEW PLANTS FROM PARTS

Seeds and transplants are not the only forms from which to raise new plants; they're the forms you'll use most often, but some vegetables are started from other plant parts — suckers, tubers, slips, crowns, sets, cloves, divisions, or cuttings. In some cases plants can be grown either from seed or from plant parts. Onions, for instance, take a very long time to germinate from seed, so it usually makes more sense to grow them from sets. Other plants grow best from plant parts. The following are ways to start vegetables from plant parts:

Suckers. Suckers, or offshoots, are plants that grow or shoot up from the root system of a mature plant. These suckers are dug up and divided from the mother plant, then transplanted to mature into new plants. Globe artichokes are usually the only vegetables grown from suckers.

Divisions. Divisions, like suckers, occur naturally in the form of small rooted plants or bulbs that grow from the mother plant, and get their name from the way you separate — or divide — them off to grow as individual plants. You can dig up the new growth as it appears and replant it. Or, as with bulbs, you can dig up the mother plant, separate the small new bulbs, and replant each unit. Horseradish and rhubarb are grown from divisions. You can divide plants in spring or in fall; fall is preferable, because the cool, moist weather gives the new plants better conditions in which to become established.

Cuttings. Cuttings are divisions that don't occur naturally. You obtain them by cutting a piece of stem or side-branch from the plant at a node — a lumpy area on the stem. The cutting is then placed in the soil and forms its own roots. You can also put the cutting in water until roots form.

Slips. Slips are young, tender, rooted cuttings or sprouts grown from roots. Sweet potatoes are the only vegetables commonly grown from slips.

Tubers. These are specialized swollen underground stems, capable of producing roots, stems, and leaves. Irish potatoes and Jerusalem artichokes are usually grown from tubers. When the tubers are cut up for planting, as in the case of Irish potatoes, they are called seed pieces.

Crowns. These are compressed stems near the soil surface that are capable of producing leaves and roots. Crowns are often planted with the roots attached, in which case they're more accurately referred to as roots. Crowns can be divided when the plants are dormant. Asparagus is usually grown from crowns.

Sets. Sets are one-year-old onion seedlings that were pulled when the bulbs were young. The bulbs are then air dried, stored for the winter, and planted the next spring. Onions are the only vegetables grown from sets.

Cloves. These are the segmented parts of a bulb; they're also called bulblets. Garlic is the only vegetable commonly grown from cloves. Each garlic bulb is made up of a dozen or more cloves, and you plant each clove separately. Don't divide the bulb until you're ready to plant; separating the cloves too early may result in lower yields.

WHEN TO PLANT YOUR VEGETABLES IN SPRING

Very hardy vegetables: *Plant 4 to 6 weeks before the average date of last frost.*	**Hardy vegetables:** *Plant 2 to 3 weeks before the average date of last frost.*	**Tender vegetables:** *Plant on the average date of last frost.*	**Very tender vegetables:** *Plant 2 to 3 weeks after the average date of last frost.*
Asparagus	Beet	Artichoke, globe	Bean, lima
Broccoli	Cardoon	Bean, broad	Chayote
Brussels sprouts	Carrot	Bean, dry	Chick pea
Cabbage	Celeriac	Bean, mung	Cucumber
Cauliflower	Celery	Bean, snap	Eggplant
Chinese cabbage	Chard	Corn	Muskmelon
Collards	Chicory	Cress	Okra
Horseradish	Dandelion	Mustard	Pea, black-eyed
Kale	Endive	Sorrel	Peanut
Kohlrabi	Jerusalem artichoke	Soybean	Pepper, hot
Leek	Lentil	Tomato	Pepper, sweet
Lettuce	Parsnip	**Herbs:**	Pumpkin
Onion	Potato, Irish	Basil	Squash, summer
Pea	Radish	Caraway	Squash, winter
Rhubarb	Salsify	Chervil	Sweet potato
Rhutabaga	Spinach, New Zealand	Coriander	Watermelon
Shallot	Turnip	Dill	
Sorrel	**Herbs:**	Sage	
Spinach	Anise	Sesame	
Herbs:	Borage		
Chives	Fennel		
Garlic	Marjoram		
Spearmint	Oregano		
Peppermint	Parsley		
Tarragon	Rosemary		
Thyme	Savory		

Planting guide: spacing

Vegetable	Inches between plants	Inches between rows	Depth of seed (inches)
Artichoke, globe	36-48	48-60	
Asparagus	12-18	36-48	1-1½
Beans, broad	8-10	36-48	1-2
Beans, dry	4-6	18-24	1-1½
Beans, lima			
bush	2-3	18-24	1-1½
pole	4-6	30-36	1-1½
Beans, mung	18-20	18-24	½
Beans, snap or green			
bush	2-3	18-24	1-1½
pole	4-6	30-36	1-1½
Beets	2-3	12-18	1
Broccoli	3	24-36	½
Brussels sprouts	24	24-36	½
Cabbage	18-24	24-36	½
Cardoon	18-24	36-48	½
Carrot	2-4	12-24	¼
Cauliflower	18-24	24-36	½
Celeriac	6-8	24-30	¼
Celery	8-10	24-30	¼
Chard	9-12	18-24	1
Chayote	24-30	60	
Chick pea	6-8	12-18	½
Chickory	12-18	24-36	1
Chinese cabbage	8-12	18-30	½
Collards	12	18-24	½
Corn	2-4	12-18	1-1½
Cress	1-2	18-24	¼
Cucumber *In inverted hills 36 inches apart**	12	18-72	½
Dandelion	6-8	12-18	¼
Eggplant	18-24	24-36	¼
Endive	9-12	18-24	⅛
Fennel	12-14	24-36	¼
Horseradish	24	18-24	¼
Jerusalem artichoke	12-18	24-36	
Kale	8-12	18-24	½
Kohlrabi	5-6	18-24	¼
Leek	6-9	12-18	⅛
Lentils	1-2	18-24	½

Note: Plants in inverted hills should be thinned to three plants in each hill

Planting guide: spacing (cont.)

Vegetable	Inches between plants	Inches between rows	Depth of seed (inches)
Lettuce	6-12	12-18	⅛
Muskmelon *In inverted hills 36 inches apart**	18-24	60-96	1
Mustard	6-12	12-24	½
Okra	12-18	24-36	½-1
Onion sets seeds	2-3 1-2	12-18 12-18	1-2 ¼
Parsnip	2-4	18-24	½
Pea, black-eyed	8-12	12-18	½
Pea, shelling	1-2	18-24	2
Peanut	6-8	12-18	1
Pepper	18-24	24-36	½
Potato, Irish	12-18	24-36	4
Pumpkin *In inverted hills 72 inches apart**	24-48	60-120	1
Radish	1-6	12-18	½
Rhubarb	30-36	36-48	
Rutabaga	6-8	18-24	½
Salsify	2-4	18-24	½
Shallot	6-8	12-18	¼
Sorrel	12-18	18-24	½
Soybean	1½-2	24-30	½-1
Spinach	2-4	12-24	½
Spinach, New Zealand	12	24-36	½
Squash, summer *In inverted hills 48 inches apart**	24-36	18-48	1
Squash, winter *In inverted hills 72 inches apart**	24-48	60-120	1
Sweet potato	12-18	36-48	3-5
Tomato	18-36	24-48	½
Turnip greens roots	2-3 3-4	12-24 12-24	½ ½
Watermelon *In inverted hills 72 inches apart*	24-72	60-120	1

*Note: Plants in inverted hills should be thinned to three plants in each hill

Points to Remember When You Plant Your Garden

1. When growing vegetables and herbs, you must first decide whether to grow from seeds or transplants. Most herbs are easy to plant from seeds or root divisions, but vegetables are a bit trickier. Cool-weather vegetables and many large-seeded vegetables should be planted from seed directly in the garden. Less hardy plants should be started indoors or in a protected environment and transplanted at the appropriate time. Some should be seeded in plantable containers because they might suffer transplant shock if moved. Corn, okra, beans, cucumbers, squashes, and watermelons are susceptible to transplant shock and should be seeded in plantable containers.

2. When growing transplants from seed it's important to use a sterilized planting medium to avoid damping-off, a disease to which very young seedlings are susceptible. Use a seed-starter medium from a good supplier, rather than regular potting soil which is too rich for seedlings.

3. Cleanliness, temperature, moisture, and light all contribute to the healthy development of seedlings grown at home. Be sure that you follow the directions for each type of plant. Also, follow the directions for planting given in the preceding pages.

4. If you plant seeds in flats rather than in individual plantable containers, you will need to thin the seedlings and transfer the strongest to individual containers before transplanting them into the garden. Thinning may seem like a waste, but failure to thin the seedlings will lead to overcrowding and poor development. Do not skip this step. The same applies to direct-seeded plants in the garden.

5. Before young seedlings are transplanted into the garden they must be hardened-off—that is, taken outside during the day and brought in again at night for at least two weeks before permanent planting. This helps them adjust gradually to outdoor life. If there's danger of frost, however, keep them inside.

6. When transplanting seedlings in peat pots, break off the lip of the pot before planting so that it does not protrude above the soil. The peat acts as a wick and will dry out the soil in the container, and this may kill the young plant.

7. When transplanting seedlings that will eventually grow into plants that must be supported with stakes, poles, or trellises, set the supports at the time of planting. If you set them later, you risk damaging the plant's developing root system.

8. Seedlings are delicate and must be protected from weather extremes. If the weather gets colder than expected, cover the plants with a protective device such as a gallon milk container with the bottom cut out, a "hat" made of newspaper, or a coffee can with both ends removed. If the weather gets too hot, protect plants with a board or some other protector angled to keep strong sunlight off the young plants, or cover them with a basket or burlap.

9. When seeding directly into the garden, be sure to space the seeds correctly to avoid having to thin heavily (and perhaps disturb the delicate roots of the remaining seedlings). Also, plant the seeds at the specified depth. Seeds that are planted too deep will not be able to struggle through the soil surface.

10. Some garden pests are particularly bothersome to transplants. Watch for danger signs and frustrate the troublemakers promptly according to the directions given in this book.

Caring for Your Garden

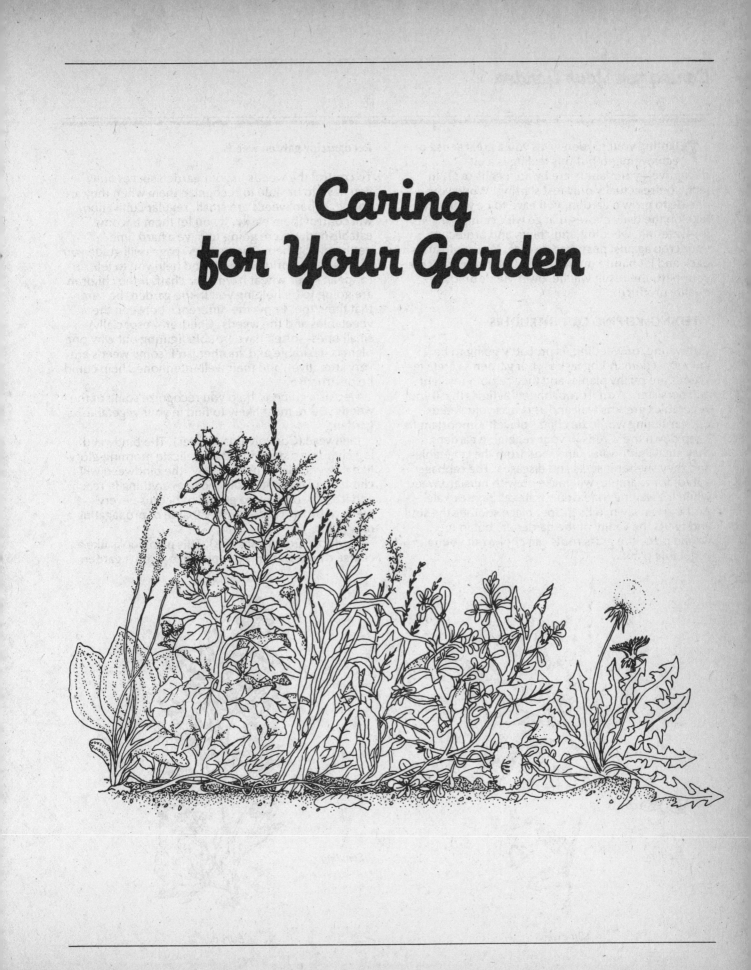

Caring for Your Garden

Planting your garden gives you a great sense of achievement, but this feeling is a bit deceptive—your labors are by no means over. In fact, you're actually only just starting. When you decide to grow a garden, you have to be willing to take on the daily chores that go with caring for it—watering, weeding, mulching, and protecting your crop against pests and disease. You could just sit back and let nature do the work. But if you don't do your part, the result will be lower yields or lower-quality produce.

WEEDING: KEEPING OUT INTRUDERS

Cultivating, or weeding, is probably going to be your most demanding task as your garden's caretaker. Weeds are pushy plants, and they're both resilient and persistent. You'll probably feel at times that if your vegetables grew as well and as fast as your weeds do, gardening would be child's play. It's important to keep down the weeds in your vegetable garden; they steal light, water, and food from the vegetables, and they shelter insects and diseases. The cabbage aphid, for example, will make do with mustard weed while it's waiting to feast on your cabbage or kale. And a green lawn in its proper place soothes the soul and feeds the vanity of the gardener; but in the wrong place the grass roots can choke out young vegetable plants.

Recognizing garden weeds

To control the weeds in your garden successfully, you have to be able to recognize them when they are young. When weeds are small, regular cultivation will control them easily. If you let them become established, you're going to have a hard time getting rid of them. The next few pages will guide you through the world of weeds and help you to tell, so to speak, your wheat from your chaff. If the children are going to be helping you in the garden, be sure that they, too, know the difference between the vegetables and the weeds. Children—especially small ones—often have trouble figuring out why one plant is desirable and another isn't (some weeds are very attractive), and their well-intentioned help could be destructive.

Here is a guide to help you recognize some of the weeds you're most likely to find in your vegetable garden:

Bindweed (Convolvulus species). The bindweed is a climbing plant with small delicate morning-glory-like flowers. Given its own way, the bindweed will climb up plants and soon choke everything in reach, and it's very difficult to get rid of because every piece of broken root seems capable of propagating a new plant.

Burdock (Arctium species). This plant looks like a coarse rhubarb. Many people have given it garden

Seedling

Bindweed

Seedling

Burdock

room only to find, late in the summer, that their only harvest will be burrs.

Canada thistle (Cirsium arvense). This is a perennial that spreads on horizontal roots. The leaves are usually crinkled, edged with spines or thorns. The flowers are spiny balls topped with purple tufts. Wear a good pair of gloves, and pull out the whole plant; try to remove as much of the root as possible.

Chickweed (Stellaria media). The chickweed is a lacy plant that spreads out over the ground like a doily. It has tiny daisylike flowers, but despite its delicate appearance it should be destroyed when quite young, because it will spread all over the place if you let it go to seed.

Dandelion (Taraxacum officinale). The dandelion is best known to nongardeners for its bright yellow flowers and its seedhead of light, feathery seeds. Gardeners know it for its long, persistent taproot. Recognize the dandelion by its rosette of jagged leaves, and remove it as soon as possible—preferably when the soil is moist. If you try to pull out the root when the soil is dry and hard you'll probably break it, leaving part of the root in the ground to grow right back into another healthy dandelion plant. The dandelion can be grown as a legitimate vegetable, but the weed in your garden won't double for its cultivated cousin.

Ground ivy or creeping charlie (Colechoma hederacea). This is a vining plant with small funnel-shaped flowers that have a purplish color. It's very adventurous and crawls along the ground on stems that may extend to a length of five feet. The leaves are almost round and grow in clumps at each node along the square stem. Ground ivy may be one of the most persistent weeds you'll have to deal with in your garden. It will choose the shadiest side of your garden first, but once it becomes established it will spread anywhere. Pull up the entire plant; each node can regenerate a whole new plant.

Lamb's-quarters or goosefoot (Chenopodium album). You can recognize lamb's-quarters by its color—greyish-green with occasional red speckles. It's an upright plant that can grow four feet tall.

Mustard (Brassica nigra). The black mustard grown for its seeds is a good example of a useful plant that escaped from a proper garden and went wild. In some parts of California mustard plants 12 feet tall have taken over whole fields and become real pests.

Pigweed (Amaranthus retroflexus). Pigweed is known as redroot, wild beet, or rough green amaranth. It is a rough plant that can grow to more than six feet in good soil.

Plantain (Plantago major and Plantago lanceolata). There are two plantains, Ruggle's plantain and buckhorn (also called English plantain or white man's footsteps). Both plants grow in rosettes and are rather similar to the plantain lily (Hosta). They have

Seedling

Chickweed

Canada thistle

Seedling

Dandelion

Ground ivy

thick clumps of roots that make them hard to pull out, except when the soil is very moist and soft.

Poison ivy (Rhus radicans). The poison ivy plant may be either a small shrub or a vine that can crawl up

anything that will support it. The large, shiny leaves (two to four inches long) are grouped in threes and pointed at the tip. Every part of this plant contains a poisonous material that can cause blisters on your

Seedling

Lamb's-quarters

Seedling

Mustard

Seedling

Pigweed

Buckhorn plantain

Seedling

Seedling

Common plantain

skin. To avoid contact with the skin, control this weed by using a herbicide.

Purslane (Portulaca oleracea). Purslane, which is also called pusley or pigweed, grows flat on the

ground. It has thick leaves and thick juicy stems, and it adores rich, freshly worked soil.

Ragweed. There are two types of ragweed: common ragweed (Ambrosia artemisiifolia) and giant

Poison ivy

Seedling

Purslane

Ragweed

Smartweed

Seedling

ragweed (Ambrosia trifida). Common ragweed is an annual that seeds itself and comes back every year. The leaves are smooth and deeply lobed. It's a much smaller plant than the giant ragweed and will grow only one to four feet tall. Pull up the entire plant before the seeds mature and assure you a return visit next year. Giant ragweed is a perennial, and as its name implies, it gets very large—it will tower to 12

Sour grass

Seedling

Seedling

Violet

to 18 feet in good soil. The leaves are large and slightly hairy, with three or occasionally five lobes. Male flowers are long spikes at the tips of the branches. As with its smaller cousin, pull up the entire plant when it is young before the seeds mature.

Smartweed (Polygonum species). Smartweed is a tough-rooted plant, with smooth stems, swollen joints, and long narrow leaves. Pull up the smartweeds and toss them on the compost pile.

Sour grass (Oxalis stricta). Sour grass is yellow wood sorrel, a delicate plant with shamrocklike three-part leaves and delicate yellow flowers. Its seed capsules are capable of shooting seeds yards away when they ripen. It also has an underground root system that can reproduce without any seeds at all.

Violet (Viola species). It's hard to look on the innocent violet as a weed, but that's what it is. This small flowering plant has deep green heart-shaped leaves and a small, succulent root system that can be easily removed.

Keeping the weeds out of your garden

Once you've identified the weeds in your vegetable garden, the best way to control them is to chop them off at soil level with a sharp hoe or knife. If a weed is close to your vegetables, don't try to dig out the whole root system of the weed; in the process you may also damage the root systems of neighboring vegetables. Persistent weeds like dandelions may have to be cut down several times, but eventually the weed will die.

Herbicides, or chemical weed-killers, can be used in some instances. Mulches, which are organic or inorganic materials laid over the soil around your plants, can also control weeds to some extent. There are advantages and disadvantages to both methods.

Herbicides need careful handling

Herbicides can be useful in helping to control weeds under certain conditions, but these conditions are not usually encountered in the small home garden. And herbicides require such careful handling that the home gardener may be well advised not to use them more than absolutely necessary.

Herbicides can be either nonselective or selective. The nonselective types kill any plant with which they come in contact. Selective herbicides may kill only broad-leaved plants or only grass plants. Both types come in forms to kill preemergent germinating seeds without harming plants that are already growing above the ground, or vice versa. Those that act below the soil surface to kill preemergent seeds usually come in granule

When you're cultivating, remove weeds carefully to avoid damaging the roots of the vegetable plants.

form. The granules are shaken on to the ground from the container. Contact herbicides that kill growing plants are usually bought in liquid form and diluted for use in a hand-sprayer or a sprayer that attaches to your hose. Whichever type you use, it's important to follow the manufacturer's instructions to the letter. It's also important to remember that herbicides may have residual effects that vary from product to product. The effect of some may last for weeks; the effect of others may last for years.

You can, if you wish, use a nonselective herbicide in the spring to clear an area for planting. If you do, carefully check that the residual effects will be gone well before your planting date—the information on the label will tell you this. If you misjudge the timing, and the effects of the herbicide persist beyond your planting date, you'll lose your whole crop for the season.

Here are some facts about herbicides you should be aware of:

- Herbicides do not kill all weeds.
- Herbicides can kill vegetables.
- Herbicides that are safe to use in a certain area can drift quite a distance and damage sensitive plants, such as tomatoes and peppers.
- No plant is entirely resistant to herbicides, so if you're using one it's important to follow the instructions exactly as they appear on the label.

If you decide to use a herbicide in your garden, follow these rules:

- If you have a problem that cannot be solved by cultivating and you want to use a herbicide, contact your local Cooperative Extension Service for a reliable recommendation.
- Read all of the label, every bit of fine print, and follow the instructions to the letter.
- Do not use a herbicide unless it is labeled for a specific crop (read the whole label).
- Be sure that the herbicide will not leave a toxic residue on the parts of the plant that you want to eat.
- Clean spray equipment carefully after each use.
- Mark your herbicide equipment and keep it separate from that used for fertilizers, insecticides, or fungicides. Use herbicide equipment *only* for herbicides.

MULCHES HAVE MANY USES IN YOUR GARDEN

Mulches are either organic or inorganic material placed on the soil around the vegetable plants.

Mulches can perform a number of useful functions. They protect against soil erosion by breaking the force of heavy rains; they help prevent soil compaction; they discourage the growth of weeds; they reduce certain disease problems. Organic mulches improve the soil texture. Mulches are also insulators, making it possible to keep the soil warmer during cool weather and cooler during warm weather.

Mulches do not eliminate weeds. They can, however, help control them if the area has been cleared of weeds to begin with. If the mulch is thick enough, the weeds that are already growing won't be able to push through, and the darkness will frustrate the germination of others. Persistent weeds can push their way through most mulch, but if they're cut off at the soil level a few times they'll die. Sometimes mulches can improve the appearance of the vegetable garden by giving it a neater, more finished look. Some mulches give the area a professional look that only a true vegetable gardener can appreciate.

Whether you use an organic or an inorganic mulch, take care not to put it down before the soil has warmed up in the spring—the mulch will prevent the soil from warming and slow down root development. In the average garden in a cool-season climate mulch should be applied about five weeks after the average date of last frost.

Organic mulches improve soil quality

Organic mulches are organic materials that, when laid on the soil, decompose to feed the microorganisms and improve the quality of the soil. If you see that the mulch you've put down is decomposing quickly, add nitrogen to make up for nitrogen used by the bacteria. Some mulches can carry weed seeds; others can harbor undesirable organisms or pests, but both diseases and pests can usually be controlled by keeping the mulch stirred up. When you're cultivating, lift the mulch a little to keep the air circulating.

To use an organic mulch, spread a layer of the material you're using on the surface of the ground around the plants after the soil has warmed up in spring; the plants should be about four inches tall so the mulch doesn't overwhelm them. If you're using a fluffy material with large particles, like bark chips, make the layer about four inches thick. If you're using a denser material like straw or lawn clippings, a two-inch layer will be enough. Be careful not to suffocate the vegetables while you're trying to frustrate the weeds.

The following are organic materials commonly used as mulches:

Buckwheat hulls. These hulls last a long time and have a neutral color, but they're lightweight and can blow away; and sometimes they smell when the weather is hot and wet.

Chunk bark. Redwood and fir barks are available in several sizes. Bark makes good-looking paths and gives the area a neat, finished appearance, but it's too chunky to be the ideal mulch for vegetables. It also tends to float away when watered or rained on.

Compost. Partly decomposed compost makes a great mulch and soil conditioner. It looks a little rough, but other gardeners will know you're giving your garden the very best.

Crushed corncobs. Crushed cobs make an excellent and usually inexpensive mulch. The cobs need additional nitrogen, unless they are partially decomposed. Sometimes corn kernels are mixed in with the crushed corncobs; this will create extra weeding later on.

Lawn clippings. Do not use clippings from a lawn that has been treated with a herbicide or weed killer—these substances can kill the vegetables you're trying to grow. Let untreated clippings dry before putting them around your garden; fresh grass mats down and smells bad while it's decomposing.

Leaves. Leaves are cheap and usually easy to find, but they blow around and are hard to keep in place. They will stay where you want them better if they're ground up or partially decomposed. Nitrogen should be added to a leaf mulch. Do not use walnut leaves; they contain iodine, which is a growth retardant.

Manure. Vintage, partially decomposed manure makes an excellent mulch. Manure has a strong bouquet that you may not appreciate, but don't use a manure that has been treated with odor-reducing chemicals; treated manures contain substances, such as boron, which are unhealthy for plants. Never use fresh, unrotted manure, it can kill your plants.

Mushroom compost (leftover, used). Where it's available, used mushroom compost is generally inexpensive. Its rich color blends in well with the colors of your garden.

Peat moss. Peat moss is expensive when large areas have to be covered. It must be kept moist or it will act like a blotter and pull moisture out of the soil and away from the plants. Once it dries, peat tends to shed water rather than letting it soak in, and the fine grades of peat have a tendency to blow away.

Poultry manure. This is potent stuff—poultry manure is about twice as strong as cow manure; proceed with caution. A good, weathered, four-year-old poultry litter can give you mulch, compost, and high-nitrogen fertilizer, all at the same time.

Sawdust. Sawdust is often available for the asking, but it needs added nitrogen to prevent microorganisms from depleting the soil's nitrogen.

Straw. Straw is very messy and hard to apply in a small area, and it's highly flammable—matches or cigarettes can result in short-order cooking. It does, however, look very professional.

Wood chips or shavings. More chips and shavings are available now that they are no longer being burned as a waste product. They decompose slowly and add needed nitrogen. Beware of maple chips, which may carry verticillium wilt into your garden.

Recycle rugs, papers as inorganic mulch

Unlikely though it may seem to the inexperienced gardener, the following materials can be used effectively as inorganic mulches.

Aluminum foil. Foil is expensive if you're dealing with more than a small area, but it does make an effective mulch. It reflects sunlight, keeps the plants clean, and scares birds away from your garden.

Backless indoor-outdoor carpet. Indoor-outdoor carpeting is ideal for the small garden and makes it easy for the fastidious gardener to keep the place neat. Water goes through it easily, and the weeds are kept down.

Newspapers. Spread a thick layer of newspapers around the plants. Keep them in place with rocks or soil. They will decompose slowly and can be turned under as a soil modifier.

Rag rugs. An old rag rug holds water and keeps the soil moist. It won't look as neat as backless carpeting, but it will be just as effective.

Plastic mulches: pros and cons

Both clear and black polyethylene are used by commercial growers as inorganic mulches. Clear plastic is not recommended for small gardens because it encourages weeds; weeds just love the cozy greenhouse effect it creates. Black plastic is sometimes used in small gardens for plants that are grown in a group or hill, such as cucumbers, squash, or pumpkins. Black plastic should not be used for crops that need a cool growing season—cabbage or cauliflower, for instance—unless it's covered with a thick layer of light-reflecting material, such as sawdust.

There are some advantages to growing with a black plastic mulch. Black plastic reduces the loss of soil moisture, raises the soil temperature, and speeds up crop maturity. Weeds are discouraged, because the black plastic cuts out their light supply, so you won't have to cultivate as much; that means less danger of root damage. The plastic also helps keep plants cleaner. And when you're making a new garden in an area where there was a lot of grass—if you've dug up a lawn, for instance—black plastic can keep the grass from coming back .

There are some disadvantages to keep in mind as well, and one of them is that you may need to water more frequently. Because of their greater growth under plastic, the plants lose more water through transpiration, especially in well-drained, sandy soils. However, you will need to water less if you use black plastic on soil that holds water or drains poorly. If you're using a black plastic mulch, keep in mind that plants can wilt and rot if the soil moisture is kept at too high a level and there isn't enough air in the soil.

You can buy black plastic from many garden centers or order it by mail from seed and garden equipment catalogs. It should be at least 1½ mil thick and about three to four feet wide. If you have a piece of wider or thicker black plastic, use it. The wider plastic is harder to handle, and the thicker type is more expensive, but it works well.

Put down black plastic mulch before the plants are set out. Try to pick a calm day; a strong wind will whip the plastic about and make laying it down hard work. Take a hoe and make a three-inch deep trench the length of the row. Lay one edge of the plastic in the trench and cover the edge with soil. Smooth the plastic over the bed and repeat the process on the other side. Be sure the plastic is anchored securely, or the wind will get under it and pull it up.

When you're ready to plant, cut holes about three inches across for the plants or seeds. After planting, anchor the edges of the holes with stones or soil. Water the plants through the holes in the mulch. After a rain, check to see if there are any spots where water is standing. If there are, punch holes through the plastic so the water can run through. After the plants are harvested, the plastic can be swept off, rolled up, and stored for use the next year.

WATER: YOUR GARDEN MUST GET ENOUGH

Some plants are composed of up to 95 percent water. Water is vital for sprouting seeds; plants need water for cell division, cell enlargement, and even for holding themselves up. If the cells don't have enough water in them, they collapse like a three-day-old balloon, and the result is a wilted plant. Water is essential, along with light and carbon dioxide, to produce the sugars that provide the plant with energy for growth. It also dissolves fertilizers and carries nutrients to the different parts of the plant.

Where the water comes from

Ideally, water for plants comes from rain or other precipitation and from underground sources. In reality, you'll often have to do extra watering by hand or through an irrigation system. (If you have too much rain about all you can do is pray). How often

Lay down black plastic mulch before you transplant, and cut holes in the plastic for the plants.

you should water depends on how often it rains, how long your soil retains moisture, and how fast water evaporates in your climate. Soil type is an important factor. Clay soils hold water very well—sometimes too well. Sandy soils are like a sieve, letting the water run right through. Both kinds of soil can be improved with the addition of organic matter. Organic matter gives clay soils lightness and air and gives sandy soils something to hold the water.

Other factors may also affect how often you need to water your garden:

- More water evaporates when the temperature is high than when it's low. Plants can rot if they get too much water in cool weather.
- More water evaporates when the relative humidity is low.
- Plants need more water when the days are bright.
- Wind and air movement will increase the loss of water into the atmosphere.
- A smooth unmulched surface will not retain water as well as one that's well cultivated.
- Water needs vary with the type and maturity of the plant. Some vegetable seeds are tolerant of low soil moisture and will sprout in relatively dry soils. These include Brussels sprouts, cabbage, cauliflower, collards, corn, kale, kohlrabi, muskmelon, peppers, radishes, squash (winter and summer), turnips, and watermelon. On the other hand, beets, celery, and lettuce seeds need very moist soil. Herbs generally do better with less water. (Trees and bushes have their own water requirements, which are detailed in the individual profiles.)
- Sometimes water is not what a wilting plant needs. When plants are growing fast, the leaves sometimes get ahead of the roots' ability to provide them with water. If the day is hot and the plants wilt in the afternoon, don't worry about them; the plants will regain their balance overnight. But if the plants are drooping early in the morning, water them right away.
- Mulches cool the roots and cut down on the amount of water needed, increasing the time that plants can go between watering. When the soil dries out, plants slow their growth—or stop growing altogether. Swift, steady growth is important for the best-tasting fruits and vegetables. Mulches keep the soil evenly moist.

There's a right and a wrong way to water

So much depends on climate and the ability of different types of soil to hold moisture that it's difficult to lay down specific directions for watering your garden. Generally, however, vegetable plants need about an inch of water a week. The best time to water your garden is in the morning. If you water at night when the day is cooling off, the water is likely to stay on the foliage, increasing the danger of disease. Some people believe that you can't water in the morning because water spots on leaves will cause leaf-burn when the sun gets hot; this isn't the case.

However hard it is to judge your garden's exact water needs, there are two hard-and-fast rules about watering that you should follow. First, always soak the soil thoroughly. A light sprinkling can often do more harm than no water at all; it stimulates the roots to come to the surface, and then they're killed by exposure to the sun. Second, never water from above. Overhead watering with a sprinkling can or a hose is easy and seems to do a fine job. But in fact, overhead watering wastes water, makes a mess, and sometimes bounces the water away from the plant so the roots do not get any at all. Furthermore, many diseases are encouraged by wet leaves. So direct water at the soil, but water gently so that the soil is not washed away or the roots exposed.

Watering with a can. Carrying water in a can or a bucket can be exhausting and extremely unsatisfying, especially if the water slops over the top into your shoes. Watering cans are easier to carry but harder to fill than buckets. They are good to use for gently moistening the soil after planting seeds and for settling dust. If you unscrew the watering can's sprinkler head and replace it with an old sock, it will be easier to concentrate the water at the base of the plant where it's needed. The sock will break the force of the water so it won't disturb the soil around the roots.

Watering with a hose. A well-placed faucet and hose can save a lot of energy. If you have a large garden, a Y-connector for the faucet makes it possible to attach two hoses at one time. Hose strategy includes having enough hose to reach all points in the garden and arranging the hose in such a way that it does not decapitate plants when you move it around.

If you have a lot of watering to do, five-eighths-inch hose will carry twice as much water as a half-inch hose. Spreading the water about can be speeded up by using basins to catch the water and by digging furrows or trenches between the plants. A length of gutter with capped ends, placed on the higher side of the garden, can be punctured at intervals to coincide with the trenches. Then when water is slowly added to the gutter it flows down all the trenches at the same time. If you want to change the placement of the holes, the ones you don't need can either be

A sock on the hose breaks the force of the water.

Keep water off the leaves of your plants.

Water gently; a sharp jet can wash away the soil.

soldered up or filled with a metal screw.

Watering with a sprinkler. Lawn sprinklers are gentle, but they waste water by covering the whole area indiscriminately and spraying water into the air where it evaporates and blows about. They also wet the leaves, which can spread disease, and often turn the whole area into a mudhole. Canvas soil-soakers are preferable. They carry water gently to the soil around the roots. A wand and water-breaker, which is a length of rigid pipe that attaches to the end of the hose, can make it much easier to put the water where you want it. This is especially useful when you're watering hanging baskets and patio containers. A water timer that measures the flow of water and shuts off automatically when the right amount has been delivered is an expensive luxury.

A capped gutter directs water into trenches to water several rows at once.

But it's an excellent device for the forgetful and can free you to do other things while the garden is being watered.

Gardening is a most satisfying occupation, because you are constantly rewarded for your efforts. All the work you put into your vegetable garden—cultivating, mulching, watering, watching, and waiting—shows dividends in the shape of healthy plants that flourish visibly under your care as the season progresses. And all the labor pays off in tangible form at harvest time.

But even when you've weathered the whole gardening season and brought your harvest home, you still have a few more tasks to complete in order to put your garden to bed for the winter.

PREPARING YOUR GARDEN FOR THE WINTER

The better the clean-up job you do in fall, the easier it will be to start in on the new growing season in spring. You may be tempted to skip some of these last-minute chores, but they're really worth doing because they can make a big difference to the success of next year's garden. True, they could be put off until spring, but come spring you'll have so much to do in the garden that it'll be a big relief to have some of the work out of the way ahead of time.

- It's a good idea to plant what farmers call a green manure or cover crop in the fall as part of your preparation for the following year. This is a crop that you don't intend to harvest. It's there simply to provide protection for the soil underneath, and when you're preparing for your spring planting you dig the whole crop into the soil. A cover crop will keep your precious topsoil from blowing or washing away, and tilling it into the soil in spring will provide valuable organic matter to enrich the texture of the soil. It's not necessary to plant the whole cover crop at one time to cover the entire garden; you can plant in each area of the garden as you harvest. Some of the best green manure or cover crops are rye, clover, oats, soybeans, and vetch. Scatter the seeds over the area you want to plant—if it's a large area a hand spreader will do the job comfortably.

- As an alternative to planting a cover crop, you can prepare the soil ahead of time. Tilling your soil in the fall can save you a lot of time and help you get an earlier start in the spring, because the soil is often too wet in early spring to let you use a spade or a rototiller. If you do till your soil in the fall, make sure to cover the soil with mulch to keep it from blowing or washing away.

- If you're growing perennial crops in a cold climate, fall is the time to protect them against winter temperatures. Apply a mulch over the whole plant when the soil first freezes, but not before then; if you mulch when the soil is still warm, you'll encourage root rot problems. Remember to remove this mulch as soon as the soil starts to thaw out in the spring. The best materials to use for this mulch are organic materials that will let the plants breathe; straw, hay, leaves, and compost are all suitable. Crops you may need to mulch for winter protection include: artichokes (in some areas); chayotes; rhubarb; and such herbs as chives, garlic, marjoram, mints, oregano, rosemary, sage, tarragon, and thyme.

When you're through with these final tasks, you have done the best you can to prepare your garden for winter. It's time to sit back and relax—and if you miss the time in your garden, you can beguile your winter hours by reading seed catalogs and planning the garden you're going to plant come spring.

Points to Remember About How to Care for Your Garden

1. You can't expect your garden to reward you as generously as you hope it will unless you give it certain basic care. Take the time to weed, water, and, if necessary, protect your plants.

2. You can't expect your vegetable crop to compete with weeds, so a working knowledge of what is a weed and what isn't is very useful. (It can also be good information for helpful kids who may pull up your seedlings by mistake.)

3. Herbicides can be helpful in controlling weeds under certain conditions, but they must be handled with care. Don't use them unless absolutely necessary, and if you do use them follow the manufacturer's instructions and the rules for use in this book.

4. Mulches can help discourage the growth of weeds, prevent soil compaction, protect against soil erosion, reduce certain disease problems, and maintain soil temperature. You can choose from organic mulches such as compost, leaves, and manure; inorganic mulches such as aluminum foil or old newspapers, or plastic mulches. You can probably use all of them in your garden at one time or another.

5. Watering your garden may sound straightforward, but there's a right and a wrong way to water. Many factors affect how often you will need to water, among them temperature, humidity, and the individual preferences of the plants. Take all these factors into account when determining how much water your garden needs—and remember that over-watering can be as much of a problem as under-watering.

6. When you've gathered in your harvest and enjoyed the results of the care you've given your garden, prepare your garden for the winter so that you'll do equally well next year. Fall clean-up may include mulching perennial plants to see them through a cold winter; tilling the soil so that you get an earlier start in spring; or planting a cover crop to keep the soil from eroding and to provide organic matter to enrich the soil before planting in the spring (you just dig it in as you prepare the soil).

7. If you have fruit trees or bushes in your yard, pruning will be a necessary part of your fall clean-up chores. Information on pruning is given in "The Home Orchard" later in this book.

Keeping Your Garden Healthy

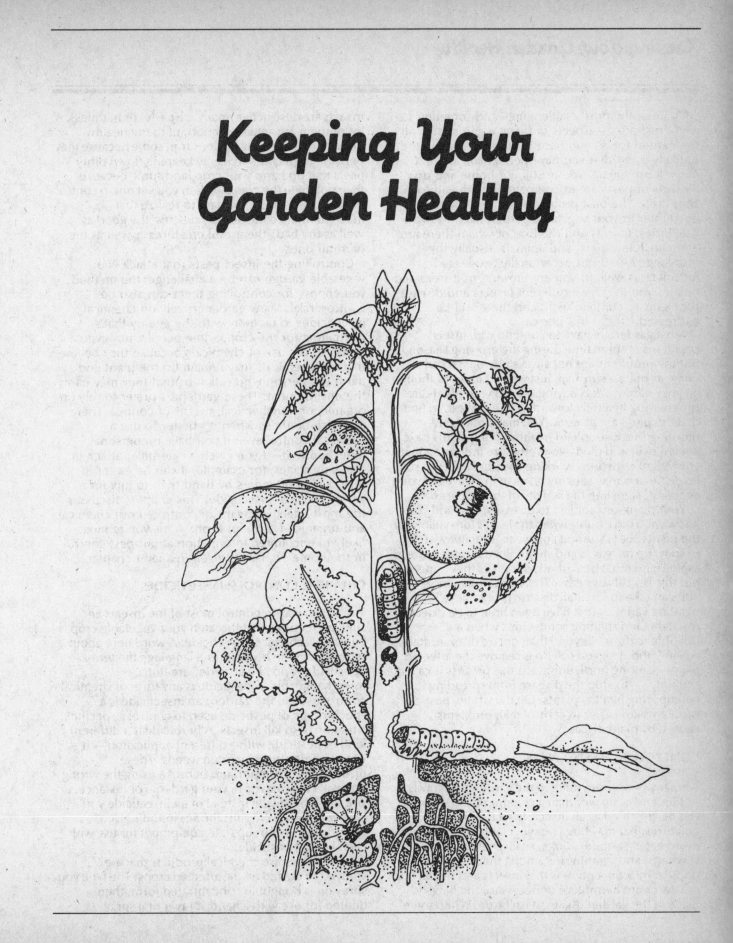

One of the most challenging—and sometimes frustrating—aspects of being a gardener is all the natural forces you have to combat. Even in the unlikely event that you have perfect soil and a marvelous climate, you're still not home and dry; all sorts of pests are in competition with you for your crop. The pest problems you're likely to encounter in your vegetable garden fall into two categories: insects and the like, of which there are a remarkable variety; and animals, usually the four-legged kind but occasionally two-legged intruders as well. (If you are growing fruit trees and bushes you may have different insects and disease problems to contend with, and these will be addressed later in this book.)

Most gardeners have to contend with insect problems at some time during the growing season, but the problems are not always obvious. It can come as quite a surprise, just when it looks as though all your hard work is paying off and your plants are progressing healthily towards a fine harvest, to find that the pests are at work. You may notice one morning that a couple of healthy young plants have keeled over and died — a pretty sure indication that you've got cutworms working away beneath the soil level. Or you may see tiny holes in the leaves of your eggplant, signaling the activity of the flea beetle.

Your plants are subject to diseases, too, and you know you're in trouble when the leaves turn yellow, or the plants seem stunted and weak, or mildew starts to show up on leaves and stems. Plant diseases spread rapidly and must be curbed as soon as they appear, but this isn't always easy. There are certain measures you can take to forestall disease problems — like planting varieties that have been bred to be disease-resistant, and rotating some crops when it's possible to do so. Beyond that, once a disease attacks a plant, about all you can do is remove the infected plant — among horticulturalists this process is called "culling" — to stop the disease from spreading to neighboring healthy plants. On the whole, pest problems are easier to control than problems caused by plant diseases.

CONTROLLING INSECT PESTS

To many people anything in the garden that crawls or flies and is smaller than a chipmunk or a sparrow can be classified as an insect. In fact, a lot of the creatures that may bug your vegetable plants are not insects at all — mites, slugs, snails, nematodes, sowbugs, and symphylans among them. Another popular misconception is that insects and similar creatures are harmful or unnecessary and have no place in the garden. Again, it isn't true. While some insects are destructive, many are perfectly harmless. A lot of them are actually important to the healthy development of your garden crop, some because they perform a specific service by keeping down other pests that do harm your crop, and some because they pollinate the plants. When you set out to control harmful pests, it's important to realize that indiscriminate controls may destroy the good as well as the bad; the useful creatures as well as the harmful ones.

Controlling the insect pests that attack your vegetable garden can be a challenge; the method you choose for controlling them can also be controversial. Many gardeners rely on chemical insecticides to do away with the enemy that's competing for the crop. Some people, however, object to the use of chemicals because they believe that the chemicals may remain on the plant and harm the person who eats it or that they may harm the environment. These gardeners prefer to rely on organic, or nonchemical, means of control. There may also be times when it's better to use a chemical control even if you have no personal objection to it—if you catch a caterpillar attack in the early stages, for example, it can be easier to pick off the offenders by hand than to mix up a whole batch of insecticide. This chapter discusses the most effective means of control—both chemical and organic—for the pest problems you're most likely to encounter. Information about pest control in the home orchard is given in a later chapter.

CHEMICAL CONTROLS: INSECTICIDES

The surest way to control most of the insects and similar creatures that threaten your vegetable crop is by using a chemical insecticide. A word here about terminology: In horticultural language the terms "pesticide" and "insecticide" are not interchangeable. A pesticide is any form of chemical control used in the garden; an insecticide is a specific type of pesticide used to control a specific situation — to kill insects. A herbicide is a different kind of pesticide with a different application — it's used to help control garden weeds. These distinctions are important, because using the wrong one will cause havoc in your garden. For instance, if you use a herbicide instead of an insecticide you'll lose your entire crop for the season. It's also important to keep separate equipment for use with each kind of pesticide.

Insecticides are chemical products that are sprayed or dusted on the affected crops. The type you spray on is bought in concentrated form, then diluted for use with a hand sprayer or a spray attachment fitted to the end of your garden hose. Dust-on insecticides are powders that you pump on to the plants. Spraying is preferable because it gives more thorough coverage, and it's easier to treat the undersides as well as the tops of leaves and plants with a spray. You can also apply insecticides directly to the soil to kill insects under the soil surface — this technique is known as applying a "soil drench."

Used correctly and responsibly, insecticides are not harmful to humans or other animals. They are toxic, but the toxicity levels are low, and their residual or carryover effect is short — the longest any of the insecticides commonly used in the home garden will remain on the plant is about 14 days. Malathion, for instance, has the same toxicity level as Scotch whiskey and breaks down faster. As to any long-lasting hazards that may be involved — nobody knows if hazards exist or what they might be; we don't know what the long-lasting hazards of *any* product might be. The choice of an organic or a synthetic pesticide is a matter of personal opinion. If you know all the options you'll be able to make your own choice.

Commonly used insecticides

The insecticides listed below for use in your home vegetable garden will provide effective control of garden insects with minimum hazard. Remember, though, that most insecticides are poisons and must be handled as such.

Diazinon. This is an organic phosphate, and it's an effective insecticide for general use. Diazinon is a contact poison. Its toxicity is low, and it's a good control for underground insects that attack the roots of cabbage family plants, onions, and radishes. You can get it as a wettable powder or in liquid form.

Malathion. This is also a phosphate insecticide; it kills sucking insects like aphids. Its effects are not as long-lasting as those of some other insecticides, but it's effective and safe in use. It's available as a dust, a wettable powder, or a liquid.

Sevin. This is also known as carbaryl and is another safe material for use in home gardens. It's an effective control for many leaf-eating caterpillars and leafhoppers, and is available as a wettable powder or a dust.

Bacillus thuringiensis. This is an organic insecticide. It's a bacterium that is considered harmless to all but insects, and you can buy it under the brand names of **Dipel, Thuricide,** or **Bactur.** It controls cabbage worms and other caterpillars and is available in wettable powder or liquid forms. This is the choice of many gardeners who prefer not to use chemical insecticides.

Cause and cure: Be sure you've got them right

Because an insecticide can't distinguish between friend and foe, it's your responsibility to make sure you're eliminating the pest, not the friendly insect that's out there working for you. Let's say, for instance, that aphids are attacking your cabbage plants, and you use carbaryl (Sevin) to try to get rid of them because you know carbaryl is a relatively safe insecticide with a short residual effect. You've overlooked the fact that carbaryl has to enter the insect's stomach in order to kill it, and since the aphid's mouth is inside the cabbage plant, none of the insecticide is going to enter the insect through the mouth and reach its stomach. Ladybugs, however, love aphids and are most helpful in keeping down their numbers. So when the ladybug eats the aphid, the carbaryl on the aphid's body enters the ladybug's stomach and kills it. Despite the best intentions in the world, you've killed off the useful insect and left the pest unharmed. In fact you've done the pest a favor by killing off its enemy — a ladybug can put away hundreds of aphids in a day.

Carbaryl can also be toxic to bees, and bees are important to your garden because they pollinate most fruiting vegetable crops. To avoid killing the bees, spray in the late evening when the flowers are closed. This way you kill the destructive pests but protect the bees.

If you use an insecticide you must always be aware also of how long its residual effect is going to last. A residue of insecticide left on the plant when it's harvested is poisonous. The residual effect of an insecticide that you use in your vegetable garden is likely to be fairly short, but the effect may vary from one type of crop to another. And because the effect is not long-lasting, you can't spray as a preventive measure; you have no way of knowing which pests are going to attack your plants before they're actually on the scene.

How to use an insecticide

Because research is constantly being done to determine the safety of insecticides and improve their effectiveness, it's difficult to give long-term recommendations about their use. Basic rules, however, always apply: Read the directions and precautions on the label and follow them meticulously, and never make the solution stronger than the label says because you think it'll work better that way. If the product would be more effective in a stronger solution the label would say so.

You need to use common sense when working with an insecticide. If there are just a few, visible insects on your plants, it may be a lot easier to remove them by hand than to go through the full routine of applying a chemical remedy. Also, weather conditions limit when you can use a product that has to be sprayed or dusted on the plants — you can't do it on a windy day because you can't control the direction of the application. The wind can take your insecticide over into your neighbor's garden; so you'll both fail to correct your own pest problem, and you'll make your neighbor mad. As the one who's using the pesticide, you are responsible for it.

You'll also defeat your own purpose by using an insecticide if rain is expected within 12 to 24 hours. The insecticide must dry on the plant in order to be effective. Whether you use a spray or a dust, make sure that you reach all parts of the plants — you're aiming for a light covering on both the tops and the undersides of all the leaves. Don't give the pests a place to hide; proper coverage is essential if the insecticide is to do its job.

The products we suggest are commonly used in the home vegetable garden as we write this. But before you go out to buy one, check with your local Cooperative Extension Service to make sure that these recommendations are still current.

If you do decide to use a pesticide to control insects in your vegetable garden, here are some important points to remember:

- Read the whole label; observe all the precautions and follow all the directions exactly.
- Check the time period that must elapse between application of the insecticide and harvesting the plant, and observe it strictly. Note all restrictions carefully — often products must be applied at a certain stage in the plant's development.
- Wear rubber gloves while handling insecticide concentrates; don't smoke while you're handling them, and take care not to breathe the spray or dust.
- Sprays usually have to be mixed before each use. Follow the directions, and use *only* the exact proportions indicated on the label. If it's not used exactly as indicated, an insecticide may be harmful to people, animals, or plants.
- Use equipment that you keep specifically for use with insecticides. Don't use equipment that has been used for herbicides.
- Do not apply an insecticide near fish ponds, dug wells, or cisterns; do not leave puddles of pesticides on solid surfaces.
- Use a spray or dust-type insecticide only when the air is still. Wind will carry the product away from your garden and, possibly, be a nuisance to someone else. Don't spray or dust within 12 to 24 hours of an expected rain — the insecticide must dry on the plants to be effective; rain will wash it off.
- After using an insecticide, wash your clothes and all exposed parts of the body thoroughly with soap and water.
- Store unused material (undiluted) in its original container out of the reach of children, irresponsible adults, or animals — preferably in a locked cabinet or storage area.
- Dispose of the empty container carefully. Do not leave it where children or animals can get to it or where it might be recycled for another use.
- Wash all treated vegetables carefully before eating them.

NONCHEMICAL CONTROLS: ORGANIC ALTERNATIVES

It's not always necessary to use a chemical insecticide in your vegetable garden even if you have no particular personal objection to its use. In some cases organic controls can give acceptable results if you don't mind putting in a little more labor for a little less reward at harvesting time. And if you're an organic gardener, there are a few things you should know about helping your vegetables survive attacks by pests.

Planting problem-free varieties

First of all, you can take the simple precaution of planting only varieties that are not susceptible to major pest problems. There are a lot of vegetables that pests usually don't attack, or don't attack in large enough numbers to cause you any real grief or require the use of nonorganic methods of control. All these are fairly problem-free vegetables: artichokes, asparagus, beets, carrots, celeriac, celery, chard, chicory, cucumbers, dandelion, horseradish, Jerusalem artichokes, leeks, okra, onions, parsnips, peas, radishes, rhubarb, salsify, soybeans, spinach, turnips, and almost all the herbs.

Some vegetables are almost always attacked by caterpillars that can be controlled by Bacillus thuringiensis, an organic product that is harmless to humans and animals. These include all the cabbage family plants — broccoli, Brussels sprouts, cabbage, cauliflower, collards, kale, and kohlrabi. The other insects that commonly attack the cabbage family plants can also usually be controlled by natural and physical methods.

Some vegetables are almost always attacked by large numbers of insects that cannot be controlled by natural or physical methods. This is not to say that you can't grow these crops without using pesticides; you can, but usually your yield will be low. These vegetables include most of the beans, Chinese cabbage, sweet corn, eggplant, lettuce, mustard, peppers, potatoes, pumpkins, rutabagas, sweet potatoes, tomatoes, and watermelons.

Squash are not included in any of these categories, because although the squash vine borer — their main enemy — cannot be effectively controlled without using a pesticide, most squash are prolific enough to give you an acceptable crop even if you do lose some to bugs.

Physical controls

Sidestepping pest problems by planting vegetables that are least likely to be seriously threatened by pests is one practical way to protect your crop. Another is the physical, do-it-yourself method of removing the offenders by hand. If you're going to do this, it's essential to identify pests in the early stages of their attack. It's not a big deal to pick a couple of dozen aphids off your broccoli; but when the attack is well under way and your plant is covered with aphids, you might as well forget about hand-picking, because it's not going to work.

If you slip up and let a pest problem get past the early stages, you can try a good blast of water from the garden hose to knock the insects off the plant. Try to do this on a dry day so that the leaves won't stay wet for too long; wet leaves make the plant more susceptible to disease and may give you a new problem to replace the one you've just solved.

Other physical control methods can be effective with specific pests. These methods are discussed in detail later in this chapter.

Natural controls

These have to be the original "organic" ways of controlling pest problems in the garden — you're simply relying on harmless insects to destroy the harmful ones. The effectiveness of these natural methods of control is questionable; in some cases you're probably just perpetuating old wives' tales. It's true that insects like ladybugs, lacewing flies, praying mantises, and aphis lions feed on bugs that are destructive to your crop and should, therefore, be protected when you find them in your garden. But it's also true that they can't offer a complete answer to a pest problem. If these helpful creatures visit your garden, welcome and protect them. But don't expect them to control all the pests that bother your plants. That's asking too much of them.

It's possible to buy ladybugs, praying mantises,

and the like through the mail from garden supply companies. However, you're likely to be wasting your time and money by doing so. All these insects are winged, and they're all very shy of people. The odds are they'll wing it away as fast as you put them out, deserting your vegetable garden for a more secluded spot. Also, the beneficial insects that you import may not consider the specific variety of pest that you have in your garden to be a particular delicacy. In this case they'll fly off in search of more appetizing fare. Either way, they're likely to let you down as far as solving your pest problem is concerned.

IDENTIFYING GARDEN PESTS

When you're talking about pest control it's an advantage to group the types of pest you may encounter in categories: Some work at night; some work underground; some chew the plant's leaves; others bore into the stems. The following is a list of pests you're most likely to meet in your vegetable garden, and chemical and nonchemical controls for each insect.

Ants

Blister beetle

Mexican bean beetle

Cucumber beetle

Underground and nocturnal pests

The pest you can't see can be the hardest to deal with. The following creatures work underground or at night, so you don't know they're around until the damage they do is visible.

Cutworms. These are the fat caterpillars of a hairless night-flying moth. They spend the day curled up just under the soil's surface, and they feed at night; in spring they cut off seedlings and transplants at ground level. Later in the season they climb up some vegetable plants and chew large holes in the fruit. Cutworms can be controlled chemically by applying carbaryl to the base of the plants at the first sign of chewing. You can discourage them without using chemicals by putting a collar around each plant when you transplant it. Thin cardboard or a Styrofoam cup with the bottom removed makes an effective collar. The collar should go down at least an inch into the soil and should stand away from the plant one and one half to three inches on all sides.

Grubs. Grubs are beetles in their immature or larva stage. They live just below the soil surface and feed on plant roots. You may suspect they're active if your plants are growing poorly for no apparent reason, or if you pull a plant and discover the damage. Grubs are normally only a problem where a lawn area has been dug up to make a new garden. Repeated tilling of the soil over a number of years will control the problem. To control grubs in the first year you will need to apply a soil drench of Diazinon.

Root maggots. Maggots are fly larvae. They are yellowish-white, legless, wormlike creatures (a quarter-inch to one and one third inches long) that feast on roots and stems just under the soil's surface. The best nonchemical control is prevention. Discourage the fly from laying eggs near the seedlings by putting shields of plastic three or four inches square around each plant. Take care not to cover the paper with soil when you cultivate. Root maggots attack beans, broccoli, Brussels sprouts, cabbage, carrots, cauliflower, radishes, spinach, squash, and turnips. You can control them chemically by drenching the soil around the plant that's under attack with Diazinon. Don't spray until you see the damage; if your plants are growing poorly, and you can't figure out why, root maggots may be the cause.

Wireworms. Wireworms are slender, hard worms about an inch long. They eat the seed in the ground and feed on underground roots and stems. After doing their damage, which appears as poor-growing, yellow, wilted plants, they grow up into click beetles. To control wireworms, apply a soil drench of Diazinon when the wireworms are present.

Chewing pests

Chewing pests are usually easy to find, especially when they have put in a good day's work, and they're easier to control by nonchemical methods than the nocturnal and underground pests are. Many of them can be hand-picked off the plant or knocked off with a blast from the hose. Almost every chewing insect that feeds on the outside of the plant can be controlled chemically by using carbaryl. Check to make sure that you have identified the guilty party; apply insecticide when the pest is first discovered, and repeat the treatment as often as necessary according to the directions on the label.

Ants. Except for the leaf-cutting varieties found in the South and West, ants generally do not create much of a problem for the home gardener. If they do nest in your garden, they can be controlled physically by digging up and destroying their nest. They can be controlled chemically by drenching their nests with Diazinon.

Beetles. Beetles come in many sizes and shapes. Some prefer one or two special vegetables; others chew on whatever looks appetizing at the time. Some get their names from their favorite delicacy.

Flea beetle

Cabbage looper

Asparagus beetles feed on asparagus; **Mexican bean beetles** love beans. **Blister beetles** feed on beans, beets, chard, corn, potatoes, tomatoes, and squash. **Cucumber beetles** (spotted and striped) often attack melons, pumpkins, squash, and watermelon, as well as cucumbers. Their eating habits may not cause much damage, but they carry cucumber bacterial wilt, which will kill any of these plants when they're older. **Flea beetles** will eat almost any garden crop. They're very small, and it's difficult to spot them, but you'll know they're there when tiny black dots jump from the plants when you come near, and when you notice that the leaves of your vegetable plants are suddenly full of small holes scattered over the entire leaf surface. **Potato beetles** chew on eggplants, potatoes, and tomatoes. If there are too many small beetles to hand-pick, try to hose them off. All these beetles can be controlled chemically with carbaryl, used according to the label directions.

Borers (squash vine borers). Cucumbers, melons, pumpkins, and squash are attacked by this borer. The egg is laid on the outside of the stem by a night-flying moth. The eggs hatch, and the borers tunnel inside the stem of the plant. As they grow inside the stem, they eat it out, and eventually the plant wilts and dies. Watch for the warning signs: stunting or unexplained wilting of the plant or — this is the surest evidence of who the culprit is — a small hole at the base of the plant and a scattering of sawdustlike material around it. A chemical control of carbaryl needs to be applied at weekly intervals to the crown of the plants before the borers get inside the stem. Once the borer gets inside the plant chemical controls will not help. You can control them physically if you slit the stem, remove all the borers, and cover the spot with earth to encourage root growth at that point. This attempt at a cure may have the opposite effect and kill the plant. But it's your only chance to get rid of the borers.

Cabbage loopers and cabbage worms. These caterpillars love to feed on all members of the cabbage family; occasionally they will make do with lettuce. To control them, spray with Bacillus thuringiensis, an organic insecticide that is available under a number of trade names including Dipel, Thuricide, and Bactur. This is a completely safe organic spray that will destroy the caterpillars without harming humans or animals.

Corn earworms. These caterpillars prefer corn, but they also feed on beans, tomatoes, peppers, and eggplant. They are also called tomato fruitworms. To effectively control them, be prepared to spray on a regular schedule with carbaryl. Hand-picking and cutting out the damaged parts of the vegetables will give limited control of this pest.

Grasshoppers. They have great appetites and will eat anything and everything. They usually appear in late summer and are more active where the winters are warm and the summers are hot. Try to control them when they are young by hand-picking them off the plants or by destroying the untended weedy spots near the garden where they begin life. Control them chemically when they are young by spraying untended weedy areas with carbaryl.

Hornworms. Hornworms are large green caterpillars three to four inches long with a hornlike growth on their rear end. They eat the foliage and fruit of your tomato plants. Since the large hornworms do not usually invade in great numbers, hand-pick them individually off the plants. If your garden is invaded by numerous hornworms spray them with Bacillus thuringiensis.

Parsley caterpillars. These feed on parsley, dill, fennel, and other members of the parsley family. They're not common enough to be a major problem, and hand-picking usually provides satisfactory control.

Leaf miners. Leaf miners are the larvae of a fly that feed on the external portions of a leaf. They will feed on cabbage and its relatives, and on chard, beets,

European corn borer

Corn earworm

Hornworm

Slug

Snail

and occasionally lettuce. The best method of controlling the leaf miner is to remove affected leaves from the plant by hand and to hand-pick egg masses that can usually be found on the backside of older leaves. Since the leaf miner is inside the leaf surface, chemical controls are ineffective.

Slugs and snails. Snails have shells and slugs don't. Both are more closely related to oysters and clams than they are to insects. You can detect their presence by the slimy trail they leave from the scene of their activity. They don't like to be out in the heat of the day; they eat and run and can be hard to control. They like to feed on cabbage and all its relatives, and on carrots, lettuce, tomatoes, and turnips. To control them remove their hiding places — old boards, cans, bricks, and other garbage. Lay scratchy sand or cinders around each plant to discourage them. Or set a saucer in the soil with the

Whiteflies

Thrip

Leafhopper

rim flush with the soil surface, and fill it with stale beer. The slugs and snails will be attracted to the beer and fall in and drown. Then you can dispose of them in the morning.

Sucking pests

Aphids, leafhoppers, mites, and thrips may be hard to see. By the time their damage is apparent it is often too late to take much action. Watch for scraped and rusty-looking places on leaves, twisted and deformed leaves and leaf-tips, and stems that look unusually thick.

Aphids. Aphids are tiny pear-shaped insects, often green, that will attack almost every vegetable crop commonly grown. They feed by sucking the sap of the tender stems and leaves, causing distortions. They also exude a sweet substance called honeydew, which is attractive to ants and can cause sooty molds. Aphids are also carriers of mosaic virus and other diseases. Ladybugs and their larvae eat aphids — provided that they're hungry and the aphids are the kind they like — and may help you control the pests. Aphids can also be controlled nonchemically by pinching out infested tips. Aphids can be chemically controlled by an application of Malathion or Diazinon (make sure to cover the underside of the leaves). Malathion generally has a shorter residue effect.

Leafhoppers. These are green, jumping, winged insects about an eighth inch long when adult. They feed on the undersides of the leaves, sucking sap and causing light-colored spotting on the upper side. They can also spread plant diseases. Populations can be discouraged organically by hosing them off the leaves. You can control leafhoppers chemically by spraying the underside of the leaves with carbaryl or Malathion. They will feed on beans, carrots, chayote, cucumbers, endive, lettuce, melons, and potatoes.

Spider mites. Spider mites are very small and difficult to see. You can be fairly sure that spider mites are to blame if the leaves are losing color in spots and turning yellowish, light green or rusty and there are silvery webs on the undersides. Spider mites are difficult to control even if you use the proper chemicals. You can spray the undersides of the foliage with Diazinon before populations get too large. If you don't want to spray or if the spraying is ineffective, remove the affected plants before the spider mites spread.

Thrips. Thrips are small, fast-moving insects that are almost invisible to the naked eye. The damage they do shows up first as white blotches, then there is a distortion of the leaf tips. When thrips attack onions, they dwarf and distort the bulbs. Thrips also attack beans, beets, carrots, cabbage and its relatives, celery, cucumbers, melons, onions, peas, squash, tomatoes, and turnips. Large populations of thrips can be discouraged by hosing them off the plants. Thrips can be controlled chemically if you spray them with Malathion or Diazinon.

Whiteflies. Whiteflies are minute sucking insects that look like tiny white moths. They live and feed on the undersides of leaves and live unnoticed until you disturb the plant, then they fly out in great white clouds. Whitefly populations can be discouraged by hosing them off the plants. Control them chemically by spraying the undersides of the leaves with Malathion or Diazinon.

PLANT DISEASES: PREVENTION BETTER THAN CURE

A number of plant diseases are the result of unfavorable growing conditions, but many are caused by parasitic bacteria and fungi that cannot produce their own food and rely on the plant for nourishment. Some diseases are airborne, and others can live for years in the soil, so it's difficult for the gardener to predict or control them.

As a matter of policy, prevention is better than cure—or attempting a cure—where plant diseases are concerned. You can try to avoid the conditions that promote disease by choosing your planting sites wisely. Primarily you want to avoid the combination of too much moisture, too much shade, and soil that's too cool—the three conditions that provide an ideal environment for the propagation of diseases. You can also plant disease-resistant varieties, rotate crops, and take steps to keep your garden clean and healthy.

If your preventive measures don't work, you'll have to cut your losses. There's little you can do to save a plant that has been attacked by a parasitic fungus or bacterial disease, and your best bet is to remove the affected plant as soon as possible before the disease has a chance to spread to healthy plants. This may seem drastic, and you may be tempted to save the plant, especially if it's near harvesttime. Don't give in to temptation—you're risking the rest of your crop. Remove the diseased plant and burn it, put it in the garbage, or dispose of it elsewhere well away from your vegetable garden. Don't leave it lying around the garden, and don't put it on the compost pile.

Protecting your garden from disease

Maintaining a healthy garden requires you to be a conscientious gardener. Here are methods you can use to keep your garden free from disease:

Prepare the soil properly. Make it easy for your plants to grow well. Plant vegetables in full sun if you can; strong sunlight is a great disinfectant, and the energy plants draw from the sun gives them extra strength. Make sure the soil is well-worked, has good drainage, and is high in organic matter so the soil moisture will remain even. Do not plant the vegetables when the soil and air are too cold. Place plants far enough apart so to avoid crowding; this will allow good air circulation, and the plants will be able to dry out after a rain.

Select disease-resistant varieties. Where possible, buy seeds that are certified as disease-free. Use seeds that have been treated with fungicide, or start your seeds in a sterile soil mix. Your local Cooperative Extension Service can supply you with a list of disease-resistant vegetable varieties for your area.

Rotate your crops. Do not grow the same plant family in the same spot year after year. Repetition of the same crop gives diseases a chance to build up strength. There are three major vegetable families: cole crops (cabbage family) — broccoli, Brussels sprouts, cabbage, cauliflower, kohlrabi, rutabaga, and turnip; cucurbits (cucumber family) — cucumber, gourds, muskmelons, pumpkins, summer and winter squash, and watermelons; and solanaceous plants (tomato and pepper family) — eggplant, Irish potato, pepper, and tomato. After growing a crop from one of these families one year, choose a variety from one of the other families to plant in the same spot the following season.

Don't work with wet plants. Do not work the soil when it is wet. When you're watering the garden, try not to splash water on the plants, especially in hot, humid weather. Handling plants when they're wet spreads diseases.

Control garden pests. Keep insects and other small pests under control. Some insects spread disease; sometimes insects just weaken the plant so that it becomes more susceptible to disease.

Don't infect your own plants. If you smoke, wash your hands well with soap and hot running water before working with tomatoes, peppers, and eggplant. Smokers can infect these plants with tobacco mosaic virus, causing them to mottle, streak, drop their leaves, and die.

Keep your garden clean. Always keep the garden clear of weeds, trash, and plants that have finished producing. Remove infected plants. If you have a sick plant in the garden, identify the problem. If it's a virus or fungus disease, remove the affected plant as quickly as possible. Destroy the plant; do not put it in the compost pile. This removal of infected plants is called "culling." Don't think of it as killing a plant;

look on it as a necessary measure for the protection of your other plants.

Common plant diseases

These are some of the common diseases that may attack your plants; if they appear in your garden, remove the diseased plant as soon as possible.

Anthracnose. Anthracnose is a fungus disease that occurs most frequently in wet weather. Look for well-defined dead areas on the leaves and fruit; these dead areas are generally depressed with a slightly raised edge around them. Anthracnose will attack beans, tomatoes, cucumbers, melons, peppers, potatoes, pumpkins, squash, and watermelons.

Blights. A blight is a bacterial disease that causes sudden and noticeable damage to the plant, but it is not a wilt disease nor a disease characterized by sharply defined spots or blotches. Blight symptoms appear as water-soaked spots that spread and fuse into irregular blotches; rot sets in shortly afterward. It attacks tomatoes, peppers, eggplant, squash, and beans.

Blossom end rot. Great variations in soil moisture, especially when wet weather is followed by dry weather, sometimes cause rot on the blossom ends of peppers, tomatoes, and squash. Calcium deficiency invites this condition, so does a soil condition that affects root growth — for example, shallow soil, poor drainage, too-deep cultivation, or too much nitrogen fertilizer.

Mildews. Powdery mildews grow on the surfaces of plants. They thrive when the weather is humid but not during rainy weather. Mildews are encouraged when plants are crowded together and air circulation is poor. Powdery mildew is common on cucumbers, melons, pumpkins, squash, peas, and beans. Downy mildews thrive in wet weather and usually grow on the undersides of the leaves and inside the tissues of the plant. Downy mildew grows on cucumbers, melons, pumpkins, squash, lima beans, and onions, and may cause unusual growth of sweet corn.

Pesticide damage. Pesticide dusts and sprays, including herbicides, can harm all vegetables. Sprays containing copper can cause reddish-brown spots, leaf drop, and stunting of cucumbers, melons, and squash. This damage is aggravated by cool, damp weather. Damage from sprays containing copper can cause the tips and edges of the leaves to burn if the temperature is 90°F or over. Herbicides are potent and their mist can drift hundreds of feet. Tomatoes, beans, and peppers are particularly sensitive to herbicides. Minute amounts left in a sprayer can distort plants badly if the sprayer is then used for applying something else. Always keep herbicide equipment entirely separate from the equipment you use for insecticides.

Rusts. A reddish or rusty appearance on the leaves is often caused by different rust fungi and is most likely to occur when growing conditions are wet, cool, and shady. Assorted rusts grow on asparagus, beans, beets, and chard.

Smuts. Masses of black spores indicate smut, which is a fungal condition. Corn smut thrives in hot weather, and the spores retain their vitality for a long time. Get rid of the infected corn, eliminate the whole plant, and try not to plant corn in the same spot for the next few years. Onion smut generally affects onions that are grown from seed. Onion smut is worse in cool summers, but only very young plants are attacked. The spores remain alive in the soil for years. To prevent onion smut, either use sets or grow the seeds in sterile soil and then transplant them, or choose only disease-resistant varieties.

Sunscale or sunburn. Peppers, tomatoes, and other fruits that are used to growing with a leaf cover can develop irregular whitish splotches that often rot when the leaves are pruned back too severely or when the leaves have been destroyed by insects or diseases.

Viruses. Yellows virus and mosaic virus are the two major virus diseases that attack crops in the home vegetable garden. The symptoms of yellows virus are stunting of the plants accompanied by an even yellow discoloration. Yellows virus will attack just about every vegetable in your garden: cabbage and the other members of the cole family, beans, carrots, celeriac, celery, cucumbers, dandelion, dill, lettuce, mustard, New Zealand spinach, onions, parsley, peas, potatoes, radishes, spinach, squash, and tomatoes. With mosaic virus the foliage is evenly mottled with green and yellow pattern; with shoestring mosaic the leaves may become distorted and stringy. Mosaic virus, like yellows virus, attacks almost everything in the garden. Virus diseases spread quickly so remove any affected plant promptly before the disease can spread.

Water. Too much or too little water can both produce stunting and poor growth. Blossom end rot in peppers, tomatoes, and squash may be due to a dry period following a wet period.

Wilts. Plants often droop because of a lack of moisture in the leaves and soft stems. This may be the result of a fungus, a bacteria, or a virus affecting the roots or the water-conducting tissues. Members of the cabbage family are affected by cabbage yellows or fusarium wilt. Celery is affected by celery yellows or fusarium wilt. The whole squash family is prone to cucurbit wilt. Wilts also attack peas, sweet potatoes, and tomatoes. The best controls are to plant resistant varieties, to destroy infected plants, and to rotate your crops.

ANIMAL PESTS IN THE GARDEN

The final types of pests that may invade your garden — animals (four-legged and two-legged) — can often be the most frustrating to deal with. Raccoons, rabbits, and birds can usually be kept in line by a fence, a net, or a scarecrow. However, you may need to use a little tact and a little forceful language with people.

Birds. Birds can usually be kept out of the garden by some type of scarecrow. If this doesn't work, you can cover seedlings and seeded areas with a net until the plants are established. If you are growing fruit trees and bushes, nets can sometimes be used to prevent damage by birds.

Rabbits. The amount of damage rabbits do is in direct proportion to how hungry they are. Usually cats and a three-foot chickenwire fence bent out at the bottom are enough to keep them away. Since rabbits are shy and don't like to run in the open, getting rid of cover — protected places where they can hide — may discourage them.

Raccoons. Raccoons are connoisseurs of fresh vegetables, especially sweet corn. A good fence and an active dog are about the best solution. Some people report that a portable radio playing loud hard-rock music will keep them away, but this is a questionable solution.

Rats. In urban areas rats can be quite destructive. Cats or dogs will keep them away if the rats are not too large. Clearing out rubbish piles in the area also helps.

Squirrels. No matter how cute they are, don't ever encourage squirrels. They are hard to get rid of except by shooting or trapping. They are as fond of sweet corn and other vegetables as raccoons. You can't fence squirrels out of the garden; you'd need a fence over the garden as well as around it.

Cats and dogs. Cats are good at keeping birds and small animals out of the garden, but they work limited hours, and they often enjoy digging in the loose earth and rolling on plants to scratch their backs. Plastic mulches and cages (for the vegetables, not the cats) are often a solution. Other people's dogs — not your own, of course — can be a nuisance, scratching or digging in your soil. Big dogs have big feet and trample your crop. Both dogs and cats are also occasionally responsible for the deposit of too much nitrogen. A good fence is the best defense against other people's dogs. Cats, of course, are a law unto themselves and have no respect for fences.

Humans. Adult humans walk around, compacting the soil, weeding the seedlings, squeezing fruits to see if they're ripe, and often pointing out that everything you're doing should be done another way. Try to be as patient as possible and explain the hows and whys of what you're doing. Try to get them interested in gardening, and maybe they'll become too busy in their own gardens to come "help" you.

Children — yours and other people's — can be a real hazard to the realization of your harvest. They pull up your seedlings by accident when they're helping you weed (just like adults), until you teach them the difference. They ride their bicycles between your rows of cabbage. They're fascinated by caterpillars and think you're mean and cruel because you won't let the caterpillars eat your plants. Let your children know that plants are living things that need care, and that do's and don'ts apply to gardens just as they do inside houses — and have them pass on the rules to their friends. Better yet, make your children your allies by giving them gardens of their own. Refer to "Planning Your Garden" for suggestions as to how to convert the least ecology-conscious youngster into a conscientious gardener.

COMMON PROBLEMS: CAUSES AND CURES

However carefully you follow all the rules, and however conscientiously you cherish and care for your garden, things still go wrong from time to time. A garden is a gathering of living things, and living things don't always live by the rules. Sometimes it's easy enough to figure out why a problem occurs and how to deal with it. Other times you'll be at a loss to know why, when you think you've done everything right, something's gone wrong. In certain circumstances you may know what the problem is, but won't be able to do anything about it except wait until next year. Don't get discouraged — remember that one prerequisite of the gardener is a generous supply of patience. Frequently, though, there's a practical solution to a garden problem. To help you decide what to do when you're not sure what to do, here's a guide to common problems that may occur in your vegetable garden, with suggestions about what caused them and what you can do to cure them.

Common problems in vegetable gardening

PROBLEM	POSSIBLE CAUSES	POSSIBLE CURES
Plants wilt	Lack of water	Water
	Too much water	Stop watering; improve drainage; pray for less rain
	Disease	Use disease-resistant varieties; keep your garden clean
Leaves and stems are spotted	Fertilizer or chemical burn	Follow instructions; read all fine print; keep fertilizer off plant unless recommended
	Disease	Use disease-resistant varieties of seed; dust or spray; remove affected plants
Plants are weak and spindly	Not enough light	Remove cause of shade or move plants
	Too much water	Improve drainage; stop watering; pray for less rain
	Plants are crowded	Thin out
	Too much nitrogen	Reduce fertilizing
Leaves curl	Wilt	Destroy affected plants; rotate crops; grow disease-resistant varieties
	Virus	Control aphids; destroy affected plants
	Moisture imbalance	Mulch
Plants are stunted — yellow and peaked	Too much water	Reduce watering
	Poor drainage	Improve drainage; add more organic matter before next planting
	Compacted soil	Cultivate soil more deeply
	Too much rubbish	Remove rubbish
	Acid soil	Test, add lime if necessary
	Not enough fertilizer	Test, add fertilizer (this should have been done before planting)

Common problems in vegetable gardening (cont.)

PROBLEM	POSSIBLE CAUSES	POSSIBLE CURES
Plants are stunted — yellow and peaked (cont.)	Insects or diseases	Identify and follow recommendations from your extension service
	Yellow or wilt disease, especially if yellowing attacks one side of the plant first	Spraying will not help; remove affected plants; plant disease-resistant seed in clean soil
Seeds do not come up	Not enough time for germination	Wait
	Too cold	Wait — replant if necessary
	Too dry	Water
	Too wet, they rotted	Replant
	Birds or insects ate them	Replant
	Seed was too old	Replant with fresh seed
Young plants die	Fungus (damping-off)	Treat seed with fungicide or plant in sterile soil
	Rotting	Do not overwater
	Fertilizer burn	Follow recommendations for using the fertilizer more closely; be sure fertilizer is mixed thoroughly with soil
Leaves have holes	Insects, birds, rabbits	Identify culprit and take appropriate measures
	Heavy winds or hail	Plan for better protection
Tortured, abnormal growth	Herbicide residue in sprayer, in grass clippings used as mulch, in drift from another location	Use separate sprayer for herbicides; spray only on still days; use another means of weed control
	Virus	Control insects that transmit disease; remove infected plants (do not put them on the compost pile)
Blossom ends of tomatoes and peppers rot	Dry weather following a wet spell	Mulch to even out soil moisture
	Not enough calcium in soil	Add lime

Common problems in vegetable gardening (cont.)

PROBLEM	POSSIBLE CAUSES	POSSIBLE CURES
Blossom ends of tomatoes and peppers rot (cont.)	Compacted soil	Cultivate
	Too-deep cultivation	Avoid cultivating too deeply
There is no fruit	Weather too cold	Watch your planting time
	Weather too hot	Same as above
	Too much nitrogen	Fertilize only as often and as heavily as needed for the variety
	No pollination	Pollinate with a brush, or by shaking plant (depending on kind); do not kill all the insects
	Plants not mature enough	Wait

The Healthy Garden: A Trouble-Shooting Record

Gardening is a process where you learn as you go along. Once you've dealt with a pest or disease problem once, you should recognize it if it occurs again. To help you keep track of the steps you have taken to keep your garden healthy, use the chart below. You shouldn't have many problems with herbs, but some vegetables need more care. Mark down the problem, the date you spotted it, what you did about it and when, and what the results were. This will give you a useful reference for the following year.

VEGETABLE (planting date)	PROBLEM (date)	TREATMENT (dates)	RESULT	NOTES

Points to Remember About Keeping Your Garden Healthy

1. Remember that a clean garden is a healthy garden. Time spent removing old or diseased plants, weeds, and garden debris is a valuable investment in keeping your garden trouble-free.

2. Do not assume that all insects are harmful. Some are harmless and some are important to the healthy development of your crop because they keep down harmful pests.

3. Watch for signs of trouble in your garden. Some of the danger signs: Suddenly some previously healthy plants keel over and die; plants seem stunted or weak; leaves of formerly healthy plants have holes in them; leaves turn yellow; mildew appears on leaves or stems. All these indicate the presence of pests or disease and should be identified promptly.

4. The surest way to control most pests in your garden (unless you are an organic gardener) is by use of chemical insecticides. A herbicide is *not* an insecticide. Different insecticides destroy different pests. Be sure you use the right one.

5. Insecticides have a residual effect, and a residue of insecticide left on the plant when it's harvested is poisonous. Always read the rules and precautions on the label and follow them very carefully. Also follow the instructions for safe use of insecticides outlined in the preceding pages.

6. Do not apply an insecticide on a windy day, or when rain is expected within 12 to 24 hours. When spraying or dusting, make sure all surfaces of the leaves are covered.

7. There are organic alternatives to chemical controls. If you do not wish to use chemical insecticides, try the following control methods:

   - Plant problem-free vegetables. Some vegetables suffer little from pest attacks; others produce so generously that you can afford to lose a few to the insects. (Herbs don't usually have many pest problems.)
   - Hand-pick large insects off the plants, or wash smaller ones off with the garden hose (do this on a dry day so the water doesn't stay on the leaves too long, making the plant more susceptible to disease).
   - Employ the "good" insects to get rid of the "bad" ones, letting the helpful insects in your garden work undisturbed. They will not, however, provide a full answer to the problem. Do not buy ladybugs, praying mantises, etc. through the mail. There's no way you can be sure they'll stay in your yard once they get there.

8. With plant diseases, prevention is better than cure. Avoid the combination of too much moisture, too much shade, and soil that's too cool.

9. Plant disease-resistant varieties, rotate crops (plant in a different area of the garden each year); and keep your garden clean.

10. If a plant does become diseased, remove and destroy it before it can infect other plants. Burn the diseased plant or put it in the garbage. Don't leave it lying in the yard, and don't put it on the compost pile.

Container and Small-Space Gardening

Container and Small-Space Gardening

Even if you don't have the land on which to plant a garden, you need not forgo the satisfaction of raising your own vegetables, herbs, and fruits for the good taste of homegrown produce. For many city or apartment dwellers who do not have access to a conventional garden plot, container gardening provides an alternative. Many vegetables can be successfully grown indoors in a sunny area or under lights, or on a sunny balcony or patio. Herbs often lend themselves obligingly to indoor life. Even dwarf fruit trees can be planted in containers and can produce an adequate crop. In fact, in cold areas, container growing may be the only way to cultivate heat-loving fruits such as peaches, which can be planted in a container outside or on a balcony and moved into a protected area during the winter months.

Container gardening is often the choice even of gardeners who do have a regular garden. It's easy, fun, and has a number of practical advantages. For one thing, some space-saving techniques lend themselves admirably to container gardening. For another, it's possible to extend the gardening season at both ends by making use of the mobility of your containers. In spring, the soil in a container—even outdoors—warms up and dries out faster than in a conventional bed, so you can plant some crops earlier and get a headstart on the growing season. And heat-sensitive crops like lettuce and some of the cabbage family benefit from being moved out of the sun on hot days. If such plants are growing in containers, all you need do is move the container. If they're growing in the garden you may need to provide sun screens or other protective devices. And in northern areas many container-grown plants can winter over comfortably in your home or apartment, although they could not survive the cold winter weather if left outside.

Many vegetables can be grown in almost any container that will hold enough soil to accommodate the mature plant comfortably and provide adequate drainage. Garden centers sell a vast assortment of containers, from ordinary clay flower

Using containers, it's possible to plant a complete vegetable garden indoors or on a sunny patio. One of the advantages of containers is that they can be moved around to accommodate the plants' heat and light preferences.

pots to half barrels. Also, many household discards can be recycled into very effective planters, among them coffee cans, plastic two- or three-liter pop bottles, plastic bags, old washtubs—whatever you have around the house. The only work you have to do on such containers is provide drainage holes (lining the bottom of the container with some type of gravel or charcoal will not provide adequate drainage).

Perhaps the easiest container of all is the plastic bag you buy your potting soil in. Leave the soil in the bag and punch a few drainage holes in the bottom of the bag (you can stand the bag upright or lay it flat). Water the soil, plant the vegetable of your choice, and put this easy "container garden" in a sunny area. Obviously, a plastic soil bag won't last more than one season.

Whether you buy or recycle your containers, it's important to correlate the size of the container to the size of the mature plant. Generally speaking, the diameter of the container should measure half the size of the full-grown plant. A tomato plant that is expected to grow two feet wide and four feet tall needs a container one foot wide and two feet tall. You could use a slightly smaller container, but you would have to fertilize and water more carefully. You can also establish a vegetable plant in a container that's larger than necessary and plant smaller vegetables, herbs, or flowers, around the edge.

A container makes a decorative feature when planted with a single large, leafy vegetable plant surrounded by smaller plants.

The soil you use in a container must be carefully chosen. Regular garden soil is usually not sufficiently well drained for container use. Also, if it's not sterilized before use it may carry weeds, diseases, or pests. The ideal soil for container use should be well balanced in that it can both retain water and nutrients and provide adequate drainage.

Most good container soils contain three elements: peat moss, perlite, and vermiculite. Peat moss is well-shredded, partially decomposed spaghnum (a plant that grows over swamps and forms peat bogs). Peat moss holds considerable water and nutrients. Vermiculite is basically a baked expanded clay material which is capable of holding one hundred times its own weight in water. Vermiculite does not hold many plant nutrients, but it helps aerate the soil because it does not compact even when dry; it's also very light, which helps reduce the weight of the soil. Perlite is white, sterilized volcanic ash. It holds neither water nor nutrients and its purpose in the soil mix is to provide drainage. Like vermiculite, it's also very light to help reduce overall weight.

These three constituents can be mixed with sterilized garden soil to make a good container soil. You can also mix them together without garden soil to make a "soil-less" container growth medium. Soil-less soils have a number of advantages over regular garden soil mixes: they're lighter, easier to handle, and more readily available, and they don't compact as solidly as soil. One disadvantage, however, is that you need to fertilize more frequently to provide the nutrients normally found in garden soil.

You can make a simple soil-less mix by combining one part (by volume) peat moss, one part perlite, and one part vermiculite. A simple soil mix consists of one third (by volume) sterilized garden soil, one third peat moss, and a final third made up of equal parts of vermiculite and perlite.

If you want to try some other mixes, here are three highly recommended mixes, each of which makes one cubic yard.

University of California Mix

11 bushels each shredded peat moss and clean sand
7½ pounds ground limestone (preferably dolomite)
2½ pounds ground calcium carbonate limestone
4 ounces powered potassium nitrate
4 ounces powered potassium sulfate

Mix all the ingredients together well. This mix will store satisfactorily for some time. Within a week of the time you want to use it, add 2½ pounds of horn and hoof meal or dried blood (13 percent nitrogen).

Cornell Peat-Lite Mix A

11 bushels shredded peat moss
11 bushels vermiculite
 5 pounds ground limestone (preferably dolomite)
 1 pound powdered superphosphate (20 percent)
 2 to 12 pounds of a 5-10-5 fertilizer

Cornell Peat-Lite Mix B

Use the same ingredients as in Mix A, but substitute perlite for the vermiculite.

If you have good garden soil available and you want a more natural soil mix, you can make your own by combining equal parts (by volume) of garden soil and clean sand.

Whatever type of soil you choose, all the ingredients should be sterilized to help prevent soil-borne weed, disease, and insect problems. Peat moss, vermiculite, and perlite are sterilized when you buy them. To sterilize your own container soil or soil ingredients, bring the temperature of the soil to 180°F and maintain this temperature for 30 minutes. You can do this in your own oven, but the smell is terrible. If possible, use an outdoor grill and a candy thermometer.

If you don't want to mess with making and fertilizing your own soil mix, you can choose from many commercial mixes. Most of these are sterilized, but check the label to make sure. Some of these commercial mixes do not contain perlite and compact easily. These mixes are not satisfactory. If you buy one accidentally, you can improve it by adding perlite. It's much easier, however, to buy a good mix to start with.

WATERING CONTAINER-GROWN PLANTS

One of the biggest disadvantages of container gardening is that you have to water more frequently. Soil type, temperature, humidity, wind, and the growth rate of the plant all determine when you need to water, so it's difficult to do it to any specific schedule. The most satisfactory way to

determine when your containers need watering is to push your finger two or three inches into the soil. If the soil at that depth is dry to the touch, water the plants. It's possible to buy all sorts of devices—probes that light up or beep when the soil is dry—to tell you when to water, but the do-it-yourself method works just as well and is much cheaper.

Don't wait for your plants to tell you they are over-dry by wilting. Once a plant wilts, it will never photosynthesize at the same rate as it did before. This damage may not be immediately recognizable, but the yield of the plant will be reduced.

Most tap water contains soluble salts which can build up in the soil and, if you are not careful, become toxic to the plant. To avoid this, water heavily when you do water, allowing the water to flow out of the drainage holes in the bottom of the container. This will help wash away the salts left in the soil by the previous watering. If you use rain or distilled water you won't have this problem with soluble salts. Distilled water, however, is expensive.

FERTILIZING CONTAINER-GROWN PLANTS

Because you water container-grown plants more frequently than garden-grown plants, you will also need to fertilize more frequently. The easiest way to fertilize container vegetables is to use a soluble house plant fertilizer, but at reduced strength. Most house plant fertilizers are much too strong for vegetables, so use them at half the rate of the label recommendation and half as often as recommended for house plants.

You can, theoretically, fertilize container-grown vegetables with regular granular-type garden fertilizer. However, it's very easy to overdo it. If you wish to use a granular fertilizer, use a half tablespoon three times in a growing season for a 12-inch diameter container. If you notice any browning on the edges of the older leaves on the plant, you have probably over-fertilized. In this case, water heavily to flush the fertilizer out of the soil.

GIVING YOUR CONTAINER GARDEN ENOUGH LIGHT

If you are growing vegetables in containers, you must provide them with the same light as in a traditional garden, which means for the most part that they should be in full sun. Fruiting vegetables need at least ten to twelve hours of sun a day in order to fruit properly. Root vegetables need eight to ten hours, and leafy vegetables need the least

Growing tomatoes in hanging pot

the plants to be of any value.

Sunlight contains the full color spectrum of light needed for plant growth, and the blue and red spectrums are the most important. Commercial plant lights produce large amounts of blue spectrum light. Incandescent light bulbs produce high amounts of red spectrum light but they also produce a lot of heat. Most incandescent bulbs get far too hot to be positioned close enough to the plants for their light to be beneficial. Fluorescent lights produce small amounts of red spectrum light, but even this small amount is adequate for vegetable plants. Cool white fluorescent lights produce as much light as regular fluorescent lights but less heat. For use with container plants, the best and most economical choices are cool white fluorescent tubes or regular fluorescent tubes.

RAISED-BED GARDENING

Raised-bed gardening is a compromise between container and traditional gardening. A raised bed is simply an enclosed area of soil that is raised above the natural level of the soil. In the garden, the bottom of the raised bed is the regular soil; when the raised bed is built on a solid base, it becomes a container. Some raised beds are constructed on wheels or rollers so that they can be moved around.

A raised bed on wheels becomes a container

amount of sun of all the vegetables—six to eight hours. Just keep in mind that the more sunlight your vegetable plants get, the better they will do. Note that the subject here is sunlight, not heat; cool-weather vegetables, like peas and lettuce, certainly need light, but will not tolerate too much heat.

If you have a choice, position your container garden, whether indoors or outdoors on a balcony, in a southern location. This will give the plants the maximum sunlight available. Next best are east and west exposures, with a northern location providing the fewest hours of sunlight.

If you can't provide sufficient light for the plants naturally, supplement the available sunlight with artificial light. Artificial light does not travel and should be within six to twelve inches of the tops of

A raised bed can be the answer to garden soil that is so poor that no amount of treatment is going to make it adequate for proper growth of your chosen plants. In such a case, you can make a raised bed simply by providing a solid frame 12 to 24 inches deep and filling it with good soil (equal parts of well-drained fertile garden soil and peat moss or compost give good results). Then you can plant as usual. The soil you use can be a commercial or homemade mix (such as the mixes described earlier), or can be transported from a spot where the soil is richer—another area of your own garden, perhaps, or a neighbor or friend's garden.

To make the frame for a raised bed, you can use any sturdy construction material that will not rot away quickly. Railroad ties and landscape timbers are ideal, and these can be purchased at most garden centers. If you're purchasing wood at the lumber yard, choose 2 × 4s or 4 × 4s; these work better than 1 × 6s, which tend to split and crack and do not last very long. Whichever size you choose, the wood should be treated with a wood preservative to prevent it from rotting.

A raised-bed garden is planted just the same way as a regular garden bed. Among its advantages are that the soil warms up faster and dries out sooner than in the garden, enabling you to start planting earlier. However, once the bed is established you will find that because the soil tends to dry out faster than in a regular bed you will need to water (and, therefore, fertilize) more often. You should also have your soil tested regularly to make sure important nutrients are not being washed away.

Another concern with a raised bed is that the small soil volume may freeze solid in cold areas, killing perennial vegetable or herb plants. Perennial crops will need additional winter protection in very cold areas. Despite these facts, however, any vegetable or herb that will grow in the garden can be grown successfully in a properly maintained raised bed.

Note, too, that raised beds offer very practical advantages to elderly or handicapped gardeners because they are easier to cultivate without excessive stooping or bending. This may not be an issue for younger, supple gardeners, but any person who has back problems or limited mobility will welcome the accessibility of a raised bed. For some handicapped gardeners or those confined to a wheelchair, raised-bed or container culture may enable them to garden productively as they could not in a regular ground-level garden.

SPACE-SAVING GARDENING TECHNIQUES

Part of the advantage of container gardening is that it makes efficient use of small spaces. Even in the traditional garden, however, it's possible to make the most of limited space by using a number of techniques which, essentially, allow you to use vertical space or "stretch" the capacity of

Raised beds are manageable, easy to cultivate, and attractive to look at. They also provide an answer to poor garden soil: the plants are grown in rich soil laid on top of the garden soil and contained within a frame of wood or some other suitable material.

A-frame

An A-frame can be constructed with narrow containers at the base, as shown, or with the supports set directly into the ground. The covering can be a trellis or simply a section of bird netting. An A-frame allows you to make use of vertical space for vining or climbing plants which, as they grow, provide shade for cool-weather vegetables planted underneath the frame.

horizontal space.

Taking advantage of vertical space is one of the easiest ways to grow more in a small area. Many gardeners already stake or cage tomatoes rather than letting them sprawl on the ground. Hanging baskets make excellent containers for some vegetables, including cherry tomatoes and bush-type cucumbers. Vining crops can be successfully trained on vertical trellises or "A" frames. An additional advantage of using an "A" frame is that the space between the supports provides an ideal bed for heat-sensitive plants like lettuce—the canopy of vines or leaves shelters the plants from the sun. Vining squash, melons, cucumbers, and pole beans can all be grown on "A" frames, with lettuce, spinach, or radishes beneath them.

You can buy an "A" frame at your garden center or make one yourself. The simplest way to build one is to make two rectangles about four to five feet high and any length you wish. Attach the rectangles at the top at an angle of about 45 degrees, and cover the frame with narrow lengths of wood to form a trellis shape or with bird netting or some similar type of netting.

Making the most of ground space means eliminating unnecessary empty space between rows, and you can do this with wide row plantings or with narrow single rows planted back to back. A wide row should be two or three feet wide (you must be able to reach halfway across from either side in order to cultivate the plants). Simply broadcast the seeds over this wide row and, when the seedlings are the appropriate size, thin them according to the directions given in the individual plant profiles in Part 2 of this book. Two narrow single rows planted back to back eliminate the empty space usually left between two rows and still give you space to maintain the plants without too much stretching.

Succession planting offers yet another way to make maximum use of your available space, and is discussed further in the earlier section on "Planting Your Garden." Succession planting is achieved by planning to replace one early crop immediately after harvesting with another crop that will mature before the growing season is over. You can also plant a crop for early harvest along with a slower-growing crop for later harvest. For instance, lettuce planted alongside tomato seedlings will be ready for harvesting long before the tomatoes grow big enough either to overshadow the lettuce too much or to need the space the lettuce occupies (in fact, the growing tomatoes will shelter the lettuce from the sun's heat). Radishes or lettuce can be planted in this manner between tomatoes, peppers, corn, or squash plants.

Even if you have plenty of garden space, you should consider using some of these space-saving techniques. The smaller the actual growing area occupied by your plants, the less weeding, watering, fertilizing, and overall maintenance will fall to your lot. Even the most devoted gardener doesn't need to make more work than necessary for himself or herself. Also, space-saving techniques allow you to save on mulch and fertilizer and to conserve water.

COMMUNITY GARDENS

Even if you're gardening successfully on your own balcony, patio, or windowsill, there's another possibility you may wish to consider. Many city and apartment dwellers are finding that community gardening—sharing a lot with friends and neighbors—is a most rewarding form of horticulture. Many cities will give prospective community gardeners permission to cultivate vacant lots free of charge, and some community groups have been able to form not-for-profit

organizations and buy their lots. Community gardening fills a number of needs: it provides space for would-be outdoor gardeners who don't have gardens of their own; it turns unattractive empty lots into welcome havens of greenery, order, and productivity; and it promotes friendship and cooperation among the people who share the project.

The ideal location for a community garden should have good soil, full sunlight, and a reliable water source. A sturdy fence is also a necessary protection from destructive elements—animal and human. Apart from these natural resources, community gardeners need a strong governing board and a well-considered set of rules. Regular meetings of those involved help keep the project running smoothly, the workload distributed fairly, and the tempers of all concerned sweet.

If you're interested in investigating the possibility of starting a community garden in your neighborhood, there are plenty of sources of help and encouragement. Many cities, park districts, and local horticultural societies have programs for beginning community gardeners. Call your city hall or check your local telephone directory for sources in your area. State Cooperative Extension Services (which are listed in Part 5 of this book) offer help to community gardeners. There is even a federal Cooperative Extensive Service program that operates in 21 cities throughout the United States for the benefit of urban gardeners. This program is located in the following cities: New York, Chicago, Los Angeles, Philadelphia, Detroit, Houston, Atlanta, Baltimore, Boston, Cleveland, Jacksonville (Florida), Memphis, Milwaukee, Newark, New Orleans, St. Louis, Indianapolis, Phoenix, Seattle, Denver, and Bridgeport.

A national organization, the American Community Gardening Association, publishes a quarterly newsletter on issues relevant to community gardeners and also sponsors a national community gardening contest. For more information, write to The American Community Gardening Association, c/o The Chicago Botanical Gardens, P.O. Box 400, Chicago, Illinois 60022.

Organic Gardening: Facts and Fallacies

Gardeners who prefer not to use chemicals to control garden pests or diseases often refer to organic methods of control. If you're interested in organic gardening it's important to know exactly what the term means, and to realize that not everything you hear is necessarily true. Organic gardening techniques, just like nonorganic practices, must be well researched and documented. Do not assume that everything you hear about a practice that someone claims to have followed successfully for years is always based on fact.

Some organic gardening practices are truly organic—that is, they make no use of chemicals of any kind. You can handpick caterpillars off your plants without using chemicals. However, using match heads (which contain sulfur) and kitchen ammonia (which is high in nitrogen) as a lawn treatment does not add up to nonchemical or organic control. The match head and ammonia system has been fairly widely recommended as a spring tonic for lawns, but the recommendation is not accompanied by specifics as to how much you should apply. The application rate, of course, would depend on the size of the lawn. Moreover, the amount of sulfur present in a few match heads is unlikely to have an effect on a lawn of any size in terms of lowering the pH—which is the intended result—and not all lawns require the same amount of nitrogen.

The significant effect of such recommendations, however, is that they encourage people to use familiar household products that are simply not designed for garden use, and have not been tested to determine how safely they can be used in the garden.

Every garden pesticide sold in the United States must meet safety standards that determine the immediate and long-term toxicity levels of the product and how long the residue remains on the plants. Many of the chemicals that you keep under the sink or in a closet for household use are, in fact, more toxic than garden pesticides. Many well-meaning gardeners have applied familiar products to their gardens, not realizing that though they are familiar with the products they know nothing at all about their effects on growing things. These same gardeners are afraid to use pesticides because of their chemical content and because they are unfamiliar with them. They do not seem to connect familiar kitchen products with toxicity and would probably be highly surprised to learn that they may be *more* toxic than an insecticide.

What is organic gardening?

One of the reasons for the confusion about organic gardening is that there is no standard definition of what the term means. Some claim that gardening organically means avoiding the use of pesticides, and others that it means using only natural pesticides; others argue about what is and is not "natural." Some organic gardeners insist that soil care will control every problem and that fertilizers destroy the soil; others think it's okay to use chemical fertilizers but not okay to apply chemical insecticides or fungicides. With so many varying views to consider, it's no wonder the organic gardener gets confused, so it's helpful to have definitions of the terms.

A pesticide is a product—chemical or natural—that's used to kill or control a pest (and "pest" does not always mean an insect). Pesticides include insecticides, fungicides, bactericides, and herbicides. Fertilizers are not usually considered pesticides.

As the names suggest, insecticides are used to control insects; bactericides to control bacterial diseases; and herbicides to control weeds.

The term toxicity measures how dangerous or poisonous a product is, and is stated as LD 50: this represents the lethal dose for 50 percent of the test population, usually rats or rabbits. The lower the number the higher the toxicity; that is, the less the amount needed to be lethal. The LD 50 is also calibrated according to body weight.

Toxicity is measured for three types of exposure to the chemical: acute oral, or ingestion by mouth; acute dermal, or absorption through the skin; and chronic or long-term exposure. Pesticides are also tested for how long their residue remains on the plants. Typical chemical pesticides are designed to break down and leave no residue within 7 to 14 days in the presence of sunlight. The pesticides break down into harmless basic elements, and after the specified time no longer present any danger of toxicity.

How poisonous are garden pesticides?

The following list details the LD 50 measures of the pesticides recommended in this book and some other garden pesticides and common household products. *Remember, the lower the number the higher the toxicity.*

Pesticides

Pesticide	Acute Oral	Acute Dermal
Captan	10,000	over 10,000
Diazinon	300-400	3600
Sevin	500	850
Benomyl	10,000	over 10,000
Zineb	over 5200	
Maneb	6750	
Dicofol	1300	5000
Thiram	780	
Ferbam	over 17,000	
Malathion	1000	4100

Bacillus thuringiensis, an organic pesticide recommended in this book, is harmless to humans and animals. Bacillus thuringiensis is also known as Dipel or Thuricide.

Common "organic" pesticides

Pesticide	Acute Oral	Acute Dermal
Rotenone	132-1500	350
Pyrethrum	1500	1800
Milky spores	harmless to mammals	

Common household products or familiar chemicals

Product	Acute Oral
aspirin	1200
ethyl alcohol	4500
common table salt	3320
caffeine	200
gasoline	150
nicotine	10 mm. per kg. body weight

It's easy to see from this information that products that we handle daily may be toxic, and that the origin of a pesticide (synthetic or organic) does not necessarily determine how safe it is. Never assume that a product can be safely used as a pesticide. Always read the *entire* label, and if a product is not specified as a pesticide for garden use, *never* use it in the garden.

Do garden pesticides cause air pollution?

Garden pesticides decompose quickly, so their use does not aggravate the problem of air pollution. You can cause more harm to the air around you by driving to the store (or, for that matter, to your community garden) than you are likely to do by spraying your plants with a pesticide. This does not mean, however, that it's safe or sensible to spray every time you see a bug. Overuse of pesticides can damage or even kill your plants. More information on pesticides is given in "Keeping Your Garden Healthy."

Sensible rules for organic gardening

If you do want to garden organically, your best plan is to select vegetables or other plants that have few pest problems; that produce so generously that you can afford to lose a few fruits to the bugs (squash, for instance); or that attract only pests that can be controlled organically or mechanically. The individual plant profiles indicate whether or not a crop is suitable for inclusion in an organic garden (herbs generally have few pest problems).

Also, try to attract beneficial insects which will help control destructive pests. (Don't buy these insects through the mail—there's no way of being sure they'll stay in your garden when you get them there.)

Finally, keep your garden very clean, and keep the soil as healthy as possible by keeping the fertility and the content of organic matter as high as possible. The following organic fertilizers can help keep your soil healthy and productive: Dried blood meal; bone meal; cow manure (use old manure because fresh manure can burn the plants); cottonseed meal; fish emulsion; granite dust; green sand; bat guano; chicken manure; leather dust; rock phosphate; seaweed (liquid); horse manure (use old manure because fresh manure can burn the plants).

These fertilizers contain different proportions of the macronutrients nitrogen, phosphorus, and potassium. Have your soil tested and use a fertilizer that will best complement the needs of the soil. Your local Cooperative Extension Service may offer a soil-testing service, or can recommend one to you. The Extension Service can also advise you on how best to improve the fertility of your soil.

One disadvantage to most organic fertilizers is that they must break down in the soil before they can be used by the plants, so they won't correct existing deficiencies in time to benefit the current crop. Keep the organic content of the soil high by adding large amounts of any of the following: Peat moss; straw; hay (note that hay may contain weed seeds); compost; grass clippings; mushroom compost; green manures; or seaweed. More information on fertilizing and soil care is given in "Spadework: The Essential Soil."

Part 2: Vegetables and Herbs

Plants, like people, often have definite likes and dislikes. Treat your vegetables and herbs right, and they'll reward you with a successful season and a healthy harvest.

Vegetables

**How your garden grows:
All the vegetables you can plant,
from seed to harvest—
you'll enjoy them all year.**

Artichoke, globe

Common names: artichoke, globe artichoke
Botanical name: Cynara scolymus
Origin: southern Europe, North America

Varieties
There are very few varieties of artichokes; Green Globe is the variety commonly grown.

Description

The artichoke is a thistlelike, tender perennial that grows three to four feet tall and three to four feet wide. It is grown for its flower buds, which are eaten before they begin to open. The elegant, architectural leaves make the artichoke very decorative, but because it is tender and hates cold weather, it's not for all gardens. Artichokes, an ancient Roman delicacy, were introduced to France by Catherine de Medici. Later they were taken to Louisiana by the French colonists.

Where and when to grow

Artichokes have a definite preference for a long, frost-free season with damp weather. They cannot handle heavy frost or snow, and in areas where the temperature goes below freezing they need special care and mulching. Artichokes grow best in the four central California counties and on the southern Atlantic and Gulf coasts. In the North, artichokes must be grown in a protected location — the temperature should not be over 70°F by day, or under 55°F at night. Plant them on the average date of last frost for your area.

How to plant

Artichokes are grown from offshoots, suckers, or seed. For best results, start with offshoots or suckers from a reputable nursery or garden center; artichoke plants grown from seed vary tremendously in quality. Artichokes need rich, well-drained

Globe artichoke seedling

Globe artichoke

soil that will hold moisture, and a position in full sunlight. When you're preparing the soil for planting, work in a low-nitrogen (5-10-10) fertilizer at the rate of one pound per 100 square feet or 10 pounds per 1,000 square feet. Too much nitrogen will keep the plant from flowering. Space the offshoots or suckers three to four feet apart in rows four to five feet apart.

Fertilizing and watering

Fertilize before planting and again at midseason, at the same rate as the rest of the garden. Detailed information on fertilizing is given in "Spadework: The Essential Soil" in Part 1.

Keep the soil evenly moist.

Special handling

For the roots to survive the winter in cooler areas, cut the plant back to about 10 inches, cover with a bushel basket, and then mulch with about two feet of leaves to help maintain an even soil temperature. Artichokes bear best the second year and should be started from new plants every three to four years.

Pests

Aphids and plume moths plague the artichoke. The plume moth is not a serious problem except in artichoke-growing areas. Aphids can be controlled chemically by spraying the foliage with Malathion or Diazinon or nonchemically by hand-picking or hosing them off the plants. Detailed information on pest control is given in "Keeping Your Garden Healthy" in Part 1.

Diseases

Crown rot may occur where drainage is poor or where the

plants have to be covered in winter. To avoid this problem, don't mulch until the soil temperature drops to 40°F, and don't leave the mulch in place longer than necessary.

Cut down on the incidence of disease by planting disease-resistant varieties when they're available, maintaining the general health of your garden, and avoiding handling the plants when they're wet. If a plant does become infected, remove and destroy it so it cannot spread disease to healthy plants. Detailed information on disease prevention is given in "Keeping Your Garden Healthy" in Part 1.

When and how to harvest

Time from planting to harvest is 50 to 100 days for artichokes grown from suckers; at least a year until the first bud forms when they're grown from seed. To harvest, cut off the globe artichoke bud with one to 1½ inches of stem before the bud begins to open.

Container growing

Globe artichokes can be container-grown provided you can find a large enough container—such as a half barrel. Each plant needs a container 36 to 38 inches wide.

Storing and preserving

Artichokes can be stored in the refrigerator for up to two weeks, or in a cold, moist place up to one month. Artichoke hearts can also be frozen, canned, or pickled. Detailed information on storing and preserving is given in Part 4.

Serving suggestions

Cook artichokes in salted water with a squeeze of lemon juice to help retain their color. With hot artichokes serve a Hollandaise sauce; a vinaigrette is delicious when they're cold. They're not as messy to eat as you may imagine—anyway, it's quite legitimate to use your fingers. Stuff artichokes with seafood or a meat mixture and bake them. To stuff, spread open the leaves and remove some of the center leaves; cut off some of the hard tips of the outer leaves. An interesting Italian-style stuffing mix is seasoned breadcrumbs with anchovies, topped with a tomato sauce. For an Armenian-style dish, try ground lamb and bulgur (cracked wheat). Baby artichokes are delicious in stews, or marinated in olive oil, vinegar, and garlic as part of an antipasto. The Romans used to bottle artichokes in vinegar and brine.

Artichoke, Jerusalem
See Jerusalem artichoke

Asparagus

Common name: asparagus
Botanical name: Asparagus officinalis
Origin: Mediterranean

Varieties
Paradise, Mary Washington, and Martha Washington are all rust-resistant varieties.

Description

Asparagus is a long-lived hardy perennial with fleshy roots and fernlike, feathery foliage. The plant grows about three feet tall, and the part you eat is the tender young stem. It takes patience to establish an asparagus bed, but it's worth it; once established, it's there for the duration. Fresh asparagus is a delicacy that commands a devoted following—the first asparagus is as welcome to the gourmet as the first crocus is to the gardener.

Where and when to grow

Asparagus grows well in most areas of the United States, with the exception of the Deep South. It likes a climate where the winters are cold enough to freeze the top few inches of soil and provide it with the necessary period of dormancy. Advance planning is essential when you're starting an asparagus bed, because it's virtually impossible to move the bed once it's established. You'll probably have to order asparagus crowns by mail through a nursery catalog; order early, and plant asparagus four to six weeks before your area's average date of last frost.

How to plant

Asparagus needs well-drained soil, with a pH over 6. Full sun is best, but asparagus will tolerate a little shade. When you're preparing the soil, spade down eight to 10 inches, and dig in one to 1½ pounds per 100 square feet of a complete, well-balanced fertilizer. Asparagus is usually

Asparagus

grown from crowns; look for well-grown, well-rooted specimens, and be sure they don't dry out. To plant asparagus crowns, dig out a trench or furrow 10 inches wide and 10 to 12 inches deep, and put in two to four inches of loose soil. Space the crowns in the prepared bed in rows 18 inches apart, leaving 12 to 18 inches between plants. Place the crowns on the soil, with the roots well spread out, and cover with two more inches of soil. As the spears grow, gradually fill in the trench to the top.

Fertilizing and watering

Apply a high-nitrogen (15-10-10) fertilizer after harvesting the spears, at the rate of one pound per 100 square feet or 10 pounds per 1,000 square feet. Detailed information on fertilizing is given in "Spadework: The Essential Soil" in Part 1.

It's important to give asparagus enough water when the spears are forming. The plant is hardy and will survive without extra watering, but the stalks may be stringy and woody if you don't keep the soil moist.

Special handling

Do not handle the plants when they are wet. Asparagus does not relish competition, especially from grass plants. Weed thoroughly by hand; control weeds conscientiously, or they will lower your yield considerably.

Pests

The asparagus beetle may attack your plants, but should not be a problem except in commercial asparagus-growing areas. If you do encounter this pest, pick it off, or spray with carbaryl. Detailed information on pest control is given in "Keeping Your Garden Healthy" in Part 1.

Diseases

Asparagus can develop rust; you can lessen the incidence of disease by opting for a rust-resistant variety. Generally, asparagus is a problem-free crop and suitable for the organic gardener. Detailed information on disease prevention is given in "Keeping Your Garden Healthy" in Part 1.

When and how to harvest

Asparagus should not be harvested until it's three years old; the crowns need time to develop fully. During the third season, cut off the spears at or slightly below soil level. Move a little soil gently aside as you cut the spears so you can see what you're doing—if you cut blind you may damage young spears that have not yet pushed through the surface. Harvest asparagus when the spears are eight to 10 inches tall; if the stalks have started to feather out, it's too late to eat them. Stop harvesting when the stalks start coming up pencil-thin; if you harvest them all, you'll kill the plants.

Container growing

Asparagus is a perennial that needs a cold period for dormancy, therefore it is extremely difficult to provide appropriate conditions in a container.

Storing and preserving

The Romans began to dry their asparagus for out-of-season dining as early as 200 B.C. These days, you can store it up to one week in the refrigerator—keep it upright in an inch or so of water, as you'd keep flowers. You can also freeze or can it, but it's best eaten fresh. Detailed information on storing and preserving is given in Part 4.

Serving suggestions

In the first century the Emperor Augustus told his minions to carry out executions "quicker than you can cook asparagus," and they knew they'd better get the job done fast. One of the earliest records of asparagus being eaten in America recommends it with "oyl and vinegar," which is still one of the best ways. Steam asparagus quickly, or cook it upright in a pan, so the stems cook faster than the tender tips. Fresh asparagus adorned with nothing but a little melted butter is superb—or try it with creamed chicken on toast or laid on toast and topped with a thin slice of prosciutto and cream sauce. Chive mayonnaise, mustard butter, or a caper butter sauce are all splendid alternative dressings for asparagus.

Q and A

Q: Why do you have to wait so long after planting before you can harvest asparagus for the first time?
A: You actually harvest the tender young shoots before they are fully developed, so the asparagus plant needs to develop a strong enough root system to compensate for the considerable damage caused by harvesting.
Q: Can I grow asparagus from the red berries on the plant?
A: Yes. Plant the dried berries early the following spring. However, growing asparagus from seed takes five to six years to first harvest. This is why most people prefer to buy established crowns.
Q: How long will an asparagus bed last once it is established?
A: A well-established and properly maintained asparagus bed will last a lifetime—30 to 40 years.
Q: Should the asparagus ferns be removed, and if so, when?
A: Yes. Remove the ferns in late fall at the first sign of frost. This will reduce disease problems.
Q: Is it true that some asparagus plants are male and some female?
A: Yes. Some plants have male flowers, while others have the female flowers that produce the red berries. There is no real difference in flavor or harvest yields.

Bean, broad

Common names: bean, broad bean, horsebean, fava bean, Scotch bean, Windsor bean
Botanical name: Vicia faba
Origin: Central Asia

Varieties
Long Pod (55 days); Broad Long Pod (57 days). Few varieties are available; grow the variety available in your area.

Description

The broad bean is a bushy, hardy annual that grows three to four feet tall; it has square stems

Broad bean

with leaves divided into leaflets. The white flowers are splotched with brown. The pods are six to eight inches long and when mature contain four to six or more light-brown seeds. The broad bean has quite a history. Upper-class Greeks and Romans thought that eating "horse beans" would cloud their vision, but the species became a dietary staple of the Roman legionnaires (who knew them as fava beans) and later of the poor people in England. In fact, they're not true beans at all but are related to the vetch, another legume.

Where and when to grow

Broad beans will grow in cool weather that would be unsuitable for snap beans. They like full sun but need cool weather to set their pods. They prefer temperatures below 70°F and should be planted very early in the growing season; they will not produce in the summer's heat. In areas where winters are mild, plant broad beans in the fall for a spring crop. In cold areas they can be grown instead of lima beans, which require a warmer and longer growing season.

How to plant

Plant broad beans very early in spring. Choose a location in full sunlight with soil that is fertile, high in organic matter, and well-drained. Broad beans prefer an alkaline soil. When you're preparing the soil for planting, work in a complete, well-balanced fertilizer at the rate of one pound per 100 square feet or 10 pounds per 1,000 square feet.

Plant broad bean seeds one to two inches deep in rows four feet apart. When the seedlings are growing strongly, thin them to stand eight to 10 inches apart.

Fertilizing and watering

Beans set up a mutual exchange with soil microorganisms called nitrogen-fixing bacteria, which help them produce their own fertilizer. Some gardeners recommend that if you haven't grown beans in the plot the previous season, you should treat the bean seeds before planting with a nitrogen-fixing bacteria inoculant to help them convert organic nitrogen compounds into usable organic compounds. This is a perfectly acceptable practice but it isn't really necessary; the bacteria in the soil will multiply quickly enough once they've got a growing bean plant to work with.

Fertilize before planting and again at midseason, at the same rate as the rest of the garden. Detailed information on fertilizing is given in "Spadework: The Essential Soil" in Part 1.

Water broad beans before the soil dries out, but don't overwater — wet soil conditions combined with high temperatures are an invitation to root diseases.

Pests

Beans are attacked by aphids, bean beetles, flea beetles, leafhoppers, and mites. Aphids, leafhoppers, and mites can be controlled chemically by spraying with Malathion or Diazinon. Bean beetles and flea beetles can be controlled chemically by spraying with carbaryl. Beans are almost always attacked by large numbers of pests that cannot be controlled by organic methods; this doesn't mean they can't be grown organically, but it does mean that yields may be lower if only organic controls are used. Detailed information on pest control is given in "Keeping Your Garden Healthy" in Part 1.

Diseases

Beans are susceptible to blight, mosaic, and anthracnose. You can cut down on the incidence of disease by planting disease-resistant varieties when they're available, maintaining the general health of your garden, and avoiding handling the plants when they're wet. If a plant does become infected, remove it and destroy it so it can't spread disease to healthy plants. Detailed information on disease prevention is given in "Keeping Your Garden Healthy" in Part 1.

When and how to harvest

Broad beans can be harvested when the beans are still the size of a pea and used like snap beans. It's more usual, however, to let them reach maturity and eat only the shelled beans. Time from planting to harvest is about 85 days.

Container growing

Beans can be grown in containers, but they need so much space to produce a reasonable crop that they're not really a practical choice for the container gardener.

Storing and preserving

Unshelled beans can be kept up to one week in the refrigerator. You can freeze, can, or dry the shelled beans. Dried shelled broad beans can be stored in a cool, dry place for 10 to 12 months. Detailed information on storing and preserving is given in Part 4.

Serving suggestions

Broad beans are good steamed and served with a light white or cheese sauce. Or top steamed broad beans with a little sautéed parsley, garlic, and onion. Use them in a casserole with onions, tomatoes, and cheese, or add them to a hearty vegetable soup along with any other vegetables you've got on hand. You can prepare broad beans any way you prepare lima beans.

Q and A

Q: I noticed small white and yellow moths in my bean patch. Are they likely to do any damage?
A: These moths are adult cabbage worms using your bean patch as shelter from the heat or predators. They will not harm your beans.
Q: Some of the bean seeds I bought for planting are pink in color. Why?
A: The pink coloring is a fungicide that protects the seeds from rotting in the cold soil.
Q: Should beans be planted in a different spot in the garden each year?
A: Beans are very susceptible to many soil-borne diseases and the incidence of disease is reduced by changing the location of the bean patch.
Q: If I plant several different beans in my garden, will they cross-pollinate and result in a poor harvest?
A: No. Beans are self-pollinating. Anyway, only the immediate offspring of a cross-pollination or the plants that grow from the crossed seeds would be affected.
Q: What can I do to stop rabbits from eating my bean plants?
A: The best way to stop rabbits is to keep them out by using some type of screen. Rabbits can also be slowed down by spraying your beans with a fungicide called Thiram. Don't use mothballs or other home remedies to deter rabbits. There is no scientific evidence that they work, and we don't know how these remedies affect the plants or the people who eat them.

Bean, dry

Common names: pinto beans, navy beans, horticultural beans, flageolet
Botanical name: Phaseolus species
Origin: South Mexico, Central America

Varieties

Dry beans are so called because the mature seeds are generally dried before they're eaten. There are many types, and some of the most common are cranberry, Great Northern, michilite, pinto, red kidney, white marrowfat, and pea beans. Horticultural beans, the genuine French flageolets, are a type of dry bean highly regarded by gourmets; they're usually eaten in the green-shell stage. Ask your Cooperative Extension Service for specific recommendations for your area.

Dry bean

Description

Dry beans are tender annuals. Their leaves are usually composed of three leaflets, and the small flowers are pale yellow or white. Dry beans are seldom planted in the home vegetable garden because it's so easy and inexpensive to buy them. They're fairly easy to grow, however, and give good yields, so if you have space in your garden you may want to try them.

You can grow either bush or pole varieties of beans. Bushes are generally easier to handle; they grow only one to two feet tall, and they mature earlier. Pole beans require a trellis for support; they grow more slowly, but produce more beans per plant.

Where and when to plant

Beans require warm soil to germinate and should be planted on the average date of last spring frost. Use the length of your growing season and the number of days the variety takes to mature to figure your latest planting date. If you need to sow before your area's average date of last frost, start the seed indoors in peat pots and transplant the seedlings when the soil has warmed up. Time your planting so that the beans will mature before very hot weather; they will not set pods at temperatures over 80°F.

You can plant bush beans every two weeks to extend the harvest, or start with bush beans and follow up with pole beans. In some parts of the country — California, for example — you can get two crops by planting in the spring and then planting again in early fall for a winter harvest.

How to plant

After the last frost is over, choose a bed in full sunlight; beans tolerate partial shade, but partial shade tends to mean a partial yield. When you're preparing the soil, mix in a pound of low-nitrogen (5-10-10) fertilizer — don't use a high-nitrogen fertilizer; too much nitrogen will promote growth of foliage but not of the beans. Bean seeds may crack and germinate poorly when the moisture content of the soil is too high. Don't soak the seeds before planting, and don't overwater immediately afterwards.

Plant the bean seeds an inch deep. If they're bush beans, plant the seeds three to four inches apart in rows at least 18 to 24 inches apart. Seeds of pole beans should be planted four to six inches apart in rows 30 to 36 inches apart. Or plant in inverted hills — five or six seeds to a hill, and 30 inches of space around each hill. When the seedlings are large enough to handle, thin the plants to four to six inches apart. Cut the seedlings with scissors at ground level; be careful not to disturb the others. Beans don't mind being a little crowded — in fact, they'll use each other for support.

Fertilizing and watering

Beans set up a mutual exchange with soil microorganisms called nitrogen-fixing bacteria, which help them produce their own fertilizer. Some gardeners recommend that if you haven't grown beans in the plot the previous season, you should treat the bean seeds before planting with a nitrogen-fixing bacteria inoculant to help them convert organic nitrogen compounds into usable organic compounds. This is a perfectly acceptable practice but it isn't really necessary; the bacteria in the soil will multiply quickly enough once they've got a growing bean plant to work with.

Fertilize before planting and again at midseason, at the same rate as the rest of the garden. Detailed information on fertilizing is given in "Spadework: The Essential Soil" in Part 1.

Keep the soil moist until the beans have pushed through the ground. Water regularly if there's no rain, but remember that water on the flowers can cause the flowers and small pods to fall off. When the soil temperature reaches 60°F you can mulch to conserve moisture.

Special handling

Don't touch bean plants when they're wet or covered with heavy dew; handling or brushing against them when they're wet

Set supports for pole beans at the time of planting.

spreads fungus spores. Cultivate thoroughly but with care, so that you don't disturb the bean plants' shallow root systems.

If you're planting pole beans, set the trellis or support in position before you plant or at the same time. If you wait until the plants are established, you risk damaging the roots when you set the supports. Make sure the support will be tall enough for the variety you're growing.

Pests

Beans may be attacked by aphids, bean beetles, flea beetles, leafhoppers, and mites. Aphids, leafhoppers, and mites can be controlled chemically by spraying with Malathion or Diazinon. Bean beetles and flea

beetles can be controlled chemically by spraying with carbaryl. Beans are almost always attacked by large numbers of pests that cannot be controlled by organic methods. This doesn't mean the organic gardener can't grow them, but yields may be lower if only organic controls are used. Detailed information on pest control is given in "Keeping Your Garden Healthy" in Part 1.

Diseases

Beans are susceptible to blight, mosaic, and anthracnose. You can cut down on the incidence of disease by planting disease-resistant varieties when they're available, maintaining the general health of your garden, and avoiding handling the plants when they're wet. If a plant does become infected, remove and destroy it so it cannot spread disease to healthy plants. Detailed information on disease prevention is given in "Keeping Your Garden Healthy" in Part 1.

When and how to harvest

Harvest dry beans when the plants have matured and the leaves have turned completely brown. At this time the seeds should be dry and hard — bite a couple of seeds; if you can hardly dent them they're properly dry and ready to harvest.

Container growing

Beans can be grown in containers, but they need so much space to produce a reasonable crop that they're not really a practical choice for the container gardener.

Storing and preserving

Unshelled beans can be kept up to one week in the refrigerator. You can freeze, can, or dry the shelled beans, and they can also be sprouted. Dried shelled beans can be stored in a cool, dry place for 10 to 12 months. Detailed information on storing and preserving is given in Part 4.

Serving suggestions

Dried beans are tremendously versatile and have the added advantage of being interchangeable in many recipes. They're also nourishing and figure prominently in vegetarian recipes. Chili and baked beans are two of the famous dishes that depend upon dried beans, and

beans are essential to the famous French cassoulet — a hearty stew that combines beans with pork, chicken, sausage, or a mixture of all three depending on the region the cook comes from. Try refried pinto beans as a filling for tacos. Add sausage or ham to a thick bean soup for a winter supper to cheer up the chilliest evening.

Q and A

Q: I noticed small white and yellow moths in my bean patch. Are they likely to do any damage?
A: These moths are adult cabbage worms using your bean patch as shelter from the heat or predators. They will not harm your beans.
Q: Some of the bean seeds I bought for planting are pink in color. Why?
A: The pink coloring is a fungicide that protects the seeds from rotting in the cold soil.
Q: Should beans be planted in a different spot in the garden each year?
A: Beans are very susceptible to many soil-borne diseases and the incidence of disease is reduced by changing the location of the bean patch.
Q: If I plant several different beans in my garden, will they cross-pollinate and result in a poor harvest?
A: No. Beans are self-pollinating. Anyway, only the immediate offspring of a cross-pollination or the plants that grow from the crossed seeds would be affected.
Q: What can I do to stop rabbits from eating my bean plants?
A: The best way to stop rabbits is to keep them out by using

some type of screen. Rabbits can also be slowed down by spraying your beans with a fungicide called Thiram. Don't use mothballs or other home remedies to deter rabbits. There is no scientific evidence that they work, and we don't know how these remedies affect the plants or the people who eat them.

Bean, green or snap

Common names: bean, green bean, snap bean, string bean, French bean, wax bean, pole bean, bush bean, stringless bean
Botanical name: Phaseolus vulgaris
Origin: South Mexico, Central America

Varieties

The most commonly grown beans are the green or snap bean and the yellow or wax variety. Since 1894, when Burpee introduced the Stringless Green Pod, most of these beans have been stringless. The following are only a few of the varieties available. Ask your Cooperative Extension Service for specific recommendations for your area.

Green bush (green snap bean, bush): Top Crop (48 days); Triumph (52 days); Gator Green (55 days); White-Seeded Provider (50 days); Astro (53 days); Blue Lake (56 days); Contender (53

Green bean

from seed to the first crop. They'll grow anywhere in the United States and are an encouraging vegetable for the inexperienced gardener. The immature pod is the part that's eaten. Beans grow as bushes or vines. Bushes are generally easier to handle; they grow only one to two feet tall, and they mature earlier. Pole beans require a trellis for support; they grow more slowly, but produce more beans per plant.

Where and when to grow

Because many varieties have a short growing season, beans do well in most areas, whatever the climate. They require warm soil to germinate and should be planted on the average date of last spring frost. You can plant bush beans every two weeks to extend the harvest, or you can start with bush beans and follow up with pole beans. In some parts of the country — California, for example — you can get two crops by planting in the spring and then planting again in early fall for a winter harvest. Use the length of your growing season and the number of days the variety takes to mature to figure your latest planting date. If you need to sow before your area's average last frost date, start the seed indoors in peat pots and transplant the seedlings when the soil has warmed up. Time your planting so the beans will mature before very hot weather; they will not set pods at temperatures over 80°F.

How to plant

After the last frost is over, choose a bed in full sunlight;

days); Provider (53 days); Tendergreen (57 days); Tender Crop (53 days)—all resistant to bean mosaic virus. **Wax bush** (yellow snap bean, bush): Cherokee Way (55 days); Early Wax (50 days)—both resistant to bean mosaic virus. **Green pole** (green snap bean, pole): Blue Lake (65 days); McCaslan (65 days)—both resistant to bean mosaic virus; Kentucky Wonder (65 days).

Description

Beans are tender annuals that grow either as bushes or vines. Their leaves are usually composed of three leaflets; their flowers are pale yellow, lavender, or white. The size and color of the pods and seeds vary. Snap beans require a short growing season — about 60 days of moderate temperatures beans tolerate partial shade, but partial shade tends to mean a partial yield. Prepare the soil by mixing in a pound of 5-10-10 fertilizer — don't use a high-nitrogen fertilizer, because too much nitrogen will promote growth of foliage but not of the beans. Work the fertilizer into the soil at the rate of one pound per 100 square feet or 10 pounds per 1,000 square feet.

Bean seeds may crack and germinate poorly when the moisture content of the soil is too high. Don't soak the seeds before planting, and don't overwater immediately afterward.

Plant seeds of all varieties an inch deep. If you're planting bush beans, plant the seeds two inches apart in rows at least 18 to 24 inches apart. Seeds of pole beans should be planted four to six inches apart in rows 30 to 36 inches apart. Or plant them in inverted hills, five or six seeds to a hill, with 30 inches of space around each hill. For pole varieties, set the supports or trellises at the time of planting.

When the seedlings are growing well, thin the plants to four to six inches apart. Cut the seedlings with scissors at ground level; be careful not to disturb the others. Beans don't mind being a little crowded; in fact, they'll use each other for support.

Fertilizing and watering

Beans set up a mutual exchange with soil microorganisms called nitrogen-fixing bacteria, which help them produce their own fertilizer. Some gardeners recommend that if you haven't grown beans in the plot the previous season, you should treat the bean seeds before planting with a nitrogen-fixing bacteria inoculant to help them convert organic nitrogen compounds into usable organic compounds. This is a perfectly acceptable practice but it isn't really necessary; the bacteria in the soil will multiply quickly enough once they've got a growing bean plant to work with.

Fertilize before planting and again at midseason, at the same rate as the rest of the garden. Detailed information on fertilizing is given in "Spadework: The Essential Soil" in Part 1.

Keep the soil moist until the beans have pushed through the ground. Water regularly if there is no rain, but remember that water on the flowers can cause the flowers and small pods to fall off. When the soil temperature reaches 60°F you can mulch to conserve moisture.

Special handling

Don't bother bean plants when they're wet or covered with heavy dew; handling or brushing against them when they're wet spreads fungus spores. Cultivate thoroughly but with care, so that you don't disturb the bean plants' shallow root systems. If you're planting pole beans, set the trellis or support in position before you plant or at the same time. If you wait until the plants are established, you risk damaging the roots when you set the supports. Make sure the support will be tall enough for the variety of beans you're growing.

Pests

Beans may be attacked by aphids, bean beetles, flea beetles, leafhoppers, and mites. Aphids, leafhoppers, and mites can be controlled chemically by spraying with Malathion or Diazinon. Bean beetles and flea beetles can be controlled chemically by spraying with carbaryl. Beans are almost always attacked by large numbers of pests that cannot be controlled by organic methods. This does not mean the organic gardener can't grow them, but yields may be lower if only organic controls are used. Detailed information on pest control is given in "Keeping Your Garden Healthy" in Part 1.

Diseases

Beans are susceptible to blight, mosaic, and anthracnose. You can cut down on the incidence of disease by planting disease-resistant varieties when they're available, maintaining the general health of your garden, and avoiding handling the plants when they're wet. If a plant does become infected, remove and destroy it so it cannot spread disease to healthy plants. Detailed information on disease prevention is given in "Keeping Your Garden Healthy" in Part 1.

When and how to harvest

Time from planting to harvest is 50 to 60 days for bush beans, 60 to 90 days for pole beans. Harvest the immature pods, and continue removing the pods before they become mature, or the plant will stop producing. Once the seeds mature, the plant dies. Do not harvest when the weather is very hot or very cold.

Container growing

Green beans can be grown in containers, but they need so much space to produce a reasonable crop that they're not really a practical choice for the container gardener.

Storing and preserving

Snap beans are a snap to store. They'll keep up to one week in the refrigerator, but don't wash them until you're ready to cook them. You can also freeze, can, dry, or pickle them. Detailed information on storing and preserving is given in Part 4.

Serving suggestions

Really fresh, tender snap beans are delicious eaten raw; they make an unusual addition to a platter of crudités for dipping. They're also good lightly cooked and tossed with diced potatoes and a little onion and bacon for a delightful hot bean salad. Try them on toast with a light cheese sauce for lunch. And vary everyone's favorite bean dish by replacing the classic Amandine sauce with a Hollandaise or mushroom sauce. Or try tossing them with a few thinly sliced mushrooms and onions that have been lightly sautéed in butter. You can also cut snap beans in lengths and sauté them all together with diced potatoes, carrots, and onions for an interesting vegetable dish. Purists will object that this means cooking the beans too long, but you can always add them halfway through the cooking time to preserve their crispness. Well-seasoned, this is a good,

filling, vegetable dish for a cold day. On their own, snap beans take well to many spices, including basil, dill, marjoram, and mint.

Q and A

Q: I noticed small white and yellow moths in my bean patch. Are they likely to do any damage?
A: These moths are adult cabbage worms using your bean patch as shelter from the heat or predators. They will not harm your beans.
Q: Some of the bean seeds I bought for planting are pink in color. Why?
A: The pink coloring is a fungicide that protects the seeds from rotting in the cold soil.
Q: Should beans be planted in a different spot in the garden each year?
A: Beans are very susceptible to many soil-borne diseases and the incidence of disease is reduced by changing the location of the bean patch.
Q: If I plant several different beans in my garden, will they cross-pollinate and result in a poor harvest?
A: No. Beans are self-pollinating. Anyway, only the immediate offspring of a cross-pollination or the plants that grow from the crossed seeds would be affected.
Q: What can I do to stop rabbits from eating my bean plants?
A: The best way to stop rabbits is to keep them out by using some type of screen. Rabbits can also be slowed down by spraying your beans with a fungicide called Thiram. Don't use mothballs or other home remedies to deter rabbits. There

is no scientific evidence that they work, and we don't know how these remedies affect the plants or the people who eat them.

Bean, lima

Common names: bean, lima bean, butter bean, civit bean
Botanical name: Phaseolus lunatus
Origin: South Mexico, Central America

Varieties

Bush lima: Burpee Improved Bush (75 days); Fordhook 242 (75 days)—both resistant to bean mosaic; Allgreen (67 days); Thorogreen (66 days); Henderson's Bush Lima (65 days). **Pole lima:** King of the Garden (90 days); Prizetaker (90 days).

Description

This tender, large-seeded annual bean grows as either a bush or a vine. With this type of bean the mature seed is eaten, not the entire pod. Lima beans need warmer soil than snap beans in order to germinate properly, and they need higher temperatures and a longer growing season for a good crop.

Bush lima beans are generally easier to handle than pole varieties; bushes grow only one to two feet tall, and they mature earlier. Pole beans require a trellis for support; they grow more slowly, but produce more beans per plant.

Lima bean

Where and when to grow

Lima beans require warm soil (five days at a minimum temperature of 65°F) to germinate, and should be planted two weeks after the average date of last spring frost. Use the length of your growing season and the number of days the variety takes to mature to figure your latest planting date. If you need to sow before your area's average last frost date, start the seed indoors in peat pots and transplant them when the soil has warmed up. Time your planting so the beans will mature before very hot weather; they will not set pods at temperatures over 80°F.

Plant bush beans every two weeks to extend the harvest, or start with bush beans and follow up with pole beans. Because limas need a long stretch of pleasant weather, the slower-growing pole varieties are difficult to raise successfully where the growing season is short.

How to plant

After the last frost is over, choose a bed in full sunlight; beans tolerate partial shade, but partial shade tends to mean a partial yield. Prepare the soil by mixing in a pound of 5-10-10 fertilizer; don't use a high-nitrogen fertilizer, because too much nitrogen will promote growth of the foliage but not of the beans.

Plant seeds of all varieties an inch deep. If you're planting bush limas, plant the seeds two inches apart in rows at least 18 to 24 inches apart. Seeds of pole beans should be planted four to six inches apart in rows 30 to 36 inches apart, or plant them in inverted hills, five or six seeds to a hill, with 30 inches of space around each hill. For pole varieties, set supports or trellises at the time of planting.

When the seedlings are growing well, thin the plants to four to six inches apart. Cut the seedlings with scissors at ground level; be careful not to disturb the others. Beans don't mind being a little crowded; in fact, they'll use each other for support.

Fertilizing and watering

Beans set up a mutual exchange with soil microorganisms called nitrogen-fixing bacteria, which help them produce their own fertilizer. Some gardeners recommend that if you haven't grown beans in the plot before, you should treat the bean seeds before planting with a nitrogen-fixing bacteria inoculant to help them convert organic nitrogen compounds into usable organic compounds. This is a perfectly acceptable practice, but it isn't really necessary; the bacteria in the soil will multiply quickly enough once they've got a growing bean plant to work with.

Fertilize before planting and again at midseason, at the same rate as the rest of the garden. Detailed information on fertilizing is given in "Spadework: The Essential Soil" in Part 1.

Bean seeds may crack and germinate poorly when the moisture content of the soil is too high. Don't soak the seeds before planting, and don't water immediately afterward. Keep the soil moist until the beans have pushed through the ground. Water regularly if there is no rain, but avoid getting water on the flowers; this can cause the

flowers and small pods to fall off. You can mulch to conserve moisture when the soil temperature reaches 60°F.

Special handling

Don't handle bean plants when they're wet or covered with heavy dew; handling or brushing against them when they're wet spreads fungus spores. Cultivate thoroughly but with care, so you don't disturb the bean plants' shallow root systems.

If you're planting pole beans, set the trellis or support in position before you plant or at the same time. If you wait until the plants are established, you risk damaging the roots when you set the supports. Make sure the support will be tall enough for the variety of beans you're planting.

The large lima bean seed sometimes has trouble pushing through the soil, although this should not happen if the soil is well worked. If your soil tends to cake, you can cover the seeds with sand, vermiculite, or a peat moss/vermiculite mix instead.

Pests

Beans may be attacked by aphids, bean beetles, flea beetles, leafhoppers, and mites. Aphids, leafhoppers, and mites can be controlled chemically by spraying with Malathion or Diazinon. Bean beetles and flea beetles can be controlled chemically by spraying with carbaryl. Beans are almost always attacked by large numbers of pests that cannot be controlled by organic methods. This doesn't mean the organic gardener can't grow them, but yields may be lower if only organic controls are used. Detailed information on

pest control is given in "Keeping Your Garden Healthy" in Part 1.

Diseases

Beans are susceptible to blight, mosaic, and anthracnose. You can cut down on the incidence of disease by planting disease-resistant varieties when they're available, maintaining the general health of your garden, and avoiding handling the plants when they're wet. If a plant does become infected, remove and destroy it so it cannot spread disease to healthy plants. Detailed information on disease prevention is given in "Keeping Your Garden Healthy" in Part 1.

When and how to harvest

Time from planting to harvest is about 60 to 75 days for bush limas and 85 to 110 days for pole limas. Harvest when the pods are plump and firm; if you leave them too long the beans will get tough and mealy. If you pick the pods promptly, limas will continue to yield until the first frost. In warmer climates, bush limas should give you two or three pickings.

Container growing

Lima beans can be grown in containers, but they need so much space to produce a reasonable crop that they're not really a practical choice for the container gardener.

Storing and preserving

Unshelled lima beans can be kept up to one week in the refrigerator. Shelled lima beans freeze satisfactorily; they can also be canned or dried. Dried shelled limas can be stored in a cool, dry place for 10 to 12 months. Detailed information on storing and preserving is given in Part 4.

Serving suggestions

Try limas raw for an unusual treat. Serve them in a salad with thinly sliced red onion, parsley, and a vinaigrette dressing, or marinate them for 24 hours in oil, lemon juice, and freshly chopped dill. Cook limas just until tender and serve with a creamy sauce. For a tangy treatment, bake them in a casserole with honey, mustard, and yogurt.

Q and A

Q: I noticed small white and yellow moths in my bean patch. Are they likely to do any damage?
A: These moths are adult cabbage worms using your bean patch as shelter from the heat or predators. They will not harm your beans.
Q: Some of the bean seeds I bought for planting are pink in color. Why?
A: The pink coloring is a fungicide that protects the seeds from rotting in the cold soil.
Q: Should beans be planted in a different spot in the garden each year?
A: Beans are very susceptible to many soil-borne diseases and the incidence of disease is reduced by changing the location of the bean patch.
Q: If I plant several different beans in my garden, will they cross-pollinate and result in a poor harvest?
A: No. Beans are self-pollinating. Anyway, only the immediate offspring of a

cross-pollination or the plants that grow from the crossed seeds would be affected.
Q: What can I do to stop rabbits from eating my bean plants?
A: The best way to stop rabbits is to keep them out by using some type of screen. Rabbits can also be slowed down by spraying your beans with a fungicide called Thiram. Don't use mothballs or other home remedies to deter rabbits. There is no scientific evidence that they work, and we don't know how these remedies affect the plants or the people who eat them.

Bean, mung

Common name: mung bean
Botanical name: Phaseolus aureus
Origin: India, Central Asia

Varieties
Few varieties are available. Grow whichever variety is available in your area, or plant the seeds that are sold for sprouting.

Description

The mung bean is a bushy annual that grows about 2½ to three feet tall, and has many branches with typical, hairy, beanlike leaves. The flowers are yellowish-green with purple streaks and produce long, thin, hairy pods containing nine to 15 small, yellow seeds. The seeds are used to produce bean sprouts.

Where and when to grow

Mung beans can be grown in any area of the United States that has 90 days of frost-free temperatures. Plant them on the average date of last frost for your area.

How to plant

Mung beans grow best in full sun, in a rich well-drained soil. When you're preparing the soil for planting, dig in a complete, well-balanced fertilizer at the rate of one pound per 100 square feet or 10 pounds per 1,000 square feet. Because the only seeds you may be able to get are not very reliable in growth, plant the seeds several at a time. Plant them an inch deep and 18 to 20 inches apart in wide rows 18 to 24 inches apart. When the seedlings are about two inches tall, thin them to leave the strongest of each group growing. Cut off the extra seedlings at ground level to avoid disturbing the survivor's roots.

Fertilizing and watering

Beans set up a mutual exchange with soil microorganisms called nitrogen-fixing bacteria, which help them produce their own fertilizer. Some gardeners recommend that if you haven't grown beans in the plot the previous season, you should treat the bean seeds before planting with a nitrogen-fixing bacteria inoculant to help them convert organic nitrogen compounds into usable organic compounds. This is a perfectly acceptable practice but it isn't really necessary; the bacteria in the soil will multiply quickly enough

Mung bean

Mung bean seedling

once they've got a growing bean plant to work with.

Fertilize before planting and again at midseason, at the same rate as the rest of the garden. Detailed information on fertilizing is given in "Spadework: The Essential Soil" in Part 1.

Mung beans don't like to dry out between waterings. If it doesn't rain, keep them well-watered.

Pests

Mung beans have no serious pest problems.

Diseases

Mung beans have no serious disease problems.

When and how to harvest

It usually takes about 90 to 100 days for mung beans to mature, and you can expect one to two pounds of seeds from a 10-foot row. Harvest them as soon as a few of the pods begin to split. If the pods are picked when they are too young they won't store or sprout. Remove the seeds from pods when you harvest them.

Container growing

Mung beans can be grown in containers, but they need so much space to produce a reasonable crop that they're not really a practical choice for the container gardener.

Storing and preserving

Mung beans are usually grown for sprouting. Unshelled beans can be kept up to one week in the refrigerator; shelled beans, naturally dried, can be stored in a cool, dry place for 10 to 12 months. Detailed information on storing and preserving is given in Part 4.

Serving suggestions

Bean sprouts turn up in all sorts of Chinese dishes. They're good in salads and sandwiches — vegetarians love them, and rightly so, because they have a high Vitamin C content.

Q and A

Q: I noticed small white and yellow moths in my bean patch. Are they likely to do any damage?
A: These moths are adult cabbage worms using your bean patch as shelter from the heat or predators. They will not harm your beans.
Q: Some of the bean seeds I bought for planting are pink in color. Why?
A: The pink coloring is a fungicide that protects the seeds from rotting in the cold soil.
Q: Should beans be planted in a different spot in the garden each year?
A: Beans are very susceptible to many soil-borne diseases and the incidence of disease is reduced by changing the location of the bean patch.
Q: If I plant several different beans in my garden, will they cross-pollinate and result in a poor harvest?
A: No. Beans are self-pollinating. Anyway, only the immediate offspring of a cross-pollination or the plants that grow from the crossed seeds would be affected.
Q: What can I do to stop rabbits from eating my bean plants?
A: The best way to stop rabbits is to keep them out by using some type of screen. Rabbits can also be slowed down by spraying your beans with a fungicide called Thiram. Don't use mothballs or other home remedies to deter rabbits. There is no scientific evidence that they work, and we don't know how these remedies affect the plants or the people who eat them.

Bean, soy

See Soybean

Beet

Common name: beet
Botanical name: Beta vulgaris
Origin: southern Europe

Varieties

Detroit Dark Red (52 days); Early Wonder (53 days); Burpee's Golden (55 days); Ruby Queen (56 days); Little Ball (56 days); Cylindra, also called Formanova or Tendersweet (60 days); Long Season, also called Winter Keeper (80 days).

Description

The beet is grown as an annual, although technically it's a biennial. It originated in the Mediterranean, where it existed first as a leafy plant, without the enlarged root we grow it for these days. Swiss chard, which is a bottomless beet, is an improved version of the early, leafy beets. The modern beet has a round or tapered swollen root — red, yellow, or white — from which sprouts a rosette of large leaves. The leaves as well as the root can be eaten.

Beet

Where and when to grow

Beets can tolerate frost and do best in the cooler areas of the country, but they'll go to seed without making roots if the plants get too cold when they're young. Plant beets two to three weeks before the average date of last frost. They're planted as a winter crop in the South. If you live in a hot climate you'll need to pay special attention to watering and mulching to give seedlings a chance to establish themselves. In very hot weather the roots become woody.

How to plant

Beets can tolerate shade and thrive in well-worked, loose soil that is high in organic matter. They don't like a very acid soil, and they need a lot of potassium. Before planting, work a complete, well-balanced fertilizer into the soil at the rate of one pound per 100 square feet or 10 pounds per 1,000 square feet. Remove stones and other obstacles, and break up any lumps in the soil that might cause the roots to become malformed.

Beets are grown from seed clusters that are slightly smaller than a pea and contain several seeds each. Plant the clusters an inch deep and an inch apart in rows spaced 12 to 18 inches apart. The seedlings may emerge over a period of time so that you've got a group of seedlings of different sizes. Since several seedlings will emerge from each seed cluster, they must be thinned to two to three inches apart when the seedlings develop true leaves. Eat thinned seedlings like spinach; they do not transplant well. Plant all the seed clusters — most seeds store well, but these clusters have only a short period of viability.

Fertilizing and watering

Fertilize before planting and again at midseason, at the same rate as the rest of the garden. Detailed information on fertilizing is given in "Spadework: The Essential Soil" in Part 1.

Be sure to provide plenty of water for the tender young roots — lack of moisture will result in stringy, tough vegetables.

Special handling

Cultivate by hand regularly; beets do not like competition from weeds. Take care, because the roots are shallow and easily damaged.

Pests

Beets have no serious pest problems. They are a good crop for the organic gardener. About the only pest that's likely to bother your beets is the leaf miner, a small wormlike insect that tunnels inside the leaf surface, leaving marks that look like irregular gray streaks on the undersides of the leaves. There's no satisfactory chemical control for leaf miners on vegetables. Your best recourse is to pick off the infected leaves and any other leaves on which you can see the tiny oblong eggs, which are white and yellow and are laid in straight rows on the undersides of the leaves.

Diseases

Beets have no serious disease problems.

Beet seedling

When and how to harvest

Time from planting to harvest is from 40 to 80 days. It takes about 60 days for a beet to reach 1½ inches in diameter — a popular size for cooking or pickling — although they'll get bigger quickly if they have plenty of water. Pull them up when they're the size you want. Twist the leaves off rather than cutting them off; this prevents "bleeding," which causes less intense color and, some people claim, less flavor.

Container growing

Most root crops need plenty of space to put down long, strong roots and therefore don't generally do well in containers. Beets, however, are an exception. They grow closer to the surface of the soil than most root vegetables and can be grown satisfactorily in containers. Beets also offer the gardener a double bonus—you can eat both the roots and the leafy tops. (In fact, chard, which is grown for its leaves, is nothing more than a leafy beet without a bottom.) Beets, therefore, are a good choice for the small-space gardener. Remember that you don't have to plant in straight rows. You can use a round container and plant the beets in concentric circles, rather like the markings on a dart board.

Storing and preserving

You can store beets in the refrigerator for one to three weeks; store the greens in a plastic bag in the refrigerator up to one week.

Beets will keep for five to six months in a cold, moist place. You can also freeze, dry, and can both the root and the greens (use the recipe for "greens"). You can even pickle the root. So there's never any problem figuring what to do with the excess crop. Detailed information on storing and preserving is given in Part 4.

Serving suggestions

Beets are more versatile than they're often given credit for. Eat them raw, or serve the tops raw as a salad green — if you don't cook them, you'll retain some of the vitamins normally lost in cooking. If you cook beets in their skins, the skins will slip off readily at the end of the cooking time. Hot, try them dressed with orange juice and topped with a few slivers of green onion, or glaze them with orange marmalade. Or keep the dressing simple: just a little butter, lemon juice, and seasoning. Beets are the basis of the thick, delicious Russian soup called borscht. Serve borscht with a dollop of sour cream.

Q and A

Q: Beet greens look a lot like Swiss chard; can you eat them?
A: Yes, beets are, in fact, closely related to Swiss chard and the greens taste very similar.
Q: Why do my beets have lush foliage but small roots?
A: The most common reason for small root crops is overcrowding or too heavy a clay soil.

Belgian endive
See Chicory

Black-eyed pea
See Pea, black-eyed

Broad bean
See Bean, broad

Broccoli

Common names: broccoli, Italian broccoli, Calabrese, brocks
Botanical name: Brassica oleracea italica
Origin: Mediterranean

Varieties

Green Comet (40 days); Packman (56 days); Premium Crop (60 days); Green Valiant (60 days); Top Star (60 days); Prominence (62 days); Royal Purple Head (90 days, resistant to disease, yellow virus).

Description

This hardy biennial, grown as an annual, is a member of the cabbage or cole family. It grows 1½ to 2½ feet tall and looks a bit like a cauliflower that hasn't quite gotten itself together. The flower stalks are green, purple, or white; when it comes to the white-budded ones, the U.S. government has trouble deciding where a broccoli stops and a cauliflower starts. The flowers of all of them are yellow, but they're usually eaten while they're still in bud, before they bloom. Americans didn't discover broccoli until the 1920s, even though this vegetable had been an Old World favorite well before that date.

Broccoli has four stages of growth: (1) rapid growth of leaves; (2) formation of the head (which is the part you eat); (3) a resting period while the embryonic blossoms are being formed; and (4) development of the stalk, flowers, and seeds. The head formation stage is essential for the production of the vegetable, but not at all necessary for the survival of the plant. Broccoli that's held in check by severe frost, lack of moisture, or too much heat will bolt, which means it will go directly to seed without bothering to form a head at all. Broccoli makes an attractive plant in a flower bed.

As with other cole family crops, you can grow broccoli in a container on the patio or indoors — a single broccoli plant in an eight-inch flower pot might make a novel houseplant. You can also grow broccoli as an accent in a flower bed.

Where and when to grow

Broccoli is frost-hardy and can tolerate low 20°F temperatures. It's a cool season crop and does best with day temperatures under 80°F and night temperatures 20°F lower. Weather that's too cold or too warm will cause the plants to bolt without forming a head. Broccoli will grow in most areas of the United States at one season or another but is not a suitable crop for very hot climates. Time planting so that you'll harvest broccoli during cool weather. In cold-winter areas, plant for summer to early fall harvest. In mild climates, plant for late spring or fall harvest; in the South, plant for harvest in late fall or winter.

How to plant

Broccoli likes fertile, well-drained soil with a pH within the 6.5 to 7.5 range — this discourages disease and lets the plant make the most of the nutrients in the soil. Broccoli is usually grown from transplants except where there's a long cool period, in which case you can sow seed directly in the garden in fall for winter harvest.

When you're preparing the soil for planting, work in a complete, well-balanced fertilizer at the rate of one pound per 100 square feet or 10 pounds per 1,000 square feet. If you have sandy soil or your area is subject to heavy rains, you'll probably need to supplement the nitrogen content of the soil. Use about a pound of nitrogen fertilizer for a 10-foot row.

Plant transplants that are four to six weeks old with four or five true leaves. If the transplants are leggy or have crooked stems, plant them deeply (up to the first leaves) so they won't grow to be top-heavy. Plant the seedlings 18 to 24 inches apart, in rows 24 to 36 inches apart. Plan for only a few heads at a time, or plant seeds and transplants at the same time for succession crops — you'll get the same result by planting early and midseason varieties at the same time. If you're planting seeds, set them half an inch deep and three inches apart, and thin them when they're big enough to lift by the true leaves. You can transplant the thinned seedlings.

Fertilizing and watering

Fertilize before planting and again at midseason, at the same rate as the rest of the garden.

Broccoli

Broccoli seedling

Detailed information on fertilizing is given in "Spadework: The Essential Soil" in Part 1.

Broccoli needs abundant soil moisture and cool moist air for the best growth. Cut down on watering as the heads approach maturity.

Pests

The cabbage family's traditional enemies are cutworms and caterpillars. However, cutworms, cabbage loopers, and imported cabbage worms can all be controlled by spraying with bacillus thuringiensis, an organic product also known as Dipel or Thungicide. Detailed information on pest control is given in "Keeping Your Garden Healthy" in Part 1.

Diseases

Such cabbage family vegetables as broccoli are susceptible to yellows, clubroot, and downy mildew. Planting resistant varieties, rotating crops from year to year, and maintaining the general health of your garden will cut down on the incidence of disease. If a plant does become infected, remove it before it can spread disease to healthy plants. Detailed information on disease prevention is given in "Keeping Your Garden Healthy" in Part 1.

When and how to harvest

Broccoli grown from seed will take 100 to 150 days to mature, and some transplants can be harvested in 40 to 80 days. Harvesting can continue over a relatively long period. Cut the central head with five to six inches of stem, when the head is well developed and before it begins to loosen and separate — if the small yellow flowers have started to show, it's past the good-eating stage. Leave the base of the plant and some outer leaves to encourage new growth. In many varieties small clusters will grow in the angles of the leaves and can be harvested later.

Container growing

Broccoli grows very well in containers, and it's worth growing because it tends to be expensive in the store. Broccoli is very sensitive to heat, so it's useful to be able to move the container into the shade on hot days. Also, the soil in a container warms up faster so you can get a head start in the spring and plant broccoli earlier than you could in a regular garden bed. Plant a single broccoli plant in an eight-inch flower pot, or place several in a large container, giving each an 18-inch diameter growing space.

Storing and preserving

Broccoli can be stored in the refrigerator up to one week, or in a cold, moist place for two to three weeks. Detailed information on storing and preserving is given in Part 4.

Serving suggestions

The good taste of broccoli has been appreciated since way back. Pliny the Elder wrote in the second century that it was much in favor with the Romans. The classically American way to serve broccoli is with a cheese or Hollandaise sauce, au gratin, or in casseroles. It's also delicious raw, broken into flowerets and used in a salad or with a dipping sauce; the small flowerets are decorative on a platter of raw vegetables. If you've got stalks left over after using the head for salads, parboil them and then sauté them in oil with a little onion and garlic. To make sure the stems cook adequately without overcooking the tender tops, cook broccoli like asparagus — upright in a tall pot so that the stems boil and the tops steam.

Q and A

Q: I saw small yellow and white moths flying around my broccoli plants. Are they doing any damage?
A: Potentially, yes. They are the adult cabbage looper and the imported cabbage worm and they're laying eggs. When the eggs hatch, the pests will damage your crop.
Q: My broccoli heads are always loose and have little yellow flowers. Why?
A: Small loose heads with premature flowering usually result from weather that's too warm. Try planting earlier in the spring.
Q: Can you eat the broccoli leaves?
A: Yes, broccoli belongs to the cabbage family and its leaves taste like cabbage, collards, or kale.
Q: Do you need to tie the leaves of a broccoli plant over its head like you do with cauliflower?
A: No. The leaves are tied over the cauliflower head to reduce light and keep the head white. With broccoli you want a green head, so this "blanching" is unnecessary.

Brussels sprout

Common names: Brussels sprouts, sprouts
Botanical name: Brawsica oleracea gemmifera
Origin: Europe, Mediterranean

Varieties
Captain Marvel (78 days); Prince Marvel (83 days); Jade Cross (90 days, is resistant to yellows virus).

Description

If you've never seen Brussels sprouts outside of a store, you may be quite impressed by the actual plant. Miniature cabbage-like heads, an inch or two in diameter, sprout from a tall, heavy main stem, nestled in among large green leaves. Brussels sprouts belong to the cabbage or cole family and are similar to cabbage in their growing habits and requirements. They're hardy and grow well in fertile soils, and they're easy to grow in the home garden if you follow the correct pest control procedures.

Brussels sprouts have four stages of growth: (1) rapid growth of leaves; (2) formation of the heads (which is the part you eat); (3) a resting period while the embryonic blossoms are being formed; and (4) development of the stalk, flowers, and seeds. The head formation stage is essential for the production of the vegetable, but not at all necessary for the survival of the plant. Brussels sprouts that are held in check by severe frost, lack

Brussels sprout

of moisture, or too much heat will bolt, which means that they'll go directly to seed without bothering to form a head at all.

Where and when to grow

Brussels sprouts are frost-hardy — in fact, they're the most cold-tolerant of the cole family vegetables — and can tolerate low 20°F temperatures. Brussels sprouts do best in a cool growing season with day temperatures under 80°F and night temperatures 20°F lower. Weather that's too cold for too long or too warm will make them taste bitter; if the sprouts develop in hot weather, they may not form compact heads, but will remain loose tufts of leaves. Brussels sprouts are not a suitable crop for very hot climates, although they will grow in most areas of the United States in one season or another. Time planting so that you harvest Brussels sprouts during cool weather. If your area has cold winters, plant for summer to early fall harvest. In mild climates, plant for late spring or fall harvest. In the South, plant for harvest in late fall or winter.

How to plant

Brussels sprouts like fertile, well-drained soil with a pH within the 6.5 to 7.5 range — this discourages disease and lets the plant make the most of the nutrients in the soil. They're usually grown from transplants, except where there's a long cool period, in which case seeds are sown directly in the garden in fall for winter harvest.

When you're preparing the soil for planting, work in a complete, well-balanced

fertilizer at the rate of one pound per 100 square feet or 10 pounds per 1,000 square feet. If you have sandy soil or your area is subject to heavy rains, you'll probably need to supplement the nitrogen content of the soil. Use about a pound of nitrogen fertilizer for a 10-foot row.

Plant transplants that are four to six weeks old, with four to five true leaves. If the transplants are leggy or have crooked stems, plant them deeply (up to the first leaves) so they won't grow to be top-heavy. Seedlings should be thinned to 24 inches apart when they're three inches tall. If you're planting seeds, set them a half inch deep, three inches apart in rows 24 to 36 inches apart. Thin them when they're big enough to lift by the true leaves and transplant the thinned seedlings.

Fertilizing and watering

Fertilize before planting and again at midseason, at the same rate as the rest of the garden. Detailed information on fertilizing is given in "Spadework: The Essential Soil" in Part 1.

Brussels sprouts need abundant soil moisture and cool moist air for the best growth. Cut down on watering as they approach maturity.

Special handling

If you live in an area with cold winters, pick off the top terminal bud when the plant is 15 to 20 inches tall. This encourages all of the sprouts to mature at once. Some gardeners believe that Brussels sprouts develop better if the lower leaves are removed from the sides of the stalk as the

Brussels sprout seedling

sprouts develop. A few more leaves can be removed each week, but the top leaves should be left intact.

Pests

The cabbage family's traditional enemies are cutworms and caterpillars. Cutworms, cabbage loopers, and imported cabbage worms can all be controlled by spraying with bacillus thuringiensis, an organic product also known as Dipel or Thungicide. It's especially important to control insects on Brussels sprouts; if they insinuate themselves into the tightly curled sprouts, you'll have a lot of trouble dislodging them. Detailed information on pest control is given in "Keeping Your Garden Healthy" in Part 1.

Diseases

Cabbage family vegetables may develop yellows, clubroot, or downy mildew. Lessen the incidence of disease by planting disease-resistant varieties when they're available, maintaining the general health of your garden, and avoiding handling the plants when they're wet. If a plant does become infected, remove and destroy it so it cannot spread disease to healthy plants. Detailed information on disease prevention is given in "Keeping Your Garden Healthy" in Part 1.

When and how to harvest

Time from planting to harvest is 85 to 95 days for Brussels sprouts grown from seed, 75 to 90 days from transplants. The sprouts mature from the bottom of the stem upward, so start from the bottom and remove the leaves and sprouts as the season progresses. Harvesting can continue until all the sprouts are gone. The leaves can be cooked like collards or cabbage.

Container growing

A single stalk of Brussels sprouts can produce two to three pounds of sprouts, so this vegetable is an excellent candidate for container planting. An eight-inch flower pot will accommodate one plant. In a larger space, allow 30 inches for each plant. Don't, however, grow the Brussels sprout as a houseplant—it's too big to domesticate.

Storing and preserving

If you have sprouts still on the stem in late fall, remove all the leaves from the plant, and hang the plant in a cool dry place; it will give you a late harvest. The plant can be kept up to one month in a cold, moist place. Sprouts will keep for about a week in the refrigerator. Remove loose or discolored outer leaves before you store them, but don't wash them until you're ready to use them. You can also freeze or dry sprouts. Detailed information on storing and preserving is given in Part 4.

Serving suggestions

Sprouts are traditionally served with turkey at an English Christmas dinner. They're also good lightly steamed and served with a lemon-butter sauce. Don't overcook them; young sprouts should be slightly crunchy, and light cooking preserves their delicate flavor. Older sprouts have a stronger taste. Brussels sprouts can also be french fried, baked, or puréed. When you trim them for cooking, cut an X in each stem so that the sprouts cook evenly; be careful not to trim the stem ends too closely or the outer leaves will fall off when you cook them. A walnut in the pot when you cook Brussels sprouts should cut down on the cabbagey smell.

Q and A

Q: Why will the flavor of Brussels sprouts be sweeter if the plant is left outside for a frost?
A: When the plant is exposed to cold temperatures, some of its carbohydrates will turn to sugar. How much this sweetens the flavor of the sprouts is a matter of opinion.
Q: Will the small yellow and white moths flying around my Brussels sprout plants do any damage?
A: Potentially, yes. The moths are the adult cabbage looper and imported cabbage worm, and are laying eggs. When the eggs hatch, the pests can damage your plants.

Cabbage

Common name: cabbage
Botanical name: Brassica oleracea capitata
Origin: South Europe

Varieties
Green: Stovehead (60 days); Jersey Wakefield (63 days); Golden Acre (65 days); Market Prize (73 days); Green Boy (75 days); Round Up (76 days); Blue Ribbon (76 days); Blue Boy (78 days); Rio Verde (79 days); Badger Ban Head (98 days); Flat Dutch (105 days). **Savoy:** Savoy Ace (80 days); Savoy King (85 days). **Red:** Red Acre (76 days); Red Ball (70 days); Red Ribbon (78 days); Ruby Perfection (90 days).

Description

Cabbage, a hardy biennial grown as an annual, has an enlarged terminal bud made of crowded and expanded overlapping leaves shaped into a head. The leaves are smooth or crinkled in shades of green or purple, and the head can be round, flat, or pointed. The stem is short and stubby, although it may grow to 20 inches if the plant is left to go to seed. Cabbage is a hardy vegetable that grows well in fertile soils, and it's easy to grow in the home garden if you choose suitable varieties and follow correct pest control procedures. Like other members of the cabbage or cole family (broccoli and kale are among them), cabbage is a cool-weather crop that can tolerate frost but not heat.

Cabbages have four stages of growth: (1) rapid growth of leaves; (2) formation of the head (which is the part you eat); (3) a resting period while the embryonic blossoms are being formed; and (4) development of the stalk, flowers, and seeds. The head formation stage is essential for the production of the vegetable, but not at all necessary for the survival of the plant. Cabbages that are held in check by severe

Cabbage

weather. If your areas have cold winters, plant for summer to early fall harvest. In mild climates, plant for late spring or fall harvest. In the South, plant for harvest in late fall or winter.

How to plant

Cabbages like fertile, well-drained soil with a pH within the 6.5 to 7.5 range — this discourages disease and lets the plant make the most of the nutrients in the soil. When you're preparing the soil for planting, work in a complete, well-balanced fertilizer at the rate of one pound per 100 square feet or 10 pounds per 1,000 square feet. If you have sandy soil or your area is subject to heavy rains, you'll probably need to supplement the nitrogen content of the soil. Use about a pound of nitrogen fertilizer for a 10-foot row. Cabbages are usually grown from transplants except where there's a long cool period, in which case you can sow seed directly in the garden in fall for winter harvest. Plant transplants that are four to six weeks old with four or five true leaves. If the transplants are leggy or have crooked stems, plant them deeply (up to the first leaves) so they won't grow to be top-heavy. Plant the seedlings 18 to 24 inches apart in rows 24 to 36 inches apart. Plan for only a few heads at a time, or plant seeds and transplants at the same time for succession crops; you'll get the same result by planting early and midseason varieties at the same time. If you're planting seeds, set them an inch deep and space them three inches apart. Thin them to 18 to 24 inches apart when they're big enough to

frost, lack of moisture, or too much heat will bolt, which means that they will go directly to seed without bothering to form a head at all. And even if the cabbage does make a head, if the weather gets too hot once it reaches that stage, the head can split.

Cabbages are decorative in the flower garden; purple cabbages and savoys look good in a mixed border. Flowering cabbages look like enormous variegated blossoms. In small spaces, grow cabbages as an accent in each corner of a flower bed or as a border. Decorative cabbages can be grown in containers on the patio or even indoors. Try growing a single cabbage in an eight-inch flowerpot; choose a flowering cabbage or a small early variety.

Where and when to grow

Cabbages are frost-hardy and can tolerate low 20°F temperatures. They do best in a cool growing season with day temperatures under 80°F and night temperatures 20°F lower. If the plants are cold for too long a period or if the weather is warm, they will bolt without forming a head. If the head has already formed, it will split in hot weather — splitting happens when the plant takes up water so fast that the excess cannot escape through the tightly overlapped leaves, and the head bursts. The cabbage is not a suitable crop for very hot climates, although it will grow in most areas of the United States at one season or another. Time planting so that you harvest cabbage during cool lift by the true leaves, and transplant the thinned seedlings.

Fertilizing and watering

Fertilize before planting and again at midseason, at the same rate as the rest of the garden. Detailed information on fertilizing is given in "Spadework: The Essential Soil" in Part 1.

Cabbages need abundant soil moisture and cool air for best growth. Cut down the watering as the heads approach maturity to prevent splitting.

Pests

The cabbage family's traditional enemies are cutworms and caterpillars. Cutworms, cabbage loopers, and imported cabbage worms can all be controlled by spraying with bacillus thuringiensis, an organic product also known as Dipel or Thungicide. Detailed information on pest control is given in "Keeping Your Garden Healthy" in Part 1.

Diseases

Yellows virus, clubroot fungus, and black rot may attack cabbage. Cut down on the incidence of

Cabbage seedling

disease by planting disease-resistant varieties when they're

available, maintaining the general health of your garden, and avoiding handling the plants when they're wet. If a plant does become infected, remove and destroy it so it cannot spread disease to healthy plants. Detailed information on disease prevention is given in "Keeping Your Garden Healthy" in Part 1.

When and how to harvest

Cabbages mature in 80 to 180 days from seed, depending on the variety, or in 60 to 105 days from transplants. A 10-foot row should give you five to eight heads. Start harvesting before the winter gets too warm, when the head is firm. To harvest, cut off the head, leaving the outer leaves on the stem. Often a few small heads will grow on the stalk, and you can harvest them later.

Container growing

Cabbage grows very easily in a container and makes an unusual house plant. Cabbage dislikes hot weather, so it's useful to be able to move the container into the shade when necessary. Also, soil warms up faster in a container, giving you a head start on the spring growing season. Plant a single standard variety cabbage plant in an eight-inch flower pot, or several in a larger container on 12-inch centers.

Storing and preserving

Cabbage stores well in the refrigerator for one to two weeks, and can be kept for three to four months in a cold, moist place. Cabbage can also be dried, and freezes fairly well; it can be canned as sauerkraut. Cabbage seeds can also be sprouted. Detailed

information on storing and preserving is given in Part 4.

Serving suggestions

Soggy cabbage is a staple of English childhood reminiscences. Actually, steamed or boiled cabbage is an excellent dish — the secret is to cut it into small pieces before you cook it so that it cooks fast and evenly. Or try braising it in a heavy-bottomed pan with butter and just a little water; toss a few caraway seeds over it before serving. Sweet and sour red cabbage is an interesting dish. Stuffed cabbage leaves are delicious, and cabbage makes a good addition to soup — the leaves add an additional texture to a hearty, rib-sticking winter soup. The Irish traditionally serve cabbage with corned beef, and a British combination of cooked cabbage and mashed potatoes sautéed together is known as "bubble-and-squeak." French country cooks stuff a whole cabbage with sausage, then simmer it with vegetables — a version known as *chou farci*. One way or another, there's a lot more to cabbage than coleslaw.

Q and A

Q: Why do my cabbage heads often split?
A: Cabbage heads split when they grow too fast and take up too much water. You can reduce this damage by breaking some of the cabbage's roots; twist the cabbage a quarter turn, and then release it.
Q: Why are my cabbage heads always so small?
A: Small, poor-quality cabbage heads may be a result of over-warm weather or of a nutrient

deficiency. Try planting earlier, and check the fertility of the soil.

Q: Will the small yellow and white moths flying around my cabbage plants do any damage?

A: Potentially, yes. They are the adult cabbage looper and imported cabbage worm and are laying eggs. When the eggs hatch, the pests can damage your plants.

Q: One year a few of my cabbage plants became diseased, and ever since I've had disease problems with my cabbages, broccoli, and cauliflower. What can I do?

A: The problem is probably black leg or black rot, both of which will attack any plant in the cabbage family, including cabbage, turnips, broccoli, cauliflower, and mustard greens. These diseases can survive in the soil for two or three years. To control them, don't grow any cabbage family plants in the affected areas of your garden for three years. Then buy seeds that have been hot water-treated. This should prevent the problem from recurring.

Cardoon

Cantaloupe

See Muskmelon

Cardoon

Common name: cardoon
Botanical name: Cynara cardunculus
Origin: Europe

Varieties
Large Smooth; Large Smooth Spanish; Ivory White Smooth. Grow any variety available in your area.

Description

Cardoon is a tender perennial grown as an annual for its young leaf-stalks, which are blanched and eaten like celery. It looks like a cross between burdock and celery but is actually a member of the artichoke family and has the same deeply cut leaves and heavy, bristled flower head. Cardoon can grow to four feet tall and two

feet wide, so it will need plenty of space in your garden.

Where and when to grow

Cardoon will grow anywhere in the United States. Plant it from transplants in the spring.

How to plant

Transplants should be moved to the garden three to four weeks after the average date of last frost in your area, so if you're growing your transplants from seed you'll need to start them six weeks ahead of your planting date. Cardoon prefers full sun but can tolerate partial shade and grows quickly in any well-drained, fertile soil. When you're preparing the soil, dig in a complete, well-balanced fertilizer at the rate of one pound per 100 square feet or 10 pounds per 1,000 square feet. Space the young plants 18 to 24 inches apart, with 36 to 48 inches between the rows.

Fertilizing and watering

Fertilize before planting and again at midseason, at the same rate as the rest of the garden. Detailed information on fertilizing is given in "Spadework: The Essential Soil" in Part 1.

Allow the plants to dry out between waterings.

Special handling

Cardoon is usually blanched to improve the flavor and to make it more tender — the stalks can get very tough. Blanch when the plant is about three feet tall, four to six weeks before harvesting. Tie the leaves together in a bunch and wrap paper or burlap around the stems, or hill up the soil around the stem.

Pests

Aphids may be a problem. Pinch out infested foliage or hose the aphids off the cardoon plants. Control aphids chemically with Malathion or Diazinon. Detailed information on pest control is given in "Keeping Your Garden Healthy" in Part 1.

Diseases

Cardoon has no serious disease problems.

When and how to harvest

Harvest the plants four to six weeks after blanching. Cut them off at ground level and trim off the outer leaves.

Container growing

Cardoons do not grow well in containers.

Storing and preserving

Keep stalks on root, wrap, and refrigerate; they will keep for one to two weeks. The plants can be kept for two to three months in a cold, moist place. Cardoon freezes fairly well and can be canned or dried; handle it like celery. Detailed information on storing and preserving is given in Part 4.

Serving suggestions

Cut the stalks into sections and parboil them until tender — the time will depend on the size of the stalks. Serve cardoon stalks cut into pieces and chilled with an oil and vinegar dressing, or hot with a cream sauce. Dip chunks into batter and deep-fry them. The Italians are fond of cardoon.

Carrot

Common name: carrot
Botanical name: Daucus carota
Origin: Europe, Asia

Varieties
Short (two to four inches):

Goldinhart (60-65 days); Amstel (60-65 days); Gold Nugget (60-65 days); Sweet and Short (60-65 days). **Finger** (three to four inches): Little Finger (60-65 days);

Carrot

Minipak (60-65 days); Tiny Sweet (60-65 days). **Half-long** (five to six inches): Danvers Half-long (75 days); Royal Chantenay (70 days); Gold King (70 days). **Cylindrical** (six to seven inches): Nantes Coreless (68 days); Tuchon Pioneer (75 days); Royal Cross Hybrid (70 days). **Standard** (seven to nine inches): Tendersweet (75 days); Spartan Bonus (77 days); Gold Pak (75 days); Imperator (75 days).

Description

Carrots are hardy biennials grown as annuals. They have a rosette of finely divided fernlike leaves growing from a swollen, fleshy taproot. The root, which varies in size and shape, is generally a tapered cylinder that grows up to 10 inches long in different shades of orange. Until the 20th century and the discovery of mechanical refrigeration techniques, root crops like carrots were almost the only vegetables available in the winter. They are cool-weather crops and tolerate the cold; they're easy to grow and have few pest problems, so they're good crops for the home gardener. The carrots we grow today originated in the Mediterranean. By the 13th century the Europeans were well aware of the carrot's food value. The first settlers brought them to America, and the Indians were quick to recognize their potential.

There are all sorts of carrots — long, short, fat, thin — but basically they differ only in size and shape. However, the sort of soil you have will influence which variety you choose. The shorter varieties will better tolerate heavy soil; the long types are more particular about their environment. Finger carrots can be satisfactorily grown in containers.

Carrot seedling

Where and when to grow

Carrots are a cool-weather crop and fairly adaptable. Plant them in spring and early summer for a continuous crop, starting two to three weeks after the average date of last frost. Although carrots are tolerant of cold, the seeds take a long time to germinate, and when they're planted in cold, raw weather they may give up before they come up. Starting two to three weeks before the average date of last frost for your area, plant successive crops every two to three weeks until three months before the average date of first fall frost.

How to plant

Carrots need a cool bed. They prefer full sun but will tolerate partial shade. Before planting, work half a cup of low nitrogen (5-10-10) fertilizer into the soil, and turn the soil thoroughly to a depth of about 10 or 12 inches. This initial preparation is vital for a healthy crop; soil lumps, rocks, or other obstructions in the soil will cause the roots to split, fork, or become deformed.

Sow the seeds in rows 12 to 24 inches apart. Wide-row planting of carrots gives a good yield from a small area. When you're planting in early spring, cover the seeds with a quarter to a half inch of soil. Later, when the soil is dryer and warmer, they can be planted a little deeper. When the seedlings are growing well, thin to two to four inches apart.

Fertilizing and watering

Fertilize before planting and again at midseason, at the same rate as the rest of the garden. Detailed information on fertilizing is given in "Spadework: The Essential Soil" in Part 1.

To keep carrots growing quickly, give them plenty of water. As they approach maturity, water less — too much moisture at this stage will cause the roots to crack.

Special handling

In areas with high soil temperatures, mulch to regulate the soil temperature; otherwise, the roots will grow

Carrots need well-worked soil, free of rocks and lumps that can cause the roots to fork or split.

short and pale. Carrot seedlings grow slowly while they're young, and it's important to control weeds especially during the first few weeks. Shallow cultivation is necessary to avoid damaging the roots.

Pests

Carrots have no serious pest problems. They're a good crop for the organic gardener.

Diseases

Carrots have no serious disease problems.

When and how to harvest

Time from planting to harvest is from 55 to 80 days, depending on the variety. Small finger carrots are usually ready to harvest in 60 days or less; other varieties need longer. When you think they're ready, pull a few samples to check on their size. If they're three quarters inch thick or more (for regular varieties), they're ready to harvest. Pull them up by hand, or use a spading fork to lift them gently out of the ground. Pull carrots when the soil is moist — if you try to pull them from hard ground you'll break the roots.

Container growing

Standard and large varieties of carrots do not thrive in containers, but short or finger varieties can be grown satisfactorily. Half-long varieties will only grow well in very deep containers. Plant carrots in wide rows in square or rectangular containers, or in concentric circles in a round container.

Storing and preserving

Carrots are most obliging vegetables when it comes to preservation — most methods can be used. They'll store for one to three weeks in plastic bags or aluminum foil in the refrigerator, or for four to five months in a cold, moist place. They can also be canned, frozen, or dried. Detailed information on storing and preserving is given in Part 4.

Serving suggestions

Carrots fresh from the garden are wonderful raw. Shredded raw carrots are delicious with a touch of oil and lemon; or add raisins and fresh pineapple for an exotic flavor. Add shredded carrots to a peanut butter sandwich. Carrot cake is a staple American confection; try it with a cream cheese frosting. There are any number of ways to cook carrots; perhaps the best treatment for very young fresh carrots is simply to boil them and toss with a respectful touch of butter. You can also try them boiled, then rolled in breadcrumbs and deep-fried, or served with a marmalade glaze. Most herbs complement the taste of carrots; parsley is the most common, but try cooked carrots and peas with a touch of mint to enhance the flavor.

Q and A

Q: My carrots have lots of green healthy foliage but skimpy roots. What can I do?
A: This problem is usually caused by overcrowding or by a very heavy clay soil. Thin your carrots properly, and add more organic matter to the soil to loosen it.
Q: My carrots had very fine roots, but the taproot and leaves were yellowish. Why?
A: This problem probably is aster yellows, a virus disease usually spread by aphids. Try growing resistant varieties, and control any insects as soon as you notice them.
Q: Why do the tops of my carrots turn green, and are they poisonous?

Grow the type of carrot best suited to your garden soil.

A: When sunlight reaches the tops of your carrots they start producing the green pigment chlorophyll. The leaves may taste bitter, but they're not poisonous.

Cauliflower

Common name: cauliflower
Botanical name: Brassica oleracea botrytis
Origin: Europe, Mediterranean

Varieties

Super Snowball (55 days); Snowball Imperial (58 days); Earli-Light (58 days); Snowball M (59 days); Snow King (60 days); White Contessa (62 days); Majestic (66 days); Self-Blanche (70 days); Greenball (95 days); Royal Purple (95 days).

Description

Cauliflower is a single-stalked, half-hardy, biennial member of the cole or cabbage family. It's grown as an annual, and the edible flower buds form a solid head (sometimes called a curd), which may be white, purple, or green. Cauliflower and broccoli are easy to tell apart until you meet a white-flowered broccoli or a green cauliflower. Both also come in purple, and even the U.S. Department of Agriculture can't always tell one from the other. Cauliflowers are prima donnas and need a lot of the gardener's attention. Mark Twain described a cauliflower as a cabbage with a college education.

Cauliflower has four stages of growth: (1) rapid growth of leaves; (2) formation of the head (which is the part you eat); (3) a resting period while the embryonic blossoms are being formed; and (4) development of the stalk, flowers, and seeds. The head formation stage is essential for the production of the vegetable, but not at all necessary for the survival of the plant. Cauliflower that's held in check by severe frost, lack of moisture, or too much heat will bolt, which means that it will go directly to seed without bothering to form a head at all.

Where and when to grow

Cauliflower is more restricted by climatic conditions than other cole family vegetables like cabbage or broccoli. It's less adaptable to extremes of temperature; it doesn't like cold weather, won't head properly if it's too hot, and doesn't tolerate dry conditions as well as broccoli.

Cauliflower needs two cool months in which to mature and is planted for spring and fall crops in most areas. Plant for a winter crop if your winters are mild. For a spring crop, plant transplants four to six weeks before the average date of the last frost in your area. If you're growing your own transplants from seed, start them about six weeks before your outdoor planting date.

How to plant

Cauliflower likes fertile, well-drained soil with a pH within the 6.5 to 7.5 range — this discourages disease and lets the

Cauliflower seedling

plant make the most of the nutrients in the soil. Like other cole crops, it's usually grown from transplants except where there is a long cool period, in which case you can sow seed directly in the garden in fall for winter harvest. When you're preparing the soil for planting, work in a complete, well-balanced fertilizer at the rate of one pound per 100 square feet or 10 pounds per 1,000 square feet. If you have sandy soil or your area is subject to heavy rains, you will probably need to supplement the nitrogen content of the soil. Use about a pound of high-nitrogen fertilizer for a 10-foot row. Plant transplants that are four to six weeks old, with four or five true leaves. If the transplants are leggy or have crooked stems, plant them deeply (up to the first leaves) so they won't grow to be top-heavy.

Plant the seedlings 18 to 24 inches apart in rows 24 to 36 inches apart. Plan for only a few heads at a time, or plant seeds and transplants at the same time for succession crops; you'll get the same result by planting early and midseason varieties at the same time. If you're planting seeds, set them half an inch deep and space them three inches apart. Thin them when they're big enough to lift by the true leaves, and transplant the thinned seedlings.

Fertilizing and watering

Fertilize before planting and again at midseason, at the same rate as the rest of the garden. Detailed information on fertilizing is given in "Spadework: The Essential Soil" in Part 1.

Abundant soil moisture and

cool moist air are needed for the best growth; do not let the ground dry out. The plants must be kept growing vigorously; if growth is interrupted by heat, cold, damage, or lack of water, the head will not form properly.

Special handling

Cultivate cauliflower regularly to diminish weed competition and prevent a crust from forming on the soil's surface. Take care not to damage the roots.

The objective with cauliflower is to achieve a perfect head, with all the flowerets pressed tightly together. Unless it's supposed to

be green or purple, the color should be untinged creamy-white, and too much sun or rain can damage the head. To prevent this, you blanch (whiten) it. Blanch the cauliflower when it gets to be about the size of an egg, by gathering three or four leaves and tying them together over the head. If you secure the leaves with colored rubber bands you can keep track of cauliflowers tied at different times. Check the heads occasionally for pests that may be hiding inside. The self-blanching cauliflower doesn't need to be tied, but it will not blanch in hot weather. Blanching cauliflower is a cosmetic

procedure; the flavor is not significantly improved, as is celery's, by blanching.

Pests

The cabbage family's traditional enemies are cutworms and caterpillars, and cauliflower is particularly susceptible to them. However, cutworms, cabbage loopers, and imported cabbage worms can all be controlled by spraying with bacillus thuringiensis, an organic product also known as Dipel or Thungicide. Detailed information on pest control is given in "Keeping Your Garden Healthy" in Part 1.

Diseases

Cauliflower may be susceptible to root rots; the first indication of this disease is yellowing of the leaves. Cut down on the incidence of disease by planting disease-resistant varieties when they're available, maintaining the general health of your garden, and avoiding handling the plants when they're wet. If a plant does become infected, remove and destroy it so it cannot spread disease to healthy plants. Detailed information on disease prevention is given in "Keeping Your Garden Healthy" in Part 1.

When and how to harvest

Time from planting to harvest is 55 to 100 days for cauliflower grown from transplants and 85 to 130 days for cauliflower grown from seed. Under good growing conditions the head develops rapidly to about six or eight inches in diameter. The mature head should be compact, firm, and white. Cut the whole head

Cauliflower

from the main stem. The leaves can be cooked like collards or cabbage.

Container growing

Cauliflower is another satisfactory container plant because, like broccoli and cabbage, it prefers cool weather and can be planted earlier in a container than in a regular bed, thus benefitting from an extended growing season. Also, it can be expensive to buy, so growing it is a good economy move. A single plant will do well in an eight-inch flower pot. In a larger container, give each plant 18 inches of space all around it.

Storing and preserving

Unwashed and wrapped in plastic, cauliflower can be stored for up to one week in the refrigerator, or for two to three weeks in a cold, moist place. Cauliflower freezes satisfactorily and can also be dried or used in relishes or pickled. Detailed information on storing and preserving is given in Part 4.

Serving suggestions

Boil the whole cauliflower head just until the base yields to the touch of a fork. Add lemon juice to the boiling water to preserve the curd's whiteness. Coat the head with a light cheese sauce or simply with melted butter and parsley. Tartar sauce is an original accompaniment to cauliflower, or sprinkle it with browned breadcrumbs for a crunchy texture. The flowerets can be separated, too, and french fried. Raw cauliflower lends a distinctive flavor to salads and is good served with other raw

Tie outer leaves of cauliflower together to blanch, or whiten, the head.

vegetables with a mustard- or curry-flavored dip. Cauliflower pickles are good, too.

Q and A

Q: My cauliflower heads have brown spots even when I blanch them. What causes this?
A: Browning on the cauliflower heads can be caused by downy mildew, which is encouraged by cool, wet conditions after the heads have formed.
Q: Will cauliflower, like broccoli, form side shoots after the main head is harvested?
A: No. Cauliflower will only form a single head.
Q: Will the small yellow and white moths flying around my cauliflower plants do any damage?
A: Potentially, yes. They are adult cabbage loopers and imported cabbage worms and are laying eggs. When the eggs

hatch, the pests can harm your plants.
Q: Can you eat the leaves of a cauliflower plant?
A: Yes. Cauliflower is a member of the cabbage family and its leaves taste like cabbage or collards.

Celeriac

Common names: celeriac, turnip-rooted celery, celery root, knob celery
Botanical name: Apium graveolens rapaceum
Origin: Europe and Africa

Varieties
Alabaster (120 days); Giant Prague (120 days).

Description

Celeriac is a form of celery, a member of the same family, and similar in growing habits and requirements. Its physical characteristics and culinary uses, however, are quite different. The edible root of celeriac is large and swollen, like a turnip, and develops at soil-level; a rosette of dark green leaves sprouts from the root. The stems are hollow. The French and Germans are more accustomed than Americans to celeriac; it's commonly used in stews or eaten raw.

Where and when to grow

Celeriac does best in cool weather and especially enjoys cool nights. To grow celeriac, start in spring in the North, in late summer in the South. In the North, start from transplants; the seeds are very slow to germinate. Plant them on the average date of last frost; set the plants six to eight inches apart in rows 24 to 30 inches apart. In the South you can grow celeriac from seed. Sometimes a second crop is grown by seeding directly outdoors in spring. Plant the seeds a quarter inch deep in rows 24 to 30 inches apart, and when the seedlings are large enough to handle, thin them to six to eight inches apart.

How to plant

Celeriac tolerates light shade and prefers rich soil that is high in organic matter, well able to hold moisture but with good drainage. It needs constant moisture and does well in wet locations. It's a heavy feeder and needs plenty of fertilizer to keep it growing quickly. When you're preparing the soil for planting, work in a complete, well-balanced fertilizer at the rate of one pound per 100 square feet or 10 pounds per 1,000 square feet.

If you're sowing seeds for transplants start indoors two to four months before your estimated planting date — the seeds germinate slowly. Cover the seeds with an eighth of an inch of soil, and then lay a material like burlap over the containers to keep the moisture in. Transplant carefully. To give the seedlings a good start, plant them in a trench three to four inches deep. Space the seedlings eight to 10 inches apart in rows two feet apart.

Fertilizing and watering

Fertilize before planting and again at midseason, at the same rate as the rest of the garden. Detailed information on fertilizing is given in "Spadework: The Essential Soil" in Part 1.

Frequent watering is important; celeriac, like celery, is shallow-rooted, and a lack of soil moisture can stop its growth. Keep the top few inches of soil moist at all times.

Special handling

Celeriac cannot compete with weeds. Cultivate conscientiously, but be careful not to disturb the

Celeriac

Celeriac seedling

shallow roots. As the tuber develops, snip off the side roots and hill up the soil over the swollen area for a short time to blanch the tubers. The outer surface will be whitened, but the interior will remain a brownish color.

Pests

Celeriac has no serious pest problems; it's a good vegetable for the organic gardener.

Vegetables

Diseases

Celeriac has no serious disease problems.

When and how to harvest

Time from planting to harvest is 110 to 120 days from seed. A 10-foot row should give you 16 to 20 roots. Pick off the lower leaves — you can use them to flavor soups and stews. Harvest celeriac when the swollen root is three to four inches wide. In warmer climates, harvest the roots when they're about the size of a baseball. Celeriac increases in flavor after the first frost, but should be harvested before the first hard freeze.

Container growing

Celeriac can be grown in a container, but not very successfully. You'll do much better with it in the regular garden.

Storing and preserving

You can dry the leaves to use as an herb in soups and stews. Keep the roots in the refrigerator up to one week, or store them in a cold, moist place for two to three months. They will keep in the ground in areas where freezing weather is not a problem. You can also freeze the roots; handle them like turnips. Detailed information on storing and preserving is given in Part 4.

Serving suggestions

Peel, dice, and cook celeriac roots; then marinate them in vinegar and oil, seasoned to your taste. Or shred the raw roots, dress them with a light

Celery

Celery seedling

vinaigrette, and add them to a salad. Celeriac makes an interesting addition to any luncheon.

Celery

Common name: celery
Botanical name: Apium graveolens dulce
Origin: Europe

Varieties

Golden Yellow (self-blanching, 82 days); Green Giant (115 days); Summer Pascal (115 days); Golden Plume (118 days); Utah 52-70 (125 days).

Description

Celery is a hardy biennial grown as an annual. It has a tight rosette of eight- to 18-inch stalks, topped with many divided leaves. The flowers look like coarse Queen Anne's lace and are carried on tall stalks. Celery is a more popular vegetable in this country than its cousin celeriac (which it doesn't resemble at all in looks or taste). Both are members of the parsley family, to which dill and fennel also belong, and probably originated in Mediterranean countries. Celery had been used earlier for medicinal purposes, but the French were probably the first to use it as a vegetable, somewhere around 1600. It was brought from Scotland to Michigan, where it was grown by Dutch farmers during the last half of the 19th century, and was not produced commercially in the United States until the 1870s. It's

a versatile vegetable — you can eat the stalks, leaves, and seeds — but it needs a lot of attention, and it's not an easy crop for the home gardener.

Where and when to grow

Celery does best in cool weather and especially enjoys cool nights. Cold weather will inhibit growth. Grow celery in spring in the North, planting transplants two to three weeks before the average date of last frost, or in the late summer in the South. Celery seeds are very slow to germinate, so it's usually more satisfactory to use transplants.

How to plant

Celery tolerates light shade and prefers rich soil that is high in organic matter, well able to hold moisture but with good drainage; it does well in wet, almost boggy locations. It's a heavy feeder and needs plenty of fertilizer for continuous quick growth. When you're preparing the soil for planting, work in a complete, well-balanced fertilizer at the rate of one pound per 100 square feet or 10 pounds per 1,000 square feet. If you're sowing seeds for transplants, start them two to four months before your estimated planting date — they germinate slowly. Cover the seeds with an eighth inch of soil, and then lay a material like burlap over the containers to keep the moisture in. Transplant them in trenches three to four inches deep and two feet apart. Space the seedlings eight to 10 inches apart, and as they grow mound the soil up around them to blanch the stems. Having the plants fairly close together will also help blanching.

Fertilizing and watering

Fertilize before planting and again at midseason, at the same rate as the rest of the garden. Detailed information on fertilizing is given in "Spadework: The Essential Soil" in Part 1.

Make sure that the plants get plenty of water at all stages of growth. Celery is a moisture-loving plant, and lack of water may slow growth and encourage the plant to send up flower stalks — it will also get very stringy.

Special handling

Celery does not like competition from weeds during the slow early growth stage, so cultivate regularly, taking care to avoid damage to the roots, which are close to the soil surface. Unlike cauliflower, which is not much affected in flavor by blanching or whitening, celery will be bitter if it isn't blanched. Blanching is achieved by covering the plants to protect them from the sun, which encourages them to produce chlorophyll and turn green. This should be started 10 days to two weeks before harvesting.

There are a number of blanching methods to choose from, but none of them should be left on more than 10 days to two weeks or the celery stalks will become pithy and rot. Soil can be mounded around each side of the celery row and built up to the tops of the stalks. Or use boards tilted to shade the celery plants. Heavy paper — freezer paper or layers of newspaper — can also be used; wrap it around each plant and fasten it with a rubber band. You can also place milk cartons with the top and bottom cut out over the plant, or gather the stalks together and fit cylinder-shaped tiles over the tops of the plants.

Pests

It's some consolation for all the work growing celery demands that the crop has no serious pest problems. This means it's a good choice for the conscientious organic gardener.

Diseases

Pink rot, black heart, and blights can all attack celery. Magnesium and calcium in the soil discourage these conditions, and with adequate fertilizing you shouldn't have a problem. If you do, check the mineral content of your soil. Detailed information on disease prevention is given in "Keeping Your Garden Healthy" in Part 1.

When and how to harvest

Time from planting to harvest is 100 to 130 days from transplants, about 20 days longer from seed. A 10-foot row should yield about 20 heads of celery. Start harvesting before the first hard frost, when the head is about two to three inches in diameter at the base. Cut off the head at or slightly below soil level.

Container growing

A container or a raised bed makes a satisfactory growing space for celery. An eight-inch pot accommodates one plant. In a larger container, allow ten inches of growing space around each plant. It's very easy to blanch a single celery plant grown in a pot: simply slip the blanching material over the pot

and pull it up around the plant.

Storing and preserving

You can refrigerate celery for up to two weeks; or if you cut the leaves to use as herbs, you can keep the leaves in the refrigerator up to one week. Celery can be dried or canned, and it freezes fairly well; or you can store it for two to three months in a cold, moist place. The leaves and seeds are used as herbs; follow the procedures given in "How To Store and Use Herbs." Detailed information on storing and preserving is given in Part 4.

Serving suggestions

Celery is versatile. You can eat the stems, the leaves, and the seeds. The stems can be boiled, braised, fried, or baked; most people are more accustomed to celery as a raw salad vegetable or relish, but celery is great creamed or baked au gratin. And what could be more elegant than cream of celery soup? The leafy celery tops that most people throw out can be made into a refreshing drink. Boil and strain them, chill the liquid, and drink it by itself or combined with other vegetable juices.

Celery cabbage

See **Chinese cabbage**

Celtuce

See **Lettuce**

Chard

Common names: chard, Swiss chard, sea kale, Swiss beet, sea kale beet
Botanical name: Beta vulgaris cicla
Origin: Europe, Mediterranean

Varieties

Lucullus (50 days); Fordhook Giant (60 days); Rhubarb (60 days).

Description

Chard is basically a beet without the bottom. It's a biennial that's grown as an annual for its big crinkly leaves. Chard is a decorative plant; with its juicy red or white leaf stems and rosette of large, dark green leaves, it can hold its own in the flower garden. It's also a rewarding crop for the home vegetable gardener — it's easy-going and very productive. If you harvest the leaves as they grow, the plant will go on producing all season. Chard has an impressive history, too; it was a popular foodstuff even before the days of the Roman Empire.

Where and when to grow

Chard prefers cool temperatures; high temperatures

Chard seedling

slow down leaf production, but chard tolerates heat better than spinach does. In a mild climate you can plant chard from fall to early spring; in the North, plant from spring to midsummer.

How to plant

Plant chard from seed clusters (which each contain several seeds) about the average date of last frost in your area. Chard tolerates partial shade and likes fertile, well-worked soil with good drainage and a high organic content; like the beet, it is not fond of acid soil. Work a complete, well-balanced fertilizer into the soil before planting, at the rate of a pound per 100 square feet or 10 pounds per 1,000 square feet.

Plant the seed clusters an inch deep and four to six inches apart in rows 18 to 24 inches apart. When they're large enough to handle, thin seedlings to stand about nine to 12 inches apart. Although you are growing from seed clusters, each of which is likely to produce several seedlings, thinning is not as important as it is when you're growing beets, which must have ample room for root development. Chard plants can stand crowding — they'll produce smaller leaves but more of them. A few extra plants will also give you replacements for any that bolt or go to seed in hot weather. Remove any plants that bolt, and let the others grow.

Fertilizing and watering

Fertilize before planting and again at midseason, at the same rate as the rest of the garden. Detailed information on fertilizing is given in "Spadework: The Essential Soil" in Part 1.

The crop does need enough water to keep the leaves growing quickly, so keep the soil moist at all times.

Pests

Aphids and leaf miners are the major pests you'll have to contend with. You can usually control aphids by pinching out the affected area; if there are a lot of them, try hosing them off the plants. Leaf miners, wormlike insects that feed inside the leaf surfaces, can also be controlled physically; pick off the older leaves where you see that miners have laid rows of pearl-white eggs. Detailed information on pest control is given in "Keeping Your Garden Healthy" in Part 1.

Chard

Diseases

Chard has no serious disease problems.

When and how to harvest

Time from planting to harvest is 55 to 60 days. A 10-foot row of chard should give you nine pounds or more of produce. Start harvesting chard when the outside leaves are three inches long; don't let them get much over 10 inches long or they'll taste earthy. Some gardeners like to take off the outside leaves a few at a time; others prefer to cut the entire plant down to three inches and let it grow back. Chard will grow and produce steadily all summer, and if the soil is fertile and the weather doesn't get too cold, harvesting may continue into a second year.

Container growing

Chard grows fairly well when planted in wide rows in a square or rectangular container. You can also space three or four plants in a eight-inch pot—chard doesn't object to being a bit crowded. Remember that if you harvest the older outside leaves, you'll give the young, tender leaves a chance to grow.

Storing and preserving

Chard can be stored for one to two weeks in the refrigerator. It can also be frozen, canned, or dried; use the recipes for greens. Detailed information on storing and preserving is given in Part 4.

Serving suggestions

Chard is delicious steamed or cooked like spinach. The leaves have a sweet taste like spinach, and they're colorful in a salad. Chard stalks can be cooked like celery. Cut them into pieces two or three inches long and simmer them until tender; serve them hot with butter or chilled with a light vinaigrette. If you're cooking the leaves and stalks together, give the stalks a five-minute head start so that both will be tender at the end of the cooking time.

Q and A

Q: Sometimes my chard plants send up a seedstalk. Why?
A: Warm temperatures and overcrowding will cause chard to bolt or go to seed prematurely.

Chayote

Common names: chayote, chocho, chuchu, sou-sou, vegetable pear, one-seeded cucumber
Botanical name: Sechium edule
Origin: Central America

Varieties

Plant whatever variety is available. You plant the whole vegetable so you can use the chayote you buy in the local Spanish *mercado*.

Description

The chayote is a tender perennial vine that grows from a tuber and can climb to 30 feet. It's a member of the gourd family, and it has hairy leaves the size and shape of maple leaves; male and female flowers are borne on the same vine. The fruit looks like a greenish or whitish flattened pear. You can eat the young shoots, the fruit, and, if the plant lives long enough, the tubers. Chayote is very popular in Mexico and Central America; it also has a place in American Creole cooking.

Where and when to grow

The chayote prefers warm to hot temperatures and cannot survive temperatures below freezing. California, Texas, and Florida have the sort of climate the chayote enjoys, but it can be grown farther north if the growing season is long. In areas where the season is short, chayote can be grown in a pot inside and then set out in the soil or kept in a pot and brought back inside when the weather turns cold.

How to plant

You plant the whole fruit with the fat side placed at an angle half way down in the soil so that the stem area is level with the soil surface. Before planting, work a complete, well-balanced fertilizer into the soil at the rate of one pound per 100 square feet or 10 pounds per 1,000 square feet. The chayote likes well-drained soil with a high content of organic matter and will tolerate partial shade. Space the plants 24 to 30 inches apart, with four or five feet between rows. You don't need to provide a support for the vines unless you want to save space.

Fertilizing and watering

Fertilize before planting and again at midseason, at the same rate as the rest of the garden. Detailed information on fertilizing is given in "Spadework: The Essential Soil" in Part 1.

Give the chayote plants plenty of water to keep them growing strongly.

Chayote seedling

Pests

Aphids may visit your chayote vines. Hand-pick or hose them off, or control them chemically by spraying with Malathion or Diazinon. Detailed information on pest control is given in "Keeping Your Garden Healthy" in Part 1.

Diseases

Chayote has no serious disease problems.

When and how to harvest

Time from planting to harvest is 120 to 150 days. Cut the chayote off the vine while the fruit is young and tender; don't wait until the flesh gets hard.

Container growing

You can grow chayote in a container, but the yield will not be impressive.

Storing and preserving

Chayotes will keep in the refrigerator up to one week. Freeze your extra chayotes either diced or stuffed like squash. Detailed information on storing and preserving is given in Part 4.

Serving suggestions

Chayote can be prepared any way you prepare squash. Chayote is best eaten young and tender. If it overripens, scoop out the flesh, remove the seed (a large seed, in what looks like a terry

Chayote

cloth bag), mash the flesh with cheese or meat, restuff the empty shell and bake. The tubers of very mature plants are edible and filling, but not very flavorful.

Chick pea

Common names: chick pea, gram, garbanzo
Botanical name: Cicer arietinum
Origin: southern Europe and India

Varieties
Few varieties are available; grow the variety available in your area.

Description

Chick peas or garbanzos are regarded as beans, but their botanical place is somewhere between the bean and the pea. They're tender annuals and grow on a bushy plant, rather like snap beans but they have a longer growing season. Chick peas have puffy little pods that contain one or two seeds each. In some areas they're grown as a field crop as a food for horses, but they're good food for people, too.

Where and when to grow

Chick peas are tender plants and can't tolerate much cold—a hard frost will damage the immature beans. You can grow them anywhere in the United States that has 90 to 100 frost-free days. Plant chick peas from seed on the average date of last frost for your area.

How to plant

Choose a bed in full sunlight; chick peas tolerate partial shade, but partial shade tends to mean a partial yield. Prepare the soil by mixing in a pound of 5-10-10 fertilizer—don't use a high-nitrogen fertilizer, because too much nitrogen will promote growth of foliage but not of the pods. Work the fertilizer into the soil at the rate of one pound per 100 square feet or 10 pounds per 1,000 square feet. The seeds may crack and germinate poorly when the moisture content of the soil is too high. Don't soak the seeds before planting, and don't overwater immediately afterward. Plant seeds an inch deep and two inches apart in rows at least 18 to 24 inches apart. When the seedlings are growing well, thin the plants to four to six inches apart. Cut the seedlings with scissors at ground level; be careful not to disturb the others. They don't mind being a little crowded; in fact, they'll use each other for support.

Fertilizing and watering

Chick peas set up a mutual exchange with soil microorganisms called

Chick pea

nitrogen-fixing bacteria, which help them produce their own fertilizer. Some gardeners recommend that if you haven't grown beans in the plot the previous season, you should treat the seeds before planting with a nitrogen-fixing bacteria inoculant to help them convert organic nitrogen compounds into usable organic compounds. This is a perfectly acceptable practice but it isn't really necessary; the bacteria in the soil will multiply quickly enough once they've got a growing plant to work with.

Fertilize before planting and again at midseason, at the same rate as the rest of the garden. Detailed information on fertilizing is given in "Spadework: The Essential Soil" in Part 1.

Keep the soil moist until the chick peas have pushed through the ground. Water regularly if there's no rain, but remember that water on the flowers can cause the flowers and small pods to fall off. When the soil temperature reaches 60°F you can mulch to conserve moisture.

Special handling

Don't bother the plants when they're wet or covered with heavy dew; handling or brushing against them when they're wet spreads fungus spores. Cultivate thoroughly but with care, so that you don't disturb the bean plants' shallow root systems.

Pests

Chick peas may be attacked by aphids, bean beetles, flea beetles, leafhoppers, and mites. Aphids, leafhoppers, and mites can be controlled chemically by

spraying with Malathion or Diazinon. Bean beetles and flea beetles can be controlled chemically by spraying with carbaryl. Chick peas are almost always attacked by large numbers of pests that cannot be controlled by organic methods. This doesn't mean the organic gardener can't grow them, but yields may be lower if only organic controls are used. Detailed information on pest control is given in "Keeping Your Garden Healthy" in Part 1.

Diseases

Chick peas are susceptible to blight, mosaic, and anthracnose. You can cut down on the incidence of disease by planting disease-resistant varieties when they're available, maintaining the general health of your garden, and avoiding handling the plants when they're wet. If a plant does become infected, remove and destroy it so it cannot spread disease to healthy plants. Detailed information on disease prevention is given in "Keeping Your Garden Healthy" in Part 1.

When and how to harvest

If you want to eat them raw, pick chick peas in the green shell or immature stage. For drying, harvest the chick peas when the plants have matured and the leaves have turned completely brown. At this time the seeds should be dry and hard — bite a couple of seeds; if you can hardly dent them they're properly dry and ready to harvest.

Container growing

Chick peas can be grown in containers, but they need so

much space to produce a reasonable crop that they're not really a practical choice for the container gardener.

Storing and preserving

Unshelled chick peas can be kept up to one week in the refrigerator. You can freeze, can, or dry the shelled chick peas, and they can also be sprouted. Dried shelled chick peas can be stored in a cool, dry place for 10 to 12 months. Detailed information on storing and preserving is given in Part 4.

Serving suggestions

Shelled chick peas can be steamed or boiled like peas, or roasted like peanuts. Vegetarian cooks often use chick peas with grains as a protein-rich meat substitute. In the Middle East they're puréed with garlic, lemon juice, and spices.

Chicory

Common names: chicory, witloof, French endive, Belgian endive, succory
Botanical name: Cichorium intybus
Origin: Asia, Europe

Varieties
For chicory root: Brunswick; Magdeburg; Zealand. For Belgian endive: Witloof.

Chicory seedling

Description

Chicory is a hardy perennial with a long, fleshy taproot and a flower stalk that rises from a rosette of leaves. It looks much like a dandelion except that the flowers grow on a branched stalk and are pale blue.

Chicory is grown either for its root, which can be roasted to produce a coffee substitute, or for its tender leaf shoots, which are known as Belgian or blanched endive. This plant is not to be confused with endive or escarole, which are grown as salad greens. Both chicory and endive belong to the same family, and the names are often used interchangeably, but they aren't the same plant. If you want to produce the chicory root or the Belgian endive, you grow chicory (*Cichorium intybus*) — you can eat the leaves, but that's not why you're growing the variety. If you're growing specifically for greens, you grow endive (*Cichorium endivia*).

Chicory has two stages of development. The first produces the harvestable root. In the second stage, you harvest the root and bury it upright in damp sand or soil until it produces sprouts or heads of pale, blanched leaves; these heads are the Belgian endives. Once you've harvested the heads, you can still use the roots, although they won't be as satisfactory as roots grown specifically for their own sake.

Where and when to grow

Chicory is very hardy, tolerates cold, and can be grown for its roots anywhere in the United States. Since the second stage that produces the heads takes place after harvesting, climate is not an issue. Plant chicory seeds in the garden two to three weeks before the average date of last frost for your area.

How to plant

Chicory tolerates partial shade. The soil should be well-drained, high in organic matter, and free of lumps that might cause the roots to fork or split. Work a complete, well-balanced fertilizer into the soil before planting, at the rate of one pound per 100 square feet or 10 pounds per 1,000 square feet. Plant the seeds an inch deep in rows 24 to 36 inches apart, and thin them to 12 to 18 inches apart when the seedlings are four inches tall. You can eat the thinnings.

Fertilizing and watering

Fertilize before planting and again at midseason, at the same rate as the rest of the garden. Detailed information on fertilizing is given in "Spadework: The Essential Soil" in Part 1.

Keep the plants evenly moist.

Special handling

If chicory is planted in well-cultivated soil that's rich in organic matter, it should develop large roots. If you're growing the plants for the roots alone, they'll be ready to harvest about 120 days after planting. If you want to produce the blanched heads, follow this procedure. Before

the ground freezes, dig up the chicory roots and cut off the tops about two inches above the crown or top of the root. Store the roots in a cool, humid place — an outdoor pit or a root cellar. In winter and spring, bury the roots to "force" them and produce the blanched sprouts — for a continuous supply repeat the procedure every few weeks.

To prepare the roots for forcing, cut off the tips so that the roots are six to eight inches long, and pack them upright in a box, pot, or other container filled with fine sand or a mixture of sand and peat moss. Cover the tops of the roots with seven or eight inches of sand or sawdust, water thoroughly, and keep at a temperature of 60° to 70°F. Put them in your basement or in a cold frame or trench in the garden. You may need to water occasionally during the three or four weeks the heads take to develop. When the heads break the surface, remove the potting material and cut the heads with a knife where they meet the root.

Pests

Chicory has no serious pest problems. It's a good crop for the organic gardener who doesn't mind doing the extra work that chicory requires in its second stage of growth.

Diseases

Chicory has no serious disease problems.

When and how to harvest

It takes more than 100 days to produce a mature chicory root. For the traditional blanched endive, you'll have to wait three or four

Chicory

weeks after starting the forcing procedure. You should be able to get 30 to 50 blanched heads from a 10-foot row of chicory plants.

Container growing

Chicory does not make a satisfactory container vegetable.

Storing and preserving

Refrigerate the cut heads until you're ready to serve them, up to one week. You can keep the entire plant — root and all — for two to three months in a cold, moist place, or you can dig up the roots and store them for 10 to 12 months. Detailed information on storing is given in Part 4.

Serving suggestions

The roots of chicory are sometimes roasted and ground to add to coffee or used as a coffee substitute. Wash and dice the root, then dry it and roast it before grinding. Blanched endive heads are good braised or in salads. Mix endive with peppers, artichoke hearts, and sardines for an Italian-style salad, or with olives, cucumbers, anchovies, and tomato wedges in the Greek manner.

Chinese cabbage

Common names: Chinese cabbage, white cabbage, flowering cabbage, celery cabbage, pakchoy, Michihli, Napa cabbage
Botanical name: Brassica chinensis
Origin: China

Varieties
What-A-Joy (65 days); China Pride (68 days); Monument (80 days); Burpee Hybrid (75 days); Crispy Choy (pakchoy type, 53 days); Michihli (heading type, 72 days).

Description

Chinese cabbage is a hardy biennial grown as an annual, and it's not a member of the cabbage family. It has broad, thick, tender leaves; heavy midribs; and can be either loosely or tightly headed and grow 15 to 18 inches tall. The variety with a large compact heart is called celery cabbage, pakchoy, or Michihli. In Chinese, call it *pe-tsai;* in Japanese, say *hakusai*. Despite the name, the appearance and taste of Chinese cabbage are closer to lettuce than to regular cabbage.

Where and when to grow

Chinese cabbage can be grown only in cool weather, because it bolts (goes to seed) quickly in hot weather and long days — it bolts much faster than the cabbage family vegetables. It's usually grown as a fall crop in the North and as a winter crop in the South. It can be started inside and transplanted outside in the spring, but Chinese cabbage shocks easily, and transplanting sometimes shocks it into going to seed.

How to plant

Chinese cabbage is difficult to grow in the home garden unless you can give it a long, cool growing season. Plant it four to six weeks before your average date of last frost. Even if the first fall frost arrives before the head forms you'll still get a crop of greens. Chinese cabbage will tolerate partial shade. The soil should be well-worked and well-fertilized, high in organic matter and able to hold moisture. When you're

Chinese cabbage seedling

Chinese cabbage

Pests

Flea beetles, aphids, and cabbage worms make Chinese cabbage difficult to grow without spraying. Aphids can be partially controlled without chemicals by hand-picking or hosing, and cabbage worms can be controlled by spraying with bacillus thuringiensis, which is an organic product. Flea beetles usually must be chemically controlled with carbaryl, which will also control cabbage loopers. Detailed information on pest control is given in "Keeping Your Garden Healthy" in Part 1.

Diseases

Yellows virus, clubroot, and black rot may attack Chinese cabbage. Cut down on the incidence of disease by planting disease-resistant varieties when they're available, maintaining the general health of your garden, and avoiding handling the plants when they're wet. If a plant does become infected, remove and destroy it so it cannot spread disease to healthy plants. Detailed information on disease prevention is given in "Keeping Your Garden Healthy" in Part 1.

preparing the soil for planting, work in a complete, well-balanced fertilizer at the rate of one pound per 100 square feet or 10 pounds per 1,000 square feet. Sow seeds in rows 18 to 30 inches apart, and when the seedlings are large enough to handle, thin them to stand eight to 12 inches apart. Don't even attempt to transplant Chinese cabbage unless you've started the seeds in peat pots or other plantable containers.

Fertilizing and watering

Fertilize before planting and again at midseason, at the same rate as the rest of the garden. Detailed information on fertilizing is given in "Spadework: The Essential Soil" in Part 1.

Water frequently to help the young plants grow fast and become tender. They'll probably go to seed if their growth slows down.

When and how to harvest

Time from planting to harvest is 50 to 80 days, and a 10-foot row should give you 10 or more heads. Harvest when the heads are compact and firm and before the seedstalks form. With a fall crop, harvest before hard-freezing weather. To harvest, cut off the whole plant at ground level.

Container growing

Chinese cabbage, like other cool-weather vegetables, appreciates getting an early start in a container—you can plant earlier than in a regular bed where the soil takes longer to warm up. Also, Chinese cabbage is sensitive to heat, so it's useful to be able to move it into the shade if necessary. One plant does well in an eight-inch flower pot. In a larger container, each plant needs ten inches of growing space all around.

Storing and preserving

Chinese cabbage stays fresh in the refrigerator up to one week, or in a cold, moist place for two to three months. You can also freeze or dry it, and the seeds of Chinese cabbage can be sprouted. Detailed information on storing and preserving is given in Part 4.

Serving suggestions

Chinese cabbage has a very delicate, mild flavor, more reminiscent of lettuce than of cabbage. It makes an interesting slaw, with a sour cream dressing and a little chopped pineapple. Or serve it in wedges like cabbage. Of course, the ideal use is in Chinese stir-fry dishes and soups. Try shredding the Chinese cabbage with a bit of carrot, flavoring it with ginger and soy sauce, and dropping it in spoonfuls into oil in the wok. It's crunchy and delicious. You can also butter-steam Chinese cabbage as an accompaniment to roast pork, or use the leaves to make cabbage rolls.

Collards

Common name: collards
Botanical name: Brassica oleracea acephalo
Origin: Europe

Varieties

Blue Max (68 days); Heavi-Crop (65 days); Georgia (75 days); Vates (75 days); Champion (78 days).

Description

A hardy biennial grown as an annual, the collard grows two to four feet tall and has tufts or rosettes of leaves growing on sturdy stems. Collard is a kind of kale, a primitive member of the cabbage family that does not form a head. The name collard is also given to young cabbage plants that are harvested before they have headed. Collards were England's main winter vegetable for centuries.

Where and when to grow

Like other members of the cole or cabbage family, collards are hardy and can tolerate low 20°F temperatures. They're also more tolerant of heat than some cole crops; they can take more heat than cabbage and more cold than cauliflower. In the South, get

Collard

ahead of the warm weather by planting collards in February or March. In the North, you can get two crops by planting in early spring and again in July or August.

How to plant

Collards like fertile, well-drained soil with a pH within the 6.5 to 7.5 range — this discourages disease and lets the plant make the most of the nutrients in the soil. Collards are usually grown from transplants planted four to six weeks before the average date of last frost, except where there is a long cool period; in this case you can sow seed directly in the garden in fall for a winter harvest.

When you're preparing the soil for planting, work in a complete well-balanced fertilizer at the rate of one pound per 100 square feet or 10 pounds per 1,000 square feet. If you have sandy soil or your area is subject to heavy rains, you'll probably need to supplement the nitrogen content of the soil. Use about a pound of nitrogen fertilizer for a 10-foot row.

If you're planting seeds, set them an inch deep and space them three inches apart. Thin them when they're big enough to lift by the true leaves. You can transplant the thinned seedlings. If you're planting transplants, they should be four to six weeks old with four or five true leaves. If the transplants are leggy or have crooked stems, plant them deeply (up to the first leaves) so that they won't grow to be top heavy. Plant the seedlings 12 inches apart in rows 18 to 24 inches apart.

Fertilizing and watering

Fertilize before planting and again at midseason, at the same rate as the rest of the garden. Detailed information on fertilizing is given in "Spadework: The Essential Soil" in Part 1.

Water them regularly to keep the leaves from getting tough.

Special handling

If collard plants get too heavy you may need to stake them.

Pests

The cabbage family's traditional enemies are cutworms and caterpillars. Cutworms, cabbage loopers, and imported cabbage worms can all be controlled by spraying with bacillus thuringiensis, an organic product also known as Dipel or Thungicide. Generally, collards have fewer pest problems than other cole crops. They are one of the best and most prolific crops for the organic gardener. Detailed information on pest control is given in "Keeping Your Garden Healthy" in Part 1.

Diseases

Collards have no serious disease problems.

When and how to harvest

Time from planting to harvest is 75 to 85 days from transplants, 85 to 95 days from seed. A 10-foot row should yield eight pounds or more of collard greens. Collards become sweeter if harvested after a frost, but you should harvest them before a hard freeze. In warmer areas, harvest the leaves from the bottom up before they get old and tough.

Container growing

Collards are good container vegetables, although a bit more demanding of space than some others. A single plant is comfortable in a ten-inch pot. In a larger container, allow 18 to 24 inches around each plant, depending on how large you want to allow the plant to grow before harvesting.

Storing and preserving

Collards can be stored in the refrigerator up to one week, or in a cold, moist place for two to three weeks. Collards can be frozen, canned, or dried; use the recipes for greens. Detailed information on storing and preserving is given in Part 4.

Serving suggestions

Collards can be steamed or boiled; serve them alone or combine them with ham or salt pork. Corn bread is a nice accompaniment.

Q and A

Q: Will the small yellow and white moths flying around my collard plants do any damage?
A: Potentially, yes. They are adult cabbage loopers and imported cabbage worms and are laying eggs. When the eggs hatch, the pests can do considerable damage to collards.
Q: Will collard greens be sweeter if harvested after a frost?
A: Technically, yes. Cool temperatures will cause some of the carbohydrates in the plants to turn to sugar, but the change

in flavor may not be very pronounced.

Q: How can I prevent collards from becoming stringy?

A: Harvest collards when they are young and tender. Under-watering may also cause collards to become stringy.

Corn

Common names: corn, sweet corn
Botanical name: Zea mays
Origin: Central America

Varieties

A large number of varieties are available. Your local extension service can give you suggestions for the best corn to grow in your area. These are just a few of the good varieties available: Polar Vee (55 days); Sugar and Gold (white and yellow kernels, 60 days); Earliking (66 days); Butter and Sugar (white and yellow kernels, 78 days); Golden Cross Bantam (84 days); Illini Chief (85 days). For late crops, try Aristogold Bantam Evergreen (90 days) or Silver Queen (92 days).

Description

Corn, a tender annual that can grow four to 12 feet tall, is a member of the grass family. It produces one to two ears on a stalk, of which only one may be harvestable. The pollen from the tassels must fall into the cornsilk to produce kernels, and if pollination does not occur, all that will grow is the cob. The kernels of sweet corn can be yellow, white, black, red, or a combination of colors. Corn is the No. 1 crop in the United States and (with rice, wheat, and potatoes) one of the top four crops in the world. But despite the popularity of sweet corn and popcorn, most corn is eaten secondhand — 80 percent of the United States corn crop goes into the production of meat. Corn is not the easiest crop to grow in your home vegetable garden, and it doesn't give you a lot of return for the space it occupies. Don't be taken in by all that lush foliage — you will generally get only one harvestable ear of corn from a stalk, although some dwarf varieties will produce two or three.

Where and when to grow

You can grow corn in any area, but the time it will take to reach maturity depends on the amount of heat it gets; corn doesn't really get into its stride until the weather warms up. You may get two crops, depending on which variety you plant.

How to plant

Corn likes well-worked, fertile soil with good drainage, and it must have full sun. Fertilize the soil before planting, using a third of a pound of a complete, well-balanced fertilizer on each side of a 10-foot row. Place the fertilizer an inch below and two inches away from where you plan to put the seed.

Plant corn when the soil temperature reaches 60°F. Plant the seeds two to four inches apart, in rows (short rows in a block, rather than one long row) or inverted hills. Planting in clumps or blocks ensures pollination. For a continuous

Corn seedling

supply, plant a dozen seeds of the same variety every two weeks (or when the previous planting shows three leaves), or plant early, midseason, and late varieties at the same time. When the corn is about six inches tall, thin short varieties to two feet apart, tall varieties to three feet apart. Corn can be grown closer together than this, but then the roots are more crowded and more watering and feeding are needed.

Fertilizing and watering

Corn is a heavy user of nitrogen. Fertilize in spring, again when the corn is eight inches tall, and again when it's 18 inches tall. Side-dress between the rows, using a third pound of complete, well-balanced fertilizer on each side of a 10-foot row. Detailed information on fertilizing is given

Protect corn from birds by tying paper bags over the ears.

in "Spadework: The Essential Soil" in Part 1.

Watering is very important. Keep the soil evenly moist. Corn often grows so fast in hot weather that the leaves wilt because the roots can't keep the leaves supplied with moisture. Although corn requires so much water, rain or water on the tassels at the time of pollination can reduce the number of kernels on a cob — and sometimes can destroy the whole crop. When watering corn, try to avoid getting water on the tassels.

Special handling

Keep the competition down. Weed early and keep the weeds cut back, but remember that corn has very shallow roots; a vigorous attack on the weeds may destroy the corn. Be sure to thin extra corn plants — crowding stimulates lots of silage, but no cobs. Protect the ears with paper bags after pollination if you're having trouble with birds.

Pests

Corn is attacked by many pests — notably cutworms, wireworms, flea beetles, corn earworms, and corn borers — and they usually attack in numbers too large to control by physical methods. Be prepared to use the appropriate insecticide at the first signs of insect damage. Cutworms and wireworms can be controlled with a soil drench of Diazinon. Spray flea beetles with carbaryl when they first appear. The corn earworm deposits its eggs on the developing silks of the corn, and the small caterpillars follow the silks down into the ears, where they feed on the tips.

Once they get inside the ear there is no effective control, so watch out for them and spray with carbaryl before the earworms get inside the protective cover of the ear. Corn borers damage stalks, ears, and tassels. They tunnel into the plant and can cause such severe damage that the stalks fall over. Watch for them, and spray with carbaryl every five days, starting when the first eggs hatch.

Raccoons and most rodents love corn and know exactly when to harvest it — usually the day before you plan to. Removing the offenders' homes and fencing in the garden are about the only ways to deter them. Because it takes up so much room and has so many pest problems, corn is not the ideal choice for either the organic gardener or the novice gardener. But for the experienced gardener with lots of room and a good spray tank, there's nothing like the taste of fresh, home-grown sweet corn. Detailed information on pest control is given in "Keeping Your Garden Healthy" in Part 1.

Diseases

Corn smut and Stewart's wilt are corn's two main disease problems. Corn smut is a fungus disease that attacks the kernels — the kernels turn gray or black and are about four times larger than normal. Destroy the affected plants, and plant your corn in a new part of the garden next time. Smut spores can survive in the soil for two years. Stewart's wilt is a bacterial disease spread by flea beetles. It causes a general yellowing of the leaves and severe stunting of the whole plant. Try to prevent it by planting resistant varieties and controlling flea beetles when they first appear. Detailed information on disease prevention is given in "Keeping Your Garden Healthy" in Part 1.

When and how to harvest

From planting to harvest takes 55 to 95 days depending on the variety and, to some extent, the weather. Your harvest won't be generous — maybe five to eight ears from a 10-foot row. Harvest your corn when the kernels are soft and plump and the juice is milky. Have the water boiling when you go out to harvest and rush the corn from the stalk to the pot, then to the table. The goal is to cook the corn before the sugar in the kernels changes to starch. A delay of even 24 hours between harvesting and eating will cause both flavor and texture to deteriorate noticeably.

Container growing

Corn looks dramatic in a container, but it's not the most practical choice for the gardener who wants to make the most of limited space. If you want to try it, sow five or six seeds in a five-gallon bucket or larger container.

Storing and preserving

If you must keep corn before eating, wrap the whole thing, ear and husk, in damp paper towels; store in the refrigerator for four to eight days. Corn can be sprouted, and it also freezes, cans, and dries satisfactorily. Detailed information on storing and preserving is given in Part 4.

Serving suggestions

After you've given your home-grown corn all that care and attention — to say nothing of a good deal of your garden space — it is almost unthinkable to do anything with it beyond boiling or steaming it quickly and annointing it with a dab of butter. You can also roast it in the husks in a hot oven or on the barbecue grill. If you have lots, make a delicate corn soup or soufflé.

Q and A

Q: How many ears of corn does each stalk bear?
A: Each stalk of corn usually produces one harvestable ear of corn.
Q: Some of my corn stalks have turned purple. Why?
A: Purple coloring on a stalk of corn usually indicates a phosphorus deficiency.
Q: Many kernels on each ear of corn do not develop. Why not?
A: There are many possible reasons for poor kernel development, including overcrowding, potassium deficiency, dry weather, or poor pollination. Poor pollination occurs when there are too few corn plants in the patch.
Q: What are the corn tassels?
A: The tassels are the male flowers of the corn plant. The ears that you eat are the female flowers.

Cress

Common names: cress, garden cress, peppergrass
Botanical name: Lepidium sativum
Origin: Asia

Varieties
Few varieties are available commercially; grow the variety available in your area.

Description

Cress is a hardy annual with finely divided tiny green leaves that have a biting flavor. You can grow cress from seed indoors or out — it will even sprout on water-soaked cotton. It takes only 15 to 20 days from planting to harvest, which means more or less instant gratification for the least patient gardener. Children love to grow it.

Cress has a peppery flavor that gives a lift to salads. There are several kinds available, but the curled variety is the most common.

Other types of cress are upland or winter cress (Barbarea vernapraecox) and watercress (Nasturtium officinale). Upland or winter cress (Barbarea vernapraecox) is a hardy biennial from Europe. You can sow it in the garden in early spring and harvest soon after midsummer. The plants are tough and will survive a cold winter if you mulch them.

Watercress is a trailing perennial of European origin with dark green peppery leaves and is usually grown in water. It's easily grown from seed but is usually propagated in temperate climates from stem-pieces, which root easily in wet soil. If you're fortunate enough to have a stream running through your garden, you can try growing watercress on the bank. You can also grow it indoors in pots set in a tray of water. Watercress adds a kick to salads and makes a pretty garnish. It's full of vitamin C and minerals.

Where and when to grow

Cress grows anywhere in the United States. Garden cress, which is the one you're most likely to grow, is started from seeds

Cress

sown every two weeks starting early in spring.

How to plant

When sown outdoors, cress likes well-worked soil with good drainage. It will flourish in shade or semishade and can tolerate a wide range of temperatures. When you're preparing the soil, dig in a complete, well-balanced fertilizer

at the rate of one pound per 100 square feet or 10 pounds per 1,000 square feet. Sow the seeds thickly, a quarter of an inch deep in wide rows, 18 to 24 inches apart, and for a continuous crop repeat the planting every 10 to 14 days.

Fertilizing and watering

Fertilize before planting and again at midseason, at the same rate as the rest of the garden. Detailed information on fertilizing is given in "Spadework: The Essential Soil" in Part 1.
    Cress needs even moisture. Try not to wet the leaves more than necessary since the soil that lodges there when water splashes on them is impossible to wash out without damaging the leaf. Cress grown indoors must have good drainage or it tends to rot.

Pests

Cress has no serious pest problems.

Diseases

Cress has no serious disease problems.

How and when to harvest

Often the plants are eaten at their very early seed-leaf stage. Cut off the cress with scissors and enjoy in salads or sandwiches.

Container growing

Cress flourishes practically anywhere, so it's a fine choice for container gardening. Sow the seeds generously over the whole planting area, or in wide rows in a large container. Don't worry about overcrowding—it won't bother the cress.

Storing and preserving

Cress does not store well, but it can be kept in the refrigerator up to one week. The seeds can be sprouted. Detailed information on storing is given in Part 4.

Serving suggestions

The English nibble "small salads" of cress and mix the young sprouts with mustard for dainty cress sandwiches. Use it in salads or for a garnish. The peppery taste is a good foil to more bland salad greens.

Cucumber

Common name: cucumber
Botanical name: Cucumis sativus
Origin: Asia

Varieties

There are dozens of varieties of cucumber, including "burpless" ones, which are supposed to be more digestible than regular cucumbers, and round yellow lemon cucumbers. In the United States cucumbers are divided into the slicing kind, which are large and stay green for a long time, the small stubby pickling varieties, and novelty varieties that are smaller than usual and suitable for containers or small gardens.
    The following are a selection of varieties in each of these categories. Talk to your local Cooperative Extension Service to find out about other varieties that will do well in your area.
Pickling: Spartan Dawn Hybrid (50-60 days); SMR-18 (50-60 days), both resistant to mosaic and

Cucumber seedling

Cucumber

scab; Liberty (48 days); Calypso (56 days); Triple Mech (52 days). **Slicing:** Slice Master (55 days) good disease resistance; Slice Nice (67 days); Universal (60 days); Setmore 100 (56 days); Poinsett (65 days) resistant to anthracnose, downy and powdery mildews, and leaf spot; Burpee Hybrid (60 days) resistant to downy mildew and mosaic; Challenger Hybrid (60 days), resistant to downy mildew and mosaic. **Burpless:** Sweet Slice Hybrid (65 days) resistant to downy and powdery mildews, mosaic, and scab. **Novelty:** Patio Pik Hybrid (50-55 days) pickling type, tolerant of downy and powdery mildews; Peppi Hybrid (50 days) pickling type, tolerant of downy and powdery mildews, mosaic, and scab. **Container varieties:** Potluck; Bush Whopper.

Description

Cucumbers are weak-stemmed, tender annuals that can sprawl on the ground or be trained to climb. Both the large leaves and the stems are covered with short hairs; the flowers are yellow. Some plants have both male and female flowers on the same vine, and there may be 10 males to every female flower, but only the female flowers can produce cucumbers. The expression "cool as a cucumber" has long been used to describe a person who is always calm in a crisis, and cucumbers do seem to give off a cool feeling. They're tender plants, however, and not at all tolerant to cold themselves.

Gulliver, in the report of his voyage to Brobdingnag, told of a project for extracting sunbeams from cucumbers, sealing them in jars, and letting them out to warm the air on raw days. Long before Gulliver, the Emperor Tiberius was so fond of cucumbers that the first greenhouses — sheets of mica in window sashes — were developed to keep the plants growing on happily indoors when it was too cold to take them outside. You can grow cucumbers in a large pot or hanging basket, or train them up a fence or over an arbor.

Where and when to grow

The cucumber is a warm-weather vegetable and very sensitive to frost. It will grow anywhere in the United States, however, because it has a very short growing season — only 55 to 65 days from planting to harvest — and most areas can provide it with at least that much sunshine. Cucumbers like night temperatures of 60° to 65°F, and day temperatures up to 90°F. Plant them when the soil has warmed up, three to four weeks after your area's average date of last frost.

How to plant

Cucumbers will tolerate partial shade, and respond to a rich, well-

Male
cucumber
blossom

Female
cucumber
blossom

worked, well-drained soil that is
high in organic matter. When
you're preparing the soil, dig in
a complete, well-balanced
fertilizer at the rate of one
pound per 100 square feet or 10
pounds per 1,000 square feet.
Plant cucumbers in inverted hills,
which you make by removing an
inch or two of soil from a circle 12
inches across and using this soil
to make a rim around the circle.
This protects the young plants
from heavy rains that might wash
away the soil and leave their
shallow roots exposed. Plant six or
eight seeds in each hill, and
when the seedlings are growing
strongly, thin them, leaving the
three hardiest plants standing six
to 12 inches apart. Cut the
thinned seedlings off with scissors
at soil level to avoid disturbing
the roots of the remaining plants.

Fertilizing and watering

Fertilize before planting and
again at midseason, at the same
rate as the rest of the garden.
Detailed information on fertilizing
is given in "Spadework: The
Essential Soil" in Part 1.

Cucumbers are 95 percent
water and need plenty of water to
keep them growing fast. Don't
let the soil dry out. In hot weather
the leaves may wilt during the
day, even when soil moisture is
high, because the plant is using
water faster than its roots can
supply. This is normal; just be
sure that the plant is receiving
regular and sufficient water.
Mulch to avoid soil compaction
caused by heavy watering.

Special handling

Cultivate to keep weeds down.
If you are growing cucumbers
inside, or in an area where there
are no insects to pollinate the
female flower — your 51st floor
balcony, for example — you may
need to help with pollination.
Take a soft-bristled brush and dust
the inside of a male flower (the
one without an immature fruit on
the stem), then carefully dust
the inside of the female flowers.
Harvest promptly; mature
cucumbers left on the vine
suppress the production of
more flowers.

Pests

Aphids and cucumber beetles
are the pests you're most likely to
encounter. To control aphids,
pinch out infested vegetation or
hose them off the cucumber
vines, or spray with Malathion or
Diazinon. Cucumber beetles
may not do much feeding damage,
but they carry cucumber

bacterial wilt. Hand-pick them off
the vines promptly, or spray
them with carbaryl. Cucumbers
are so prolific that the organic
gardener who doesn't want to use
chemical controls can afford to
lose a few to the bugs. Detailed
information on pest control is
given in "Keeping Your Garden
Healthy" in Part 1.

Diseases

Cucumber plants are
susceptible to scab, mosaic, and
mildew. Planting disease-
resistant varieties and maintaining
the general cleanliness and
health of your garden will help cut
down the incidence of disease.
If a plant does become infected,
remove and destroy it before it
can spread disease to healthy
plants. Cucumbers are not
tolerant to air pollution; a high
ozone level may affect their
development. Detailed
information on disease
prevention is given in "Keeping
Your Garden Healthy" in Part 1.

When and how to harvest

Time from planting to harvest is
55 to 65 days, and a 10-foot row
should give you as many
cucumbers as you can use. Pick the
cucumbers while they're
immature — the size will depend
on the variety. When the seeds
start to mature the vines will stop
producing.

Container growing

The introduction of varieties
specially developed for small-
space use means you can now
grow cucumbers successfully in
containers. However, there's a
great disparity in size among
even the bush-type cucumbers,

In a small garden, save space by growing cucumbers on a fence.

so choose carefully. A single Potluck cucumber will be quite at home in a six-inch pot. Varieties such as Patio Pik or Bush Whopper need larger containers. The use of a trellis or some other type of support will increase yields even with container-grown cucumbers.

Storing and preserving

Cucumbers can be stored in the refrigerator up to one week, but if the temperature is too low they'll freeze and turn soft. You can pickle them or use them for relish if they're the right variety. Detailed information on storing and preserving is given in Part 4.

Serving suggestions

In the Gay '90s the hallmark of an elegant tea party was cucumber sandwiches, open-faced on thin-sliced bread. In England the sandwiches are closed and cut into small squares or triangles. Slice cucumbers thinly and dress them with plain yogurt and a little dill. Don't peel them — cucumbers are mostly water anyway, and most of the vitamins they do contain are in the skin. Instead of eating them, you can make them into a refreshing face cleanser — cucumbers are an ingredient in many cosmetic products.

Q and A

Q: Why do so many early cucumber flowers fall off without setting fruit, then begin to set a week or two later?
A: Cucumbers have separate male and female flowers. The early flowers you see are probably male flowers, which usually show first but never set fruit.

Q: A few of the cucumber seeds in the package were pink. Why?
A: Some hybrid cucumbers have only female flowers, but need some male flowers in order to produce. The pink seeds were probably those that produce the male flowers. These hybrids are usually more productive and set earlier than other varieties.

Q: Why do some of my cucumber plants suddenly wilt and die just when they start producing?
A: The problem is probably bacterial wilt, which is spread by cucumber beetles. To prevent this disease, control the beetles as soon as they appear.

Q: Why do some cucumber leaves turn a gray-white color late in the season?
A: This is powdery mildew, a fungus disease which can be controlled by selecting resistant varieties. Correct spacing will also help reduce the problem.

Q: Is it true that watermelons, cantaloupes, or squash will cross-pollinate with cucumbers and make them taste bitter?
A: No; the popular idea that cross-pollination causes a bitter taste is completely false. Cross-pollination will not affect the current crop in any way. However, plants grown from seed saved from the affected plants will show the effects of the cross-pollination.

Dandelion

Common name: dandelion
Botanical name: Taraxacum officinale
Origin: Europe and Asia

Varieties
Thick-leaved; Improved Thick-leaved.

Description

The dandelion is a hardy perennial that's grown as an annual for its foliage and as a biennial for its roots. The jagged green leaves grow in a short rosette attached by a short stem to a long taproot. Bright yellow flowers one to two inches wide grow on smooth, hollow flower stalks. The dandelion is best known — and feared — by gardeners as a remarkably persistent lawn weed, but its leaves are actually high in vitamin A and four times higher in vitamin C than lettuce. It's also versatile: Dandelion leaves are used raw in salads or boiled like spinach, and the roots can be roasted and made into a coffeelike drink.

Where and when to grow

Dandelions grow well in any soil anywhere. They prefer full sun but will do fine in partial shade. They're very hardy and will survive both the hottest summers and the coldest winters. Plant the seeds in early spring, four to six weeks before the average date of last frost.

How to plant

Dandelions grow best in a well-drained fertile soil from which you've removed all the stones and rubble. If you're growing dandelions for their foliage only, they'll tolerate soil in poorer physical condition. When you're preparing the soil, dig in a complete, well-balanced fertilizer at the rate of one pound per 100 square feet or 10 pounds per 1,000 square feet. Plant seeds in the garden a quarter inch deep in rows or wide rows 12 to 18 inches apart. Thin plants six to eight inches apart after the true leaves appear.

Fertilizing and watering

Don't bother to fertilize dandelions at midseason. Detailed information on fertilizing is

Dandelion

given in "Spadework: The Essential Soil" in Part 1.

Keep the plants supplied with water; the dandelion's foliage may become even more bitter than it is naturally if it's subjected to long periods of drought.

Pests

Pests don't bother dandelions. If you let the dandelions produce their delicate clocklike seed heads, however, they may well become pests themselves by seeding all over your and your neighbors' lawns.

Diseases

Dandelions have no serious disease problems.

When and how to harvest

Harvest dandelion greens at your pleasure throughout the growing season. Harvest the roots in the fall of the second year; pull the whole root from the ground — or lift the roots with a fork to avoid breaking them.

Container growing

Dandelions, as any gardener with a lawn knows only too well, flourish in the most inhospitable conditions—so you'll have no trouble growing dandelions in a container. Broadcast the seeds over the surface and cover with a quarter inch of soil—you then have a ready-made wide row bed.

Storing and preserving

You can refrigerate the greens up to one week, or store the roots for 10 to 12 months in a cold, moist place, as you do with chicory. Detailed information on storing and preserving is given in Part 4.

Serving suggestions

Dandelion wine is a brew much beloved of do-it-yourself vintners. Or make dandelion tea, and drink it well-chilled. Remove the stalks from the dandelions and toss the leaves in a vinaigrette dressing. Or try a hot dressing, as for a wilted spinach salad. Cook the leaves quickly and serve them with lemon and oregano, Greek-style. To use the roots, wash and dice them, then dry and roast them before grinding.

Dry bean,
See **Bean, dry**

Eggplant

Common names: eggplant, aubergine, guinea squash
Botanical name: Solanum melongena
Origin: East Indies, India

Varieties
Dusky (61 days); Black Bell (70 days); Black Magic Hybrid (73 days); Jersey King Hybrid (75 days); Black Nite (78 days); Black Beauty (80 days). **Long slender fruits:** Tyeoon (54 days); Imperial (63 days); Ichiban (70 days); Slim Jim (75 days).

Description

Eggplant is a very tender perennial plant with large, hairy, grayish-green leaves. The star-shaped flowers are lavender with yellow centers, and the long, slender or round, egg-shaped fruit is creamy-white, yellow, brown, purple, or sometimes almost black. Eggplants will grow two to six feet tall, depending on the variety. They belong to the solanaceous family, are related to tomatoes, potatoes, and peppers, and were first cultivated in India.

Where and when to grow

Eggplant is very sensitive to cold and needs a growing season with day temperatures between 80° and 90°F and night temperatures between 70° and 80°F. Don't plant eggplant seedlings until two to three weeks after your average date of last frost, or when daytime temperatures reach 70°F.

How to plant

You can grow eggplant from seed, but you'll wait 150 days for a harvest. It's easier to grow from transplants, started inside about two months before your outside planting date. Don't put your transplants into the garden until two or three weeks after the average date of last frost for your area — eggplants won't be rushed, and if you plant them too early they won't develop. Eggplants must have full sun. They'll grow in almost any soil, but they do better in rich soil that is high in organic matter, with excellent drainage. When you're preparing the soil, dig in a complete, well-balanced fertilizer at the rate of one pound per 100 square feet or 10 pounds per 1,000 square feet. Set the plants 18 to 24 inches apart in rows 24 to 36 inches apart.

Fertilizing and watering

Fertilize before planting and again at midseason, at the same rate as the rest of the garden. Detailed information on fertilizing is given in "Spadework: The Essential Soil" in Part 1.

Eggplants are very fussy about temperature and moisture and must be treated with solicitude until they're well established. Try to maintain even soil moisture to ensure even growth; eggplants are susceptible to root rot if there's too much moisture in the soil.

Special handling

If you live in an area where an unpredictable late frost may occur, provide protection at night until all danger of frost is past. In hot climates the soil temperature may become too warm for the roots; in this case, mulch the plants about a month after you set them outside. Plants that are heavy with fruit may need to be staked.

Pests

Eggplants are almost always attacked by one pest or another, so they're not the ideal crop for the organic gardener. The pests you're most likely to encounter are cutworms, aphids, flea beetles, Colorado potato bugs, spider mites, and tomato hornworms. Hand-pick hornworms off the plants; control aphids and beetles by hand-picking or hosing them off the plants and pinching out infested areas. Collars set around the plants at the time you transplant them will discourage cutworms. Spider mites are difficult to control even with the proper chemicals; spray the

Eggplant

Eggplant seedling

undersides of the foliage with Diazinon before the populations get too large. Detailed information on pest control is given in "Keeping Your Garden Healthy" in Part 1.

Diseases

Fungus and bacterial diseases may attack eggplants. Planting disease-resistant varieties when possible and maintaining the general cleanliness and health of your garden will help lessen the incidence of disease. If a plant does become infected, remove it before it can spread disease to healthy plants. Protect the plants against soilborne diseases by rotating your crops and planting vegetables from a different plant family in the eggplants' spot the following season. Detailed information on disease prevention is given in "Keeping Your Garden Healthy" in Part 1.

When and how to harvest

Time from planting to harvest is 100 to 150 days from seed, 70 to 85 days from transplants. Harvest the fruit young, before the flesh becomes pithy. The fruit should be firm and shiny, not streaked with brown. The eggplant fruit is on a sturdy stem that does not break easily from the plant; cut it off with a sharp knife instead of expecting it to fall into your hand.

Container growing

Being able to protect the plant from cold (a single frost will kill eggplant) makes eggplant an ideal container vegetable. In cold areas, you can extend the season considerably by planting eggplant in a container and moving it

around for warmth. An eight-inch pot will house a single plant; in larger containers allow a 12-inch diameter area for each plant.

Storing and preserving

Whole eggplant will store up to one week at 50°F; don't refrigerate it. You can also freeze or dry it. Detailed information on storing and preserving is given in Part 4.

Serving suggestions

Eggplant is very versatile and combines happily with all kinds of other foods — cheese, tomatoes, onions, and meats all lend distinction to its flavor. The French use it in a vegetable stew called *ratatouille*, with tomatoes, onions, peppers, garlic, and herbs. Ratatouille is a good hot side dish or can be served cold as a salad. Eggplant is also a key ingredient of the Greek moussaka, layered with ground meat and topped with a béchamel sauce. Or coat slices in egg and breadcrumbs and deep-fry them. To remove excess moisture from eggplant slices before you cook them, salt them liberally, let them stand about half an hour, wash them, and pat them dry. Or weight the slices with a heavy plate to squeeze out the moisture.

Q and A

Q: Why do the leaves of my eggplants suddenly get riddled with small holes every summer?
A: These holes are made by flea beetles, which can be controlled with Sevin.
Q: Is there such a thing as a white-fruited eggplant?
A: Yes, but the fruits are small and usually taste bitter.

Q: Last year my eggplant leaves suddenly wilted, turned brown, and died. Why did this happen?
A: Verticillium wilt is a common disease that causes those symptoms, and only a few varieties of eggplants are resistant to it. Try planting Blackjack or Superhybrid, which are somewhat resistant.

Endive

Common names: endive, escarole
Botanical name: Cichorium endivia
Origin: South Asia

Varieties

Full Heart Batavian (90 days) has smooth leaves. Salad King (98 days) has curled leaves.

Description

Endive is a half-hardy biennial grown as an annual, and it has a large rosette of toothed curled or wavy leaves that are used in salads as a substitute for lettuce. Endive is often known as escarole, and they're varieties of the same plant; escarole has broader leaves. Endive should not be confused with Belgian endive, which is the young blanched sprout of the chicory plant. Both endive and chicory, however, belong to the genus Cichorium.

Where and when to grow

Like lettuce, endive is a cool-season crop, although it's more tolerant of heat than lettuce. Grow it fom seed planted in your garden four to six weeks before your average date of last frost. Long, hot summer days will force the plants to bolt and go to seed. If your area has a short, hot growing season, start endive from seed indoors and transplant it as soon as possible so that the plants will mature before the weather gets really hot. Sow succession crops, beginning in midsummer. In a mild-winter climate, you can grow spring, fall, and winter crops.

How to plant

Endive needs well-worked soil with good drainage and moisture retention. When you're preparing the soil, dig in a complete, well-balanced fertilizer at the rate of one pound per 100 square feet or 10 pounds per 1,000 square feet. If you're using transplants, start them from seed eight to 10 weeks before the average date of last frost in your area. If you're direct-seeding endive in the garden, sow seeds a quarter inch deep in wide rows 18 to 24 inches apart, and when the seedlings are large enough to handle, thin them to nine to 12 inches apart. Thinning is important because the plants may bolt if they're crowded. Plant transplants nine to 12 inches apart in rows 18 to 24 inches apart.

Fertilizing and watering

Fertilize before planting and again at midseason, at the same rate as the rest of the garden. Detailed information on fertilizing is given in "Spadework: The Essential Soil" in Part 1.

Water regularly to keep the plants growing quickly; lack of

Endive

water will slow growth and cause the leaves to become bitter.

Special handling

Endive tastes better in salads if you blanch it to remove some of the bitter flavor. Blanching deprives the plants of sunlight and

Endive seedling

discourages the production of chlorophyll. Blanch two to three weeks before you're ready to harvest the plants. You can do this in several ways: Tie string around the leaves to hold them together; lay a board on

supports over the row; or put a flowerpot over each plant. If you tie the endive plants, do it when they're dry; the inner leaves may rot if the plants are tied up while the insides are wet.

Pests

Cutworms, slugs, and snails can be troublesome. You may also have to deal with aphids. Put a collar around each plant to discourage cutworms, and trap slugs and snails with a saucer of stale beer set flush to the soil. To control aphids, pinch out infested foilage, or hose the aphids off the plants. You can also spray them with Malathion or Diazinon, taking care to spray the undersides of the leaves. Detailed information on pest control is given in "Keeping Your Garden Healthy" in Part 1.

Diseases

Endive has no serious disease problems.

When and how to harvest

Time from planting to harvest is 90 to 100 days from seed. To harvest, cut off the plant at soil level.

Storing and preserving

Like lettuce, endive can be stored for up to two weeks in the refrigerator, but you can't freeze, can, or dry it. Share your harvest with friends. Detailed information on short-term storage is given in Part 4.

Container growing

Like other leafy vegetables, endive takes kindly to container growth. Grow one in a six-inch pot, or several on ten-inch centers in a larger container.

Serving suggestions

Chill endive and serve it with an oil-and-vinegar dressing; add chunks of blue cheese or croutons. Mix it with other salad greens to add a distinctive flavor. The French use endive in a salad with heated slices of mild sausage, diced bacon, and croutons.

Escarole,
See **Endive**

Fennel

Common names: fennel, Florence fennel, finocchio, fenucchi
Botanical name: Foeniculum vulgare dulce
Origin: Mediterranean

Varieties
Grow the variety available in your area.

Description

Florence fennel or finocchio is the same as the common or sweet fennel that is grown for use as a herb. The leaves and seeds of both are used the same way for seasoning, but Florence fennel is grown primarily for its bulbous base and leaf stalks, which are used as vegetables. Florence fennel is a member of the parsley family. It's a stocky perennial grown as an annual, and looks rather like celery with very feathery leaves. The plant grows four to five feet tall and has small, golden flowers, which appear in flat-topped clusters from July to September. The whole plant has an anise flavor.

Where and when to grow

Fennel will grow anywhere in the United States. It tolerates both heat and cold, but should mature in cold weather. Grow it from seed sown two to three weeks before your average date of last frost.

How to plant

Fennel needs well-drained soil that's high in organic matter. When you're preparing the soil for planting, work in a complete, well-balanced fertilizer at the rate of one pound per 100 square feet or 10 pounds per 1,000 square feet.

Plant the seeds a quarter of an inch deep, in rows two to three feet apart, in full sun. When the seedlings are growing strongly, thin them to 12 inches apart.

Fertilizing and watering

Fertilize before planting and again at midseason, at the same rate as the rest of the garden. Detailed information on fertilizing is given in "Spadework: The Essential Soil" in Part 1.

Keep fennel on the dry side.

Special handling

Fennel plants grow four to five feet tall; you may need to stake them if they are becoming unwieldy.

Pests

Since fennel is a member of the parsley family, the parsley caterpillar may appear. Remove it by hand. It has no other serious pest problems, so fennel is a good bet for the organic gardener.

Diseases

Fennel has no serious disease problems.

When and how to harvest

You can start harvesting a few sprigs as soon as the plant is well-established and growing steadily; use them for flavoring. Harvest the bulbous stalk when it is three inches or more in diameter; cut the whole stalk like celery, just below the point where the individual stalks join together.

Container growing

Fennel grows as well in a container as in a traditional garden bed, but spring plantings will not produce a large bulb. Plant in fall, placing a single plant in a six-inch pot or several on eight-inch centers in a larger container.

Storing and preserving

Fennel leaves can be frozen or dried as herbs; crumble the dried leaves and store them in an airtight container. You'll probably want to eat the stalks fresh; store them in the refrigerator up to one week or in a cold, moist place for two to three months. The stalks can also be frozen or dried; handle them like celery.

Serving suggestions

Fennel is featured in many Italian dishes. The leaves add flavor to soups and casseroles, and fennel goes well with fish. You can prepare Florence fennel in many ways as you do celery. Cut the fennel stalks into slices, simmer them in water or stock until tender, and serve buttered. Bake slices of fennel with cheese and butter as an accompaniment to a roast, or eat the stalks raw as a dipping vegetable. French and Italian cooks have been using fennel for generations — hence the variety of names by which it's known. The French served grilled sea bass on a bed of flaming fennel stalks, and the dried stalks can be used for barbecuing, too.

Fennel

Garbanzo,
See Chick pea

Garden pea,
See Pea

Gourd,
See Squash, winter

Green bean,
See Bean, green or snap

Greens,
See Beet, Chard, Collard, Kale, Turnip

Honeydew melon,
See Muskmelon

Horseradish

Common name: horseradish
Botanical name: Armoracia rusticana
Origin: Eastern Europe

Varieties
New Bohemian.

Horseradish

Description

Horseradish looks like a giant, two-foot radish. In fact, it's a hardy perennial member of the cabbage family. Ninety-eight percent of all commercial horseradish is grown in three Illinois counties near St. Louis. Horseradish has a very strong flavor and — like the animal for which it's named — can deliver a powerful kick when you're not expecting it.

Where and when to grow

Horseradish is a very cold-hardy plant, which does well in the North and in cool, high-altitude areas in the South. Grow it from crowns or roots planted four to six weeks before the average date of last frost for your area.

How to plant

Horseradish tolerates partial shade and needs rich, well-drained soil. Turn over the soil to a depth of 10 to 12 inches, and remove stones and lumps that might cause the roots to split. When you're preparing the soil, dig in a complete, well-balanced fertilizer at the rate of one pound per 100 square feet or 10 pounds per 1,000 square feet. Plant the roots in a trench, and place them 24 inches apart with the narrow end down. Fill in the trench until the thicker end is just covered.

Fertilizing and watering

Fertilize before planting and again at midseason, at the same rate as the rest of the garden. Detailed information on fertilizing is given in "Spadework: The Essential Soil" in Part 1.

Keep the soil evenly moist so that the roots will be tender and full of flavor; horseradish gets woody in dry soils.

Pests

Horseradish has no serious pest problems.

Diseases

Horseradish has no serious disease problems.

When and how to harvest

Plants grown from roots cannot be harvested until the second year. A 10-foot row should give you six to eight roots. Horseradish makes its best growth in late summer and fall, so delay harvesting until October or later. Dig the roots as needed, or in areas where the ground freezes hard, dig them in the fall. Leave a little of the root in the ground so that you'll have horseradish the following year, too.

Container growing

Horseradish needs plenty of downward space to accommodate its long, woody root, so it's not a suitable candidate for container growing.

Storing and preserving

Store in a glass jar in the refrigerator one to two weeks. To freeze, grate the roots and mix with vinegar and water, as specified in "How to Freeze Vegetables." You can also dry horseradish or store the roots in a cold, moist place for 10 to 12 months. Detailed information on storing and preserving is given in Part 4.

Plant horseradish roots narrow end down.

Serving suggestions

Horseradish is a classic accompaniment to beef roasts and steaks. Serve it solo, freshly grated, to brave souls who appreciate its full flavor. For the less stern of stomach, calm the flavor with whipped or sour cream. Serve it as one of the dipping sauces with a beef fondue. Since the fumes are very strong, grate horseradish outdoors if you can. If you must do it indoors, use a blender.

Q and A

Q: My horseradish roots are never very large in diameter. What can I do to get larger roots?

A: Pruning off the side roots will force the horseradish to develop a large taproot. Slice a spade straight down around the plant about three to four inches from the base. Do this in midsummer and late fall the first year, and in midsummer the second year.

Q: What causes small white cottony blotches on the upper surfaces of the leaves and corresponding yellow discoloration on the undersides?

A: This is caused by white rust, a fungus disease which seldom causes enough damage to horseradish to require any control.

Hot pepper,
See Pepper

Jerusalem artichoke

Common names: Jerusalem artichoke, sunchoke
Botanical name: Helianthus tuberosus
Origin: North America

Varieties

Few varieties are available; grow the varieties available in your area. You may find Jerusalem artichokes growing wild by the side of the road. Commercial Jerusalem artichokes are sometimes sold in supermarkets; use these to start your own crop.

Description

Jerusalem artichokes are large, upright, hardy perennials, with small yellow flowers two to three inches across and rough, hairy leaves four to eight inches long. This plant, which grows five to 10 feet tall, was grown by the North American Indians for its tubers, which look like small potatoes. The tubers are low in starch and taste a bit like water chestnuts.

The Jerusalem artichoke isn't an artichoke, and it didn't come from Jerusalem. It's related to the sunflower, and the name is probably derived from the Italian name for a sunflower, *girasole*, which means turning to the sun.

Where and when to grow

Jerusalem artichokes will grow anywhere, and in almost any soil as long as it's warm and well-drained. Plant the tubers two to three weeks before the average date of last frost for your area.

How to plant

Give Jerusalem artichokes the least productive soil in your garden (provided the location is sunny); they'll probably love it, and they'll take over areas where nothing else will grow. Plant them as a screen or windbreak. Be sure you know where you want them before you plant, however, because once Jerusalem artichokes become established little short of a tornado will shift them. It's not necessary to fertilize the soil before planting. Plant the tubers two to six inches deep, 12 to 18 inches apart. You won't need to cultivate because

Jerusalem artichoke

weeds are no competition for a healthy Jerusalem artichoke.

Fertilizing and watering

Don't fertilize Jerusalem artichokes at midseason — they'll do fine on their own.

Water only during extremely dry periods. The plants themselves can survive long dry spells, but the tubers will not develop without a regular supply of water.

Pests

Aphids occasionally visit the Jerusalem artichoke, but they don't present any significant problem. If they do appear, pinch out infested foliage or hose the aphids off the plants. Chemically aphids can be controlled with Malathion or Diazinon. Detailed information on pest control is given in "Keeping Your Garden Healthy" in Part 1.

Diseases

Tuber rot may occur if the soil is not properly drained. Maintaining the general health and

Jerusalem artichoke seedling

cleanliness of your garden lessens the incidence of disease. If a plant does become infected, remove it before it can spread disease to healthy plants. Detailed information on disease prevention is given in "Keeping Your Garden Healthy" in Part 1.

When and how to harvest

Time from planting to harvest is 120 to 150 days, and a 10-foot row should yield about 20 pounds of tubers. As the plant grows, cut off the flower stalks as soon as they appear; this will encourage tuber production. If the plant is using its energy to produce seeds, it won't produce tubers. (The flowers, in fact, are cheerful. If you're growing Jerusalem artichokes for decorative as well as practical purposes, you may be willing to sacrifice a few tubers so you can enjoy the flowers). Harvest the tubers when the leaves die back; dig them up with a spading fork, leaving a few in the ground for next year.

Container growing

This is a big, space-hungry plant and does not take kindly to container growing—unless, perhaps, you have a loft, a spare bathtub, and a sense of the dramatic.

Storing and preserving

Store Jerusalem artichokes in the refrigerator for seven to 10 days, or store in a cold, moist place for two to five months. You can also freeze Jerusalem artichokes or leave them in the ground as long as possible, and dig them up as you need them. Detailed information on storing and preserving is given in Part 4.

Serving suggestions

The slightly nutty flavor of the Jerusalem artichoke goes well with mushrooms. Serve them cooked until tender then cooled and sliced, in a salad with mushrooms and a vinaigrette dressing. They can also be used raw, peeled, and thinly sliced, in a mushroom salad. Cooked, you can puree

them, sauté slices with tomatoes, or simply toss them with butter and seasonings as a side dish with meat or poultry. They can also be used as an extender in meat loaf.

Kale

Common names: kale, borecole, collards, green cabbage, German greens
Botanical name: Brassica oleracea acephala
Origin: horticultural hybrid

Varieties
Dwarf Blue Curled (55 days); Dwarf Blue Scotch (55 days); Vates (55 days); Dwarf Green Curled (60 days).

Description

Kale is a hardy biennial plant grown as an annual. It's a member of the cabbage family and looks like cabbage with a permanent wave. Scotch kale has gray-green leaves that are extremely crumpled and curly; Siberian or blue kale usually is less curly and is a bluer shade of green. There are also decorative forms with lavender and silver variegated leaves.

Where and when to grow

Kale is a cool-weather crop that grows best in the fall and will last through the winter as far north as Maryland and central Indiana. Frost even improves the flavor, and kale is better adapted for fall planting throughout a wide area

of the United States than any other vegetable. Kale doesn't tolerate heat as well as the collard—which it resembles in being one of the oldest members of the cabbage or cole family. All cole crops are frost-hardy and can tolerate low 20°F temperatures. Kale does best in a cool growing season with day temperatures under 80°F. Time plantings so that you can harvest kale during cool weather. If your area has cold winters, plant for summer to early fall harvest. In mild climates, plant for late spring or early fall harvest. In the South, plant for harvest in late fall or winter. Plant kale from transplants early in the spring and again in the midsummer if your summers aren't too hot. Direct-seed in the fall.

Flowering varieties of kale can be planted in containers or as accent points in a flower bed. The leaves are attractive, and their color is at its best in cool fall weather.

How to plant

Kale likes fertile, well-drained soil with pH within the 6.5 to 7.5 range; this discourages disease and lets the plant make the most of the nutrients in the soil. Kale is usually grown from transplants except where there is a long cool period, in which case seed can be sown directly in the garden in fall for winter harvest.

When you're preparing the soil for planting, work in a complete, well-balanced fertilizer at the rate of one pound per 100 square feet or 10 pounds per 1,000 square feet. If you have sandy soil or your area is subject to heavy rains, you'll probably need to supplement the nitrogen content of the soil. Use

Kale

Kale seedling

about a pound of nitrogen fertilizer for a 10-foot row.

Plant transplants that are four to six weeks old, with four or five true leaves. If the transplants are leggy or have crooked stems, plant them deeply (up to the first leaves) so they won't grow to be top-heavy. Plant the seedlings eight to 12 inches apart, in rows 18 to 24 inches apart. If you're planting seeds, set them half an inch deep and space them three inches apart. Thin them when they're big enough to lift by the true leaves, and either transplant the thinned seedlings or eat them right away.

Fertilizing and watering

Fertilize before planting and again at midseason, at the same rate as the rest of the garden. Detailed information on fertilizing is given in "Spadework: The Essential Soil" in Part 1.

Abundant soil moisture and cool moist air are needed for the best growth. Regular watering keeps kale growing strongly and prevents it from getting tough.

Pests

The cabbage family's traditional enemies are cutworms and caterpillars. Cutworms, cabbage loopers, and imported cabbage worms can all be controlled by spraying with bacillus thuringiensis, an organic product also known as Dipel or Thungicide. Kale does not suffer too much from pests, so it's a good choice for the organic gardener. Detailed information on pest control is given in "Keeping Your Garden Healthy" in Part 1.

Diseases

Kale has no serious disease problems.

When and how to harvest

Time from planting to harvest is 55 days from transplants, 70 to 80 days from seed. A 10-foot row will produce about 10 plants. Leave kale in the garden until needed. As the plants mature, take outside leaves, leaving the inner ones to grow, or cut off the entire plant. But harvest kale before it gets old and tough.

Container growing

Kale grows and produces well in a container. It is a cool-weather vegetable and benefits from being moved out of the heat into cooler temperatures. You can extend the growing season noticeably at both ends by planting early in spring—before regular garden soil has warmed up—and moving the plants out of the sun as the weather gets warmer. Plant a single kale in a six-inch pot, or allow eight inches all around plants in a larger container.

Storing and preserving

If possible, leave kale in the garden until you want to eat it. It will store in the refrigerator in a plastic bag for up to one week, or in a cold, moist place for up to three weeks. You can also freeze, can, or dry it; use the recipes for greens. Detailed information on storing and preserving is given in Part 4.

Serving suggestions

Young kale makes a distinctive salad green; dress it simply with oil and vinegar. You can also cook it in a little water and serve it with butter, lemon juice, and chopped bacon. Instead of boiling, try preparing it like spinach steamed with butter and only the water that clings to the leaves after washing. The Italians steam kale until tender, then add olive oil, a little garlic, and breadcrumbs, and sprinkle it with Parmesan cheese in the last minute or two of cooking. You can also prepare kale Chinese-style, stir-fried with a few slices of fresh gingerroot.

Q and A

Q: Will the white and yellow butterflies flying around my kale plants do any damage?
A: These butterflies are actually moths, and they are adult cabbage loopers or imported cabbage worms. They are laying eggs and when the eggs hatch the pests can do a lot of damage.
Q: Will kale taste sweeter if it is harvested after a frost?
A: Yes; cold temperatures will change some of the carbo-hydrates to sugar and will improve the flavor of the kale greens.
Q: What is flowering kale, and can you eat it?
A: Flowering kale is a small leafy plant that looks like a loose-headed cabbage. It has green outer leaves and pink or white inner leaves. Yes, you can eat it.

Kohlrabi

Common names: kohlrabi, turnip-rooted cabbage, stem turnip, turnip cabbage
Botanical name: Brassica caulorapa
Origin: horticultural hybrid

Varieties

Grand Duke (50 days); Purple Danube (52 days); Early White Vienna (55 days); Early Purple Vienna (60 days).

Description

Kohlrabi is a hardy biennial grown as an annual and is a member of the cabbage clan. It has a swollen stem that makes it look like a turnip growing on a cabbage root. This swollen stem can be white, purple, or green, and is topped with a rosette of blue-green leaves. In German, *kohl* means cabbage and *rabi* means turnip—a clue to the taste and texture of kohlrabi, although it is mild and sweeter than either of them. Kohlrabi is a fairly recent addition to the vegetables grown in northern Europe. In this country, nobody paid it any attention until 1800.

Where and when to grow

All cole crops are hardy and can tolerate low 20°F temperatures. Kohlrabi tolerates heat better than other members of the cabbage family, but planting should be timed for harvesting during cool weather. Kohlrabi has a shorter growing season than cabbage. It grows best in cool weather and produces better with a 10° to 15°F difference between day and night temperatures. If your area has cold winters, plant for summer to early fall harvest. In the South, plant for harvest in late fall or winter. With spring plantings, start kohlrabi early so that most growth will occur before the weather gets too hot.

How to plant

Kohlrabi likes fertile, well-drained soil with a pH within the 6.5 to 7.5 range; this discourages disease and lets the plant make the most of the nutrients in the soil. The soil should be high in organic matter. When you're preparing the soil for planting, work in a complete, well-balanced fertilizer at the rate of one pound per 100 square feet or 10 pounds per 1,000 square feet. Cole crops are generally grown from transplants except where there's a long cool period. Kohlrabi, however, can be grown directly from seed in the garden. Sow seeds in rows 18 to 24 inches apart and cover them with a quarter to a half inch of soil. When the seedlings are growing well, thin them to five or six inches apart—you can transplant the thinnings. Cultivate carefully to avoid harming the shallow roots.

Fertilizing and watering

Fertilize before planting and again at midseason, at the same rate as the rest of the garden. Detailed information on fertilizing is given in "Spadework: The Essential Soil" in Part 1. Kohlrabi should have even moisture or it will become woody.

Pests

The cabbage family's traditional enemies are cutworms and caterpillars. Cutworms, cabbage loopers, and imported cabbage worms can all be controlled by spraying with bacillus thuringiensis, an organic product also known as Dipel or Thungicide. Detailed information on pest control is given in "Keeping Your Garden Healthy" in Part 1.

Kohlrabi

Kohlrabi seedling

Diseases

Cabbage family crops are susceptible to yellows, clubroot, and downy mildew. Lessen the incidence of disease by planting disease-resistant varieties when they're available; maintaining the general health of your garden; and avoiding handling the plants when they're wet. If a plant does become infected, remove and destroy it so it cannot spread disease to healthy plants. Detailed information on disease prevention is given in "Keeping Your Garden Healthy" in Part 1.

Container growing

Kohlrabi does not grow well in a container.

Storing and preserving

Kohlrabi will store for one week in a refrigerator or for one to two months in a cold, moist place. Kohlrabi can also be frozen. Detailed information on storing and preserving is given in Part 4.

Serving suggestions

Small, tender kohlrabi are delicious steamed, without peeling. As they mature you can peel off the outer skin, dice them, and boil them in a little water. Kohlrabi can also be stuffed, like squash.

Try young kohlrabi raw, chilled, and sliced; the flavor is mild and sweet, and the vegetable has a nice, crisp texture. You can also cook kohlrabi, then cut it into strips and marinate the strips in an oil and vinegar dressing; chill this salad to serve with cold cuts. Cooked kohlrabi can be served just with seasoning and a little melted butter or

mashed with butter and cream. For
a slightly different flavor, cook it
in bouillon instead of water.

Leek

Common name: leek
Botanical name: Allium porrum
Origin: Mediterranean, Egypt

Varieties
Titan (120 days); American Flag
(120 days); Leader (120 days);
Catalina (120 days); Broad London
(130 days); Tivi (115 days).

Description

The leek is a hardy biennial
grown as an annual. It's a member
of the onion family, but has a
stalk rather than a bulb and leaves
that are flat and straplike
instead of hollow. The Welsh
traditionally wear a leek on St.
David's day (March 1) to
commemorate King
Cadwallader's victory over the
Saxons in A.D. 640, when the
Welsh pulled up leeks and wore
them as ID's. The more
decorous now wear a daffodil
instead.

Where and when to grow

Leeks are a cool-weather crop.
They'll tolerate warm
temperatures, but you'll get
better results if the days are cool;
temperatures under 75°F
produce the best yields. Plant
leeks from seed in the spring
four to six weeks before the
average date of last frost and

Leek

Leek seedling

from transplants in fall for a late harvest. Plant transplants in spring if you want to speed up the crop to avoid a hot summer.

How to plant

Leeks like a place in full sun and thrive in rich, well-worked soil with good drainage. When you're preparing the soil, dig in a complete, well-balanced fertilizer at the rate of one pound per 100 square feet or 10 pounds per 1,000 square feet. Plant the seeds an eighth inch deep in rows 12 to 18 inches apart, and thin them six to nine inches apart. To plant transplants, make holes six inches deep, about six to nine inches apart, in well-worked soil. Double rows save space; to make them, stagger the plants with their leaves growing parallel to the rows so they will not grow into the pathway. Drop the leeks in the holes, but do not fill in with soil. Over a period of time, watering will slowly collapse the soil around the leeks and settle them in.

Special handling

In order to grow a large, white, succulent leek, blanch the lower part of the stem by hilling the soil up around the stalk as it develops.

Fertilizing and watering

Fertilize before planting and again at midseason, at the same rate as the rest of the garden. Detailed information on fertilizing is given in "Spadework: The Essential Soil" in Part 1.
   Give leeks plenty of water to keep them growing strongly.

Pests

Onion thrips may show up on leeks in dry weather. Discourage them by hosing them off the plants, or spray them with Malathion or Diazinon. Leeks will do well in the organic garden despite the thrips. More detailed information on pest control is given in "Keeping Your Garden Healthy" in Part 1.

Diseases

Leeks have no serious disease problems.

When and how to harvest

Time from planting to harvest is about 80 days from transplants and 120 days or more from seed. A 10-foot double row should give you about 20 leeks. Around midsummer, start removing the top half of the leaves. This will encourage greater growth of the leek stalk. Pull the leeks as you need them, but harvest them all before frost.

Container growing

Leeks do not grow satisfactorily in containers.

Storing and preserving

Store leeks in the refrigerator for up to one week or in a cold, moist place for two to three months. You can also freeze them. Detailed information on storing and preserving is given in Part 4.

Serving suggestions

Leeks don't develop bulbs as onions do, but they belong to the same family, and leeks have a delicate onion flavor. Grit and sand get trapped in the wrap-around leaves, so slice the leeks or cut them lengthwise, and wash them thoroughly under running water before you cook them. Serve leeks steamed or braised, chilled in a salad, or in a hot leek and potato soup—keep the soup chunky or puree it for a creamy texture. The French call leeks the "asparagus of the poor."

Lentil

Common name: lentil
Botanical name: Lens culinaris
Origin: Mediterranean region

Varieties

There are three varieties of lentil seeds: flat brown ones, small yellow ones, and larger pea-shaped ones. Choose the variety that's available or that tastes best to you.

Description

Lentils are a hardy annual member of the pea family. They grow on small weak vines 18 to 24 inches tall, and the small whitish to light purple pealike flowers are followed by flat, two-seeded pods.

Where and when to grow

Lentils need a cool growing season of 70 to 80 days and can be grown in most areas of the United States. Plant them early in spring, two to three weeks before the average date of last frost.

How to plant

Lentils grow best in a sunny area with a fertile well-drained soil. When you're preparing the soil, dig in a complete, well-balanced fertilizer at the rate of one pound per 100 square feet or 10 pounds per 1,000 square feet. Plant seeds an inch apart and a half inch deep in rows 18 to 24 inches apart. Thin to stand one to two inches apart.

Fertilizing and watering

Lentils will probably be harvested before your midseason fertilizing of the vegetable garden. Detailed information on fertilizing is given in "Spadework: The Essential Soil" in Part 1.
   Keep the lentils fairly moist.

Special handling

Give your lentil plants a low trellis for support.

Pests

Aphids may show interest in your lentils. Control them by pinching out infested areas of the plants or, if there are a lot of them, hose them off the lentil vines. You can also spray them with Malathion or Diazinon. Detailed information on pest control is given in "Keeping Your Garden Healthy" in Part 1.

Diseases

Lentils have no serious disease problems.

When and how to harvest

The growing season for lentils is 70 to 80 days. Harvest them when the pods are plump and full.

Lentil

Container growing

Lentils can be grown in containers, but they need so much space to produce a usable yield that they're not really a practical proposition for the container gardener.

Storing and preserving

Store fresh lentils in the refrigerator, unshelled, for up to one week. Or dry the shelled lentils and store them in a cool, dry place for 10 to 12 months. Lentils can also be sprouted. Detailed information on storing and preserving is given in Part 4.

Serving suggestions

Cooked lentils with a little onion and seasonings, chilled, make a good salad. You can also serve them in a hearty soup; one good soup seasons lentils and tomatoes with thyme and marjoram for a delicate and unusual flavor combination. Try lentils curried with apples and raisins.

Lettuce

Common names: lettuce, crisphead lettuce, butterhead lettuce, stem lettuce (celtuce), leaf lettuce, cos, romaine
Botanical name: Lactuca sativa
Origin: Near East

Leaf lettuce

Varieties

The following are only a few of the varieties available. Ask your Cooperative Extension Service for specific recommendations for your area. Lettuce varieties are basically of two types—one forms a tight head, and the other has a head of loose, more open leaves. A less usual type is stem lettuce, which has thicker stems and far less prominent leaves. **Head lettuce** (iceberg or crisphead): Great Lakes (90 days). **Butterhead lettuce:** Summer Bibb (62 days); Buttercrunch (75 days). **Leaf lettuce:** Black-Seeded Simpson (45 days); Ruby (45 days); Red Sails (45 days). **Cos lettuce** (romaine): Parris Island Cos (73 days). **Stem lettuce:** Celtuce (80 days).

Description

Lettuce is a hardy, fast-growing annual with either loose or compactly growing leaves that range in color from light green through reddish-brown. When it bolts, or goes to seed, the flower stalks are two to three feet tall, with small, yellowish flowers on the stalk. The lettuce most commonly found in supermarkets (iceberg or head lettuce) is the most difficult to grow in the home vegetable garden. Butterhead and bibb lettuces, which are often so extravagantly expensive in the store, are easier to grow. Butterhead lettuces have loose heads and delicate crunchy leaves. Stem lettuce (celtuce) might fool you into thinking you're eating hearts of palm and makes a crunchy addition to a salad. Celtuce is grown in the same way as lettuce, except that you *want* celtuce to bolt or go to seed, because you're going to harvest the thickened stem. You use the leaves of celtuce as you would regular lettuce; the heart of the stem is used like celery. Cos or romaine lettuce forms a loose, long head and is part way between a butterhead and leaf lettuce in flavor. Leaf lettuce is delightfully easy to grow, grows fast, and provides bulk and color to salads.

Leaf lettuce and butterhead lettuce make attractive borders or accents in a flower garden, and either kind can be grown singly in a four-inch pot or in a window box. With a little planning you can grow an entire salad garden in containers on a balcony or terrace.

Historically, King Nebuchadnezzar grew lettuce in his gardens in ancient Babylon. The Romans used lettuce as a sedative.

Where and when to grow

Lettuce is a cool-season crop, usually grown from seed planted in the garden four to six weeks before your average date of last frost. Long, hot summer days will make the plants bolt, or go to seed; when this happens the plant sends up a flower stalk and becomes useless as a vegetable. If your area has a short, hot growing season, start head lettuce from seed indoors eight to 10 weeks before your average date of last frost and transplant it as soon as possible so that the plants will mature before the weather gets really hot. Sow succession crops, beginning in midsummer. In a mild-winter climate, grow spring, fall, and winter crops.

Vegetables

Bibb lettuce

Leaf lettuce

How to plant

Lettuce needs well-worked soil with good drainage and moisture retention. When you're preparing the soil, dig in a complete, well-balanced fertilizer at the rate of one pound per 100 square feet or 10 pounds per 1,000 square feet. Start transplants from seed eight to 10 weeks before your average date of last frost. If you are direct-seeding lettuce in the garden, sow seeds a quarter inch deep in wide rows, and when the seedlings are large enough to handle, thin leaf lettuce to stand six to eight inches apart and head lettuce 12 inches apart. Thinning is important; heading lettuce won't head, and all lettuce may bolt if the plants are crowded. Transplant the thinnings.

Fertilizing and watering

Give the entire garden a midseason application of fertilizer. Your successive crops of lettuce will benefit from it, even though you will already have harvested an early crop. Detailed information on fertilizing is given in "Spadework: The Essential Soil" in Part 1.

Always keep the soil evenly moist but not soggy, and don't let the shallow-rooted lettuce plants dry out. Heading lettuce

Lettuce seedling

needs careful watering when the head is forming. Try not to splash muddy water on the lettuce plants — the cleaner they are, the easier they are to prepare for eating. Use a light mulch of straw or hay to keep soil off the leaves.

Pests

Cutworms, slugs, and snails can be troublesome. You may also have to deal with aphids. Put a collar around each plant to discourage cutworms, and trap slugs and snails with a saucer of stale beer set flush to the soil. To control aphids, pinch out infested foliage, or hose the aphids off the plants. Control aphids chemically with Malathion or Diazinon, taking care to spray the undersides of the leaves. Detailed information on pest control is given in "Keeping Your Garden Healthy" in Part 1.

Diseases

Lettuce has no serious disease problems.

When and how to harvest

As the lettuce grows, either pick the outer leaves and let the inner leaves develop, or harvest the whole plant at once by cutting it off at ground level. Try to harvest when the weather is cool; in the heat of the day the leaves may be limp. Chilling will crisp up the leaves again.

Container growing

Lettuce grows very well in any container, and in northern areas can easily be grown all winter in an indoor container. Head lettuce Is very heat-sensitive, so container-grown plants benefit from being moved to a cooler spot as the weather warms up—hot sun encourages the plants to go to seed. A single head lettuce does well in a six-inch pot; in a larger container allow ten inches all around each plant. Leaf lettuce seeds should be sown liberally over the surface of the container and covered with a quarter inch of soil. In a larger container, plant in wide rows. Leaf lettuce can handle some overcrowding, and the extras can be thinned out for your salad.

Storing and preserving

Don't harvest lettuce until you're ready to use it. It can be stored for up to two weeks in the refrigerator, and everyone has a favorite way of keeping it crisp. Some suggest washing the lettuce first, then wrapping it in a cotton or linen towel and keeping it in the refrigerator. Others suggest storing the whole lettuce in a plastic bag. You can't freeze, dry, or can lettuce, but you can sprout lettuce seeds. If you've got lots, share your bounty with friends. Detailed information

Celtuce

Head lettuce

Head lettuce

on short-term storage is given in Part 4.

Serving suggestions

Yes, salads, of course — but there are other ways to serve lettuce. Braise it in butter with seasoning to taste — the French use nutmeg. Make a wilted salad or cream of lettuce soup, or stir-fry it with mushrooms and onions. Cook peas and shredded lettuce together in a little butter — throw in the lettuce just before you take the peas off the heat. Use several varieties of lettuce together for an interesting combination of shades and textures. Serve a very plain salad — a few leaves of lettuce dressed with oil and a good wine vinegar — to cleanse the palate between courses of a fancy dinner.

Q and A

Q: What causes lettuce plants to flower early?
A: Long, hot sunny days cause lettuce to bolt, that is, go to seed prematurely.
Q: Why does my lettuce taste so bitter?
A: Lettuce will taste bitter if it matures and begins to flower, or if it is grown in very warm temperatures. If you store the lettuce in the refrigerator for a couple of days before use, it will taste much less bitter.
Q: What causes a brown watery rot inside a head of lettuce?
A: The most common cause is sclerotenia rot, and the only control is to plant the lettuce in a different area of your garden each year.
Q: Does red leaf lettuce taste the same as green lettuce?
A: Yes, green and red oak leaf lettuce have exactly the same

somewhat bitter taste. Ruby leaf lettuce tastes just as good as any green lettuce.
Q: Lettuce seeds are so small that it's difficult to space them properly when planting. Is there an easy way?
A: Yes, seed companies are now selling seeds which are coated with a soluble material that washes away in the soil. These enlarged seeds are easier to handle than the tiny uncoated seeds.

Lima bean,
See **Bean, lima**

Melon,
See **Muskmelon; see also Watermelon**

Mung bean,
See **Bean, mung**

Mushroom

Common name: mushroom
Botanical name: Agaricus species
Origin: Mushrooms are found all over the world.

Varieties
Although there are many varieties of edible mushrooms, only a few are available for home production; grow the varieties that are available commercially.

Description

Mushrooms are the fruiting bodies of a fungus organism, and there are between 60,000 and 100,000 species of fungus that produce mushrooms. Because many mushrooms are poisonous, and it's extremely difficult to tell the edible variety from the poisonous kind, gathering wild mushrooms to eat is a very risky pastime. There are, however, many good books on the market that will help you recognize some of the 50 or more edible varieties that grow wild in the United States; so if you do want to go mushroom-hunting, do a little homework first. You can also grow mushrooms at home from prepared trays, kits, and spawn that are available commercially through seed catalog companies and garden suppliers. It's not too difficult, and it can be both productive and fun.

Where and when to grow

Because you're growing them indoors, the type of climate you live in is a matter of indifference to your mushrooms. You can also grow them at any time of the year, but the trays or kits are usually available commercially only from October through April.

How to plant

Mushrooms grow best in a dark, humid, cool area. In most homes the best places are the basement and the cabinet under the kitchen sink. A little light won't hurt the mushrooms, but they do need high humidity — 80 to 85 percent — and a cool temperature — 55° to 60°F.

Mushrooms for growing at home are available in two different forms — in kits or as spawn. You can buy prepared trays and kits already filled with the growing medium and the mushroom spores. All you have to do is remove the tray from the package, add an inch of topsoil, and water. Keep them in a dark, humid, cool place, and you should be harvesting mushrooms within about four weeks.

Many seed companies also sell mushroom spawn; growing from spawn is less expensive, but it does require a little more care. Plant half-inch pieces of the spawn about two inches deep and eight to 10 inches apart in a well-rotted strawy horse or cow manure. Keep the planted spawn in a dark, humid room with the temperature at about 70°F for the first 21 days; then lower the temperature to about 60°F and cover the bed with a one-inch layer of good, sterilized topsoil. If the conditions are right, you should be able to start harvesting in about four weeks.

Fertilizing and watering

You don't need to fertilize mushrooms.

Keep them moist; don't let the mushrooms dry out, but don't allow water to stand on the soil.

Pests

Pests present no serious problems when you're growing mushrooms at home.

Diseases

Mushrooms grown at home have no serious disease problems.

When and how to harvest

Whether you're growing mushrooms from a kit or from spawn, you'll wait about four weeks for results. You can harvest the mushrooms as immature buttons, before the caps open, or when the cap is fully open and the gills exposed — at this stage the mushrooms are ripe and their flavor is at its highest level. Never pull the mushrooms out of the soil; cut them off at soil level with a sharp knife. Check and harvest your mushrooms every day; if you leave mature mushrooms in the planting bed your yield will be lower, but if you pick them regularly the bed will produce continuously for as long as six months.

Container growing

As described above, container growing is the only way to produce mushrooms at home.

Storing and preserving

Mushrooms can be stored in the refrigerator up to one week. You can also freeze, can, or dry them. Detailed information on storing and preserving is given in Part 4.

Serving suggestions

Fresh mushrooms are wonderful raw, sliced thinly and eaten alone or tossed in a green salad. Simmer them in red wine and tomatoes with parsley and herbs for a delicious vegetarian supper dish. Stuff them with herbed breadcrumbs and broil them, or sauté them lightly and toss them in with a dish of plain vegetables — try them with zucchini. Use mushrooms in your stir-fry Oriental dishes; the quick cooking preserves their flavor and texture. You can also fold them into an omelette topped with sherry sauce for an elegant lunch dish.

Mushroom

Muskmelon

Common names: muskmelon, cantaloupe, cantaloup
Botanical name: Cucumis melo
Origin: South Asia, tropical Africa

Varieties

Muskmelons are very dependent on climate and growing conditions. Check with your garden center or local extension office for the varieties that grow best in your area.

Description

The muskmelon is a long, trailing annual that belongs to the cucumber and watermelon family. The netted melon or muskmelon is usually called a cantaloupe, but it should not be confused with the real cantaloupe, which is a warty or rock melon. The word cantaloupe means "song of the wolf" and was the name of an Italian castle. In 1885, when William S. Ross brought two barrels of muskmelons into the South Water Market in Chicago, everyone laughed at the little melons. Ross, however, laughed all the way to the bank. The U.S. Department of Agriculture spells it cantaloup, without the final "e."

Another type of melon you may like to try in your garden is the honeydew. It's sometimes referred to as a winter melon, but again the name is inaccurate — the true winter melon is a Chinese vegetable. Honeydews have a smoother surface than muskmelons, and lack their distinctive odor. They also ripen later and require a longer growing season, which means that they will not ripen fully in short-season areas. Your Cooperative Extension Service will advise you on growing honeydews in your area. The following growing information for muskmelons applies also to honeydews.

Where and when to grow

Muskmelon is a tender, warm-weather plant that will not tolerate even the slightest frost. It also has a long growing season, which means that you must be careful to select a variety suited to your area's climate. In cool areas you'll do better with small-fruited varieties; in warmer areas, where you can accommodate their need for a longer season, you can grow the large varieties. In cool areas grow muskmelons from transplants, using individual, plantable containers at least four inches in diameter so that the root systems are not disturbed when you plant them. Set the plants in the garden when the ground is thoroughly warm, two to three weeks after your average date of last frost.

How to plant

Muskmelons must have full sun and thrive in well-drained soil that is high in organic matter. When you're preparing the soil, dig in a complete, well-balanced fertilizer at the rate of one pound per 100 square feet or 10 pounds per 1,000 square feet. Grow muskmelons in inverted hills spaced four to six feet apart. If you're planting from seed, plant six to eight seeds in each hill; when

Muskmelon

the seedlings have developed three or four true leaves, thin them to leave the strongest two or three seedlings in each hill. Cut the thinned seedlings with scissors at soil level to avoid damaging the survivors' root systems. Where cucumber beetles, other insects, or weather are a problem, wait a bit before making the final selection. If you're using transplants, put two or three in each hill.

Fertilizing and watering

Fertilize before planting and again at midseason, at the same rate as the rest of the garden. Detailed information on fertilizing is given in "Spadework: The Essential Soil" in Part 1.

Muskmelons need a lot of water while the vines are growing. Be generous with water until the melons are mature, then stop watering while the fruit ripens.

Special handling

To keep competitive plants weeded out, cultivate carefully until the vines cover the ground. The roots are very shallow and extend quite a distance, so proceed with caution. You can grow muskmelons three feet apart on fences instead of in inverted hills. As the fruits develop, they may need support if you're growing them on a fence. A net or bag will do the job — try using old pantyhose. If the muskmelons are growing in a hill, put a board under each melon to keep it off the ground.

Pests

Aphids and cucumber beetles are the pests you're most likely to encounter. To control aphids,

Muskmelon seedling

pinch out infested vegetation, hose them off the vines, or spray the aphids with Malathion or Diazinon. Cucumber beetles may not do much feeding damage, but they carry cucumber bacterial wilt. Hand-pick them off the vines promptly, or spray them with carbaryl. Detailed information on pest control is given in "Keeping Your Garden Healthy" in Part 1.

Diseases

Muskmelon vines are susceptible to wilt, blight, mildew, and root rot. Planting disease-resistant varieties when possible and maintaining the general cleanliness and health of your garden will help cut down the incidence of disease. If a plant does become infected, remove and destroy it before it can spread disease to healthy plants. Detailed information on disease prevention is given in "Keeping Your Garden Healthy" in Part 1.

When and how to harvest

Time from planting to harvest is 60 to 110 days, depending on type, and in a good season you might get 10 melons from a 10-foot row. Leave melons on the vine until they're ripe; there is no increase in sugar after harvesting. Mature melons slip easily off the stem; a half-ripe melon needs more pressure to remove than a ripe melon, and often comes off with half the stem attached.

Container growing

Muskmelons are usually too large to grow in a container, but you could try one of the bush-type varieties, using a trellis or other support to save space and increase yields. In northern areas with a short growing season, you can start muskmelons earlier in a container than in a regular garden bed, and you can extend the growing season even more by bringing the container-grown plants inside on cold fall evenings.

Storing and preserving

You can store muskmelons up to one week in the refrigerator or, if you have a lot, for two to three weeks in a cool, moist place. You can also freeze your extras or make pickles with them. Detailed information on storing and preserving is given in Part 4.

Serving suggestions

Muskmelon or honeydew is delicious by itself. A squeeze of lemon or lime juice brings out the flavor nicely. Or fill the halves with fruit salad, yogurt, or ice cream. You can also scoop out the flesh with a melon-baller, and freeze the balls for future use. Mix balls or chunks of different types of melon for a cool dessert. Serve wedges of honeydew with thinly sliced prosciutto as an appetizer.

Q and A

Q: What causes some muskmelon plants to suddenly wilt and die?
A: The cause is bacterial wilt, which is spread by cucumber beetles. To prevent this disease,

control the beetles as soon as they appear.

Q: What causes muskmelon leaves to turn a gray-white color late in the season?

A: The cause is powdery mildew, a fungus disease which can be controlled by selecting resistant varieties and improving air circulation by spacing the plants properly.

Q: Is it true that watermelons, cucumbers, or squash will cross-pollinate with muskmelons and cause them to taste bitter?

A: No, the popular idea that cross-pollination causes a bitter taste is completely false. Cross-pollination will not affect the current crop in any way. However, plants grown from seed saved from the affected plants will show the effects of the cross-pollination.

Mustard

Mustard

Common names: mustard, Chinese mustard, leaf mustard, spinach greens
Botanical name: Brassica juncea
Origin: Asia

Varieties
Tendergreen (spinach mustard, 30 days); Green Wave (45 days); Southern Giant Curled (40 days).

Description

Mustard is a hardy annual with a rosette of large light or dark green crinkled leaves that grow up to three feet in length. The leaves and leaf stalks are eaten. The seeds can be ground and used as a condiment. If you had lived in ancient Rome, you would have eaten mustard to cure your lethargy and any pains you suffered.

Where and when to grow

Mustard is a cool-season crop; it's hardy, but the seeds will not germinate well if you sow them too early, so plant seeds in the garden on your average date of last frost. Mustard is grown like lettuce; it is more heat-tolerant than lettuce, but long hot summer days will force the plants to bolt and go to seed. As mustard has a very short growing season, most areas of the United States can accommodate it without any problems.

How to plant

Mustard tolerates partial shade and needs well-worked soil, high in organic matter, with good drainage and moisture retention. When you're preparing the soil, dig in a complete, well-balanced fertilizer at the rate of one pound per 100 square feet or 10 pounds per 1,000 square feet. Plant the seeds half an inch deep in rows 12 to 24 inches apart, and when the seedlings are large enough to handle, thin them to stand six to 12 inches apart. Transplant the thinned seedlings, or eat them in soups or as greens. For a continuous harvest, plant a few seeds at intervals, rather than an entire row at one time. As soon as the plants start to go to seed, pull them up or they will produce a great number of seeds and sow themselves all over the garden. Plant mustard again when the weather begins to cool off.

Fertilizing and watering

Fertilize before planting and again at midseason, at the same rate as the rest of the garden. Detailed information on fertilizing is given in "Spadework: The Essential Soil" in Part 1.

Water mustard before the soil dries out to keep the leaves growing quickly.

Pests

Mustard is almost always attacked by flea beetles or aphids. Handpick or hose the insects off the plants, or use a chemical spray of Malathion to control the aphids. Flea beetles can be discouraged somewhat by being washed off the plants, but to control them entirely you need to use a chemical spray of carbaryl (Sevin). Because of its pest problems, mustard is less than ideal for organic gardeners. Detailed information on pest control is given in "Keeping Your Garden Healthy" in Part 1.

Diseases

White rust is the only serious disease problem to which mustard is subject. If white rust

is prevalent in your area, treat the plants with a fungicide containing Maneb or Sinab when the first three or four leaves are half grown. Controls are effective if started early. Detailed information on disease prevenion is given in "Keeping Your Garden Healthy" in Part 1.

When and how to harvest

Pick off individual leaves as they grow, or cut the entire plant. Harvest when the leaves are young and tender; in summer the leaf texture may become tough and the flavor strong. Harvest the whole crop when some of the plants start to go to seed.

Container growing

Growing mustard in a container is easy and productive. Sow the seeds liberally over the surface of the container and cover lightly with soil. In a large container, plant in wide rows. Mustard grows well even if overcrowded, and the thinnings can be eaten.

Storing and preserving

You can store mustard in the refrigerator for up to one week, or you can freeze, can, or dry your excess crop; use the recipes for greens. You can also sprout mustard seeds. Detailed information on storing and preserving is given in Part 4.

Serving suggestions

Use young, tender leaves of mustard in a salad, alone or mixed with other greens. Boil the older leaves quickly in just the water that clings to them after washing; dress them with a little olive oil and vinegar, or add some crumbled

bacon. Substitute mustard greens for spinach in an omelette or *frittata*.

Q and A

Q: What causes small white cottony blotches on the upper surfaces of the leaves and corresponding yellow discoloration on the undersides?
A: The cause is white rust, a fungus disease that seldom causes enough damage to mustard plants to require control.
Q: Why do some mustard greens flower prematurely?
A: Hot weather, overcrowding, poor soil fertility, or under-watering can all cause mustards to bolt, that is, go to seed prematurely.
Q: Why do mustard leaves get riddled with small holes as soon as they emerge from the soil?
A: The holes are made by flea beetles, which must be controlled immediately to save these young mustard plants.
Q: Is it true that mustards taste hotter if grown when the summer temperatures are high?
A: Yes; mustards will taste somewhat hotter if grown during very hot periods. They will taste even hotter if they are slightly under-watered.
Q: Can mustard greens be eaten raw?
A: Yes; they add a snappy flavor to a tossed salad.

New Zealand spinach,
See Spinach

Okra

Common names: okra, lady's fingers, gumbo
Botanical names: Hibiscus esculentus
Origin: Africa

Varieties

Blondy (48 days); Emerald (56 days); Clemson Spineless (58 days); Dwarf Green Long Pod (52 days).

Description

Okra, a member of the cotton and hibiscus family, is an erect, tender annual with hairy stems and large maplelike leaves. It grows from three to six feet tall, and has large flowers that look like yellow hibiscus blossoms with red or purplish centers. When mature, the pods are six to 10 inches long and filled with buckshotlike seeds. Okra is used in Southern cooking, in gumbo or mixed with tomatoes.

Where and when to grow

Okra is very sensitive to cold; the yield decreases with temperatures under 70°F, but it has a short season, which permits it to be grown almost anywhere in the United States. Plant okra from seed in the vegetable garden about four weeks after your average date of last frost. Okra does not grow well in containers.

How to plant

Okra will grow in almost any warm, well-drained soil and needs a place in full sun. When you're

Okra

Okra seedling

preparing the soil, dig in a complete well-balanced fertilizer at the rate of one pound per 100 square feet or 10 pounds per 1,000 square feet. Plant the seeds a half inch to an inch deep in rows 24 to 36 inches apart, and when the seedlings are growing strongly, thin them to stand 12 to 18 inches apart.

Fertilizing and watering

Fertilize before planting and again at midseason, at the same rate as the rest of the garden. Detailed information on fertilizing is given in "Spadework: The Essential Soil" in Part 1.

Keep the plants on the dry side. The stems rot easily in wet or cold conditions.

Special handling

Don't work with okra plants when they're wet. You may get an allergic reaction.

Pests

Flea beetles and aphids may visit okra. Spray flea beetles with carbaryl. Pinch out aphid-infested vegetation, control the aphids chemically with Malathion or Diazinon. Detailed information on pest control is given in "Keeping Your Garden Healthy" in Part 1.

Diseases

Okra may be attacked by verticillium or fusarium wilt. Okra varieties are not resistant to these diseases, but maintaining the general cleanliness and health of your garden will help cut down the incidence of disease. If a plant does become infected, remove it before it can spread

disease to healthy plants. Rotate crops to prevent the buildup of diseases in the soil. Detailed information on disease prevention is given in "Keeping Your Garden Healthy" in Part 1.

When and how to harvest

Time from planting to harvest is 50 to 65 days, and a 10-foot row will yield about six pounds of pods. When the plants begin to set their pods, harvest them at least every other day. Pods grow quickly, and unless the older ones are cut off the plant will stop producing new ones. Okra will grow for a year if not killed by frost and if old pods are not left on the plant. Keep picking the pods while they are quite small; when they're only about two inches long they are less gluey. If you let the pods mature you can use them in winter flower arrangements; the pods and the stalks are quite dramatic.

Container growing

Okra does not grow well in containers.

Storing and preserving

Pods will store in the refrigerator for seven to 10 days. You can also freeze, can, or dry them. Detailed information on storing and preserving is given in Part 4.

Serving suggestions

Many people are disappointed because their first mouthful often tastes like buckshot in mucilage. A taste for okra is perhaps an acquired one. Try it in gumbo, mixed with tomatoes, or sautéed.

Q and A

Q: Will okra stop producing if it's not picked continuously?
A: Yes; if you keep picking the okra pods before the seeds mature, the plant will continue to produce more pods. If you let the seeds mature, the plant will slow or stop its production of pods.
Q: What causes okra plants to suddenly wilt, dry up, and die in midsummer just as they begin to produce?
A: Okra plants are susceptible to verticillium or fusarium wilt, either of which will cause the described symptoms. To prevent these diseases, plant okra in a different part of the garden each year.

Onion

Common name: onion
Botanical name: Allium cepa
Origin: Southwest Asia

Varieties

Soil and growing conditions affect the flavor of an onion as much as the variety, so check with a garden center or with your Cooperative Extension Service for specific varieties that will do well in your area.

Description

Onions are hardy biennial vegetables usually grown as annuals. They have hollow leaves, the bases of which enlarge to form a bulb. The flower stalk is also hollow, taller than the leaves, and topped with a cluster of white or lavender flowers. The bulbs vary in color from white through yellow to red. All varieties can be eaten as green onions, though spring onions, bunching onions, scallions, and green onions are grown especially for their tops. Green onions take the least time to grow. Bermuda and Spanish onions are milder than American onions. American and Spanish onions generally take longer to mature than Bermuda onions.

Where and when to grow

Most onions are sensitive to day length. The American and Spanish onions need long days to produce their bulbs, and the Bermuda onion prefers short days. Onions are also sensitive to temperature, generally requiring cool weather to produce their tops and warm weather to produce their bulbs. They're frost-hardy, and you can plant whichever variety you're using four weeks before your average date of last frost. In the South, onions can be planted in the fall or winter, depending on the variety.

How to plant

Onions are available in three forms — seeds, transplants, and sets. Sets are onions with a case of arrested development — their growth was stopped when they were quite small. The smaller the sets are, the better; any sets larger than the nail of your little finger are unlikely to produce good bulbs. Sets are the easiest to plant and the quickest to produce a green onion, but they

are available in the least number of varieties, and are not the most reliable for bulb production — sometimes they'll shoot right on to the flowering stage without producing a bulb. Transplants are available in more varieties than sets and are usually more reliable about producing bulbs. Seeds are the least expensive and are available in the greatest variety, but they have disease problems that sets don't have and take such a long time to grow that the forces of nature often kill them before they produce anything.

In limited space you can grow onions between other vegetables, such as tomatoes or cabbages, or tuck them in among flowers — they don't take much room. They can also be grown in containers. An eight-inch flowerpot can hold eight to 10 green onions.

Onions appreciate a well-made, well-worked bed with all the lumps removed to a depth of at least six inches. The soil should be fertile and rich in organic matter. Locate most bulbs in full sun — green onions can be placed in a partially shady spot. When you're preparing the soil, dig in a complete, well-balanced fertilizer at the rate of one pound per 100 square feet or 10 pounds per 1,000 square feet.

When you plant transplants and sets, remember that large transplants and large sets (over three quarters inch in diameter) will often go directly to seed and should be grown only for green or pulling onions. Grow smaller transplants or sets for bulbs. Plant transplants or sets an inch to two inches deep, and two to three inches apart, in rows 12 to 18 inches apart. The final size of the onion will depend on

Onion

how much growing space it has. The accompanying illustration shows how to plant onion transplants or sets. If you're planting onions from seed, plant the seeds a quarter inch deep in rows 12 to 18 inches apart, and thin to one to two inches apart.

Fertilizing and watering

Fertilize before planting and again at midseason, at the same rate as the rest of the garden. Detailed information on fertilizing is given in "Spadework: The Essential Soil" in Part 1.

The soil should not be allowed to dry out until the plants have started to mature — at this stage the leaves start to get yellow and brown and to droop over. Then let the soil get as dry as possible.

Special handling

Onions are not good fighters; keep the weeds from crowding in and taking all their food and water. Keep the weeds cut off from the very beginning since they are hard to remove when they snuggle up to the onion. Thin conscientiously; in a crowded bed

Plant large sets close together for green onions, and small sets farther apart for dry onions.

onions will mature when very small without growing a bulb.

Pests

Onion thrips and maggots are the pests to watch for. Discourage thrips by hosing them off the

plants, or control them chemically with Malathion or Diazinon. Prevention is the best nonchemical control for maggots — put a three- or four-inch square of plastic around the plants to discourage flies from laying their eggs near the plants.

Plant large onion sets deeper than small sets.

Space onion transplants to allow room for growth.

To control maggots chemically, drench the soil around the plants with Diazinon at the first sign of damage. Detailed information on pest control is given in "Keeping Your Garden Healthy" in Part 1.

Diseases

In areas that produce onions commercially, onions are susceptible to bulb and root rots, smut, and downy mildew. Planting disease-resistant varieties when possible and maintaining the general cleanliness and health of your garden will help cut down the incidence of disease. If a plant does become infected, remove it before it can spread disease to healthy plants. Detailed information on disease prevention is given in "Keeping Your Garden Healthy" in Part 1.

When and how to harvest

Harvest some leaves for flavoring throughout the season, and harvest the green onions when the bulb is full but not much larger in diameter than the leaves. Harvest dry onion bulbs after the leaves have dried. Lift them completely out of the soil; if the roots touch the soil they may start growing again and get soft and watery.

Container growing

Onions are a satisfactory container crop. Large sets of green onions can be planted side by side in a container. Bulb onions can be planted in wide rows in square or rectangular containers on six-inch centers (choose smaller sets). Or, plant bulb onions six inches apart in circular rows in a round container.

Storing and preserving

Store green onions in the refrigerator for up to one week. Let mature bulbs air-dry for about a week outside; then store them in a cold, dry place for up to six or seven months. Do not refrigerate mature onions. You can also freeze, dry, or pickle onions. Detailed information on storing and preserving is given in Part 4.

Serving suggestions

Onions are probably the cook's most indispensable vegetable. They add flavor to a huge variety of cooked dishes, and a meat stew or casserole without onions would be a sad thing indeed. Serve small onions parboiled with a cream sauce, or stuff large ones for baking. Serve onion slices baked like scalloped potatoes. Perk up a salad with thin onion rings, or dip thick rings in batter and deep-fry them. Serve onions as one of the vegetables for a tempura. Add chopped, sautéed onion to a cream sauce for vegetables, or fry a big panful of slices to top liver or hamburgers. Serve pickled onions with cheese and crusty bread for a "farmer's lunch." It's virtually impossible to run out of culinary uses for your onion crop.

Q and A

Q: How long does it take to produce onion bulbs from seed?
A: Two growing seasons.
Q: Does climate affect the flavor of onions?
A: Yes. Cool temperatures tend to sweeten the onions; hot temperatures and dry conditions tend to strengthen their flavor.

Parsnip

Common name: parsnip
Botanical name: Pastinaca sativa
Origin: Europe

Varieties
Hollow Crown improved (95 days), All American (105 days), Harris Model (120 days).

Description

Parsnips are biennals grown as annuals and belong to the same family as celery, carrots, and parsley. A rosette of celerylike leaves grows from the top of the whitish, fleshy root. Parsnips taste like sweet celery hearts. Roman Emperor Tiberius demanded annual supplies of parsnips from Germany. Parsnips were the potato of medieval and Renaissance Europe.

Where and when to grow

Parsnips need a long, cool growing season. They will tolerate cold at both the start and the end of their growing season, and they can withstand freezing temperatures. Plant them from seed two to three weeks before the average date of last frost.

How to plant

Parsnips prefer full sun but will tolerate partial shade. Before planting, work a 5-10-10

Parsnip

Parsnip seedling

fertilizer into the soil at the rate of half a cup to 100 square feet. Turn the soil thoroughly to a depth of 10 to 12 inches, and remove all lumps and rocks. This initial soil preparation is essential for a healthy crop; soil lumps, rocks, or other obstructions in the soil will cause the roots to split, fork, or become deformed. Don't use manure in the soil bed for root crops unless it is very well-rotted; it may also cause forking. Plant seeds a half inch deep in wide rows 18 to 24 inches apart. When the seedlings develop two true leaves, thin them to two to four inches apart. Thinning is very important; parsnips must have adequate space for root development. Do not pull out the thinned seedlings; cut them off at ground level to avoid disturbing the remaining seedlings.

Fertilizing and watering

Fertilize before planting and again at midseason, at the same rate as the rest of the garden. Detailed information on fertilizing is given in "Spadework; The Essential Soil" in Part 1.

To keep parsnips growing quickly, give them plenty of water. As they approach maturity, water less; too much moisture at this stage may cause the roots to crack.

Special handling

In areas with high soil temperature, roots will grow short unless you mulch to regulate the soil temperature. Control weeds, especially during the first few weeks, but cultivate shallowly to avoid damaging the young roots.

Pests

Parsnips have few enemies, but root maggots may be troublesome. Discourage flies from laying eggs near the plants by putting a three- or four-inch square of plastic around each plant. Control maggots chemically by drenching the soil around the plants with Diazinon. Detailed information on pest control is given in "Keeping Your Garden Healthy" in Part 1.

Diseases

Parsnips have no serious disease problems.

When and how to harvest

Leave the parsnips in the soil as long as possible or until you need them. The roots are not harmed by the ground's freezing. In fact, some people think this makes them taste better. The low temperatures convert the roots' starch to sugar. Dig them up before the ground becomes unworkable.

Container growing

The leafy tops of parsnips produce well in a container, but the roots do not grow satisfactorily. Since it's the root you eat, you probably won't want to grow parsnips just for their greenery.

Storing and preserving

Store parsnips in the refrigerator for one to three weeks, or in a cold, moist place for two to six months. You can also freeze them. Detailed information on storing and preserving is given in Part 4.

Serving suggestions

Parsnips can be cooked like carrots. If the roots are very large, remove the tough core after cooking. Put parsnips around a beef roast so that they cook in the meat juices, or puree them and add butter and seasonings.

Pea

Common names: pea, sweet pea, garden pea, sugar pea, English pea
Botanical name: Pisum sativum
Origin: Europe, Near East

Varieties
Shelling types: Little Marvel (62 days); Frosty (64 days); Wando (75 days); Dwarf Grey Sugar (65 days).
Edible-pod types: Giant Melting (65 days); Melting Sugar (69 days); Oregon Sugar Pod (75 days); Sugar Snap (65 days); Sugar Bon (58 days); Sugar Ann (58 days); Sugar Daddy (62 days).

Description

Peas are hardy, weak-stemmed, climbing annuals that have leaflike stipules, leaves with one to three pairs of leaflets, and tendrils that they use for climbing. The flowers are white, streaked, or colored. The fruit is a pod containing four to 10 seeds, either smooth or wrinkled depending on the variety. Custom has it that you can make a wish if you find a pea pod with nine or more peas in it.

Edible-pod peas are a fairly recent development. Grow them the same way as sweet peas, but harvest the immature pod before the peas have developed to full size. Peas have traditionally been a difficult crop for the home gardener to grow, with yields so low that it was hardly worth planting them. The introduction of the new easy-to-grow varieties of edible-pod peas has made growing peas a manageable undertaking for the home gardener, and no garden should be without them. All you need to grow peas is cool weather and a six-foot support trellis.

Where and when to grow

Peas are a cool-season crop that must mature before the weather gets hot. Ideal growing weather for peas is moist and between 60° and 65°F. Plant them as soon as the soil can be worked in spring — about six weeks before the average date of last frost.

How to plant

Peas tolerate partial shade and need good drainage in soil that is high in organic material. They produce earlier in sandy soil, but yield a heavier, later crop if grown in clay soil. Although soaking seeds can speed germination, a lot of seed can be ruined by oversoaking, and peas are harder to plant when they're wet, because the seeds tend to break. Before planting, work a complete well-balanced fertilizer into the soil at the rate of one pound per 100 square feet or 10 pounds per 1,000 square feet. Plant the peas two inches deep, one to two inches apart, in rows 18 to 24 inches apart.

Fertilizing and watering

Fertilize before planting and again at midseason, at the same rate as the rest of the garden. Detailed information on fertilizing is given in "Spadework: The Essential Soil" in Part 1.
Peas need ample moisture; don't let the soil dry out. When the vines are flowering, avoid getting water on the plants; it may damage the flowers and reduce the crop.

Special handling

Provide trellises to support the pea vines. Cultivate very gently to avoid harming the fragile roots.

Pests

Aphids, rabbits, birds, and people are attracted to pea vines. Control aphids by pinching out infested foliage or by hosing them off the vines. Fence out the rabbits, and discourage birds with a scarecrow. Stern words may do the trick with human trespassers. Despite this competition, peas are an excellent crop for any garden. Detailed information on pest control is given in "Keeping Your Garden Healthy" in Part 1.

Diseases

Peas are susceptible to rot, wilt, blight, mosaic, and mildew. New, highly disease-resistant varieties are available; use them to cut down on disease problems in your garden. You will also lessen the incidence of disease if you avoid handling the vines when they're wet, and if you maintain the general health and cleanliness of the garden. If a plant does

Pea

nowhere near as tasty as young ones; as peas increase in size, the sugar content goes down as the starch content goes up. Sugar will also begin converting to starch as soon as peas are picked. To slow this process, chill the peas in their pods as they are picked and shell them immediately before cooking.

Harvest edible-pod peas before the peas mature. Pods should be plump, but the individual peas should not be competely showing through the pod.

Container growing

Like beans, peas will grow in a container. However, it takes so much space to produce a reasonable crop of peas in a container that you probably won't consider it worth your while.

Pea seedling

Storing and preserving

Storing fresh shelling peas is seldom an issue for home gardeners; there are seldom any left to store but they can be stored in the refrigerator, unshelled, up to one week. You can sprout, freeze, can, or dry peas. Dried peas can be stored in a cool, dry place for 10 to 12 months. Edible-pod peas are also

so good raw that you may not even get them as far as the kitchen. If you do have any to spare, you can store them in a plastic bag in the refrigerator for seven to 10 days. Edible-pod peas also freeze well and, unlike shelling peas, lose little of their flavor when frozen. Detailed information on storing and preserving is given in Part 4.

Serving suggestions

Freshly shelled peas are a luxury seldom enjoyed by most people. Cook them quickly in a little water and serve them with butter and chopped mint. Or add a sprig of mint during cooking. Fresh peas and boiled new potatoes are the perfect accompaniment for a lamb roast. Toss cold, cooked peas into a salad, or add them to potato salad — throw in diced cooked carrots as well, and you've got a Russian salad. Simmer peas in butter with a handful of lettuce tossed in at the end of the cooking time. Or try lining the pot with lettuce leaves and cooking the peas briefly over low heat. Add a few sautéed mushrooms or onions for a sophisticated vegetable dish. Add edible pod peas to a stir-fry dish — the rapid cooking preserves their crisp texture and delicate flavor. Eat them raw, or use them alone, lightly steamed, as a side dish.

Q and A

Q: Is it necessary to inoculate pea seeds with a nitrogen-fixing bacteria?
A: No. This bacteria does help produce healthier peas, but it is already in the soil and will multiply quickly enough once peas or beans are growing there.

become diseased, remove and destroy it before it can spread disease to healthy plants. Detailed information on disease prevention is given in "Keeping Your Garden Healthy" in Part 1.

When and how to harvest

Time from planting to harvest is from 55 to 80 days. A 10-foot row may give you about three pounds of pods. Pick shelling peas when the pods are full and green, before the peas start to harden. Overmature peas are

Q: Do peas need a trellis to grow and produce properly?
A: Peas can be grown without a trellis or other support system. However, they will grow and produce much better if they have some type of support.

Q: What causes pea plants to suddenly wilt and turn yellow? This yellowing starts with the lower leaves and works up, and seems to start just as the plants begin to produce peas.
A: Fusarium wilt and root-rot disease can cause these symptoms. Grow resistant varieties to control fusarium wilt. Plant peas in well-drained soil to eliminate most root-rot disease problems.

Pea, black-eyed

Common names: pea, black-eyed pea, cowpea, chowder pea, southern pea, black-eyed bean, China bean
Botanical name: Gigna sinensis
Origin: Asia

Varieties
Queen Anne (68 days); California Black Eye (75 days); Pink Eye Purple Hull (78 days); Mississippi silver (80 days).

Description

Black-eyed peas are tender annuals that can be either bushy or climbing plants, depending on the variety. The seeds of the dwarf varieties are usually white with a dark spot (black eye) where they're attached to the pod; sometimes the spots are brown or purple. Black-eyed peas originated in Asia. Slave traders brought them to Jamaica, where they became a staple of the West Indies' diet.

Where and when to grow

Unlike sweet peas, black-eyed peas tolerate high temperatures but are very sensitive to cold — the slightest frost will harm them. They grow very well in the South, but they don't grow well from transplants, and some Northern areas may not have a long enough growing season to accommodate them from seeds. If your area has a long enough warm season, plant black-eyed peas from seed four weeks after the average date of last frost.

How to plant

Black-eyed peas will tolerate partial shade and will grow in very poor soil. In fact, like other legumes, they're often grown to improve the soil. Well-drained, well-worked soil that's high in organic matter increases their productivity. When you're preparing the soil for planting, work in a complete, well-balanced fertilizer at the rate of one pound per 100 square feet or 10 pounds per 1,000 square feet. Sow seeds half an inch deep and about two inches apart in rows two to three feet apart; when the seedlings are large enough to handle, thin them to three or four inches apart.

Fertilizing and watering

Fertilize before planting and again at midseason, at the same

Black-eyed pea

rate as the rest of the garden. Detailed information on fertilizing is given in "Spadework: The Essential Soil" in Part 1.

Don't let the soil dry out, but try to keep water off the flowers; it may cause them to fall off, and this will reduce the yield.

Pests

Beetles, aphids, spider mites, and leafhoppers attack black-eyed peas. Control aphids and beetles physically by hand-picking or hosing them off the plants, pinch out aphid-infested vegetation, or using a chemical spray of Diazinon or Malathion. Hose leafhoppers off the plants or spray with carbaryl. Spider mites are difficult to control even with the proper chemicals; remove the affected plants before the spider mites spread, or spray the undersides of the foliage with Diazinon. Detailed information on pest control is given in "Keeping Your Garden Healthy" in Part 1.

Diseases

Black-eyed peas are susceptible to anthracnose, rust, mildews, mosaic, and wilt. Planting disease-resistant varieties when possible and maintaining the general cleanliness and health of your garden will help cut down the incidence of disease. To avoid spreading disease, don't work with the plants when they're wet. If a plant does become infected, remove it before it can spread disease to healthy plants. Detailed information on disease prevention is given in "Keeping Your Garden Healthy" in Part 1.

When and how to harvest

Time from planting to harvest is from 70 to 110 days. You can eat either the green pods or the dried peas. Pick pods at whatever stage of maturity you desire — either young and tender or fully matured to use dried.

Container growing

Black-eyed peas can be grown in containers, but they need so much space to produce a reasonable crop that they're not really a practical choice for the container gardener.

Storing and preserving

Unshelled black-eyed peas can be kept up to one week in the refrigerator. Young black-eyed peas can be frozen, pod and all; the mature seeds can be dried, canned, or frozen. Dried shelled black-eyed peas can be stored in a cool, dry place for 10 to 12 months. Detailed information on storing and preserving is given in Part 4.

Serving suggestions

Eat young black-eyed peas in the pod like snap beans; dry the shelled peas for use in casseroles and soups. Combine cooked black-eyed peas and rice, season with red pepper sauce, and bake until hot; or simmer the peas with pork or bacon for a classic Southern dish.

Peanut

Common name: peanut
Botanical name: Arachis hypogaea
Origin: South America

Varieties

Few varieties are available. Try either Virginia or Spanish peanuts, whichever is available in your area. If you can find raw peanuts at the grocery store, plant those.

Description

The peanut is a tender annual belonging to the pea family. It grows six inches to 2½ feet tall, depending on whether it's the bunch type, which grows upright, or the runner type, which spreads out over the ground. Small clusters of yellow, sweet-pea-like flowers grow on stems called pegs. The pegs grow down and push into the soil, and the nuts develop from them one to three inches underground. You can grow a peanut plant indoors if you give it lots of sunlight; it's a novel and entertaining houseplant.

Peanuts are 30 percent protein and 40 to 50 percent oil. George Washington Carver made over 117 separate products out of peanuts.

Where and when to grow

Peanuts need a frost-free growing season four to five months long. They're not grown commercially north of Washington, D.C., but they can be grown for fun much farther north. If your growing season is short, start the peanuts in pots inside, and then transplant them outdoors when the weather warms up. Start them two weeks before your average date of last frost, and transplant them outside two to three weeks after your average date of last frost.

Peanut

the plants start to flower, then water less. Blind (empty) pods are the result of too much rain or humidity at flowering time.

Special handling

Use a heavy mulch to keep the soil surface from becoming hard — the peanut pegs will not have to work so hard to become established in the soil. Mulching will also make harvesting easier.

Pests

Local rodents will be delighted that you've become a peanut farmer. Discourage them by removing their hiding places and fencing them out of your garden. Peanuts have no other serious pest problems. In warm climates they are a good crop for the organic gardener. Detailed information on control is given in "Keeping Your Garden Healthy" in Part 1.

Diseases

Peanuts have no serious disease problems.

When and how to harvest

Time from planting to harvest is 120 to 150 days. Your yield depends on the variety of peanut and the weather at the time of flowering, but usually there are not as many peanuts as you might imagine. Start harvesting when the plants begin to suffer from frost. Pull up the whole plant and let the pods dry on the vine.

Container growing

Peanuts grow well in a container and make an attractive plant.

How to plant

Peanuts like well-worked sandy soil that is high in organic matter. The pegs have difficulty penetrating a heavy clay soil. When you're preparing the soil for planting, work in a complete, well-balanced fertilizer at the rate of one pound per 100 square feet or 10 pounds per 1,000 square feet. Plant either shelled raw peanuts or transplants six to eight inches apart, in rows 12 to 18 inches apart. If you're growing from seed, plant the seeds one to three inches deep. Grow them in double rows to save space.

Fertilizing and watering

Fertilize before planting and again at midseason, at the same rate as the rest of the garden. Detailed information on fertilizing is given in "Spadework: The Essential Soil" in Part 1.

Keep soil moisture even until

However, if you're growing them for practical purposes, you'll be out of luck—peanuts need plenty of soil space in which to bury the nuts, and do not produce well in a container.

Storing and preserving

Shelled peanuts can be sprouted, frozen, or used for peanut butter, or roasted for snacks. Dried shelled peanuts can be stored in a cool, dry place for 10 to 12 months. Detailed information on storing and preserving is given in Part 4.

Serving suggestions

You probably won't be able to resist eating your peanuts as snacks, but if you've got lots, make peanut butter. Run the nuts

Peanut seedling

through a meat grinder for crunchy peanut butter; for the smooth kind put them in the blender. And imagine homemade peanut butter cookies with homegrown peanuts — you'll be one up on everyone at the school bazaar. Add peanuts and candied orange peel to a fudge recipe — it makes a delicious crunchy candy.

Pepper

Common names: pepper, bell pepper, sweet pepper, hot pepper, wax pepper, chili pepper, pimento
Botanical names: Capsicum frutescens (hot pepper), Capsicum annuum (sweet and hot peppers)
Origin: New World tropics

Varieties

Peppers come in bell (sweet) or hot varieties. The bell peppers are the most familiar; most are sweet, but there are a few hot varieties. They're usually harvested when green, but will turn red (or occasionally yellow) if left on the plant. Hot peppers — sometimes called chili peppers — are intensely flavored, and there are more than a hundred varieties. Ask your Cooperative Extension Service for specific recommendations for your area.

The following are reliable varieties for general use; the initials TM indicate resistance to tobacco mosaic disease. **Bell (sweet) peppers:** Bell Boy (TM, 75 days); Big Bertha (TM, 72 days); California Wonder (73 days); Yolo Wonder (TM, 73 days). **Hot peppers:** Chile Jalapeno (72 days); College 6-4 Chile (78 days); Hungarian Wax (67 days); Large Cherry (78 days).

Description

Peppers are tender erect perennials that are grown as annuals. They have several flowers growing in the angle

between the leaf and stem. Sweet peppers are erect annuals that have only a single flower growing from the space between the leaf and the stem.

When Columbus was looking for the black pepper — the dried berries of the Piper nigrum vine — he found the fruit of the Capsicums; it wasn't related in any way to the peppers he'd started out to find, but that did not stop him from using the name.

The American peppers are members of the solanaceous family, which includes tomatoes, potatoes, eggplants, and tobacco. Peppers range in size from the large sweet bullnose or mango peppers to the tiny, fiery bird or devil peppers. Peppers also grow in many shapes: round, long, flat, and twisted. Some like them hot, some like them sweet. The large sweet ones are used raw, cooked, or pickled, and the hot ones are used as an unmistakable flavoring or relish. In Jamaica, there are some peppers so hot that people claim a single drop of sauce will burn a hole in the tablecloth. Choose peppers carefully when you make a selection to be sure the variety you're growing suits your palate.

Where and when to grow

Peppers prefer a soil temperature above 65°F. They don't produce well when the day temperature gets above 90°F, although hot peppers tolerate hot weather better than sweet peppers. The ideal climate for peppers is a daytime temperature around 75°F and a nighttime temperature around 62°F.

The easiest way to grow peppers is from transplants. You can also grow them from seed,

Bell pepper

Pepper seedling

patio; individual plants can be grown in a cubic foot of soil. A single chili (hot pepper) plant is very decorative and can fill many people's hot pepper requirements for a whole year.

How to plant

Peppers do best in a soil that is high in organic matter and that holds water but drains well. When you're preparing the soil for planting, work in a complete, well-balanced fertilizer at the rate of one pound per 100 square feet or 10 pounds per 1,000 square feet. Plant the pepper transplants in full sun, 18 to 24 inches apart, in rows 24 to 36 inches apart.

Fertilizing and watering

Fertilize before planting and again at midseason, at the same rate as the rest of the garden. Do not overfertilize peppers; too much nitrogen will cause the plants to grow large but to produce few peppers. Detailed information on fertilizing is given in "Spadework: The Essential Soil" in Part 1.

Keep the soil evenly moist but not wet.

Special handling

Peppers are shallow-rooted, so cultivate them gently to eliminate weeds. Use a mulch to keep soil temperature and moisture even.

Pests

Peppers are almost always attacked by some pest and may not be a good choice for the organic gardener. Aphids, cutworms, flea beetles, and hornworms will attack peppers. Discourage cutworms by placing a collar

starting seven to 10 weeks before your outdoor planting date. And if you have a very long growing season, you can seed peppers directly in the garden. Set

transplants in the garden two to three weeks after the average date of last frost for your area.

Try growing peppers in a large pot or container indoors or on the around each transplant at the time of planting, and hand-pick hornworms off the plants. You can partially control flea beetles and aphids by hosing them off the plants and pinching out aphid-infested foliage. Chemically, control aphids with Malathion or Diazinon, and flea beetles with carbaryl. Carbaryl can also be used to control cutworms; apply it to the base of the plants. Detailed information on pest control is given in "Keeping Your Garden Healthy" in Part 1.

Diseases

Pepper plants are susceptible to rot, blossom end rot, anthracnose, tobacco mosaic virus, bacterial spot, and mildew. Planting disease-resistant varieties and maintaining the general cleanliness and health of your garden will help cut down the incidence of disease. If a plant does become infected, remove it before it can spread disease to healthy plants. If you smoke, wash your hands before working with the plants to avoid spreading tobacco mosaic virus. Detailed information on disease prevention is given in "Keeping Your Garden Healthy" in Part 1.

When and how to harvest

If you want sweet red peppers, leave your sweet green peppers on the vine until they ripen and turn red. Cut the peppers off the vine; if you pull them off half the plant may come up with the fruit. Hot peppers can irritate skin, so wear gloves when you pick them.

Container growing

Peppers grow and produce well in a container, and in cold northern areas they can be grown all year around if you bring them in and let them winter over in a sunny window. Peppers need warm soil temperatures, so you can start them earlier in a container than in the garden where the soil is slower to warm up in spring. An eight-inch pot will accommodate

Hot pepper

a single plant. In a larger container, each plant needs 12 inches of growing space all around.

Storing and preserving

Peppers will keep up to one week in the refrigerator or for two to three weeks in a cool, moist place. Sweet or hot peppers can be pickled whole or in pieces, or they can be chopped and frozen or dried. Whole peppers can be strung up to dry — a wreath of hot peppers makes a great kitchen decoration. Detailed information on storing and preserving is given in Part 4.

Serving suggestions

Stuffed, raw, pickled, or roasted, sweet and hot peppers add lively flavor to any meal. Stuff sweet peppers with tuna, chicken, a rice and meat mixture, or chili con carne. For a vegetarian dish, stuff them with rice and chopped vegetables, a cheese mixture, or seasoned breadcrumbs. Stuff raw peppers with cream cheese, slice into rings, and serve in a salad. Use thick rings in a dish of vegetables for tempura. French-fry peppers, or fry them Italian-style in oil and garlic. Use chopped peppers in chili and spaghetti sauce recipes, and add a spoonful of chopped hot pepper to a creamy corn soup for an interesting flavor contrast.

When you're preparing raw hot peppers, cut and wash them under running water and wash your hands well when you're finished. Avoid rubbing your eyes while handling hot peppers. Milk is more soothing than water for washing the hot pepper's sting from your skin.

Q and A

Q: My pepper plants are large, dark green, and very healthy looking, yet they fail to set fruit. Why is this?
A: Too much nitrogen fertilizer will create large leafy pepper plants with few or no fruits. Warm windy nights also contribute to failure to set fruit.
Q: Will a mulch help increase the productivity of peppers?
A: Yes, a gray or black plastic mulch will improve pepper yields. Organic mulches work just as well as plastic mulches in reducing weeding and watering chores, but they won't increase the yield as effectively.
Q: Why do some green peppers turn red, and do they taste the same after they change color?
A: Green peppers turn red when the seeds inside mature. The color change does not alter the taste.
Q: Is it true that weather affects the flavor of peppers?
A: Yes; hot peppers will taste hotter if they develop during hot, dry weather.
Q: Can I pot up my pepper plants in the fall and bring them inside for the winter?
A: Yes. Make sure you use a large enough container. Bring the pepper plants inside only for a few hours a day at first until they get used to the lower light available indoors. Also, consider planting a few peppers in containers at the beginning of the season and then bringing them inside in the fall.

Potato

Common names: potato, white potato, Irish potato
Botanical name: Solanum tuberosum
Origin: Chile, Peru, Mexico

Varieties
There are more than 100 varieties of potatoes in the United States, and they fall into four basic categories: long whites, round whites, russets, and round reds. The most important variety is Russet Burbank, but it does not grow successfully in all areas. Good white varieties for general use are Irish Cobbler (75 days) and Norchip (90 days). Good red varieties for general use are Norland (75 days) and Red La Soda (110 to 120 days). Because there are so many varieties, and the results you get will vary according to growing conditions in your area, ask your Cooperative Extension Service for specific recommendations for your area.

Description

The potato is a perennial grown as an annual. It's a weak-stemmed plant with hairy, dark green compound leaves that look a little like tomato leaves, and it produces underground stem tubers when mature. The potato is a member of the solanaceous family, and is related to the tomato, the eggplant, and the pepper; it originated at high altitudes and still prefers cool nights.

Potatoes haven't always been as commonplace as they are now. They grew in temperate regions along the Andes for a couple of thousand years before Spanish explorers introduced them to Europe in the 16th century. To encourage the growing of potatoes, Louis XVI of France wore potato flowers in his buttonhole, and Marie Antoinette wore a wreath of potato flowers in her hair to a ball. But the people didn't become interested in potatoes until an armed guard was assigned to watch the royal potato patch.

Where and when to grow

Potatoes need a frost-free growing season of 90 to 120 days. They're a cool- weather crop, and they grow best in areas with a fairly cool summer; the ideal potato-growing temperature is 60° to 70°F. Hot weather cuts down on the production of tubers. Grow potatoes in summer in the North, and in fall, winter, and spring in the South. Plant early varieties just before your average date of last frost, and plant fall crops 120 days before the average date of the first fall frost. If your season is short, plant as soon as possible for a late crop.

How to plant

Potatoes are grown from whole potatoes or pieces of potatoes — these are called seed pieces; each piece must have at least one eye. Always plant certified disease-free seed pieces, and don't try to use supermarket potatoes, which have been chemically treated to prevent sprouting. Some suppliers are experimenting with potatoes

Potato   Potato seedling

grown from actual seed, but these have yet to prove themselves, and the use of potato seed is not recommended at this stage.

Potatoes need well-drained fertile soil, high in organic matter,

with pH of 5.0 to 5.5. Adding lime to improve the soil and reduce acidity usually increases the size of the crop, but it also increases the incidence of scab — a condition that affects the skin of the potato but not the eating quality. When you're preparing the soil for planting, work in a complete, well-balanced fertilizer at the rate of one pound per 100 square feet or 10 pounds per 1,000 square feet. Plant potatoes or potato pieces in full sun, four inches deep, 12 to 18 inches apart, in rows 24 to 36 inches apart. You can also plant in a trench or on top of the ground and cover them with a thick mulch, such as 12 inches of straw or hay. For a very compact plant, you can grow potatoes in barrels, old tires, or large bags — as the plant grows you add layers of soil to cover the leaves and stems. This encourages the plant to produce new tubers.

Fertilizing and watering

Fertilize before planting and again at midseason, at the same rate as the rest of the garden. Detailed information on fertilizing is given in "Spadework: The Essential Soil" in Part 1.

For the best production, try to maintain even soil moisture; watering before the soil dries out. A thick mulch will conserve soil moisture, keep down weeds, and keep the soil from getting too warm.

Pests

Colorado potato bugs, leafhoppers, flea beetles, and aphids attack potatoes. Spray Colorado potato bugs, leafhoppers and flea beetles with carbaryl. Spray aphids with Malathion. Detailed information on pest control is given in "Keeping Your Garden Healthy" in Part 1. Potatoes have so many pest problems they may

not be a good choice for the organic gardener.

Diseases

Potatoes are susceptible to blight and to scab, which causes a curly roughness of the skin but does not affect the eating quality of the potato. Plant resistant varieties for the best results, especially for large plantings, and use seed certified as true to type and free of disease. Maintaining the general health and cleanliness of your garden will also lessen the incidence of disease. If a plant does become infected, remove and destroy it to avoid spreading disease to healthy plants. Detailed information on disease prevention is given in "Keeping Your Garden Healthy" in Part 1.

When and how to harvest

Time from planting to harvest is 75 to 130 days, and a 10-foot row will give you eight to 10 pounds of potatoes. Each plant will probably produce three to six regular-size potatoes and a number of small ones. Potatoes are fun to grow, and the young new potatoes are delicious. Dig up new potatoes after the plant blooms, or if it doesn't bloom, after the leaves start to yellow. For potatoes that taste like store-bought ones, dig up the tubers two weeks after the vine dies in fall. Use a spading fork to dig the potatoes, and be as gentle as possible to avoid bruising or damaging the skins.

Container growing

Potatoes don't produce well in traditional containers, but they

do even better than in the ground in a contraption made of several car tires. Fill the first tire with soil and plant four or five seed pieces. When the potato vines are 8 to 10 inches tall, place the second tire over the first and fill with soil, allowing 2 or 3 inches of vine to protrude above the soil. As the vines grow, continue to build up the tire stack until the growing season is over. New potatoes will be set at every tire level. At the end of the growing season, knock the tires down and harvest the potatoes. You can buy manufactured potato barrels, but the stacked tires work better because sunlight reaches the plants at each level.

Storing and preserving

Cure potatoes in a dark, humid place for 10 days at 60° to 65°F; then store them in a cold, moderately moist place for four to six months. Be careful not to let them get wet, or they'll rot. Do not refrigerate them. Prepared or new potatoes freeze well and potatoes can also be dried. Detailed information on storing and preserving is given in Part 4.

Serving suggestions

Potatoes are wonderfully versatile in the kitchen — you can boil, bake, roast, fry, puree, sauté, and stuff them. The enterprising cook can serve a different potato dish every day for a month. Small new potatoes are delicious boiled and tossed in butter and parsley or mint; don't peel them. Stuff potatoes with tuna and spinach for a nourishing all-in-one dish. Enjoy low-calorie fries by brushing the fries all over with oil and baking them in a single layer on a cookie sheet. Pipe pureed potatoes around the edge of a dish for an elegant garnish. Add cubed, cooked potatoes with other vegetables to an omelette or frittata. Don't throw away potato skins — they're full of goodness. Deep fry them, or simmer them to make stock. When you're mashing potatoes use hot milk, not cold — they'll be lighter and fluffier; a teaspoon of baking powder will have the same effect.

A nonedible use for potatoes: Cut a potato in half, and carve a picture or design on the cut surface; ink it, and press on paper for an instant block print. It's a splendid way of keeping the children busy on a wet afternoon.

Q and A

Q: Can I use potato pieces from store-bought or homegrown potatoes as seed for next season?
A: No. This practice can lead to serious disease problems. Always plant certified disease-free seed potatoes.
Q: What causes green potatoes, and are they poisonous?
A: Green potato skins result when the potatoes are exposed to sunlight during growing or curing. If potatoes protrude from the soil while they're growing, cover them with a mulch. Never cure potatoes in bright sunlight; either cover them with burlap or keep them in a dark basement or garage. Green potatoes are not really poisonous, but they taste bitter and may make you sick.
Q: Even though I plant certified seed, the skins of my potatoes are rough and scabby. What can I

do to prevent this?
A: Potato scab disease does not develop when the pH of the soil is 5.5 or lower. Lower the pH of the soil and grow resistant varieties.
Q: How do you grow new potatoes?
A: New potatoes are simply harvested earlier, before the vines die and when the potatoes are only one or two inches in diameter. You'll also find some small new potatoes when you harvest the mature potatoes.

Potato, sweet

See Sweet potato

Pumpkin

Common name: pumpkin
Botanical names: Cucurbita maxima, Cucurbita moschata, Cucurbita pepo
Origin: tropical America

Varieties
Small pumpkins are grown primarily for cooking; intermediate and large sizes for cooking and for making jack-o'-lanterns; and the very large jumbo ones mainly for exhibition. The bush and semi-vining varieties are best suited to small home gardens. The following are a few of the varieties available, and unless otherwise indicated they are the vining kind. Ask your Cooperative Extension Service for other specific

recommendations for your area. **Small (four to six pounds, 100-110 days):** Early Sweet Sugar; Luxury; Spookie; Sugar Pie.
Intermediate (eight to 15 pounds, 100-110 days): Cinderella (bush); Green-Striped Cushaw; Jack-O'-Lantern; Spirit (semi-vining).
Large (15 to 25 pounds, 100 days): Big Tom; Connecticut Field; Halloween; White Cushaw.
Jumbo (50 to 100 pounds, 120 days): Big Max; King of the Mammoths.

Description

Pumpkins are tender annuals with large leaves on branching vines that can grow 20 feet long. The male and female flowers — sometimes as large as eight inches in diameter — grow on the same vine, and the fruit can weigh as much as 100 pounds. The name pumpkin is also given to a number of other squashes and gourds — anything that's orange and hard. The harvest poem reference, "when the frost is on the pumpkin," means the first light frost, not a hard freeze. The first pumpkin pies were made by pouring milk into a pumpkin and baking it.

Where and when to grow

Pumpkins need a long growing season; they will grow almost anywhere in the United States, but in cooler areas you'll do better with a smaller variety. Pumpkins are sensitive to cold soil and frost. Plant them from seed two to three weeks after your average date of last frost when the soil has warmed up. Pumpkins are relatively easy to grow so long as you have space to accommodate them. They're not the vegetable to grow in a small home garden, although you can train them on a fence or trellis, and the bush type requires less space than the vining varieties.

How to plant

Pumpkins can tolerate partial shade and prefer well-drained soil, high in organic matter. Too much fertilizer tends to encourage the growth of the vines rather than the production of pumpkins. When you're preparing the soil for planting, work in a complete, well-balanced fertilizer at the rate of one pound per 100 square feet or 10 pounds per 1,000 square feet. Plant pumpkins in inverted hills, made by removing an inch of soil from a circle 12 inches in diameter and using the soil to build up a rim around the circle; leave six feet between hills. Plant six to eight seeds in each hill, and thin to two or three when the seedlings appear. When the seedlings have four to six true leaves, thin to

only one plant in each hill. Cut off the thinned seedlings at soil level to avoid disturbing the roots of the chosen survivor. One early fruit can suppress the production of any more pumpkins. Some people suggest removing this first pumpkin, but this is a gamble because there's no guarantee that others will set. If you remove it, eat it like squash.

Fertilizing and watering

Fertilize before planting and again at midseason, at the same rate as the rest of the garden. Detailed information on fertilizing is given in "Spadework: The Essential Soil" in Part 1.

Be generous with water; pumpkins need plenty of water to keep the vines and fruit growing steadily.

Pests

Squash vine borers attack pumpkins, and if the plant is wilting it may be that borers are to blame. Prevention is better than cure with borers, because once the pest is inside the plant chemical controls won't help. If you suspect borers are at work, apply carbaryl to the crown of the plant at weekly intervals. If the vine wilts from a definite point onward, look for a hole or a thinning of the wall near the point where the wilting starts. The culprit may still be there, but you may still be able to save the plant. Slit the stem, remove the borer and dispose of it, then cover the stem with soil to encourage rooting at that point. Detailed information on pest control is given in "Keeping You Garden Healthy" in Part 1.

Pumpkin seedling

Pumpkin

Diseases

Pumpkins are susceptible to mildew, anthracnose, and bacterial wilt. Planting disease-resistant varieties when possible, maintaining the general cleanliness and health of your garden, and not handling the vines when wet will help cut down the incidence of disease. If a plant does become infected, remove it before it can spread disease to healthy plants. Detailed information on disease prevention is given in "Keeping Your Garden Healthy" in Part 1.

When and how to harvest

Time from planting to harvest is 95 to 120 days. A 10-foot row may give you one to three pumpkins—when you're talking pumpkins, your back yard starts to look like small potatoes. Leave the pumpkins on the vine as long as possible before a frost, but not too long—they become very soft when they freeze. Cut off the pumpkin with one or two inches of stem.

Container growing

Space-hungry pumpkins do not grow well in containers.

Storing and preserving

Cure pumpkins in a dark, humid place for 10 days at 80° to 85°F; then store them at 50° to 55°F, in a dry place for three to six months. Do not refrigerate. Stored pumpkins will shrink as much as 20 percent in weight; they'll still make good pies, but they look sad if kept too long. You can dry or pickle pumpkin, or freeze or can the cooked pulp. You can also sprout pumpkin seeds. Detailed information on storing and preserving is given in Part 4.

Serving suggestions

Spice up the cooked pumpkin flesh for pie fillings, breads, or muffins; or use it in custards, or as a stuffing for meats or vegetables. Roast the seeds for a nutritious snack. If a pumpkin has served only briefly as a jack-o'-lantern, you can still use the flesh for cooking.

Q and A

Q: Why do some pumpkin plants suddenly wilt and die just when they have started to produce pumpkins?
A: The cause is probably bacterial wilt, which is spread by cucumber beetles. Control the beetles as soon as they appear.
Q: Why do pumpkin leaves turn a gray-white color in late summer or early fall?
A: The cause is powdery mildew, a fungus disease that can be controlled by planting resistant varieties and spacing the pumpkins correctly so they are not overcrowded.
Q: Why do some of the first flowers on my pumpkins die without setting fruit?
A: This is a natural occurrence and not a problem. The first flowers are male and do not produce fruit.
Q: Is it true that watermelons, cantaloupes, cucumbers or squash will cross-pollinate with pumpkins and make them taste bitter?
A: No; the popular idea that cross-pollination causes a bitter flavor is completely false. Cross-pollination will not affect the current crop in any way.

However, plants grown from seed saved from the affected plants will show the effects of the cross-pollination.

Radish

Common name: radish
Botanical name: Raphanus sativus (spring radish), Raphanus sativus longipinnatus (winter radish)
Origin: temperate Asia

Varieties
Radishes can be grown for a spring or winter crop. Spring varieties are the commonly known small red varieties. Winter radishes are larger and more oval and can grow eight or nine inches long. The following are a few of the varieties available.
Spring crop: Cherry Belle (22 days); Burpee White (25 days).
Winter crop: Black Spanish (55 days); White Chinese (60 days).

Description

Radishes are hardy annuals or biennials that produce white, red, or black roots and stems under a rosette of lobed leaves. They're fun to grow, and youngsters get hooked on gardening after growing radishes more than any other vegetable. A bunch of radishes, well washed, makes a great posy to give away. Radishes are distantly related to horseradish.

Where and when to grow

Radishes are cool-season crops and can take temperatures below freezing. You can grow them anywhere in the United States, and they mature in such a short time that you can get two to three crops in spring alone. Start planting them from seed in the garden two or three weeks before the average date of last frost for your area. Radishes germinate quickly and are often used with slower-growing seeds to mark the rows. Spring radishes produce a crop so fast that in the excitement very few people ask about the quality of the crop. Radishes can also be grown in six-inch pots in a bright, cool window. They will grow in sand if watered with liquid, all-purpose fertilizer diluted to quarter strength.

How to plant

Radishes tolerate partial shade and like well-worked, well-drained soil. When you're preparing the soil for planting, work in a complete, well-balanced fertilizer at the rate of one pound per 100 square feet or 10 pounds per 1,000 square feet. If you're planting winter radishes, be sure to loosen the soil well and remove soil lumps or rocks that might cause the roots to become deformed. Plant seeds half an inch deep in rows or wide rows 12 to 18 inches apart. When the seedlings are large enough to handle, thin them according to the variety; thin small spring varieties one to three inches apart, and give winter varieties a little more space.

Fertilizing and watering

Fertilize before planting and again at midseason, at the same rate as the rest of the garden. Detailed information on fertilizing

is given in "Spadework: The Essential Soil" in Part 1.

Give radishes enough water to keep the roots growing quickly. If the water supply is low, radishes become woody.

Special handling

Radishes sometimes bolt, or go to seed, in the summer, but this is more often a question of day length than of temperature. Cover the plants in midsummer

so they only get an eight-hour day; a 12-hour day produces flowers and seeds but no radishes.

Pests

Aphids and root maggots occasionally attack radishes, but you harvest radishes so quickly that pests are not a serious problem. You can pinch out aphid-infested foliage, and drench the soil around the plants with Diazinon to control root maggots.

Radish seedling

Radish

Detailed information on pest control is given in "Keeping Your Garden Healthy" in Part 1.

Diseases

Radishes have no serious disease problems.

When and how to harvest

Time from planting to harvest is 20 to 30 days for spring radishes, 50 to 60 days for winter radishes. Pull up the whole plant when the radishes are the right size. Test-pull a few or push the soil aside gently to judge the size, and remember that the biggest radishes aren't necessarily the best. If you wait too long to harvest, the centers of spring radishes become pithy.

Container growing

Radishes do well in containers, and in cold northern areas they can be grown indoors. Because radishes are sensitive to heat, it's helpful to be able to move them out of the sun as necessary. In a round container, plant radishes in concentric circles; in a larger container, plant in wide rows.

Storing and preserving

Radishes will store for one to two weeks in the refrigerator. You can also sprout radish seeds. Detailed information on storing and preserving is given in Part 4.

Serving suggestions

Radishes can be sculptured into rosettes or just sliced into a salad. They are low in calories and make good cookie substitutes when you have to nibble. Put radishes on a relish tray, or on a platter of vegetables for dipping. Try "pickling" the excess crop by mincing them and marinating in vinegar.

Q and A

Q: Why do some of my spring radishes develop plenty of leaves and small skinny roots?
A: Spring radishes will only produce large roots in cool weather. Warm temperatures or overcrowding will result in small roots.
Q: Why do spring radishes sometimes flower and produce only small roots?
A: Long sunny days will force spring radishes to flower. Plant when days are short—early in spring or fall.
Q: Why do radishes get pithy and crack or split?
A: These radishes are old; harvest them earlier.
Q: What makes radishes taste hot?
A: Slow growth and inadequate water cause this hot taste.

Overcrowding can ruin your root vegetable crops; thin radishes so that the roots have room to develop.

Rhubarb

Common names: rhubarb, pie plant
Botanical name: Rheum rhaponticum
Origin: southern Siberia

Varieties

Canada Red; MacDonald; Valentine; Victoria (green stalks).

Description

A hardy perennial, rhubarb grows two to four feet tall, with large, attractive leaves on strong stalks. The leaf stalks are red or green and grow up from a rhizome or underground stem, and the flowers are small and grow on top of a flower stalk. Don't allow the plant to reach the flowering stage; remove the flower stalk when it first appears. You eat only the rhubarb stalks; the leaves contain a toxic substance and are not for eating.

Where and when to grow

Rhubarb is very hardy and prefers cool weather. In areas where the weather is warm or hot, the leaf stalks are thin and spindly. Rhubarb can be grown from seed, but the plants will not grow "true" — which means they won't be the same variety as the parent plant. Grow from the divisions that grow up from the parent stems for a close or exact copy of the parent plant. Buy divisions or divide your own plants in spring, about four to six weeks before the average date of last frost. The timing is not

Rhubarb

crucial, because you won't harvest rhubarb the first year. Refer to "Planting Your Garden" in Part 1 for information on dividing plants.

How to plant

Rhubarb likes rich, well-worked soil that is high in organic matter and drains well. Give it a place in full sun or light shade. When you're preparing the soil for planting, work in a complete, well-balanced fertilizer at the rate of one pound per 100 square feet or 10 pounds per 1,000 square feet. Plant the divisions about three feet apart in rows three to four feet apart, with the growing tips slightly below the soil surface.

Fertilizing and watering

Fertilize before planting and again at midseason, at the same rate as the rest of the garden. Detailed information on fertilizing is given in "Spadework: The Essential Soil" in Part 1.

Rhubarb does best with even soil moisture. Water it thoroughly before the soil dries out, but don't let the soil get soggy.

Special handling

Keep grass and other competitors away from rhubarb and mulch it, especially in winter. To get earlier and longer leaf stalks, cover the plants with bottomless boxes in the early spring. Remove the flower stalks when they appear to keep the leaf stalks growing strongly; divide the plant every three to four years. Rhubarb can be forced or made to produce before its natural maturity. To do this dig up roots that are at least two years old and pile them on the ground

so they will be frozen with the first hard frost. After the freeze, put them into pots or boxes filled with sand, and surround the containers with sand to keep the roots moist. Store the containers in a cold place but not where the temperature could fall more than a couple of degrees below freezing. When you move the roots to a dark cellar at 60°F, the stalks will grow tall with very small, pale, folded-up leaves. Rhubarb can also be forced in a cold frame later in the year; these stalks will be greener and more nutritious, and the leaves will be almost

Rhubarb seedling

normal size. Information on making and using a cold frame is given in "Planning Your Garden" in Part 1.

Pests

Rhubarb has no serious pest problems. It's a trouble-free crop for any garden.

Diseases

Rhubarb has no serious disease problems. Some old clumps may develop crown rot, but this can be avoided by dividing the clumps before they get too large.

When and how to harvest

Don't expect quick results from your rhubarb crop; you'll have to wait two to three years from the time of planting while the roots establish themselves. You can sneak a single leaf stalk the first year, if the plant has four or more leaves. A 10-foot row of rhubarb should give you nine to 10 pounds of mature stems. To harvest, twist off the leaf stalk at the soil line. To keep the plant going strong, do not cut more than a third of the leaves in any year.

Container growing

Rhubarb is a perennial that needs a cold dormancy period. Therefore it is not suitable for container gardens.

Storing and preserving

Rhubarb can be stored in the refrigerator for up to two weeks; cut off the leaves first. Freeze or make preserves from any extra rhubarb. It can also be canned or dried. Detailed information on storing and preserving is given in Part 4.

Serving suggestions

Botanically, rhubarb is a vegetable, but for culinary purposes it is a fruit. It's good in pies, jams, and jellies, and can be eaten baked or stewed as a topping for a cooked breakfast cereal. It has a tart taste and needs to have sugar added. The sweetened juice makes a refreshing cold drink. Add finely chopped rhubarb to any nut bread recipe.

Rutabaga

Common names: rutabaga,
   Swedish turnip, Swede, Russian
   turnip, yellow turnip
Botanical name: Brassica
   napobrassica
Origin: northern Europe

Varieties

American Purple Top (90 days);
Laurentian (90 days).

Description

Rutabaga is a hardy biennial
grown as an annual. It has a rosette
of smooth, grayish-green leaves
that grow from the swollen stem,
and it has a root that can be
yellow, purple, or white. The
rutabaga can be distinguished
from the turnip by the leaf scars on
its top, and the leaves are more
deeply lobed than the turnip's. As
vegetables go, rutabagas are a
fairly modern invention. They
were created less than 200 years
ago by crossing a cabbage with a
turnip (probably Swedish).

Where and when to grow

Rutabagas are very hardy and
grow better in cool weather. They
like a definite difference
between day and night
temperatures. In hot weather
they produce lots of leaves, but
small stringy roots. Plant them
in late summer in the North, and in
the fall in the South or where the
weather gets very hot. Start spring
plantings from seed four to six
weeks before the average date of
last frost.

Rutabaga

How to plant

Rutabagas do best in well-
drained soil that's high in organic
matter. Although they're less
likely than carrots to fork or split,
they need well-worked soil with

all the rocks and soil lumps
removed. When you're
preparing the soil for planting,
work in a complete, well-
balanced fertilizer at the rate of
one pound per 100 square feet
or 10 pounds per 1,000 square feet.
Plant the seeds half an inch deep
in rows 18 to 24 inches apart, and
when the seedlings are large
enough to handle, thin them to six
to eight inches apart. Thinning
is important; like all root crops,
rutabagas must have room to
develop.

Fertilizing and watering

Fertilize before planting and
again at midseason, at the same
rate as the rest of the garden.
Detailed information on fertilizing
is given in "Spadework: The

Rutabaga seedling

Essential Soil" in Part 1.
   Water thoroughly before the
roots dry out, and water often
enough to keep the rutabagas
growing steadily. If their growth
slows down, the roots will be
tough.

Pests

Aphids attack rutabagas and can
be persistent. Try to control them
physically by pinching out
infested foliage or hosing the
aphids off the plants.
Chemically, control them with
Malathion or Diazinon, being
sure to spray the undersides of the
foliage. Detailed information on

pest control is given in "Keeping Your Garden Healthy" in Part 1.

Diseases

Rutabagas have no serious disease problems.

When and how to harvest

Time from planting to harvest is 90 to 100 days, and a 10-foot row may give you over 10 pounds of rutabagas if the weather has been right. To harvest, dig up the whole roots when the rutabagas are three to five inches in diameter. In cold areas, mulch heavily to extend the harvesting period.

Container growing

Like many other root crops, rutabagas do not grow well in containers.

Storing and preserving

Leave the rutabagas in the ground for as long as possible until you're ready to use them; in very cold areas, mulch them heavily. Store rutabagas in a cold, moist place for two to four months; do not refrigerate. They can also be frozen. Detailed information on storing and preserving is given in Part 4.

Serving suggestions

Peel rutabagas and steam or boil until tender; then mash them for use in puddings and pancakes. They can also be served sliced or diced. Add rutabagas to vegetable soups and stews. Sauté them in butter with apples and brown sugar. Rutabaga is very good with lots of butter or sour cream; low-calorie alternatives are yogurt or low-fat cream cheese.

Q and A

Q: What causes small white cottony blotches on the upper surfaces of the leaves of rutabagas and corresponding yellow discoloration on the undersides?
A: The cause is white rust, a fungus disease that seldom causes enough damage to rutabagas to require control.
Q: What causes small holes that riddle the entire surface of rutabaga leaves?
A: The holes are made by flea beetles, which should be controlled as soon as any damage is noticed.
Q: Why are homegrown rutabagas smaller and more bitter than store-bought ones?
A: Rutabagas should be grown in cool temperatures to develop the proper size and flavor.

Salsify

Common names: salsify, oyster plant
Botanical name: Tragopogon porrifolius
Origin: southern Europe

Varieties
Few varieties are available; grow the variety available in your area.

Salsify

Salsify seedlings

Description

Salsify is a hardy biennial grown as an annual. It's related to dandelion and chicory, and its flowers look like lavender chicory blossoms. The edible part is the long taproot. This salsify should not be confused with black salsify (Scorzonera hispanica) or Spanish salsify (Scolymus hispanicus); both of these are related to the radish. Some people claim that salsify has a slight oyster flavor — hence the name "oyster plant." In fact, it tastes rather like artichoke hearts.

Where and when to grow

Salsify is hardy and tolerates cold. Like its prolific cousin, the dandelion, it's very easy to grow and will grow anywhere in the United States. Plant salsify from seed two or three weeks before your area's average date of last frost.

How to plant

Plant salsify seeds in full sun in rich, well-worked soil. When you're preparing the soil for planting, work in a complete, well-balanced fertilizer at the rate of one pound per 100 square feet or 10 pounds per 1,000 square feet. Work the soil thoroughly to a depth of eight to 12 inches, and remove all stones, soil lumps, or rocks that might cause the roots to fork and split. Plant the seeds half an inch deep in rows 18 to 24 inches apart, and when the seedlings are large enough to handle, thin them to stand two to four inches apart.

Fertilizing and watering

Fertilize before planting and again at midseason, at the same rate as the rest of the garden. Don't overfertilize salsify; it will cause the roots to fork and split. Detailed information on fertilizing is given in "Spadework: The Essential Soil" in Part 1.

Keep salsify evenly moist to prevent the roots from getting stringy.

Pests

Salsify has no serious pest problems.

Diseases

Salsify has no serious disease problems.

When and how to harvest

Time from planting to harvest is about 120 days, and a 10-foot row should yield 20 to 40 roots. Salsify roots can take freezing, so leave them in the ground as long as possible until you want them. The longer they're out of the ground, the less they taste like oysters. To harvest, dig up the whole root.

Container growing

Salsify does not grow well in a container.

Storing and preserving

Cut the tops off salsify and store the roots in the refrigerator for one to three weeks, or store in a cold, moist place for two to four months. For freezing, handle salsify like parsnips. Detailed information on storing and preserving is given in Part 3.

Serving suggestions

Salsify roots should not be peeled before cooking; they can "bleed." Scrub them clean, steam, and slice them, then dip the slices in batter or breadcrumbs and fry; serve with tartar sauce. People who have never had oysters can't tell them apart. Try salsify braised with lemon and butter — the lemon helps preserve the color. Or serve it with a white sauce; add chopped parsley for color.

Shallot

Common name: shallot
Botanical name: Allium cepa
Origin: Asia

Varieties
Few varieties are available; grow the variety available in your area.

Description

The shallot is a very hardy biennial grown as an annual, and it's a member of the onion family. It's believed that French knights returning from the Crusades introduced them to Europe, and that De Soto brought them to America in 1532. Shallot plants grow about eight inches tall in a clump, with narrow green leaves, and look very much like small onions; they're favorites with gourmets. The roots are very shallow and fibrous, and the bulbs are about a half inch in diameter when mature. The small bulbs have a more delicate flavor than regular onions. Use the young outer leaves like chives.

Where and when to grow

Shallots are easy to grow and very hardy. You can grow them

Shallot

Diseases

Shallots have no serious disease problems.

When and how to harvest

Cut the green shallot leaves throughout the growing season, but be careful not to cut away any new growth coming from the central stem. Dig up bulbs when the tops wither and fall over.

Container growing

Shallots are a good choice for container growing. They like to be cool, and therefore thrive from being moved out of the heat as necessary. An eight-inch pot will accommodate two or three shallot cloves.

Storing and preserving

Store shallots in the refrigerator for up to one week or store the bulbs like onions in a cold, dry place for two to eight months. You can also freeze or dry them like onions. The greens can be chopped and frozen like chives. Detailed information on storing and preserving is given in Part 4.

Serving suggestions

Shallots have a delicate flavor and are less overpowering than many onions. They're very good stirred into sour cream as a dressing for vegetables or fish, or chopped and added to an oil-and-vinegar dressing for salads. Use the small bulbs in the classic French beef stew, *boeuf bourguignonne*.

Snap bean,
See **Bean, green or snap**

anywhere in the United States from cloves planted early in spring.

How to plant

Shallots can be grown in any soil but may have less flavor when they're grown in clay soils. Shallots are very shallow-rooted plants and need little soil preparation. Although they prefer full sun, they'll survive in partial shade. Shallots seldom form seed, so they're usually grown from cloves, which should be planted four to six weeks before your average date of last frost. When you're preparing the soil for planting, work in a complete, well-balanced fertilizer at the rate of one pound per 100 square feet or 10 pounds per 1,000 square feet. Plant the cloves six to eight inches apart in rows 12 inches apart, and set them so that the tops of the cloves are even with the soil, but no deeper. Keep them carefully cultivated when they're small; the shallow root systems don't like to compete with weeds.

Fertilizing and watering

Fertilize before planting and again at midseason, at the same rate as the rest of the garden. Detailed information on fertilizing is given in "Spadework: The Essential Soil" in Part 1.

Water the shallots regularly; do not allow the soil to dry out.

Pests

Shallots have no serious pest problems.

Sorrel

Common names: garden sorrel, herb patience or spinach dock, French sorrel, spinach rhubarb.
Botanical name: Rumex acetosa, Rumex patientia, Rumex scutatus, Rumex abyssinicus.
Origin: Europe

Varieties

Few varieties are available commercially; grow the variety available in your area. Garden sorrel, French sorrel, and herb patience or spinach dock are all good for eating.

Description

Several varieties of sorrel will do well in your garden. Garden sorrel (R. acetosa) grows about three feet tall and produces leaves that are good used fresh in salads; herb patience or spinach dock (R. patientia) is a much taller plant, with leaves that can be used either fresh or cooked. French sorrel (R. scutatus) grows only six to 12 inches tall; its fiddle-shaped leaves make good salad greens. Spinach rhubarb (R. abyssinicus) is a lofty plant — it grows up to eight feet tall. As the name suggests, you can cook the leaves like spinach and the stalks like rhubarb. Avoid other varieties — they're weeds and not good for eating.

Where and when to grow

All the sorrels are very hardy and can be grown in almost every area of the United States. Start them from seed in the early spring before your average date of last frost.

How to plant

All the sorrels require a sunny location with well-drained, fertile soil. When you're preparing the soil, dig in a complete, well-balanced fertilizer at the rate of one pound per 100 square feet or 10 pounds per 1,000 feet. Plant sorrels from seed two to three weeks before the average date of last frost. Plant the seeds a half inch deep in rows 18 to 24 inches apart, and when the plants are six to eight weeks old, thin them to 12 to 18 inches apart.

Fertilizing and watering

Fertilize before planting and again at midseason, at the same rate as the rest of the garden. Detailed information on fertilizing is given in "Spadework: The Essential Soil" in Part 1.

Sorrel

Sorrel plants should be kept moist; water them more often than the rest of the garden.

Pests

Aphids will probably show interest in your sorrel. Control them by pinching out infested areas or hosing the aphids off the plants; or spray with Malathion or Diazinon. Detailed information on pest control is given in "Keeping Your Garden Healthy" in Part 1.

Diseases

Sorrel has no serious disease problems.

When and how to harvest

Pick the fresh leaves of the sorrel throughout the growing season. Pick off the flowers before they mature to keep the plants producing new leaves long into the fall.

Container growing

Sorrel does very well in a container. Plant a single sorrel plant in a six-inch pot, or several in a larger container on eight-inch centers.

Storing and preserving

Use sorrel fresh, or store sorrel leaves in the refrigerator for one to two weeks. You can also freeze or dry the leaves as herbs, but you'll lose some flavor. Detailed information on storing and preserving is given in Part 4.

Serving suggestions

You can use sorrel leaves raw, as salad greens or very lightly steamed or boiled and tossed in butter. Sorrel soup is a classic French favorite, and the Russians use sorrel in a green borscht soup. In the time of Henry VIII, sorrel was used as a spice and to tenderize meat. The English also mashed the leaves with vinegar and sugar as a dressing for meat and fish — hence the name green sauce.

Soybean

Common name: soybean
Botanical name: Glycine max
Origin: East Asia

Varieties

A number of varieties have been bred to adapt to certain types of climate. Ask your Cooperative Extension Service for specific recommendations for your area.

Description

The soybean is a tender, free-branching annual legume. Though it can grow five feet tall, it's usually only two to 3½ feet tall. The stems and leaves are hairy; the flowers are white with lavender shading, and the pods are one to four inches long and grow in clusters. The soybean is extremely high in protein and calcium and is a staple of a vegetarian diet. It's also very versatile and can be used to make milk, oil, tofu, or a meat substitute. The ancient Chinese considered the soybean their most important crop. The United States now produces about 75 percent of the world's soybeans.

Where and when to grow

Soybeans are sensitive to cold and most varieties have a narrow latitude range in which they will mature properly and produce a good crop. Plant a variety suited to your area about two to three weeks after the average date of last frost. Don't plant before the soil has warmed up.

How to plant

After the last frost is over, choose a bed in full sunlight; soybeans tolerate partial shade, but partial shade tends to mean a partial yield. Prepare the soil by mixing in a pound of 5-10-10 fertilizer — don't use a high-nitrogen fertilizer, because too much nitrogen will promote growth of foliage but not of the beans. Work the fertilizer into the soil at the rate of one pound per 100 square feet or 10 pounds per 1,000 square feet. The seeds may crack and germinate poorly when the moisture content of the soil is too high. Don't soak the seeds before planting, and don't overwater immediately afterwards.

Plant seeds an inch deep, one to two inches apart in rows 24 to 30 inches apart. When the seedlings are growing well, thin the plants to two inches apart. Cut the seedlings with scissors at ground level; be careful not to disturb the others. Soybeans don't mind being a little crowded; in fact, they'll use each other for support.

Fertilizing and watering

Soybeans set up a mutual exchange with soil microorganisms called nitrogen-fixing bacteria, which

Soybean

Fertilize before planting and again at midseason, at the same rate as the rest of the garden. Detailed information on fertilizing is given in "Spadework: The Essential Soil" in Part 1.

Keep the soil moist until the soybeans have pushed through the ground. Water regularly if there's no rain, but remember that water on the flowers can cause the flowers and small pods to fall off. When the soil temperature reaches 60°F you can mulch to conserve moisture.

Special handling

Don't handle soybean plants when they're wet or covered with heavy dew; handling or brushing against them when they're wet spreads fungus spores. Cultivate thoroughly but with care, so that you don't disturb the plants' shallow root systems.

Pests

Soybeans do not have many pest problems, unless you're growing them in an area where soybeans are produced commercially. Flea beetles may appear; hand-pick or hose them off the vines, or spray with carbaryl. Rabbits, raccoons, and woodchucks love soybeans and can be strong competitors for your crop. Discourage them by removing places where they can nest or hide or by fencing them out of your garden. Detailed information on pest control is given in "Keeping Your Garden Healthy" in Part 1.

Diseases

Soybeans have no serious disease problems.

help them produce their own fertilizer. Some gardeners recommend that if you haven't grown soybeans or beans in the plot the previous season, you should treat the seeds before planting with a nitrogen-fixing bacteria inoculant to help them convert organic nitrogen compounds into usable organic compounds. This is a perfectly acceptable practice, but it isn't really necessary; the bacteria in the soil will multiply quickly enough once they've got a growing plant to work with.

When and how to harvest

Time from planting to harvest is 45 to 65 days, and a 10-foot row will supply one to two pounds of beans. The yield is not generous, so except for novelty value, soybeans are not the ideal crop for a small home garden. Harvest when the pods are about four inches long or when they look plump and full.

Container growing

Soybeans can be grown in containers, but they require so much room to produce a usable crop that they are not really a practical choice for the container gardener.

Storing and preserving

Store fresh unshelled soybeans in the refrigerator up to one week. Shelled soybeans can be frozen, canned, or dried. They can also be sprouted. Dropping the pods into boiling water for a minute or two makes shelling easier. Dried, shelled soybeans can be stored in a cool, dry place for 10 to 12 months. Detailed information on storing and preserving is given in Part 4.

Serving suggestions

The Japanese cook soybeans in salted water, serve them in the shell, and then squeeze out the seeds and eat them. Soybeans are extremely versatile; they can be made into oil, milk, or tofu — a major foodstuff among vegetarians. Soybeans are also used as a high-protein meat substitute or ground into flour. Soybeans supply about half the vegetable fats and oils used in this country.

Spinach

Common name: spinach
Botanical name: Spinacla oleracea
Origin: Asia

Varieties

Spinach: Skookum (41 days); Bloomsdale Long Standing (43 days); America (52 days). **New Zealand Spinach:** Only a few varieties of New Zealand spinach are available; use the variety available in your area.

Description

There are two kinds of spinach — the regular kind which is a hardy annual, and the less well-known New Zealand spinach, which is a tender annual and is not really spinach at all. Spinach, the regular kind, is a hardy annual with a rosette of dark green leaves. The leaves may be crinkled (savoy leaf) or flat. Spinach is related to beets and chard. The cartoon character Popeye made spinach famous with young children because he attributed his great strength to eating spinach — probably with some justification, because spinach has a very high iron content. Spinach was brought to America by the early colonists; the Chinese were using it in the sixth century, and the Spanish used it by the 11th century.

New Zealand spinach (Tetragonia expansa) comes — as the name indicates — from New Zealand. It's a tender annual with weak, spreading stems two to four feet long, sometimes longer, and it's covered with dark green leaves that are two to four inches long. New Zealand spinach is not really spinach at all, but when it's cooked the two are virtually indistinguishable. The leaves of New Zealand spinach are smaller and fuzzier than those of regular spinach, and it has the advantage of being heat-tolerant and able to produce all summer. Heat makes regular spinach bolt, or go to seed, very quickly.

Where and when to grow

Spinach is very hardy and can tolerate cold — in fact, it thrives in cold weather. Warm weather and long days, however, will make it bolt, or go to seed. Ideal spinach weather is 50° to 60°F. Spinach grows well in the winter in the South, and in early spring and late summer in the North. Plant it about four weeks before your area's average date of last frost.

New Zealand spinach likes long warm days. It grows best at 60° to 75°F and won't start growing until the soil warms up. It has a short season, however (55 to 65 days), so it can be grown successfully in most areas of the United States. Plant it on the average date of last frost for your area. Plant New Zealand spinach to supply you with a summer harvest long after it's too hot for regular spinach.

How to plant

Both spinach and New Zealand spinach are grown — like beets and chard — from seed clusters that each produce several seedlings. This means they must be thinned when the seedlings appear. Both types tolerate partial shade and require well-drained soil that's rich in organic matter. Spinach does not like acid soil. When you're preparing the soil for planting, work in a complete, well-balanced fertilizer at the rate of one pound per 100 square feet or 10 pounds per 1,000 square feet. Plant spinach seed clusters half an inch deep, two to four inches apart, in rows 12 to 14 inches apart, and when the seedlings are large enough to handle, thin them to leave the strongest seedling from each cluster.

For New Zealand spinach, plant the seed clusters half an inch deep, 12 inches apart, in rows 24 to 36 inches apart. Thin when the seedlings are large enough to handle, leaving the strongest seedling from each cluster to grow. Cut off the others with scissors at soil level.

Fertilizing and watering

Fertilize both types before planting and again at midseason, at the same rate as the rest of the garden. Detailed information on fertilizing is given in "Spadework: The Essential Soil" in Part 1.

Spinach does best when the soil is kept uniformly moist. Try not to splash muddy water on the leaves — it will make the spinach difficult to clean after harvesting. Mulch to avoid getting soil on the leaves. New Zealand spinach especially needs a regular supply of water to keep it producing lots of leaves.

Special handling

Spinach does not like competition from weeds. Cut weeds at ground level to avoid damaging the shallow roots of the spinach plants.

Pests

Aphids and, occasionally, leafminers may attack spinach. Pinch out aphid-infested foliage, and remove leaves on which leafminers have laid their eggs — look for the eggs on the undersides of the leaves. Control aphids chemically with Malathion or Diazinon; chemical controls are ineffective on leafminers once they're inside the leaf. New Zealand spinach has no serious pest problems and is a good crop for the organic gardener. Detailed information on pest control is given in "Keeping Your Garden Healthy" in Part 1.

Diseases

Spinach is susceptible to rust, but most varieties are rust-resistant. Planting disease-resistant varieties and maintaining the general cleanliness and health of your garden will help cut down the incidence of disease. If a plant does become infected, remove it before it can spread disease to healthy plants. New Zealand spinach has no serious disease problems. Detailed information on disease prevention is given in "Keeping Your Garden Healthy" in Part 1.

When and how to harvest

For spinach, time from planting to harvest is 40 to 52 days, and a 10-foot row should yield about five pounds of spinach leaves. To harvest, either pick the outside leaves periodically, or pull up the

Spinach seedling   *New Zealand spinach seedling*

Spinach

whole plant at one time. Be sure to wash spinach thoroughly to eliminate the grit that sometimes sticks to the crinkled leaves.

For New Zealand spinach, time from planting to harvest is 55 to 65 days, and a 10-foot row will produce about five to 10 pounds of leaves. To harvest keep cutting the tender tips off the ends of the stems; this will encourage new growth, and you can harvest until the first frost.

Container growing

Spinach grows very well in a container. Because spinach is so heat-sensitive, it is an advantage to be able to move the container into the shade on hot days. Also, because the soil in a container warms up faster than regular garden soil in spring, you can give your spinach a longer cool growing period by starting it in a container. Plant four of five seeds in an eight-inch pot. In larger containers, plant in wide rows.

Storing and preserving

Both types of spinach can be refrigerated for up to one week. They can also be frozen, canned, or dried. Spinach seeds can also be sprouted. Detailed information on storing and preserving is given in Part 4.

Serving suggestions

Both spinach and New Zealand spinach can be used in the same ways, and the following suggestions apply to both. Fresh spinach is wonderful in salads, and its dark green leaves add color and variety to lettuce. Add orange segments and almonds to a salad of fresh spinach, and toss

New Zealand spinach

in a sweet-sour dressing. Or add crumbled bacon, hard-cooked egg, and croutons. Add cubes of cheese to spinach, peppers, and sliced fresh mushrooms for an appealing lunch-time salad. Children who hate cooked spinach on principle often enjoy it raw. Cooked spinach is delicious creamed or in a soufflé, in crepes or topped with poached eggs. Try it with a horseradish sauce, or with melted butter and a little garlic. Spinach is an attractive ingredient for a quiche; add flaked salmon for a more substantial meal.

Q and A

Q: What causes small white cottony blotches on the upper surfaces of spinach leaves and corresponding yellow discoloration on the undersides?
A: The cause is white rust, a fungus disease that can be controlled on spinach by spraying with Bravo.
Q: What causes spinach to become stunted and yellow, with twisted leaves and stems?
A: The problem is a virus disease called spinach blight or spinach yellows, which is spread by aphids. Grow resistant varieties and control aphids immediately when they appear.
Q: What causes spinach to flower before it's ready to harvest?
A: Long days and warm summer temperatures force spinach to flower prematurely. Plant earlier in the spring or in fall, when days are shorter.

Sprouts

See Brussels sprout; see also "How to Sprout Vegetables," Part 3

Squash, summer

Common names: summer squash, crookneck, pattypan, straightneck, scallop, zucchini
Botanical name: Cucurbita species
Origin: American tropics

Varieties

Crookneck: Golden Summer Crookneck (53 days). **Scallop or pattypan:** Peter Pan (60 days); Scallopini hybrids (60 days); St. Patrick Green Tint (60 days). **Straightneck:** Early Prolific Straightneck (50 days). **Zucchini:** Gold Rush (60 days); Zucchini hybrids (60 days). These are only a few of the varieties available. Ask your Cooperative Extension Service for other specific recommendations for your area.

Summer squash

Description

The cucumber family, to which squashes belong, probably has the greatest diversity of shapes and sizes of any vegetable family except the cabbages. It's the genus Cucurbita and includes certain gourds and pumpkins, as well as squashes. Most are trailing or climbing plants with large yellow flowers (both male and female); the mature fruits have a thick skin and a definite seed cavity. "Summer squash," "winter squash," and "pumpkin" are not definite botanical names. "Pumpkin," which any child can tell you is a large vegetable used for jack-o'-lanterns and pies, is applied to long-keeping varieties of *C. moschata, C. pepo,* and a few varieties of *C. maxima.* Summer squashes are eaten when they are immature; winter squashes are eaten when mature.

Squashes are hard to confine. A bush-type zucchini will grow well in a tire planter if kept well-watered and fertilized; a vining squash can be trained up a fence. Summer squashes are weak-stemmed, tender annuals, with large, cucumberlike leaves and separate male and female flowers that appear on the same plant. Summer squash usually grows as a bush, rather than as a vine; the fruits have thin, tender skin and are generally eaten in the immature stage before the skin hardens. The most popular of the many kinds of summer squashes are crookneck, straightneck, scallop, and zucchini.

Where and when to grow

Squashes are warm-season crops and very sensitive to cold and frost. They like night temperatures of at least 60°F. Don't plant the seeds until the soil has warmed up in spring, about two to three weeks after the average date of last frost for your area. Direct-seeding is best for squashes, but if you're planting a variety that requires a longer growing season than your area can provide, use transplants from a reputable nursery or garden center, or grow your own. To grow your own transplants, start four to five weeks before your outdoor planting date, and use individual plantable containers to lessen the risk of shock when the seedlings are transplanted. Make sure that the plantable containers are large enough for the variety of squash you're planting.

How to plant

Squash varieties like well-worked soil with good drainage. They're heavy feeders, so the soil must be well fertilized. When you're preparing the soil for planting, work in a complete, well-balanced fertilizer at the rate of one pound per 100 square feet or 10 pounds per 1,000 square feet. Two to three weeks after your area's average date of last frost, when the soil is warm, plant squash in inverted hills. Make inverted hills by removing an inch of soil from an area about 12 inches across and using this soil to form a ring around the circle. Make the inverted hills three to four feet apart, and plant four or five seeds in each one. When the seedlings are large enough to handle, thin them to leave the two or three strongest young plants standing. Cut the thinned seedlings off at soil level with scissors; if you pull them out you'll disturb the roots of the remaining seedlings.

Fertilizing and watering

Fertilize before planting and again at midseason, at the same rate as the rest of the garden. Detailed information on fertilizing is given in "Spadework: The Essential Soil" in Part 1.

Keep the soil evenly moist; squashes need a lot of water in hot weather. The vines may wilt on hot days because the plant is using water faster than the roots can supply; if the vines are getting a regular supply of water, don't worry about the wilting — the plants will liven up as the day gets cooler. If squash vines are wilting first thing in the morning, water them immediately.

Special handling

If you grow squashes indoors, or in an area where there are no insects to pollinate the female flowers — your 51st-floor balcony, for instance — you may need to pollinate the flowers yourself. Take a soft-bristled brush and dust the inside of a male flower (the one without an immature fruit on the stem), then carefully dust the inside of the female flowers.

Pests

Squash bugs, squash borers, and cucumber beetles are the major pests that squash plants attract. They don't usually show up until you have a good harvest, so squash is still a good choice for the organic gardener. Squashes are prolific, so you can afford to lose a few of your crop to the bugs. Beetles can often be controlled by hand-picking or hosing them off

Zucchini

the plants. Control them chemically with carbaryl. To control borers, apply carbaryl to the crowns of the plants at weekly intervals. Do this as soon as there's any suspicion of damage — once the borers get inside the plants, chemical controls are ineffective. If a small hole in the stem tells you borers are already inside, you may still be able to save the plant. Slit the stem, remove the borers, and dispose of them. Then cover the area with soil to encourage root development at that point.

Squash seedling

Detailed information on pest control is given in "Keeping Your Garden Healthy" in Part 1.

Diseases

Squashes are susceptible to bacterial wilt, mosaic virus, and mildew. Planting disease-resistant varieties when they're available and maintaining the general cleanliness and health of your garden will help lessen the incidence of disease. When watering, try to keep water off the foliage, and don't handle the plants when they're wet — this can cause powdery mildew and spread disease. If a plant does become infected, remove and destroy it before it can spread disease to healthy plants. Detailed information on disease prevention is given in "Keeping Your Garden Healthy" in Part 1.

When and how to harvest

Time from planting to harvest depends on the variety, as does the yield you can expect. Harvest summer squashes when they're young — they taste delicious when they're small, and if you leave them on the plant too long they will suppress flowering and reduce your crop. Harvest summer squashes like the zucchini and crookneck varieties when they're six to eight inches long; harvest the round types when they're four to eight inches in diameter. Break the squashes from the plant, or use a knife that you clean after cutting each one; if the knife is not perfectly clean, it can spread disease to other plants.

Container growing

Bush-type summer squash can be grown satisfactorily in containers. Plant two or three seeds in the center of a 10-inch container and thin when the seedlings have two true leaves, leaving the strongest seedling to grow. Move the pot indoors on cool nights when frost is expected. This will both extend the growing season and increase yields.

Storing and preserving

Summer squashes can be stored in the refrigerator for up to one week; don't wash them until you're ready to use them. They can also be frozen, canned, pickled, or dried. Detailed information on storing and preserving is given in Part 4.

Serving suggestions

Summer squashes lend themselves to a good variety of culinary treatments. Sauté slices of summer squash with onions and tomatoes for a robust but delicately flavored side dish. Add sliced zucchini and mushrooms to a thick tomato sauce for spaghetti. Halve summer squashes and stuff with a meat or rice mixture, or bake them with butter and Parmesan cheese. Pan-fry slices of summer squash, or simmer them with fruit juice for a new flavor. Use the popular zucchini raw on a relish tray and among vegetables for a tempura, or slice it thinly in salads. Use the larger fruits for making zucchini bread.

Q and A

Q: What causes the first flowers to die without setting fruit?
A: Squash have separate male and female flowers. The first flowers you see are probably male flowers which do not produce fruit.
Q: Why do squash leaves turn a gray-white color late in the season?
A: The cause is powdery mildew, a fungus disease that can be controlled on squash by spraying with Kelthane. Proper spacing will also help reduce this problem.
Q: Is it true that watermelons, cantaloupes, cucumbers, or pumpkins can cross-pollinate squash and make them taste bitter?
A: No, the popular idea that cross-pollination will cause a bitter taste is completely false. Cross-pollination will not affect the taste, size, or shape of the current crop. However, seed saved from these fruits will produce plants affected by the cross-pollination.
Q: What causes squash plants to suddenly wilt and die just as they begin to produce?
A: The cause may be either vine borers or bacterial wilt. Bacterial wilt is spread to the plant by cucumber beetles, which must be controlled immediately as they appear. Controlling vine borers is more difficult; for more information see "Keeping Your Garden Healthy."
Q: Are squash flowers really edible?
A: Yes, they can be dipped in a batter and deep-fried. (Eat only the male flowers so as not to reduce the productivity of the plants.)
Q: What makes squash plants mottled yellow and stunted?
A: The probable cause is mosaic virus, which is spread by aphids. Control aphids, and remove affected plants.
Q: What causes squash fruit to rot away from the blossom end?
A: The cause is blossom end rot, which results from continuous fluctuations in soil moisture. To control blossom end rot, water regularly and use a mulch around the plants.

Squash, winter

Common names: acorn, banana, buttercup, butternut, cushaw, delicious, hubbard, spaghetti, Turk's turban
Botanical name: Cucurbita species
Origin: American tropics

Varieties

Not every type of winter squash has specific recommended varieties. These are some of the varieties available; ask your Cooperative Extension Service for other specific recommendations for your area.
Acorn: Ebony (80 days); Table Ace (85 days); Table King (bush-type, 85 days). **Butternut:** Waltham (95 days); Butterbush (small-fruited bush, 90 days); Hercules (95 days). **Delicious:** Golden Delicious (100 days). **Hubbard:** Kinred (100 days); Blue Hubbard (100 days).

Description

The cucumber family, to which squashes belong, probably has the greatest diversity of shapes and sizes of any vegetable family, except the cabbages. It's the genus Cucurbita, and includes certain gourds, and pumpkins, as well as squashes. Most are trailing or climbing plants with large yellow flowers (both male and female); the mature fruits have a thick skin and a definite seed cavity. "Summer squash," "winter squash," and "pumpkin" are not definite botanical names. "Pumpkin," which any child can tell you is a large vegetable used for jack-o'-lanterns and pies, is applied to long-keeping varieties of *C. moschata*, *C. pepo*, and a few varieties of *C. maxima*. Summer squashes are eaten when they are immature; winter squashes are eaten when mature. Squashes are hard to confine. A bush-type squash will grow well in a tire planter if kept well-watered and fertilized; a vining squash can be trained up a fence.

Gourds are a close relation of squash. They're warm-season vining crops that are grown primarily for decorative uses; you can also make cooking utensils out of them, and some of them can be eaten when immature. They have the same growing requirements as winter squash, and they're harvested in fall when the shells are hard and glossy. The importance of the gourd was recognized by Henri Christophe, who fought in the American Revolution under Lafayette and was a leader of the slave revolt in Haiti in the early 19th century. As Henry I, he used gourds as a medium of exchange, and Haitian currency is still called *gourde*, which is also Louisiana slang for a dollar.

Winter squashes are weak-stemmed, tender annuals, with large, cucumberlike leaves and separate male and female flowers that appear on the same plant. Most winter squashes grow as vines, although some modern varieties have been bred to have a more compact, bushy habit of growth. Winter squash varieties have hard skins when they're harvested and eaten. Popular types of winter squash include hubbard, butternut, acorn, delicious, banana, Turk's turban, buttercup, and cushaw. Spaghetti squash is technically a small pumpkin and is planted and cared for like pumpkins. Vining types of winter squash can be caged or trained to climb up a fence or trellis to save space. If you're growing a variety that will need support, set the support in place at the time of planting. If you do it later, you risk damaging the plants' roots.

Where and when to grow

Squashes are warm-season crops and very sensitive to cold and frost. They like night temperatures of at least 60°F. Don't plant the seeds until the soil has warmed up in spring, about two to three weeks after the average date of last frost for your area. Direct-seeding is best for squashes, but if you're planting a variety that requires a longer growing season than your area can provide, use transplants from a reputable nursery or garden center, or grow your own. To grow your own transplants, start four to five weeks before your outdoor planting date, and use

Winter squash

individual plantable containers to lessen the risk of shock when the seedlings are transplanted. Make sure that the plantable

Squash seedling

containers are large enough for the variety of squash you're planting.

How to plant

Squash varieties like well-worked soil with good drainage. They're heavy feeders, so the soil must be well-fertilized. When you're preparing the soil for planting, work in a complete, well-balanced fertilizer at the rate of one pound per 100 square feet or 10 pounds per 1,000 square feet. Two to three weeks after your area's average date of last frost, when the soil is warm, plant squash in inverted hills. Make inverted hills by removing an inch of soil from an area about 12 inches across and using this soil to form a ring around the circle. Make the inverted hills three to four feet apart, and plant four or

five seeds in each one. When the seedlings are large enough to handle, thin them to leave the two or three strongest young plants standing. Cut the thinned seedlings off at soil level with scissors; if you pull them out you'll disturb the roots of the remaining seedlings.

Fertilizing and watering

Fertilize before planting and again at midseason, at the same rate as the rest of the garden. Detailed information on fertilizing is given in "Spadework: The Essential Soil" in Part 1.

Keep the soil evenly moist; squashes need a lot of water in hot weather. The vines may wilt on hot days because the plant is using water faster than the roots can supply; if the vines are getting a regular supply of water, don't worry about the wilting — the plants will liven up as the day gets cooler. If squash vines are wilting first thing in the morning, water them immediately.

Special handling

If you grow squashes indoors or in an area where there are no insects to pollinate the female flowers — your 51st-floor balcony, for instance — you may need to pollinate the flowers yourself. Take a soft-bristled brush and

dust the inside of a male flower (the one without an immature fruit on the stem), then carefully dust the inside of the female flowers.

Pests

Squash bugs, squash borers, and cucumber beetles are the major pests that squash plants attract. They don't usually show up until you have a good harvest, so squash is still a good choice for the organic gardener. Squashes are prolific, so you can afford to lose a few of your crop to the bugs. Beetles can often be controlled by hand-picking or hosing them off the plants. Control them chemically with carbaryl. To control borers, apply carbaryl to the crowns of the plants at weekly intervals. Do this as soon as there's any suspicion of damage — once the borers get inside the plants, chemical controls are ineffective. If a small hole in the stem tells you borers are already inside, you may still be able to save the plant. Slit the stem, remove the borers, and dispose of them. Then cover the area with soil to encourage root development at that point. Detailed information on pest control is given in "Keeping Your Garden Healthy" in Part 1.

Diseases

Squashes are susceptible to bacterial wilt, mosaic virus, and mildew. Planting disease-resistant varieties when they're available and maintaining the general cleanliness and health of your garden will help lessen the incidence of disease. When watering, try to keep water off foliage, and don't handle the plants when they're wet — this

Female squash blossom

Male squash blossom

can cause powdery mildew and spread disease. If a plant does become infected, remove and destroy it before it can spread disease to healthy plants. Detailed information on disease prevention is given in "Keeping Your Garden Healthy" in Part 1.

When and how to harvest

Leave winter squashes on the vine until the skin is so hard that it cannot be dented with your thumbnail, but harvest before the first frost. Break it off the vine, or cut it off with a knife that you clean after cutting each one; if the knife is not perfectly clean, it can spread disease to other plants.

Container growing

Space-hungry squash plants get claustrophobia in containers. Give them the run of the yard.

Storing and preserving

Cure squashes in a dark, humid place for 10 days at 80° to 85°F; then store them at 50° to 60°F in a moderately dry, dark place for five to six months. Winter squashes can also be frozen or dried, and the seeds can be sprouted. Detailed information on storing and preserving is given in Part 4.

Serving suggestions

Winter squashes lend themselves to a good variety of culinary treatments and have the flexibility of adapting to both sweet and savory uses. Cut winter squashes into halves and bake them; serve them with honey or brown sugar and butter. Fill the halves with browned sausages, or mash the pulp and season well with salt and pepper. As a treat for the children, top mashed squash with marshmallow and brown it under the grill. Use the pulp of winter squash as a pie filling — it makes a pleasant change from pumpkin.

Q and A

Q: What causes the first flowers of winter squash to die without setting fruit?
A: Squash have separate male and female flowers. The first flowers you see are probably male flowers, which do not produce fruit.
Q: Why do squash leaves turn a gray-white color late in the season?
A: The cause is powdery mildew, a fungus disease that can be controlled on squash by spraying with Kelthane. Proper spacing will also help reduce this problem.
Q: Is it true that watermelons, cantaloupes, cucumbers, or pumpkins can cross-pollinate squash and make them taste bitter?
A: No, the popular idea that cross-pollination will cause a bitter taste is completely false. Cross-pollination will not affect the taste, size, or shape of the current crop. However, seed saved from these fruits will produce plants affected by the cross-pollination.
Q: What causes squash plants to suddenly wilt and die just as they begin to produce?
A: The cause may be either vine borers or bacterial wilt. Bacterial wilt is spread to the plant by cucumber beetles, which must be controlled immediately as they appear. Controlling vine borers is more difficult; for more information see "Keeping Your Garden Healthy."
Q: Are squash flowers really edible?
A: Yes, they can be dipped in a batter and deep-fried. (Eat only the male flowers so not to reduce the productivity of the plants.)
Q: What makes squash plants mottled yellow and stunted?
A: The probable cause is mosaic virus, which is spread by aphids. Control aphids, and remove affected plants.
Q: What causes squash fruit to rot away from the blossom end?
A: The cause is blossom end rot, which results from continuous fluctuations in soil moisture. To control blossom end rot, water regularly and use mulch around the plants.

Sweet corn,
See Corn

Sweet pepper,
See Pepper

Sweet potato

Common names: potato, sweet
potato, yam
Botanical name: Ipomoea
batatas
Origin: tropical America and
Caribbean

Varieties
Centennial (150 days); Goldrush
(140 days); Jasper (150 days).

Description

The sweet potato is a tender
vining or semi-erect perennial
plant related to the morning
glory. It has small white, pink, or
red-purple flowers and swollen,
fleshy tubers that range in color
from creamy-yellow to deep
red-orange. There are "dry" and
"moist" kinds of sweet
potatoes, which describes the
texture when they're eaten;
some dry varieties have a higher
moisture content than some
moist ones. The moist varieties are
often called yams, but the yam is
actually a different species that is
found in tropical countries.
Sweet potato vines are
ornamental, so this vegetable is
often grown as ground cover or in
planters or hanging baskets.
You can even grow a plant in water
in your kitchen — suspend the
sweet potato on toothpicks in a jar
of water, and watch it grow.

Where and when to grow

Sweet potatoes are extremely
sensitive to frost and need warm,
moist growing weather. They
have a long growing season —
about 150 days — and in areas
with a shorter growing season,
tend to produce small potatoes.
Don't try to hurry sweet potatoes;
plant them four weeks after the
average date of last frost for
your area, or when the soil is
thoroughly warm.

How to plant

Sweet potatoes are planted
from rooted sprouts, or slips,
taken from a mature tuber. To
grow your own slips, place several
sweet potato roots about an
inch apart in a hotbed and cover
with two inches of sand or light
soil. Add another inch of soil when
the shoots appear, keep the bed
at a temperature between 70° and
80°F, and don't let it dry out. In
about six weeks you will have
rooted slips that can be planted
in the garden. Refer to "Planning
Your Garden" for information
on making and using a hotbed. If

Sweet potato

you don't want to go to the trouble of growing your own, buy slips from a reputable garden center or supplier.

A good, sandy soil is best for sweet potatoes. Over-rich soil produces luxuriant vines but small tubers. The soil should be moderately fertile, rich in organic matter, and well-worked to ensure looseness. Remove all soil lumps, rocks, or other obstacles that might cause deformity of the tubers, and work in a complete, well-balanced fertilizer at the rate of one pound per 100 square feet or 10 pounds per 1,000 square feet. For good tuber production sweet potatoes must have full sun; in partial shade the vine will be handsome but not very productive. Set the slips on ridges made by mounding up the soil about eight inches high along rows three feet apart. Make the ridges about 12 inches wide, and set the slips at 12-inch intervals.

Fertilizing and watering

Fertilize before planting and again at midseason, at the same rate as the rest of the garden. Detailed information on fertilizing is given in "Spadework: The Essential Soil" in Part 1.

If the soil is too wet, the roots of sweet potatoes may rot; in well-worked, loose soil this should not be a problem. Although sweet potatoes will survive dry seasons, the yield is much higher if they get an inch of water every week until three or four weeks before harvesting. Do not water during the last three or four weeks.

Pests

Insects and diseases are not much of a problem in the North. In the South, sweet potato weevils and wireworms are common pests. The damage they do appears in the form of stunting or weakening of the plants. Both pests can be controlled by a soil drench of Diazinon. Detailed information on pest control is given in "Keeping Your Garden Healthy" in Part 1.

Diseases

Fungus diseases and root rot may attack sweet potatoes. Planting disease-resistant varieties and maintaining the general cleanliness and health of your garden will help cut down the incidence of disease. If a plant does become infected, remove it before it can spread disease to healthy plants. Detailed information on disease prevention is given in "Keeping Your Garden Healthy" in Part 1.

When and how to harvest

The tubers are damaged by freezing or cold soils, so dig up sweet potatoes early rather than late, before the first frost. Be careful when you dig — these potatoes are thin-skinned and bruise easily.

Container growing

Sweet potatoes do not grow very well in containers.

Storing and preserving

Cure sweet potatoes in crates in a dark, humid place for 10 days at 80° to 85°F; then store them at 55° to 60°F in a moderately moist place for four to six months. You can also freeze, can, or dry them.

Detailed information on storing and preserving is given in Part 4.

Serving suggestions

Sweet potatoes are very versatile; you can boil, steam, fry, or bake them, and they take well to either sweet or savory seasoning. Use pureed sweet potatoes in bread or cookies. Candy them, or stuff them and bake them in their skins. Include slices of raw sweet potato with the vegetables for a tempura. Cinnamon, cloves, nutmeg, and allspice all go well with sweet potatoes.

Tomato

Common names: tomato, love apple
Botanical name: Lycopersicon esculentum
Origin: tropical America

Varieties

The varieties of tomatoes available would fill a book. Choose them according to your growing season, whether you plan to stake or cage them or let them sprawl, and what you want to do with the fruit. Some varieties are specially suited to canning and preserving, others are better for salads. Beefsteak varieties are the large kind with rather irregularly shaped fruits. Patio varieties are suited to growing in containers or small spaces, and cherry tomatoes are the very small, round ones. Ask your

Cooperative Extension Service for specific recommendations for your area.

The following are just a few of the varieties available and are well-adapted for use in most areas. The initials V, F, and N refer to disease resistance; some varieties are resistant to verticillium (V), fusarium (F), and/or nematodes (N). If you've never had any problem with any of these, you can try any variety. If you have had difficulty growing tomatoes in the past you'll do better to stay with resistant varieties.

Varieties for general use: Better Boy (VFN, 72 days); Burpee's Big Boy (78 days); Early Girl (V, 62 days); Fantastic (70 days); Heinz 1350 (VF, 75 days); Terrific (VFN, 70 days); Wonder Boy (VFN, 80 days); Champion (VFNT, 62 days); Heartland (VFN, 68 days, suitable for containers). **Beefsteak varieties:** Beefmaster (VFN, 80 days); Pink Ponderosa (90 days). **Patio varieties:** Pixie (52 days); Toy Boy (68 days); Tiny Tim (55 days). **Cherry varieties:** Small Fry (VFN, 60 days); Tumblin' Tom (72 days). **Canning tomatoes:** Roma VF (VF, 75 days); Chico III (F, 75 days); Royal Chico (75 days).

Description

Tomatoes are tender perennials grown as annuals. They have weak stems and alternate lobed and toothed leaves that have a distinctive odor. The yellow flowers grow in clusters. Most tomatoes have vining growth habits and need a fair amount of space. Some are advertised as bush varieties that save space, but they'll still sprawl if you let them, and you may still have to stake or cage them. Depending on the variety, the

Tomato plants take up a lot of space if you let them sprawl. A strong stake supports the plant and keeps the fruit clean.

fruit varies in size and in color—red, yellow, orange, and white.

Tomatoes can be divided into two main groups, according to growth habits: determinate and indeterminate. On the determinate tomato (bush tomato), the plant stops growing when the end buds set fruit— usually at about three feet tall. It seldom needs staking. On the indeterminate tomato (vine tomato), the end buds do not set fruit; the plant can grow almost indefinitely if not stopped by

Tomatoes in a cage are easy to take care of.

frost. Most of the varieties that are staked or caged are indeterminate tomatoes.

Tomatoes are also classified by the size and shape of their fruit (currant, cherry, plum, pear, etc.), by their color (red, pink, orange, yellow, and cream), and by their use (eating, canning, pickling). When you're short on garden space, grow tomatoes in a large pot or container. Dwarf tomatoes can be grown in one cubic foot of soil, and standard tomatoes can be grown in two to three cubic feet of soil. The small-fruited tomatoes do very well in hanging baskets or window boxes. Plants growing in containers may easily exhaust the available moisture, in which case the leaves will wilt. However, the plants will revive when they're watered.

Vining tomatoes can be staked or caged to support the fruit, or can be left to sprawl naturally on the ground. Naturally sprawling tomatoes require less work than staked or caged plants; they are less likely to develop blossom end rot, and they produce more fruit per plant. In dry areas, sprawling on the ground protects the fruit from sunburn. But sprawling tomatoes are harder to cultivate than staked or caged plants, and they need mulching under the fruit to keep them clean to reduce disease. Staked tomatoes give you cleaner fruit, less loss from rot, and less loss from problems that occur in warm humid areas. They require less room for each individual plant. On the negative side, they produce less fruit per plant, are much more susceptible to blossom end rot, and are more work. Caged tomatoes require less work than staked tomatoes, but slightly more effort than doing

nothing. Caged tomatoes conserve space, keep the fruit cleaner, and are easier to work around in small areas.

Where and when to grow

Tomatoes grow best when the day temperature is between 65° and 85°F. They stop growing if it goes over 95°F, and if the night temperature goes above 85°F the fruit will not turn red. The flowers will not set fruit if the temperature goes below 55°F at night. Start tomatoes either from seed planted in the garden on the average date of last frost for your area or from transplants set in the garden two to three weeks after the average date of last frost, when the soil has warmed up.

How to plant

Tomatoes must have full sun and need warm, well-drained, fertile soil. Although they will produce earlier in sandy soils, they will have a larger yield in clay soils. When you're preparing the soil for planting, work in a complete, well-balanced fertilizer at the rate of one pound per 100 square feet or 10 pounds per 1,000 square feet. Plant seeds half an inch deep in rows 24 to 48 inches apart (depending on how large the variety will grow). When the seedlings are large enough to handle, thin them to 18 to 36 inches apart.

Set the plants out on a cloudy day or in the late afternoon. If the sun is very hot, protect the plants with hats made of newspapers. Disturb the roots as little as possible when transplanting. Plants should be gently slipped out of clay and plastic pots. If they're planted in peat pots, plant the entire container. Make sure the tops of the containers are below the soil's surface or the peat will act like a wick and evaporate the soil moisture. If the plants are growing together in a flat, cut the plants apart several days before transplanting them.

Put the plant in the soil so that it's deeper than it was growing before, up to the first leaves. If the stem is very long or spindly, lay it on a slant so that only the leaves are above soil level. The roots will grow from the submerged stem, making a sturdier plant. Set the transplants 18 to 36 inches apart in rows 24 to 48 inches apart, depending on the variety.

Fertilizing and watering

Fertilize before planting and again at midseason, at the same rate as the rest of the garden. Detailed information on fertilizing is given in "Spadework: The Essential Soil" in Part 1.

Tomatoes need lots of water, but they don't like to swim. Water thoroughly before the soil dries out. During the hot days of summer the leaves sometimes wilt because they use more water than their roots can supply. Don't worry about this if the tomatoes are receiving a regular supply of water. If the plants are wilting first thing in the morning, however, water them at once. Sometimes tomato plants curl their leaves as a survival tactic on hot days or during a long period of no rain. This is nothing to worry about; just water them.

Special handling

To stake tomatoes, use six-foot stakes (one by two inches) or reinforcing rods, and set the

Staked tomatoes should be pruned to grow one straight stem.

supports at the time of transplanting. Staked tomatoes should be pruned so that they grow one straight stem. Prune by removing any suckers that appear below the first fruiting cluster — the accompanying illustration shows how to prune a staked tomato plant. The suckers are not productive, so you don't affect the yield by pruning, and pruned plants have more energy to develop fruit. Let the suckers develop two leaves above the first fruiting cluster and then pinch out the rest of the sucker; the extra leaves will provide shade for the fruit. To cage tomatoes, use six-by-six-inch mesh concrete reinforcing wire. A five-foot width can be cut five feet long and bent into a cylinder by locking the ends. Remove the bottom strand and push the whole cage into the ground six inches deep around the tomato plant. If the area is windy, drive in a supporting stake. Or use commercially produced cages — you can now buy square cages that have the advantage of folding flat for storage.

Tomato plants will not set fruit in rainy or very humid weather. Sometimes a plant that has plenty of water and fertilizer produces a lot of foliage but no tomatoes. As a last resort, try giving the plant a shock by pruning it back and cutting down on water; it may start producing.

Pests

Aphids, tomato hornworms, cutworms, tomato fruitworms, and whiteflies are the major problems. Tomatoes are almost always attacked by some insect and may not be the best choice for the organic gardener; however, the fresh taste of a ripe tomato may overpower the logical choice. Collars placed around the plants at the time of transplanting help to discourage cutworms, and hornworms can be hand-picked off the plants. Aphids and whiteflies can be discouragd by hosing them off the plants or pinching out infested foliage. Malathion or Diazinon chemically control aphids and whiteflies. Detailed information on pest control is given in "Keeping Your Garden Healthy" in Part 1.

Diseases

Verticillium wilt, fusarium wilt, early blight, septoria leafspot, tobacco mosaic virus, and blossom end rot are diseases that can attack tomatoes. Planting disease-resistant varieties and maintaining the general cleanliness and health of your garden will help cut down the incidence of disease. Keep moisture off the leaves as far as possible, and avoid handling the plants when they're wet. If you smoke, wash your hands thoroughly before working with tomato plants to avoid spreading tobacco mosaic virus. If a plant does become infected with any disease, remove it before it can spread disease to healthy plants. Detailed information on disease prevention is given in "Keeping Your Garden Healthy" in Part 1.

When and how to harvest

Time from planting to harvest is 40 to 180 days from transplants, depending on variety, and several weeks longer from seed. Transplants usually produce earlier than tomatoes grown from seed. A 10-foot row will give you anywhere from 10 to 45 pounds of tomatoes. The color when ripe depends on the variety; ripe tomatoes should feel firm — neither squashy nor too hard. When the temperature is high during the day, the fruit may get soft but not red. Take hard green tomatoes inside at the end of the season to ripen; don't leave them on the plants.

Container growing

Smaller determinate varieties of tomatoes grow very well in containers. Because tomatoes are so sensitive to frost, you can extend the harvest by bringing the plants inside on cool nights when frost is expected. You can grow tomatoes indoors all winter long in cold northern areas. Grow a single plant in a 12- to 24-inch container depending on the expected full-grown size of the variety. Be sure to provide each plant with a support—a trellis, cage, or stake. Set the support when you plant the seed to avoid the risk of damaging the growing roots later on.

Storing and preserving

Ripened tomatoes will keep up to one week in the refrigerator. You can also freeze, can, or dry them whole, sliced, as juice, paste, relish, or pickles. Green tomatoes harvested before a frost can be held in a cool, moist place up to one month to ripen. Detailed information on storing and preserving is given in Part 4.

Serving suggestions

Fresh tomatoes from your garden are wonderful with very little embellishment — slice them, and dress them with a touch of olive oil and lemon juice and a pinch of basil; or eat them as fruit, with a little sugar. Alternate slices of fresh tomato and cooked potato for an interesting side dish — add olive oil and parsley. Add tomatoes to almost any salad, or serve them alone, sliced with bread and cheese for an instant lunch. Stuff raw tomatoes with tuna, chicken, or rice, or broil them plain or topped with breadcrumbs. Serve broiled tomatoes with bacon and sausages for a hearty breakfast. Use cherry tomatoes, whole or halved, in salads or on relish trays; the green kind are delicious fried or pickled. Cooked tomatoes, whole, pureed, or as a paste, are indispensable to all sorts of dishes — spaghetti sauces, stews, and casseroles — and fresh tomato sauce, seasoned with a little basil, is a delightfully simple topping for pasta. Make an unusual pie by alternating layers of sliced tomatoes with chopped chives and topping with pastry. Oregano, sage, tarragon, and thyme all go beautifully with tomatoes.

Q and A

Q: What causes tomato plants to suddenly wilt, turn brown, and die? This seems to happen in a week or less.
A: The cause is either verticillium or fusarium wilt, and the only way to control these diseases is to grow resistant varieties of tomatoes.
Q: What causes tomato flowers to die without setting fruit?
A: Night temperatures colder than 55°F or day temperatures above 95°F will keep the flowers from setting fruit.
Q: What causes tomato leaves to be distorted, twisted, and stunted?
A: The cause may be either mosaic virus or herbicide injury. An herbicide may travel half a mile from the site of application and still damage tomato plants. To control virus diseases, always buy healthy transplants from a reliable dealer. Remove affected plants from the garden as soon as possible to prevent spreading disease.
Q: What causes young tomatoes to start rotting on the bottom of the fruit?
A: The problem is blossom end rot, which is caused by continuous fluctuations in soil moisture. To control blossom end rot, water regularly and use a mulch around the plants.
Q: Is it better to cage or stake tomato plants?
A: Whether you cage, stake, or simply let your tomatoes trail on the ground is a matter of

preference. Caging is probably the most satisfactory of the three methods in terms of ease and convenience.

Turnip

Common name: turnip
Botanical name: Brassica rapa
Origin: northeastern Europe, Siberia

Varieties

Shogin (30 days); Foliage Turnip (30 days); Tokyo Cross (35 days); Tokyo Market (35 days); Just Right (40 days); Purple Top White Globe (57 days).

Description

The turnip, a hardy biennial grown as an annual, sports a rosette of hairy, bright green leaves growing from a root—which is not really a root, but a swelling at the base of the stem. The turnip is more commonly grown for use as a root vegetable, but can also be grown for the leaves, which are used as greens. Turnips originated in the Mediterranean in prehistoric times. The rutabaga, a younger cousin, is believed to have come about in the Middle Ages from a cross between a turnip and a cabbage. Englishmen have been known to refer to each other as "turniphead"; this is not a compliment, as turnips are often considered to be rather dull. In fact, they're quite versatile.

Where and when to grow

Turnips are a cool-weather crop, grown in the fall, winter, and spring in the South and in the spring and fall in the North. They don't transplant well, so grow them from seed, and plant them two to three weeks before the average date of last frost for your area.

How to plant

Turnips tolerate partial shade and need soil that's high in organic matter and well-drained but able to hold moisture. Too much nitrogen in the soil encourages the plant to produce leaves and a seed stalk rather than a good-sized root, so when you're preparing the soil for planting, work in a low-nitrogen (5-10-10) fertilizer at the rate of one pound per 100 square feet or 10 pounds per 1,000 square feet. Plant seeds half an inch deep in rows or wide rows 12 to 24 inches apart. When the seedlings are large enough to handle, thin them to three or four inches apart; if you're growing turnips primarily for greens, thin to two to three inches apart.

Fertilizing and watering

Fertilize before planting and again at midseason, at the same rate as the rest of the garden. Detailed information on fertilizing is given in "Spadework: The Essential Soil" in Part 1. Water is important to keep turnips growing as fast as possible, so water regularly, before the soil dries out. If growth is slow the root gets very strong-flavored and woody, and the plant will often send up a seed stalk.

Turnip seedling

Pests

Aphids and flea beetles attack turnips, and the flea beetles make this a difficult crop for the organic gardener. Control aphids by pinching out infested foliage and hosing large populations off the plants; control them chemically with Malathion or Diazinon. Carbaryl will control flea beetles. Detailed information on pest control is given in "Keeping Your Garden Healthy" in Part 1.

Diseases

Time from planting to harvest is 30 to 60 days, and a 10-foot row of turnips should give you five pounds of leaves and 10 pounds of roots. You can eat the tops as you thin the seedlings, or when the root is ready to be pulled. Harvest the roots when they're one to two inches across.

Container growing

Turnips do not produce satisfactorily when grown in a container.

Storing and preserving

Store turnip greens in the refrigerator up to one week, or in a cold, moist place for two to three weeks. Store the roots in a cold, moist place for four to five months; do not refrigerate. You can also freeze both the roots

Turnip

and the greens, and can or dry the greens; use the recipes for greens. Turnip seeds can also be sprouted. Detailed information on storing and preserving is given in Part 4.

Serving suggestions

When small, turnips make a great substitute for radishes. They're also easier to carve than radishes if you feel the urge to sculpture roses or daisies for decorative garnishes. Sliced raw turnips give a nice crunch to salads. Steam or boil turnips and serve them with butter or cream—add a little sugar to the cooking water to improve the flavor. They're very good in soups or stews or cooked around a roast. You can use the tops in a salad or cooked as greens.

Q and A

Q: Why do turnip leaves suddenly become riddled with small holes?
A: The holes are made by flea beetles, which can be controlled with Sevin.
Q: Why do my turnips have plenty of leaves but small roots?
A: Overcrowding or heavy clay soil can cause this problem.
Q: What causes small white cottony blotches on the upper surfaces of the leaves and corresponding yellow discoloration on the undersides?
A: The cause is white rust, a fungus disease that seldom causes enough damage to turnips to require control.

Watercress,

See Cress

Watermelon

Common name: watermelon
Botanical name: Citrullus vulgaris
Origin: tropical Africa

Varieties

The traditional watermelon takes up too much space to be practical in a small home garden, but new smaller watermelon varieties are now available and are more suited to a limited garden patch. **Small watermelons:** Petite Sweet (75 days); New Hampshire Midget (77 days); Sugar Baby (79 days). **Standard-size watermelons:** Charleston Gray (90 days); Crimson Sweet (90 days). Ask your Cooperative Extension Service for specific recommendations for your area.

Description

The watermelon is a spreading, tender annual vine related to the cucumber. It produces round, oval, or oblong fruits that can weigh five to 100 pounds and have pink, red, yellow, or greyish-white flesh. Male and female flowers appear on the same vine. Watermelon was Dr. Livingston's favorite African fruit. Although smaller varieties are now available, you still need to give watermelons a lot of headroom. They're space-consuming, and they take a lot of nutrients from the soil, so they're still not the ideal crop for some gardens.

When and where to grow

Watermelons require warm soil and warm days; night temperatures below 50°F will cause the flavor of the fruit to deteriorate. In warm areas, direct-seed watermelons two to three weeks after the average date of last frost. In cold areas, start from transplants grown in peat pots; watermelons don't transplant too easily.

How to plant

Watermelons must have full sun, and prefer well-drained soil that holds moisture well. When you're preparing the soil for planting, work in a complete, well-balanced fertilizer at the rate of one pound per 100 square feet or 10 pounds per 1,000 square feet. Grow watermelons in inverted hills, made by removing an inch of soil from a circle 12 inches across and using the soil to form a rim around the circle. Space the hills six feet apart, and plant four to five seeds in each hill. When the seedlings have developed three or four true leaves, thin them to leave the strongest one or two seedlings in each hill. Cut the thinned seedlings with scissors at soil level to avoid damaging the survivors' root systems. Where cucumber beetles, other insects, or weather are a problem, wait a bit before making the final selection. If you're using transplants, put two or three in each hill.

Fertilizing and watering

Fertilize before planting and again at midseason, at the same rate as the rest of the garden. Detailed information on fertilizing is given in "Spadework: The Essential Soil" in Part 1.

Watermelons are 95 percent water, so make sure they have enough to keep them growing well. Do not let the soil dry out, and use a mulch to keep the soil moisture even.

Special handling

As the watermelons develop, provide a support for the fruit. If they're growing on a fence or trellis, support the fruit with a net. If the vines are trailing on the ground, put a board under the fruit to keep it off the ground. Mulch helps keep the fruit clean as well as regulating soil moisture.

Pests

Cucumber beetles may visit your watermelon vines. They don't cause much feeding damage, but they carry cucumber bacterial wilt; hand-pick them off the

Watermelon seedling

vines as soon as they appear. Watermelons are a good crop for the organic gardener who has lots of space. Detailed information on pest control are given in "Keeping Your Garden Healthy" in Part 1.

Diseases

Watermelons are susceptible to anthracnose and wilt. Planting disease-resistant varieties when they're available and maintaining the general cleanliness and health of your garden will help cut down

the incidence of disease. Don't handle the vines when they're wet. If a plant does become infected, remove it before it can spread disease to healthy plants. Detailed information on disease prevention is given in "Keeping Your Garden Healthy" in Part 1.

When and how to harvest

If one watermelon gets an early start on a vine it can suppress all further activity until it matures. Some people suggest pinching out this first watermelon to encourage more melons, but this is a gamble because, sometimes no more watermelons will set. It's easier to judge when a watermelon is ripe than it is with some other types of melon; a watermelon is ready to harvest when the vine's tendrils begin to turn brown and die off. A ripe watermelon will also sound dull and hollow when you rap it with your knuckles.

Watermelon

Container growing

Space-hungry watermelons are not a practical proposition for the container gardener.

Storing and preserving

A watermelon will store for up to one week in the refrigerator — it takes about 12 hours to chill a large one thoroughly before you eat it. If you have a lot of melons, store them in a cool, moderately moist place for two to three weeks. You can freeze the flesh of the watermelon and make pickles with the rind.

Serving suggestions

Slices of fresh watermelon make a wonderful summer cooler. Scoop out the flesh with a melon baller and add to other types of melon for a cool fruit salad — pile the fruit into a muskmelon half. For a great party dish, serve a big fruit salad in the scooped out half-shell of the watermelon—or carve the shell into a basket. Make pickles with the rind.

Q and A

Q: What causes watermelon fruit to rot away from the blossom end?
A: This problem is blossom end rot, which is caused by continuous fluctuations in soil moisture. To control blossom end rot, water regularly and use a mulch around the plants.
Q: Is it true that cantaloupes, cucumbers, squash or pumpkins can cross-pollinate with watermelons and make them taste bitter?
A: No, the popular idea that cross-pollination causes a bitter taste is completely false. Cross-pollination will not affect the taste, size, or shape of the current crop. However, seed saved from these fruits will produce plants affected by the cross-pollination.

Q: What causes the first watermelon flowers to die without setting fruit?
A: Watermelons have separate male and female flowers. The first flowers are probably the male flower, which do not produce fruit.
Q: Why do some watermelon plants suddenly wilt and die just as they begin to produce fruit?
A: The cause is bacterial wilt, which is spread to the plants by cucumber beetles. The beetles must be controlled immediately as they appear.

Yam,
See Sweet potato

Zucchini,
See Squash, summer

Counting the Calories in Vegetables

Food	Portion	Calories
ARTICHOKES		
Cooked	1 medium	86.5
Hearts, frozen	3 oz	20
ASPARAGUS		
Raw	1 spear	2.5
Frozen	4 spears	15
Canned	4 spears	15

Food	Portion	Calories
BEANS		
Lima		
Cooked	1 cup	189
Frozen	1 cup	163
Canned	1 cup	176
Snap		
Cooked	1 cup	31
Frozen	3 oz	22

Food	Portion	Calories
BEETS		
Cooked	1 cup	54
Canned	1 cup	109
Sliced	1 cup	479
Harvard	1 cup	140
Pickled	1 cup	150
Beet greens, cooked	1 cup	26
BROCCOLI		
Raw	1 stalk	48
Frozen		
Cooked	1 cup	48
With cheese sauce	3.3 oz	198
With hollandaise sauce	3.3 oz	100
BRUSSELS SPROUTS		
Raw	1 medium	9
Frozen		
Cooked	1 cup	51
In butter sauce	3.5 oz	56
CABBAGE		
Green		
Raw	1 cup	36
Cooked	1 cup	29
Red, raw	1 cup	22
CARROTS		
Raw	1 carrot	30
Frozen		
Cut or whole	3.3 oz	33
In butter sauce	3.3 oz	75
Canned	1 cup	69
CAULIFLOWER		
Raw	1 cup	27
Cooked	1 cup	28
Frozen		
Cooked	1 cup	32
With cheese sauce	3 oz	109

Food	Portion	Calories
CELERY		
Raw	1 stalk	7
CHARD		
Cooked	1 cup	26
COLLARDS		
Cooked	1 cup	63
Frozen	3 oz	51
CORN		
Cooked	1 ear	70
Frozen	1 cup	135
Canned		
Creamed style	1 cup	210
CUCUMBER		
Raw	7 slices	4
DANDELION GREENS		
Cooked	1 cup	35
EGGPLANT		
Cooked	1 cup	38
ENDIVE		
Raw	1 cup	10
KALE		
Cooked	1 cup	43
Frozen	3 oz	40
KOHLRABI		
Cooked	1 cup	40
LETTUCE		
Iceburg	1 cup	8

Vegetables

Food	Portion	Calories
MUSHROOMS		
Raw	1 cup	20
Canned	2 oz	13
MUSTARD GREENS		
Raw	1 cup	45
Cooked	1 cup	30
Frozen	3.3 oz	20
OKRA		
Cooked	10 pods	31
ONIONS		
Mature, dry	1 cup	66
Green	2 medium	14
PARSLEY		
Raw	1 tbsp	2
PARSNIPS		
Cooked	1 cup	139
PEAS		
Cooked	1 cup	114
Frozen	3 oz	73
In butter sauce	3.5 oz	79
Canned	1 cup	164
PEPPERS		
Hot, raw	1 pod	31
Sweet, raw or cooked	1 pod	36
POTATOES		
Baked or boiled	1 medium	145
Frozen		
French fried	10 strips	170
Canned	1 cup	90

Food	Portion	Calories
PUMPKIN		
Canned	1 cup	81
RADISH		
Raw	4 small	6
RUTABAGA		
Cooked	1 cup	84
SHALLOT		
Raw	1 tbsp	7
SPINACH		
Raw	1 cup	14
Cooked	1 cup	41
Frozen		
Regular	3.3 oz	22
Creamed	3 oz	63
Canned	1 cup	44
SQUASH		
Summer		
Cooked	1 cup	29
Canned	1 cup	18
Winter		
Baked, mashed	1 cup	113
Frozen	1 cup	91
SWEET POTATOES		
Baked or boiled in skin	1 potato	20
Canned	1 potato	45
Candied	1 potato	143
Yam, raw	1 cup	253
TOMATOES		
Raw	1 tomato	27
Cooked	1 cup	63
Canned		
Whole	1 cup	51
Stewed	1 cup	70
Juice	1 cup	46

Herbs

**Add fragrance to your garden
and flavor to your food.
Outdoors or in, easy-to-grow herbs
are a delight in any garden.**

Herbs are quite possibly the easiest of all horticultural crops to grow. Given poor soil, poor light, and general neglect, most of them actually thrive. In fact, careful fertilizing and watering—which are essential to the growth of most plants—often cause herbs to lose some of their flavor: the young, succulent growth encouraged by over-maintenance has fewer of the oils which give herbs their distinctive flavors.

PLANNING YOUR HERB GARDEN

The easiest way to plan your herb garden is to go to your kitchen cabinet and make a list of the herbs you use most. Clearly, those are the ones you should plant. The ideal location for a herb garden is right outside your door, so that you can practically reach out the kitchen door and pick the herbs you need for the dish you are preparing. If such an ideal location isn't available, you can plant herbs in a flower border or in your vegetable garden. Most herbs don't need much room to produce enough for average family needs. Some, like the mints, are so easy to grow that you must contain them or they'll take over the garden.

When making your plan, pay attention to the growth patterns of the herbs you have chosen. Perennials continue to grow year after year without re-seeding, and these herbs need room to spread. They should also be planted where they won't be

disturbed. The middle of your garden where you rototill every year is not the place to plant perennial herbs. They might do well, however, in borders or flower beds where you can cultivate around them without disturbing the plants themselves.

Annual herbs complete their life cycle in a single growing season. Some will re-seed themselves, but this should not be relied upon as a sure way of replenishing the crop for next year. Annuals can be planted anywhere—if you make a mistake or want to change your garden plan you can start over next year.

There are a few biennial herbs which grow vegetatively for one season, flower in the second season, and then die. Caraway and parsley are the only biennial herbs you are likely to encounter. With caraway, you want to harvest the seeds that appear the second year, so position it where it will be undisturbed for two seasons. Parsley for table use should be considered an annual; after it flowers the leaves get very bitter. Plan to replant your parsley bed every year.

PLANTING HERBS

Annual herbs should be planted as early as possible so that they can make full use of the growing season and produce flavorful foliage. Most perennial herbs can be planted at any time, but will suffer the least transplant shock if they are planted in cool, moist spring or fall weather. The exception to this rule is garlic, which must be planted in fall. Parsley and caraway should be planted in early spring.

With the exception of tarragon, the herbs listed in these pages can be grown from seed, transplants, or root or stem cuttings. True French tarragon can be grown only from root cuttings. Tarragon grown from seed is Russian tarragon and has an inferior flavor.

CARING FOR HERBS

The care of most herbs is amazingly simple, and many of them thrive on benign neglect. Most herbs have no, or few, disease or pest problems, and those few problems that do occur can usually be controlled organically without the use of chemical sprays. The few insects that attack herbs can be handpicked off the plants, and rare disease problems can be prevented by correct watering. Most herbs need to be watered only occasionally once they are established, and over watering is more of a problem than the under-watering. If it is necessary to water herbs, water deeply so that the roots are encouraged to grow deep in the soil.

GROWING HERBS INDOORS

Most herbs are so flexible in their growing requirements that they can be raised easily indoors.

Annual herbs can be planted in a container a month before the first frost is expected in your locality. This will ensure a continuous fresh harvest. Perennial herbs that are grown for their foliage adapt well to indoor conditions, but will usually survive only for a year. So if you are growing perennial herbs indoors, treat them as annuals.

Indoor containers for herbs should be large enough to accommodate the mature plant without crowding. The diameter of the container should be half the size of the mature height of the plant (the height to which each plant can be expected to grow is listed in the individual plant profiles). For instance, a herb you expect to grow to 12 inches in height should be planted in a pot with a six-inch diameter. The container should have drainage holes in the bottom; do not use glass or ceramic containers that do not have drainage holes.

When growing herbs indoors, use well-drained, sterilized soil. A soil mix that contains approximately one third perlite drains well. Sterilization prevents insect, weed, and disease problems. If you're using a store-bought mix, check the packet to make sure the mix is sterilized. If you are using garden soil, bake it at 180°F for 30 minutes on your outdoor barbecue grill. Theoretically you can bake it indoors, but the smell is terrible. For more information on soil and soil mixes see the sections on "Spadework: The Essential Soil" and "Container and Small-Space Gardening."

Herbs grown outdoors can tolerate partial shade, but indoors they should be given as much sun as possible. A south-facing window will provide the maximum amount of sunlight; if you don't have a south-facing window, try a bright east or west window. Indoor herbs need six to 12 hours of sunlight a day. If there's no area of your home that's sufficiently well lit to meet these criteria, you can supplement the available light by artificial means. Any type of light bulb can be used, but cool white bulbs may be the best because they generate light but not much heat. Lights should be positioned six to eight inches from the tops of the plants.

Indoor herbs prefer rather cool temperatures. Optimum temperatures are 65° to 70°F during the day and 55° to 60° at night. Warmer temperatures tend to produce weak, spindly plants.

Overwatering can cause severe damage to indoor herbs or even kill them. Temperature, humidity, soil quality, and the rate at which the plant is growing all determine how often you will need to water. The only accurate way to tell if an herb plant needs water is to push your finger two or three inches into the soil; if the soil at this depth is dry to the touch, the plant needs water. Water heavily so that the water comes out of the drainage holes in the bottom of the pot; this will help remove excess salts from the soil.

More detailed growing information is given in the following herb profiles.

Anise

Common name: anise
Botanical name: Pimpinella anisum
Origin: Europe

Varieties
Few varieties are available; grow the variety available in your area.

Description

Anise is a slow-growing annual with low, spreading, bushy plants that grow 12 to 14 inches tall and almost as wide. The flowers are yellowish-white in umbrella-shaped clusters and appear about 10 weeks after planting. The licorice-flavored seeds are most commonly used in baking, candy, or to flavor liquors. Anise used to be credited with warding off the evil eye; the Romans flavored their cakes with it on special occasions. Anise was one of the first European herbs to become popular in America.

Where and when to grow

Anise needs a long growing season — at least 120 days free of frost. It also prefers a moderate and uniform rainfall, especially at harvest time.

How to plant

Anise prefers a well-drained fertile soil. Work a complete, well-balanced fertilizer into the soil before planting at the rate of one pound per 100 square feet. Give anise a location in full sun, and plant it from seed in early spring, two weeks after the average date of last frost. Plant the seeds a quarter inch deep in rows 18 to 24 inches apart, and when the seedlings are six weeks old, thin them to six to 12 inches apart.

Fertilizing and watering

Fertilize before planting and again at midseason, at the same rate as the rest of the garden. Detailed information on fertilizing is given in "Spadework: The Essential Soil" in Part 1.

Anise prefers uniform moisture especially at or just before harvesting. Alternate rainy and dry periods when the seed is near maturity can cause it to turn brown, reducing quality and yield.

Pests

Anise has no serious pest problems.

Anise

Diseases

Anise has no serious disease problems.

When and how to harvest

Harvest the anise seed heads approximately 100 days after planting, while they are still green and immature. Be sure to harvest before the first frost.

Container growing

Anise makes an attractive container plant. It grows and yields well in a container.

Storing and preserving

The dry seeds can be stored for months in airtight containers. Detailed information on storing and preserving is given in Part 4.

Serving suggestions

Add anise to bouillon for fish or veal stews. Sprinkle anise seeds on an apple crisp. Aniseed balls are an old-fashioned favorite children's candy.

Basil

Common name: basil
Botanical names: Ocimum basilicum, Ocimum crispum, Ocimum minimum
Origin: India, Central America

Varieties
Citriodorum (lemon-scented); Dark Opal (purple-red leaves and rose-colored flowers); Minimum (dwarf variety). Or grow the variety available in your area.

Description

These tender annuals grow one to 2½ feet tall, with square stems and opposite leaves. Basil may have either green or purple-red soft-textured leaves, and spikes of small whitish or lavender flowers. In India basil is considered a holy herb. In Italy it is a love gift, and in Romania an engagement token. In Greece the connotation is less romantic; there basil is a symbol of death and hatred. Basil has the distinction of being fragrant at all stages of its development.

Where and when to grow

Like most herbs, basil can be grown quite easily anywhere in the United States. It prefers a

Basil seedling

climate that does not run to extremes of temperatures, but it tolerates heat better than cold. The first fall frost will kill the plant. It's grown from seed or transplants, and you can plant either in spring, a week or two after your area's average date of last frost.

How to plant

Basil needs a well-drained soil that's high in organic matter. It does well in soil that many other plants wouldn't tolerate; and too-fertile soil is actually a disadvantage, because it encourages lush foliage but a low oil content, which affects the aromatic quality of the herb. If you grow from seed, sow the seed a quarter inch deep in rows 18 to 24 inches apart. When the seedlings are growing strongly, thin them to stand four to six inches apart. A sunny spot is best, but basil will tolerate light shade. Basil seeds itself and will often produce good plants if the soil is not disturbed too much in the spring. Using transplants in the spring will mean you can harvest your basil sooner. You can also buy a healthy plant from a nursery or farmers' market stand and plant that. If you want to grow basil indoors, put it in a sunny window or under lights.

Fertilizing and watering

Do not fertilize basil; overfertilizing is a disadvantage to most aromatic herbs. If the soil is very acid, sweeten it with some lime. Otherwise, let it be. Detailed information on fertilizing is given in "Spadework: The Essential Soil" in Part 1.

If basil needs water the leaves will wilt — give it enough water to prevent this.

Special handling

Pinch off the terminal shoots to encourage branching and slow down flower production. If you don't, the plants will get tall and leggy.

Pests

Basil has no serious pest problems.

Diseases

Basil has no serious disease problems.

When and how to harvest

Pick the basil as you need it by cutting a few inches off the top. This will encourage the plant to become bushy instead of going to flower.

Container growing

Basil makes a charming houseplant—put it in a sunny window.

Storing and preserving

Store the crushed dry leaves in an airtight container. You can also freeze the leaves. Detailed information on storing and preserving is given in Part 4.

Serving suggestions

Fresh basil gives a wonderful flavor to sliced tomatoes dressed with a little oil and lemon juice, and it's good in other salads, too. Fresh basil is the essential ingredient in pesto, a luxuriously aromatic pasta dish. You can also use the leaves — fresh or dried — with fish, game and meat dishes, on eggs, and in stews and sauces. Try herbed butter with basil, or make basil vinegar.

Borage

Common name: borage
Botanical name: Borago officinalis
Origin: Europe

Basil

Varieties

Few varieties are available; grow the variety available in your area.

Description

Borage is a tender annual that grows two to three feet tall. The stems and leaves are grey-green and covered with velvety hair, and the light blue flowers grow in drooping clusters. When borage is in flower it's a striking plant, especially if you set it high — on a wall, for instance — because the nodding flowers are seen to best advantage from below. The flowers are used to add color to potpourri. Borage, like thyme, is supposed to give courage. An old English jingle goes: "I, Borage, Bring Courage."

Where and when to grow

Borage will grow almost anywhere in the United States. It tolerates a wide range of temperatures but will not survive a hard frost. Because of its striking coloring and unusual flowers, it makes an attractive indoor plant.

How to plant

Borage prefers well-drained sandy soil in full sun. When you're preparing the soil, dig in a complete, well-balanced fertilizer at the rate of one pound per 100 square feet. Plant borage from seed in early spring after the average date of last frost. Plant the seeds (which germinate readily) a quarter inch deep in rows 18 to 24 inches apart, and when the plants are six to eight inches tall, thin them to stand 12 inches apart.

Fertilizing and watering

Do not fertilize borage again at midseason. Detailed information on fertilizing is given in "Spadework: The Essential Soil" in Part 1.

Let borage dry out between waterings.

Pests

Borage has no serious pest problems. Like most herbs, it's a good choice for the organic garden.

Diseases

Borage has no serious disease problems.

When and how to harvest

Harvest young leaves as needed throughout the growing season, and harvest the entire plant in the fall before frost.

Container growing

Borage makes an attractive container plant. It grows and yields well in a container.

Borage

Storing and preserving

Refrigerate the stems and leaves for fresh use, or freeze them. Detailed information on storing and preserving is given in Part 4.

Serving suggestions

Fresh borage leaves have a cucumberlike taste and can be used in salads, soups, and stews, or cooked like spinach. You can peel the stems and use them in salads. Borage flowers are sometimes candied for use as a garnish in fruit drinks.

Caraway

Common name: caraway
Botanical name: Carum carvi
Origin: Europe

Varieties
Few varieties are available; grow the variety available in your area.

Description

Caraway is a biennial grown for its leaves and seeds. It has fine feathery leaves that grow in a short rosette; the second year the plant produces white, dill-like flowers on fine, two-foot flower stalks. The finely cut foliage makes the caraway plant a charming foil to flowers in a garden border.

When and where to grow

If you only want the foliage, you can grow caraway anywhere in the United States. In some colder areas, however, it may need winter protection in order to produce flowers and seeds in the second year.

How to plant

Caraway prefers full sun but will tolerate partial shade; it grows best in a well-drained sandy soil. When you're preparing the soil, dig in a complete, well-balanced fertilizer at the rate of one pound per 100 square feet. Caraway has a taproot, which makes it difficult to transplant, so grow it from seed sown in early spring in the South or in fall in cooler northern areas. Plant the seeds a quarter inch deep in rows 18 to 24 inches apart, and thin the plants to stand 12 to 18 inches apart.

Caraway will reseed itself in most areas, assuring you a constant supply.

Fertilizing and watering

Fertilize before planting and again at midseason, at the same rate as the rest of the garden. The second year do not fertilize at midseason. Detailed information on fertilizing is given in "Spadework: The Essential Soil" in Part 1.

Allow caraway plants to dry out between waterings.

Pests

Caraway is a member of the parsley family, so you may encounter a parsley caterpillar. Handpick it off the plant.

Caraway

Diseases

Caraway has no serious disease problems.

When and how to harvest

Harvest caraway leaves as needed throughout the growing season for use in soups and salads. Harvest the seeds in the fall of the second growing season. Harvest when they dry out and turn brown or before the first frost.

Container growing

Caraway does not grow very well in a container.

Storage and preserving

It's best to use caraway leaves fresh, but they can be stored in the refrigerator for a few weeks. The seeds can be stored for months in a sealed jar. Detailed information on storing and preserving is given in Part 4.

Serving suggestions

Caraway seeds have all kinds of uses—in breads, cakes, and cookies; in sauerkraut; or to flavor cheeses. They add a nice crunch, as well as a distinctive flavor.

Chervil

Common name: chervil
Botanical name: Anthriscus cerefolium
Origin: Europe and Asia

Varieties
Few varieties are available; grow the variety available in your area.

Description

Chervil is a hardy annual of the parsley family, and its lacy, bright green leaves resemble those of parsley, although its flavor is more subtle. The plant grows one to two feet tall, and the tiny white flowers appear in umbels— umbrellalike clusters. In folk medicine, chervil was soaked in vinegar and the liquid administered as a cure for hiccups.

Where and when to grow

Chervil prefers a cool climate, but will grow anywhere in the United States. Plant it early in spring.

How to plant

Chervil grows best in a moist and partially shaded environment. When you're preparing the soil, dig in a complete, well-balanced fertilizer at the rate of one pound per 100 square feet. In spring, about the average date of last frost, plant chervil seeds half an inch deep in rows 18 to 24 inches apart. When the plants are six weeks old, thin them to stand three to four inches apart. To encourage thicker foliage, cut the flower stems before they bloom.

Chervil

Fertilizing and watering

Fertilize before planting and again at midseason, at the same rate as the rest of the garden. Detailed information on fertilizing is given in "Spadework: The Essential Soil" in Part 1.

For best growth, keep chervil moist.

Pests

Chervil is a member of the parsley family, so you may encounter an occasional parsley caterpillar. Hand-pick it off the plant.

Diseases

Chervil has no serious disease problems.

When and how to harvest

Pick fresh leaves as you need them during the growing season. In the fall before a hard frost, harvest all the stems and leaves and dry them rapidly in a shady area.

Container growing

Chervil is a good addition to your container garden. It grows and produces well in a container.

Storing and preserving

Store crushed dry leaves in a tightly sealed container. You can also freeze the leaves. Detailed information on storing and preserving is given in Part 4.

Serving suggestions

Add fresh chervil leaves to salads; it also makes an attractive alternative to parsley as a garnish. Chervil is an especially appropriate seasoning for fish, chicken, and egg dishes.

Chives

Common name: chives
Botanical name: Allium schoenoprasum
Origin: Europe

Varieties

Few varieties are available; grow the variety available in your area.

Description

This hardy perennial relative of the onion has tufts of thin hollow leaves six to 10 inches long. In the late spring, it produces striking flowers — rounded soft purple globes. The chive blossom appears, dried or fresh, in many Japanese dishes. Chives are perennials that will remain in your garden for years once they're established.

Where and when to grow

Chives are hardy and will grow anywhere in the United States. They do well in cool weather but can survive extremes of temperature.

How to plant

You can grow chives from seed or divisions — small bulbs separated from clumps. The seeds take a long time to germinate and need a very cool temperature, not above 60°F; after their slow start they grow quickly. Plant either seeds or divisions about four to six weeks before your average date of last frost — a late frost won't hurt them. Chives tolerate partial shade, and prefer sandy soil with plenty of organic matter — this is important for perennial herbs — and good drainage. When you're preparing the soil, dig in a low nitrogen (5-10-10) fertilizer at the rate of a half pound per 100 square feet. Plant seeds a quarter inch deep in rows 12 inches apart. The plants can be fairly close together; small clumps (25 plants) can be set out six to eight inches apart in rows. They'll fill in and make an attractive array.

Fertilizing and watering

Don't fertilize chive plants at midseason. Detailed information on fertilizing is given in "Spadework: The Essential Soil" in Part 1.

Watering is important for good growth; the plants will survive neglect, but if you let the soil dry out, the tips of the leaves — the part you want to eat — will become brown and unappetizing.

Special handling

Chives will take care of themselves without much help from you. Separate the clumps from time to time. If you grow chives indoors, grow several pots so you can take turns clipping from them when you need chives for cooking and flavoring.

Pests

Chives are trouble-free. Onion thrips may be a problem in a commercial onion-producing area, but they shouldn't bother plants that have enough water.

Diseases

Chives have no serious disease problems.

When and how to harvest

If you start from seed, you can start snipping chives after 90 days; from transplanted divisions, after 60 days. Either way, the plants will produce much better the second year. To harvest, it's usual to just snip the tops off the leaves, but if you harvest from the base you'll avoid unattractive stubble.

Container growing

Chives can be container-grown as an annual, or can be grown in the garden and taken into a protected area such as an unheated garage or patio to winter over.

Storing and preserving

If you're growing chives on the windowsill or on the border of your flowerbed, you may not need to store any — you've got a regular supply right there. However, chives can be satisfactorily frozen or dried. Detailed information on storing and preserving is given in Part 4.

Serving suggestions

Try a little chopped chives and parsley in an omelette — it's quick and a little different for breakfast. Used raw, chives add a mild onion flavor to any dish. They are often mixed with cottage cheese, sour cream, or cream cheese. The blossoms can be eaten too and are best when just coming into bloom.

Chives

Chives seedling

Coriander

Common name: coriander
Botanical name: Coriandrum sativum
Origin: Europe, Asia Minor, and Russia

Varieties

Few varieties are available; grow the variety available in your area.

Description

Coriander is a fast-growing annual that grows to about 12 to 18 inches in height. It has tall slender stems with fine feathery leaves; the flowers are pale pink and grow in clusters. The seeds are used for flavoring candies, sauces, and soups. Coriander has a strong odor that many people don't like; it's one of the oldest known herbs. It was grown in ancient Egyptian gardens, and its seeds have been found in Egyptian tombs. Coriander is also mentioned as a food source in the Old Testament. The Spanish for coriander is *cilantro*, and the herb is sometimes known by this name.

Where and when to grow

Coriander grows almost anywhere that has a growing season of at least 100 days. It's not very hardy and will not survive hard frost, so plant it in the spring after all danger of frost.

How to plant

Coriander grows best in a fertile, well-drained soil. It prefers a sunny location but will survive in a slightly shaded area. When you're preparing the soil, dig in a complete, well-balanced fertilizer at the rate of one pound per 100 square feet. Plant coriander from seed in the early spring, two to three weeks after the average date of last frost. Plant the seeds a quarter inch deep in rows eight to 12 inches apart, and thin the plants to stand 12 inches apart when the seedlings are growing strongly.

Fertilizing and watering

Do not fertilize coriander at midseason. Detailed information on fertilizing is given in "Spadework: The Essential Soil" in Part 1.

Coriander should be kept evenly moist throughout the

Coriander

growing season, but when the seeds are nearing maturity too much rain can reduce the yield.

Pests

Coriander has no serious pest problems.

Diseases

Coriander has no serious disease problems.

How to harvest

You can pick a few coriander leaves any time after the plants are about six inches tall — the fresh leaves are known as cilantro. Harvest the coriander seeds when they turn a light brown, two to three weeks after flowering. The seeds are small — only an eighth inch in diameter — and are split in half and dried after harvesting.

Container growing

Coriander can be container-grown as an annual, or can be grown in the garden and taken into a protected area such as an unheated garage or patio to winter over.

Storing and preserving

The dried seeds can be stored for months in an airtight container. You can freeze or dry the leaves. Detailed information on storing and preserving is given in Part 4.

Serving suggestions

Add a little coriander to guacamole or to Chinese soups. The dried seeds are good in bread, cookies, potato salad, and fruit dishes. Coriander is used a lot in sausages.

Dill

Common name: dill
Botanical name: Anethum graveolens
Origin: Southeast Europe

Varieties
Few varieties are available; grow the variety available in your area. Bouquet is a dwarf variety.

Description

Dill, a member of the parsley family, is an annual herb that grows two to four feet tall. Dill has finely cut leaves and small yellow flowers growing in a flat-topped cluster; it has a delicate feathery look and makes a good background for flowers or vegetables. Carrying a bag of dry dill over the heart is supposed to ward off the evil eye. Dill water was once used to quiet babies and get rid of gas.

Dill seedling

Where and when to grow

Dill, like most herbs, can be grown pretty much anywhere, and can withstand heat or cold. Grow it from seed sown in the spring or fall. Once established, dill will seed itself and return year after year.

How to plant

Poor, sandy soil is an advantage when you're growing dill — the herb will have stronger flavor — but the soil must drain well. Dill will tolerate partial shade; in light shade the plants won't get as bushy as in full sun, so they can be closer together. Plant the seeds two or three weeks before your average date of last frost in rows two to three feet apart; they germinate quickly. When the seedlings are growing well, thin them to 12 inches apart. You can also thin dill to form a clump or mass rather than a row. Make sure you know where you want the plants, because dill has a taproot and is not easy to transplant. Dill is short-lived, so make successive sowings to give you a continuous crop.

Fertilizing and watering

Fertilizing is unnecessary for dill. Detailed information on fertilizing is given in "Spadework: The Essential Soil" in Part 1.

It doesn't need too much water and seems to do better if it's kept on the dry side.

Special handling

The stems are tall and fine; you may need to stake them.

Pests

Dill, like most herbs, is a good choice for the organic gardener.

It's a member of the parsley family, so you may encounter a parsley caterpillar; handpick it off the plant.

Diseases

Dill has no serious disease problems.

When and how to harvest

Time from planting to harvest is 70 days for foliage, 90 days for seeds. To harvest, snip off the leaves or young flower heads for use in soups or salads. For pickling, cut whole stalks when the plant is more mature. Gather the mature seeds for planting (although the dill will do its own planting without your help if you leave it alone) or for drying.

Container growing

Dill makes an attractive container plant. It grows and yields well in a container.

Storing and preserving

Dill seeds can be sprouted if they are allowed to dry naturally; store the dried seeds in an airtight jar. Crumble the dried leaves, and store them the same way. Detailed information on storing and preserving is given in Part 4.

Serving suggestions

Dill pickles, obviously. You can also make a marvelous leek and potato soup seasoned with dill, and dill adds a new kick to rye bread. Dill is very good with fish or potatoes, and you can use it for garnish if you run out of (or are bored with) parsley.

Dill

Fennel

Common names: fennel, Florence fennel, finnochio
Botanical name: Foeniculum vulgare dulce
Origin: Mediterranean

Varieties
Few varieties are available; grow the variety available in your area.

Description

Fennel is a stocky perennial grown as an annual, and looks a bit like celery with very feathery leaves. Ordinary fennel (F. vulgare) is also a perennial. Its leaves are picked for soups, sauces, and salads. The whole herb has an anise flavor. The plant will grow four to five feet tall, and the small, golden flowers appear in flat-topped clusters from July to September. A variant called "Copper" has charcoal-gray foliage and makes an interesting contrast to other colors in a flower bed. In folk medicine all sorts of good results have been attributed to fennel; at one time or another it has been credited with sharpening the eyesight, stopping hiccups, promoting weight loss, freeing a person from "loathings" and acting as an aphrodisiac.

Where and when to grow

Fennel will grow anywhere, and tolerates both heat and cold. Grow it from seed sown two to three weeks before your average date of last frost.

How to plant

Like most herbs, fennel needs well-drained soil that is high in organic matter. Plant seeds in full sun, in rows two to three feet apart. When seedlings are growing strongly, thin them to stand 12 inches apart. Fennel is a difficult herb to transplant because of its taproot.

Fertilizing and watering

Do not fertilize fennel. Detailed information on fertilizing is given in "Spadework: The Essential Soil" in Part 1.

Fennel

Keep fennel on the dry side; it just needs enough moisture to keep it going.

Fennel seedling

Special handling

The plants grow four to five feet tall; you may need to stake them.

Pests

Since fennel is a member of the parsley family, the parsley caterpillar may appear. Remove it by hand. Like most herbs, fennel is a successful bet for the organic gardener.

Diseases

Fennel has no serious disease problems.

When and how to harvest

You can start harvesting a few leaves as soon as the plant is well-established and growing steadily; use them for flavoring. Harvest the bulbous stalk when it is three inches or more in diameter for use as a vegetable.

Container growing

Fennel is a good choice for a container, where it will grow as well as in a traditional garden bed. Plant in fall—spring planting will not produce a large bulb.

Use a six-inch pot for a single plant; in a larger container, plant several on eight-inch centers.

Storing and preserving

The leaves of fennel can be frozen or dried. Crumble the dried leaves, and store them in an airtight container. Detailed information on storing and preserving is given in Part 4. You'll probably want to eat the stalks fresh, but they can also be frozen.

Serving suggestions

Fennel is featured in many Italian dishes. The leaves add flavor to soups and casseroles, and fennel is a good seasoning with fish. Add the seeds to rye bread or a creamed cheese spread.

Common name: garlic
Botanical name: Allium sativum
Origin: South Europe

Varieties
Few varieties are available; grow the variety available in your area.

Description

Garlic is a hardy perennial plant that looks a lot like an onion, except that the bulb is segmented into cloves. The flower head looks like a tissue paper dunce cap and is filled with small flowers and bulblets. There is an old story that when the Devil walked out of the Garden of Eden after the fall of Adam and Eve, onions sprang up from his right hoof-print and garlic from his left.

Where and when to grow

Garlic must have cool temperatures during its early growth period, but it's not affected by heat in the later stages. Plant garlic in spring in the North; in the South you can get good results with fall plantings.

How to plant

You grow garlic from cloves or bulblets, which are planted with the plump side down. Use the plumpest cloves for cooking and plant the others. They need full sun and well-worked soil that drains well and is high in organic matter. Do not fertilize the soil. Plant the cloves four to six weeks before the average date of last frost. Plant them an inch or two deep, four to six inches apart, in rows about a foot apart.

Fertilizing and watering

The organic content of the soil is important, but fertilizing isn't; don't fertilize because it will decrease the flavor of the garlic bulbs. Detailed information on fertilizing is given in "Spadework: The Essential Soil" in Part 1.

Keep the garlic slightly dry, especially when the bulbs are near maturity; this also improves the flavor. Keep the area cultivated.

Pests

Occasionally onion thrips may attack garlic, but they don't constitute a real problem; hose them off the plants if they do appear. Garlic is a good crop for the organic gardener. Detailed information on pest control is given in "Keeping Your Garden Healthy" in Part 1.

Diseases

Mildew may occur in a warm, moist environment, but it's not

Garlic seedling

common enough to be a problem. Keep the garlic fairly dry.

When and how to harvest

Harvest the bulbs when the tops start to dry—that's the sign that the bulbs are mature.

Container growing

Garlic cannot be grown satisfactorily in a container.

Storing and preserving

Store the mature bulbs under cool, dry conditions. Braid the tops of the plants together with twine and hang them to dry — very Gallic; in France you can still see rural vendors on bicycles with strings of garlic slung over their handlebars. Detailed information on storing and preserving is given in Part 4.

Serving suggestions

Garlic is indispensable to French cooking, and its use is now generally accepted in this country. If you still know anyone who disapproves of the strong flavor of garlic, try to convert him—he'll thank you later. Spice up your next spaghetti dinner with garlic bread. Rub a salad bowl with a cut clove of garlic before tossing the salad. Add a clove of garlic to a homemade vinaigrette; let the dressing stand for a while before use if you like your salad good and garlicky. Insert slivers of garlic into small slits in a roast, or rub a cut clove over a steak before grilling.

Garlic

Garlic chives

Common name: garlic chives
Botanical name: Allium species
Origin: Asia

Varieties

Plant the variety available in your area.

Description

Garlic chives are hardy perennials that grow in short, thick tufts like regular chives. Unlike chives, however, garlic chives have long, flat, grass-like leaves. The white flowers grow in large clusters on stems that rise above the leaves. The tips of the leaves have a mild garlic and onion flavor.

Where and when to grow

Garlic chives are hardy and will grow anywhere in the United

States. They do well in cool weather but can survive extremes of temperature.

How to plant

You can grow garlic chives from seeds or divisions—small bulbs separated from clumps. The seeds take a long time to germinate and need a very cool temperature, not above 60°F; after their slow start they grow quickly. Plant either seeds or divisions about four to six weeks before your average date of last frost—a late frost won't hurt them. Garlic chives tolerate partial shade, and prefer sandy soil with plenty of organic matter—this is important for perennial herbs—and good drainage. When you're preparing the soil, dig in a low nitrogen (5-10-10) fertilizer at the rate of a half pound per 100 square feet. Plant seeds a quarter inch deep in rows 12 inches apart. The plants can be fairly close together; small clumps (25 plants) can be set out six to eight inches apart in rows. They'll fill in and make an attractive array.

Fertilizing and watering

Don't fertilize garlic chive plants at midseason. Detailed information on fertilizing is given in "Spadework: The Essential Soil" in Part 1.

Watering is important for good growth; the plants will survive neglect, but if you let the soil dry out the tips of the leaves—the part you want to eat—will become brown and unappetizing.

Special handling

Garlic chives will take care of themselves without much help from you. Separate the clumps from time to time. If you grow garlic chives indoors, grow several pots so you can take turns clipping from them when you need them for cooking and flavoring.

Pests

Garlic chives are trouble-free. Onion thrips may be a problem in a commercial onion-producing area, but they shouldn't bother plants that have enough water.

Diseases

Garlic chives have no serious disease problems.

When and how to harvest

If you start from seed, you can start snipping garlic chives after 90 days; from transplanted divisions, after 60 days. Either way, the plants will produce

Garlic chives

much better the second year. To harvest, it's usual to just snip the tops off the leaves, but if you harvest from the base you'll avoid unattractive stubble.

Container growing

Garlic chives can be container-grown as an annual, or can be grown in the garden and taken into a protected area such as an unheated garage or patio to winter over.

Storing and preserving

If you're growing garlic chives on the windowsill or in the border of your flowerbed, you may not need to store any—you've got a regular supply right there. However, garlic chives can be satisfactorily frozen or dried. Detailed information on storing and preserving is given in Part 4.

Serving suggestions

Garlic chives can be used in any recipe that calls for regular chives. They add a mild garlic and onion flavor. The garlic chive blossoms are not usually eaten.

Lemon balm

Common name: lemon balm
Botanical name: Melissa officinalis
Origin: Europe and Asia

Varieties

Few varieties are available. Grow the variety available in your area.

Description

Lemon balm is a shallow-rooted, fast-spreading perennial. The toothed leaves have an opposite arrangement on square stems, and the small white flowers are borne in tight clusters at the leaf axles.

Where and when to grow

Lemon balm is a hardy perennial and can be grown almost anywhere in the United States. Plants can be grown from seeds started in early spring, or from root divisions planted at any time during the growing season.

How to plant

Lemon balm will take over the garden if it gets the chance, so each plant should be set in the soil in a container that will keep the roots in place. A two-pound coffee can with both ends removed works well. Lemon balm grown from seed also spreads rapidly, so unwanted young plants should be weeded out before they have a chance to spread.

Lemon balm

Lemon balm will grow in almost any soil. It prefers full sun but will tolerate fairly heavy shade. Work a complete, well-balanced (10-10-10) fertilizer into the soil before planting at the rate of a pound per 100 square feet.

Although root divisions of lemon balm can be planted at any time during the growing season, they will become established faster if planted in cool spring or fall weather. Seeds should be planted early in spring in rows 18 to 24 inches apart. Seedlings should be thinned to six to eight inches apart.

Fertilizing and watering

Don't fertilize lemon balm in midseason; it will never miss it. Detailed information on fertilizing is given in "Spadework: The Essential Soil" in Part 1. Lemon balm prefers moist soil, so it will require more watering than the rest of the garden. Keep it evenly moist until root divisions are established.

Pests

Lemon balm has no serious pest problems.

Diseases

Lemon balm is susceptible to verticillium wilt and mint rust. Prevent these diseases by removing all the dead stems and leaves from the bed before winter. Detailed information on disease prevention is given in "Keeping Your Garden Healthy" in Part 1.

When and how to harvest

The more lemon balm you pick, the better the plants will grow, and you can pick sprigs throughout the growing season. Harvest more fully as the plants begin to bloom, just as the lower leaves start to yellow. Cut the entire plant down two or three inches above the soil. You'll get a second, smaller harvest the same season.

Container growing

Lemon balm can be container-grown as an annual, or can be grown in the garden and brought into a protected area such as an unheated garage or patio for the winter. Note that even when growing it in the garden, it's a good idea to plant lemon balm in a container that will keep the roots from spreading too enthusiastically.

Storing and preserving

Strip the leaves from the stem and let them dry in a warm shady area. The dried leaves can be stored in a sealed jar. Detailed information on storing and preserving is given in Part 4.

Serving suggestions

Lemon balm leaves can be used to make tea, or a fresh sprig used to flavor other prepared teas. The leaves are also added to soups. Lemon balm is also used in toilet waters and soaps.

Common names: marjoram, sweet marjoram
Botanical name: Marjorana hortensis
Origin: Mediterranean

Varieties

Few varieties are available; grow the variety available in your area.

Description

A tender branching perennial, usually grown as an annual, marjoram grows 10 to 15 inches tall. It has greyish opposite leaves and lavender or whitish flowers growing up most of the stem. Marjoram means "joy of the mountain." Venus was reputed to be the first to grow this herb. Its leaves and flowering heads, steeped and made into a tea, have been said to relieve indigestion and headaches.

Where and when to grow

Marjoram will grow in most areas of the United States, but it's sensitive to frost and needs winter protection to survive the winter in very cold areas. Plant marjoram from seeds or transplants on your average date of last frost.

How to plant

Marjoram tolerates light shade and thrives in poor soil with good drainage. Don't fertilize the soil before planting; over-fertile soil will produce lots of leaves, but they'll have little flavor. One of the attractive qualities of many herbs is that they'll thrive in the kind of soil conditions that a lot of other plants won't tolerate. Marjoram is started from seed or transplants. On your average date of last frost, sow seeds a quarter inch deep in rows 18 to 24 inches apart. Thin the seedlings about six inches apart when they're growing sturdily, or plant transplants that are two or three inches tall, and set them about six inches apart. If the weather

Marjoram

Fertilizing and watering

Don't fertilize marjoram. Detailed information about fertilizing is given in "Spadework: The Essential Soil" in Part 1.

Water sparingly. The less water marjoram gets, the better the flavor will be.

Special handling

About all the special attention marjoram requires is a protection of mulch to help it weather very cold winters.

Pests

Marjoram has no serious pest problems. Like most herbs, it's a good plant for organic gardens.

Diseases

Marjoram has no serious disease problems.

When and how to harvest

When the first blooms appear, cut the plants back several inches;

Marjoram seedling

you can do this several times without harming the plant. Fresh leaves can be harvested at any time.

Container growing

Marjoram can be container-grown as an annual, or can be

warms up quickly, mulch transplants to protect the roots from too much heat until they're acclimated. If you're afraid marjoram won't survive the winter, dig up the plants in the fall, let them winter as houseplants, and plant again in spring — divide the clumps before replanting.

grown in the garden and taken into a protected area such as an unheated garage or patio to winter over.

Storing and preserving

Dry leaves and flower tops quickly. Store the crumbled, dry leaves for winter use. Detailed information on storing and preserving is given in Part 4.

Serving suggestions

Marjoram is one of the traditional components of a *bouquet garni*. The leaves are good with veal and liver, in meat and egg dishes, and in poultry stuffings. Try them in soups or on roast beef sandwiches. Make herb butter with them. Add chopped marjoram leaves in melted butter to spinach just before serving.

Mint

Common name: mint
Botanical names: Mentha piperita (peppermint); Mentha spicata (spearmint).
Origin: Europe

Varieties

There are many varieties of mint, of which the best known are spearmint and peppermint. Other varieties have different flavors, like golden apple mint or orange mint. Grow the variety available in your area or the scent and flavor you like best.

Description

A number of different varieties go by the collective name of mint; peppermint and spearmint are probably the two most popular. Both are hardy perennials, and both are very prolific—once you set them in a corner of the garden they'll quietly take over. Peppermint (Mentha piperita) is a tall, shallow-rooted, fast-spreading perennial with square stems and leaves that usually have a purple tinge. The light lavender flowers appear in terminal spikes and bloom through most of the growing season. The plant grows to about three feet tall. Spearmint (M. spicata) is a perennial that grows two to 2½ feet tall, with square stems and leaves that are slightly curled and deeply veined. The flowers are light purple to white and grow in spikes two to four

Mint

inches long that start blooming in early summer and continue well into fall. You may also come across varieties like golden apple mint, which has a more delicate flavor than spearmint. This plant also has pale purple flowers, but the leaves are dark green streaked with gold. Orange mint, sometimes known as bergamot mint, gets its name from its delicate scent of oranges. Orange mint has reddish-green leaves edged with purple; the flowers are lavender.

Where and when to grow

Both peppermint and spearmint are very hardy and can be grown almost anywhere in the United States. Plant them from root divisions any time during the growing season.

How to plant

Mint varieties from seed will not grow "true." So it's generally more satisfactory to use root divisions. An innocuous little plant of mint will wander all over the garden if it gets half a chance, so plant each one in a container that will keep the roots in one place — a two-pound coffee can with both ends removed is good. Peppermint and spearmint grow well in any soil; they prefer sun but will tolerate partial shade. For spearmint, work a complete, well-balanced fertilizer into the soil before planting at the rate of a pound per 100 square feet. Don't fertilize before planting peppermint — you'll get all the peppermint you can use without it. Although you can plant mints anytime during the growing season, root divisions will be established faster if planted on a cool, moist day in spring or fall.

Space plants two or three inches apart in rows 18 to 24 inches apart.

Fertilizing and watering

Don't fertilize mints in midseason; they'll never miss it. Detailed information on fertilizing is given in "Spadework: The Essential Soil" in Part 1.

Both peppermint and spearmint prefer moist soil, so they'll require more watering than the rest of the garden. Keep them evenly moist until root divisions are established.

Pests

Mints have no serious pest problems.

Diseases

Mints are susceptible to verticillium wilt and mint rust. Prevent these diseases by removing all the dead stems and leaves from the bed before winter. Detailed information on disease prevention is given in "Keeping Your Garden Healthy" in Part 1.

When and how to harvest

The more mint you pick, the better the plants will grow, and you can pick sprigs throughout the growing season. Harvest more fully as the plants begin to bloom, just as the lower leaves start to yellow. Cut the entire plant down two or three inches above the soil. You'll get a second smaller harvest the same season.

Container growing

Mint can be container-grown as an annual, or can be grown in

the garden and brought into a protected area such as an unheated garage or patio for the winter. Note that even when growing it in the garden, it's a good idea to plant mint in a container that will keep the roots from spreading too enthusiastically—mint will take over the garden if you let it.

Storing and preserving

Strip the mint leaves from the stem and let them dry in a warm shady area. The dried leaves can be stored in a sealed jar. Detailed information on storing and preserving is given in Part 4.

Serving suggestions

A sprig of fresh mint is a pretty garnish for summer drinks — and you can't have a mint julep without it. Cook peas in a very little water to which you've added a couple of sprigs of mint. Toss boiled new potatoes with butter and chopped mint—a nice change from parsley. Instead of mint jelly with a lamb roast, try the traditional English mint sauce. Add a little sugar to a couple of tablespoons of chopped fresh mint leaves, add boiling water to bring out the flavor, then top off with vinegar to taste.

Oregano

Common names: oregano, wild marjoram
Botanical names: Origanum vulgare, Origanum heracleoticum
Origin: Mediterranean (O. vulgare), Cyprus (O. heracleoticum)

Oregano

shape, and the flowers are pink, white, or purple. O. heracleoticum is a tender perennial that grows only a foot high. The leaves are very hairy and oval in shape, and the plant bears small white flower clusters on tall stems. Oregano's reputed medicinal powers are varied. A tea made from the leaves and flowers was believed to relieve indigestion, headaches, and nervousness. Oil extracted from the plant was used as a cure for toothache.

Where and when to grow

O. vulgare can be grown anywhere in the United States from root divisions or seed planted early in spring. O. heracleoticum can also be grown anywhere in the United States from seed or root divisions if planting is delayed until all danger of frost is past; it should be grown as an annual or given winter protection in colder northern areas. O. heracleoticum can also be grown in a container — it makes an attractive houseplant.

How to plant

Don't fertilize the planting bed for oregano—lack of nutrients even enhances the flavor. Both varieties need well-drained soil in a sunny location, although O. vulgare will tolerate partial shade. Plant both varieties from root divisions or seeds and space plants about a foot apart. Plant O. vulgare on your average date of last frost, and O. heracleoticum two to three weeks later. Plant seeds a quarter inch deep in rows 12 to 18 inches apart, and thin to six to 12 inches apart. Plant divisions six to

Varieties

In cold northern areas grow any variety of O. vulgare. In warmer areas grow any variety of either O. vulgare or O. heracleoticum.

Description

The name "oregano" is more accurately applied to a flavor than to a plant, and there are two varieties that you can grow for seasoning called oregano. O.

vulgare is usually grown; it's hardier and easier to propagate than the alternative, O. heracleoticum—also known as wild marjoram. The name "oregano" itself has been traced back to an ancient Greek word translated as "delight of the mountains," which suggests that the plants once grew wild on the hillsides of Greece. Oregano (O. vulgare) is a very hardy perennial that may grow 2½ feet tall.

The leaves are greyish-green, slightly hairy, and oval in

12 inches apart in rows 12 to 18 inches apart.

Fertilizing and watering

Don't fertilize oregano at all. Detailed information on fertilizing is given in "Spadework: The Essential Soil" in Part 1.

Keep the oregano plants on the dry side.

Pests

Oregano varieties have no serious pest problems.

Diseases

These plants have no serious disease problems.

When and how to harvest

Oregano is ready to harvest when it begins to flower; cut the stems down to a few inches above the soil. Leaves can be harvested for fresh use throughout the growing season if you cut off the flowers before they open—this encourages fuller foliage.

Container growing

Oregano makes an attractive houseplant. It can be container-grown as an annual or grown in the garden and taken into a protected area such as an unheated garage or patio to winter over.

Storing and preserving

Hang oregano in bunches to dry; when they're dry, remove the leaves and store them in an airtight container. Detailed information on storing and preserving is given in Part 4.

Serving suggestions

Oregano is essential to lots of Italian dishes. Add it to spaghetti sauce, and sprinkle it on pizza. Try oregano and a touch of lemon on lamb chops or steak. Sprinkle oregano on cooked vegetables for a lively flavor.

Parsley

Common name: parsley
Botanical name: Petroselinum crispum
Origin: Mediterranean

Varieties

Moss Curled (70 days); Perfection (75 days); Hamburg or Parsnip-Rooted parsley (90 days).

Description

Parsley is a hardy biennial that is treated as an annual. (In the early spring of its second year, parsley will flower, causing the flavor to be very bitter.) It has finely divided, fernlike leaves that are either flat or curly. The leaves grow in a rosette from a single taproot that in some varieties is quite large and can be eaten like parsnips. Parsley has flat-topped clusters of greenish-yellow flowers, similar to those of dill, which belongs to the same family. The Romans wore parsley wreaths to keep from becoming intoxicated. Parsley is probably the best known of the herbs used for flavoring and for garnish. It is also very nutritious

and is high in vitamins A and C, potassium, and iron.

Where and when to grow

Parsley will grow anywhere and can survive cold. It tolerates heat, but very hot weather will make the plant go to seed. Plant parsley

Parsley seedling

two to three weeks before your average date of last frost. Parsley also does well as a houseplant; some gardeners bring parsley in from the garden in fall and let it winter in a bright window.

How to plant

Parsley likes well-worked, well-drained soil with moderate organic content. Don't fertilize before planting. Plant from seed two to three weeks before your average date of last frost. The seeds take a long time to germinate, but you can speed up the process by soaking them in warm water overnight before planting. Even so, the seeds will take four weeks to germinate. Plant the seeds a quarter-inch deep in rows 18 to 24 inches apart. Thin the seedlings to 12 to 18 inches apart when they're growing strongly. Or start seeds indoors six weeks before the average date of last frost.

Fertilizing and watering

Fertilize parsley only once, in early spring, using a pound of a well-balanced (10-10-10) fertilizer per 100 square feet, or a quarter handful sprinkled round a few plants. Detailed information on fertilizing is given in "Spadework: The Essential Soil" in Part 1.

It's important to keep the soil moderately moist; parsley needs a regular supply of water to keep producing new leaves.

Pests

The parsley caterpillar is the only pest you're likely to have to contend with. Handpick it off the plants. Rabbits may take a fancy to your parsley, in which case your only recourse is to use a fence or screen around the garden.

Diseases

Parsley has no serious disease problems.

When and how to harvest

From planting to harvest is about 70 to 90 days, and a ten-foot row of parsley will keep you—and all your neighbors—well supplied. Harvest parsley leaves any time during the growing season; cut them off at the base of the plant. Pick the outside leaves so that the heart can continue to grow and produce new leaves. To encourage the growth of new foliage, cut off the flower stalk when it appears. The flower stalk shoots up taller than the leaves, and the leaves on it are much smaller. The plant will retain its rich color until early winter. Many gardeners harvest the entire parsley plant in fall and dry it; you can also bring the whole plant inside for the winter.

Container growing

Parsley makes an attractive container plant. It grows and yields well in a container.

Storing and preserving

Parsley lends itself well to freezing and drying. Store the dried leaves in an airtight container. Detailed information on storing and preserving is given in Part 4.

Parsley

Serving suggestions

Parsley's reputation as a garnish often does it a disservice—it gets left on the side of the plate. In fact it's been known for thousands of years for its excellent flavor and versatility. Add chopped parsley to buttered potatoes and vegetables; toss a little on a sliced tomato salad along with a pinch of basil. Add it to scrambled eggs or an omelette aux fine herbs. Parsley is a natural breath-freshener.

Rosemary

Common name: rosemary
Botanical name: Rosemarinus officinalis
Origin: Mediterranean

Varieties
Albus; Collingwood Ingram; Tuscan Blue; Prostratus; Lockwood de Forest.

Description

Rosemary is a half-hardy, evergreen, perennial shrub with narrow, aromatic, grey-green leaves. It can grow six feet tall, and the flowers are small and light blue or white. It's a perennial, but in areas with very cold winters it's grown as an annual. It is said that rosemary got its name when the Virgin Mary draped her cloak over a rosemary plant during the flight from Jerusalem, and the plant turned the same color as her cloak. Rosemary is also one of the traditional strewing herbs; in the language of flowers its message is "remember." In Shakespeare's play, Ophelia gives Hamlet a sprig of rosemary "for remembrance." Keep up the old tradition of an herb of remembrance by tying a sprig of rosemary to a gift.

Rosemary

Where and when to grow

Rosemary can handle temperatures a bit below freezing and tolerates cold better in a sandy, well-drained location. Less-than-ideal conditions improve its fragrance, but it's not really hardy north of Washington,

D.C. Grow it in a cold-winter area if you're willing to mulch it for winter protection. Mulch after the soil has frozen.

How to plant

Like most herbs, rosemary is most fragrant and full of flavor if it's grown in well-drained, sandy soil that's high in organic matter but not over-rich. Very fertile soil will produce beautiful plants but decrease the production of the aromatic oils on which the plant's fragrance depends. Don't fertilize the soil if you're planting rosemary, except if you're growing it as a perennial in a mild winter climate; in this case, work a low-nitrogen (5-10-10) fertilizer into the soil before planting at the rate of about a half pound to 100 square feet. To grow rosemary from seed, start the seeds indoors or in a cold frame four to six weeks before your average date of last frost. Two weeks after the average date of last frost, transplant them to a location in full sun with a foot or more between the plants and 18 to 24 inches between rows. You can also grow rosemary from stem cuttings. Pot a rosemary plant from the garden in fall and bring it into the house for winter use. In the spring take stem cuttings to propagate your new crop. To take stem cuttings, cut six- to eight-inch long tips from the plant and strip the leaves from the lower two or three inches. Stick the cuttings in sand and keep them well watered. They should root in two to four weeks. Cuttings can be taken at any time, but usually do best if taken in spring.

Fertilizing and watering

Do not fertilize at midseason.

Detailed information on fertilizing is given in "Spadework: The Essential Soil" in Part 1.

If the weather is dry, water regularly to keep the soil moist, and don't let the roots dry out. However, rosemary has a better flavor if kept slightly on the dry side.

Rosemary seedling

Pests

Rosemary has no serious pest problems. Like most herbs, it does well in the organic garden.

Diseases

Rosemary has no serious disease problems.

When and how to harvest

You can take some of the leaves, which look like short pine needles, and use them fresh any time you want them. Growth can be pruned back several times during a season.

Container growing

Rosemary can be container-grown as an annual, or can be grown in the garden and taken into a protected area such as an unheated garage or patio to winter over.

Storing and preserving

Dry the leaves and store them in airtight containers. Detailed information on storing and preserving is given in Part 4.

Serving suggestions

Treat rosemary with respect; it can easily overpower more delicate herbs. Rosemary is traditionally used with lamb or pork; it's also excellent combined with a little lemon juice and chopped parsley and sprinkled on chicken before it's baked.

Rue

Common name: rue
Botanical name: Ruta graveolens
Origin: Southern Europe

Varieties

Few varieties are available. Grow the variety available in your area.

Description

Rue is a grayish-blue hardy perennial that has small yellow flowers. The evergreen leaves are fragrant and lacy. The base of the plant gets woody as the plant ages. Rue is the national plant of Lithuania.

Where and when to grow

Rue is very adaptable and will grow almost anywhere in the United States. Plant seeds or (if you can find them) transplants in early spring.

Rue

How to plant

Rue does best in well-drained, preferably not-too-fertile soil. Rich soil produces large but less well-flavored plants. Seeds should be planted a quarter inch deep in rows 12 to 18 inches apart, and the seedlings thinned to about a foot apart when they are an inch tall. Rue transplants should only be planted in spring, on or around the average date of last frost.

Fertilizing and watering

The first year, work a low-nitrogen (5-10-10) fertilizer into the soil before planting at the rate of a half pound per 100 square feet. Once it's established, rue seldom needs watering. In fact, it does better if kept slightly on the dry side.

Special handling

Rue does not compete well with weeds and should be cultivated conscientiously. The plant tends to get very woody after a few years, and should be replanted after six to ten years.

Pests

Rue has no serious pest problems. Like most herbs, it does well in the organic garden.

Diseases

Rue has no serious disease problems.

When and how to harvest

You may cut small sprigs of rue at any time during the growing season after the plant is large enough to handle. Don't cut back more than half the plant (you are not likely to do so—a little rue goes a long way). It's not necessary to remove the flowers in order to retain the full flavor of the herb. Rue has such a strong flavor that flowering will make little noticeable difference.

Container growing

Rue can be container-grown as an annual, or can be grown in the garden and taken into a protected area such as an unheated garage or patio to winter over.

Storing and preserving

Dry the rue, crumble it, and put into tightly capped jars. Detailed information on storing and preserving is given in part 4.

Serving suggestions

Rue is generally used in poultry or pork dishes, and in some sausage recipes. It has a very strong taste and should be used with discretion.

Sage

Common name: sage
Botanical name: Salvia officinalis
Origin: Mediterranean

Varieties
Albiflora (white flowers); Aurea (variegated leaves); Purpurea (reddish-purple upper leaves).

Description

Sage is a hardy, perennial shrub that grows to two feet tall and gets quite woody. The leaves, which grow in opposite pairs on square stems, are usually oval- to lance-shaped, sometimes five inches long. Grayish-green leaves are more common but several varieties have variegated leaf color: purple, yellow and green, or green and white. The flowers are bluish-lavender and grow on spikelike stems. Traditionally, sage was considered a panacea for many ills, particularly those linked with aging. It was also supposed to improve the memory and intelligence (and occasionally is still credited with these properties), and keep the hair from falling out. The purple or golden varieties make delightful ornamental houseplants. They're smaller plants than the green or gray varieties, but they're prettier, and the flavor is just as good. Most garden shops and catalog lists offer only the gray varieties. Go to a herb specialist for the less common types.

Sage seedling

Where and when to grow

Sage, like most herbs, is an accommodating plant that will grow almost anywhere in the United States from root divisions or seeds. It thrives in soil that is nutritionally poor but well-drained. It prefers full sun but will tolerate partial shade. In northern areas, it may be necessary to mulch to help the plants survive the winter. Mulch should be applied after the soil freezes.

How to plant

Sage can be reproduced by layering, by division, or by using stem cuttings. You can also start it from seed. Seeds should be started indoors and the seedlings transplanted into the garden as soon as the soil warms up. Stem cuttings and layerings should be taken in early spring when the plants are actively growing. Sage thrives in poor soil as long as the drainage is good, and it's not normally necessary to fertilize—if the soil is too rich the flavor will be poorer. If you're planting sage as a perennial, fertilize the first year only with a low-nitrogen fertilizer. When you're preparing the soil for planting, work a 5-10-10 fertilizer into the soil at the rate of half a pound per 100 square feet. To improve drainage, add organic matter such as grass clippings, peat moss, compost, manure, straw, or hay. Plant sage

Sage

seeds or divisions on your average date of last frost. Plant seeds a quarter inch deep in rows 18 to 24 inches apart, and thin 12 inches apart. Plant divisions or cuttings 12 inches apart in rows 18 to 24 inches apart. They should be in full sun; the plants will tolerate partial shade, but the flavor will be impaired.

Fertilizing and watering

Don't fertilize at midseason. Detailed information on fertilizing is given in "Spadework: The Essential Soil" in Part 1.

Sage should be kept well watered during the first season. Once it is established it should be kept on the dry side. Lack of water will actually improve the flavor. However, never let the plant wilt from lack of moisture.

Pests

Sage has no serious pest problem. Like most herbs, it does well in the organic garden.

Diseases

Sage has no serious disease problems. If the area is too damp or shady, rot may occur, and the plants may not survive the winter in northern areas. Avoid this by planting sage in a dry, sunny location and improving the soil drainage. Detailed information on disease prevention is given in "Keeping Your Garden Healthy" in Part 1.

When and how to harvest

Sage usually takes 75 days from planting to harvest, and a few plants will supply you and a lot of other people, too. At least twice during the growing season, cut six to eight inches from the top of the plants. Pick the leaves as desired as long as you don't cut back more than half the plant—if you do, the plant will stop producing and may die.

Container growing

Sage can be container-grown as an annual, or can be grown in the garden and taken into a protected area such as an unheated garage or patio to winter over.

Storing and preserving

Store dried sage leaves in an airtight container. Detailed information on storing and preserving is given in Part 4.

Serving suggestions

Sage and onion make a good combination and are traditionally used together in stuffings for pork, turkey, or duck. Sage can overwhelm other seasonings, so handle it with care. Some people steep dried sage leaves to make an herb tea.

Savory

Common names: summer savory, winter savory
Botanical names: Satureja hortensis (summer savory); Satureja montana (winter savory)
Origin: Mediterranean, Southern Europe

Varieties

Few varieties are available; grow the variety available in your area.

Description

Both types of savory belong to the mint family. Summer savory is a bushy annual with needle-shaped leaves and stems that are square when the plant is young and become woody later. The flowers are light purple to pink, and the plant grows to a height of about 18 inches. Winter savory is a bushy hardy perennial that grows about a foot tall. The small flowers are white or purple and, like the summer variety, winter savory has needle-shaped leaves and square stems that become woody as they develop. The winter variety has sharper-flavored leaves than the summer kind.

Where and when to grow

Both varieties grow anywhere in the United States from seeds planted two to three weeks after the average date of last frost.

How to plant

Summer savory can be grown in almost any soil; winter savory prefers soil that is sandy and well-drained. Both need full sun. Before planting, work a complete, well-balanced fertilizer into the ground at the rate of one pound to 100 square feet. Plant seeds of both summer and winter varieties half an inch deep in rows 12 to 18 inches apart. When the seedlings are four to six weeks old thin summer savory plants to stand three to four inches apart. Winter savory needs more room; thin the plants to 12 to 18 inches apart.

Savory

Fertilizing and watering

Do not fertilize at midseason. Detailed information on fertilizing is given in "Spadework: The Essential Soil" in Part 1.

Both varieties do better if kept on the dry side.

Special handling

Summer savory has a tendency to get top-heavy; stake the plants if necessary.

Pests

Savory has no serious pest problems.

Diseases

Savory has no serious disease problems.

When and how to harvest

Pick fresh leaves and stems of both summer and winter savory at any time during the growing season. In areas with a long growing season you may get two harvests. For drying, cut off the top six to eight inches of the plant as soon as it begins to flower.

Container growing

Winter savory can be container-grown as an annual, or can be grown in the garden and taken into a protected area such as an unheated garage or patio to winter over.

Storing and preserving

Store the dried leaves in an airtight container. Detailed information on storing and preserving is given in Part 4.

Serving suggestions

Savory has a peppery flavor that is good with fish, poultry, and in egg dishes. Try it in vinegars, or add a little to a cheese soufflé.

Sesame

Common name: sesame
Botanical name: Sesamum indicum
Origin: Africa

Varieties
Few varieties are available; grow the variety available in your area.

Description

Sesame is a hardy annual that has a unique drought-tolerant root system composed of a long taproot and a large number of fibrous secondary roots. It's an attractive plant, with cream or pale orchid-colored flowers that grow in the angles of the leaves. Sesame used to be credited with magic powers and was associated with Hecate, queen of witches. Its uses today are less dramatic; the dried seeds are used to flavor breads, candy, and baked goods, and the oil extracted from the seeds is used for cooking and in salad dressings.

Where and when to grow

Sesame is easy to grow if you can give it a growing season of about 120 days; it grows well in the warm, dry areas of the South and Southwest. Plant it when danger of frost is over.

How to plant

Give sesame a place in the sun in well-drained, fertile soil. When you're preparing the soil, dig in a complete, well-balanced fertilizer at the rate of one pound per 100 square feet. Four to six weeks after the average date of last frost, plant the seeds a half inch deep in rows 12 to 18 inches apart. Thin the plants to 12 to 18 inches apart when they are four to five weeks old.

Fertilizing and watering

Fertilize before planting and again at midseason, at the same rate as the rest of the garden. Detailed information on fertilizing is given in "Spadework: The Essential Soil" in Part 1.

Allow the plants to dry out between waterings.

Pests

Sesame has no serious pest problems.

Diseases

Sesame has no serious disease problems.

When and how to harvest

Harvest about 90 to 120 days after planting when the mature seed pods are about the size of a peanut. Crack the pods open carefully, and remove the seeds.

Container growing

Sesame does not grow very well in a container.

Storing and preserving

Store the dried sesame seeds in an airtight container. Detailed information on storing and preserving is given in Part 4.

Serving suggestions

Toast sesame seeds and toss them over vegetable dishes or soups. They give an extra crunch to pan-fried fish. Or, just eat the roasted seeds as a snack. Sesame is used a lot in Oriental dishes and the seeds, untoasted, are added to cookies, cakes, and breads before baking.

Sesame

Tarragon

Common name: tarragon
Botanical name: Artemisia
   dracunulus
Origin: Caspian Sea, Siberia

Varieties

Few varieties are available.
Grow the variety available in your
area, but try to make sure that
it's the French, not the Russian,
kind.

Description

Tarragon is a half-hardy
perennial that grows two to four
feet tall; it has slender stems
and thin narrow leaves that taste a
bit like licorice, and it rarely
produces flowers—they're small
and whitish in color. True
French tarragon is a sterile clove
and cannot be grown from
seed; use rooted divisions or
stem cuttings. There is also a
Russian variety of tarragon, which
has a stronger flavor that most
people don't like. Many herbs are
decorative, but tarragon is not
glamorous. However, its finely
textured dark-green foliage
makes an attractive background
for small, bright flowers. The
word tarragon comes from the
Arabic word for dragon. The
French translation, *estragon* (little
dragon), might reflect either
the way tarragon was used
medicinally to fight pestilence
during the Middle Ages, or the
snakelike appearance of its
roots.

Tarragon

Tarragon seedling

Where and when to grow

Tarragon can be grown anywhere in the United States and will survive cold winters if it's given adequate protection. It's hardy in well-drained, sandy soils, but is less tolerant of cold in compacted or wet soil.

How to plant

Seeds of the Russian variety are available commercially, but are likely to produce plants of inferior flavor. Instead, use divisions or stem cuttings of French tarragon. Tarragon tolerates poor, rather dry soil. Fertilize the soil the first year only with a low-nitrogen (5-10-10) fertilizer; before planting, work the fertilizer well into the soil at the rate of a half pound to 100 square feet. Plant cuttings or divisions on your area's average date of last frost, and set them 18 to 24 inches apart in rows 24 to 36 inches apart. Give them a place in full sun; the plant will tolerate partial shade, but the flavor will be impaired.

Fertilizing and watering

Don't fertilize at midseason. Detailed information on fertilizing is given in "Spadework: The Essential Soil" in Part 1.

Keep tarragon on the dry side to encourage the flavor to develop.

Special handling

If you live in an area where the ground freezes and thaws often in the winter, mulch after the first freeze so that a thaw will not push the plant up and out of the ground. Mulching also helps the tarragon survive the cold.

Subdivide the plants every three or four years.

Pests

Tarragon has no serious pest problems. It does well in the organic garden.

Diseases

Tarragon has no serious disease problems.

When and how to harvest

Time from planting to harvest is about 60 days, and you don't need a lot of tarragon. One plant supplies the average family, so if you're growing a lot you will be able to supply the whole neighborhood. Pick the tender top leaves of tarragon as you need them. Cut back the leafy top growth several times during the season to encourage the plant to bush out.

Container growing

Tarragon does not grow very well in a container.

Storing and preserving

Tarragon is best fresh, but can be dried or frozen. Detailed information on storing and preserving is given in Part 4.

Serving suggestions

Put a fresh stem or two of tarragon into bottles of good cider vinegar or wine vinegar and, *voila*, tarragon vinegar; allow a couple of weeks for the flavor to develop before you use it. Since the flavor of tarragon is so distinctive, use it with a light touch. Use the leaves to decorate cold dishes glazed with aspic. It's tarragon that gives a kick to a good *sauce tartare*, and, of course, you can't have chicken tarragon without it.

Thyme

Common name: thyme
Botanical name: Thymus vulgaris
Origin: Mediterranean

Varieties

Argentens; Aureus; Rosens; Broadleaf English; Narrowleaf French.

Description

Thyme is a fragrant, small, perennial evergreen shrub with six- to eight-inch stems that often spread out over the ground. It's a member of the mint family and has square stems with small opposite leaves and pale lavender mintlike flowers. Thyme is a charming, cheerful little plant and will last for years once it's established. It's a good plant for a border or rock garden. There are more than 200 species and many hybrids, but the common form is the one grown for flavoring. The Greeks and Romans believed that thyme gave courage and strength; their highest compliment was to tell a man that he smelled of thyme. In the Middle Ages ladies embroidered sprigs of thyme on the scarves they gave their knights. Linnaeus, the father of modern botany, recommended thyme as a hangover cure.

Thyme seedling

Thyme

How to plant

Thyme likes well-drained soil, preferably low in fertility; rich soils produce plants that are large but less fragrant. The first year, work a low-nitrogen (5-10-10) fertilizer into the soil before planting at the rate of about a half pound per 100 square feet. This is generous of you, because in adverse soil conditions thyme, like many herbs, will have better flavor. Whatever the soil's like, it's important to give thyme a place in the sun. Plant seeds in early spring, two to three weeks before your average date of last frost. Plant the seeds a quarter inch deep in rows 16 to 24 inches apart, and when the seedlings are two to three inches tall thin them about a foot apart. You can also plant thyme cuttings or root divisions. Plant them at the same time, and space them a foot apart.

Fertilizing and watering

Don't fertilize at midseason. Detailed information on fertilizing is given in "Spadework: The Essential Soil" in Part 1.
   Thyme seldom needs watering; it does best on the dry side.

Special handling

Some herbs, like mints, grow like weeds whatever the competition. Thyme can't handle competition, especially from grassy weeds, and needs an orderly environment; cultivate conscientiously.
   Start new plants every three to four years, because thyme gets woody; reduce the clump greatly. If you've no room in the garden for extra plants, plant them in a hanging basket.

Where and when to grow

Thyme prefers a mild climate but can survive temperatures below freezing. It tolerates cold better in well-drained soil. Plant thyme from seed anywhere in the United States two to three weeks before your average date of last frost.

Pests

Thyme has no serious pest problems. Like most herbs, it's ideal for the organic gardener.

Diseases

Thyme has no serious disease problems.

When and how to harvest

Pick thyme as needed. For drying, harvest when the plants begin to bloom. Cut off the tops of the branches with four to five inches of flowering stems.

Container growing

Thyme can be container-grown as an annual, or can be grown in the garden and taken into a protected area such as an unheated garage or patio to winter over.

Storing and preserving

After drying, crumble the thyme and put into tightly capped jars.

Detailed information on storing and preserving is given in Part 3.

Serving suggestions

Thyme is usually blended with other herbs and used in meat dishes, poultry, stuffings (parsley and thyme is a happy combination), and soups. It adds a nice flavor to clam chowder and is often used along with a bay leaf to give a delicate lift to a white sauce or a cheese soufflé.

Planting guide: spacing herbs

Herb	Inches between plants	Inches between rows	Depth of seed (inches)
Anise	6-12	18-24	1/4
Basil	4-6	18-24	1/4
Borage	12	18-24	1/2
Caraway	12-18	18-24	1/4
Chervil	3-4	18-24	1/2
Chives	8-10	12	1/4
Coriander	12	12-18	1/4
Dill	12	24-36	1/4
Fennel	12	2-3	1/4
Garlic	3-6	24-36	1/4
Garlic Chives	8-12	12-18	2-3
Lemon Balm	8-12	18-24	1/4
Marjoram	6-12	18-24	1/4
Mint	2-3	18-24	1/4
Oregano	6-12	12-18	1/4
Parsley	12-18	18-24	1/4
Rosemary	18	18-24	1/4
Rue	8-12	12-18	1/4
Sage	12	18-24	1/4
Savory	6-18	12-18	1/4
Sesame	6	12-18	1/4
Tarragon	18-24	24-36	1/4
Thyme	12-16	16-24	1/4

Part 3: The Home Orchard

It's easier than you think to grow fruits and berries yourself for a luscious, homegrown harvest. Here's all you need to know about planning, planting, and caring for a home orchard, and a garden plot of berries and other small fruits.

Growing a home orchard is a gratifying achievement, but fruit trees and bushes demand a considerable investment in terms of space, equipment, and the gardener's time and effort. Most modern fruit trees are self-unfruitful, which means they cannot pollinate themselves, so it's necessary to plant another tree of an appropriate variety nearby to provide the necessary pollination. So, for starters, you're probably looking at two trees where you thought you needed one. Even if you intend to grow dwarf varieties, space is a significant factor.

PLANNING A HOME ORCHARD

Before you go to the garden center or send in your catalog order for fruit trees, it's important to put some thought into planning your orchard. First, list the types of fruit trees you wish to grow, and the varieties you favor. Check how big they'll be when fully mature. Find out which are self-fruitful and which will require another tree nearby for cross-pollination. With this information before you, make an orchard plan on paper—just as you did for your vegetable garden. It's easier to erase a tree when it's a pencil outline on paper than to dig it up and move it when it's growing lustily in your yard.

Another factor to consider is time. Most fruit trees won't produce a normal crop for three to five years after planting, so don't plan a home orchard unless you intend to stay in your home long enough to see your plans come to (literal) fruition.

You will also need to invest time and equipment in maintaining your orchard. All fruit trees need to be pruned at least annually, so you will need pruning and/or lopping shears and a pruning saw. If you want a worthwhile crop you will also have to spray the trees regularly—often weekly, so a good sprayer is a must. If you are using chemical sprays, you must also take into account the cost of these products.

Where and when to grow

Before planting fruit trees you should examine your available planting space. Fruit trees like soil that is well drained and rich in organic matter, and it's wise to have a soil test done to detect any nutrient deficiencies that need to be supplemented. Some state Cooperative Extension Services do soil tests, and those that don't will direct you to a soil-testing agency. There will be a fee for the test. The test will identify the soil content of the three macronutrients (nitrogen, potassium, and phosphorus) and a number of micronutrients, and the testing agency will make recommendations (if necessary) for improving the balance of these substances in the soil.

All fruit trees will fruit best in full sun; some will tolerate a certain amount of shade, but their productivity will be reduced. Trees should be spaced according to the chart given at the end of this section. In the case of citrus fruits, which require a great deal of water, it's wise to form a depression around each tree in which water can collect. This basin should extend to the drip-line (outer branch canopy) of the tree.

drip line

When fertilizing fruit trees, fertilizer should be applied about a foot from the trunk and extending to the drip line, or outer canopy, of the tree. Also, to make the best use of available rainfall, make a saucer-shaped depression in the soil extending to the drip line to retain water.

Most fruit trees can be planted at any time during the growing season; however, they will suffer less transplant stress if planted in the cool, moist spring and fall seasons. The trees can be purchased bareroot or balled and burlapped or, sometimes, in a container. Bareroot trees are the least expensive and are only available early in spring. Specific planting instructions for bareroot, balled and burlapped, or container-grown trees are given in the individual plant profiles.

When selecting fruit trees, look for medium to small varieties. Large trees require more pruning at first planting and suffer more from transplant shock. Also, they are more difficult to train later.

Controlling pests and diseases

Fruit trees are susceptible to many insect pests, and these pests must be controlled if the trees are to produce high-quality crops. Many of the insects that attack fruit trees must be controlled early, before they damage the immature fruits. Apple maggot flies, for example, lay eggs on the surface of the fruit; when the egg is laid the surface of the fruit is damaged and a dimpled area appears. The eggs hatch and the young worms or maggots eat their way to the center of the fruit. To control this insect, the tree must be sprayed before the adult fly lays its eggs, so that the fruit is already protected. Therefore the home gardener must use preventive sprays. Your Cooperative Extension

Service or local garden center can provide a specific spraying schedule for your area.

Appropriate fertilizing, watering, and pruning all help keep fruit trees healthy, but the trees are also susceptible to diseases which, like the pests discussed above, need to be prevented by chemical means. Many fruit tree diseases can be prevented by spraying with fungicides. These fungicides do not cure diseases, but they do prevent them from spreading and therefore must be applied before the disease organisms attack. Again, it is necessary to follow a spraying schedule especially formulated for your locality, and information is available from your state Cooperative Extension Service or local garden center. Fortunately, most insecticides and fungicides can be mixed together, so that you can apply them at the same time. This cuts down considerably on the number of times you actually have to spray. Most spray schedules call for applications every seven to ten days from the time the trees come into leaf almost until the fruit is harvested.

Pruning fruit trees

All fruit trees need some pruning. Without it, they would become overcrowded and yield poorly. Most pruning should be done in late fall or in winter, at which times the trees are dormant. Some pruning—to remove dead, diseased, or damaged wood or to remove suckers—should be done as necessary.

Unwanted growth saps a tree's energy, inhibits light penetration, and reduces yields, so correct pruning to remove this growth is essential. This illustration shows a mature apple tree before and after pruning. Orchardists say that a bird should be able to fly through the branches of a properly pruned apple tree without scratching a feather.

When pruning, the cut should be made close to the main trunk, as shown on the left. Such a cut heals quickly, whereas a cut that leaves a stub like the one shown on the right takes longer to heal.

Apple trees need more pruning than any other fruit trees, and cherries need the least. The following list indicates how much pruning fruit trees need (most to least):

1. Apple (most)
2. Pear
3. Peach
4. Apricot
5. Nectarine
6. Orange
7. Grapefruit
8. Lemon
9. Lime
10. Plum
11. Cherry (least)

Further information on pruning is given in the individual plant profiles.

Fertilizing fruit trees

With the possible exception of pears, all fruit trees require regular annual fertilizing. (In some areas pears do better without being fertilized because over-fertilization heightens the risk of fireblight disease.) Most fruit trees grown in average soils require about a half pound of a well-balanced (10-10-10) fertilizer per year of the tree's age, to a maximum of ten pounds for a fully-grown standard-size tree. Fertilize in the spring as soon as the leaf buds begin to swell; spread the fertilizer under the tree, starting one foot away from the trunk and continuing out to the drip line of the tree.

When pruning, remove watersprouts, which are the vertical shoots that grow from a horizontal branch.

Harvesting your fruit

It may seem that a lot of time and effort is required to grow fruit trees, but the reward is quite encouraging. A dwarf apple tree may give you five bushels of fruit; a standard apple tree may produce up to 15 bushels. Of course, the quantity produced by homegrown fruit trees is not your only consideration—what matters most is the delicious, fresh flavor of your own tree-ripened fruits.

The following chart gives you a rough idea of how much produce to expect from an average-sized fruit tree.

Apple (standard)	up to 15 bushels
Apricot	up to 5 bushels
Cherry	up to 16 pecks
Figs	up to 10 bushels
Grapefruits	up to 10 bushels
Lemon	up to 7 bushels
Lime	up to 7 bushels
Nectarine	up to 5 bushels
Orange	up to 10 bushels
Peach	up to 6 bushels
Pear	up to 10 bushels
Plum	up to 5 bushels

GROWING SMALL FRUITS

Small fruits such as raspberries and blueberries don't need as much space in your home garden as regular trees, but they do need considerable room and it's just as important to make a ground plan as it is when planting any other part of your garden. In fact, small fruits can be very rewarding.

If possible, try planting more than one type of small fruit—preferably a selection that will give you fruit throughout the growing season. For instance, you could plant strawberries for a spring crop, blueberries to produce in midsummer, and grapes for fall.

You can extend your harvesting season somewhat by planting everbearing strawberries and raspberries. Despite the name, however, these varieties do not actually bear fruit continuously. Everbearing strawberries and raspberries both produce fruit in early spring and again in fall, and you do pay a certain price for this double yield in terms of smaller and slightly less well-flavored fruit.

When and where to grow

For best results, all small fruits need a sunny location and well-drained, fertile soil. Any work that you put in on soil improvement before planting will be well rewarded, because properly maintained small fruit canes and bushes continue to yield indefinitely. Fruit grown in full sunlight tastes better than that grown in partial sun; however, small fruits will tolerate some shade although yields will be less generous and, as we have said, somewhat less flavorful.

All small fruits can be planted any time during the growing season. However, they will suffer less transplant stress if planted in the cool, moist spring or fall seasons. Most small fruits will begin to bear earlier if planted in spring.

Controlling pests and diseases

Small fruits generally need much less spraying than fruit trees. The insects that attack small fruits can generally be controlled as soon as they put in an appearance with little or no lasting damage to the plants or crops. Most of the diseases that attack small fruits can be prevented by following these simple horticultural practices:

1. Choose disease-resistant varieties.
2. Buy healthy, disease-free plants from a reliable nursery or garden center.
3. Renovate plants by pruning properly.
4. Remove any diseased plants as soon as possible and destroy them.
5. Fertilize properly.
6. Water properly.
7. Eliminate weed competition.

Pruning small fruits

Pruning is one of the most important practices in raising successful small fruit crops. It's also the most overlooked and least understood by the average home gardener. Although most small fruits need less pruning than regular fruit trees, all need some type of attention. Pruning grapes is a complex matter, but most small fruits are a lot easier to handle. Nothing could be simpler, for instance, than removing spent strawberry leaves after harvesting. If you don't prune small fruits, they will become overgrown and both fruit yield and flavor will be adversely affected. Specific pruning recommendations are given in each plant profile.

Fertilizing small fruits

All small fruits require regular annual fertilizing. Given good, fertile soil, most small fruits need one and one half to two pounds of a well balanced (10-10-10) fertilizer per 100 square feet. This fertilizer should be applied in spring in the case of raspberries, blackberries, currants, gooseberries, and grapes. Strawberries should be fertilized in midsummer after harvesting and renovation. Specific information is given in the plant profiles.

Most small fruits require a soil pH of about 6.5 to 7.0, which is slightly acid to neutral. The exceptions are blueberries, which require very acid soil with a pH of 4.5 to 5.5. You can reduce the pH of the soil be applying ammonium sulfate. Never use the more common aluminum sulfate on any edible crop; the aluminum could build up in the fruit and become toxic.

Any work you put into your small fruit garden is definitely worthwhile when you consider the yields you can expect. The following table tells you approximately how much fruit you can expect from a well maintained plant each year:

Blackberries	up to 5 to 10 quarts
Blueberries	up to 3 to 4 quarts
Currants	up to 3 to 4 quarts
Gooseberrie	up to 5 to 10 quarts
Grapes	up to 5 to 10 quarts
Raspberries:	
standard red	up to 1 to 2 quarts
everbearing red	up to 1 to 2 quarts
black	up to 1 to 1½ quarts
purple	up to 1 to 1½ quarts
Strawberries	up to 1 to 3 quarts
	per 10 plants

Apple

Common name: apple
Botanical name: Malus pumiia
Origin: southwestern Asia

Varieties

There are so many varieties of apples that the following list offers only a few suggestions. Early summer varieties: Redfree, Jerseymac, Earliblaze. Early fall varieties: Red Delicious, Sir Prize, Jonathan, Golden Delicious, Priscilla, Empire, Jonafree, McIntosh. Late fall varieties: Winesap, Rome. Avoid novelty varieties like 5 in 1 (five apple varieties grafted on to one tree).

Description

The apple is a hardy, deciduous, woody perennial tree that needs a cold dormancy period. Most modern varieties of apple are grafted; that is, their root system is different from the fruit-producing portion. Some varieties have not only a different root system but also a different trunk.

Dwarf, semi-dwarf, and standard apples

Apple trees are dwarfed basically by the type of root system onto which they are grafted. Root systems are identified by such names as MM9, M9, or EM26. Most apple dwarfing rootstocks were originated in England at the Malling Research Station (hence all the "M's" in their names).

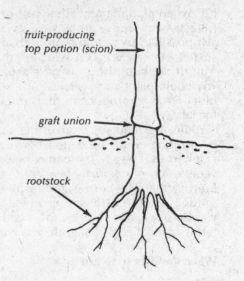

Many fruit trees are grafted; that is, the fruit-producing top portion of one variety is grafted onto the root system of another variety.

A tree that is grafted onto a dwarfing rootstock will be reduced in size by a certain percentage.

Each rootstock dwarfs a tree by a certain percentage: an apple variety that would normally grow to 30 feet would only grow to 18 feet if grafted onto a dwarfing rootstock. Another apple variety that would normally grow to 25 feet would only grow to 15 feet if grafted onto the same rootstock. Therefore the total height depends on the natural vigor of the variety and the percentage of dwarfing caused by the rootstock. A new development in recent years has been "spur type" apple varieties. These trees are less vigorous in their growth and are naturally smaller than nonspur-type varieties. They also develop fruit spurs in greater numbers and usually begin to bear fruit earlier in their lives.

Where and when to grow

Apples need a climate where the winters are cold enough to freeze the top few inches of soil and provide the necessary period of dormancy. Keep in mind that many types of apples are self-unfruitful: they will not produce a normal crop when pollinated by their own pollen or pollen from another tree of the same variety. A self-unfruitful tree should have another apple tree of a suitable variety within 300 feet.

The pollen of some apple trees is sterile and will not pollinate either itself or another apple variety. Of the varieties listed above, Winesap and Sir Prize are sterile. Check with your local Cooperative Extension Service or local garden center for advice on a fruitful combination.

How to plant

Apple trees dislike "wet feet" and should be planted in well-drained soil. They grow best in full sunlight. They will tolerate partial shade although the yield will not be as generous. Apple trees can be purchased either bareroot, balled and burlapped, or in a container.

A balled and burlapped tree may be planted any time during the growing season. The soil ball should be positioned in the planting hole at the same depth that the tree was growing at in the nursery. After positioning the ball in the hole, remove all twine or rope used to hold the ball together. Then open the top of the burlap so that water can penetrate the soil ball.

A bareroot tree should be planted only in early spring, and the planting hole should be large enough for the roots to be spread out completely. A bareroot tree should be planted two inches deeper than in the nursery. The grey soil line on the trunk will help you determine this depth.

A container-grown tree can be planted any time during the growing season. Remove the container carefully and plant the ball at the same depth as in the container.

After planting, water each tree in thoroughly and fertilize with a high-phosphorus liquid starter fertilizer.

The size of a mature apple tree depends on the varieties which have been grafted to produce the tree. In grafting, the root portion of one variety is combined with the upper fruit-producing portion (scion) of another variety. The combination not only controls the size of the mature tree, but improves hardiness, disease resistance, and fruit quality.

Fertilizing and watering

Apple trees should be fertilized with a half pound of a well-balanced (10-10-10) fertilizer for every year of age, to a maximum of 10 pounds per tree per year.

During the first summer they may need weekly watering. Once the trees are established they should only need infrequent watering during prolonged dry periods.

Special handling

During the first two growing seasons, apple trees should not be allowed to produce fruit. Handpick flowers or young fruit before they sap the energy the tree needs for growth. After the first two seasons, the trees may be allowed to bear small crops. If they bear large crops, limb damage may result, so thin out the fruit. Mature trees should have apples thinned to about six to eight inches apart.

Pruning is very important if apple trees are to produce a quality crop. Experienced growers will tell you that "a bird should be able to fly directly through a properly pruned tree without scratching a feather." Light pruning may be done at any time of the year, but heavy pruning should be done in the fall when the tree is dormant. When pruning, follow these rules:

1. Remove all diseased, dead, or broken branches.

2. Remove all watersprouts. Watersprouts are fast-growing, vertical branches that usually have no side branches.

3. Remove suckers. These are the fast-growing shoots that grow from the root below the soil surface.

4. Remove V-branching crotches. These are narrow crotches that will

Apples

not support the weight of a full crop of fruit.

5. Remove rubbing branches. If two branches cross and rub against each other they can cause a wound that offers an opportunity for invasion by insects or disease. Remove the least desirable branch.

6. Never remove more than one third of the total tree in a single growing season.

7. Always prune to a growth bud or flush to a main branch or trunk.

8. Maintain pruning annually.

Pests

Apples are attacked by a number of insects that are very difficult to control without using preventive chemical sprays. Among the pests that attack apples are scale, apple maggots, codling moths, and mites. Proper control of these pests requires timely intervention. The following is a general schedule. For more specific spraying instructions for your area consult your local Cooperative Extension Service.

1. Apply a dormant oil spray before buds open and when the temperature has been above 33°F for 48 hours.

2. Apply a multipurpose fruit tree spray when the buds begin to break.

3. Do not spray when the tree is in bloom.

4. When almost all the flower

petals have fallen, begin applying a multipurpose fruit tree spray every ten to 14 days.

5. Discontinue all spraying two weeks before harvest.

Diseases

Apple trees are attacked by many diseases that are almost impossible to control without the use of preventive chemical sprays. For this reason apples are not a good choice for the organic gardener. Apple trees are attacked by apple scab, blotch, cedar-apple rust, fireblight, and powdery mildew. To reduce fireblight potential, do not grow apples in the vicinity of pear trees. To reduce cedar-apple rust, keep cedars and junipers 300 yards from apples. For proper disease control, follow the spray schedule outlined earlier under "Pests".

When and how to harvest

For best flavor, apples should be harvested at full color. With green apple varieties, simply taste a couple to determine ripeness. Mature apples should come away from the tree easily; it should not be necessary to cut the stem.

Container growing

Apple trees cannot be grown satisfactorily in containers.

Q and A

Q: How long after an apple tree is planted will it produce fruit?
A: If they are watered, fertilized, and pruned properly, most apple varieties will begin producing after three or four years.
Q: Is it all right to grow grass around an apple tree?

A: The major problem caused by growing grass under an apple tree occurs when the grass is mown: the constant knocking of the mower against the trunk of the tree causes considerable damage and may even kill the tree. Also, the grass will use up a lot of the fertilizer intended for the use of the tree.
Q: Is there anything that can be done for a neglected, 30-year-old apple tree to make it productive again?
A: It would take three to four years to rejuvenate such a tree, which is probably not a practical proposition for the average home orchardist. It would be a lot easier to start all over with a new apple tree.
Q: What causes the leaves to turn brown and fall off an apple tree early in the fall?
A: This cause is a fungus disease called apple scab. Preventive spraying with a fungicide will help discourage this disease.

Apricot

Common name: apricot
Botanical name: Prunus armenica
Origin: Korea and Manchuria

Varieties

Royal Blenheim, Tilton, Moor Park, Riland, Perfection, Robust, Scout, Doty, Henderson, Geneva. Container varieties: Aprigold, Goldenglo.

Description

Apricot trees are semi-hardy, deciduous woody perennials. Most modern apricot varieties are grafted: the root system and the fruit-producing portion are different.

Where and when to grow

Apricots need a climate where the winters are cold enough to provide them with the necessary period of dormancy, but they will not produce reliably and may not even survive where temperatures drop below 0°F consistently. Most modern apricot varieties are self-fruitful and will pollinate themselves. Riland and Perfection are the only listed varieties that are not self-fruitful; in order to produce a normal crop they require another apricot tree of a suitable variety within 300 feet.

How to plant:

Apricot trees, like most fruit trees, dislike "wet feet" and should be planted in well-drained soil. Apricot trees grow best in full sunlight. They can tolerate partial shade, but the yield will be less generous.

Apricot trees may be purchased either bareroot, balled and burlapped, or in a container.

A balled and burlapped tree may be planted any time during the growing season. The soil ball should be positioned in the planting hole at the same depth that the tree was growing at in the nursery. After positioning the ball in the hole, remove all twine or rope used to hold the ball together. Then open the top of the burlap so that water can penetrate the soil ball.

A bareroot tree should be

planted only in early spring, and the planting hole should be large enough for the roots to be spread out completely. A bareroot tree should be planted at the same depth as in the nursery.

A container-grown tree can be planted any time during the growing season. Remove the container carefully and plant the ball at the same depth as in the container.

After planting, water each tree in thoroughly and fertilize with a high-phosphorus liquid starter fertilizer.

Fertilizing and watering

Apricot trees should be fertilized with one pound of a well-balanced (10-10-10) fertilizer for every year of the age of the tree, to a maximum of ten pounds per year per tree.

During the first summer after planting, apricot trees may need weekly waterings; once the trees are established, they should only need infrequent waterings during prolonged dry periods.

Special handling

During the first two growing seasons, apricots should not be allowed to flower or fruit. Handpick any flowers or young fruit before they use the energy the tree needs for growth. After the first two growing seasons, the trees may be allowed to bear a small crop. If they bear a large crop, limb damage may result, so the fruit should be thinned. On mature trees, apricots should be thinned to an average of two to three inches apart.

Pruning is a very important practice in producing a quality crop of apricots. Light pruning may be done at any time of the

Apricots

year. Heavy pruning should be done in the fall when the tree is dormant. When pruning, follow these basic rules.

1. Remove all diseased, dead, or broken branches.

2. Remove all watersprouts. Watersprouts are fast-growing, vertical branches that usually have no side branches.

3. Remove suckers. These are the fast-growing shoots that grow from the root below the soil surface.

4. Remove V-branching crotches. These are narrow crotches that will not support the weight of a full crop of fruit.

5. Remove rubbing branches. If two branches cross and rub against each other they can

cause a wound that offers an opportunity for invasion by insects or disease. Remove the least desirable branch.

6. Never remove more than one third of the total tree.

7. Always prune to a growth bud or flush to a main branch or trunk.

8. Maintain pruning annually.

Pests

Apricots are attacked by a number of insects that are very difficult to control without using chemical sprays, and for this reason are not a good choice for the organic gardener. Among the insects that attack apricots are scales, borers, Oriental fruit moths, and plum curculios. Proper pest control is dependent on timely seasonal applications of the correct insecticides. The following is a general spray schedule; for a more specific spray schedule for your area contact your local Cooperative Extension Service.

1. Apply a dormant oil spray before buds open and when the temperature is expected to stay above 33°F for 48 hours.

2. Apply Captan or Benomyl when the fruit buds show color as they start to open. Repeat the application seven days later when the flowers are in bloom.

3. After the fruit is established, spray every ten to 14 days with a multipurpose fruit tree spray until four weeks before harvest.

4. Starting four weeks before harvest, apply Captan every ten to 14 days until one week before harvest.

5. To control borers, spray or paint the trunk and lower limbs with Sevin in mid-July, and mid-August.

Diseases

Apricots are also attacked by brown fruit rot, which is nearly impossible to control without preventive chemical sprays—another reason why apricots are not a very good choice for the organic gardener. For proper disease control, follow the spray schedule outlined earlier under "Pests".

When and how to harvest

Apricots will ripen quickly when temperatures reach 80° to 90°F. They taste best when they are allowed to ripen on the tree; however, they can be harvested when they are full size and fully colored, and then allowed to ripen at room temperature. Ripe apricots will come away from the tree easily. It should not be necessary to cut the stem.

Container growing

Container growing may be the only way to produce apricots in very cold climates. Aprigold and Goldenglo apricot varieties can be grown in containers. Plant a single tree in a container three feet or more in diameter (for instance, a half wine or whiskey barrel). In cold climates, bring the tree into a protected, unheated area such as an unheated garage when it goes into dormancy in the fall. In the spring, bring the tree out as soon as possible. When it is in bloom, however, the tree should be moved back into the protected area on evenings when frost is expected.

Q and A

Q: How soon after planting will an apricot tree bear a full crop of fruit?
A: If properly watered, fertilized, and pruned, apricot trees will begin bearing three to five years after planting.
Q: Are apricots more sensitive to cold than peaches?
A: Yes; apricots are more sensitive to cold than any other tree fruit.
Q: Do you need to plant more than one apricot tree or apricot variety to produce fruit?
A: No; apricots are basically self-fruitful. However, a second variety can improve yields.

Cherry

Common name: cherry, sour cherry, sweet cherry
Botanical name: Prunus cerasus (sour cherries) Prunus avium (sweet cherries).
Origin: Korea

Varieties

Sour cherries: Early Richmond, English Morello, Montmorency. Sweet cherries: Bing, Black Tatarian, Emperor Francis, Hendelfingen, Lambert, Lyons, Napoleon, Royal Ann, Windsor, Yellow Spanish.

Description

The cherry is a hardy, deciduous, woody, perennial tree that needs a cold dormancy period. Most modern cherries are grafted: their root system is different from the fruit-producing portion. All cherries bloom in early spring.

Where and when to grow

Cherries need a climate where the winters are cold enough to freeze the top few inches of soil and provide the necessary period of dormancy. Keep in mind that sour cherries are usually self-fruitful, but sweet cherries are usually self-unfruitful: they will not produce a normal crop when pollinated by their own pollen or pollen from another tree of the same variety. A self-unfruitful tree should have another cherry tree of a suitable variety within 300 feet. The

Cherries

pollen of some cherries is sterile and will not pollinate itself or other varieties. Of the varieties listed, Bing, Lambert, Napoleon, and Emperor Francis are sterile. Check with your local Cooperative Extension Service to find a combination of sweet cherries that will be fruitful. Because all cherries bloom early in the spring, the flowers are susceptible to being killed by late frost even before the leaves appear. Sour cherries are slightly less susceptible to frost than sweet cherries. Where late frosts are common, it's advisable not to grow cherries.

How to plant

Cherry trees dislike "wet feet" and should be planted in a well-drained soil. They grow and produce best in full sunlight, but will tolerate partial shade, although the yield will not be as generous. Cherry trees can be purchased either bareroot, balled and burlapped, or in a container.

A balled and burlapped tree may be planted any time during the growing season. The soil ball should be positioned in the planting hole at the same depth that the tree was growing at in the nursery. After positioning the ball in the hole, remove all twine or rope used to hold the ball together. Then open the top of the burlap so that water can penetrate the soil ball.

A bareroot tree should be planted only in the early spring, and the planting hole should be large enough for the roots to be spread out completely. A bareroot cherry tree should be planted at the same depth as in the nursery.

A container-grown tree can be planted any time during the growing season. Remove the container carefully and plant the ball at the same depth as in the container.

After planting, water each tree in thoroughly and fertilize with a high-phosphorous liquid starter fertilizer.

Fertilizing and watering

Cherry trees should be fertilized with a half pound of a well-balanced (10-10-10) fertilizer for every year of age, to a maximum of 10 pounds per tree. During the first summer after planting, cherry trees may need weekly waterings. Once the trees are established, they should need only infrequent waterings during prolonged dry periods.

Special handling

One of the major problems with cherries is that birds will eat all or a large portion of the crop. Bird nets can be used to prevent bird damage, but most bird nets are not large enough to cover a full-size cherry tree, and covering entire trees with netting is not very practical.

During the first two growing seasons, cherry trees should not be allowed to produce fruit. Handpick any flowers or young fruit before they use the energy the tree needs for growth. After the first two seasons of growth, cherries may be allowed to bear a normal crop.

Pruning is an important factor in producing a satisfactory crop of cherries. Light pruning may be

The gardener can lose an entire cherry crop to birds unless the fruit is protected. Bird nets, though cumbersome, effectively protect the crop. Nets are also used to protect some small fruits from birds.

done at any time, but heavy pruning should be done in the fall when the tree is dormant. When pruning, follow these basic rules:

1. Remove all diseased, dead, or broken branches.

2. Remove all watersprouts. Watersprouts are fast-growing, vertical branches that usually have no side branches.

3. Remove suckers. These are the fast-growing shoots that grow from the root below the soil surface.

4. Remove V-branching crotches. These are narrow crotches that will not support the weight of a full crop of fruit.

5. Remove rubbing branches. If two branches cross and rub against each other they can cause a wound that offers an opportunity for invasion by insects or disease. Remove the least desirable branch.

6. Never remove more than one third of the total tree.

7. Always prune to a growth bud or flush to a main branch or trunk.

8. Maintain pruning annually.

Pests

Cherry trees are attacked by a number of insects that are very difficult to control without resorting to chemical sprays, so cherries are generally not a good choice for the organic gardener. Among the pests that attack cherries are aphids, scales, borers, and plum curculios. The following is a general spraying schedule. For more specific spraying instructions for your area, consult your local Cooperative Extension Service.

1. Apply a dormant oil spray before the buds begin to open and when the temperatures are expected to stay above 33°F for 48 hours.

2. After the fruit is set, apply a multi-purpose fruit tree spray every seven to ten days until two weeks before harvest.

3. After harvest, apply Captan, Dodine, or Benomyl. Repeat the application two weeks later.

4. If aphids appear, spray with Malathion.

5. To control borers, spray or paint the trunk and lower limbs with Sevin in mid-June, mid-July, and mid-August.

Diseases

The diseases that commonly attack cherries are brown rot and cherry leaf spot. To control these diseases, follow the spraying schedule outlined earlier under "Pests."

When and how to harvest

Cherries achieve the best flavor when they are allowed to ripen fully on the tree. Determining when cherries are fully mature is simple, because all cherries undergo obvious color changes when they mature. If you can't tell when your cherries are ripe the birds certainly can—and they'll eat them all unless you get there first.

Container gardening

Cherry trees do not grow well in containers.

Fig

Q and A

Q: How long after planting will cherry trees begin producing fruit?
A: Sour cherries will produce fruit three to five years from the time of planting, sweet cherries four to seven years from the time of planting.
Q: Do you need to plant more than one cherry tree in order to produce fruit?
A: Sour cherry trees are basically self-fruitful and don't need another tree in order to produce fruit. Most sweet cherry trees are self-unfruitful and do need a different variety of cherry tree planted within 30 feet if they are to produce fruit.
Q: What causes small black dots and yellowing of cherry leaves?
A: The problem is a disease called cherry leaf spot, which can only be controlled by regular sprayings with a fungicide.

Figs

Common name: fig
Botanical name: Ficus carica
Origin: Asia

Varieties

Adriatic, Brown Turkey, Celeste, Dottato.

Description

Fig trees are tender, deciduous, woody perennials that need a cool period of dormancy in order to fruit.

Where and when to grow

Figs can only be grown outside and unprotected in areas where temperatures do not drop below 32°F. Figs are grown in much colder climates, but only with the use of elaborate protective measures. In some areas, figs are buried every winter. In colder areas they are grown in tubs and moved indoors for the winter.

Many figs must undergo an involved process of pollination in order to produce fruit. The varieties listed above will produce fruit without this process.

How to plant

Figs grow well only in well-drained soil. They grow best in full sunlight. They can tolerate partial shade but yields will be less generous. Fig trees can usually be purchased either balled and burlapped or in a container. Both balled and burlapped and container-grown trees can be planted any time during the growing season. Place the ball in the planting hole at the same depth it was grown at in the nursery. Once the ball is in the hole at the correct depth, remove all the twine or rope used to hold the ball together. Open the top of the burlap so that water can penetrate the soil ball.

When planting container-grown figs, remove the container carefully, then place the ball in the hole at the same depth as in the container.

After planting, water each tree in thoroughly and fertilize with a high-phosphorous liquid starter fertilizer.

Fertilizing and watering

Fig trees should not be over-fertilized. Over-fertilizing encourages heavy foliage which inhibits light penetration and air circulation. Fertilize fig trees with a quarter pound of a well-balanced (10-10-10) fertilizer for every year of growth to a maximum of five pounds per year per tree.

During the first growing season fig trees may need weekly waterings. Once the trees are established, they should only need infrequent waterings during prolonged dry periods.

Special handling

During the first two growing seasons fig trees should not be allowed to fruit. Handpick all young fruit before they use any of the energy the tree needs for growth. After the first two seasons the trees may be allowed to bear a small crop. As they mature, they may be allowed to bear larger, and then full, crops.

Pruning is also very important in producing a quality crop of figs. Light pruning may be done any time of the year. Heavy annual pruning should be done in the fall when the tree is dormant.

When pruning, follow these basic rules:

1. Remove all diseased, dead, or broken branches.

2. Remove all watersprouts. Watersprouts are fast-growing, vertical branches that usually have no side branches.

3. Remove suckers. These are the fast-growing shoots that grow from the root below the soil surface.

4. Remove V-branching crotches. These are narrow crotches that will not support the weight of a full crop of fruit.

5. Remove rubbing branches. If two branches cross and rub against each other they can cause a wound that offers an opportunity for invasion by insects or disease. Remove the least desirable branch.

Pests

Figs are attacked by scales, four-legged mites, and spider mites, which are impossible to control without the use of chemical sprays. For this reason figs may not be the best choice for the organic gardener. The following is only a general spraying schedule. For a more specific spraying schedule for your area contact your local Cooperative Extension Service.

1. Apply a dormant oil spray before the buds open.

2. Apply Zineb, Ferbam, or Kelthane every 10 to 14 days until four weeks before harvest.

3. Apply Malathion when scale crawlers are present.

Diseases

Fig trees are susceptible to rust, leaf spot, anthracnose, souring, black smut, internal rot, and botrytis twig dieback. For proper disease control follow the spray schedule outlined above for controlling pests on fig trees.

When and how to harvest

Figs develop their best flavor when they are allowed to ripen fully on the tree. Figs show obvious signs when they ripen. They turn from green to a brown or purplish color and begin to soften slightly. Ripe figs fall easily from the tree, breaking off naturally at the node where they are attached to the tree branch. It should not be necessary to cut them from the tree.

Container growing

Container growing may be the only way to produce figs in colder climates. Plant a single fig tree in a container three feet or more in diameter; for instance, a half wine or whiskey barrel. In cold climates, bring the fig tree into an area where the temperature will remain above 33°F, and keep the tree there for the winter. In the spring, bring the tree outside as soon as any chance of frost is past.

Q and A

Q: Is it necessary to grow more than one fig tree in order to produce fruit?
A: A few fig varieties will produce fruit on their own. These are not high-yield varieties, but they do produce enough for the home gardener. These varieties include Adriatic, Brown Turkey, and Celeste.
Q: How long does it take for figs to begin producing fruit?
A: Fig trees can often be purchased already bearing immature fruits. This is fine if you plan to keep the tree growing in a container. If not, remove the fruit for two to three years to allow the tree to mature

before letting it bear a normal crop.

Q: Is it normal for fig trees to lose all their leaves when they are brought in for the winter?
A: Yes. Fig trees are deciduous and lose their leaves even under the best conditions.

Grapefruit

Common name: grapefruit
Botanical name: Citrus paradisi
Origin: West Indies

Varieties

White flesh: Duncan, Indian River, McCartney; pink flesh: Foster, Thompson, Ruby

Description

Grapefruit trees are tall, tender perennials that can grow to 25 to 30 feet. The leaves are dark, shiny green. Grapefruit may be seeded or seedless, with white or pink flesh. The fruit varies from six to twelve inches in diameter. Grapefruit trees are usually grafted: the root system and the fruit-producing portion are different.

Where and when to grow

Grapefruit trees can be grown in any region where temperatures never fall below 20°F. They will not fruit well if temperatures drop below 27°F after the tree has flowered. Grapefruit trees should be planted in early spring.

Grapefruit

Grapefruit trees can be purchased either balled and burlapped or bareroot. In either case, the tree should be planted at the same depth it was growing at time of purchase. The grey soil line on the trunk will help you determine this depth.

When planting a balled and burlapped tree, remove all the rope or twine that holds the ball together. If left in place, this rope or twine might constrict the growth of the tree. Also, open the top of the burlap so that water can penetrate the soil ball.

When planting a bareroot tree, make the planting hole large enough to accommodate the spread-out roots without crowding. Prune the top of the tree heavily by removing approximately one-third of the upper branches. This will reduce water loss, because as the tree develops there will be fewer leaves through which the tree's moisture can evaporate.

When planting either a balled and burlapped or a bareroot tree, water the tree in thoroughly. Paint the trunk white or wrap it in burlap or a commercial tree wrap to protect it from sunburn.

Grapefruit trees should be planted 25 to 35 feet apart, preferably in full sun. In shaded areas, fruit yield will be reduced.

Fertilizing and watering

Fertilizing grapefruit trees is a

tricky undertaking. First you should have your soil tested. Some Cooperative Extension Services test soil, and those that don't can recommend a testing service. Following the recommendations of the testing organization, adjust the balance of the major nutrients (nitrogen, phosphorus, and potassium) in the soil. You may also need to adjust the soil content of minor nutrients such as zinc, iron, magnesium, manganese, copper, etc. Contact your local Cooperative Extension Service for specific recommendations for your area.

Grapefruit trees need watering all year around and should receive up to four to six inches of water every two weeks. If the rainfall is less than this, you will have to provide the extra water. It's helpful to provide a catch basin around each tree to retain the available water; to do this, shape the soil around the tree into a saucer-shaped depression that extends to the drip line (or outer branches) of the tree. Grapefruit trees need slightly less water in the winter months.

Special handling

Grapefruit trees need only limited pruning. During the first few years all you need do is remove the watersprouts and any dead wood. Older trees may be "topped" to keep them from growing unduly tall. Cut off eight to twelve inches of the top branches to control the tree's height and encourage lateral branching.

Pests

Grapefruit trees have so many pest problems that it is

impossible to list them all; because these pests cannot be controlled without chemical means, grapefruit are not a suitable crop for the organic grower. The pests that attack grapefruit trees vary according to region, but the most common are armored scales, mites, thrips, and ant-protected aphids. It will be necessary to use chemical sprays to control these pests; however, do not spray during the blooming period or within a week of harvesting. Contact you local Cooperative Extension Service for a specific spraying schedule for your area.

Diseases

Grapefruit trees are also subject to many disease problems. Like the pests listed above, these diseases vary according to region and must be chemically controlled—another reason why grapefruit are not a good crop for the organic grower. Scab and melanose are two of the most common diseases of grapefruit trees. Contact your local Cooperative Extension Service for a specific spraying schedule for your area.

When and how to harvest

Grapefruit can be picked as soon as they have reached full color. You can also use the taste test to judge the ripeness of the fruit. When harvesting, cut rather than pull the fruit from the tree.

Container growing

Grapefruit trees cannot be grown satisfactorily in a container.

Q and A

Q: Will a sweeter soil sweeten the flavor of my grapefruit crop?
A: No. the pH of the soil will not affect the flavor of any fruit.
Q: I've heard that grapefruit will cross with other citrus fruits and that this has an adverse effect on the flavor of the crop. Is this true?
A: No. The popular notion that different types of citrus fruits can cross-pollinate and cause the resulting fruit to be bitter is completely false. Only the offspring of such a cross would be affected.
Q: How long from the time of planting will it take for my grapefruit tree to begin producing fruit?
A: Grapefruit will begin bearing a normal crop in four to five years.
Q: Should I plant more than one grapefruit tree in order to get a crop?
A: No. Grapefruit trees are self-fruitful and do not need another tree for pollination.

Lemon

Common name: lemon
Botanical name: Citrus limonia
Origin: West Indies

Varieties

Eureka, Lisbon, Villafranca, Meyer, Ponderosa, Millsweet, Dorshapo

Description

Lemon trees are tall, tender perennials that can grow to 15 to 25 feet. The leaves are dark, shiny green. Lemons are usually egg-shaped and pointed at each end, and vary from three to seven inches in diameter.

Where and when to grow

Lemon trees can be grown in any region where temperatures never fall below 20°F. They will not fruit well if temperatures drop below 27°F after the tree has flowered. Lemon trees should be planted in early spring or late fall.

Lemon trees can be purchased either balled and burlapped or bareroot. In either case the tree should be planted at the same depth it was growing at time of purchase. The grey soil line on the trunk will help you determine this depth.

When planting a balled and burlapped tree, remove all the rope or twine that holds the ball together. If left in place, this rope or twine might constrict the growth of the tree. Also, open the top of the burlap so that water can penetrate the soil ball.

When planting a bareroot tree, make the planting hole large enough to accommodate the spread-out roots without crowding. Prune the top of the tree heavily by removing approximately one-third of the upper branches. This will reduce water loss, because as the tree develops there will be fewer leaves through which the tree's moisture can evaporate.

When planting either a balled and burlapped or a bareroot tree, water the tree in thoroughly. Paint the trunk white or wrap it in burlap or a commercial tree

Lemon

wrap to protect it from sunburn.

Lemon trees should be planted 25 to 35 feet apart, preferably in full sun. In shaded areas, fruit yield will be reduced.

Fertilizing and watering

Fertilizing lemon trees is a tricky undertaking. First you should have your soil tested. Some Cooperative Extension Services test soil, and those that don't can recommend a testing service. Following the recommendations of the testing organization, adjust the balance of the major nutrients (nitrogen, phosphorus, and potassium) in the soil. You may also need to adjust the soil content of minor nutrients such as zinc, iron, magnesium, manganese, copper, etc. Contact your local Cooperative Extension Service for specific recommendations for your area.

Lemon trees need watering all year around and should receive up to four to six inches of water every two weeks. If the rainfall is less than this, you will have to provide the extra water. It's helpful to provide a catch basin around each tree to retain the available water; to do this, shape the soil around the tree into a saucer-shaped depression that extends to the drip line (or outer branches) of the tree. Lemon trees need slightly less water in the winter months.

Special handling

Lemon trees need only limited pruning. During the first few years all you need do is remove the watersprouts and any dead wood. Older trees may be "topped" to keep them from growing unduly tall. Cut off eight to twelve inches of the top branches to control the tree's height and encourage lateral branching.

Pests

Lemon trees have so many pest problems that it is impossible to list them all; because these pests cannot be controlled without chemical means, lemons are not a suitable crop for the organic grower. The pests that attack lemon trees vary according to region, but the most common are armored scales, mites, thrips, and ant-protected aphids. It will be necessary to use chemical sprays to control these pests; however, do not spray during the blooming period or within a week of harvesting. Contact your local Cooperative Extension Service for a specific spraying schedule for your area.

Diseases

Lemon trees are also subject to many disease problems. Like the pests listed above, these diseases vary according to region and must be chemically controlled— another reason why lemons are not a good crop for the organic grower. Scab and melanose are two of the most common diseases of lemon trees. Contact your local Cooperative Extension Service for a specific spraying schedule for your area.

When and how to harvest

Lemons can be picked as soon as they have reached full color. You can also use the taste test to judge the ripeness of the fruit. When harvesting, cut rather than pull the fruit from the tree.

Container growing

Dwarf lemon trees that will bear fruit are available, but they are extremely difficult to grow indoors, and although they will grow somewhat more satisfactorily in an outdoor container the flavor of the fruit will still be inferior to that of fruit from an orchard-grown tree. You can try growing one of the smaller varieties if you live in a Northern area where you couldn't grow citrus fruits in your garden anyway, or if you're more interested in the appearance of the tree than in the flavor of the fruit. Breeders are working on developing dwarf citrus varieties that will yield well-flavored fruits.

Q and A

Q: Will a sweeter soil sweeten the flavor of my lemon crop?
A: No. The pH of the soil will not affect the flavor of any fruit.
Q: I've heard that lemons will cross with other citrus fruits and that this has an adverse effect on the flavor of the crop. Is this true?
A: No. The popular notion that different types of citrus fruits can cross-pollinate and cause the resulting fruit to be bitter is completely false. Only the offspring of such a cross would be affected.
Q: How long from the time of planting will it take for my lemon tree to begin producing fruit?
A: Lemons will begin bearing a normal crop in two to three years.
Q: Should I plant more than one lemon tree in order to get a crop?

A: No. Lemon trees are self-fruitful and do not need another tree for pollination.

Lime

Common name: lime
Botanical name: Citrus aurantifolia
Origin: Mexico and Tahiti

Varieties

Rangpur, Bearss, Palestine, Sweet, Otaheite

Description

Lime trees are tall, tender perennials that can grow to 15 to 20 feet. The leaves are dark, shiny green. The fruit, which is usually round, varies from three to four inches in diameter.

Where and when to grow

Lime trees can be can be grown in any region where temperatures never fall below 20°F. They will not fruit well if temperatures drop below 27°F after the tree has flowered. Lime trees should be planted in early spring or late fall.

Lime trees can be purchased either balled and burlapped or bareroot. In either case the tree should be planted at the same depth it was growing at time of purchase. The grey soil line on the trunk will help you determine this depth.

When planting a balled and burlapped tree, remove all the

rope or twine that holds the ball together. If left in place, this rope or twine might constrict the growth of the tree. Also, open the top of the burlap so that water can penetrate the soil ball.

When planting a bareroot tree, make the planting hole large enough to accommodate the spread-out roots without crowding. Prune the top of the tree heavily by removing approximately one-third of the upper branches. This will reduce water loss, because as the tree develops there will be fewer leaves through which the tree's moisture can evaporate.

When planting either a balled and burlapped or a bareroot tree, water the tree in thoroughly. Paint the trunk white or wrap it in burlap or a commercial tree wrap to protect it from sunburn.

Lime trees should be planted 25 to 35 feet apart, preferably in full sun. In shaded areas, fruit yield will be reduced.

Lime

Fertilizing and watering

Fertilizing lime trees is a tricky undertaking. First you should have your soil tested. Some Cooperative Extension Services test soil, and those that don't can recommend a testing service. Following the recommendations of the testing organization, adjust the balance of the major nutrients (nitrogen, phosphorus, and potassium) in the soil. You may also need to adjust the soil content of minor nutrients such as zinc, iron, magnesium, manganese, copper, etc. Contact your local Cooperative Extension Service for specific recommendations for your area.

Lime trees need watering all year around and should receive up to four to six inches of water every two weeks. If the rainfall is less than this, you will have to provide the extra water. It's helpful to provide a catch basin around each tree to retain the available water; to do this, shape the soil around the tree into a saucer-shaped depression that extends to the drip line (or outer branches) of the tree. Lime trees need slightly less water in the winter months.

Special handling

Lime trees need only limited pruning. During the first few years all you need do is remove the watersprouts and any dead wood. Older trees may be "topped" to keep them from growing unduly tall. Cut off eight to twelve inches of the top branches to control the tree's height and encourage lateral branching.

Pests

Lime trees have so many pest problems that it is impossible to list them all; because these pests cannot be controlled without chemical means, limes are not a suitable crop for the organic grower. The pests that attack lime trees vary according to region, but the most common are armored scales, mites, thrips, and ant-protected aphids. It will be necessary to use chemical sprays to control these pests; however, do not spray during the blooming period or within a week of harvesting. Contact you local Cooperative Extension Service for a specific spraying schedule for your area.

Diseases

Lime trees are also subject to many disease problems. Like the pests listed above, these diseases vary according to region and must be chemically controlled— another reason why limes are not a good crop for the organic grower. Scab and melanose are two of the most common diseases of lime trees. Contact your local Cooperative Extension Service for a specific spraying schedule for your area.

When and how to harvest

Limes can be picked as soon as they have reached full color. You can also use the taste test to judge the ripeness of the fruit. When harvesting, cut rather than pull the fruit from the tree.

Container growing

Dwarf lime trees that will bear fruit are available, but they are extremely difficult to grow indoors, and although they will grow somewhat more satisfactorially in an outdoor container the flavor of the fruit will still be inferior to that of fruit from an orchard-grown tree. You can try growing one of the smaller varieties if you live in a Northern area where you couldn't grow citrus fruits in your garden anyway, or if you're more interested in the appearance of the tree than in the flavor of the fruit. Breeders

are working on developing dwarf citrus varieties that will yield well-flavored fruits.

Q and A

Q: Will a sweeter soil sweeten the flavor of my lime crop?
A: No. the pH of the soil will not affect the flavor of any fruit.
Q: I've hear that limes will cross with other citrus fruits and that this has adverse effect on the flavor of the crop. Is this true?
A: No. The popular notion that different types of citrus fruits can cross-pollinate and cause the resulting fruit to be bitter is completely false. Only the offspring of such a cross would be affected.
Q: How long from the time of planting will it take for my lime tree to begin producing fruit?
A: Lime trees will begin bearing a normal crop in two to three years.
Q: Should I plant more than one lime tree in order to get a crop?
A: No. Lime trees are self-fruitful and do not need another tree for pollination.

Nectarine

Common name: nectarine, smooth peach
Botanical name: Prunus persica
Origin: China

Varieties

Yellow-fleshed fruit: Lexington, Redchief, Cavalier, Pocahontas, Cherokee, Redbud. White-fleshed fruit: Nectarose, Nectaheart, Nectacrest, Nectacate.

Description

The nectarine is an interesting horticultural phenomenon. It is different from the peach in appearance and flavor, but is still the same genus and species. In fact, a nectarine tree will occasionally grow from a peach seed and a peach tree from a nectarine seed. Nectarine trees are semi-hardy, deciduous, woody perennials. Most modern nectarines are grafted: the root system and the fruit-producing portion are different.

Where and when to grow:

Nectarines will not produce reliably (and may not even survive) in areas where winter temperatures drop below 0°F. Most modern nectarine varieties are self-fruitful and will pollinate themselves.

How to plant

Nectarine trees dislike "wet feet" and should be planted in well-drained soil. They grow best in full sunlight. They can tolerate partial shade, but the yield will be less generous. Nectarine trees may be purchased either bareroot, balled and burlapped, or in a container.

A balled and burlapped tree may be planted any time during the growing season. The soil ball should be positioned in the planting hole at the same depth that the tree was growing at in the nursery. After positioning the ball in the hole, remove all twine or rope used to hold the ball together. Then open the top of the burlap so that water can penetrate the soil ball.

A bareroot tree should be planted only in early spring, and the planting hole should be large enough for the roots to spread out completely. A bareroot nectarine tree should be planted at the same depth as in the nursery.

A container-grown tree can be planted any time during the growing season. Remove the container carefully and plant the ball at the same depth as it had been in the container. After planting, water each tree in thoroughly and fertilize with a high-phosphorus liquid starter fertilizer.

Fertilizing and watering

Nectarine trees should be fertilized with one pound of a well-balanced (10-10-10) fertilizer for every year of age to a maximum of 10 pounds per year per tree. During the first summer nectarine trees may need weekly waterings. Once the trees are established they should only need infrequent waterings during prolonged dry periods.

Special handling

During the first two growing seasons nectarine trees should not be allowed to flower or fruit. Handpick any flowers or young fruit before they use the energy the tree needs for growth. After the first two seasons the trees may be allowed to bear a small crop. If they bear large crops, limb damage may result, so thin out the fruit, leaving nectarines

Nectarine

an average of six to eight inches apart on mature trees.

Pruning is an important practice in producing a quality crop of nectarines. Light pruning may be done at any time, but heavy pruning should be done in the fall when the tree is dormant.

When pruning, follow these basic rules:

1. Remove all diseased, dead, or broken branches
2. Remove all watersprouts. Watersprouts are fast-growing, vertical branches that usually have no side branches.
3. Remove suckers. These are the fast-growing shoots that grow from the root below the soil surface.
4. Remove V-branching crotches. These are narrow crotches that will not support the weight of a full crop of fruit.
5. Remove rubbing branches. If two branches cross and rub against each other they can cause a wound that offers an opportunity for invasion by insects or disease. Remove the least desirable branch.
6. Never remove more than one third of the total tree.
7. Always prune to a growth bud or flush to a main branch or trunk.
8. Maintain pruning annually.

Pests

Nectarines are attacked by a number of insects that are very difficult to control without chemical sprays, and may therefore be a poor choice for organic gardeners. Nectarines are attacked by scales, borers, mites, Oriental fruit moths, and plum curculios. Proper control of these pests is dependent on timely seasonal applications of the appropriate insecticides. The following is a general schedule. For more specific spraying instructions for your area contact your local Cooperative Extension Service.

1. Apply a dormant oil spray before the buds open and when the temperature is expected to stay above 33°F for 48 hours.

2. Apply Captan or Benomyl when the fruit buds show color as they start to open, and again seven days later when they are in bloom.

3. After the fruit is established, spray every 10 to 14 days with a multi-purpose fruit tree spray. Discontinue spraying four weeks before harvest.

4. Apply Captan every 10 to 14 days until one week before harvest.

5. To control borers, spray or paint the trunk and lower limbs with Sevin in mid-June, mid-July, and mid-August.

Diseases

Netarine trees are also attacked by numerous diseases that are nearly impossible to control without chemical sprays. For this reason also, nectarines may not be a good choice for the organic gardener. Nectarines are attacked by brown fruit rot, peach leaf curl and peach scab. For proper disease control follow the spray schedule outlined earlier under "Pests."

When and how to harvest

Nectarines are best harvested when the fruit shows full color but before it begins to soften. Ripe nectarines will come away from the tree easily; it should not be necessary to cut the stem.

Container Growing:

Container growing may be the only way to produce nectarines in very cold climates. Stark Honeyglo, Stark Sweet Melody, and Mericrest nectarine varieties can be grown in containers. Plant a single nectarine tree in a container three feet or more in diameter (e.g., a half wine or whiskey barrel). In cold climates bring the nectarine tree into a protected, unheated area such as an unheated garage in the winter. In the spring bring the tree out as soon as possible. When the nectarine tree is in bloom, bring it into a protected, unheated area on evenings when frost is expected.

Q and A

Q: How soon after planting will nectarine trees begin producing fruit?
A: Most modern nectarine varieties will begin to produce normal crops two to three years after planting.
Q: Is it necessary to plant more than one nectarine tree to produce fruit?
A: No; nectarines are self-fruitful, and only one tree is necessary to produce fruit.
Q: Each year my tree produces plenty of nectarines, but very few develop to full size. How can I get the tree to produce larger fruits?
A: Nectarine trees usually

overproduce and need to be thinned. The fruits should be thinned to approximately eight inches apart as soon after the fruit sets as possible, and not later than a month after blooming.

#

Common name: orange
Botanical name: Citrus sinensis
Origin: West Indies

Varieties

Parson Brown, Hamlin, Jaffa, Homossasa, Valencia; in the dry southwest, Washington Navel.

Description

Orange trees are tall, tender perennials that can grow to 25 to 35 feet. The leaves are dark, shiny green. Oranges may be seeded or seedless, varying in diameter from two to three inches to as large as eight inches.

Where and when to grow

Orange trees can be can be grown in any region where temperatures never fall below 20°F. They will not fruit well if temperatures drop below 27°F after the tree has flowered. Orange trees should be planted in early spring or late fall.

Orange trees can be purchased either balled and burlapped or bareroot. In either case the tree should be planted at the same depth it was growing at time of purchase. The grey soil line on the trunk will help you determine this depth.

When planting a balled and burlapped tree, remove all the rope or twine that holds the ball together. If left in place, this rope or twine might constrict the growth of the tree. Also, open the top of the burlap so that water can penetrate the soil ball.

When planting a bareroot tree, make the planting hole large enough to accommodate the spread-out roots without crowding. Prune the top of the tree heavily by removing approximately one-third of the upper branches. This will reduce water loss, because as the tree develops there will be fewer leaves through which the tree's moisture can evaporate.

When planting either a balled and burlapped or a bareroot tree, water the tree in thoroughly. Paint the trunk white or wrap it in burlap or a commercial tree wrap to protect it from sunburn.

Orange trees should be planted 25 to 35 feet apart, preferably in full sun. In shaded areas, fruit yield will be reduced.

Fertilizing and watering

Fertilizing orange trees is a tricky undertaking. First you should have your soil tested. Some Cooperative Extension Services test soil, and those that don't can recommend a testing service. Following the recommendations of the testing organization, adjust the balance of the major nutrients (nitrogen, phosphorus, and potassium) in the soil. You may also need to adjust the soil content of minor nutrients such as zinc, iron, magnesium, manganese, copper, etc. Contact your local Cooperative Extension

Service for specific recommendations for your area.

Orange trees need watering all year around and should receive up to four to six inches of water every two weeks. If the rainfall is less than this, you will have to provide the extra water. It's helpful to provide a catch basin around each tree to retain the available water; to do this, shape the soil around the tree into a saucer-shaped depression that extends to the drip line (or outer branches) of the tree. Orange trees need slightly less water in the winter months.

Orange

Special handling

Orange trees need only limited pruning. During the first few years all you need do is remove the watersprouts and any dead wood. Older trees may be "topped" to keep them from growing unduly tall. Cut off eight to twelve inches of the top branches to control the tree's height and encourage lateral branching.

Pests

Orange trees have so many pest problems that it is impossible to list them all; because these pests cannot be controlled without chemical means, oranges are not a suitable crop for the organic grower. The pests that attack orange trees vary according to region, but the most common are armored scales, mites, thrips, and ant-protected aphids. It will be necessary to use chemical sprays to control these pests; however, do not spray during the blooming period or within a week of harvesting. Contact your local Cooperative Extension Service for a specific spraying schedule for your area.

Diseases

Orange trees are also subject to many disease problems. Like the pests listed above, these diseases vary according to region and must be chemically controlled—another reason why oranges are not a good crop for the organic grower. Scab and melanose are two of the most common diseases of orange trees. Contact your local Cooperative Extension Service for a specific spraying schedule for your area.

Container growing

Dwarf orange trees that will bear fruit are available, but they are extremely difficult to grow indoors, and although they will grow somewhat more satisfactorily in an outdoor container the flavor of the fruit will still be inferior to that of fruit from an orchard-grown tree. You can try growing one of the smaller varieties if you live in a Northern area where you couldn't grow citrus fruits in your garden anyway, or if you're more interested in the appearance of the tree than in

the flavor of the fruit. Breeders are working on developing dwarf citrus varieties that will yield well-flavored fruits.

When and how to harvest

Oranges can be picked as soon as they have reached full color, but determining this requires watchfulness and some experience because some varieties color and then re-green as they become overripe (re-greening is actually caused by sunburn). You can also use the taste test to judge the ripeness of the fruit. When harvesting, cut rather than pull the fruit from the tree.

Q and A

Q: Will a sweeter soil sweeten the flavor of my orange crop?
A: No. The pH of the soil will not affect the flavor of any fruit.
Q: I've heard that oranges will cross with other citrus fruits and that this has an adverse effect on the flavor of the crop. Is this true?
A: No. The popular notion that different types of citrus fruits can cross-pollinate and cause the resulting fruit to be bitter is completely false. Only the offspring of such a cross would be affected.
Q: How long from the time of planting will it take for my orange tree to begin producing fruit?
A: Orange trees will begin bearing a normal crop in three to four years.
Q: Should I plant more than one orange tree in order to get a crop?
A: No. Orange trees are self-fruitful and do not need another tree for pollination.

Peach

Common name: peach
Botanical name: Prunus persica
Origin: China

Varieties

Yellow-fleshed fruit: Cresthaven, Earliglo, Garnet Beauty, Redhaven, Compact Redhaven, Biscoe, Elberta, Redskin, Reliance, Madison. White-fleshed fruit: Belle of Georgia.

Description

Peaches are semi-hardy, deciduous, woody perennial trees. Most modern peach varieties are grafted: their root system is different from the fruit-producing portion.

Where and when to grow

Peaches will not produce reliably (and may not even survive) in areas where winter temperatures drop below 0°F. Most modern peach varieties are self-fruitful and will pollinate themselves.

How to plant

Peach trees dislike "wet feet" and should be planted in well-drained soil. They grow best in full sunlight. They can tolerate partial shade, but the yield will be less generous. Peach trees may be purchased either bareroot, balled and burlapped, or in a container.

A balled and burlapped tree may be planted any time during the growing season. The soil ball should be positioned in the planting hole at the same depth that the tree was growing at in the nursery. After positioning the ball in the hole, remove all twine or rope used to hold the ball together. Then open the top of the burlap so that water can penetrate the soil ball.

A bareroot tree should be planted only in early spring, and the planting hole should be large enough for the roots to be spread out completely. A bareroot peach tree should be planted at the same depth as in the nursery.

A container-grown tree can be planted any time during the growing season. Remove the container carefully and plant the ball at the same depth as in the container.

After planting, water each tree in thoroughly and fertilize with a high-phosporus liquid starter fertilizer.

Peach

Fertilizing and watering

Peach trees should be fertilized with one pound of a well-balanced (10-10-10) fertilizer for every year of age to a maximum of 10 pounds per year per tree. During the first summer, peach trees may need weekly waterings. Once the trees are established they should only need infrequent waterings during prolonged dry periods.

Special handling

During the first two growing seasons, peach trees should not be allowed to flower or fruit. Handpick any flowers or young fruit before they use the energy the tree needs for growth. After the first two seasons the trees may be allowed to bear a small

crop. If they bear large crops, limb damage may result, so thin out the fruit, leaving peaches an average of six to eight inches apart on mature trees.

Pruning is an important practice in producing a quality crop of peaches. Light pruning may be done at any time, but heavy pruning should be done in the fall when the tree is dormant. When pruning, follow these basic rules:

1. Remove all diseased, dead, or broken branches.
2. Remove all watersprouts. Watersprouts are fast-growing, vertical branches that usually have no side branches.
3. Remove suckers. These are the fast-growing shoots that grow from the root below the soil surface.

4. Remove V-branching crotches. These are narrow crotches that will not support the weight of a full crop of fruit.
5. Remove rubbing branches. If two branches cross and rub against each other they can cause a wound that offers an opportunity for invasion by insects or disease. Remove the least desirable branch.
6. Never remove more than one third of the total tree.
7. Always prune to a growth bud or flush to a main branch or trunk.
8. Maintain pruning annually.

Pests

Peaches are attacked by a number of insects that are very difficult to control without chemical sprays, and may therefore be a poor choice for organic gardeners. Peaches are attacked by scales, borers, mites, Oriental fruit moths, and plum curculios. Proper control of these pests is dependent on timely seasonal applications of the appropriate insecticides. The following is a general schedule. For more specific spraying instructions for your area contact your local Cooperative Extension Service.

1. Apply a dormant oil spray before the buds open and when the temperature is expected to stay above 33°F for 48 hours.

2. Apply Captan or Benomyl when the fruit buds show color as they start to open, and again seven days later when they are in bloom.

3. After the fruit is established, spray every 10 to 14 days with a multi-purpose fruit tree spray. Discontinue spraying four weeks before harvest.

4. Apply Captan every 10 to 14 days until one week before harvest.

5. To control borers, spray or paint the trunk and lower limbs with Sevin in mid-June, mid-July, and mid-August.

Diseases

Peach trees are also attacked by numerous diseases that are nearly impossible to control without chemical sprays. For this reason also, peaches may not be a good choice for the organic gardener. Peaches are attacked by brown fruit rot, peach leaf curl and peach scab. For proper disease control follow the spray schedule outline earlier under "Pests."

When and how to harvest

Peaches develop the best flavor when they are allowed to mature on the tree. Peaches should be picked when they have reached full color. It may be difficult to tell when some peach varieties have reached full color, so test for the slight softening which also indicates ripeness. Periodic taste-testing will also help you determine when the major part of the crop is ripe. Ripe peaches will come away from the tree easily; it should not be necessary to cut the stem.

Container growing

Container growing may be the only way to produce peaches in very cold climates. Stark Sensation and Garden Gold peach varieties can be grown in containers. Plant a single peach tree in a container three feet or more in diameter (e.g., a half wine or whiskey barrel). In cold climates bring the peach tree into a protected, unheated area such as an unheated garage in the winter. In the spring bring the tree out as soon as possible. When the peach tree is in bloom, bring it into a protected, unheated area on evenings when frost is expected.

Q and A

Q: Why aren't white peaches sold in most northern states?
A: White-fleshed peaches are so soft-bodied that they cannot be shipped successfully.
Q: All the leaves on my peach tree curled up and died, and a few weeks later new leaves appeared. What happened?
A: These are symptoms of the disease known as peach leaf curl, which weakens the tree and reduces yields. Preventive spraying with a fungicide will help control the disease.
Q: Is it necessary to whitewash the trunk of a peach tree to discourage ants?
A: The only reason for whitewashing the trunk of a peach tree is to protect it from sunburn in early spring. Whitewashing the trunk will not discourage ants.

Pear

Common name: pear
Botanical name: Pyrus communis
Origin: Western Asia

Varieties

Maxine, Starking Delicious, Peckel, Morgan, Magness, Moonglow, Anjou, Bosc, Comice, Dana Hovey, Gorham, Bartlett.

Description

Pears are hardy, deciduous, woody perennial trees that need a cold dormant period. Many modern pear varieties are grafted. This means the root system and the fruit-producing portions are different.

Where and when to grow

Pears need a climate where the winters are cold enough to freeze the top few inches of soil and provide the necessary period of dormancy. Keep in mind that some varieties of pears are self-unfruitful: they will not produce a normal crop when pollinated by their own pollen or pollen from another tree of the same variety. A self-unfruitful tree should have another pear tree of a suitable variety within 300 feet. Maxine and Starking Delicious pears will not pollinate either themselves or each other. Seckel and Moonglow will pollinate each other, and will also pollinate Maxine and Starking Delicious.

How to plant

Pear trees dislike "wet feet" and should be planted in well-drained soil. They grow and produce best in full sunlight. They will tolerate partial shade, although the yield will not be as generous. Pear trees can be purchased bareroot, balled and burlapped, or in a container.

A balled and burlapped tree may be planted any time during the growing season. The soil ball should be positioned in the planting hole at the same depth that the tree was growing at in the nursery. After positioning the ball in the hole, remove all twine or rope used to hold the ball together. Then open the top of the burlap so that water can penetrate the soil ball.

A bareroot tree should be planted only in early spring, and the planting hole should be large enough for the roots to be spread out completely. A bareroot tree should be planted at the same depth as in the nursery.

A container-grown tree can be planted any time during the growing season. Remove the container carefully and plant the ball at the same depth as in the container.

After planting, water each tree in thoroughly and fertilize with a

Pear

high-phosphorus liquid starter fertilizer.

Fertilizing and watering

Pear trees should be fertilized with a quarter pound of a well-balanced (10-10-10) fertilizer for every year of age, to a maximum of five pounds per tree per year. Do not over-fertilize. Over-fertilizing may cause excessive shoot growth which can lead to fireblight. With pears, it's better to fertilize too little than too much.

During the first summer, pear trees may need weekly waterings. Once the trees are established, they should need only infrequent waterings during prolonged dry periods.

Special handling

During the first two growing seasons, pear trees should not be allowed to flower or fruit. Handpick any flowers or young fruit before they sap the energy the tree needs for growth. After the first two seasons, the trees may be allowed to bear small crops. If they bear large crops, limb damage may result, so thin out the fruit. Mature trees should have pears thinned to average of six to eight inches apart.

Pruning is very important in producing a quality crop of pears. According to a traditional saying, "A bird should be able to fly directly through the center of a properly pruned tree without scratching a feather." Light pruning may be done at any time, but heavy pruning should be done in the fall when the tree is dormant. When pruning, follow these basic rules:

1. Remove all diseased, dead, or broken branches.

2. Remove all watersprouts. Watersprouts are fast-growing, vertical branches that usually have no side branches.

3. Remove suckers. These are the fast-growing shoots that grow from the root below the soil surface.

4. Remove V-branching crotches. These are narrow crotches that will not support the weight of a full crop of fruit.

5. Remove rubbing branches. If two branches cross and rub against each other they can cause a wound that offers an opportunity for invasion by insects or disease. Remove the least desirable branch.

6. Never remove more than one third of the total tree in a single growing season.

7. Always prune to a growth bud or flush to a main branch or trunk.

8. Maintain pruning annually.

Pests

Pear trees are usually only attacked by San Jose scales, which can be controlled by spraying the tree with a dormant oil spray. Apply the dormant oil spray when the tree is in dormancy and when the temperature is expected to remain above 33°F for 48 hours.

Diseases

Fireblight is the only major disease problem to which pear trees are subject. Fireblight damage can be reduced by pruning off damaged twigs at least six inches beyond the damaged area. You can reduce the incidence of fireblight by preventing the excessive shoot growth caused by over-pruning or over-fertilizing.

When and how to harvest

Pears taste best if you pick them when they are immature and allow them to ripen in a cool dark place. When the first few pears begin to mature, harvest the rest and store them in a garage, basement, or other cool spot. Check the pears weekly and remove the ripe ones for immediate use.

Container growing

Pear trees do not grow well in containers.

Q and A

Q: In midsummer the leaves on the twig tips of my pear trees suddenly appeared burned, as if in a fire. Why?
A: The cause is fireblight, a disease that can only be controlled by pruning six to eight inches below the damage.
Q: Is it true that you should not plant pears and apples together?
A: Yes, apple trees rarely get fireblight unless they are planted near pears. Fireblight becomes more destructive when apples and pears are planted together.
Q: The pear tree in my backyard has never fruited in seven years even though it shows no signs of disease or insect problems. Why won't it fruit?
A: Pear trees are basically self-unfruitful. Plant another variety of pear nearby so that cross-pollination can take place.

Plum

Common names: European plum; Japanese plum; American plum
Botanical name: Prunus domestica; Prunus americana
Origin: As their common names indicate, European plums originated in Europe, Japanese plums in China, and American plums in the United States.

Varieties

European: Agen, Arctic, Bradshaw, French, Grand Duke, California Blue, Green Gage, Italian Prune, Reine, Claude, Stanley, Yellow Egg. Japanese: Kaga, South Kakota, Abundance, Beauty, Burbank, Methley, Santa Rosa, Shiro. American: Desoto, Hawkeye, Cheney, Wayland, Golden Beauty, Miner, Compass, Oha, Opata, Sapa. Red-fruited American: Superior, Underwood, Monitor, Redcoat, Red Glow, Pipestone.

Description

European and American plum trees are hardy and Japanese plum trees are semi-hardy, deciduous, woody perennials that need a cold period of dormancy. Most modern plum varieties are grafted: the root system and the fruit-producing portion are different.

Plum. This illustration shows how fruit is thinned on the branch to encourage full development of the remaining fruit.

Where and when to grow

European and American plums will grow anywhere apples will grow. Japanese plums will grow anywhere peaches will grow. When planting plums, it is important to pay attention to their pollination requirements. Many plums are self-unfruitful and will not produce a normal crop when pollinated by their own pollen or by the pollen of another tree of the same variety. A self-unfruitful plum tree should have another plum tree of a suitable variety within 300 feet. The pollen of many European plum trees is sterile and will not pollinate itself or any other plum variety of the European type. Stanley, Agen, Reine, Claude, Italian Prune, California Blue, and Yellow Egg are all self-fruitful and will pollinate another

European-type plum. Most Japanese and American plum trees are self-unfruitful and it is advisable to plant two or three different varieties to ensure pollination. Check with your local Cooperative Extension Service or garden center to find a combination that will be fruitful.

How to plant

All plum trees dislike "wet feet" and should be planted in well-drained soil. Plum trees grow best in full sunlight. They can tolerate partial shade, but the yield will be less generous. Plum trees can be purchased bareroot, balled and burlapped, or in a container.

A balled and burlapped tree may be planted any time during the growing season. The soil ball should be positioned in the

planting hole at the same depth that the tree was growing at in the nursery. After positioning the ball in the hole, remove all twine or rope used to hold the ball together. Then open the top of the burlap so that water can penetrate the soil ball.

A bareroot tree should be planted only in early spring, and the planting hole should be large enough for the roots to be spread out completely. A bareroot plum tree should be planted two inches deeper than in the nursery. The grey soil line on the trunk will help you determine this depth.

A container-grown tree can be planted any time during the growing season. Remove the container and plant the ball at the same depth as in the container.

After planting, water each tree in thoroughly and fertilize with a high-phosphorus liquid starter fertilizer.

Fertilizing and watering

Plum trees should be fertilized with a half pound of a well-balanced (10-10-10) fertilizer for every year of the age of the tree, to a maximum of 10 pounds per year per tree.

During the first summer after planting, plum trees may need weekly waterings. Once the trees are established they should only need infrequent waterings during prolonged dry periods.

Special handling

During the first two growing seasons, plum trees should not be allowed to flower or fruit. Handpick any flowers or fruit before they use the energy the tree needs for growth. After the first two growing seasons the trees may be allowed to bear a small crop. If they bear a large crop, limb damage may result, so the fruit should be thinned. Mature trees should have the plums thinned to an average of two to three inches apart. Do not thin plums until the end of June.

Pruning is a very important practice in producing a quality crop of plums. Light pruning may be done at any time of the year. Heavy pruning should be done in the fall when the trees are dormant. When pruning, follow these basic rules:

1. Remove all diseased, dead, or broken branches.
2. Remove all watersprouts. Watersprouts are fast-growing, vertical branches that usually have no side branches.
3. Remove suckers. These are the fast-growing shoots that grow from the root below the soil surface.
4. Remove V-branching crotches. These are narrow crotches that will not support the weight of a full crop of fruit.
5. Remove rubbing branches. If two branches cross and rub against each other they can cause a wound that offers an opportunity for invasion by insects or disease. Remove the least desirable branch.
6. Never remove more than one third of the total tree.
7. Always prune to a growth bud or flush to a main branch or trunk.
8. Maintain pruning annually.

Pests

Plums are attacked by numerous insects that are almost impossible to control without the use of chemical sprays. For this reason, plums are not a good choice for the organic gardener. Among the pests that attack plums are scales, apple maggots, borers, mites, Oriental fruit moths, and plum curculios. Proper control of these pests is dependent on timely seasonal applications of the correct insecticides. The following is only a general spray schedule. For a more specific spray schedule for your area contact your local Cooperative Extension Service.

1. Apply a dormant oil spray before the buds open in spring and when the temperature is expected to stay above 33°F for 48 hours.
2. Apply Captan or Benomyl when the fruit buds show color as they start to open, and again seven days later when the flowers are in bloom.
3. After the fruits are established, spray every 10 to 14 days with a multipurpose fruit tree spray; spray until four weeks before harvest.
4. Starting four weeks before harvest, apply Captan every 10 to 14 days until one week before harvest.
5. To control borers, spray or paint the trunk and lower limbs with Sevin in mid-June, mid-July and mid-August.

Diseases

Plums are attacked by brown fruit rot and peach scab. To control these diseases it is necessary to use preventive chemical sprays. For proper disease control follow the spray schedule outlined above under "Pests."

When and how to harvest

Plums achieve the best flavor when they are allowed to ripen on the tree. Both Japanese and European types of plums show obvious color changes when they ripen: Japanese plums turn from green to red, European plums from green to blue. Harvest both types as soon as they are ripe.

Container growing

Plums do not grow well in containers.

Q and A

Q: How soon after planting will plums begin to bear fruit?
A: Both Japanese and European types of plums will begin bearing fruit three to five years from the time of planting.
Q: Is it necessary to plant two plum trees in order to produce fruit?

A: Yes; both types of plums are self-unfruitful and will not produce fruit unless other suitable varieties are planted in the vicinity.

Q: Will Japanese plums pollinate European-type plums or vice versa?

A: No. To ensure fruiting, plant two varieties of the same type.

Q: What causes some plums to drop from the tree in early summer?

A: This is called June drop, and is the tree's natural way of dropping excess fruit. It's nothing to be concerned about.

Blackberry

Blackberry

Common name: blackberry
Botanical name: Rubus
    allegheniensis
Origin: America

Varieties

Darrow, Bailey, Eldorado, Evergreen, Cheyenne, Ranger, Raven. Thornless varieties: Black Satin, Dirksen, Thornless, Thornfree, Thornless Evergreen, Thornless Boysenberry.

Description

Blackberries are large, semi-hardy, deciduous, perennial shrubs. The fruit is borne on biennial canes which grow for one year, produce fruit the second year, and then die and should be removed. Most standard blackberry canes have large, sharp thorns. The new thornless varieties are less hardy than the thorned varieties.

Where and when to grow

Blackberries produce fruit in climates where the winters are cold enough to freeze the top few inches of soil and provide the necessary period of dormancy. They should not be planted, however, where winter temperatures drop below 5 to 10°F. Blackberries should be planted in the spring.

How to plant

Blackberries grow best in well-drained soil and in full sunlight. They can tolerate partial shade, but yields will be less generous. Blackberries are normally sold in containers. Plant container-grown blackberries at the same depth as in the nursery. They can also be started by simply bending the tip of a cane and burying it in the soil in the fall; in the spring, the rooted stem can be dug up and transplanted.

Blackberries also produce numerous suckers that can be dug up in the spring and transplanted. Blackberries should be planted about four to five feet apart at the same depth that they were growing at previously.

After planting, water each plant in thoroughly and fertilize with a high-phosphorous liquid starter fertilizer.

Fertilizing and watering

During the first growing season,

blackberries should be fertilized with two ounces of a well-balanced (10-10-10) fertilizer for each plant. After the first year, fertilize with one and one half to two pounds of a well-balanced fertilizer per 100 square feet. Apply this fertilizer in the early spring before the plants begin to grow.

During the first growing season blackberries may need weekly waterings. Once they are established, they should only need infrequent waterings during prolonged dry periods.

Special handling

Pruning is very important to the production of a quality crop of blackberries. As mentioned earlier, blackberries bear fruit on biennial canes, which grow for one summer, produce flower buds in the fall, overwinter, and produce fruit the next summer. After fruiting, the canes dry up and die. (During the summer when these canes are fruiting, new canes are growing for the following year's crop.) After the canes have finished fruiting they should be completely removed; as these canes die they are usually infected with a disease which can spread to the healthy young canes. Unwanted canes (suckers) should be removed in the early spring. Each blackberry plant should be allowed to produce five or six new canes each year. If all of the canes were allowed to grow, they would soon become overcrowded, decreasing yields and making the weakened plants more susceptible to disease.

Pests

Birds can completely eliminate your blackberry harvest, but you can discourage them by simply covering the plants with a bird net. In some areas blackberries are attacked by numerous insects, which cannot be controlled effectively without the use of preventive chemical sprays. Follow the spray schedule listed here if you have problems with the following insects: sawflies, borers, psyllids, mites, scales, or tarnished plant bugs. If you are an organic gardener and these insects are very common in your area, blackberries are not the ideal crop for you.

The following is a general spray schedule for blackberries. For a more detailed spray schedule for your area, consult your local Cooperative Extension Service.

1. If mites are present, spray with Kelthane before fruit forms and again after harvest.

2. If sawflies are present, spray with Methoxychlor or Sevin.

3. If psyllids or rose scales are present, spray with Malathion.

4. Tarnished plant bugs can be controlled by spraying with Methoxychlor just before the first flowers open.

Cane borers sometimes produce irregularly-shaped galls on the canes. Affected canes should be pruned off and destroyed.

Diseases

Blackberries are attacked by rust and sterility. Rust causes large

To encourage lateral branching, the tips of some fruiting canes and bushes are pinched back; that is, the top few inches of the mature cane are removed. Raspberries and blackberries are pruned in this manner.

orange spots on the undersides of the leaves. Blackberries affected by sterility grow and bloom normally but do not produce any normal berries. The best way to control these diseases is to remove and destroy affected plants before the diseases can spread to healthy plants.

When and how to harvest

Blackberries develop their best flavor when they are allowed to ripen on the plant. Blackberries turn from red to black as they ripen, and are ripe when they are firm and black. Blackberries ripen over a period of six or seven weeks rather than all at once. Check the canes frequently and harvest the ripe berries.

Container gardening

Blackberries do not grow well in containers.

Q and A

Q: Are there thornless blackberry plants?
A: Yes, but these are the least hardy of the blackberry varieties and should not be grown in cold northern climates.
Q: How long after planting will bushes begin producing fruit?
A: Properly grown blackberries will begin to produce a normal crop the second growing season.
Q: A few of my blackberries grow and flower well but produce only a few malformed berries. Why is this?
A: The problem is blackberry sterility. It's best to destroy these plants and plant recommended varieties.

Blueberry

Common name: blueberry
Botanical name: Vaccinium corymbosum
Origin: America

Varieties

Angela, Atlantic, Berkeley, Blue Crop, Blueray, Burlington, Collins, Concord, Coville, Dixi, Earliblue, Ethel, Gem, Herbert, Ivanhoe, Jersey, Katharine, Keweenaw, Murphy, Olympia, Pacific, Pemberton, Pioneer, Rubel, Sam, Satilla, Scammell, Stanley, True-Blue, Walker, Wareham, Washington, Weymouth, Wolcott.

Description

Blueberries are tall, very hardy, deciduous perennial shrubs. The shiny leaves turn an attractive red color in fall and can be enjoyed for their ornamental value as well as for their fruit.

Where and when to grow

Blueberries need a climate where winters are cold enough to freeze the top few inches of the soil and provide the necessary period of dormancy. They also require fairly acid soil. Most blueberries are self-unfruitful. They will not pollinate either themselves or another blueberry of the same variety. It is advisable, therefore, to plant several varieties. Contact your local Cooperative Extension Service for advice on combinations

that will be fruitful. Blueberries are best planted in the spring.

How to plant

Blueberries grow best in a soil with a high content of organic matter and a pH of 4.5 to 5.0, which is on the acid side of neutral. Blueberries grow best in full sunlight. They can tolerate partial shade, but the yields will not be as generous.

Blueberries are normally sold in a container. To plant a container-grown blueberry, remove the container carefully, and then plant the ball at the same depth as in the container. Blueberries should be planted at least five feet apart.

After planting, water each plant in thoroughly and fertilize with a high-phosphorus liquid starter fertilizer.

Fertilizing and watering

Blueberries grown in naturally acid soils should be fertilized in early spring with one and one half pounds of a well-balanced (10-10-10) fertilizer per 100 square feet. Blueberries grown in a neutral pH soil should be fertilized with one ounce of ammonium sulfate midway through the first summer after planting. In succeeding years the ammonium sulfate should be increased by two ounces per year to a maximum of eight ounces per plant. Do not substitute aluminum sulfate for ammonium sulfate. Any fertilizer prepared for acid-loving plants like azaleas or rhodondendrons can be used for blueberries at the same rate as long as it contains no aluminum sulfate.

Blueberries

In order to produce a healthy crop, blueberry bushes must have unwanted growth pruned out. This illustration shows a blueberry bush before and after pruning.

During the first growing season blueberries will need watering at least once a week. When they are established, they need to stay consistently moist in order to produce large, succulent berries. Water as often as necessary to keep the soil moist.

Special handling

Pruning is about the only special handling necessary to produce large blueberries. During the first two growing seasons, remove all weak, broken, or diseased branches. During the first two growing seasons it is also important to remove the flowers. This will improve both vegetative growth and future harvests. Once the plants are established, remove the top three to four inches of new canes when the canes are about four to five feet tall. This "tipping" will encourage strong lateral branching where the fruit is borne, and should be done before August. After the plants are five to six years old, it is important to remove older, less productive branches. In the fall, when the plants are dormant, remove these branches completely, all the way down to the ground.

Pests

Birds are a serious hazard to blueberries. While the berries are ripening, the plants can be covered with bird netting. In northern areas, blueberry maggots may attack blueberries in June and July. They can be controlled by spraying with Malathion in early June and July. Cranberry fruit worms, cherry fruit worms, and plum curculios all attack the fruits. They can be controlled by spraying with Methoxychlor every 10 to 14 days after the flower blossoms fall. Leafhoppers not only feed on blueberry leaves but also spread virus diseases; they should be sprayed with Sevin as soon as they appear. Cranberry weevils eat into leaf and fruit buds and destroy them. They can be controlled by spraying with Malathion when the buds swell in the spring. Because of all these pest problems, which require chemical controls, blueberries are not a good choice for the organic gardener.

Diseases

Stunt is a virus which dwarfs plants and reduces both the size and the number of the berries. Stunt is spread by leafhoppers, so complete control of leaf-hoppers is necessary to avoid it. Once plants become affected by stunt, the condition cannot be cured and the plants should be destroyed. Mummy berry, stem cankers, and double leaf spot are other diseases that afflict blueberries. These diseases can best be prevented by planting resistant varieties and spraying with Benomyl or Ferbam and copper sulfate every 10 to 14 days. Spray as soon as the buds break, until the blossoms form, the again after the blossoms have fallen.

When and how to harvest

Blueberries should be harvested when they are fully ripe. They will have little flavor if they are picked too early. Blueberries turn from green to blue as they ripen, and are fully ripe when they are a deep shiny blue in color. Because the berries do not ripen all at the same time, berries need to picked individually, not in clusters. Handpick only the ripe berries.

Container growing:

Blueberries should not be grown in containers.

Q and A

Q: How long after planting will blueberries begin bearing fruit?
A: Properly grown blueberries can begin producing a normal crop in the third growing season.
Q: Is it true that blueberry plants make attractive landscape plants?
A: Yes, blueberry plants are often used as ornamentals and they take on a beautiful color in fall. The only drawback to using blueberries as landscape plants is that the netting used to protect the berries from birds is not particularly scenic.
Q: What causes pale yellow leaves with reddish streaks on some blueberry plants?
A: Blueberries need soil with a low pH and the problem you describe may result from a high pH content. Have the soil tested, and use ammonium sulfate to lower the pH if necessary.
Q: Is there any chemical that will control birds on blueberries?
A: No, there is no effective chemical control for birds on blueberries.

Currant

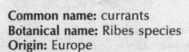

Common name: currants
Botanical name: Ribes species
Origin: Europe

Varieties

Red Lake, Wilder, White Imperial, Minnesota, White Grape.

Description

Currants are very hardy, deciduous, perennial shrubs. Most currants grow three to five feet tall. Currants grow on a very neat and attractive shrub; some nonfruiting varieties are grown as ornamentals.

Where and when to grow

Currants are an alternate host of blister rust, which is a serious problem on white pines. In areas where this disease is a problem, it may actually be illegal to grow currants. If you want to grow currants, first contact your local Cooperative Extension Service to find out if it is permissible to do so in your area. Currants need a climate where winter temperatures are cold enough to freeze the top few inches of soil and provide the necessary period of dormancy. Currants are best planted in the spring.

How to plant

Currants will grow well in just about any ordinary garden soil. They grow best in full sunlight. They can tolerate partial shade, but the yields will be less generous. Currants are sold bareroot or in a container. To plant a container-grown currant, remove the container carefully and plant the ball at the same depth that is was grown at in the container. Bareroot currants should be planted in a hole large enough for the roots to be spread out completely. Plant bareroot currants at the same depth as in the nursery. Currants should be planted four to five feet apart. After planting, water each plant in thoroughly and fertilize with a high-phosphorus liquid starter fertilizer.

Fertilizing and watering

In the first growing season, currants should be fertilized with two ounces of a well-balanced (10-10-10) fertilizer for each plant. After the first year, fertilize with one to one and one half pounds of a well-balanced fertilizer per 100 square feet. Apply this fertilizer in the early spring before the plants begin to grow.

During the first growing season, currants may need weekly watering. Once they are well established they should only need infrequent watering during prolonged dry periods.

Special handling

Currants need very little care and, once the plants are well established, only minimal pruning. After the currants are established, completely prune out any cane over three years old. This will encourage vigorous young canes that are more disease-resistant and more productive than the older canes.

Pests

Currants are attacked by currant aphids, San Jose scales, currant borers, currant stem girdlers, currant worms, and sawflies. These insects can be controlled by spraying with a dormant oil spray. Apply the dormant oil spray in the spring when the plants are dormant and when the temperature is expected to

Currants

remain above 33°F for 48 hours. It is also necessary to spray with Malathion every 10 to 14 days (except when the currants are in bloom), and again two weeks before harvest. Currants don't have these pest problems in every area; where these pests are not prevalent, currants are a good choice for the organic gardener. Birds may also present a threat to your currants, but you can protect the plants by covering them with bird netting.

Diseases

Currants are attacked by blister rust and anthracnose. These diseases can be controlled with weekly sprayings of Ferbam or

Benomyl. Begin spraying as soon as the leaf buds open in the spring. Don't spray during the blooming period, or for two weeks before harvest.

When and how to harvest

Currants will only develop full flavor if they are allowed to ripen on the plant. Currants ripen over a period of five or six weeks rather than all at once, but can remain on the plant for a week or so after ripening. Currants are ripe when they show full color, and should be handpicked so that only the ripe berries are harvested.

Container Growing

Currants should not be grown in a container.

Q and A

Q: Why is it against the law to grow currants in some areas of the United States?
A: Currants are an alternate host of white pine blister rust, and there are restrictions against growing them in many states.
Q: How long after planting will currants begin producing a normal crop?
A: Currants will begin · producing normal crops two to three years after planting.
Q: What causes currant leaves to curl early in summer?
A: The problem is currant aphids, which suck the juice from the leaves, causing them to curl. You may not notice the aphids because they hide on the undersides of the leaves. Look for them and control them at once.

Gooseberries

Gooseberry

Common name: gooseberry
Botanical name: Ribes uvacrispa
Origin: Europe

Varieties

Pixwell, Poorman, Downing, Fredonia, Welcome.

Description

Gooseberries are very hardy, deciduous, perennial shrubs. They are neat, attractive shrubs and most varieties grow to four to five feet tall.

Where and when to grow

Gooseberries are an alternate host of blister rust, which is a serious problem on white pines. In areas where this disease is a problem it may actually be illegal to grow gooseberries. If you want to grow gooseberries, first contact your local Cooperative Extension Service to find out if it is permissible to do so in your area. Gooseberries need a climate where winter temperatures are cold enough to freeze the top few inches of soil and provide the necessary period of dormancy. They are best planted in the spring.

How to plant

Gooseberries will grow well in just about any ordinary garden soil. They grow best in full sunlight. They can tolerate partial shade, but the yields will be less generous. Gooseberries are sold bareroot or in a container. To plant a container-grown gooseberry, remove the container carefully and plant the ball at the same depth that it was grown in the container.

Bareroot gooseberries should be planted in a hole large enough for the roots to be spread out completely. Plant bareroot gooseberries at the same depth as in the nursery.

Gooseberries should be planted four to five feet apart. After planting, water each plant in thoroughly with a high-phosphorous liquid starter fertilizer.

Fertilizing and watering

In the first growing season, gooseberries should be fertilized with two to three ounces of a well-balanced (10-10-10) fertilizer per plant. After the first year, fertilize with a one to one and one half pounds of a well-balanced fertilizer per 100 square feet. Apply this fertilizer in the early spring before the plants begin to grow.

During the first growing season gooseberries may need weekly waterings. Once they are well established they should only need infrequent waterings during prolonged dry periods.

Special handling

Gooseberries need very little care and, once the plants are well established, only minimal pruning. After they are established, completely prune out any canes over three years old. This will encourage vigorous young canes that are more disease-resistant and more productive than older canes.

Pests

Gooseberries are attacked by currant aphids, San Jose scales, currant borers, currant stem girdlers, currant worms, and sawflies. These insects can be controlled by spraying with a dormant oil spray. Apply the dormant oil spray in the spring when the plants are still dormant, but when the temperature is expected to remain above 33°F for 48 hours. It is also necessary to spray with Malathion every 10 to 14 days (except when the bushes are in bloom), and two weeks before harvest. Birds may also be a threat to your crop, but you can protect the plants by covering them with bird netting. Gooseberries do not always have these pest problems in every area, and in those areas where these pests are not prevalent, gooseberries are a good choice for the organic gardener.

Diseases

Gooseberries are attacked by blister rust and anthrancnose. These diseases can be controlled with weekly sprayings of Ferbam or Benomyl. Begin spraying as soon as the leaf buds open in the spring. Don't spray when the flowers are in bloom, and stop spraying altogether two weeks before harvest.

When and how to harvest

Gooseberries will only develop full flavor if they are allowed to ripen on the plant. Gooseberries ripen over a period of five or six weeks rather than all at once, but can remain on the plant for a week or so after ripening. Gooseberries are ripe when they show full color, and should be handpicked so that only the ripe berries are harvested.

Container growing

Gooseberries should not be grown in containers.

Q and A

Q: Can gooseberries be eaten raw or must they be cooked?
A: Gooseberries are delicious either raw, or made into jams and jellies.
Q: Why is it against the law to grow gooseberries in some areas of the United States?
A: Gooseberries are an alternate host of white pine blister rust, and there are restrictions against growing them in many states.

Grape

Common name: grape, fox grape, muscadine grape
Botanical name: Vitis vinifera, Vitis labrusca, Vitis rotundifolia
Origin: V. vinifera are native to Europe. V. labrusca and V. rotundifolia are native to America.

Varieties

V. labrusca, Northern American type: Concord, Niagara, Catawba, Delaware, Fredonia, Worden, Interlaken, Golden Muscat, Erie, Ontario. V. rotundifolia (muscadine grapes): Burgaw, Duplin, Pender, Tarheel, Wallace, Willard, Scuppernong, Thomas, James, Mish, Flowers. V. vinifera (European types for table use): Almeria, Cardinal, Emperor, Italia, Malaga, Perlette, Ribier, Tokay, Thompson Seedless.

Description

Grapes are deciduous, perennial, woody, vining shrubs. They bear fruit in large clusters on the current season's growth.

Where and when to grow

European-type grapes can be grown only in California and on the Northwest Pacific coast and, recently, in small areas of Arizona. Northern American-type grapes need a climate where the winter temperatures are cold enough to freeze the top few inches of soil and provide the necessary period of dormancy. Unlike Northern American-type grapes, muscadine-type grapes can be grown in the warmer southern areas. Grapes are best planted in the spring.

Grapes

How to plant

Grapes need very well-drained soil and grow best in full sunlight. They can tolerate partial shade, but they will not produce nearly as well as in full sun. Grapes are usually sold bareroot or in a container. To plant a container-grown grape, remove the container carefully and plant the ball at the same depth that it was grown at in the container. Bareroot grapes should be planted in a hole large enough for the roots to be spread out completely. Plant bareroot grapes at the same depth as in the nursery. For best results, plant either one- or two-year-old vines. Grapes should be planted about eight feet apart, depending on the support system used (supports are discussed later in this section).

Fertilizing and watering

The best fertilizer for grapes is well-rotted manure, but grapes should not be fertilized at all during the first few growing seasons. After that, apply approximately 10 pounds of manure around each mature vine, at least a foot from the trunk. The manure should not be too close to the vines. If manure is not available, apply one pound of a well-balanced (10-10-10) fertilizer per mature vine. This fertilizer also should be applied at least one foot away from the vine.

During the first growing season grapes may need weekly waterings. Once they are well established they should only need infrequent waterings during prolonged dry periods. In fact, some drought stress actually improves the flavor of the grapes.

Special handling

Grapes should be provided with some type of trellis or arbor for support. The most common type of support is called the four-arm Kniffin system, which consists of two wires attached to posts about 10 feet apart. The lowest wire should be about 30 inches off the ground, and the second 30 inches above the first. The vine is pruned as a single trunk that branches off to the left and right on each wire.

Grapes produce fruit only on one-year-old canes. If grapes are not pruned annually, they will become woody and will produce far too many small, poorly-developed, poor-tasting grape clusters. Annual pruning should remove the canes that fruited the previous season and limit the number of buds, thus adjusting the number of grape clusters. Pruning should be done in mid-winter. If pruning is done in the spring the new cuts will "bleed" profusely. This bleeding does not cause extensive damage, but neither does it help the vines.

When pruning, first remove the canes that fruited the previous season. Then limit the number buds according to the vigor of the vine. There are many different rules of thumb that determine the number of buds that should be left. Some growers make an estimate by weighing the prunings of last year's growth, but it's extremely difficult to make an accurate

After planting, a grape vine is pruned to leave two buds on a single stem. The illustration shows the young vine before and after pruning.

Grapes can be trained by the Kniffin method, which involves the use of two horizontal wire supports, one about 30 inches above the ground and the second another 30 inches above the first. The supports are held in place by upright posts set at intervals.

assessment of the weight of sprawling vines. The best way to determine the number of buds that should be left requires a mix of experience and guesswork: leave 45 to 60 buds on vigorous vines, and 30 to 40 buds on less vigorous vines. The canes that remain should be about pencil-size in diameter and should start as close as possible to the main trunk. A renewal spur of two buds should be left near the trunk. The branches grown from these renewal spurs will be the canes selected to remain on the vine to produce fruit the following year. After pruning, and during the summer, it may be necessary to tie the vines to the wire supports.

Pests

Birds will attack grapes but can be controlled by covering the vines with bird netting. Grapes are also attacked by flea beetles, plume moths, scales, Japanese beetles, rose chafers, and grape berry moths. Plume moths, grape scales and cottony maple scales can be controlled with a dormant oil spray. Apply the spray in the spring while the vines are still dormant and when the temperature is expected to remain above 33°F for 48 hours. Control flea beetles, Japanese beetles, rose chafers, and grape berry moths by spraying every 10 to 14 days with Sevin or Mexthoxychlor, starting as soon as buds open. Do not spray when the flowers are in bloom, and stop spraying altogether two weeks before harvest. Because of all the serious pest problems to which they are subject, grapes are not a good choice for the organic gardener.

Diseases

Black rot, downy mildew, and powdery mildew are all serious diseases of grapes. They can be controlled by spraying with Ferbam every 10 to 14 days. Do not spray when the flowers are in bloom, and stop spraying altogether two weeks before harvest.

When and how to harvest

Grapes will only develop full flavor if allowed to ripen on the vine. They are ripe when they reach full color, and grapes in a cluster will ripen at the same time. When harvesting, you can pick either whole fruit clusters or individual ripe grapes. When harvesting whole fruit clusters, use a knife or a pair of clippers to make a clean cut.

Container growing

Grapes should not be grown in a container.

Q and A

Q: How long does it take grape vines to produce fruit?
A: Vines will take at least two years to begin producing grapes.
Q: How important is it to prune grapes every year?
A: Pruning is the most important cultural practice in growing grapes. Without pruning, grape vines become overgrown and produce only small, poor-tasting grapes.
Q: What causes grape leaves to become distorted, curled, and discolored?
A: Grapes are extremely sensitive to herbicides containing 2, 4-D, which is the main ingredient in most lawn herbicides. If this substance comes in contact with the vines, it will produce the described effect.
Q: Is it necessary to girdle some varieties in order to produce grapes?
A: Girdling means removing a small ring of bark around the fruiting vine. This is done to produce larger grapes. Home gardeners do not need to follow this practice unless they are growing fruits for the county fair.

Raspberry

Common name: raspberry
Botanical name: Rubus occidentalis
Origin:

Varieties

Red single bearing: Bristol, Canby, Latham, Milton, Newburgh, Taylor. Red everbearing: Indian Summer, September, Fall Red, Heritage. Black: Munger, Plum Farmer, Black Pearl, Maples. Purple single-bearing: Purple Autumn. Yellow: Amber, Fallgold.

Description

Raspberries are very hardy, deciduous, perennial shrubs. The fruit is borne on biennial canes which grow one year, produce fruit the second year, and then die and should be removed. Single-bearing raspberries usually fruit in July. Everbearing varieties begin fruiting in July, stop for a couple of weeks, and then fruit

Raspberry

until frost. Everbearing fruit is a little smaller then single-bearing varieties, but it's just as sweet and produces more generously. Red-, purple-, black-, and yellow-fruited varieties of raspberries are available.

Where and when to grow:

Raspberries need a climate where winters are cold enough to freeze the top few inches of soil and provide them with the necessary period of dormancy. Raspberries will grow well in the northern half of the United States and in southern Canada. They can be planted in spring or fall. If you have a choice, plant in spring.

How to plant

Raspberries grow best in well-drained soil and in full sunlight. They can tolerate partial shade,

To produce a healthy crop, raspberry canes must be pruned of unwanted growth. The illustration shows a mature raspberry plant before and after pruning.

but yields will be reduced. Raspberries are normally sold already started in a container. To plant a container-grown raspberry, remove the container carefully, then plant the ball at the same depth as it was grown in the container. After planting, water each plant in thoroughly and fertilize with a high-phosphorus liquid starter fertilizer.

Fertilizing and watering

During the first growing season, raspberries should be fertilized with two ounces of well-balanced (10-10-10) fertilizer per plant. After the first year, fertilize with one and one half to two pounds of a well-balanced fertilizer per 100 square feet. Fertilize in early spring before the plants begin to grow.

During the first growing season, raspberries may need weekly waterings. Once they are well established they should only need infrequent waterings during prolonged dry periods.

Special handling

Pruning is very important in producing a quality crop of raspberries. As mentioned earlier, single-bearing raspberries bear fruit on biennial canes which grow for one year, produce flower buds in the fall, overwinter, and produce fruit the next summer. After fruiting, the canes dry up and die. At the same time that these canes are fruiting, new canes are growing for the following year's fruit. After the canes have finished fruiting they should immediately be removed altogether; as the old canes die, they are usually infected with a disease which can

spread to the healthy young canes.

Everbearing raspberries bear a crop in the fall on the tips of first-year canes. In the second year the same canes bear a second crop lower down on the stem. Remove these canes after this second crop. Pruning in the fall would remove the next summer's crop.

Black and purple raspberries produce fruit on lateral branches. The more lateral branches, the more fruit produced. To encourage more lateral branches, prune off the top three to four inches of these raspberry canes when they are three to four feet tall. Also remove unwanted canes in the early spring. Each raspberry plant should be allowed to produce five or six new canes each year; the rest of the canes should be completely removed. If all the canes were allowed to grow they would become overcrowded, yields would be decreased, and diseases would attack the weakened plants.

Pests

In some areas, raspberries are attacked by numerous insects which can only be controlled by chemical means. The following insects may attack raspberries: raspberry cane borers, rednecked cane borers, raspberry maggots, raspberry fruit worms. If these insects are common to your area, and you are an organic gardener raspberries would not be a good choice for you. If you are willing to use chemical controls, follow the spray schedule given here. Birds can also destroy your raspberry crop, but can be controlled by covering the plants with a bird net. Aphids may also attack rasp-

berries, and need to be controlled immediately. Not only do the aphids suck the sap from the plants; they also transmit viruses from sick plants to healthy ones. When aphids attack, spray as soon as possible with Malathion. The following is a general spray schedule for raspberries. For more specific information, consult your local Cooperative Extension Service.

1. Spray with Methoxychlor or Ferbam just before the plants bloom.

2. If Japanese beetles attack your raspberry canes, spray with Malathion, Rotenone, or Sevin. Handpick the insects from the plants.

3. If mites are present, spray with Kelthane before fruit forms and again after harvest.

Diseases

Mosaic viruses, anthracnose, and powdery mildew may attack raspberries. Planting disease-resistant varieties and controlling aphids will usually control mosaic viruses. Anthracnose can be controlled by pruning out weak and overcrowded canes and canes that have finished fruiting. Powdery mildew, which appears as a white powdery growth on the tips of new canes, can be controlled by spraying with Karathane.

Never plant black or purple raspberries within 500 feet of red raspberries. Red raspberries can transmit viruses, to which they are resistant themselves, to black or purple raspberries.

When and how to harvest

Raspberries develop their best flavor when they are allowed to ripen on the plant. Raspberries are ripe when they are fully colored and come away from the plant easily. It should not be necessary to cut them from the plant.

Container growing

Raspberries cannot be grown in a container.

Q and A

Q: How long after planting will raspberry canes begin producing fruit?
A: Everbearing raspberries will produce a few berries in the fall of the first year. Spring-bearing raspberries will begin bearing fruit in the spring of the second year.
Q: Are yellow raspberries as satisfactory as red, purple, or black raspberries?
A: No. Yellow raspberries are smaller and produce far less generously. They also taste different from the rest of the raspberries.
Q: Is it really important to prune raspberries?
A: Yes. Without pruning, raspberries become overcrowded and yields are greatly reduced. Pruning also reduces disease problems.
Q: What causes raspberry leaves to become discolored, twisted, and curled?
A: This is caused by mosaic virus disease, which is best controlled by planting resistant varieties and removing infected plants. Mosaic virus is spread by aphids, which should be controlled as soon as they appear.
Q: Are black raspberries and blackberries the same thing?

A: No, they are entirely different. They taste different and have different growth characteristics.

Common name: strawberry
Botanical names: Fragaria virginiana; Fragaria chiloenis
Origin: Europe and the Americas

Varieties

Many strawberry varieties are adaptable to wide areas (both cold and warm climates); others are not so adaptable. Contact your local Cooperative Extension Service for information about the varieties best suited to your area.

Description

Strawberries are low-growing, very hardy, broadleaf evergreen perennials. Some strawberries are everbearing and produce fruit in the early spring and again in the fall. Others are spring-bearing, and only produce fruit in the early spring. Everbearing strawberries would appear to be the obvious choice for the home gardener, but their fruit is generally smaller and not quite as sweet.

Where and when to grow

No matter where you live, there is a strawberry that will grow in your area. Most strawberries are started from young bareroot plants, which can be planted as soon as the soil can be worked in the spring.

How to plant

Many gardeners plant bareroot strawberries either too deep or too close to the surface. In fact, the soil should just cover the tops of the strawberry roots. Strawberries can also be purchased already started in containers. These can be planted any time during the growing season. Plant them at the same depth at which they were growing in the container.

Recently, the introduction of the Sweetheart strawberry enabled growers to grow strawberries from seed. In colder climates, Sweetheart strawberry seeds can be started indoors in early February, and the young plants can be transplanted into the garden around the average date of last frost. In warmer climates they can be planted directly in the garden. Sweetheart strawberries will bear fruit in the fall. After planting, water the strawberry plants in well and fertilize with a high-phosphorus liquid starter fertilizer. The developers advise that seeded strawberries be treated as annuals rather than as perennials, and should be started anew each year.

Fertilizing and watering

After the spring harvest, strawberry plants should be fertilized with a half pound of a well-balanced (10-10-10) fertilizer per 100 square feet. This fertilizer may be broadcast over the plants, but only when the leaves are dry. After broadcasting the fertilizer, brush the leaves with a broom or rake to remove the particles, which will burn the leaves if they are allowed to remain on them. Do not over-fertilize. Over-fertilizing can lead to disease problems.

During the first year, strawberries may need weekly waterings. Once the plants are established they should only need infrequent watering during prolonged dry periods.

Special handling

The first year after planting, strawberries should not be allowed to bear fruit. Remove all flowers before they use the energy the plants need for growth. Removing the flowers encourages the plants to produce more runners, thus increasing the following year's crop. Flowers that develop after July 1 on everbearing strawberries can be left on for a fall crop.

After four or five years of production, strawberry beds need to be renovated. The easiest method for the home gardener is

Strawberry plant and runners

to simply run a power mower set at its highest level over the strawberry bed. This should remove all the leaves about an inch above the crowns. This renovation should be done immediately after the spring harvest. If you can't do it within a week of harvesting, postpone it until the following year. After mowing off the leaves, water and

fertilize as outlined earlier under "Fertilizing and watering."

Pests

Strawberries can be attacked by a large number of different insects, but they usually aren't, so they are a good choice for the organic gardener. Birds, however, can do considerable damage to your harvest. Nets over the plants provide effective protection from birds.

Diseases

Strawberries can be attacked by numerous diseases, but if they are properly renovated and fertilized these disease problems can usually be avoided. If you do have a disease problem, it is generally best to take the line of least resistance and start a new strawberry patch in a new location.

Planted too low   Planted too high   Planted just right

To make use of a small area, plant strawberries in a circular, raised, pyramid planter. These planters are available at garden centers.

Strawberries may be grown satisfactorily in a barrel. Each plant is set in one of a series of staggered holes in the barrel.

When and how to harvest

Strawberries develop their best flavor when they are allowed to ripen on the plant. It's easy to judge when strawberries are ripe. Strawberry fruits start out green, turn white, and finally turn red when they are ripe. They should be picked when they are red, firm, and shiny. Soft, dull red strawberries are over-mature and have poor flavor. Fully ripe strawberries "pop" easily from their stems. It should not be necessary to cut them from the plant.

Container growing

Strawberries grow well in containers. Choose an everbearing variety and make use of available vertical space. Plants will produce fruit when planted in strawberry barrels and pyramid containers, which are available commercially, but these containers are somewhat difficult to manage. An easier system is to space planting holes 10 to 12 inches apart on a full-size whisky barrel. Offset the holes vertically so that sunlight can reach all the plants. Plant a single strawberry plant in each hole. Commercial pyramids come with planting instructions.

Q and A

Q: How long after planting will strawberries begin to produce fruit?
A: If allowed to do so, strawberries will bear a few berries the first year. However, blossoms should be picked off during the first growing season so that they do not form fruit. Effectively, therefore, strawberries begin bearing fruit in their second year.
Q: Which are better, spring-bearing or everbearing strawberries?
A: For size and flavor, spring-bearing strawberries are superior to everbearing strawberries. However, everbearing strawberries are slightly more productive because they fruit twice a year.
Q: What are climbing strawberries, and do they really climb?
A: Climbing strawberries simply have slightly longer runners and can be trained to climb by being tied to a structure. In fact, any strawberry variety can be trained this way.

Planting guide: spacing fruits

Fruit	Feet between plants	Feet between rows
Apple		
dwarf	6-8	10-12
semi-dwarf	10-12	15-17
standard	20-22	25-30
Apricot	15-18	20-25
Cherry		
sour	8-15	20-25
sweet	18-20	20-25
Fig		
standard	15-20	25-30
dwarf	4-6	8-10
Grapefruit	24-30	30-36
Lemon	20-25	20-25
Lime	20-25	20-25
Nectarine	8-12	16-18
Orange	24-30	30-36
Peach		
standard	14-18	20-25
dwarf	8-10	13-15
Pear		
standard	20-22	25-30
dwarf	8-12	14-20
Plum	8-14	16-18
Blackberry	6-8	8-10
Blueberry	6-8	8-10
Currant	6-8	8-10
Gooseberry	4-5	6-8
Grape	6-9	8-10
Raspberry	2-3	5-8
Strawberry	6-12 inches	24-30 inches

Counting the Calories in Fruit

Food	Portion	Calories
APPLES		
Raw or baked	1 apple	80
Frozen, slices	1 cup	211
Dried, sulfured	8 oz	314
APPLESAUCE		
Sweetened, canned	1 cup	232
Unsweetened, canned	1 cup	100
Sweetened, jar	1 cup	180
APRICOTS		
Raw	3 apricots	55
Unpeeled, canned	1 cup	222
Dried	1 cup	332
BERRIES		
Blackberries (Boysenberries)		
Raw	1 cup	85
Canned	1 cup	88
Blueberries		
Raw	1 cup	90
Frozen	1 cup	91
Raspberries		
Raw	1 cup	98
Strawberries		
Raw	1 cup	55
Frozen, sliced	1 cup	278
CHERRIES, SWEET		
Raw	1 cup	82
Canned	1 cup	105
CITRUS		
Grapefruit		
Raw	½ grapefruit	40
Frozen, unsweetened	1 cup	178
Canned, sweetened	1 cup	180
Lemon, raw	1 medium	22
Oranges, raw	1 medium	64
CRANBERRY		
Raw	1 cup	44
Cranberry sauce	1 cup	404

Food	Portion	Calories
CURRANT		
Raw	1 cup	3
Dried	1 cup	8
Canned	1/2 cup	190
FIGS		
Raw	1 fig	40
Canned	1 cup	119
Dried	1 fig	2
GRAPES		
Thompson seedless	10 grapes	34
MUSKMELON		
Cantaloup	1/2 melon	82
Casaba	1/5 melon	38
Honeydew	1/5 melon	49
NECTARINES		
Raw	1 nectarine	88
PEACHES		
Raw	1 peach	38
Frozen	1 cup	220
Canned	1 cup	76
Dried, uncooked	1 cup	340
PEARS		
Raw	1 pear	100
Canned	1 cup	78
Dried	1 cup	482
PLUMS		
Raw	1 plum	66
Canned	1 cup	114
RHUBARB		
Cooked, sugared	1 cup	381
Frozen	1 cup	386
WATERMELON		
Fresh	1/16 melon	111

Points to Remember When Planting Your Home Orchard

1. It's as important to plan your home orchard on paper as it is to plan your vegetable garden. Fruit trees and bushes constitute quite an investment of space, equipment, and effort, so it makes sense to plan ahead rather than to dig up and move a tree or bush.

2. Self-unfruitful fruit trees cannot pollinate themselves and need another tree of an appropriate variety within 300 feet if they are to produce crops. Keep this in mind when selecting varieties for your garden. Your state Cooperative Extension Service can advise you on which trees to plant.

3. Have your soil tested before you plant fruit trees; they require well-drained soil with plenty of organic matters.

4. Fruit trees will produce more generously in full sun. Some will tolerate partial shade, but the crop will be reduced.

5. Citrus fruits require a great deal of water. In order to make full use of rainwater, form a depression in the soil around the trunk of each tree. Extend the depression to the outer canopy, or drip line, of the tree.

6. Choose medium to small fruit tree varieties. They require less initial pruning than large varieties, are less susceptible to transplant shock, and are easier to train later.

7. Fruit trees are susceptible to many diseases that can be prevented by spraying with fungicides. Fungicides don't actually cure a disease that has taken hold, so they must be applied before the disease organisms strike.

8. Pruning is essential to ensure that fruit trees produce a good crop. Follow the instructions for pruning given in the individual plant profiles. Of the most popular fruit trees, apples need the most pruning and cherries the least.

9. Most fruit trees require regular annual fertilizing. The exceptions are pear trees, which in some areas become more susceptible to fireblight disease if they are over-fertilized.

10. When fertilizing fruit trees, keep the fertilizer one foot away from the trunk and extend it to the outer canopy or drip line.

11. When you plant small fruits, try to plant different types to give you successive crops throughout the growing season.

12. The name might lead you to believe that everbearing varieties of strawberries and raspberries produce fruit continuously. This is not the case; in fact, they produce in spring and again in fall.

13. Small fruits are usually attacked only by pests that can be controlled without chemical sprays. The diseases to which they are susceptible can usually be prevented by following simple horticultural practices such as choosing disease-resistant varieties, and pruning, fertilizing, and watering properly.

14. Pruning is probably the least-understood practice of those required for small-fruit gardening. Small fruits (except for grapes) need less pruning than fruit trees, but will become overgrown if not pruned at all. Follow the pruning recommendations in the individual plant profiles.

Part 4
The Kitchen

Enjoy your homegrown produce all year around. The right storing and preserving methods make it happen. You can store, freeze, can, or dry your crop for good eating in all seasons.

How to Store Fruits and Vegetables

Once you've harvested your crops, you may find yourself with a big surplus. What do you do with all those fruits and vegetables? Well, you can—and will—enjoy them fresh; and you can also give a lot of them away. You can keep them in the refrigerator for a few days. You can freeze, can, or dry them for the months ahead, as detailed in the following chapters. But in some cases, cold storage—not freezing—can be your best bet. It's a low effort, electricity-free choice that can keep you supplied with fresh vegetables all winter long. Both refrigerator storage and cold storage are discussed below, and the accompanying charts show you which methods of storing or preserving work best for each fruit or vegetable.

Vegetable preserving methods

Vegetable	Cold Storage	Freezing	Canning	Drying
Artichoke	✔	✔	✔	
Asparagus		✔	✔	
Bean, broad	✔ (dried)	✔	✔	✔
Bean, dry	✔ (dried)	✔	✔	✔
Bean, green		✔	✔	✔
Bean, lima	✔ (dried)	✔	✔	✔
Bean, mung				✔
Beet				
root	✔	✔	✔	✔
greens		✔	✔	✔
Broccoli	✔	✔		
Brussels sprout	✔	✔		✔
Cabbage	✔	✔		✔
Cardoon	✔	✔	✔	✔
Carrot	✔	✔	✔	✔
Cauliflower	✔	✔	✔ (pickled)	✔
Celeriac	✔	✔		
Celery	✔	✔		✔
Chard		✔	✔	✔
Chayote		✔		✔
Chick pea	✔ (dried)	✔	✔	✔
Chicory	✔			
Chinese cabbage	✔	✔		✔
Collard	✔	✔	✔	✔
Corn		✔	✔	✔
Cress, garden				
Cucumber			✔ (pickled)	
Dandelion				
Eggplant		✔		✔
Endive				
Fennel	✔	✔	✔	✔
Horseradish	✔	✔		✔
Jerusalem artichoke	✔	✔		
Kale	✔	✔	✔	✔
Kohlrabi	✔	✔		

Vegetable preserving methods continued

Vegetable	Cold Storage	Freezing	Canning	Drying
Leek	✔	✔		
Lentil	✔ (dried)	✔	✔	✔
Lettuce				
Mushroom		✔	✔	✔
Muskmelon	✔	✔	✔ (pickled)	
Mustard		✔	✔	✔
Okra		✔	✔	✔
Onion				
mature	✔	✔	✔	✔
green		✔		✔
Parsnip	✔	✔		
Peanut	✔ (dried)	✔	✔	✔
Pea	✔ (dried)	✔	✔	✔
Pea, black-eyed	✔ (dried)	✔	✔	✔
Pepper	✔	✔	✔	✔
Potato	✔	✔	✔	✔
Pumpkin	✔	✔		✔
Radish				
Rhubarb		✔	✔	✔
Rutabaga	✔	✔		
Salsify	✔			
Shallot	✔		✔	✔
Sorrel				
Soybean	✔ (dried)	✔	✔	✔
Spinach, New Zealand spinach		✔	✔	✔
Squash, summer		✔	✔	✔
Squash, winter	✔	✔		✔
Sweet potato	✔	✔	✔	✔
Tomato	✔ (green)	✔	✔	✔
Turnip				
root	✔	✔		
greens	✔	✔	✔	✔
Watermelon	✔	✔	✔ (pickled)	

SHORT-TERM REFRIGERATOR STORAGE

Most fruits and vegetables keep best for a short time when stored in the refrigerator, at high humidity and a constant temperature, just above freezing. A temperature of about 40°F and a humidity of 95 percent are ideal for storing fresh fruits and vegetables, and these conditions are most likely to be found in the crisper or hydrator sections of the refrigerator. For the best results, the crisper should be at least two-thirds full; if it's empty or almost empty, vegetables placed in it will dry out.

To keep fruits and vegetables moist and fresh, follow these simple rules for refrigerator storage:

- Store vegetables in the crisper or hydrator, and keep the crisper full.
- When storing only a few vegetables, put them into airtight plastic bags or plastic containers, then into the crisper.
- Store apples in a separate compartment, away from vegetables. Apples absorb odors from strong-flavored vegetables. Also, they hasten the ripening of other fruits.
- When storing vegetables in other parts of the

Fruit preserving methods

Fruit	Cold Storage	Freezing	Canning	Drying
Apples	✓	✓	✓	✓
Apricots	✓ (dried)	✓		✓
Blackberries		✓		✓
Blueberries		✓		✓
Cherries		✓	✓	✓
Currants		✓	✓	✓
Figs		✓	✓	✓
Gooseberries		✓	✓	✓
Grapes		✓	✓	✓
Grapefruit	✓			
Lemons	✓			
Limes	✓			
Peaches		✓	✓	✓
Pears	✓		✓	✓
Plums		✓	✓	✓
Nectarines		✓	✓	✓
Oranges	✓			
Raspberries		✓	✓	✓
Strawberries		✓	✓	✓

refrigerator, put them into airtight plastic bags or plastic containers to prevent moisture loss.

Almost all vegetables store well in the refrigerator, but there are a few that don't. Mature onions, peanuts (dried), potatoes, sweet potatoes, pumpkins, winter squash, and such root vegetables as rutabagas, salsify, and turnips keep better in cold storage outside the refrigerator, in a basement storage room or root cellar. This type of storage is discussed in the next section. Most other vegetables, regardless of whether they *can* be kept in cold storage, keep very well for a short time in the refrigerator.

Preparing vegetables for refrigerator storage

Refrigerator storage is the simplest type of storage to prepare for — all you have to do is sort the vegetables, remove damaged or soft ones for immediate use or discard, and remove as much garden soil as you can. Some vegetables should be washed before they're stored; others keep better when they're not washed until you're ready to use them. The directions below tell you how to prepare each type of vegetable for refrigerator storage. For the best results, discard damaged vegetables or use them immediately; perfect vegetables keep best.

Artichokes

Do not wash until ready to use. Store in plastic bag up to 2 weeks.

Asparagus

Do not wash until ready to use. Slice off bottoms of stalks and stand upright in 1 to 2 inches of water. Store up to 1 week.

Beans, green or snap

Do not wash until ready to use. Store in plastic bag up to 1 week.

How to Store Fruits and Vegetables

Beans, broad, dry, lima, or mung

Do not shell or wash until ready to use. Store in plastic bag up to 1 week.

Beets

Cut off tops, leaving about 1 inch of stem. Do not wash roots until ready to use. Store in plastic bag for 1 to 3 weeks. Wash greens thoroughly in cold water; drain well and store in plastic bag up to 1 week.

Broccoli

Do not wash until ready to use. Remove any damaged leaves. Store in plastic bag up to 1 week.

Brussels sprouts

Do not wash until ready to use. Remove any damaged leaves. Store in plastic bag up to 1 week.

Cabbage

Do not wash until ready to use. Remove any damaged leaves. Store in plastic bag for 1 to 2 weeks.

Cardoon

Trim roots and cut off leaves. Wash thoroughly in cold water; drain well. Store stalks attached to root in plastic bag for 1 to 2 weeks.

Carrots

Cut off tops. Wash thoroughly in cold water; drain well. Store in plastic bag for 1 to 3 weeks.

Cauliflower

Do not wash until ready to use. Remove any damaged leaves. Store in plastic bag up to 1 week.

Celeriac

Cut off leaves and root fibers. Do not wash until ready to use. Store in plastic bag up to 1 week.

Celery

Trim roots and wash thoroughly in cold water; drain well. Cut off leaves and store in plastic bag for 3 to 5 days. Store stalks attached at root in plastic bag for 1 to 2 weeks.

Chard

Wash thoroughly in cold water; drain well. Trim any bad spots on leaves and cut off tough stalks. Store in plastic bag for 1 to 2 weeks.

Chayote

Do not wash until ready to use. Store in plastic bag up to 1 week.

Chick peas

Do not shell or wash until ready to use. Store in plastic bag up to 1 week.

Chicory

Do not wash until ready to use. Store in plastic bag up to 1 week.

Chinese cabbage

Trim roots and wash thoroughly in cold water; drain well. Store in plastic bag up to 1 week.

Collards

Wash thoroughly in cold water; drain well. Remove any damaged leaves. Store in plastic bag up to 1 week.

Corn

Do not husk or wash; store in plastic bag for 4 to 8 days. For best flavor, do not store; use immediately.

Cress, garden

Wash thoroughly in cold water; drain well. Store in plastic bag up to 1 week.

Cucumbers

Wash thoroughly in cold water and pat dry. Do not cut until ready to use. Store in plastic bag up to 1 week.

Dandelion

Cut off roots and remove any damaged leaves. Wash thoroughly in cold water; drain well. Store in plastic bag up to 1 week.

Eggplant

Store eggplant at about 50°F, up to 1 week. Do not refrigerate.

Endive

Wash thoroughly in cold water; drain well. Remove any damaged leaves. Store in plastic bag up to 1 week.

Fennel

Do not separate stalks or wash until ready to use. Store in plastic bag up to 1 week.

Horseradish

Cut off leaves and trim root; wash thoroughly in cold water and pat dry. Mix with vinegar and water according to recipe in "How to Freeze Vegetables." Store in airtight glass jar in refrigerator for 1 to 2 weeks. For stronger flavor, grate as soon as possible after picking; store in airtight glass jar.

Jerusalem artichokes

Wash tubers thoroughly in cold water and pat dry. Store in plastic bag for 7 to 10 days.

Kale

Wash thoroughly in cold water; drain well. Remove any damaged leaves. Store in plastic bag up to 1 week.

Kohlrabi

Cut off leaves and trim root; wash thoroughly in cold water and pat dry. Store in plastic bag up to 1 week.

Leeks

Cut off roots and all but 2 inches of leaves. Do not wash until ready to use. Store in plastic bag up to 1 week. Wash very thoroughly in cold water before using.

Lentils

Do not shell or wash until ready to use. Store in plastic bag up to 1 week.

Lettuce

Wash thoroughly in cold water; drain well. Store in plastic bag up to 2 weeks.

Mushrooms

Do not wash until ready to use. Store in open plastic bag or spread on a tray and cover with damp paper towels. Store up to 1 week. Wash quickly in cold water before using; pat dry.

Muskmelon

Do not wash. Store in plastic bag up to 1 week; cover cut surfaces with plastic wrap.

Mustard

Wash thoroughly in cold water; drain well. Remove any damaged leaves. Store in plastic bag up to 1 week.

Okra

Do not wash until ready to use. Store in plastic bag for 7 to 10 days.

Onions, green

Wash thoroughly in cold water; drain well. Store in plastic bag up to 1 week. Do not refrigerate mature onions.

Parsnips

Cut off tops, leaving about 1 inch of stem. Do not wash until ready to use. Store in plastic bag for 1 to 3 weeks.

Peas, black-eyed

Do not shell or wash until ready to use. Store in plastic bag up to 1 week.

Peas, shelling

Do not shell or wash until ready to use. Store in plastic bag up to 1 week. For best flavor, do not store; use immediately.

Peppers

Do not wash until ready to use. Store in plastic bag up to 1 week.

Radishes

Cut off tops. Do not wash until ready to use. Store in plastic bag 1 to 2 weeks.

How to Store Fruits and Vegetables

Rhubarb

Cut off leaves. Wash stalks thoroughly in cold water; drain well. Store in plastic bag up to 2 weeks.

Salsify

Cut off tops, leaving about 1 inch of stem. Do not wash roots until ready to use. Store in plastic bag for 1 to 3 weeks.

Shallots

Wash thoroughly in cold water; drain well. Store in plastic bag up to 1 week.

Sorrel

Wash thoroughly in cold water; drain well. Remove any damaged leaves. Store leaves or stalks in plastic bag for 1 to 2 weeks.

Soybeans

Do not shell or wash until ready to use. Store in plastic bag up to 1 week.

Spinach, New Zealand spinach

Trim roots and tough stalks. Wash very thoroughly in cold water; drain well. Store in plastic bag up to 1 week.

Sprouts (sprouted vegetable seed, any type)

Store in plastic bag up to 1 week. Use sprouts as soon as possible.

Squash, summer

Do not wash until ready to use. Store in plastic bag up to 1 week.

Tomatoes

Wash thoroughly in cold water; pat dry. Store uncovered up to 1 week, depending on ripeness. Let green tomatoes ripen at room temperature, out of direct sun or in cold storage; then store as above.

Turnips

Cut off tops, leaving about 1 inch of stem on roots. Do not wash roots until ready to use. Store in plastic bag for 1 to 3 weeks. Wash greens thoroughly in cold water; drain well. Store in plastic bag for up to 1 week. Do not refrigerate turnip roots; keep in cold storage.

Watermelon

Wash thoroughly in cold water; pat dry. Store uncovered up to 1 week; cover cut surfaces with plastic wrap.

Preparing fruits for refrigerator storage

Apples

Wash thoroughly in cold water; pat dry. Store in a separate compartment away from tomatoes and other fruits. Apples hasten the ripening of other produce. Refrigerate 1 to 2 weeks. Sort; check for signs of spoilage.

Apricots

Apricots are extremely delicate. Store in the refrigerator for 2 to 3 days. Use promptly.

Berries

For gooseberries, blueberries, strawberries, raspberries, and blackberries, sort, then wrap and refrigerate for 2 to 3 days. Use as soon as possible. Do not wash until ready to use.

Cherries

Wrap loosely and refrigerate for 1 to 2 days. Use as soon as possible. Do not wash until ready to use.

Cranberries

Wash, drain on paper towels, then refrigerate for up to a week to 10 days. Use plastic bags.

Currants

Wash, drain on paper towels, then refrigerate for up to a week to 10 days. Use plastic bags.

Figs

Ripen at room temperature. Refrigerate for a day or two.

Grapes

Wrap loosely and refrigerate for 2 to 3 days. Use as soon as possible. Do not wash until ready to use.

Lemons and limes

Refrigerate for 7 to 9 days. Do not wash until ready to use.

Nectarines

Age at room temperature in a paper bag with an apple added. Tear a few holes in the bag. Keep nectarines in bag until softened and sweet-smelling. Refrigerate 1 to 2 days. Do not wash until ready to use.

Oranges

Bag and store in refrigerator 1 to 2 weeks. Store unwashed.

Peaches

Age at room temperature in a paper bag with an apple added. Tear a few holes in the bag. Keep peaches in bag until softened and sweet-smelling. Refrigerate 1 to 2 days. Do not wash until ready to use.

Plums

Refrigerate 1 to 2 days. Do not wash until ready to use.

COLD STORAGE

Cold storage is an old-fashioned but time-tested method for keeping raw, whole vegetables through the winter. If you've planted a big vegetable garden and if you've got (or can construct) the storage space, storing can be the most practical way to go.

You'll find many vegetables from your garden well-suited to cold storage, including beets, carrots, onions, parsnips, potatoes, pumpkins, sweet potatoes, turnips, winter squash, and many others. For a complete list, see "Directions for storing vegetables," later in this chapter. Other vegetables should be used fresh or preserved. Vegetables that are not suitable for cold storage include asparagus, fresh shelling beans, green beans, chayote, corn, cucumbers, eggplant, fresh greens — beet greens, chard, cress, dandelion, endive, lettuce, mustard, and sorrel — fresh lentils, mushrooms, okra, green onions, fresh peas and chick peas, fresh peanuts, new potatoes, radishes, rhubarb, fresh soybeans, spinach and New Zealand spinach, summer squash, and ripe tomatoes. Shelled dried beans, lentils, peas and chick peas, soybeans, and dried peanuts can be kept up to one year in cold storage.

Late-ripening and maturing vegetables are the best choices for cold storage. Certain varieties take better to this method than others — late cabbage, for example. Check seed catalogs and packets before you buy and plant, and talk to the specialists at your County or State Extension Service Office. They can help you decide what vegetables to plant when you're planning your garden, and what storage methods work best in your area.

Few fruits store well. Apples store best of the popular fruits. Like vegetables, late-ripening fall varieties store most successfully. Because apples absorb odors from potatoes, turnips, and other strong vegetables, they should be stored in a distant corner away from other vegetables or fruits. Apples give off high quantities of gases which will hasten the ripening of pears and other vegetables. Apples can be kept for 4 to 6 months in a root cellar if individually wrapped in crumpled newspaper.

Pears can be stored in the same manner as apples for 4 to 5 months. Store them in another area, away from apples.

Although grapes have a short life in cold storage, they are next in line as far as successful cold storage is concerned. They will last 1 to 2 months in a cool root cellar.

Other fruits are best frozen, canned, or dried.

How cold storage works

Like any other method of food preservation, cold storage keeps food from decomposing by stopping or slowing down the activity of enzymes, bacteria, yeasts, and microbes that can eventually spoil food. In cold storage, this is done by keeping fresh, raw, whole vegetables at temperatures between 32°F and 40°F. In this range, the food won't freeze, but it stays cold enough to stop the spoilers. The length of storage time varies with each vegetable, from a few weeks for broccoli or cauliflower to four to six months for potatoes. Dried beans and peas will keep the longest — 10 to 12 months.

One of the advantages of storing your vegetables is that you don't risk eating unwholesome, spoiled food. If the food goes bad, you can tell almost immediately by the way it looks, smells, or feels. But there's still a lot to learn about storage. For example, squash have to be kept warmer than do carrots, so these two vegetables can't be stored in the same spot. Or, if you plan to keep cabbages or turnips, don't store them indoors in the basement; you'll soon find their strong, distinctive odor penetrating up into the house. And, if you live in a climate where heavy snow is common in winter, outdoor storage of vegetables in mounds or barrels isn't going to be practical for you, because deep snow will make them inaccessible in winter.

Although storing vegetables may sound easy, it's a lot more complex than at first meets the eye. Although you don't have to do any chopping, blanching, or processing of vegetables to be stored, each vegetable does have to be handled in a special manner. Perhaps the trickiest part of all is that you've got to keep a weather eye on your stored food. Since the temperature of cold storage depends on the temperature outdoors, you may sometimes have to move or change the location of stored vegetables, open windows or vents, or adjust the humidity level. When storing food indoors, keep a thermometer as well as a humidity gauge in the storage area so you can accurately monitor temperature and moisture conditions.

Because it's harder to control the temperature of stored food, spoilage can happen more easily than with any other form of food preservation. Routine checks for spoilage will help you prevent food losses when storing vegetables indoors — but, once you open up an outdoor mound or barrel, you'll have to empty it of all the stored vegetables at once.

Storage methods for vegetables

Before the days of refrigerators, freezers, and supermarkets, most families depended on cold storage to keep a supply of vegetables all year long. In colonial times, a certain portion of every harvest was kept in cool caves or in straw-lined pits that could withstand freezing temperatures. In later times, most houses were built to include root cellars or cold, damp basements intended as storage areas. These chilly spots were perfect for keeping root vegetables, celery, pumpkin, squash, potatoes, and other vegetables through the cold months.

Compared to houses of a century ago, our modern dwellings are snug, warm, and dry. Today, very few homes offer the cool, damp basement corners, outdoor sheds, or attics that formerly served as food storage areas. That means you'll have to plan, and perhaps construct, one or more special spots for cold storage of your garden's bounty — particularly if you plan to store a variety of vegetables.

In milder climates, where frost is infrequent and doesn't penetrate too deeply, vegetables can be kept in specially prepared outdoor locations. In colder areas, you'll have to store the vegetables indoors as an extra precaution against freezing. In the directions for storing vegetables that follow, you'll find the proper storage method for each vegetable.

Four vegetable groups

Where and how you store each vegetable will depend on how much or how little cold it can take and the amount of humidity it needs to keep fresh. Vegetables to be stored fall into four groups: cold-moist, cool-moist, cold-dry, and cool-dry.

Vegetables that should be cold-moist stored make up the largest group, and include beets, broccoli, Brussels sprouts, cabbage, carrots, cauliflower, celery, turnips, and many others. These vegetables require the coldest storage temperatures — 32°F — and the highest humidity — 95 percent — of all vegetables that can be stored.

The second group of vegetables requires cool-moist: melons, peppers, potatoes, and green tomatoes. These vegetables can be kept at temperatures ranging from 38°F to 60°F and at humidity levels of 80 to 90 percent.

Dry onions and shallots require cold-dry storage temperatures of 32°F to 35°F and humidity of 60 to 75 percent.

The cool-dry group is composed of pumpkin and winter squash, dried peas and beans, and live seeds, all of which must be stored at temperatures of 50°F to 55°F and at a humidity of 60 to 70 percent.

Vegetables in the cold-moist and cool-moist groups can be stored outdoors in a mound or barrel, or indoors in a specially insulated basement storage room that is partitioned off from the central heating area or a root cellar. Vegetables in the cold-dry and cool-dry groups can be stored indoors in a cool area of a heated basement, but they must be kept away from water that might condense and drip down from overhead pipes. Cold-dry storage can also be provided by a dry shed or attic, window wells, or cellar stair storage.

The accompanying chart shows how vegetables in each of these four groups should be stored — at what temperature, at what humidity, and for how long. Any one of the storage methods discussed in this chapter can be used if it supplies the necessary conditions of temperature and humidity. For some vegetables in the cool-moist group, the refrigerator is an ideal storage area. And when cold storage doesn't add significantly to the length of time you can keep a vegetable from the cold-moist group, you may prefer just to refrigerate your crop.

Recommended storage conditions for vegetables

Vegetable	Temperature	Humidity	Storage Period
Cold-moist group:			
Artichokes	32°-34°F	90-95%	1 month
Beets (roots only)	32°-34°F	90-95%	5-6 months
Broccoli	32°-34°F	90-95%	2-3 weeks
Brussels sprouts	32°-34°F	90-95%	1 month
Cabbage	32°-34°F	90-95%	3-4 months
Cardoon	32°-34°F	90-95%	2-3 months
Carrots	32°-34°F	90-95%	4-5 months
Cauliflower	32°-34°F	90-95%	2-3 weeks
Celeriac	32°-34°F	90-95%	2-3 months
Celery	32°-34°F	90-95%	2-3 months
Chicory			
roots and greens	32°-34°F	85-90%	2-3 months
roots only	32°-34°F	90-95%	10-12 months
Chinese cabbage	32°-34°F	90-95%	2-3 months
Collards	32°-34°F	90-95%	2-3 weeks
Fennel	32°-34°F	90-95%	2-3 months
Horseradish	32°-34°F	90-95%	10-12 months
Jerusalem artichokes	32°-34°F	90-95%	2-5 months
Kale	32°-34°F	90-95%	2-3 weeks
Kohlrabi	32°-34°F	90-95%	1-2 months
Leeks	32°-34°F	90-95%	2-3 months
Parsnips	32°-34°F	90-95%	2-6 months
Rutabagas	32°-34°F	90-95%	2-4 months
Salsify	32°-34°F	90-95%	2-4 months
Turnips			
roots	32°-34°F	90-95%	4-5 months
greens	32°-34°F	90-95%	2-3 weeks
Cool-moist group:			
Muskmelons	45°-50°F	85-90%	2-3 weeks
Peppers, sweet or hot	45°-50°F	85-95%	2-3 weeks
Potatoes	38°-40°F	85-90%	4-6 months
Sweet potatoes	55°-60°F	85-90%	4-6 months
Tomatoes, green	55°-60°F	85-90%	1 month
Watermelons	45°-55°F	80-85%	2-3 weeks
Cold-dry group:			
Onions (mature)	32°-34°F	60-75%	6-7 months
Seed, live	32°-40°F	65-70%	10-12 months
Shallots	32°-34°F	60-75%	2-8 months
Cool-dry group:			
Beans, dried (broad, dry, horticultural, or lima)	32°-50°F	65-70%	10-12 months

Recommended storage conditions for vegetables continued

Vegetable	Temperature	Humidity	Storage Period
Chick peas, dried	32°-50°F	65-70%	10-12 months
Lentils, dried	32°-50°F	65-70%	10-12 months
Peas, dried (shelling, black-eyed)	32°-50°F	65-70%	10-12 months
Peanuts, dried	32°-50°F	65-70%	10-12 months
Pumpkins	50°-55°F	60-75%	3-6 months
Soybeans, dried	32°-50°F	65-70%	10-12 months
Squash, winter	50°-60°F	70-75%	5-6 months

Recommended storage conditions for fruits

Fruit	Temperature	Humidity	Storage Period
Apples	32°F	80-90%	4-6 months
Grapes	32°F	80-90%	1-2 months
Pears	32°F	85-90%	4-5 months

OUTSIDE STORAGE

Where winters are mild and there isn't much snow, outside storage is an easy answer to holding large crops. You can store vegetables in well-insulated mounds or barrels, or in little underground lean-tos. Both cold-moist and cool-moist vegetables can be stored in these outdoor locations.

Mound storage

When planning mound storage, first find a spot in your garden where the mound will have good drainage. Dig a shallow, dish-shaped hole six to eight inches deep, and line it with straw or leaves. Spread the straw bed with some metal screening (to keep out burrowing animals), and then stack your vegetables in a cone on the prepared bed. Wrap the individual pieces and separate the layers of food with packing material.

Making a cone or volcano shape, cover the mound with more straw or leaves, then shovel on three or four inches of dirt. Cover all but the top of the cone. Pack the dirt firmly with the back of your shovel. Pile on another thick (six- to eight-inch) layer of straw, but don't cover the top of the cone — it must be left open for ventilation. Put a piece of board on top of each mound to protect it from the weather. If necessary, weight the board with a stone or a brick to keep it in place. Finally, dig a

shallow drainage ditch around the mound.

You can store several kinds of vegetables in the same mound, if they're separated by packing material — that way you can enjoy a bushel of mixed vegetables instead of all carrots or all potatoes. However, several small mounds are more practical than one large mound. Once you've opened a mound, it can't be repacked again — which means you'd have to take out all the vegetables at one time. With several smaller mounds, you can bring manageable portions of vegetables into the house, without having to disturb the whole store. The U.S. Department of Agriculture recommends changing the location of the pits every year to avoid contamination.

Cabbage mound storage

If you want to be able to remove cabbages a few at a time, you can store heads in a mound that's rectangular rather than volcano-shaped. Prepare a long, narrow, rectangular mound with the same base of straw or leaves, metal screening, and more straw, as directed for mound storage. Then put in the individual heads of cabbage head-down in one layer, more straw, and a final layer of dirt. Dig a small trench along each long side of the mound to drain off water. With this type of mound, you can remove just a few cabbages at a time, because there's only one layer of heads.

Barrel storage

Choose a well-drained spot in your garden for barrel storage. Dig out a hole deep enough to cradle the barrel on its side — the barrel doesn't have to be completely buried. Line the hole with straw, and nest the barrel into it. Pack in the vegetables, cover the barrel opening with metal screening or tight-fitting wood covers to keep out rodents, then cover the whole barrel with several insulating layers of straw and dirt. Be sure to mark the location of the barrel mouth, so you can find it easily when you're ready to dig out the vegetables.

Frame storage

Frame storage is a special method that works best for celery and celerylike vegetables, such as Chinese cabbage and fennel. In this little underground lean-to, you store the celery bunches upright with their roots in the ground. Dig a trench about one foot deep, two feet wide, and as long as needed to hold the celery you've grown. Harvest the celery, leaving the roots intact, and stand the bunches up — closely together — in the trench. Water the roots, and leave the trench open until the celery tops are dry. Build a lean-to over the celery with the boards — set a wide board on edge along one side of the trenched celery, and prop another wide board against this support to make a slanted roof over the bunches of celery. Finally, cover the lean-to with straw and then with dirt.

INDOOR STORAGE — THE ROOT CELLAR

If you live in a region where freezing or very snowy weather is common in winter, you'll need to store your vegetables indoors. Your house (or possibly another building on your property) may offer several of the storage areas described in this section, or you may decide to build a basement cold storage room. If you live in an older house, there may be a fruit cellar or cold corner that could easily be closed off to stay cold and moist. Or, your newer house may have a crawl space that's cold and damp. However it's done, indoor storage calls for a bit more upkeep than outdoor storage, since you've got to keep an eye on the temperature, the ventilation, and the humidity to which your vegetables are exposed, as well as make routine checks for spoilage.

A storage mound in a garden provides safe keeping for your vegetables. A ground-level screen discourages burrowing animals; layers of straw and dirt topped by a board shelter the vegetables inside the cone-shaped mound.

An alternative to the traditional mound method of storage is a barrel placed on its side and set in a well-drained outdoor location. Screens or wood over the opening keep out animal intruders; straw and dirt provide insulation.

Vegetables like celery, Chinese cabbage, or lettuce store well in frames. To make a frame, stand the vegetables in bundles in a trench about one foot deep. Cover them with a lean-to of boards and mound straw and dirt over the top.

A basement area, crawl space, or---in older houses---fruit cellar can be closed off to stay cold and moist to make an effective root cellar for your vegetables. Many vegetables can be stored all winter in a well-planned root cellar.

Check around your property to see if it offers storage areas like those described in this section. Test the temperature and humidity in any area you're considering *before* you use it for storing your vegetables. The ideal time to plan your storage area is in winter before you plant.

Temperature. You'll need to put up a reliable indoor/outdoor thermometer in your storage area. Most vegetables are stored at temperatures below 40°F but above freezing. However, there are some exceptions; watery vegetables such as tomatoes, green peppers, winter squash, and pumpkins must all be cool-stored at temperatures above 40°F to keep from spoiling.

Fruits that store well (apples, pears, and grapes) are best stored at 32°F. Store fruits for short periods and check often for signs of spoilage.

Humidity. Unless extra humidity is provided, your cold-moist and cool-moist stored fruits and vegetables will dry up and shrivel when stored indoors. Keep a humidity gauge in your storage area to be sure the vegetables are getting neither too much nor too little humidity, and make any necessary adjustments from time to time. You don't need fancy equipment or techniques for maintaining the right humidity. You might put pans of water or a tub of dampened sand on the floor; cover the floor with damp straw, sand, or sawdust; use damp sand or sawdust for packing the food; or line packing boxes with plastic bags.

Ventilation. You need ventilation in your storage area in case the indoor temperature grows too warm for the vegetables you're keeping. If that should happen, you must let in some cold winter air to cool things off. Good ventilation can be provided by a vent to the outside, a window, or a door. Although it's simple enough to open a window or a door to lower the temperature of your storage place, you must also protect your stored vegetables from contact with the air. Oxygen reacts with other substances in food to cause changes that will spoil the food. Since whole vegetables "breathe," they must be wrapped or packed in materials that will prevent oxidation. You must also keep the vegetables separate from one another so any spoilage won't be able to spread. To do this, layer the vegetables with clean, dry leaves, sand, moss, or dirt, or wrap each vegetable individually in paper.

Apples and pears must be individually wrapped and placed in clean, stout cartons or crates. A special section must be partitioned off for fruit storage. Apples absorb odors from potatoes and turnips and other strong vegetables. Also, apples give off high amounts of gases which will cause your vegetables to ripen too quickly and spoil before winter is over.

When storing apples and pears, insulate boxes with clean straw or hay. If plastic bags are used for storage, breathing holes must be made in them.

Pick pears when mature but still green. Store in the same way as apples. Use Anjou for longest storage life, followed by Bosc and Comice. Pears break down and start to decay in the centers while the outsides still look healthy. Check often for signs of spoilage.

Grapes can be stored for 1 to 2 months in an indoor root cellar but, like apples and pears, they absorb odors from other fruits and vegetables. Store grapes in a separate corner of the fruit section of your root cellar. As underripe grapes start to mature they create their own humidity.

Cellar steps storage

If your house has an outside basement entrance with stairs going down, you can use it as a storage area — the stairs become your shelves. You'll need a door at the top of the stairs, and probably another door at the bottom of the stairs, over the existing house door, to hold in the basement's heat. Which door you use as access depends on the climate. In a mild climate, you could use either door to get to the

The outside stairs to your basement can make a good vegetable storage area. Set a plank on each step for insulation and check the temperature on each step.

vegetables. In colder climates, you may need to go through the basement. Cover the outside door to keep your vegetables from freezing.

Use a thermometer to check the temperature on each step and put barrels or boxes of food where the temperature is right for each item. It's a good idea to set a wooden plank as insulation on each step. If you need to add more humidity, set a bucket of damp sand on one of the steps.

Window well storage

Window wells can make nifty little storage areas, if they don't collect and hold water. Line the wells with

Line dry window wells with straw or bedding, put in the vegetables, then cover with a board or more bedding.

straw or bedding, put in the vegetables and add packing material, if necessary. Then cover the wells with boards or more bedding. If the windows open inward, you may be able to take vegetables out from the basement, without ever having to go outside and dig!

Dry shed or attic storage

Dry shed or attic storage provides cold, dry storage — just right for onions, shallots, pumpkins, and winter squash. By "dry shed," we mean any location that offers constant low temperatures and low humidity. This could be a garage, an unheated breezeway, a shed or storage building, even an unused doghouse. (If your garage or storage shed is fragrant with oil and gasoline, it's no good for storing vegetables. Some vegetables will absorb the oil and gasoline fumes and odors.) In milder winter zones, shelves in a storage shed or boxes on the floor may work well. If you live in a very cold region, you may have to insulate the corner of the shed to keep the vegetables from freezing.

Attic storage is convenient *only* if temperatures can be held somewhat constant. Since many attics will warm up quickly on a sunny day, you'll have to construct a special little storage area in it. Choose a spot that's well-insulated and near ventilation in the coldest part of the attic. Partition and roof it off from the rest of the attic, and use it for storing winter squash and onions.

Basement storage room

You can go all out and build a cold storage room in your basement. What you'll be doing is creating a separate little room, insulated from heat. You can get plans for constructing indoor cold storage rooms from agricultural extension offices, lumberyards, or gardening magazines.

Basically, you'll have to partition off an area that has no heating pipes or ducts. For ventilation, there should be a window — two or more windows if the room is partitioned. For air circulation, plan to have removable slatted flooring and shelves. Slatted flooring makes it easier to use dampened sawdust or other wet material to raise the humidity.

BASIC EQUIPMENT FOR STORING VEGETABLES

In addition to the proper indoor or outdoor storage areas, you'll need the following equipment to store your vegetables:

- Containers, such as wooden boxes, crates, barrels, or plastic garbage bags — cardboard boxes are only suitable for storing vegetables that need dry conditions.
- Newspapers or other paper for wrapping vegetables.
- Packing and insulating materials, such as sand, sawdust, peat, sphagnum moss, leaves, straw, or wood shavings.
- An indoor/outdoor thermometer for monitoring temperatures in an indoor storage area.
- A humidity gauge for monitoring the humidity in an indoor storage area.
- Metal screening for use as protection against contamination by rodents in outdoor storage areas.
- Wood slats for constructing lean-to and frames.
- A shovel for digging out mound, frame, or barrel storage areas.

BASIC COLD-STORING TECHNIQUES

Your vegetables must be harvested at just the right moment so they'll take well to storing and won't decay before you're ready to use them. Damaged or imperfect vegetables will spoil quickly, so you must be very careful when handling them prior to storing. *Never* store bruised or damaged vegetables; they can cause spoilage of your whole crop. It's usually better to clean off but not wash vegetables before storing, because washing can lead to the development of soft rot.

With methods of food preservation, you can process the food and then forget about it until you're ready to use it. Not so with storage. Since the temperature outdoors is the major factor affecting the storage of your vegetables, you have to be constantly alert to the changes in weather. If it turns suddenly colder, warmer, or wetter, you must make whatever adjustments are needed to maintain the proper conditions in your storage area. You must also make regular spoilage checks of the boxes, bags, or bins of vegetables stored indoors.

Handling

Harvest vegetables as late as possible. For many vegetables, this means plant later than usual in order to get a late harvest. You should wait until the first frost warnings to harvest. Carrots, parsnips, potatoes, and turnips, for example, can stay in the ground even after the first frost or two, if the ground is well mulched.

Pick only perfect vegetables for cold storage and handle them carefully to avoid bruising. One bad item can spread decay to others and ruin the whole box, barrel, or mound.

Harvest on a dry day, if possible, and let the vegetables dry on the ground, in the sun, for several hours before packing them away. Onions often need several days of drying; potatoes, however, shouldn't be exposed to hot sun or strong wind. Produce should be cool when packed.

Wash vegetables, if you must, but most experts agree that all you really need to do is brush off excess dirt. The vegetables should be dry before you pack them.

Curing

Potatoes, pumpkins, and most types of winter squash have to be cured before storing. Curing is holding the vegetables at a warm temperature — 70°F to 85°F — in a dark, humid place for about 10 days. Curing hardens the skins and rinds and helps heal surface cuts, reducing mold and rot damage.

How to Store Fruits and Vegetables

Packing

Some vegetables — potatoes, onions, and squash — can go from the garden right into boxes, barrels, plastic bags, or other containers. Root vegetables — such as beets, carrots, turnips, and parsnips — are better packed in some material such as newspaper that will insulate them, slow down their breathing, and keep them from touching one another, so decay can't spread from root to root.

You can wrap the vegetables separately in newspaper, then pack them loosely in boxes, barrels, or plastic bags. If you use plastic bags, poke a few holes in the bags to allow some ventilation. Other packing materials include damp or dry sand, sawdust, peat, sphagnum moss, leaves, straw, or wood shavings. Line the container with a layer of packing wood material, then arrange a layer of vegetables, leave space around each vegetable for packing material. Fill in around each vegetable and then again on top with a layer of packing material. Repeat these steps until the container is full. Be careful to leave enough room for examining the produce at the bottom of the container when you're making routine spoilage checks.

Moist sand is sometimes suggested for packing certain vegetables. You'll know the sand is just the right consistency if it feels cold and falls apart in your hand when squeezed, leaving just a few particles sticking to your skin.

DIRECTIONS FOR COLD-STORING VEGETABLES

If you plan to store a variety of vegetables, you'll probably have to arrange several different kinds of storage. The following directions for storing vegetables tell you which methods are best suited to each vegetable. Choose the one that works best for your climate and your available space.

Artichokes

Cut the fleshy, tight buds before they open. Artichokes are best stored in the refrigerator, but they can be kept in cold storage. Store on shelves or loosely packed in open boxes at 32°F to 34°F and 90 to 95 percent humidity (moist), with some air circulation. Store in a basement storage room or root cellar up to 1 month.

Beans, dried (broad, dry, or lima)

Dried beans won't freeze, and will store well when properly dried and packaged. Dry them according to the instructions in "How to Dry Vegetables." Then store them at 32°F to 50°F and 65 to 70 percent humidity (dry), with some air circulation. Store in a dry shed or attic for 10 to 12 months.

Beets

Choose late-maturing varieties and leave them in the ground until after the first few frosts. Dig them up when the soil is dry, and leave them on the ground for 3 or 4 hours. Remove the tops, leaving about ½ inch of the crowns. Don't remove the roots. Pack in packing material in wooden boxes, barrels, plastic bags with air holes, or in a mound or buried barrel. Store at 32°F to 34°F and 90 to 95 percent humidity (moist), with just a little air circulation. Beets will freeze at 30°F. Store in a basement storage room, root cellar, mound, or buried barrel for 5 to 6 months.

Broccoli

Harvest in late fall. Remove the root, but leave the leaves on as protection. Pack in boxes; separate and cover the stalks with moist sand. Store at 32°F to 34°F and 90 to 95 percent humidity (moist), with some air circulation. Broccoli will freeze at about 30°F. Store in a basement storage room or root cellar up to 3 weeks.

Brussels sprouts

Leave Brussels sprouts in the ground and mulch them heavily to protect the sprouts. Brussels sprouts plants can be stored in a frame, like celery, or in a mound, like cabbage, but often the size of the plants makes this impractical. Store Brussels sprouts plants at 32°F to 34°F and 90 to 95 percent humidity (moist), with just a little air circulation. Store in a basement storage room or root cellar up to 1 month.

Cabbage

Choose late-maturing varieties. For storage in a root cellar, remove the roots, then cover the heads in moist dirt or sand in a bin. For outdoor mound storage, don't remove the stem or root. Place the cabbages head-down, pack straw between the heads, then cover with a final layer of dirt. Store at 32°F to 34°F and 90 to 95 percent humidity (moist), with just a little air circulation. Cabbage will freeze at 30°F. Store in a mound, buried barrel, or root cellar for 3 to 4 months. Do *not* store cabbages in a basement storage room; their strong odor can escape up into the house.

Cardoon

Harvest the plants with roots intact. Don't remove the tops. Set the roots firmly in moist sand or dirt so the plants stand upright, and construct a frame over the plants, as detailed earlier in this chapter. Keep the roots moist during storage, but don't water the leaves of the plants. Store at 32°F to 34°F and 90 to 95 percent humidity (moist), with just a little air circulation. Cardoon will freeze at just under 32°F. Store in a basement storage room, outside frame, or root cellar for 2 to 3 months.

Carrots

Choose late-maturing varieties, and leave them in the ground until after the first couple of frosts. After harvesting, leave them on the ground for 3 to 4 hours. Remove the tops, leaving about ½ inch of the crown. Don't remove the roots. Pack in packing material in wooden boxes, barrels, plastic bags with air holes, or bury in a mound. Store at 32°F to 34°F and 90 to 95 percent humidity (moist), with just a little air circulation. Carrots will freeze at about 30°F. Store in a basement storage room, mound, buried barrel, or root cellar 4 to 5 months.

Cauliflower

Harvest in late fall. Remove the root, but leave on the outer leaves as protection. Pack in boxes; separate and cover the heads with moist sand. Store at 32°F to 34°F and 90 to 95 percent humidity (moist), with a little air circulation. Cauliflower will freeze at about 30°F. Store in a basement storage room or root cellar for 2 to 3 weeks.

Celeriac

Dig up the roots when the soil is dry, and leave them on the ground for 3 or 4 hours. Cut off the tops, leaving 2 or 3 inches of the crown; don't remove the root fibers. Pack in wooden boxes, barrels, or plastic bags with air holes, or in a mound or buried barrel. Store at 32°F to 34°F and 90 to 95 percent humidity (moist), with just a little air circulation. Celeriac will freeze at just under 32°F. Store in a basement storage room, buried barrel, mound, or root cellar for 2 to 3 months.

Celery

Harvest the plants with roots intact. Don't remove the tops. Set the roots firmly in moist sand or dirt so the celery stands upright, and construct a frame over the plants, as detailed earlier in this chapter.

Keep the roots moist during storage, but don't water the leaves of the plants. Store at 32°F to 34°F and 90 to 95 percent humidity (moist), with just a little air circulation. Celery will freeze at just under 32°F. Store in a basement storage room, outside frame, or root cellar for 2 to 3 months.

Chick peas, dried

Dried chick peas won't freeze, and will store well when properly dried and packaged. Dry them according to the instructions in "How to Dry Fruits and Vegetables." Then store them at 32°F to 50°F and 65 to 70 percent humidity (dry), with some air circulation. Store in a dry shed or attic for 10 to 12 months.

Chicory

Harvest the plants with the roots intact, and don't trim the leaves. Tie all the leaves together, then stand the plants upright in moist sand or dirt and construct a frame over the plants, as detailed earlier in this chapter. Store at 32°F to 34°F and 85 to 90 percent humidity (moderately moist), with just a little air circulation. Chicory will freeze at just under 32°F. Store in a basement storage room, outside frame, or root cellar for 2 to 3 months.

To store the roots only, dig them up when the soil is dry, and leave them on the ground for 3 to 4 hours. Remove the tops, leaving about ½ inch of the crowns. Pack in packing material in wooden boxes, barrels, plastic bags with air holes, or in a mound or buried barrel. Store at 32°F to 34°F and 90 to 95 percent humidity (moist), with just a little air circulation. Chicory roots freeze at about 30°F. Store in a basement storage room, mound, buried barrel, or root cellar for 10 to 12 months.

Chinese cabbage

Harvest the plant with roots intact. Don't remove the tops. Set the roots firmly in moist dirt so the cabbage stands upright and construct a frame over the plants, as detailed earlier in this chapter. Keep roots moist during storage but don't water the leaves of the plants. Store at 32°F to 34°F and 90 to 95 percent humidity (moist), with just a little air circulation. Chinese cabbage will freeze at just under 32°F. Store in a basement storage room, outside frame, or root cellar for 2 to 3 months.

Fennel

Harvest the plants with roots intact. Don't remove the tops. Set the roots firmly in moist sand or dirt so the plants stand upright, and construct a frame over the plants, as detailed earlier in this chapter. Keep the roots moist during storage, but don't water the leaves of the plants. Store at 32°F to 34°F and 90 to 95 percent humidity (moist), with just a little air circulation. Fennel will freeze at just under 32°F. Store in a basement storage room, outside frame, or root cellar for 2 to 3 months.

Horseradish

Choose late-maturing plants and leave them in the ground until after the first few frosts. Dig them up when the soil is dry, and leave them on the ground for 3 or 4 hours. Remove tops, leaving about ½ inch of the crown. Don't remove the roots. Pack in packing material in wooden boxes, barrels, plastic bags with air holes, or in a mound or buried barrel. Store at 32°F to 34°F and 90 to 95 percent humidity (moist), with a little air circulation. Horseradish freezes at about 30°F. Store in a basement storage room, mound, buried barrel, or root cellar for 10 to 12 months.

Greens (collard, kale, and turnip)

Harvest the plant with roots intact. Don't remove the tops. Set the roots firmly in moist dirt so it stands upright. Keep the roots moist during storage, but don't water the leaves of the plant. Store at 32°F to 34°F and 90 to 95 percent humidity (moist), with some air circulation. Greens freeze at just below 32°F. Store in a frame for 2 to 3 weeks.

Jerusalem artichokes

Dig the roots when the soil is dry, and leave them on the ground for 3 or 4 hours. Remove the tops, leaving about ½ inch of the crowns. Then pack into boxes or other well-ventilated containers, but without additional packing material. Store at 32°F to 34°F and 90 to 95 percent humidity (moist), with little air circulation. Jerusalem artichokes will freeze at just below 31°F. Store in a basement storage room or root cellar for 2 to 5 months.

Kohlrabi

Choose late-maturing varieties and leave in the ground until after the first few frosts. Dig when the soil is dry, and leave on the ground for 3 or 4 hours. Remove the tops, leaving about ½ inch of the crown. Don't remove the roots. Pack in packing material in wooden boxes, barrels, plastic bags with air holes, or in a mound or buried barrel. Store at 32°F to 34°F at

90 to 95 percent humidity (moist), with just a little air circulation. Kohlrabi freezes at 30°F. Store in a basement storage room, mound, buried barrel, or root cellar for 1 to 2 months.

Leeks

Harvest with roots intact. Don't remove the tops. Set the roots firmly in moist dirt so the leeks stand upright. Keep the roots moist during storage, but don't water the leaves of the plant. Store at 32°F to 34°F and 90 to 95 percent humidity (moist), with some air circulation. Leeks freeze at just below 32°F. Store in a basement storage room, outside frame, or root cellar for 2 to 3 months.

Lentils, dried

Dried lentils won't freeze and will store well when properly dried and packaged. Dry them according to "How to Dry Fruits and Vegetables." Then store them at 32°F to 50°F and 65 to 70 percent humidity (dry), with some air circulation. Store in a dry shed or attic for 10 to 12 months.

Muskmelon

Harvest melons slightly immature; they will continue to ripen during storage. Store at 45°F to 50°F and 85 to 90 percent humidity (moderately moist), with some air circulation. Pile or stack melons loosely, with no packing material, on shelves in a basement storage room or root cellar for 2 to 3 weeks.

Onions

Dig up mature onion bulbs and leave them on the ground to dry completely, usually about a week. Cut off the tops, leaving ½ inch of stem. Pack the bulbs loosely, without any packing material, in well-ventilated containers. If you like, braid the tops together and hang the onions from hooks in a cold storage area. Store at 32°F to 34°F and 60 to 75 percent humidity (dry), with some air circulation. Onions freeze at just under 31°F. Store in a dry shed or attic for 6 to 7 months.

Parsnips

Choose late-maturing varieties and leave them in the ground until after the first few frosts. Dig them up when the soil is dry, and leave them on the ground for 3 or 4 hours. Remove the tops, leaving about ½ inch of the crown. Don't remove the roots. Pack in packing material in wooden boxes, barrels, plastic bags with air holes, or in a mound or buried barrel. Store at 32°F to 34°F and 90 to 95 percent humidity (moist), with a little air circulation. Parsnips freeze at 30°F. Store in a basement storage room, mound, buried barrel, or root cellar for 2 to 6 months.

Peanuts, dried

Dried peanuts won't freeze, and will store well for 10 to 12 months when properly dried and packaged. Dry them according to "How to Dry Fruits and Vegetables." Then store them at 32°F to 50°F and 65 to 70 percent humidity (dry), in a dry shed or attic.

Peas, dried
(shelling, black-eyed)

Dried peas won't freeze, and will store well when properly dried and packaged. Dry them according to "How to Dry Fruits and Vegetables." Then store them at 32°F to 50°F and 65 to 70 percent humidity (dry), with some air circulation. Store in a dry shed or attic for 10 to 12 months.

Peppers

Harvest before the first frost. Choose only the firmest peppers for storing, since they're easily damaged. Pack into plastic bags punched with air holes; then place in boxes. Peppers must be monitored very carefully during storage to be sure they don't become too moist or too cold. Store at 45°F to 50°F and 85 to 95 percent humidity (moderately moist), with a little air circulation. Peppers will freeze at just below 31°F. Store in a basement storage room or root cellar for 2 to 3 weeks.

Potatoes

Choose late-maturing varieties. Early potatoes are difficult to keep in cold storage. Dig the potatoes when the soil is dry, and leave them on the ground for 3 or 4 hours. Avoid sun and wind damage. Cure by storing them at regular basement temperatures — 60°F to 65°F—in moist air for 10 days. Then pack them into boxes or other well-ventilated containers, but without additional packing material. Store at 38°F to 40°F, and 85 to 90 percent humidity (moderately moist), with a little air circulation. Potatoes will freeze at just below 31°F. Store in a basement storage room or root cellar for 4 to 6 months.

Pumpkins

Harvest just before the first frost, leaving an inch or so of stem. Cure at 80°F to 85°F for 10 days, or for 2 to 3 weeks at slightly lower temperatures. After curing, move them to a cooler spot for long-term storage. Store at 50°F to 55°F and 60 to 75 percent humidity (dry), with a little air circulation. Pumpkins will freeze at just above 30°F. Store on shelves in a basement storage room, dry shed, or attic for 3 to 6 months.

Rutabagas

Choose late-maturing varieties and leave them in the ground until after the first few frosts. Dig them up when the soil is dry, and leave them on the ground for 3 or 4 hours. Remove the tops, leaving about ½ inch of the crowns. Don't remove the roots. Pack in packing material in wooden boxes, barrels, or plastic bags with air holes, or in a mound or buried barrel. Store at 32°F to 34°F and 90 to 95 percent humidity (moist), with a little air circulation. Rutabagas will freeze at about 30°F. Store in a basement storage room, mound, buried barrel, or root cellar for 2 to 4 months.

Salsify

Harvest in late season. Dig them up when the soil is dry, and leave them on the ground for 3 or 4 hours. Remove the tops, leaving about ½ inch of the crowns. Don't remove the roots. Pack in packing material in wooden boxes, barrels, plastic bags with air holes, or in a mound or buried barrel. Store at 32°F to 34°F and 90 to 95 percent humidity (moist), with a little air circulation. Salsify freezes at about 30°F. Store in a basement storage room, mound, buried barrel, or root cellar for 2 to 4 months.

Seed, live

Most gardeners buy seeds to plant, but you may want to harvest seeds to sprout when your vegetables mature. Cabbage and lettuce seeds, for instance, can both be sprouted, as detailed in "How to Sprout Vegetables." Leave the seeds on the plant until they're dry and fully mature; then harvest them. Store dried seeds in airtight plastic bags in a metal container, or in airtight glass jars; keep glass jars in a bag or wrap in newspaper to keep light from reaching the seeds. Store at 32°F to 40°F and 65 to 70 percent humidity (dry). Store in a dry shed or attic for 10 to 12 months.

How to Store Fruits and Vegetables

Shallots

Dig up mature bulbs and leave them on the ground to dry completely, usually about a week. Cut off the tops, leaving about ½ inch of stem. Pack the bulbs loosely, without any packing materials, in well-ventilated containers. Store at 32°F to 34°F and 60 to 75 percent humidity (dry), with some air circulation. Shallots freeze at just under 31°F. Store in a dry shed or attic for 2 to 8 months.

Soybeans, dried

Dried soybeans won't freeze, and will store well when properly dried and packaged. Dry them according to "How to Dry Fruits and Vegetables." Then store them at 32°F to 50°F and 65 to 70 percent humidity (dry), with some air circulation. Store in a dry shed or attic for 10 to 12 months.

Squash, winter

Harvest just before the first frost, leaving on an inch or so of stem. Cure at 80°F to 85°F for 10 days, or for 2 to 3 weeks at slightly lower temperatures. After curing, store at 50°F to 60°F and 70 to 75 percent humidity (moderately dry), with some air circulation. Squash freezes at just above 30°F. Store in a basement storage room, root cellar, dry shed, or attic for 5 to 6 months.

Sweet potatoes

Choose late-maturing varieties. Put sweet potatoes directly into storage containers when you harvest them. Cure them under moist conditions at 80°F to 85°F for 10 days. At lower temperature, curing takes longer—2 to 3 weeks. Stack storage crates and cover them to hold in the humidity while curing. After curing, store at 55°F to 60°F and 85 to 90 percent humidity (moderately moist), with some air circulation. Sweet potatoes freeze at just below 30°F. Store in a basement storage room or dry shed for 4 to 6 months.

Tomatoes, green

Plant late so the vines will still be vigorous when you pick the tomatoes for storage. Harvest green tomatoes just before the first killing frost. When you harvest, remove the stems from the tomatoes, then wash and dry them before storing. Be careful not to break skins.

Separate the green tomatoes from those that are showing red. Pack green tomatoes 1 or 2 layers deep in boxes or trays; you can also ripen a few tomatoes for immediate use by keeping them in closed paper bags in the house and out of the direct sun. Store green tomatoes at 55°F to 60°F and 85 to 90 percent humidity (moderately moist), with good air circulation. At room temperature mature green tomatoes ripen in 2 weeks; at 55°F, ripening will be slowed down to nearly 1 month. Immature green tomatoes will take longer to ripen at either temperature; tomatoes showing some red will ripen faster, and can't be held in storage as long as totally green ones. Check your tomatoes once a week to monitor the ripening; remove the ripe ones and any that have begun to decay. Tomatoes will freeze at about 31°F. Store in a basement storage room or dry shed up to 1 month.

Turnips

Choose late-maturing varieties and leave them in the ground until after the first few frosts. Dig them up when the soil is dry, and leave them on the ground for 3 or 4 hours. Remove the tops, leaving about ½ inch of the crown. Don't remove the roots. Pack in packing material in wooden boxes, barrels, plastic bags with air holes, or in a mound or buried barrel. Since the strong odor of turnips can escape from the basement up into the house, it's wisest to store them separately and outdoors. Store at 32°F to 34°F and 90 to 95 percent humidity (moist), with a little air circulation. Turnips will freeze at about 30°F. Store in a mound or buried barrel for 4 to 5 months.

Watermelon

Harvest melons when fully ripe; they will not continue to ripen during storage. Store at 45°F to 50°F and 80 to 85 percent humidity (moderately moist), with some air circulation. Pile or stack melons loosely, with no packing material, on shelves in a basement storage room or root cellar for 2 to 3 weeks.

DIRECTIONS FOR COLD-STORING FRUITS

Apples

Choose late varieties: Winesap, Northern Spy, Jonathan, McIntosh, Cortland, and Golden and Red Delicious. Select apples that are mature but hard. Wrap each apple individually in a crumpled sheet of newspaper. Store in wooden crates or barrels. Insulate the bottom of each storage container with a layer of clean straw or hay. Store apples in a corner away from other fruits and vegetables. Store at 80 to 90 percent relative humidity for up to 6 months. Check often for signs of spoilage.

Grapes

Catawba grapes keep best. Second in line are Tokay and Concord grapes. Pick underripe bunches and store between layers of clean straw and hay. You should make the stacks no more than three layers deep. Store grapes away from other fruits and vegetables from which they might absorb odors. Store at 80 to 90 percent relative humidity for 1 to 2 months.

Pears

Select dessert pears for storage. Anjou pears keep best, followed by Bosc or Comice. Harvest mature green pears that are still hard. Store in the same manner as apples (see above). Caution: Pears that have begun to ripen will decay quickly. Pears rot from the core; although they look fine on the outside, the inside may be rotting. Store for 4 to 6 months, checking often for signs of spoilage.

How to Freeze Fruits and Vegetables

Freezing foods is one of the fastest and simplest methods of food preservation. It's easy to prepare food for the freezer and easy to prepare food for the table from the freezer. Best of all, foods preserved by freezing taste more like fresh than their canned or dried counterparts, and they retain more color and nutritive value.

Almost all vegetables take well to freezing. In fact, some vegetables shouldn't be preserved and stored by any other method. The list of better-frozen vegetables includes broccoli, Brussels sprouts, cabbage, cauliflower, eggplant, mushrooms, parsnips, edible-pod peas, pumpkins, rutabagas, and winter squash.

The natural flavor, color, and texture of many fruits are best retained by freezing. Also, sugar syrups preserve the color of light fruits that might otherwise darken when exposed to air. Although the additional sugar adds calories, the results are excellent, and you don't need to add any more sugar when you thaw the fruits for use in desserts or pies.

Although the techniques are simple and easy, freezing is a more expensive form of storage than canning. The freezer itself is an investment, and it takes electricity to run. But if you manage your freezer wisely, it can still help save on food costs.

Frozen vegetables and fruits can be stored a lot longer than many other foods, but shouldn't be kept stored for more than 12 months. By keeping your frozen foods in a constant state of turnover, the freezer space is being given maximum use. To get the most value from your freezer, use up the foods you've stored and replace them with others in season. The higher the rate of turnover, the lower the cost per pound of food.

Keep a list near the freezer to indicate what you've used, what's left, and what new foods you may be adding from time to time. By keeping track of what you have and how long it's been in the freezer, you'll be sure to use up all your frozen foods within the recommended storage period.

Getting started

Freezing is a simple method of food preservation and requires only a few steps. Having selected good-quality fruits and vegetables, then prepared and packaged them for freezing, you can sit back and let cold temperatures do the rest of the work.

Starting with the highest-quality produce is the single most important factor in guaranteeing the quality of your frozen foods, but you must follow the directions for all freezing procedures exactly. Select the most perfect foods, and always exercise the strictest sanitary conditions and precautions when handling them. You can never be too careful about properly packaging and sealing foods for freezer storage.

If you follow freezing directions to the letter and keep food in a well-managed freezer, your frozen fruits and vegetables will be as delicious when you serve them as when you preserved them.

STOPPING THE SPOILERS

Extreme cold — and that means temperatures of 0°F or lower — is what stops the growth of the microorganisms in or around food that can cause spoilage. Zero temperatures also slow down enzyme activity and oxidation, which are chemical changes affecting the color, flavor, and texture of food. Although cold doesn't kill off these spoilers the way heating at high temperatures for canning does, freezing halts their activity during the time the food is stored.

There are five major spoilers that can affect frozen food if it isn't handled properly:

● **Bacteria, yeasts, and molds** are normally present in all fresh foods. When these begin to multiply rapidly, spoilage occurs. You can stop these spoilers in their tracks by using the highest-quality produce, by preparing it under the most sanitary conditions, and by storing food at the specified, very cold temperatures.

● **Enzymes,** also normally present in all food, work to bring about chemical changes in it. These changes result in spoilage — unless enzyme activity is stopped before food is frozen, enzymes can destroy the fresh flavor of vegetables and cause them to take on an off-color. You can stop enzyme activity by blanching vegetables (a brief heat treatment) before freezing them.

● **Freezer burn** affects foods that haven't been wrapped carefully enough. If exposed surfaces on the food come in contact with the dry air of the freezer, moisture is lost, and dry, tough surfaces develop. You can control freezer burn by using moisture/vaporproof packaging materials that are airtight when sealed.

● **Large ice crystals** occur when food isn't frozen quickly enough. Quick-freezing means storing foods at 0°F or even subzero temperatures. If foods freeze too slowly, moisture from the cells in the food fibers forms ice crystals between the fibers, and the product loses liquid and may darken. Quick-freezing at zero temperatures locks the cells in the food fiber in their proper places.

● **Oxidation** is a chemical change that occurs when frozen foods are exposed to oxygen. The oxygen reacts chemically with other substances in the foods to create changes that affect the quality of that food. To prevent loss of quality due to oxidation, fill and seal your freezer containers correctly and carefully.

BASIC FREEZING EQUIPMENT

Except for the freezer and proper packaging materials, your kitchen is probably already supplied with most of the other pots, pans, and utensils you'll need for home freezing. This section is a guide to the tools and materials necessary for proper freezing of vegetables. (Information on freezing fruits will follow later in this chapter.) Always remember that no matter how good your equipment, it must be spotlessly clean and sanitary while you work, to prevent bacterial contamination.

Freezer containers

Preserving food by freezing is based on the principle that extreme cold (0°F) halts the activity of microorganisms, enzymes, oxidation, and other changes that cause food spoilage. When preserving foods by the heat treatment method of canning, containers must be hermetically sealed. Although that's not necessary for frozen storage, the packages you use *must* be airtight, as well as moisture/vaporproof, odorless, tasteless, and greaseproof.

The best package size for you depends on your freezer and your family. Pack food in containers that will take care of your crew for one meal. You can plan on two servings to a pint container; three or four servings from a quart-size. It's quicker to thaw two single pint containers than one large container.

There are two kinds of freezer containers suitable for freezing foods at home—rigid containers and flexible bags or wrappers. Some delicate vegetables like asparagus or broccoli might be damaged if packaged immediately after blanching. To protect them, these vegetables are tray frozen briefly before being packaged in freezer containers. Some fruits should also be tray frozen before storage.

Rigid containers. Rigid containers are best for vegetables or foods that are liquid or don't have a distinct shape. Rigid containers include plastic freezer containers with tight-fitting lids or can-or-freeze jars with wide mouths and tight-fitting lids. Square or rectangular containers use freezer space more efficiently than round containers or those with flared sides or raised bottoms. Freezer containers can be reused. Wash them and their lids in hot suds; then rinse, drain, and cool.

Can-or-freeze jars come in three sizes: ½ pint, 1 pint, and 1½ pints. Plastic freezer boxes come in 1-pint, 1½-pint, 1-quart, and 2-quart sizes.

Freezer bags and pouches. Bags made from polyethylene or heavy-duty plastic or the new boilable pouches that can be heat sealed are also good for freezing vegetables. Liquid foods are safest in plastic bags that are then placed in

You probably already have in your kitchen much of the basic equipment needed for freezing foods. You will also need freezer containers and bags. When freezing vegetables in twist-tie plastic bags, the bags should always be filled to the top and excess air gently pressed out (use your hands) before freezing.

protective cardboard boxes. Although bags aren't always easy to stack, they're great for tray-frozen foods and bulky or odd-shaped items.

Plastic freezer bags come in many sizes: 1 pint, 1½ pints, 1 quart, 2 quarts, 1 gallon, and 2 gallons. You close these bags by pressing out the air, twisting the top and doubling it over, then wrapping the top several times with a twist tie.

Other packaging materials. Never use empty, plastic-coated milk cartons or cottage cheese or ice cream containers for freezing, since these aren't airtight enough to be reused as freezer containers. Lightweight plastic wrap, butcher paper, and waxed paper aren't tough enough to protect food in the freezer, either. Freezer wrap — specially laminated or coated freezer paper, heavy-duty plastic wrap, or heavy-duty aluminum foil — is seldom used for freezing vegetables. Reserve it for meats, fish, game, casseroles, and cakes.

Tray freezing. Cranberries, blueberries, and raspberries are often tray frozen for convenience. When using this method, simply wash the berries, drain them, and freeze them on a cookie sheet or tray. Then pour the frozen berries into freezer bags or rigid containers, label them, and return them to the freezer.

The freezer

In this book, all references to a freezer mean a separate appliance for freezing only. The ice-cube section of a refrigerator is good for very short-term storage only, and "short-term" means days, not weeks or months. The separate freezing compartment of a refrigerator can hold food for weeks; a side-by-side freezer section can hold food for a few months. But for long-term storage at 0°F, a separate household freezer is still your best bet.

Three types of freezers. There are three types of home freezers from which to choose. *Upright freezers* range in size from 6 to 22 cubic feet and may have 3 to 7 shelves. *Chest freezers* run from 6 to 32 cubic feet. *Refrigerator-freezer combinations* range in size from 2 to 16 cubic feet of freezer space. Freezers with the frostless feature save you the work of annual defrosting, and keep frost from building up on food packages. (Frostless freezers should be cleaned annually.)

The freezer size and type you buy will depend on your needs and available space. A chest freezer usually costs less to buy, and to run, but an upright may fit into your home more easily. Most folks agree that it's easier to find and remove foods from an upright freezer, too. In a combination model, the freezer is separated from the refrigerator section, having a separate door either at the top, bottom, or side of the refrigerator. Check your space and your budget to decide which type is best for you.

Plan on 6 cubic feet of freezer space per person in your family. Then, if you can manage it, buy a freezer bigger than that. Once you get used to having a freezer, you'll have no trouble filling it.

Whichever freezer type you choose, place it in a cool, dry, and well-ventilated location. Before you start shopping, scout out a good location in your home, measure it, and check your doorway measurements to be sure the freezer you buy will fit through them.

Adjusting freezer temperature. Keep track of your freezer's temperature with a refrigerator-freezer thermometer. Put it toward the front of the storage area, fairly high up in the load of food. Leave it overnight — without opening the freezer — before you check it for the first time. If the thermometer reads above 0°F, adjust the freezer's temperature control to a lower setting. Wait another day and check the thermometer again to see if you adjusted the temperature correctly. When you've got the temperature just right, check the thermometer once a day. But, if your freezer has an automatic defrost, don't take a reading during the defrost cycle — it won't be an accurate reflection of normal freezer temperature.

Managing your freezer. For the most efficient use of your freezer, you must be organized. Think of your freezer as a warehouse or a food depository. You need to keep track of what's inside, when it went in, and when it should come out. "First in, first out" is the byword for the best in flavor and appearance in frozen food. The food is still safe to eat after 12 months, but may not be at the peak of its quality. As a rule of thumb, rotate your entire stock about every six months, or freeze only enough vegetables to last until the next growing season.

By grouping like with like in your freezer, your inventory will be more organized and your searching simplified. One shelf or section can keep vegetables, another fruits, another cooked foods or main dishes. Devise an inventory form to help you keep track of where each category of food is. You might put the chart on a clipboard hung on the freezer door handle or nearby. Then note what goes in, out, how much, and when. Don't forget to label each and every package clearly — in writing or symbols someone besides yourself can read! Legible labels and good packing in the freezer make inventory and food selection easy.

As you use your frozen food, keep a running

check on your methods and packaging. If you notice that a particular bag, container, or sealing method isn't doing the job, make a mental note of it and try another procedure or packaging next time.

Caring for your freezer. Take care of your freezer according to the manufacturer's directions. By keeping the freezer defrosted, free of ice, and clean, it'll work better and cost you less to operate. A full or almost-full freezer is cheaper to run than an empty or almost-empty one. The higher the turnover — the more you use and replace frozen foods — the less your freezer "warehouse" costs per item.

If your freezer needs annual or semi-annual defrosting, do it while the weather is cold, preferably before you start planning your garden. During a defrosting in cold weather, not only can the food wait outside (in well-insulated boxes or coolers), but you can take a thorough inventory and then determine how much to plant in spring. If you have lots of green beans left in March, that's a clue that supply is exceeding demand. Put up less the coming year and fill that freezer space with something else.

To defrost your freezer, follow manufacturer's directions. If you don't have directions, remove food to a cold place — outdoors in a cooler, if the weather is very cold or placed in a neighbor's freezer, or a locker. Unplug or turn off the freezer, and put in a pan or two of hot water or a blowing fan to help hurry the melting. DON'T use a hair dryer or other heating appliance, because the heat could melt or warp some of the materials on the inside of the freezer. As the ice loosens, scrape it off with a plastic windshield scraper or other similar tool. When all the ice is gone, wash the inside of the freezer with a solution of three tablespoons baking soda dissolved in a quart of warm water. Wipe dry, turn the freezer on, and put the food back in. Clean frostless freezers with a baking soda solution annually.

If your freezer develops an odor, put a piece or two of charcoal on a paper towel and set them in the freezer for a few days.

What to do when the freezer goes out. If your freezer quits or the power goes out, there are several steps you can take to protect your frozen foods. First, set the freezer temperature at the lowest setting, then shut the freezer and DON'T OPEN IT UNLESS ABSOLUTELY NECESSARY. If kept closed, a full freezer will keep food frozen for 15 to 20 hours and food will stay below 40°F for up to 48 hours. A half-full freezer may keep foods frozen for just under a day.

If the freezer will be off for longer, dry ice could save the day, if you act quickly. (It's a good idea to locate a source of dry ice in advance and keep the name and number handy for just such an emergency.) A 25-pound chunk of dry ice, carefully handled with gloves and placed on a piece of heavy cardboard on top of the packages of food, should hold a half-full freezer (10 cubic feet) for two to three days; if the freezer is full, it will carry you over for three to four days. (Use two-and-a-half pounds of dry ice for each cubic foot.) Be sure the room is well-ventilated when you're working with dry ice.

If dry ice is unavailable, pack up the food and use a locker or a neighbor's freezer.

If the food's temperature rises above 40°F — ordinary refrigerator temperature — check it over carefully and immediately cook it completely. It's always better to use thawed foods immediately. If you do refreeze thawed foods, use them as soon as possible. If the food shows any signs of spoilage — color or texture change, slipperiness, or off-odor — and has been over 40°F, don't take any chances — toss it out. A freezer thermometer is an excellent guide to freezer safety. If you don't have a thermometer, feel the food and take a guess. Anything that's still frozen solid, and still has ice crystals throughout, is safe to refreeze or use if you're quick about it.

Vegetables are precooked slightly before freezing to arrest chemical changes caused by enzyme activity. This precooking is called blanching.

After blanching, it's necessary to arrest the cooking process by transferring the vegetables quickly to a large pan of ice water.

The blancher

Vegetables are precooked slightly before freezing in order to arrest the chemical changes that are caused by enzyme activity. This brief heat treatment is called blanching, and you'll need a blancher to do it properly. A blancher is a large pot, with a cover and a perforated insert or basket insert for lifting vegetables out of the boiling water. You can buy one in the housewares section of most stores, or you can make your own from a large (6- to 8-quart) pot with a cover and something (a colander, sieve, deep frying basket, or cheesecloth bag) to lift the vegetables from the boiling water.

When you aren't using the blancher for freezing vegetables, it won't gather dust. It can also be used as a spaghetti cooker, steamer, or even a deep-fat fryer.

Other basic equipment

Besides the freezer and blancher, the basic equipment for freezing consists of whatever kitchen implements you'll need to prepare the food for packaging. Remember that it's essential to keep equipment, work area, and hands clean.

To freeze vegetables successfully, you'll need:

Rigid freezer containers with airtight lids for
  liquid foods: plastic freezer containers;
   freezer cans or jars with wide mouths
Bags: plastic storage bags; heavy-duty plastic
bags; or boilable pouches
String, rubber bands, pipe cleaners, or twist
  ties to fasten freezer bags
Shallow tray, cookie sheet, or jelly-roll pan for
  tray freezing
Additional heavy-duty plastic wrap or heavy-
  duty aluminum foil
Sharp paring knife
Chopping knife
Colander, sieve, strainer, or paper towels
Stiff vegetable scrubbing brush
Teakettle for extra boiling water
Ricer, food mill, or blender for mashing or
  pureeing
Freezer tape to seal wrapped foods and to
  make labels
Grease pencil or felt-tip marker or
  pressure-sensitive labels for labeling
  packages

BASIC INGREDIENTS

Choose vegetables that are tender, ripe but just barely ready to eat, and just as fresh as possible. Slightly under-mature vegetables are better for freezing than those that are past their prime. (Different rules apply to fruit.) For peak flavor, rush vegetables from the garden to the freezer within two hours. If you can't freeze vegetables within that time limit, cool the vegetables quickly in ice water, drain well, and keep refrigerated until ready to prepare for freezing.

Ice. Since cooling is an important part of preparing vegetables for freezing, you need plenty of ice at hand to keep the cooling water really cold. Estimate one pound of ice for each pound of vegetables you're going to freeze. Keep a good store of ice in reserve for your home freezing needs by filling heavy-duty plastic bags with ice cubes, or freezing water in empty milk cartons. Keep adding to your stored ice from time to time, and you won't be caught short in the midst of a big freezing job.

Butter and seasonings. Most vegetables are frozen without any flavoring or seasoning added. However, if you want to freeze pouched vegetables in butter sauce, we suggest a combination of butter, salt, and herbs (oregano, basil, savory, chervil, tarragon, thyme, sage, or marjoram).

BASIC FREEZING TECHNIQUES

Although freezing food is one of the easiest methods for putting food by, that doesn't mean there's nothing to it. If you approach the project carefully and scientifically, you'll be able to get the best frozen food possible and to use energy wisely.

Most vegetables take well to freezing, and, when you serve them at a later date, they'll be as close to fresh as any preserving method can guarantee. In fact, some vegetables shouldn't really be stored by any other method, since freezing has proven to be the best method for preserving them. These include broccoli, Brussels sprouts, cabbage, cauliflower, eggplant, mushrooms, parsnips, edible-pod peas, pumpkins, rutabagas, and winter squash. The only vegetables that don't freeze well are lettuce and other fresh greens for salads, and watery vegetables like radishes and cucumbers.

Other than those, almost anything can be frozen. When you aren't sure whether you'll like a certain vegetable frozen, try a sample batch of just a few packages, bags, or containers. Freeze for a couple of weeks, then taste. If you hate it, not much has been lost.

Fruits are best frozen in pieces, with sugar or sugar syrup added. The addition of ascorbic acid or lemon juice, or a commercial preparation containing vitamin C, can be added to fruits to retard browning. Peaches and apricots brown less readily if first treated with one of these products.

Fruit syrups may be light or heavy depending on personal preference and the use to which you intend to put the fruit. Blueberries freeze well without the addition of sugar or syrup.

When freezing fruit with syrup, always allow adequate head space for expansion. Pint-size containers require ½ inch head space; quarts require 1 inch.

It's a good idea to check with your local Cooperative Extension Service Office for advice on the best vegetables to plant for freezing. Knowledgeable produce people, either in the supermarket or at a stand, can be excellent sources of information, too.

Selecting fruits and vegetables

Rule number one is to select the highest-quality food possible. The fruits and vegetables you choose should be tender, fresh, and ripe enough to be eaten right away. NEVER use produce that has become overripe either before or after harvesting.

As with any preserving method, you must clean vegetables carefully before freezing. Wash, scrub, rinse, and drain them just as if you were going to eat and serve them right away.

Blanching

Blanching is a brief heat treatment given to vegetables before they're packaged and frozen. Its purpose is to stop the action of enzymes, which can destroy the fresh flavor of vegetables and cause off-colors. If you want to successfully freeze vegetables, it's generally necessary to blanch them before freezing. This simple technique also helps seal in vitamins, brightens the color of vegetables to be frozen, and shrinks them slightly to make packing easier. When freezing herbs or vegetables such as green onions or hot peppers, which are to be used for flavoring only, blanching *isn't* necessary.

When preparing fruits and vegetables for freezing, wash them in several changes of cold water (clean vegetables with a brush if necessary), then lift them from the water and drain in a colander.

Follow blanching times given in the freezing recipes precisely. Blanching for too short a time is worse than not blanching at all — enzyme action will be stimulated instead of stopped. And if blanched for too long a time your vegetables will cook, losing vitamins, minerals, flavor, and color.

Use one gallon of water per pound of vegetables, or two gallons for leafy greens. Blanching water must be boiling when you lower the vegetables into it. Fill the blancher with vegetables and lower it into boiling water; start timing as soon as the vegetables have gone into the boiling water. You may keep the blancher covered during the blanching period or keep the heat on high and stir frequently. If you live at 5,000 feet or more above sea level, blanch one minute longer than the times specified in each recipe. You can also blanch vegetables in a microwave oven. Follow the directions in the manufacturer's instruction book.

When blanching a large quantity of vegetables, start with only the amount that can be blanched and cooled in a 15-minute period, and put the rest in the refrigerator. Package, label, and freeze each blanched group before starting on the next. You can use the same blanching water for several batches of vegetables, adding additional boiling water from a teakettle to replace water lost through evaporation. If you wish, change the water when it becomes cloudy. Keep a second pot or large teakettle boiling, so you won't be delayed when the time comes to change the blanching water.

Cooling

After vegetables have been precooked the exact amount of time, remove them immediately from the boiling water and cool them. This is crucial for keeping the heating process from continuing past the proper period for each vegetable or food. Transfer the vegetables quickly from the blancher to the ice water. The kitchen sink is a good spot for holding ice water to cool vegetables, but if you want it free for other uses, put the ice water in a plastic dishpan or other large, clean container.

Be sure to add new ice to the ice water frequently, so it stays as cold as possible. You'll need plenty of ice on hand to keep the cooling water really cold. Plan on one pound of ice for every pound of vegetables you're going to freeze. To have a ready supply when you need it, you'll have to stock up in advance.

Packing and sealing

The secret to successful freezer packaging is to seal the air out and keep it out. Immediately after blanching and cooling, pack vegetables loosely in proper containers. Plastic freezer bags and boxes or can-and-freeze jars are all excellent. Freezer containers must be airtight, moisture/vaporproof, odorless, tasteless, and greaseproof.

Head space. Since food expands as it freezes, you must allow room — or head space — for this expansion. Otherwise the lids will pop off, bags will burst, and you'll have wasted food, time, and money.

Food expands as it freezes, so it's important to leave head space at the top of each freezer container to allow for this expansion. Check your recipe carefully to determine how much head space to allow for each type of produce.

Foods that are dry need no head space. Food that's packed in liquid or is mostly liquid needs ¼ inch of head space for pints, ½ inch for quarts. If you pack foods in containers with narrow mouths, the food expands upward in the container even more, requiring ¾ inch of head space for pints and 1½ inches for quarts. We suggest you stick to wide-mouth containers. The recipes in this book give you head space needs for each particular food for wide-mouth containers only.

Sealing. How you seal food for the freezer is just as important as how you package it. After wiping the mouths of your freezer containers with a clean, damp cloth, seal rigid containers by following the manufacturer's instructions (if there are any), or by snapping, screwing, or fitting the lid tightly on the container. If the lid doesn't seem tight, seal it with freezer tape.

Seal bags or boilable pouches with a heat-sealing appliance; follow the instructions that come with the heat sealer. Or seal bags by pressing out the air, then twisting the bag close to the food. Fold the twisted section over and fasten it with a rubber band, pipe cleaner, or twist tie. To get air out of an odd-shaped bag, lower the filled bag into a sink full of water and let the water press the air out. Twist the bag top, lift it out, double the twisted area backward, and fasten.

Labeling. A good freezer label should tell what food is in the package, the amount of food or number of servings, and when it went into the freezer. Better yet, it should tell how the food was packed, and when, for example, "Sugar Pack Strawberries — June, 1986." You might want to include an "expiration" or "use by" date. Frozen main dishes, sauces packed in boilable pouches, and other more complex items call for a label with description, number of servings, perhaps even heating and thawing instructions.

Select labeling materials that will last. A grease pencil or felt tip marker may write directly on the container. Freezer tape makes a quick label, as do pressure-sensitive labels from a stationery store. Print legibly and use standard abbreviations.

Tray freezing. This technique is used with more delicate vegetables — asparagus for example — to keep them from being damaged during packaging. Since individual stalks are frozen separately first, tray freezing allows you to remove serving portions from the pouch when you need them. To tray freeze, blanch the vegetables, cool them in ice water, drain well, and then spread in a single layer on a cookie

Many berries can be successfully tray frozen before being stored in plastic bags in the freezer. It takes about one hour to tray freeze berries or small pieces of fruit. Always fill the bags to the top before sealing and freezing. Fruit is easily measured from this free-flow pack, and the unused portion can be resealed tightly and returned promptly to the freezer.

sheet, jelly-roll pan, or special tray. Freeze until just solid — usually about an hour. As soon as the vegetables are frozen solid, transfer them to containers, bags, or pouches. Seal the containers and store them in the freezer.

The tray-freezing technique is used with asparagus, green beans, lima beans, soybeans, broccoli, Brussels sprouts, cauliflower, whole-kernel corn, kohlrabi, peas, sweet or hot peppers, prepared potatoes, rutabagas, and summer squash. The recipes that follow indicate if tray freezing is recommended.

Cranberries and blueberries freeze well by this method also. They may then be measured from a large bag as needed, and the unused portion resealed and returned to the freezer. The section on freezing fruits indicates when tray freezing is desirable.

Quick-freezing

Put your sealed freezer packages in the coldest spot in your freezer, which should be set at 0°F. Place the containers in a single layer, leaving a little space between each package for heat to escape — or follow any specific freezing directions given by the manufacturer. Be sure to set the freezer temperature control to the lowest setting several hours *before* you'll be preparing food for freezing.

Look back to the use-and-care book that came with your freezer to locate the coldest sections. If you have an upright freezer, the shelves are the coldest places; in a chest freezer, the coldest places are near the walls. In a combination refrigerator-freezer, the shelves inside the freezer — not the door shelves — are the coldest places.

After arranging packages in a single layer, shut the freezer and leave it alone for 24 hours. When that time has elapsed, the food should be frozen solid. Stack it up and move it away from the coldest part to another area in the freezer for storage. Then you can add another batch to be frozen.

Your freezer can only freeze a limited amount of food at a time, usually two to three pounds of food for each cubic foot of freezer space. Don't try to freeze any more than that or the food will freeze too slowly and quality will be lowered. The amount of food your freezer can freeze at once helps you determine how much food to prepare for the freezer on any particular day. If you have more food to be frozen than your freezer can take, either refrigerate packages for a day or so (not much longer), or cart it all to a locker to be frozen, then transfer it to your home freezer. Always try to keep a cold spot free to quickly freeze additional food.

Delicate vegetables like asparagus should be briefly tray frozen before they're packaged. Spread the blanched vegetables in a single layer on a cookie sheet or tray, and freeze them until just solid. Then transfer the frozen vegetables to containers and store them in the freezer.

When you're done freezing food in quantity, reset the control to the setting that will maintain 0°F.

Serving frozen vegetables

Most frozen vegetables should be cooked without thawing. Corn-on-the-cob is a major exception; it must be thawed completely before cooking. Greens should be *partially* thawed in order to separate the individual leaves before cooking. Vegetables fully cooked before freezing should also be partially thawed before heating. Once they're thawed, use your vegetables as quickly as possible. Food that's been frozen spoils more quickly than fresh food.

Cooking frozen vegetables. For best results, cook frozen vegetables just as you would fresh ones — but cook them for a shorter period, since blanching shortens cooking times. Prepare only the amount of vegetables you'll consume at one meal, and use as little cooking water as possible.

For each pint of frozen vegetables, heat ¼ to ½ cup water to boiling in a small or medium saucepan. Add the vegetables and keep them over high heat until the water returns to a boil. Break vegetables into individual pieces with a fork as they heat. When the

water boils again, cover the pan, reduce the heat, and simmer just until the vegetables are tender. The recipes in this book give specific postfreezing cooking times for each vegetable. Begin timing when the cooking water returns to a boil. When crisp-tender, add butter or margarine, salt, pepper, or other seasonings to taste. Serve vegetables immediately after cooking, so they won't lose nutrients.

For tray-frozen vegetables, just remove the amount you need from the freezer. Increase cooking water to a little more than ½ cup if you plan to serve more than 2 cups of vegetables. Cook as above.

For pouched vegetables, follow the cooking directions that come in the heat-sealer's instruction book.

Butter sauce for pouched vegetables. For each 1 to 1½ cups vegetables in small boilable pouches, add 2 tablespoons water, 1 tablespoon butter, ¼ to ½ teaspoon salt, and a dash oregano, basil, savory, chervil, tarragon, thyme, sage, marjoram, or other herbs appropriate to your vegetable. Seal, label, and freeze. Heat as the manufacturer directs.

Soups, casseroles, sauces, gravies, dips, and other mixtures need only be heated to serving temperatures. Baked goods such as zucchini bread or carrot bread can be served just after thawing.

Rules for safe freezing

For clean and safe-to-eat foods, always follow the freezing recipe directions exactly, use the containers and equipment called for, and keep in mind the following Do's and Don'ts:

DO

- Work in a clean kitchen with clean floors, counter tops, cabinets and range, and clean equipment.
- Keep utensils that handle raw meat and poultry scrupulously clean. That means scrubbing, washing, and rinsing knives and cutting boards between each type of cutting or chopping task.
- Work with clean food. Wash, scrub, and rinse fruits and vegetables in several changes of water, lift food out of the water to drain, and don't let water drain off over food.
- Work with clean dishcloths and towels, clean hands, and clean clothes.
- Wash your hands each time you touch something other than food, such as your hair, your face, the phone, a child, or a pet.
- Get out all the necessary equipment. Wash it and ready all ingredients before you start to follow recipe directions, so there'll be no delays and no chance for food to spoil.
- Remember to protect your hands when working with hot foods. Use hot pads and tongs.
- Be extra cautious with large pots or kettles of boiling water or food. Don't move them, but keep them on the range and work there.
- Avoid any sudden changes in temperatures when working with can-or-freeze jars. Putting a hot jar on a counter or in a cold draft could cause it to break.
- Always read and follow manufacturer's directions for special equipment or appliances.
- Use the very best, most perfect food for freezing. Spending time and money to freeze less than the best is a waste.
- Blanch all vegetables before freezing. Blanching destroys enzymes that can cause chemical changes in foods, and is an essential step.
- Use moisture/vaporproof containers and seal properly, following recipe directions exactly. Poor packaging can cause freezer burn, off-flavors, and less-than-the-best foods.
- Freeze foods quickly to prevent large ice crystals from forming. Follow the directions for quick-freezing.
- Treat fruits with ascorbic acid to retard browning. Most fruits freeze best with sugar added by the dry pack method, or the use of a sugar syrup.

- Buy a freezer thermometer and check it regularly. It should read 0°F at all times — any higher temperature and you're shortening the freezer life of the food.
- Keep an inventory of your frozen vegetables, so you can use them within the best part of their freezer life. Most vegetables will maintain quality for a year. Vegetables that have been fully cooked before freezing should be stored for a much shorter time — no more than a month.
- Cook and serve vegetables as each recipe directs. Vegetables are best cooked directly from the frozen state, in a very small amount of water and just until tender.
- Put your freezer in a convenient, cool, dry, well-ventilated location and clean and/or defrost it once a year.

DON'T

- Don't use your hands when a kitchen tool will do the job. Keep fingers out of food if at all possible.
- Don't try shortcuts or substitutions or time-saving gimmicks. There's only one correct way to prepare food for freezing, and the techniques and recipes that follow are based on it.
- Don't cook or prepare food for preserving when you're sick.
- Don't prepare food if you have sores on your hands, unless you wear rubber gloves.

BASIC FREEZING STEPS FOR VEGETABLES

By now you can see that preparing vegetables for the freezer isn't too different from preparing them for dinner. However, you must always follow the freezing recipes exactly. The recipes in the next section give you specific instructions for each vegetable, but here is a summary of the basic steps:

1. Check your freezer's size and estimate how much food you can freeze in a 24-hour period (3 pounds of food for each cubic foot of space), then check the recipe for the vegetable you want to freeze to see how much to pick for a single preparation session.
2. Select tender, young, fresh vegetables that are unblemished.
3. Wash vegetables well in plenty of cold water, scrubbing with a brush whenever necessary. Lift the vegetables out of the water to drain. Don't let them stand in water any longer than necessary, because they lose nutrients. Sort

by size and handle like sizes together for even heating and cooling.

4. Put 1 gallon of water (2 gallons for greens) in the blancher; cover, and place it over high heat.
5. Prepare the sink or dishpan full of ice cubes and ice water.
6. Cut or prepare the vegetables, about 1 pound or 4 cups at a time, as the recipe directs.
7. Put 1 pound of prepared vegetables in the blancher's insert and lower it into rapidly boiling water. Keep the heat high. Cover and begin timing immediately.
8. When the time is up, remove the cover, lift the blancher's insert up out of the blancher for a few seconds to drain, then immediately put the insert of vegetables into ice water.
9. Keep vegetables in the ice water for about the same length of time as they were in the boiling water, or until cold. Stirring will help cool the vegetables.
10. Lift the vegetables from the ice water and drain them well in a colander, sieve, or on paper towels.
11. Pack into containers, bags, or freeze on trays.
12. Label each package with contents, number of servings, and date frozen. You might also wish to list an expiration date.
13. Freeze, following the directions for quick-freezing, or any special manufacturer's directions for your freezer.
14. Most vegetables will keep for 12 months at 0°F.

RECIPES FOR FREEZING VEGETABLES

Most vegetables take well to freezing. And when your garden produces an extra big crop of zucchini or tomatoes, for example, you can also cook up and freeze batches of spaghetti sauce, soup, zucchini bread, and other hearty dishes.

The recipes that follow give you specific directions for freezing vegetables. It's a good idea to read through the whole recipe before you begin preparing foods for freezing. Follow the directions exactly, and don't try to shortcut or skip any steps. A few of the following recipes don't call for blanching — except in these instances, you must always blanch vegetables before freezing, and the recipes will specify for how long. Similarly, if no head space is specified, you can assume that the food will not expand during freezing. All our recipes have been designed by food experts to insure proper safety standards and the most successful food preserving.

ARTICHOKES

20 to 25 1¼-inch trimmed = 1 pint

1. Choose artichokes that are uniformly green, with a compact globe shape and tightly adhering leaves. Size doesn't affect quality or flavor, but do handle artichokes of similar size together.
2. Remove the outer leaves until you come to light yellow or white leaves or bracts. Cut off the tops of the buds and trim the heart and stem to a cone shape. Wash each heart in cold water just as soon as you've finished trimming it. Drain.
3. Blanch 7 minutes. Cool; drain well.
4. Pack into containers.
5. Seal, label, and freeze.
6. Cook frozen artichokes about 5 to 10 minutes or until tender.

ASPARAGUS

1 to 1½ pounds = 1 pint
1 crate (24 pounds) = 15 to 22 pints

1. Choose very fresh stalks that are brittle and beautifully green. The tips should be compact and tightly closed.
2. Wash well and sort by size. Remove scales with a sharp knife.
3. Break off the tough ends. Leave the stalks whole or cut into 1- or 2-inch lengths.
4. Blanch small stalks for 1½ to 2 minutes; medium stalks 2 to 3 minutes; large stalks 3 to 4 minutes. Cool; drain well.
5. Tray freeze or pack into containers, alternating tip and stem ends.
6. Seal, label, and freeze.
7. Cook frozen asparagus 5 to 10 minutes.

BEANS, GREEN OR SNAP

⅔ to 1 pound = 1 pint
1 bushel (30 pounds) = 30 to 45 pints

1. Choose young, tender beans that snap easily. The beans in the pods should not be fully formed.
2. Wash well, snip the ends, and sort by size.
3. Leave the beans whole, cut in even lengths, or cut French-style (lengthwise).
4. Blanch 2 to 3 minutes, depending on the size of the beans. Cool; drain well.
5. Tray freeze or pack into containers. Seal, label, and freeze.

6. Cook frozen whole or cut beans 12 to 18 minutes; French-style beans 5 to 10 minutes.

BEANS, BROAD OR LIMA (young)

²/₃ to 1 pound = 1 pint

1. Choose wide, flat beans that are tender, meaty, and stringless.
2. Wash well, snip off the ends, and cut or break them into 1½-inch pieces.
3. Blanch 3 minutes. Cool; drain well.
4. Tray freeze or pack into containers. Seal, label, and freeze.
5. Cook frozen beans about 10 minutes.

BEANS, BROAD, DRY, OR LIMA (shelled)

2 to 2½ pounds in pods = 1 pint
1 bushel (32 pounds) in pods = 12 to 16 pints

1. Choose well-filled pods of young, green, tender beans.
2. Wash, shell, and wash again. Sort by size.
3. Blanch small beans 1 minute; medium beans 2 minutes; large beans 3 minutes. Cool; drain well.
4. Tray freeze or pack into containers. Seal, label, and freeze.
5. Cook large beans 15 to 20 minutes; small beans 6 to 10 minutes.

BEETS

1¼ to 1½ pounds without tops = 1 pint
1 bushel (52 pounds) without tops = 35 to 42 pints

1. Choose young, tender, evenly colored beets no more than 3 inches in diameter.
2. Remove tops, leaving ½ inch of stem. Wash.
3. Cook in boiling water to cover, 25 to 30 minutes for small beets; 45 to 50 minutes for medium.
4. Cool and slip off skins. Leave whole or slice, cube, or dice.
5. Pack into containers. Seal, label, and freeze.
6. Cook frozen beets just until heated through.

BROCCOLI

1 pound = 1 pint
1 crate (25 pounds) = 24 pints

1. Choose compact, dark green heads. Stalks should be tender not woody.
2. Wash well, then soak heads of broccoli in 1 cup salt per gallon of water for ½ hour to get rid of bugs. Rinse in fresh water; drain.
3. Cut stalks to fit into containers. Split stalks so that heads are about 1 to 1½ inches in diameter.
4. Blanch 3 minutes. Cool; drain well.
5. Pack into containers. Seal, label, and freeze.
6. Cook frozen broccoli 5 to 8 minutes.

BRUSSELS SPROUTS

1 pound = 1 pint
4 one-quart boxes = 6 pints

1. Choose firm, compact, dark green heads.
2. Wash thoroughly, then soak in salt water as for broccoli. Rinse in fresh water; drain. Sort by size.
3. Blanch small sprouts 3 minutes; medium sprouts 4 minutes; large sprouts 5 minutes. Cool; drain well.
4. Tray freeze or pack into containers. Seal, label, and freeze.
5. Cook frozen sprouts 4 to 9 minutes.

CABBAGE

Frozen cabbage can only be used as a cooked vegetable, not in slaw.

1 to 1½ pounds = 1 pint

1. Choose fresh, solid heads with crisp leaves.
2. Trim the coarse outer leaves.
3. Cut medium-coarse shreds, thin wedges, or separate into leaves.
4. Blanch 1 to 1½ minutes for shreds; 3 minutes for wedges or leaves. Cool; drain well.
5. Pack into containers, leaving ¼-inch head space. Seal, label, and freeze.
6. Cook frozen cabbage about 5 minutes, or thaw leaves to use for stuffed cabbage or cabbage rolls.

CARROTS

1¼ to 1½ pounds without tops = 1 pint
1 bushel (50 pounds) without tops = 32 to 40 pints

1. Choose tender, small to medium, mild-flavored carrots.
2. Remove tops, wash well, and pare.

3. Cut in cubes, slices, or lengthwise strips, or leave small carrots whole.

4. Blanch small whole carrots 5 minutes; blanch diced or sliced carrots and lengthwise strips 2 minutes. Cool; drain well.

5. Tray freeze or pack into containers, leaving ¼-inch head space. Seal, label, and freeze.

6. Cook frozen carrots 5 to 10 minutes.

CAULIFLOWER

1⅓ pounds = 1 pint
2 medium heads = 3 pints

1. Choose compact, white, tender heads.

2. Break into flowerets about 1 inch in diameter.

3. Wash well, then soak in salt water as for broccoli. Rinse with fresh water; drain.

4. Blanch 3 minutes. Cool; drain well.

5. Tray freeze or pack into containers. Seal, label, and freeze.

6. Cook frozen cauliflower 5 to 8 minutes.

CELERY

Use frozen celery in cooked dishes only.

1 pound = 1 pint

1. Choose crisp, tender stalks without coarse strings.

2. Wash well, trim, and cut into 1-inch lengths.

3. Blanch 3 minutes. Cool; drain well.

4. Tray freeze or pack into containers.

5. Cook frozen celery with other vegetables in soups, stews, and casseroles.

CHICK PEAS

2 to 2½ pounds in pods = 12 to 16 pints

1. Choose pods of young, tender chick peas.

2. Wash, shell, and wash again.

3. Blanch chick peas 2 to 3 minutes. Cool, drain well.

4. Tray freeze or pack into containers. Seal, label, and freeze.

5. Cook frozen chick peas 10 to 15 minutes.

CHINESE CABBAGE

Use frozen Chinese cabbage in cooked dishes only.

1 to 1½ pounds = 1 pint

1. Choose fresh, solid heads with crisp leaves.

2. Trim coarse or shriveled leaves.

3. Cut into medium-coarse shreds, thin slices, or separate into leaves.

4. Blanch 1 to 1½ minutes for shreds; 3 minutes for slices or leaves. Cool; drain well.

5. Pack into containers, leaving ¼-inch head space. Seal, label, and freeze.

6. Cook frozen Chinese cabbage about 5 minutes, or thaw leaves to stuff.

CORN, WHOLE–KERNEL

2 or 2½ pounds in husks = 1 pint
1 bushel (35 pounds) in husks = 14 to 17 pints

1. Choose well-developed ears with plump, tender kernels and thin, sweet milk. Press a kernel with a thumbnail to check the milk. Corn must be fresh to freeze.

2. Husk, remove the silk, and trim the ends. Sort by size.

3. Blanch small ears (1½ inches or less in diameter) 1 minute; medium ears (2 inches in diameter) 8 minutes; large ears (more than 2 inches in diameter) 10 minutes. Cool; drain well.

4. Cut kernels from the cob at ⅔ the depth of the kernel.

5. Tray freeze or pack in containers, leaving ¼-inch head space. Seal, label, and freeze.

6. Cook frozen corn 3 to 4 minutes.

CORN, CREAM–STYLE

2 to 2½ pounds in husks = 1 pint
1 bushel (35 pounds) in husks = 14 to 17 pints

1. Prepare as for whole-kernel corn, but cut the kernels from cob at ½ the depth of the kernel. Then scrape the cob with the back of a knife to remove the milk and heart of the kernel.

2. Pack with liquid in containers as for whole-kernel corn. Seal, label, and freeze.

3. Cook as for whole-kernel corn.

CORN, PRECOOKED

2 to 2½ pounds in husks = 1 pint
1 bushel (35 pounds) in husks = 14 to 17 pints

1. Choose, husk, and sort corn. Don't blanch.

2. Cut corn from cob as for cream-style corn.

3. Heat corn with about ¼ cup water for each pint of corn over low heat, stirring frequently, just until thick.

4. Pour hot corn into another pan and set pan into ice water to cool. Stir frequently to hurry cooling.

5. Pack in containers, leaving ¼-inch head space. Seal, label, and freeze.

6. Cook just until heated to serving temperature. Note: Don't cook more than 3 quarts of corn at one time.

CORN-ON-THE-COB

1. Choose corn and prepare as for whole-kernel corn.

2. Blanch small ears (1½ inches or less in diameter) 6 minutes; medium ears (2 inches in diameter) 8 minutes; large ears (more than 2 inches) 10 minutes. Cool thoroughly; drain well.

3. Pack in containers or wrap ears individually or in family-size amounts in freezer paper, plastic wrap, or foil, then in plastic freezer bags. Seal, label, and freeze.

4. Thaw frozen corn-on-the-cob before cooking, then cook about 4 minutes.

EGGPLANT

1 to 1½ pounds = 1 pint

1. Choose plump, firm, evenly and darkly colored eggplant and harvest before inner seeds mature.

2. Wash, peel, and slice ⅓-inch thick. Work quickly because eggplant discolors if allowed to stand.

3. Blanch 4 minutes. Add ½ cup lemon juice or 4½ teaspoons citric acid to 1 gallon blanching water. Cool; drain well.

4. Tray freeze or pack into containers. Seal, label, and freeze. To make slices easier to separate, pack with a piece of freezer wrap between them.

5. Cook frozen eggplant about 5 to 10 minutes. It's best cooked in a sauce, or thawed to be coated and fried, or used as an ingredient in Ratatouille or Moussaka.

GREENS, BEET

1 to 1½ pounds greens = 1 pint
1 bushel (12 pounds) = 8 to 12 pints

1. Choose young, tender leaves.
2. Wash well, in several changes of water.

3. Remove tough stems and bruised leaves.

4. Blanch each pound of greens in 2 gallons boiling water for 2 minutes. Stir to keep greens from sticking together. Cool; drain well.

5. Pack into containers, leaving ¼-inch head space. Seal, label, and freeze.

6. Cook frozen beet greens 6 to 12 minutes.

GREENS (chard, collard, kale, mustard, and turnip)

1 to 1½ pounds = 1 pint
12 pounds (1 bushel) = 8 to 12 pints

1. Choose young, tender leaves.
2. Wash well in several changes of water.
3. Remove tough stems or bruised leaves.
4. Blanch each pound of greens in 2 gallons boiling water for 2 minutes; collard greens, 3 minutes. Stir to keep greens from sticking together. Cool, drain well.
5. Pack into containers, leaving ¼-inch head space. Seal, label, and freeze.
6. Cook frozen greens 8 to 15 minutes.

HORSERADISH

Yield varies widely depending on the size of the root and the method of preparation.

1. Choose tender small to medium roots.
2. Wash well and remove small roots and stubs.
3. Pare and grate root outdoors, if possible; or if you must work indoors, pare, cube, and grate the root in a blender or food processor with tap water to cover or with a couple of ice cubes. Add water until horseradish reaches desired consistency. Add 2 to 3 tablespoons of white vinegar and ½ teaspoon salt to each cup of grated horseradish to stop enzyme action. (The earlier in grating process you add vinegar, the milder horseradish will be.)
4. Pack into jars, screw on lids, and freeze. Horseradish prepared in this fashion can also be kept in jars in the refrigerator for a long time. To use frozen horseradish, thaw to desired temperature.

JERUSALEM ARTICHOKES

2 to 4 pounds = 1 pint

1. Choose fresh, firm roots with no bad spots.
2. Scrub well; if necessary, cut into chunks.

3. Blanch 3 to 5 minutes, depending on size. Cool, drain well.

4. Pack in containers. Seal, label, and freeze.

5. Cook frozen Jerusalem artichokes just until tender.

KOHLRABI

1¼ to 1½ pounds = 1 pint

1. Choose young, tender small to medium kohlrabi.

2. Cut off tops and roots and wash well.

3. Pare, leave whole, or slice ¼-inch thick or dice into ½-inch cubes.

4. Blanch whole kohlrabi 3 minutes; blanch diced or sliced kohlrabi 1 to 2 minutes.

5. Tray freeze or pack in containers, leaving ¼- inch head space. Seal, label, and freeze.

6. Cook frozen kohlrabi 8 to 10 minutes.

LEEKS

1 pound = 1 pint

1. Select fresh, firm leeks. Trim off the roots and all but 2 inches of the leaves.

2. Wash leeks well, then split lengthwise, and wash again.

3. Slice leeks or chop them.

4. Package in recipe-size amounts. Or, tray freeze them and then pack or bag the leeks so you can pour out what you need. Leeks don't require blanching, but they shouldn't be stored in the freezer more than 3 months at 0°F.

LENTILS

2 to 2½ pounds in pods = 12 to 16 pints

1. Choose pods of young, tender lentils.

2. Wash, shell, and wash again.

3. Blanch lentils 1 minute. Cool; drain well.

4. Pack into containers. Seal, label, and freeze.

5. Cook frozen lentils 6 to 10 minutes.

MUSHROOMS

1 to 2 pounds = 1 pint

1. Choose young, firm, medium mushrooms with tightly closed caps.

2. Wash well, trim off ends, and sort by size. Slice larger mushrooms, if desired.

3. Blanch small mushrooms 3 minutes; large mushrooms 4 minutes. Add 1 tablespoon lemon juice to each quart of blanching water. Cool; drain well. Or, cook mushrooms in a frying pan with a small amount of butter until almost done. Cool.

4. Pack in containers. Seal; label, and freeze.

5. Cook frozen mushrooms just until heated through.

MUSKMELON

1 to 1¼ pounds = 1 pint

1. Select fully ripe, but firm melons.

2. Cut in half, scoop out seeds, and cut off rind.

3. Cut into ¾-inch cubes, slices, or balls. Pack into freezer containers or freezer bags, seal, and freeze.

4. Thaw only until still slightly frozen and serve.

OKRA

1 to 1½ pounds = 1 pint

1. Choose young, tender, green pods.

2. Wash well. Cut off the stems, but don't cut open the seed cells. Sort by size.

3. Blanch small pods 3 minutes; large pods 4 minutes. Cool; drain well.

4. Slice crosswise in ½- to ¾-inch slices, or leave whole.

5. Tray freeze or pack into containers, leaving ¼-inch head space. Seal, label, and freeze.

6. Cook frozen okra about 5 minutes.

ONIONS

1 to 3 medium chopped or sliced = 1 pint

1. Choose the highest-quality, fully mature onions. Freeze only chopped or sliced onions. Store whole onions in a cool, dry place.

2. Peel, wash, and chop or slice.

3. Package onions in recipe-size amounts. Or, tray freeze them and then pack or bag the onions in recipe-size amounts so you can pour out what you need. Onions don't need to be blanched, but they shouldn't be stored in the freezer longer than 3 to 6 months at 0°F.

PARSNIPS

1¼ to 1½ pounds without tops = 1 pint
1 bushel (50 pounds) without tops = 32 to 40 pints

1. Choose small to medium, tender, not woody, parsnips.
2. Remove tops, wash, pare, and cut in ½-inch cubes or slices.
3. Blanch 3 minutes. Cool; drain well.
4. Pack in containers, leaving ¼-inch head space. Seal, label, and freeze.
5. Cook frozen parsnips about 10 to 12 minutes.

PEANUTS

3 to 6 pounds in shell = 1 quart
1 bushel (30 pounds) = 5 to 10 quarts

1. Select fully mature peanuts.
2. Wash, drain, shell, and wash again. Sort by size.
3. Blanch small peanuts 1 minute; medium peanuts 2 minutes; large peanuts 3 minutes. Cool; drain well.
4. Tray freeze or pack into containers. Seal, label, and freeze.
5. Cook peanuts in water to cover until very tender, about 2 hours.

PEAS, EDIBLE–POD

⅔ to 1 pound = 1 pint
1 bushel (30 pounds) = 35 to 40 pints

1. Choose very fresh, tender pods of the same size.
2. Wash well, then snip off the ends, if you wish.
3. Blanch 1½ minutes. Cool; drain well.
4. Tray freeze or pack into containers. Seal, label, and freeze.
5. Cook edible-pod peas just until heated through and crisp-tender, about 2 to 3 minutes.

PEAS, BLACK–EYED

2 to 3 pounds in pods = 1 pint

1. Choose pods with tender and barely grown seeds.
2. Wash, shell, and pick over peas. Discard too mature or insect-damaged peas. Wash again.
3. Blanch small peas 1 minute; larger peas 2 minutes. Cool; drain well.
4. Tray freeze or pack peas in containers,

leaving ¼-inch head space. Seal, label, and freeze.
5. Cook frozen peas 15 to 20 minutes.

PEAS, SHELLING

2 to 3 pounds in pods = 1 pint

1. Choose young pods containing tender peas.
2. Wash, shell, and wash again.
3. Blanch 2 minutes in boiling water or steam blanch 3 minutes. Cool; drain well.
4. Tray freeze or pack into containers. Seal, label, and freeze.
5. Cook frozen peas 3 to 5 minutes until heated through.

PEPPERS, SWEET OR HOT

⅔ pound fresh = 1 pint

1. Choose shapely, firm, evenly colored peppers.
2. Cut out the stems; remove seeds of sweet peppers.
3. Leave whole, cut in half, slice, or dice. It's not necessary to blanch peppers.
4. Tray freeze or pack into containers. Seal, label, and freeze.
5. Add frozen chopped pepper to uncooked or cooked dishes, or cook about 5 minutes.

PEPPERS, HOT

Yield varies widely depending on the size of the peppers.

1. Choose firm, crisp, deep-red hot peppers with thick walls.
2. Roast hot peppers in 400°F oven 3 to 4 minutes.
3. Rinse in cold water to remove charred skins. Drain.
4. Tray freeze or pack into containers, leaving ¼-inch head space. Seal, label, and freeze.
5. Chop frozen peppers and add them to cooked dishes.

POTATOES, BAKED

1. Bake potatoes, then let cool. Scoop out potato and mash. Season and stuff mashed potato back into shells, if desired.
2. Tray freeze, then wrap shells individually. Seal, label, and freeze.
3. Cook by unwrapping and reheating in a 400°F oven until hot, about 30 minutes.

4. Freeze leftover baked potatoes unstuffed, then thaw and slice or cube them for creamed or scalloped potatoes, potato salad, or American fries.

POTATOES, FRENCH−FRIED

Yield varies widely depending on the size of the potatoes.

1. Choose large, mature potatoes.
2. Wash, pare, and cut them in sticks about ½- inch thick.
3. Rinse well in cold water; drain. Pat dry.
4. Fry small amounts at a time in deep fat (360°F) for 5 minutes or until tender but not brown.
5. Drain well on paper towels. Cool.
6. Pack into containers. No head space is necessary. Seal, label, and freeze.
7. Cook frozen French fries in deep fat (375°F) until browned. Or spread them in single layer on cookie sheet and heat in 450°F oven, 5 to 10 minutes or until browned.

POTATOES, NEW

2 to 4 pounds = 1 pint

1. Choose smooth, tiny new potatoes.
2. Scrub well.
3. Blanch 3 to 5 minutes, depending on size. Cool; drain well.
4. Pack in containers. Seal, label, and freeze.
5. Cook frozen new potatoes just until tender.

PUMPKIN

3 pounds = 2 pints

1. Choose finely textured, ripe, and beautifully colored pumpkins.
2. Wash, cut in quarters or small pieces, and remove seeds.
3. Cook in boiling water, steam, pressure-cook, or oven-cook until tender.
4. Scoop the pulp from the skin. Mash in a saucepan, or press through a ricer, sieve, or food mill into a saucepan.
5. Cool by putting the saucepan in ice water and stirring the pumpkin occasionally until cold.
6. Pack into containers, leaving a ¼-inch head space for pints, ½-inch for quarts. Seal, label, and freeze.
7. Cook frozen pumpkin just until heated through.

PUMPKIN PIE FILLING

1. Prepare the pumpkin as above.
2. Combine measured amounts of mashed pumpkin with the remaining ingredients in your favorite pumpkin pie filling recipe (omit cloves, if used, and add after thawing, because freezing will change the flavor).
3. Pour the pumpkin into containers in single pie amounts. Seal, label, and freeze.
4. Thaw, add cloves, turn into a pastry shell, and bake as your recipe directs.

RHUBARB

This spring fruit will probably be the garden's first contribution to your freezer.

⅔ to 1 pound = 1 pint
15 pounds = 15 to 22 pints

1. Select colorful, firm but tender stalks with few fibers.
2. Wash and trim off leaves and woody ends.
3. Cut in 1- or 2-inch lengths.
4. Blanch 1 minute. Cool quickly in cold water to save color and flavor; drain well.
5. **Unsweetened pack:** Pack rhubarb pieces tightly in containers. Seal, label, and freeze. **Syrup pack:** * Pack rhubarb pieces tightly in containers. Cover with cold 40 percent syrup, leaving ¼-inch head space for pints, ½-inch for quarts. Crumple a small piece of plastic wrap, waxed paper, or freezer paper and put it on top of rhubarb in each container. Seal, label, and freeze.

*For 40 percent syrup, mix 3 cups sugar with 4 cups water until sugar dissolves. Chill in refrigerator until ready to use. This makes 5½ cups. You'll need about ½ cup of syrup for each pint of rhubarb.

RUTABAGAS

1¼ to 1½ pounds = 1 pint

1. Choose young, tender, medium rutabagas.
2. Cut off tops, wash, and pare. Cut in ½-inch cubes.
3. Blanch for 3 minutes. Cool; drain well.
4. Tray freeze or pack into containers. Seal, label, and freeze.
5. Cook frozen rutabagas 12 to 15 minutes.
6. **Mashed rutabagas:** proceed as above until step 2. Then cook cubed rutabagas in just enough water to cover until tender, instead of blanching.

Drain, then mash in saucepan. Pack in containers, leaving ¼-inch head space for pints, ½-inch for quarts. Seal, label, and freeze. Cook mashed rutabagas just until heated through.

SOYBEANS

2 to 2½ pounds in pods = 12 to 16 pints

1. Choose well-filled pods of young, tender, green beans.
2. Wash pods well.
3. Blanch beans in pods 5 minutes. Cool; drain well.
4. Squeeze beans out of pods and pick over, discarding any bad beans.
5. Tray freeze or pack into containers. Seal, label, and freeze.
6. Cook frozen soybeans 10 to 20 minutes.

SPINACH, NEW ZEALAND SPINACH

1 to 1½ pounds = 1 pint
1 bushel (12 pounds) = 8 to 12 pints

1. Choose young, tender leaves.
2. Wash well in several changes of water.
3. Remove tough stems and bruised leaves.
4. Blanch each pound of spinach in 2 gallons boiling water for 2 minutes. For very tender spinach, blanch only 1½ minutes. Stir to keep leaves from sticking together. Cool; drain well.
5. Pack into containers, leaving ¼-inch head space. Seal, label, and freeze.
6. Cook frozen spinach 8 to 12 minutes.

SQUASH, SUMMER

1 to 1¼ pounds = 1 pint
1 bushel (40 pounds) = 32 to 40 pints

1. Choose young, tender squash.
2. Wash, cut off the ends, and slice the squash ½-inch thick.
3. Blanch 3 minutes. Cool; drain well.
4. Tray freeze or pack into containers. Seal, label, and freeze.
5. Cook frozen summer squash about 10 minutes.

SQUASH, WINTER

3 pounds = 2 pints

1. Choose firm, mature squash with hard skins.

2. Wash. Cut squash in half or in quarters. Bake, simmer, or pressure-cook until tender.
3. Scoop pulp from the skin. Mash the pulp in saucepan, or press through a sieve, ricer, or food mill into a medium saucepan.
4. Cool by placing the saucepan in ice water and stirring the squash occasionally until cold.
5. Pack into containers, leaving ¼-inch head space for pints, ½-inch for quarts. Seal, label, and freeze.
6. Cook frozen squash just until heated through.

SWEET POTATOES

3 to 4 medium potatoes (⅔ pound) = 1 pint

1. Choose medium or large, mature potatoes that have been cured for at least a week.
2. Wash well and sort by size.
3. Simmer, bake, or pressure-cook potatoes until tender. Cool.
4. **Baked:** Grease outside of potatoes with oil. Bake in a preheated 350°F oven until soft. Cool, then wrap individually in moisture/vaporproof wrapping and freeze. Heat through to serve. **Candied:** Cook unpared potatoes in water to cover at just below simmering for about 30 minutes. Pare and cut lengthwise or crosswise into ½-inch-thick slices. For each ⅔ pound potato slices, prepare syrup by heating to boiling 1½ cups water, 1 cup sugar, and 1 tablespoon lemon juice in saucepan. (There should be enough syrup to cover sweet potato slices). Add sweet potato slices to boiling syrup and cook 3 minutes. Don't drain. Cool quickly by pouring slices and syrup into another pan and placing that pan in ice water. Pack tightly in containers, covering slices with syrup, and leaving ¼-inch head space for pints, ½-inch for quarts. Seal, label, and freeze. Heat through to serve. **Mashed:** Simmer, bake, or pressure-cook potatoes until tender. Cool, pare, and put through food mill. Add ½ cup sugar, ½ cup cold water, and 1 tablespoon lemon juice for each 5 pounds of mashed potatoes. Pack tightly into containers, leaving ¼-inch head space for pints, ½-inch for quarts. Seal, label, and freeze. Heat through to serve.

TOMATOES

1 bushel (53 pounds) = 30 to 40 pints

1. Choose ripe, firm, red tomatoes, free of blemishes.

2. Wash well.

3. **Whole:** Remove stems after washing. Wrap each tomato in plastic wrap or small plastic bag, then freeze. To use in cooked dishes, run under lukewarm water for a few seconds to loosen skin, then remove skin and blossom end. Add tomato, along with other ingredients, and cook. **Stewed:** Dip whole, washed tomatoes in boiling water 2 minutes to loosen skins. Peel and core. Cut in quarters or pieces; simmer 10 to 20 minutes or until tender. Cool. Pack in containers, leaving ¼-inch head space. Seal, label, and freeze. **Pureed:** Peel tomatoes as for stewed tomatoes. Core and cut them in quarters into a blender container. For each 4 medium tomatoes, add ½ onion, chopped; 1 green pepper (seeded, stemmed, and cut in quarters); 1 tablespoon salt, and 1 tablespoon sugar. Blend on low or medium speed until onion and pepper are chopped. Pack the puree in containers, leaving ¼-inch head space for pints, ½-inch for quarts. Seal, label, and freeze.

TOMATOES, GREEN

Yield varies widely depending on the size of the tomatoes.

1. Select firm, sound, green tomatoes.
2. Wash, core, and slice ¼-inch thick.
3. Tray freeze, without blanching, then pack in containers or bags with layer of freezer wrap between slices. Seal, label, and freeze.
4. Thaw and coat to fry.

TOMATO JUICE

3 to 3½ pounds whole = 1 quart
1 bushel (53 pounds) whole = 12 to 16 quarts

1. Select firm, sound, ripe tomatoes.
2. Wash well, core, and cut into quarters or chunks.
3. Simmer until tender, about 5 to 10 minutes.
4. Put through a food mill or strainer. Cool.
5. Pour into containers, leaving ¼-inch head space for pints, ½-inch for quarts. Seal, label, and freeze.
6. Thaw and stir to serve.

TURNIPS

1 to 1½ pounds = 1 pint

1. Choose young, tender, small to medium turnips.

2. Remove tops, wash, pare, and cut in ½-inch cubes or slices.
3. Blanch 3 minutes. Cool; drain well.
4. Pack in containers, leaving ¼-inch head space. Seal, label, and freeze.
5. Cook frozen turnips about 10 to 12 minutes.

VEGETABLE PUREES

Freeze a puree to have on hand for casseroles, cream soups, special diets, or for baby food. Yields vary widely depending on your selection of vegetables.

1. Choose and prepare vegetables as directed in specific recipes.
2. Cook in just enough boiling water to cover, or steam, bake, or pressure-cook until tender.
3. Mash in saucepan; or press through sieve, ricer, or food mill into saucepan; or puree in blender or food processor and pour into saucepan.
4. Cool by putting the saucepan in ice water and stirring the puree occasionally until cold.
5. Pack in recipe-size amounts in containers, leaving ¼-inch head space. Seal, label, and freeze.
6. Thaw in the refrigerator, microwave oven, or in a double boiler. **Baby food:** Pour puree into ice cube trays and freeze solid. Transfer to plastic bags, seal, and store in the freezer. Thaw in a custard cup over boiling water or in a microwave oven.

WATERMELON

1 to 1¼ pounds = 1 pint

1. Select fully ripe, firm melons.
2. Cut in half, remove seeds, and cut off rind.
3. Cut into ¾-inch cubes, slices, or balls. Pack into freezer containers or freezer bags, seal, and freeze.
4. Thaw only until still slightly frozen and serve.

BASIC STEPS FOR FREEZING FRUITS

Freezing fruits requires a few steps in addition to those listed earlier in this chapter for freezing vegetables. (However, blanching is required for vegetables only.) Low temperatures (0°F or below) plus the addition of ascorbic acid and/or sugar are necessary for freezing fruits. The recipes in this section will give you specific instructions on how to treat each fruit for best results. The following is a summary of the basic steps.

1. Check your freezer's size and estimate how much you can freeze in 24 hours (3 pounds of food per each cubic foot of space). Then check your recipe to see how much fruit you should pick or purchase to freeze in one session.
2. Do not use over-soft fruit. Fruits ripened on the tree (or bush or plant) freeze better than fruits picked before they are ripe and allowed to ripen after harvesting. Fruit picked at a less-mature stage will have less flavor.
3. Wash fruit. Scrub firm fruits such as apples, peaches, and pears before peeling. Wash berries in several changes of cool water, but don't allow the berries to stand in the water because they will both lose nutritional value and absorb excess water.
4. Sort fruit. Handle it gently. Discard any fruit that is damaged, bruised, or over-mature. Also discard soft berries and under-mature fruits. Take care in sorting. A few spoiled pieces of fruit can ruin the flavor of several containers of the finished product.
5. Prepare fruit syrups in advance. Sugar will dissolve best in hot or boiling water. Always allow syrup to cool completely before using it.
6. Cut, peel, and prepare fruits according to recipe directions. Do not work with more than 1 pound or 4 cups at a time. Work quickly.
7. Use ascorbic acid, lemon juice, or a commercial preparation to prevent browning, especially when freezing light-colored fruit. (These agents are discussed later in this chapter.)
8. Pack fruit into freezer containers or bags, or freeze on trays.
9. Label each container with method of freezing, date, name of product, and number of servings.
10. Freeze, following the directions for quick freezing and any special manufacturer's directions for your freezer.
11. Most fruits will keep for 12 months at 0°F.
12. When placing cartons of food in the freezer, remember to leave an inch of space around packages. The circulating cold air will help fruits freeze quickly, producing a higher-quality result upon thawing.

PREPARING SUGAR SYRUP

Type of syrup:	sugar	water
30 percent (light)	1 cup	2 cups
40 percent (medium light)	1 cup	1¼ cup
50 percent (medium)	1 cup	⅞ cup
60 percent (heavy)	1 cup	½ cup

Note: ½ cup corn syrup may be substituted for 1 cup of sugar in the above solution.

Dissolve the sugar in water by stirring or heating (do not allow the mixture to boil). Cool the syrup completely before covering fruit.

Making syrup

Low-sugar pectic syrup

1 cup water
1 box powdered fruit pectin
½ cup sugar
cold water

Combine 1 cup water and powdered fruit pectin in a saucepan and bring to a boil over medium high heat. Boil for one minute to dissolve pectin, then stir in sugar until dissolved. When sugar is dissolved, remove mixture from heat and add enough cold water to make 2 cups. Chill.

This syrup may be used with any fruit suitable for freezing. Prepare the fruit by washing, peeling, pitting or coring, and slicing as necessary. Put the prepared fruit in a large bowl. Add enough syrup to glaze each piece of fruit. Gently fold the fruit through the syrup glaze, so that each piece of fruit has a thin coating of syrup. Pack into freezer containers, seal, label, and freeze. Fruits frozen by this method will keep for up to 12 months at 0°F or below.

KEEPING FRUIT FROM BROWNING

Most fruits will brown or darken when the cut or peeled surfaces are exposed to air. This can be prevented by the use of an anti-darkening agent. There are several ways of keeping fruit from browning, and a number of commercial products are available.

Ascorbic acid. Ascorbic acid in crystalline form is the antioxidant most often used to keep fruit from browning. It is vitamin C, so it's not a harmful food additive. Ascorbic acid is available in crystalline, tablet, or powdered forms in most drugstores or health food stores. Don't use the tablets; they are very expensive and they do not dissolve easily. Ascorbic acid in crystalline form comes in quantities from 25 to 1,000 grams. One teaspoon weighs about 3 grams. Buy as much as you need according to the amount of fruit you plan to process.

Ascorbic acid mixtures. Commercial products for keeping fruit from browning are available from supermarkets. These products are not pure ascorbic acid but are usually a combination of citric acid or ascorbic acid and sugar. These products are usually expensive, because the active ingredient that prevents browning has been diluted with sugar. If you use a commercial product, follow the manufacturer's directions.

Lemon juice. Lemon juice contains ascorbic acid and prevents browning to some extent. However, it's not as effective as ascorbic acid in crystalline form. Also, lemon juice is not suitable for use with all fruits, and when used in large quantities can alter the natural flavor of the fruit or give it a sour taste.

Light-colored fruits will darken unless pretreated. To prevent darkening, dissolve ascorbic acid in a little water, and sprinkle over the fruit before adding sugar.

When to add ascorbic acid

Peaches, apricots and nectarines darken quickly during preparation. To prevent these and other light fruits from darkening during peeling and slicing, drop them into a solution of ¼ teaspoon crystalline ascorbic acid dissolved in 1 quart water. Drain before freezing or before adding sugar. This process will help keep the fruit its original light color.

When preserving fruit by the dry sugar pack method, mix the sugar with a small amount of fruit at a time. As the sugar dissolves, juice will begin to form.

When freezing fruits without sugar, use ¼ teaspoon ascorbic acid dissolved in ¼ cup water. Sprinkle this mixture over 1 quart prepared fruit. Mix gently. Pack into freezer containers and freeze.

Unsweetened pack. Sprinkle ascorbic acid dissolved in 1 to 2 tablespoons of water over the fruit and mix gently.

Dry sugar pack. Sprinkle ascorbic acid dissolved in 1 to 2 tablespoons water over the fruit just before adding the sugar. Then fold the sugar gently over the fruit.

Syrup pack. Add the dissolved ascorbic acid to cold syrup just before use.

Crushed fruits. Add the dissolved ascorbic acid to the fruit preparation and mix.

RECIPES FOR FREEZING FRUITS

Follow the directions given in each specific recipe for best results. Some fruits freeze well without the addition of sugar. Read the entire recipe before you begin preparation. Assemble all equipment and ingredients. Make sure you have enough containers on hand.

APPLES (in syrup)

Choose Jonathan or Stayman apples. Prepare 40 or 50 percent syrup and cool. Add ½ teaspoon crystalline ascorbic acid to each quart of syrup. If using a commercial anti-darkening product, follow label directions.

1 to 1½ pounds = 1 pint
1 bushel = 32 to 40 pints

1. Choose full-flavored apples that are crisp and firm. Do not use soft or mealy-textured apples.
2. Wash, peel, and core apples.
3. Pour ½ cup ascorbic acid syrup into each pint-size container.
4. Slice apples in sixteenths, and drop slices immediately into ascorbic acid syrup to prevent browning.
5. Press fruit down in containers and add enough syrup to cover.
6. Leave 1 inch head space in each container.
7. Seal, label, date, and freeze.

APPLESAUCE

Apple sauce keeps well when frozen or canned. Suggested apple varieties for sauce include: Rome Beauty, McIntosh, Jonathan, Baldwin, or Greening. Sweeten your apple sauce with honey or sugar to taste. This recipe will yield approximately 4 pints.

4 pounds apples
1½ cups water
¼ cup lemon juice
¾ cup honey
cinnamon (optional)

1. Wash and core apples. Peel if desired.
2. Cut apples into chunks or slices.
3. In a large, heavy stainless steel or enamel kettle, cook apples with water, lemon juice, and honey until tender (about 15 minutes).
4. Put apple mixture through a food mill or sieve if desired.
5. If desired, add ½ teaspoon cinnamon powder to applesauce for added flavor.
6. Allow applesauce to cool.
7. Pack into pint-size freezer jars or freezer containers, leaving ½ inch head space.
8. Seal, label, date, and freeze.

Using a crumpled piece of waxed paper to keep fruit submerged in syrup helps avoid having fruit float to the top of the container and become discolored. You simply discard the paper when you thaw the fruit.

APPLES (in low-sugar pectin syrup)

Prepare low-sugar pectin syrup and cool. Syrup pack is preferred for apples to be used for fruit salad or uncooked desserts. Two cups low-sugar syrup will coat 3 to 4 quarts sliced apples.

3 to 4 medium apples = 1 pound (2²/₃ cups sliced)
12 medium apples = 4 pounds (3 quarts sliced)

1. Choose full-flavored, firm, ripe apples.
2. Wash, peel, and core about 1 pound of apples
3. Slice apples to desired thickness directly into low-sugar pectin syrup.
4. Fold apple slices gently until each is covered with a light coating of syrup. Lift apples from syrup with a slotted spoon. Allow excess syrup to drain.
5. Pack apples into freezer containers or freezer jars, leaving ½ inch head space.
6. Wash, peel, and core another pound of apples, repeat steps 3 to 5. Repeat until all apples are prepared for freezing.
7. Seal freezer containers, label, date, and freeze before proceeding with the next batch of apples.

APPLES (dry sugar pack)

Apples packed in sugar are good for pies or cooked apple desserts. Allow to thaw in the refrigerator for 4 to 6 hours before use. The sealed container can be immersed in cold water for faster thawing.

3 medium apples = 1 pound (2²/₃ cup sliced)
12 medium apples = 4 pounds (3 quarts sliced)

1. Select firm, ripe apples that are free of bruises
2. Wash, peel, and core.
3. Slice into sixteenths and drop immediately into ascorbic acid water (1 teaspoon ascorbic acid dissolved in 1 quart water).
4. After preparing all of the apples, drain off water. Allow to drain thoroughly before adding sugar.
5. Sprinkle ½ cup sugar evenly over each quart of apples and stir gently.
6. Pack apples in rigid containers or freeze on a tray first for free-flow pack.
7. Seal, label, date, and freeze.

APRICOTS (syrup pack)

It is necessary to treat cut apricots to prevent darkening. Select firm, ripe, uniformly yellow apricots. If you want to freeze apricots without peeling, heat them in boiling water for 30 seconds to keep peel from toughening during freezer storage.

²/₃ to ⁴/₅ pounds apricots = 1 pint
1 bushel apricots = 32 to 40 pints

1. Prepare 40 percent syrup or low-sugar pectin syrup. Cool. Set aside.
2. Select firm fruit. Sort, wash, halve, and pit. Peel and slice if desired.
3. Add ¾ teaspoon crystalline ascorbic acid to each quart of syrup.
4. Pour ½ cup syrup into 1-pint freezer container. Fill to within 1½ inch of top with prepared fruit.
5. Crumple a piece of waxed paper and place over the fruit and syrup to keep apricots immersed in the syrup. Leave ½ inch head space above waxed paper.
6. Seal, label, date, and freeze.

APRICOTS (dry sugar pack)

When using the dry sugar or sugar-free methods, prepare an ascorbic acid treatment to prevent browning. Sweeten to taste.

²/₃ to ⁴/₅ pounds apricots = 1 pint
1 bushel apricots = 32 to 40 pints

1. Prepare ascorbic acid treatment by dissolving ¼ teaspoon crystalline ascorbic acid in ¼ cup cold water. Refrigerate until ready to use.
2. Sort, wash, peel, halve, and pit apricots.
3. Sprinkle ascorbic acid mixture over 1 quart prepared fruit and mix gently.
4. Mix ½ cup sugar with each quart of apricots.
5. Pack fruit into freezer containers.
6. Seal, label, date, and freeze.

In the following recipes the term berries includes blackberries, huckleberries, blueberries, elderberries, gooseberries, and boysenberries.

BERRIES IN SYRUP

The following freezing methods are suitable for blueberries, gooseberries, or blackberries. You will need 50 percent syrup or low-sugar pectin syrup.

1 pound = 1¹/₂ pints
1 crate (24 quarts) = 32 to 36 pints

1. Choose fully ripe, firm berries. Sort, and remove stems. Handle fruit gently to prevent bruising.
2. Wash carefully in cold water. Discard soft, underripe, or defective fruit.
3. Place in colander to drain.
4. Prepare 50 percent syrup. If possible use berry juice from crushed fruit instead of water to prepare syrup. Cool syrup.
5. Pack berries in freezer containers, and cover with 50 percent syrup to within ¹/₂ inch of tops of containers.
6. Seal, label, date, and freeze.

BERRIES (unsweetened)

Unsweetened berries are excellent for use in cooked desserts or jams. This method is also excellent for use in muffins and coffee cakes. Pre-measure whole berries and tray freeze for free-pour packages.

1 pound = 1¹/₂ pints
1 crate (24 pints) = 32 to 36 pints

1. Choose fully bush-ripened berries. Sort, and discard soft berries. Remove stems.
2. Wash berries carefully in cold water. Drain in colander.
3. Measure and place in freezer bags. Or pre-freeze on trays or cookie sheets, then pour into freezer bags for free-flow pack.
4. Seal bags by pushing as much air out as possible with your hands before closing.
5. Label, date, record amounts, and freeze.

BERRIES (dry sugar pack)

2²/₃ pounds = 1 quart
1 crate (24 pints) = 32 to 36 pints

1. Choose fully ripened berries. Sort, removing soft berries. Remove stems.
2. Wash berries carefully in cold water. Drain in colander.
3. Measure 1 quart berries. Add ¹/₂ cup sugar per quart.
4. Toss berries in sugar until berries are coated and sugar begins to dissolve.
5. Place berries in rigid pint-size freezer containers or freezer jars.
6. Seal, label, date, and freeze.

SOUR CHERRIES (unsweetened)

Sweet cherries and sour cherries freeze well, but the red varieties freeze better than the black varieties. Pit cherries before freezing. Unpitted cherries take on an undesirable almond-like flavor, so take the time to remove all pits before freezing cherries.

1 bushel = 36 to 44 pints
1¹/₄ to 1¹/₂ pounds = 1 pint cherries

1. Select fully ripened, firm, red cherries. Sort, and discard soft fruit. Remove stems.
2. Wash carefully in cold water. Drain in colander. Pit each cherry.
3. Place cherries in a single layer on a tray or cookie sheet. Freeze.
4. Measure, and fill freezer bags, pushing as much air as possible out of bags with your hands.
5. Seal, label, date, record amounts, and freeze.

SOUR CHERRIES IN SYRUP

Prepare 60 percent syrup or low-sugar pectin syrup in advance, and chill. Cherries packed in syrup are best served uncooked.

1 bushel = 36 to 44 pints
¹/₄ to 1¹/₂ pounds = 1 pint

1. Select fully ripened red cherries. Sort, and discard soft fruit. Remove stems.
2. Wash cherries carefully in cold water. Drain in colander.
3. Pit each cherry.
4. Pour ¹/₂ cup cold 60 percent syrup into each pint-size freezer container.
5. Add cherries and enough syrup to cover, leaving 1¹/₂ inches head space.
6. Crumple a piece of wax paper and place on top of cherries to keep fruit immersed in syrup during freezing. Leave ¹/₂ inch head space above waxed paper.
7. Seal, label, date, and freeze.

SOUR CHERRIES (dry sugar pack)

Use this method of freezing for cherries to be used in cooked desserts. Cherries preserved in this manner also make excellent pie filling.

1¹/₃ pound = 1 quart
1 bushel = 18 to 22 quarts

1. Select tree-ripened red cherries. Sort, and discard soft fruit. Remove stems.
2. Wash cherries carefully in cold water. Drain in colander.
3. Pit each cherry.
4. Add ½ cup sugar per quart of cherries. Fold sugar into fruit.
5. Fill freezer bags or freezer containers.
6. Seal, label, date, and freeze.

SWEET CHERRIES IN SYRUP

Sweet cherries are more delicate than their sour counterparts. Use ascorbic acid and work quickly to avoid color and flavor changes. Sweet cherries are best in a 40 percent sugar syrup or coated with a low-sugar pectin syrup. Serve uncooked or in uncooked dessert dishes.

1¼ to 1½ pounds = 1 pint

1. Select even-colored, tree-ripened fruit.
2. Taste the fruit; it should have a natural sweet flavor.
3. Sort, and discard soft cherries. Remove stems.
4. Wash cherries carefully in cold water. Drain in colander.
5. Pit each cherry.
6. Pack cherries into freezer containers. Add ½ teaspoon crystalline ascorbic acid to each container and mix well.
7. Cover cherries with syrup to within 1½ inch of top, or cover with cold low-sugar pectin syrup.
8 Crumple a piece of waxed paper and press into freezer container to keep cherries immersed in syrup during storage. Leave ½ inch head space above waxed paper.
9. Seal, label, date, and freeze.

CURRANTS IN SYRUP

1 pound = 1 pint

1. Select fully ripe currants. Sort, and remove stems.
2. Wash carefully in cold water. Drain in colander.
3. Crush the fruit slightly and combine 3 parts fruit with 1 part sugar.
4. Allow to stand until sugar dissolves (about 20 minutes).
5. Pack into pint-size freezer containers, leaving ½ inch head space.

6. Crumple a piece of waxed paper and put on top of currants.
7. Seal, label, date, and freeze.

CURRANTS (unsweetened)

Unsweetened currants are good for use in cooked desserts.

1 pound = 1 pint

1. Select fully ripe currants. Sort, and remove stems.
2. Wash carefully in cold water. Drain in colander.
3. Pack into rigid containers or freezer bags.
4. Seal, label, date, and freeze.

FIGS IN SYRUP

Take care in selecting figs. They should be soft to the touch when ripe. A sour odor in the center of the fig indicates that the juices have started to ferment. Cut whole figs in half and check that no sour odor is present. Do not freeze figs with a sour center. Prepare and chill 40 percent syrup or low-sugar pectin syrup.

3 pounds = 2½ pints

1. Select tree-ripened, soft figs. Sort and wash figs. Peel if desired. Cut off stems.
2. Cut each fig in half and check centers for sour odor. Discard sour fruit.
3. Slice figs or leave in halves.
4. Add ¾ teaspoon crystalline ascorbic acid or ½ cup lemon juice to each quart of syrup.
5. Pack figs into rigid freezer containers or freezer jars. Cover with cold syrup, leaving ½ inch head space, or coat pieces with low-sugar pectin syrup.
6. Seal, label, date, and freeze.

FIGS (unsweetened)

3 pounds = 2½ pints

1. Select tree-ripened, soft figs. Sort and wash figs. Peel if desired. Cut off stems.
2. Cut figs in half and check centers for sour odor. Discard sour fruit.
3. Slice figs or leave in halves.

4. Pack into freezer bags or tray-freeze first for free-pour pack.
5. Seal, label, date, and freeze.

GRAPES (unsweetened)

Grapes to be used in jelly-making or for juice are best frozen whole without sugar. You can purchase large quantities during the peak season and freeze them. They will keep for a year if properly frozen.

3½ pounds = 4½ to 5 cups juice
3½ pounds = 6 pints whole grapes

1. Select firm, ripe, fully colored grapes.
2. Wash bunches and remove individual grapes from stem.
3. Pack into freezer bags.
4. Seal, label, date, and freeze.

GRAPES IN SYRUP

Freeze Thompson seedless red or green grapes or Muscadine grapes whole in 40 percent syrup.

3 pounds = 6 pints

1. Select firm, ripe, fully colored grapes.
2. Wash, and remove from stems.
3. Pack into pint-size rigid freezer containers or freezer jars.
4. Cover with cold 40 percent syrup to within ½ inch of top.
5. Seal, label, date, and freeze.

KIWI FRUIT

Select fruit that is slightly soft to the touch but not mushy. Avoid rock-hard fruit; it is not ripe.

6 medium kiwi = 1 pound
1 pound = 1 pint

1. Select fully ripe, firm kiwi fruit. Peel.
2. Cut kiwi into ¼-inch slices.
3. Pack the slices of fruit into rigid freezer containers, sprinkling sugar over each layer as you go.
4. Seal, label, date, and freeze.

LEMONS

Buy lemons in large quantities when they are at bargain prices. The juice can be frozen for lemonade or for cooking. Freeze the whole fruit. Wash and dry the fruit, twist freezer bag tightly around fruit, seal, label, date, and freeze. This freezing method can also be used for limes.

8 to 10 lemons = approximately 1½ cups juice

1. Select firm, thick-skinned, yellow-colored lemons with no green spots. (A green spot is the result of faulty curing.)
2. Wash, using a vegetable brush to scrub the peel.
3. To freeze whole lemons (or limes), remove zest or peel, being careful to remove only the yellow part of the peel. Freeze each lemon in a small freezer jar or bag. Label, date, and freeze.
4. For juice, follow these steps: After removing peel, roll each lemon gently but firmly, pressing with the palm of your hand. This will make the lemons yield more juice.
5. Cut each lemon in half and either squeeze or use juicer to remove juice. Strain juice. Pour into ½-pint freezer jars, or measure by tablespoons into ice trays. If using ice trays, remove the juice cubes when frozen and pack in freezer bags. Seal, label, date, and store in freezer.
6. To freeze lemon slices for use in drinks or as garnishes, wash and slice the lemons and freeze on trays. When frozen, remove to freezer bags. Label, date, and freeze.

ORANGES (dry sugar pack)

Valencia, Temple, King, and blood oranges are the sweetest; navel oranges and tangerine types are good eating oranges. Seville oranges are bitter and are often used in drinks or marmalades. The variety you choose to freeze depends on how you want to use the oranges. Peel oranges before freezing, and dry or freeze the peel for other uses.

3 medium oranges = 1 pint
1 bushel = approximately 34 pints

1. Select firm, uniformly shaped oranges free of soft spots. Wash and dry.
2. Peel, holding each orange over a large bowl to catch the juice. Using a sharp paring knife, pare away rind and white skin. Pare the orange with a circular motion, as when peeling apples.

3. Slice across the sections or loosen sections by cutting down along the membrane. Lift out each section in one piece. Remove seeds.

4. Layer orange sections alternately with sugar in rigid pint-size freezer containers. Use about ¼ cup sugar per orange.

5. Seal, label, date, and freeze.

ORANGES IN SYRUP

Use navel oranges, or Valencia, Temple, or King oranges for freezing in syrup. Prepare 30 percent syrup or low-sugar pectin syrup. Chill. (When preparing 30 percent syrup use orange juice instead of water if possible.)

3 medium oranges = 1 pint
1 bushel = approximately 34 pints

1. Select firm, uniformly shaped oranges free of soft spots. Wash and dry.

2. Peel, holding each orange over a large bowl to catch the juice. Using a sharp paring knife, pare away rind and white skin. Pare the orange with a circular motion, as when peeling apples.

3. Slice across sections. Pack slices into pint-size, rigid freezer containers.

4. Cover with cold syrup, leaving ½ inch head space, or fold sections in low-sugar pectin syrup so that each piece is coated.

5. Seal, label, date, and freeze.

PEACHES/NECTARINES IN SYRUP

When buying large quantities of peaches or nectarines try to taste one first (ask the storekeeper if you may do so). Quite often the flavor of the fruit does not measure up to its appearance. Buy only well-flavored fruit. Prepare 40 percent syrup and have ascorbic acid on hand.

1 bushel peaches or nectarines = 32 to 48 pints
1 to 1½ pounds peaches or nectarines = 1 pint

1. Select fully ripened, well-flavored peaches for freezing. Sort. Discard fruit with green patches on the skin. Wash the fruit.

2. Blanch peaches by dipping in boiling water to loosen skins, then immersing in ice water for 30 seconds to stop the cooking process.

3. Peel fruit, cut in halves, and remove pits; or slice wedges around the pit.

4. Add ½ teaspoon crystalline ascorbic acid to cold syrup. Mix gently.

5. Pour ½ cup syrup into quart- or pint-size rigid freezer containers. Slice fruit into cold syrup to within 1½ to 2 inches of tops of containers.

6. Crumple waxed paper and fit into each container, pressing to push fruit under syrup. Leave ½ inch head space above waxed paper.

7. Seal, label, date, and freeze.

PEARS IN SYRUP

Pears freeze best after being poached in 40 percent syrup. A vanilla pod or a few hard cinnamon candies may be added if desired for extra flavor. Commice pears are excellent when prepared in this manner.

1 to 1½ pounds = 1 pint
1 bushel = 32 to 45 pints

1. Select firm, well-ripened (but not hard) pears.

2. Wash fruit in cold water. Peel.

3. Cut in half. Remove core with small melon baller. Leave cored fruit in halves, or cut in slices.

4. Heat pears in 40 percent syrup for 1½ to 2 minutes. Cool.

5. Pack into pint- or quart-size freezer containers. Leave ½ inch head space for pints and 1 inch head space for quarts.

6. Crumple waxed paper and fit into each container, pushing pears under syrup. Leave ½ inch head space for pints and 1 inch head space for quarts above waxed paper.

7. Seal, label, date, and freeze.

PLUMS IN SYRUP

Use large sugar plums for freezing. Save Damson plums for making jellies and sauces. Plums must be peeled and the stones removed before freezing. As with cherries, the stone imparts an off flavor to the fruit during long-term freezer storage. Prepare 40 percent syrup or low-sugar pectin syrup. Chill.

2 pounds = 1 quart
1 bushel = 28 pints

1. Select large, firm plums. Sort. Discard any fruit that feels mushy.

2. Wash carefully in cold water, peel, and remove stones. Slice.

3. Add ½ teaspoon crystalline ascorbic acid to each quart of 40 percent syrup.

4. Pack plums into pint- or quart-size rigid freezer containers.

5. Add syrup, or coat fruit with low-sugar pectin syrup. Leave ½ inch head space for pints and 1 inch head space for quarts.

6. Seal, label, date, and freeze.

RASPBERRIES (dry sugar pack)

Take care in handling these berries; they are soft and bruise easily.

1⅓ to 1½ pounds = 1 pint
1 crate = 34 pints

1. Select large, firm berries.

2. Sort, wash carefully in cold water, and drain thoroughly.

3. Arrange berries in a single layer on a tray, leaving space between each berry.

4. Sprinkle with sugar. Cover tray and freeze for 1 to 2 hours.

5. Transfer frozen berries to freezer bags. Use your hands to push as much air out of the bags as possible. Twist tops of bags.

5. Seal, label, date, and freeze.

RASPBERRIES IN SYRUP

Raspberries in syrup are good used in uncooked desserts. Handle these delicate berries with care. Prepare 40 percent syrup or low-sugar pectin syrup. Chill.

1⅓ to 1½ pounds = 1 pint
1 crate = 34 pints

1. Select firm, ripe, juicy berries.

2. Sort, remove stems, wash, and drain.

3. Fold berries carefully into 40 percent or low-sugar pectin syrup, being careful not to crush them.

4. Pack berries in rigid pint-size containers and cover with cold syrup to within ½ inch of tops of containers.

5. Seal, label, date, and freeze.

STRAWBERRIES IN SYRUP

Strawberries are the most popular of the berry family. Freeze plenty to cheer up cold winter days. The best method uses chilled low-sugar pectin syrup. Freeze whole or sliced strawberries, using 2 cups syrup to coat about 3 pounds berries.

1 pound = 1½ pints

1. Select firm, fully ripe, red berries with no white or green spots.

2. Wash berries in cold water and drain.

3. Remove hulls and slice berries into a shallow dish. Fold syrup into berries so that each piece is coated.

4. Remove berries from syrup with a slotted spoon.

5. Pack into rigid pint-size freezer containers, leaving ½ inch head space.

6. Seal, label, date, and freeze.

STRAWBERRIES (dry sugar pack)

Slightly tart berries are excellent frozen by the dry sugar pack method. Slice large berries. Leave small ones whole.

1⅓ pounds = 1 quart

1. Select firm, fully ripe, red berries with no white or green spots.

2. Wash berries in cold water and drain.

3. Remove hulls and slice large berries, leaving small ones whole.

4. Place in shallow dish and add ¾ cup sugar per quart of prepared strawberries.

5. Turn berries over and over to coat with sugar until juice is formed.

6. Pack berries and juice in rigid freezer containers, leaving ½ inch head space.

7. Crumple waxed paper and press firmly into freezer containers to keep berries immersed in juice during storage.

8. Seal, label, date, and freeze.

FREEZER JAMS AND JELLIES

Freezer jams and jellies have a wonderful fresh fruit flavor and are easy to make. The most tedious step, cooking the mixture, has been eliminated, and the results are excellent.

The basic equipment needed for freezer jams and jellies is simple. Remember to keep equipment, hands, and work surfaces clean.

Basic equipment

To freeze jams and jellies successfully you'll need the following:

> 1- to 4-cup measuring cup for liquids
> Standard set of dry measuring cups
> Measuring spoons
> Small saucepan
> Shallow glass baking dish
> Potato masher to crush fruit
> Blender or food processor
> Large and small bowls
> Cutting board
> Paring knives
> Colander to drain
> Wide mouth funnel
> 8-ounce glass freezer jars with two piece lids, rigid plastic freezer containers, or zip-closure pint-size plastic bags
> Mixing spoons and ladle
> Kitchen timer

Basic instructions

● Choose fully ripened fruit.

● Never alter the amount of sugar or fruit called for in the recipe. Freezer jams and jellies require exact proportions of fruit, sugar, and pectin. Altering any ingredient may mean you get a syrupy product instead of a firm, set product. Sugar also helps to preserve these products, so the danger of spoilage is increased if less sugar is used.

● Always make a single recipe at a time. Do not double recipes or use more fruit than called for in the recipe. You will be more successful preparing a recipe twice.

● Prepare fruit just as you are ready to use it.

● Do not interchange liquid or powdered fruit pectin in the recipe. Although liquid and powdered fruit pectin are very similar they are not interchangeable in freezer jam and jelly preparation.

● Follow the recipe to the letter for a perfect product.

● Since food expands as it freezes, head space must be allowed for this expansion. It is very disappointing and a waste of time and money to skimp on head space and find popped lids and broken bags when you come to use the product. For pint-size containers of freezer jam and jellies, allow 1/2 inch head space. Half-pint jars and rigid containers require 1/4 inch head space. If glass jars are used for these recipes, stick to wide-mouth jars.

APRICOT FREEZER JAM

2 cups finely mashed apricots
1 teaspoon ascorbic acid powder
4 cups sugar
1 package powdered pectin
1 cup water

Yield: approximately six 1/2-pint jars

1. Combine ascorbic acid with mashed apricots to prevent browning of the fruit.
2. Mix in sugar, and allow this mixture to set 20 minutes to dissolve sugar. Stir occasionally.
3. In a small saucepan combine powdered pectin and water. Boil for 1 minute, stirring constantly.
4. Remove from heat. Add apricots, and stir about 2 minutes.
5. Pour into sterilized jelly jars or freezer containers, leaving 1/4 inch head space for half-pint containers and 1/2 inch for pints.
6. Cover containers and let stand at room temperature for 24 to 48 hours to allow jelly to set.
7. Freeze. (Small amounts will keep in the refrigerator for several weeks.)
8. To thaw for use, put in your refrigerator for 6 to 8 hours. Always return opened products to the refrigerator after use.

BERRY FREEZER JAM

3 cups fresh or frozen berry juice
4 1/2 cups sugar
1 box powdered pectin
1/2 cup water

Yield: about six 1/2 pint jars

1. Combine sugar with 1 1/4 cups of the berry juice. Stir thoroughly to dissolve the sugar.
2. In a saucepan combine pectin with 1/2 cup water. Heat almost to boiling, stirring constantly. Remove from heat.

3. Pour the pectin mixture into the remaining 1³/₄ cups berry juice. Stir until pectin is completely dissolved. Let stand 15 minutes. Stir occasionally.

4. Combine juice mixture with pectin mixture and stir, making sure all the sugar is dissolved.

5. Pour into ¹/₂-pint freezer jars or freezer containers, leaving ¹/₄ inch head space.

6. Let stand at room temperature for at least 6 hours or overnight. Freeze.

BLACKBERRY OR RED RASPBERRY FREEZER JAM

3 cups finely mashed or sieved red raspberries or
  blackberries
5¹/₂ to 6 cups sugar
1 cup water
1 package powdered pectin

Yield: about nine ¹/₂-pint jars

1. Combine red raspberries with 5¹/₂ cups sugar. Use 6 cups sugar for blackberries. Let stand 20 minutes. Stir occasionally.

2. In a small saucepan combine water and powdered pectin. Bring to a boil and boil for 1 minute, stirring constantly.

3. Remove from heat, add berries, and stir about 2 minutes.

4. Pour into jelly jars. Cover and let stand at room temperature for 24 to 48 hours to allow jelly to set.

5. Freeze, or store small amounts in the refrigerator for several weeks.

Note: To use liquid pectin for this jam, omit powdered pectin and water and use 1 pouch liquid pectin. Do not cook.

CHERRY FREEZER JAM

3 cups pitted and ground cherries
5 cups sugar
1 box powdered pectin and 1 cup water,
  or 1 pouch liquid pectin

Yield: about 7 ¹/₂-pints

1. Put cherries through a food grinder or food processor.

2. Mix cherries with sugar. Let stand 20 minutes, stirring occasionally.

3. If powdered pectin is used, combine it with 1 cup water, and bring to a boil for 1 minute,

stirring constantly. Combine with cherries and sugar.

4. Stir together pectin and fruit mixtures for 2 minutes.

5. Pour into freezer jars or freezer containers leaving ¹/₄ inch head space for ¹/₂ pints and ¹/₂ inch head space for pints.

6. Cover containers and refrigerate 24 to 48 hours or until set. Freeze.

GRAPE FREEZER JAM

6 ounces frozen grape juice concentrate
2 cups lukewarm water
1 box powdered pectin
3¹/₄ cups sugar

Yield: about six ¹/₂-pint jars

1. Mix the powdered pectin slowly into the lukewarm water in a 2-quart mixing bowl.

2. Stir constantly until pectin is completely dissolved. Let stand 45 minutes. Stir occasionally but do not heat.

3. Thaw juice by placing can in cold water. When juice is thawed, pour into a 1-quart mixing bowl.

4. Add 1³/₄ cups sugar to juice. Mix thoroughly. All the sugar will not be dissolved.

5. Add the remaining 1¹/₂ cups sugar to the pectin mixture. Stir until all sugar is dissolved.

6. Combine juice mixture with pectin mixture. Stir constantly until all sugar is dissolved.

7. Pour into ¹/₂-pint freezer jelly jars, leaving ¹/₄ inch head space. Cover with lids and let stand at room temperature overnight or until set. Freeze.

PEACH FREEZER JAM

3 cups mashed peaches
3 tablespoons lemon juice
5 cups sugar
1 box powdered pectin and 1 cup water,
  or 1 pouch liquid pectin

Yield: about seven ¹/₂-pint jars

1. To mash peaches, use a potato masher, blender, or food processor. Add lemon juice.

2. Add sugar and let mixture stand for 20 minutes.

3. If powdered pectin is used, combine pectin

and water in a small saucepan. Bring to a boil and boil for 1 minute, stirring constantly.

4. Add pectin to peach/sugar mixture. If using liquid pectin, add directly to peach/sugar mixture without cooking. Stir 2 minutes.

5. Pour jam into freezer jars or freezer containers, leaving head space. Refrigerate 24 to 48 hours or until set. Freeze.

STRAWBERRY FREEZER JAM

Follow recipe for apricot freezer jam, substituting 2 cups strawberries for the apricots and omitting the ascorbic acid.

Yield: about six ½-pint jars

How to Can Fruits and Vegetables

Canning is a method of preserving and storing food. Sealing food in containers and processing it at boiling or above boiling temperatures destroys the molds, yeasts, bacteria, and enzymes that are in or on the food — and that can make the food unsafe to eat, as well as change its flavor, color, and texture. In canning, heating destroys microorganisms; sealing keeps new ones from getting to the food.

A Frenchman named Nicholas Appert is credited with the discovery of canning when he sealed and heated food in glass bottles to help Napoleon feed his troops. For this ingenious work, Appert won a prize of 12,000 francs, as well as the gratitude of generations to follow. In 1810 Monsieur Appert didn't really know why his techniques worked, but in the last 170 years, both home and commercial canning techniques have advanced considerably.

Today we know the exact whys and hows of food preservation techniques and have equipment to help us do the job safely and easily in our home kitchens. Canning — or "putting food by," as our great-grandmothers called it — was once a necessity for every household. It has now become a particularly satisfying craft, especially as more and more cooks of all ages venture into the kitchen for fun and fulfillment. Learning the proper procedures, and the reasons behind those procedures, can make canning as safe and simple as it is satisfying. New methods of preserving foods safely are constantly being researched by the U. S. Department of Agriculture. Methods that were considered safe 40 years ago are not recommended for today's home canning. Processing times, equipment, and preparation procedures have been updated, assuring the production of high-quality foods that retain the highest nutritional value, are safe to eat, and, of course, are delicious.

Although you'll find it easy to can most vegetables successfully, there are a few varieties that are better frozen instead. These are broccoli, Brussels sprouts, cabbage, cauliflower, eggplant, parsnips, edible-pod peas, pumpkins, rutabagas, and winter squash. When you want to preserve any of these vegetables, turn to "How to Freeze Fruits and Vegetables" for complete step-by-step directions and delicious recipes.

TWO TYPES OF CANNING

Since Appert first started his experiments, two distinct types of canning have been developed — heating, or processing, in boiling water; and processing under steam pressure. These two methods are used for different types of foods, and are not interchangeable.

The acidity of a food is what determines how it should be canned, because acidity determines what microorganisms can spoil the food. So it's important to understand two things before you start canning: what causes food to spoil, and why some foods spoil differently than others. Once you know these two things, you can figure out which canning method should be used to preserve any particular food.

Why food spoils

Food spoilage is caused by molds, yeasts, enzymes, and bacteria. Heating food and then sealing it in a container destroys these spoilers, and, at the same time, prevents new ones from getting to the food.

Mold is a form of fungus, often recognizable as a fuzzy area on food. Some molds produce alfatoxins. All alfatoxins are highly toxic and some have been found to be carcinogens (substances that cause cancer). Therefore, unsuccessful home-canned products which contain mold growth cannot be eaten and should be discarded immediately. Jellies are no longer sealed with paraffin, because the old method grandmother used did not always prevent mold growth.

Some molds produce mycotoxins, which can be harmful to humans if eaten. An acid environment, as in tomatoes or pickles, can support mold, but heat will destroy it.

Yeasts (also fungi) can cause food to ferment. But both yeasts and molds are killed when the food is heated to temperatures between 140°F and 190°F.

Enzymes are substances in all living things that assist in chemical and organic changes. Although very necessary to life, enzymes can cause flavor, texture, and color changes in food, some of them less than pleasant. Enzymes, like molds and yeasts, are destroyed by heat at temperatures above 140°F.

Bacteria are the most difficult of the spoilers to destroy, because some of them may thrive at temperatures that kill molds, yeasts, and enzymes. Heating food to boiling, sealing it in jars, and then processing it in boiling water destroy molds, yeasts, and enzymes, but not all bacteria. That's where steam-pressure canning comes in. The most dangerous bacteria, *Clostridium botulinum*, produce spores which, in turn, produce a deadly toxin. These bacteria are found just where vegetables grow—in the soil. And they thrive in a low-acid, moist, air-free environment—which describes exactly the conditions inside a sealed canning jar. All vegetables can be contaminated by these botulism bacteria.

Botulism bacteria can be destroyed by boiling,

but the spores of the bacteria are not destroyed until the temperature of the food reaches 240°F. Since water boils at only 212°F, any food that will support the botulism bacteria must be processed in a steam-pressure canner, where the pressure creates temperatures above boiling.

As a further safety precaution, we recommend boiling home-canned foods before consuming them. Most food should be boiled for 10 minutes to destroy any possible botulism toxins that may have been produced in the jar. Vegetables that are more dense (corn and greens such as spinach, chard, etc.) should be boiled for 20 minutes because it takes longer for heat to completely penetrate the thicker mass of the food.

If you follow canning procedures and processing times exactly, and if you keep your pressure canner in good operating condition, the food you preserve should be safe to eat.

Acid and low-acid foods

Botulism bacteria thrive only in foods that have a low acid content, so for all practical purposes, the acidity of a food determines which canning method must be used to preserve it. Some foods are high in acid. These acid foods—fruits, some tomatoes, sauerkraut, rhubarb, and foods with vinegar added, such as pickles and relishes—are not popular with these bacteria, and so can be processed by the boiling water bath method. Low-acid foods—all vegetables, as well as meat, poultry, seafoods, and soups—can support the botulism bacteria, and must be steam-pressure canned. This method of canning destroys these bacteria and their by-products.

Choosing the right canning method

Never take shortcuts in safe canning procedures. Follow the directions precisely. To make sure your home-canned foods are safe, always process low-acid foods—all vegetables except tomatoes—in a steam-pressure canner, following the instructions specified in each recipe. When you're canning any combination of acid and low-acid foods, such as tomatoes and corn, treat the mixture as a low-acid food. It doesn't pay to take chances.

Don't try to shortcut either of the correct canning methods by using substitutions or gimmicks such as preserving powders, aspirin, dishwasher canning, oven canning, "steam" canning in a shallow pan over boiling water, or microwave oven canning. Taking any shortcuts is

asking for trouble—spoiled food, sickness, even death.

Also, don't use old-fashioned recipes that call for open-kettle processing. This method has you cook food in an open kettle, then pack it into jars and seal it without any processing. Because of the lack of processing, the chances of spoilage are great.

Both steam-pressure canning and boiling water bath canning are described in this book, along with step-by-step directions for each. All of our recipes also indicate which processing method is required. Be sure to follow the instructions in each recipe exactly.

BASIC CANNING EQUIPMENT

The most important piece of equipment for canning is the processor. This is either a boiling water bath canner, for acid foods, or a steam-pressure canner, for low-acid foods. By not fastening the lid securely, a steam-pressure canner can also be used as a water bath. But a water bath canner cannot be used for steam-pressure processing. See the sections on "Steam-pressure canning" and "Boiling water bath canning" for full descriptions of these techniques.

After the canner itself, the most important part of your equipment is the jars in which you pack the foods. The other tools you'll need are, for the most part, probably already included among your everyday kitchen equipment.

Jars and lids

Standard ½-pint, 1-pint, 12-ounce, 1½-pint, or 1-quart jars with two-piece self-sealing lids are the only proper containers for canning vegetables, or any other foods. These are often called Mason jars, after the man who patented a glass canning jar with a threaded top. The two-piece metal lid consists of a flat metal cap, rimmed with sealing compound, and an accompanying metal screw band to hold the lid in place for sealing and processing. The lids now come in bright colors, especially nice for making gifts of the foods you've canned.

Canning jars come in a wide variety of sizes and styles and are carefully made so the home canning closures will seal well. The glass in the jars is tempered to withstand the heat of the steam-pressure canner or the subzero temperatures of the food freezer.

Wide-mouth jars make it easier to pack large pieces of food and are also easier to clean. Some jars have measurement levels marked on them. Some

The whys and whats of canning

● **Why must I follow the recipe directions and processing times exactly?**
The recipes in this book have been developed and tested by experts to allow for enough heat and time to destroy the microorganisms that would spoil food or cause illness. Never substitute ingredients, jar sizes, or methods in home canning recipes. Shortcuts are dangerous.

● **Why do different recipes have different processing techniques, times, and temperatures?**
Foods vary in their physical characteristics. Some take longer to heat through, and others may be susceptible to certain types of bacteria or spoilage. The different times and temperatures are related to the type of food being canned.

● **Why do I need to know about acid and low-acid foods?**
Because the acidity of the food determines how bacteria can affect it, thus determining the processing method you must use.

● **Why can't I use the boiling water bath method for both acid and low-acid foods?**
The temperature food reaches in a boiling water bath isn't high enough to kill the spores of the botulism bacteria. Illness is caused by the toxin produced when these particular bacterial spores are present in foods in the absence of air. This may occur in foods that are low-acid or that have become low-acid. All vegetables except tomatoes are low-acid. Other low-acid foods are **meats, poultry, fish (seafoods), soups, and mixed canned foods.** Acid foods such as **fruits, tomatoes, sauerkraut, pickles and relishes, jams and preserves, and fruit juices** may become low-acid by using overripe fruit, by adding excess water, or through the growth of mold. **Sweet peppers** are particularly low-acid foods and require special precautions in processing. Follow the recipes exactly!

● **Why is the timing of the processing so important?**
The processing time must be long enough for the food in the center of the jar to reach the temperature necessary to destroy all the harmful microorganisms. Don't shorten the time or take shortcuts. Begin counting processing time only after the water in a boiling water bath canner has returned to a full rolling boil or after the pressure in a steam-pressure canner has reached 10 pounds pressure. Use an accurate timer or watch.

of the fancier home canning jars add a nice touch to vegetables and jellies. Can-or-freeze jars can be used for either preservation method, and are tapered so that partially frozen food can easily be removed.

Most canners like to choose the size and types of jars that fit in well with their meal planning. Remember, however, that processing times differ according to the sizes of the containers. Follow the recipes for processing times. The recipes tell you how many of which size jars you'll need, too.

Tin containers are used for commercial canning of fruits, meats, and vegetables. Home canning in tin cans (actually steel with tin coating) is still done in some areas, but supplies are difficult to find. You must match types of cans to the food being processed, and you need an expensive device for sealing the cans. Tin cans don't display the food as glass jars do and are not reusable. Tin cans for home canning do not come in the 1-quart, 1½-pint, 1-pint, and ½-pint sizes that are common for glass jars. For this reason, the processing times given in all the recipes do not apply to tin cans. The processing times given in this book are for glass jars only.

Sterilizing jars. Your hot-water bath canner can be used to sterilize canning jars. All food items which require less than 15 minutes processing time must be placed in sterilized canning jars. Jars are sterilized by simply boiling them for 15 minutes and holding them in the hot water until ready to use. In areas where hard water is a problem, add ¼ cup vinegar to the boiling jars to prevent white mineral deposits from settling on the jars.

Reusing jars. As long as they aren't damaged — and even a nick is enough to disqualify them — you can reuse canning jars year after year. You can also reuse the screw bands used to fasten them. Lids cannot be reused; they must be new each time.

The basic equipment for either steam-pressure or boiling water bath canning includes canning jars and lids, a jar lifter, a narrow spatula, a scale, and a timer.

Don't try to use jars other than those especially made for canning. Peanut butter, mayonnaise, instant coffee, or other food jars are not tempered to withstand the heat of processing, and their top rims may not be right for the lids. Don't risk losing food or cutting yourself on a cracked jar by using substitutes for canning jars.

Sealing jars properly. You must always follow the manufacturer's instructions for sealing jars properly. They usually instruct you to put the lid over the mouth of the jar so that the sealing compound rests on the rim. Screw the band down firmly, so that it is hand-tight. Don't use a jar wrench or other device to tighten the screw band.

During processing, there's enough "give" in the lid to allow air to exhaust from the jar. Don't tighten or loosen it after processing. As the jar cools, the vacuum created inside the jar will pull the lid down in the center until it's slightly concave. You'll hear a slight pinging sound as the seal is formed. When each jar has cooled for 12 to 24 hours, the screw bands should be removed, since the lid will be held in place by the vacuum. The lid must be discarded after one use, but the screw bands are reusable. Store the bands in tightly sealed plastic bags. Do *not* save the flat lids after they've been removed from the jars; they cannot be reused. In fact, it's a good idea to open sealed jars with a pointed opener, piercing the lid so that it can't be saved and reused.

Old-fashioned canning jars. Although they haven't been manufactured for years, there are still some old-fashioned, even antique, jars around. These jars

Safe canning jars have a two-piece closure, with a flat metal lid and a metal screw band to hold the lid in place. Never use bailing-wire closures or zinc lids for canning.

have wire bails and glass lids. The lids are not the screw-on type, but instead use a rubber ring sitting on a ledge around the top of the jar, a domed glass lid, and a wire clamp to seal the contents.

Some old canning jars are sealed with a glass lid and wire bails. These jars may be used for storage or decoration, but they are not safe for home canning.

Some jars have zinc caps lined with porcelain. The zinc cap screws on over the rubber tubing. These jars should not be used for home canning.

Use these jars for storing pasta, grain products, or dried herbs. In fact, there are many practical uses for these lovely old jars, but home-canning is not one of them. These jars are dangerous because it is almost impossible to tell if the jars have been properly sealed. If the jars are not properly sealed, mold growth and toxin-producing bacteria can destroy the product. Do not take the risk of causing illness or possible death by using outdated canning equipment.

Other canning equipment

The other equipment you'll need for canning is mostly equipment you already have on hand. The following items are essential:

- A wide-mouth funnel and a ladle with a pouring lip make jar filling neat and easy. Many funnels sit down ½ inch inside the jar, so in some instances you can use the bottom for a head space guide.
- A large preserving kettle, saucepan, or pot will be needed for most hot-packed foods. Don't use iron, copper, brass, aluminum, galvanized zinc, or tin pans — they may discolor food or cause bad flavors.
- Spoons will be needed for stirring, spooning, and packing. Use wooden spoons for stirring, slotted spoons for lifting, and smaller spoons for filling. Accurate measuring spoons are essential.
- Knives are a necessity. A sharp chopping knife or chef's knife and a good paring knife will handle most tasks.
- Kitchen scissors and a vegetable parer will come in handy for many jobs.
- Long-handled tongs and/or special jar lifters are not expensive, and they are very helpful for taking jars in and out of boiling water. Don't try to manage without these helpers.
- Measuring equipment should include both dry (metal) and liquid (glass) measuring cups. It's handy to have a full set — ¼-, ⅓-, ½-, and 1-cup — dry measures along with a 2-cup measurer. A set of 1-cup, 1-pint, and 1-quart liquid measurers will simplify canning. Household scales that can weigh from ¼ pound (4 ounces) up to 10 to 25 pounds will help you measure produce.
- A timer saves you from clock-watching cooking and processing times.
- A strainer or colander helps hold vegetables after they have been washed or rinsed, and may also be necessary for draining.
- A teakettle or large saucepan will boil the extra water you may need to cover jars in a boiling water

A wide-mouth funnel, large spoons, and hot pads are all essential equipment for canning. Prepare your jars and get your equipment ready before you start to work.

bath, to fill a pressure canner, or to cover vegetables in jars.

- Hot pads, oven mitts, wire cooling racks, or folded dish towels protect your hands and counter tops from the hot jars. Some canners keep a pair of old cotton gloves clean and at hand to wear while filling and sealing hot jars.
- A non-metal spatula or tool with a slim handle, such as a rubber spatula, wooden spoon, specially made plastic bubble-freer, or even a plastic knife, is needed to run down along the insides of filled jars to release air bubbles. Metal knives or spatulas could nick the jars.
- A stiff brush will help you get vegetables really clean. And you'll need a sink or large dish pan for rinsing.
- A food chopper, grinder, food mill, shredder, or blender or food processor may be helpful for some pickle and relish recipes.
- A crock is needed in which to ferment some pickles and sauerkraut. Be sure the crock is clean, unchipped, and uncracked. Brand-new, clean plastic buckets can be used in place of crocks. You may also need a large mixing bowl, new and clean plastic dishpan, unchipped enamel or stainless steel bowl, or another large container for short-term brining of some pickles.

- Labels help you keep track of the type of food and when it was canned.
- Cheesecloth helps to hold together the whole spices often used in pickling. And a cheesecloth lining can turn a colander into a strainer.

BASIC CANNING TECHNIQUES

Once you've learned the procedures and precautions of canning, it's then just a matter of getting it all together. If you're about to can for the first time, read through the rest of this section, including the step-by-step directions, and always read through any recipe before beginning to prepare it. If you're an experienced canner, you'll want to refresh your memory at the start of each canning season and perhaps learn something new to refine your techniques even more.

Always check your recipe to determine the number of jars you'll need. Buy the jars and lids well in advance so you're sure of an ample supply. Check all jars by eye and by feel for any cracks, nicks, or sharp edges, and check to be sure screw bands are unbent and free from rust. Don't reuse lids. The sealing compound on the underside of the lid is only good for one use. Discard old lids immediately so that you don't confuse them with new ones.

Next, wash and rinse all the other equipment you'll need. Be sure everything is in working order — especially the dial gauge in your steam-pressure canner — then assemble and prepare your ingredients.

Time and space required

Canning need not take hours and hours out of your day. You can prepare and process food as it ripens in your garden, perhaps putting away a canner-full each day. You shouldn't prepare more food at one time than will fill one group of jars in the canner, anyway. So, organize canning to fit your schedule. Perhaps do one canner-load in the morning, and another in the cool of the evening. Or you might find it more convenient to devote a whole day to several canning sessions. How about setting up your own canning co-op? A group of people can divide the cost of a pressure canner and the other equipment involved, and also share in the work and its results. However you schedule it, work fast with small amounts at each canning session.

And don't try to do anything else while you're canning. Though it can be difficult, avoid delays. That means avoiding other kitchen chores, children, or the ringing phone. You should keep small children out of the kitchen. Older children can help by preparing food, washing jars, and sealing containers, but the little ones may be in danger.

Once you've started the process, you can't stop; you must continue all the way through to the finish. If you stop in the middle for some reason, food can begin to spoil — and that's asking for trouble.

Canning takes ample work space, so plan ahead. You'll need:

- Sink room for washing and preparing food.
- Counter space for sorting, chopping, or cutting.
- Range space for cooking, processing, and heating water.
- Additional counter space for cooling jars. A sturdy table, set away from traffic and drafts, makes a good cooling area for jars.
- Shelf space in a clean, cool, dark, dry storage area where the food will not freeze.

If you've canned before, take an inventory to see how much you should put up this year. Take stock before you plan your garden, too, so you'll know how much and what to plant to put up this season. A look at what's left from last year will help you determine the size of your crops.

Be sure to move last year's jars to the front of the shelf so they'll be used first.

Rules for safe food handling

Did you know that a bout with the "24-hour bug" might actually have been caused by something you ate? Food-borne illness is surprisingly common, and is caused by poor handling practices in the kitchen.

Food cleanliness and safety are important for every kitchen job. Cleanliness and safety are even more important in food preservation, where microorganisms have the time, and the right conditions, to grow and do their dirty work.

For clean and safe-to-eat foods, always follow canning recipe directions exactly, use the containers and equipment called for, and keep in mind the Do's and Don'ts that follow:

DO

1. Work in a clean kitchen, with clean floors, counter tops, cabinets, and range, and clean equipment.
2. Keep utensils scrupulously clean. That means sterilizing jars in boiling water for 15 minutes if the recipe calls for less than 15 minutes processing time, and washing and rinsing the knives and cutting board between each cutting or chopping task.
3. Work with clean food. Wash, scrub, and rinse vegetables in several changes of water, lifting food out of the water to drain and not letting water drain off over food.
4. Work with clean dishcloths and towels, clean hands, and clean clothes.
5. Wash your hands each time you touch something other than food, such as your hair, your face, the phone, a child, or a pet.
6. Set out and wash all equipment and assemble ingredients before you start to follow recipe directions so there'll be no delays, no chance for food to spoil.
7. Remember to protect your hands when working with hot foods and jars. Use hot pads, tongs, and jar lifters.
8. Be extracautious with large pots or kettles of boiling water or food. Don't move them, but keep them on the range and work there.
9. Avoid any sudden changes in temperature when working with hot jars of hot food. Putting a hot jar on a cool counter or in a cold draft could break it.
10. Always read and precisely follow the manufacturer's directions for all equipment.
11. Avoid the open-kettle method. All home-canned products must be processed for a specified length of time to sterilize the jar and its contents and to produce a partial vacuum inside the jar. No product can be safely stored without first being processed.
12. If you have any doubts about the safety of home-canned foods, boil acid food 10 minutes and low-acid foods 20 minutes before tasting or serving.

DON'T

1. Don't use your hands when a kitchen tool will do the job. Keep fingers out of food, if at all possible.
2. Don't try shortcuts or substitutions or time-saving gimmicks. There's only one right way to prepare food for preserving, and all the techniques and recipes in this book are based on it. Follow the recipes exactly.
3. Don't cook or prepare food for preserving when you're sick.
4. Don't prepare food if you have sores on your hands, unless you wear rubber gloves.
5. Don't use home-canned foods without

checking carefully for signs of spoilage. Discard the contents of any jar showing these signs.

6. Don't use old-fashioned canning jars, or old peanut butter or mayonnaise jars for home canning.

Handling jars

Always start with clean, perfect jars. Be sure to examine them carefully for nicks, scratches, or even the slightest imperfections and run your finger over the rims as well. If a jar isn't perfect, don't use it. Next, wash the jars in hot sudsy water, rinse them well and keep them in hot water until you're ready to use them. Jars may be held in your dishwasher on the dry setting in some cases. If your recipe calls for processing the product for less than 15 minutes, a sterilized jar and screw band are required. Sterilize jars and screw bands by boiling them for 15 minutes and holding them in the hot water until ready to fill. Do not warm them in the oven. The oven's heat cannot be substituted for sterilizing jars and screw bands. Do not boil lids for canning; the sealing compound may be destroyed by the long boiling process.

Remember that you are working with glass, and that sudden changes of temperature can cause cracking or breakage. That means you must always be sure the jar and the food being canned are close to the same temperature and that the jar is set on wood, a cloth, or a rack as you fill it. Never

← HEAD SPACE

Headspace at the top of the jar allows for expansion of food during processing.

pour boiling water or hot food into a room-temperature jar, never put a room-temperature jar full of food into boiling water, and never put a hot, processed jar on a cold, wet surface; it could break.

Take care to protect your jars from contact with metal. Don't use steel wool to clean them and never use a knife or other metal utensil to remove air bubbles or loosen food from the jar. This could cause nicks or scratches that lead to breakage.

Finally, use only jars made specifically for canning. No other jars are designed to withstand the heat and pressure of processing.

Lids and caps should always be washed in hot, soapy water and rinsed well. You must follow the manufacturer's directions to the letter. Generally, you put vacuum lids and screw bands in a pan with water to cover and bring them to a simmer (180°F). Having done this, remove them from the heat and keep them in the water until ready for use to protect them from microorganisms.

Hot and cold pack

There are two ways to pack food into jars—the cold pack method and the hot pack method. The cold (or raw) pack is used for fruits and some vegetables. Pare and cut raw fruits or vegetables, pack them into hot jars, and then cover them with boiling liquid, usually syrup, fruit juice, or water. Uncooked foods shrink slightly after processing, and some fruits float to the top of the jar during processing, so you must pack firmly, leaving the recommended head space. The cold pack method is for foods like whole tomatoes, which might not hold their shape if cooked before being packed into jars.

The hot pack method is generally preferred for foods that are relatively firm and easy to handle even after processing. With this method, you pare and cut the fruits or vegetables and then precook them briefly before putting them into jars; the cooking liquid is used to cover the fruits and vegetables. As an alternative, you can use boiling water—or add boiling water to the other liquid to make up the necessary quantity. Foods prepared this way are more pliable, so they're easier to pack in jars. They don't shrink as much as cold-packed foods do.

Processing times in a steam-pressure canner are the same for hot-packed and cold-packed foods. In a boiling water bath canner, hot-packed foods require less processing time than foods that are cold-packed.

Jars of cold-packed foods shouldn't go directly into boiling water in either the boiling water bath or steam-pressure canner. Because the food and the jars are much lower in temperature, the jars could break. Put cold-packed jars in the canner, add hot water, and then heat to boiling.

Head space. You'll note that the recipes in this chapter direct you to pack food and liquid into the jars to within 1½, 1, ½, or ¼ inch of the tops of the jars. This room is called head space, and is necessary for expansion of the food during processing.

If you leave too little room at the top of the jar, the food may expand and bubble when air is being forced out from the lid during processing. The bubbling food may leave a deposit on the rim of the jar or the lid seal and keep the jar from sealing properly. If you leave too much room at the top, the surface of the food may discolor, or the jar may not seal properly because there won't be enough processing time to drive a sufficient amount of air out of the jar. Each recipe in this book gives you the proper head space.

High-altitude canning

Higher altitudes and thinner air mean boiling points and pressure are affected, so you must make adjustments in timing and pressure. The times given in this book's recipes are for altitudes of less then 1,000 feet above sea level for boiling water bath, 2,000 feet for steam-pressure. If you live at a higher altitude than that, you'll need to increase times or pressures. Check the charts on pages 398 and 413 to find what adjustments are necessary at your altitude. If your steam-pressure canner has a weighted gauge, use 15 pounds pressure instead of 10 when foods are processed at any altitude above 2,000 feet.

How to prevent problems

There are so many factors involved in canning that sometimes things can go wrong. Here are some common problems, causes, and solutions:

- **Spoilage** is caused by improper handling, faulty seals, or underprocessing. Follow all directions carefully and use the proper equipment and the right kind of food, as directed in the recipes. **The signs of spoilage are bulging lids, broken seals, leakage, changes in color, foaming, unusual softness or slipperiness, spurting liquid when jars are opened, mold, and off-odor.** If you notice any of these signs, don't use the food. Discard it where humans and animals won't be able to get to it. You can salvage the jars by washing them well, rinsing, and then boiling them for 15 minutes.

- **Jars can lose liquid** during processing because the food was not hot enough before packing; because the jars were filled too full and liquid boiled out; because air bubbles were not released; because the jars weren't covered with boiling water during the boiling water bath processing; because pressure fluctuated during steam-pressure processing; because you tried to hurry the pressure reduction and liquid was forced out of jars by the sudden change in pressure; or because starchy food can absorb liquid during processing. Don't try to add more liquid to the jars — the food is safe as it is. If you add more liquid, you must put food in clean, hot jars, seal with new lids, and reprocess.

- **Underprocessing** can be caused by skimping on processing time, not having an accurate gauge on your pressure canner, not reducing the canner pressure as the manufacturer directs, or not following head space guides (especially for foods like corn, peas, or lima beans, which expand a great deal during processing).

- **Jars that don't seal** could be the result of flaws in the jar or lids, inadequate heat, excess air in the jar, or food on the rim of the jar. The seal could have been broken by tightening the screw band after removing the jar from the canner or by turning the jar over as it's removed from the canner, or by leaving too much or too little head space in the jar, or by failing to release air bubbles before sealing. Foods in jars that don't seal can be repacked immediately in clean jars with new lids and reprocessed. Or, if just a jar or two fail to seal, refrigerate the contents of these, and use as quickly as possible.

- **Cloudy liquids inside jars** do not necessarily indicate spoilage; they may be the result of minerals in the water, starch in the vegetable, or fillers added to table salt. But if canned foods show any signs of spoilage, discard them.

- **Vegetables that float** can be the result of overcooking or using too few vegetables for the amount of liquid. Check carefully for signs of spoilage.

- **Discolored food** in jars may mean the jars have not been filled full enough (air at the top of the jar causes the food to darken), or that processing time wasn't long enough to destroy enzymes. Iron or copper in the water or storage in light can also cause discoloration. Green vegetables may lose their bright color during processing through the natural reaction of heat breaking down the chlorophyll;

but they're still all right to eat.

Some green vegetables may turn brown from overcooking or because they were too ripe to be canned. Yellow crystals on canned green vegetables are due to glucoside, a natural and harmless substance. White crystals on spinach are also natural and harmless. Some foods may turn a blackish brown or gray from natural chemical substances such as tannins, sulfur compounds, and acids reacting with hard water, copper, iron, or chipped enameled utensils. Some varieties of corn and overmature or overprocessed corn can also discolor. Hard white crystals or flakes in home-canned tomatoes, tomato juice, or tomato paste are harmless calcium nitrate crystals. Color changes don't always mean that food has spoiled, although spoiled food may be discolored. Check for other signs of spoilage.

● **The underside** of the jar's lid may discolor from chemicals in the food or water. This is common and represents no danger.

● **Jars that break** in a canner may have had hairline cracks before they were filled, or may not have been hot enough. The jars may have bumped each other during processing, or were placed directly on the bottom of the canner without a rack.

● **A scum or milky powder** on the outside of jars, noticeable after processing or cooling, is due merely to minerals in the water. Wipe it off with a cloth and don't worry about it. Next time, add a tablespoon or two of vinegar or a teaspoon of cream of tartar to the water in the canner. This helps prevent staining the inside of the canner.

STEAM - PRESSURE CANNING

Steam-pressure canning is the method used for home canning of low-acid foods, such as vegetables, meat, poultry, seafood, and soup. Mixed-vegetable recipes that contain tomatoes are also considered low-acid. In steam-pressure canning, you pack jars with hot or cold food and place them on a rack in a pressure canner. Then you add water (as the manufacturer directs), seal the canner, and heat it. The steam created is under pressure and reaches the superheated temperature of 240° F, which is capable of killing the harmful by-products of the botulism bacteria.

Next time your vegetable garden produces a bumper crop, a steam-pressure canner will help you preserve high-quality canned supplies of zucchini, corn, beans, peas, and other vegetables. The fresher the vegetable, the tastier (and safer) it will be when canned. In fact, produce rushed from your own garden to your pressure canner is the best for canning. Most vegetables may be either cold- or hot-packed.

Remember, too, that altitude can affect the pressure in your steam-pressure canner. Check the

Altitude adjustment — steam-pressure canner	
Altitude (feet):	**Process at pressure of:**
2,000- 3,000	11½ pounds
3,000- 4,000	12 pounds
4,000- 5,000	12½ pounds
5,000- 6,000	13 pounds
6,000- 7,000	13½ pounds
7,000- 8,000	14 pounds
8,000- 9,000	14½ pounds
9,000-10,000	15 pounds

chart above to find what adjustments may be necessary at your altitude. If your pressure canner has a weighted gauge, use 15 pounds pressure at all altitudes over 2,000 feet.

The steam-pressure canner

A pressure canner is a large, heavy metal utensil that heats water under pressure to create steam. The steam is hotter than boiling water and can cook food to the 240° F needed to kill dangerous botulism bacteria.

To process low-acid foods like vegetables, you'll have to purchase a steam-pressure canner. Although the initial expense of a canner may seem high, it should last you through many, many years of gardening and canning. In addition, it can be used for quick-cooking many other foods.

Types of pressure canners

Steam-pressure canners come in several sizes, ranging from eight to 22 quarts in capacity and holding four to seven one-quart jars, or many more pint jars of food. You may already have a pressure cooker, or saucepan pressure cooker. You can use this for processing if it will hold pint jars, if it has an accurate gauge, and if it will maintain 10 pounds of pressure. Add 20 minutes to the processing time given in the

Vent   Pressure gauge

The steam-pressure canner is a large heavy pot that locks to keep steam inside. A rack in the pot holds the canning jars.

recipe if using a pressure cooker or saucepan pressure cooker.

Pressure canners (and cookers) differ slightly in construction — one type has a dial gauge, another a weighted gauge. Always read and follow the instructions that come with your canner to the letter. Before you start to prepare food to be processed in a pressure canner, take out your canner and book and become acquainted with all parts, controls, and instructions. (If you've lost the instruction book, write to the manufacturer for another, giving the model number of your canner.) Study the base, handles, and rack that fits inside, then look over the cover carefully, noting the dial or pressure control vents. Check the gasket and locking mechanism and clean all parts as the manufacturer directs.

Get acquainted with your pressure canner. Familiarity breeds confidence and dispels fear!

Testing the dial gauge

Dial gauges must be checked each canning season. The home economist at your local Cooperative Extension Service Office can tell you where and when you can have the dial tested. If the dial varies more than five pounds per square inch either way, get a new one. If the variation is less than five pounds, adjust pressure using the chart below. Weighted gauges don't need to be tested, but they must be kept clean. Handle the dial gauges with care — never rest the cover on the gauge and never turn the cover upside down over a full pan with the gauge

attached, because moisture could enter the gauge and rust it.

Maintaining proper heat levels

Big pressure canners may cover the range burners completely. Set the pressure canner on the burner to be sure there's enough air space to keep gas burners on or to prevent the enamel of the range surface around the electric unit from growing too hot. If a pressure canner seems too snug against a burner, lift it up ¼ to ½ inch on blocks so that heat and air can circulate.

Adjustment for inaccurate dial gauges			
If gauge reads low by:	Process at pressure of:	If gauge reads high by:	Process at pressure of:
1 pound	11 pounds	1 pound	9 pounds
2 pounds	12 pounds	2 pounds	8 pounds
3 pounds	13 pounds	3 pounds	7 pounds
4 pounds	14 pounds	4 pounds	6 pounds

Note: If gauge is inaccurate by more than 5 pounds, replace the gauge.

BASIC EQUIPMENT FOR STEAM–PRESSURE CANNING

The basic equipment needed for steam-pressure canning includes the following, as detailed earlier in this chapter:

Steam-pressure canner (read instructions!)
Standard jars with 2-piece self-sealing lids
Preserving kettle
Teakettle
Strainer
Spoons (wooden and slotted)
Knives
Measuring cups

Measuring spoons
Wide-mouth funnel
Ladle with pouring lip
Jar-lifter and tongs
Timer
Hot pads
Plastic bubble-freer, narrow spatula, or other slim, non-metal tool
Wire cooling racks or folded dish towels

BASIC INGREDIENTS

Fresh, perfect, uniformly sized vegetables should be selected for canning. That means you have to spend time picking over the vegetables, discarding poor-quality pieces, and sorting canning-quality vegetables by size. For many vegetables, uniform size is important for even, thorough processing. Asparagus, green beans, carrots, lima beans, beets, corn, greens, okra, peas, and summer squash should all be tender, young, just-ripe, and as freshly picked as possible.

Water and salt, or a salt-sugar mixture, are the only other ingredients used in the recipes for vegetable canning given in this book. Always use canning or pickling salt. Table salt contains additives and/or an anti-caking ingredient. These additives may cause clouding in otherwise clear liquids, making it difficult to distinguish signs of spoilage. Since the salt in these recipes is for flavoring only, you may omit it without affecting the canning process in any way. The salt-sugar mixture is used to enhance the flavors of peas, beets, and corn. Simply mix one part salt with two parts sugar and add two teaspoons of the salt-sugar mixture to each pint jar before sealing. Double the amount for quarts.

BASIC STEPS FOR STEAM-PRESSURE CANNING

The canning steps described in this section will give you an idea of the proper sequence of steam-pressure canning procedures, but you must *always* follow the manufacturer's instructions for heating, venting, and general operation of your canner. It's a good idea to review the manufacturer's directions at the start of each canning season.

Always check the dial gauge of your canner at the beginning of each canning season to be sure it's accurate. Your Cooperative Extension Service home economist can tell you where and how to have this done. Be sure to clean the petcock and safety valve, too. This can be done by drawing a string through the openings. When processing foods, never skimp on the processing times. Even the most perfect vegetables can be spoiled if not heated long enough. Keep the heat even under your canner, so that the temperature and pressure won't vary. For perfect steam-pressure canned vegetables, follow these basic steps:

1. Select perfect, just-mature, and very fresh vegetables that are free from blemishes or decay. Sort them by size and maturity and handle the ones that are alike together. Prepare only enough for one canner-load at a time.
2. Set out all the ingredients and equipment. Wash and dry all the equipment, counter tops, working surfaces, and your hands. Check jars for nicks and cracks, then wash and rinse the jars, lids, and screw bands. Keep the jars hot in hot water or in the dishwasher on its "dry" cycle. Prepare the lids as the manufacturer directs (usually simmer at 180° F and keep in hot water until ready to use).
3. Wash the vegetables very carefully, using several changes of washing and rinsing water and scrubbing them with a brush before breaking the skin. Remember that botulism bacteria are in the soil, and only thorough washing will eliminate them from the vegetables. Be sure that you lift the vegetables out of the rinse water to drain.
4. Prepare the vegetables as each recipe directs — cutting, paring, or precooking only enough for one canner-load of jars at a time.
5. Completing one jar at a time, pack the vegetables into the jars, leaving head space as the recipe directs. (This varies from ½ to 1 inch, depending on the vegetable and how much it expands during processing.) Stand the hot jar on a wood surface or on a cloth while filling it.
6. Pour boiling water, cooking liquid, or juice into the packed jars to the level given in the recipe.
7. Release air bubbles by running a slim non-metal tool or plastic bubble-freer down along the inside of each jar. Pour in additional boiling water, if necessary, to bring the liquid back up to the level specified in the recipe.
8. Wipe the tops and threads of each jar with a clean, damp cloth.
9. Put on lids and screw bands as the manufacturer directs. Tighten bands firmly by hand. Never use a jar wrench or any other device to tighten them.
10. Put the rack in the canner and pour in the boiling water as the manufacturer directs.
11. Carefully lower the filled and sealed jars into the canner (arranging them on the rack so steam can flow around the jars).
12. Put on the cover, gauge, and lock according to the manufacturer's directions.
13. Heat the canner, following the manufacturer's directions for the steam flow and the time to exhaust the canner. Put on the control or close the vent.
14. When the canner reaches the required pressure (usually 10 pounds of pressure, adjusting for higher altitudes, if needed), start timing for the exact length of time given in each recipe. Do *not* start timing until the correct pressure is reached. Keep pressure constant for entire processing time. If you live at a high

altitude, make adjustments according to the chart on page 398.

15. When the processing time is up, remove the canner from the heating element to the range top and let it stand until the pressure is reduced to zero. Don't try to hurry this step — it's very important for the pressure to go down slowly. A canner with a weighted gauge may take up to 45 minutes; nudge the control with a pencil and, if you don't see any steam, it means the pressure is at zero. A dial gauge will show the pressure is at zero when the jars are ready to be removed. But once the pressure is down, wait 2 minutes more.

16. Remove the weight control (if you have that type of canner), open the vent, and unlock the cover. Open by lifting the cover away from you so the steam will come out on the far side, or

After filling the canning jars, run a narrow spatula down along the inside of each jar to release air bubbles.

according to the manufacturer's directions. Let stand 10 minutes.

17. Using long-handled tongs or a special jar lifter, carefully lift out the jars and put them several inches apart on a folded towel or rack in an out-of-the-way, draft-free spot. Don't

tighten the screw bands on the jars after processing.

18. Let the jars cool undisturbed for 24 hours. Don't cover the jars while they cool.

19. When the jars are completely cooled, check the seals. The lids should be slightly depressed and, when jar is tipped slightly, there should be no leakage. If the center of the lid can be pushed down and springs back up, the canning process didn't work. Use the food immediately (store it in the refrigerator) or pour the food into another clean, hot jar, seal with a new lid, put a screw band on, and reprocess.

20. Wipe the jars with a clean, damp cloth, then label clearly with contents, date, hot or cold pack method, seasoning or any other pertinent information, and batch (if more than one canner-load is done in 1 day).

21. Remove the screw bands. If they are left on, they may rust in place. To remove stuck screw bands, wring out a cloth in hot water, then wrap around the band for a minute or 2 to help loosen it. Clean and dry the screw bands and, store them in a sealed plastic bag in a dry place.

22. Store the jars in a cool, dark, dry place where they will not freeze. You can put the jars in the boxes they came in to protect them from light.

23. Before using canned food, check for signs of spoilage. If you notice bulging lids, broken seals, leakage, spurting liquid, mold, off-odor, or food that looks slimy, discard the food where humans and animals can't get to it. You can salvage the jars. Wash them thoroughly, rinse, and then boil for 15 minutes.

24. As a further safety precaution, before using them, heat home-canned acid food to boiling and boil for 10 minutes. Boil low acid foods for 20 minutes before tasting or serving. If the food foams, smells bad, or shows other signs of spoilage, discard immediately. (Read "Disposing of Spoiled Foods" on p. 402 .)

If you've followed directions, and if your pressure canner is in good working order, home-canned foods should be safe. We recommend boiling only as extra insurance.

STEAM–PRESSURE CANNING RECIPES

When choosing produce for these home-canning recipes, freshness is extremely important. Once foods are picked, they begin to lose flavor and can also start to spoil quite quickly. Rush foods from the garden to the kitchen and into the jars. Experts say two hours from harvest to jar is the best time span for capturing flavor. If you can't prepare foods right away, be sure to refrigerate them immediately, but don't let them remain in the refrigerator for too long.

Canning for special diets

Except in recipes for sauces, pickles, relishes, and preserves, sugar and salt aren't crucial to the canning process. Since they're only added for flavor, you may omit the sugar and/or salt from our recipes if someone in your family is on a special diet.

Processing times

The times in the recipes that follow are given for both pints and quarts. If you use ½-pint jars, follow the times for pints; if using 12-ounce or 1½-pint jars, process as for quarts. Never skimp on processing times. The correct times are given in each recipe.

ARTICHOKES

Artichoke hearts are a real treat out of season. They're precooked and canned in an acid solution, so you'll need a large kettle as well as the basic equipment for steam-pressure canning.

20 to 40 whole artichokes (about a 23-pound crate), trimmed = 1 quart

1. Choose evenly sized, uniformly green artichokes, with a compact globe shape and tightly closed leaves.
2. Organize and prepare equipment and work area.
3. Remove outer leaves of each artichoke until you come to light yellow or white leaves or bracts. Cut off tops of buds and trim heart and stem to a cone shape. Wash each heart in cold water as soon as you've finished trimming it. Drain.
4. Cook artichoke hearts for five minutes in a large kettle of boiling water mixed with ¾ cup vinegar per gallon. Drain.
5. Pack hearts into hot pint or quart jars to within ½ inch of tops.
6. Prepare canning liquid of 1 gallon water, 3 tablespoons salt, and ¾ cup vinegar or lemon

juice; bring to boil. Pour boiling canning liquid into jars to within 1 inch of tops; make sure hearts are covered.
7. Run a slim, non-metal tool down along the inside of each jar to release air bubbles. Add more boiling liquid to within ½ inch of tops.
8. Wipe tops and threads of jars with damp cloth.
9. Put on lids and bands as manufacturer directs.
10. Process at 10 pounds pressure, 25 minutes for quarts and pints. Process very large hearts 10

Disposing of Spoiled Foods

Check all home-canned products for signs of spoilage before tasting or serving. When you discover a jar that does show spoilage signs you should dispose of the contents immediately. If the product is contaminated with botulism toxins, then pets, farm animals, and people can be killed. These toxins are not necessarily destroyed by sewage treatment plants, so use one of the following methods to destroy the spoiled food:

- **Bury it.** Bury it deeply enough that dogs or other animals cannot dig it up, and that none of the product can seep to the surface.

- **Boil it.** Boiling for 10 minutes will produce a foul odor but will destroy the toxins. The food can then be disposed of safely.

- **Chemically inactivate it.** Put the food in a glass container and mix in ½ to 1 cup chlorine bleach or several tablespoons of strong lye. Let it stand overnight out of reach of children and animals.

Caution: Use rubber or plastic gloves to handle the spoiled food. Do not taste. Once the food has been boiled or chemically treated it can be flushed down the toilet or wrapped in newspaper and put into the garbage.

Boil the jars and screw bands hard for 15 minutes in a strong detergent solution, then wash and rinse. They can then be reused safely. Lids cannot be reused anyway, so dispose of lids along with the spoiled food. Wash your hands carefully, and clean any area where food may have spilled with chlorine bleach and water.

minutes longer. Follow manufacturer's directions for your canner.

11. Follow basic steps for steam-pressure canning, 10 through 24.

ASPARAGUS

Home-canned asparagus is handy for cold salads, as well as for hot vegetable dishes. You'll need the basic equipment for steam-pressure canning.

2¹/₂ to 4¹/₂ pounds = 1 quart
1 bushel (45 pounds) = 10 to 18 quarts

1. Choose tender, evenly sized, tight-tipped fresh spears.
2. Organize and prepare equipment and work area.
3. Wash asparagus spears thoroughly. Trim off scales and tough ends and wash them again.
4. Leave spears whole or cut into 1-inch lengths.
5. **Cold pack:** Gently but firmly pack asparagus as tightly as possible without breaking the spears into hot jars to within ¹/₂ inch of tops. If desired add ¹/₂ teaspoon salt to pints, 1 teaspoon salt to quarts. Pour boiling water into jars to within ¹/₂ inch of tops. **Hot pack:** Cook asparagus pieces two or three minutes in enough boiling water to cover them. Pack the pieces loosely into hot pint or quart jars to within ¹/₂ inch of tops. Add ¹/₂ teaspoon salt to pints, 1 teaspoon salt to quarts, if desired. Pour boiling cooking water into jars to within ¹/₂ inch of tops. Add boiling water if you run out of cooking water.
6. Run a slim, non-metal tool down along the inside of each jar to release air bubbles. Add more boiling liquid to fill to within ¹/₂ inch of tops.
7. Wipe tops and threads of jars with damp cloth.
8. Put on lids and screw bands as manufacturer directs.
9. Process at 10 pounds pressure, 25 minutes for pints, 30 minutes for quarts. Follow manufacturer's directions for your canner.
10. Follow basic steps for steam-pressure canning, 10 through 24.

BEANS, GREEN OR SNAP

Even a small plot of beans can produce a surprisingly large crop. Canned, the beans from your garden can be enjoyed all year. All the basic equipment for steam-pressure canning is used.

1¹/₂ to 2¹/₂ pounds = 1 quart
1 bushel (30 pounds) = 15 to 20 quarts

1. Choose young, tender beans that snap easily.
2. Organize and prepare equipment and work area.
3. Wash beans very well in several changes of water.
4. Trim off ends, string, and cut or break beans into 2-inch pieces.
5. **Cold pack:** Pack beans tightly into jars, to within ¹/₂ inch of tops. Add ¹/₂ teaspoon of salt to each pint jar, 1 teaspoon to quarts, if desired. Pour in boiling water to within ¹/₂ inch of tops of jars. **Hot pack:** Cook beans in boiling water to cover for 5 minutes. Pack into hot jars to within ¹/₂ inch of tops. Add ¹/₂ teaspoon salt to pint jars, if desired. Pour in boiling cooking water to within 1 inch of tops of jars. Add boiling water if you run out of cooking water.
6. Run a slim, non-metal tool down along the inside of each jar to release air bubbles. Add more boiling liquid to fill to within 1 inch of tops.
7. Wipe tops and threads of jars with a damp cloth.
8. Put on lids and screw bands as manufacturer directs.
9. Process at 10 pounds pressure, 20 minutes for pints, 25 minutes for quarts. (This time is for tender, young beans. More mature beans require 15 to 20 minutes more processing time.) Follow manufacturer's directions for your canner.
10. Follow basic steps for steam-pressure canning, 10 through 24.

BEANS, BROAD OR LIMA

Perhaps you can employ some young helpers to shell and sort the beans. While they shell, you can organize the basic equipment you'll need.

3 to 5 pounds in pods = 1 quart
1 bushel (32 pounds) in pods = 6 to 10 quarts

1. Choose only young, tender beans.
2. Organize and prepare equipment and work area.
3. Wash, drain, and shell beans. Sort them according to size. Wash again.
4. **Cold pack:** Pack small beans loosely into hot

jars to within 1 inch of tops of pint jars, 1½ inches of tops of quarts. Pack larger beans to ¾ inch of tops of pint jars and 1¼ inches of tops of quarts. Don't press down or shake beans to pack more in the jars. They need space to expand as they cook. If desired, add ½ teaspoon salt to pint jars, 1 teaspoon to quarts. Pour in boiling water to within ½ inch of tops of jars. **Hot pack:** Cook beans in just enough boiling water to cover for 3 minutes. Pack beans into hot jars to within 1 inch of tops. Add ½ teaspoon salt to pints, 1 teaspoon to quarts, if desired. Pour in boiling water to within 1 inch of tops of jars.

5. Run a slim, non-metal tool down along the inside of each jar to release air bubbles. Add more boiling liquid to fill to within ½ inch of tops.

6. Wipe tops and threads of jars with damp cloth.

7. Put on lids and screw bands as manufacturer directs.

8. Process at 10 pounds pressure, 40 minutes for pints, 50 minutes for quarts. (If beans are large, process 10 minutes longer.) Follow manufacturer's directions for your canner.

9. Follow basic steps for steam-pressure canning, 10 through 24.

BEANS, DRIED

Mature pinto, kidney, and other shelled beans are usually preserved by drying; they may also be canned successfully. Canning dried beans requires rehydration to ensure a safe product. You'll need all the basic equipment for steam-pressure canning.

1 pound dried beans = 6 cups cooked
3 to 5 pounds in pod = 1 quart

1. Shell beans, discard damaged or diseased beans and rinse in cold water.

2. Cover beans with cold water and soak 12 to 18 hours in a cool place, making sure there is enough water to cover the beans at all times.

3. Drain off soaking water. Cover with fresh water and boil 30 minutes.

4. Pack hot beans into jars, leaving 1 inch of head space.

5. If desired, add ½ teaspoon salt per pint, or 1 teaspoon salt per quart.

6. Add boiling water; work out air bubbles with a plastic knife or rubber spatula and adjust water level to leave 1 inch head space.

7. Wipe rims and adjust two-piece canning lids.

8. Process in a pressure canner at 10 pounds pressure for 75 minutes for pint jars, 90 minutes for quarts. Follow manufacturer's directions for your canner.

9. Follow basic steps for steam-pressure canning, 10 through 24.

BEETS

Beets have to be cooked before they're processed, so be sure to have a large kettle ready, along with the rest of the basic equipment.

2 to 3½ pounds without tops = 1 quart
1 bushel (52 pounds) with tops = 15 to 24 quarts

1. Choose young, tender beets.

2. Organize and prepare equipment and work area.

3. Sort beets by size. Cut off tops, leaving the root and 2 inches of stem.

4. Wash very well.

5. Put beets in a large saucepan or kettle, cover with boiling water, and cook until tender, about 15 to 25 minutes depending on size.

6. Drain, slip off skins, and trim ends and root.

7. Leave tiny beets whole; slice or cube medium or large beets.

8. Pack beets into hot pint or quart jars to within ½ inch of tops. Pour in boiling cooking water to within ½ inch of tops of jars.

9. Add ½ teaspoon salt to pints, 1 teaspoon to quarts, if desired.

10. Run a slim non-metal tool down along the inside of each jar to release air bubbles. Add more boiling liquid to within ½ inch of tops.

11. Wipe tops and threads of jars with a damp cloth.

12. Put on lids and screw bands as manufacturer directs.

13. Process at 10 pounds pressure, 30 minutes for pints, 35 minutes for quarts. Follow manufacturer's directions for your canner.

14. Follow basic steps for steam-pressure canning, 10 through 24.

CARROTS

Large, mature carrots don't can well. For canning young, tender carrots, use all the basic equipment.

2 to 3 pounds without tops = 1 quart
1 bushel (50 pounds) without tops = 16 to 25 quarts

1. Choose only young, tender carrots.
2. Organize and prepare equipment and work area.
3. Wash carrots well, scrape or pare, and wash again: Cut off tops and tips.
4. Slice or dice carrots or leave whole.
5. **Cold pack:** Pack carrots tightly into hot pint or quart jars to within 1 inch of tops. Add ½ teaspoon salt to pints, 1 teaspoon to quarts, if desired. Pour in boiling water to within ½ inch of tops of jars. **Hot pack:** Put carrots in a large saucepan, cover with boiling water and heat to boiling. Pack them into hot pint or quart jars to within 1 inch of tops. Add ½ teaspoon salt to pints, 1 teaspoon to quarts, if desired. Pour in boiling cooking water to within ½ inch of tops of jars. Add boiling water if you run out of cooking water.
6. Run a slim, non-metal tool down along the inside of each jar to release air bubbles. Add more boiling liquid to within 1 inch of tops.
7. Wipe tops and threads of jars with a damp cloth.
8. Put on lids and screw bands as manufacturer directs.
9. Process at 10 pounds pressure, 25 minutes for pints, 30 minutes for quarts. Follow manufacturer's directions for your canner.
10. Follow basic steps for steam-pressure canning, 10 through 24.

CELERY AND TOMATOES

Use equal amounts of celery and tomatoes in this combination. It's nice for use in soups, stews, sauces, and casseroles. You'll need the basic equipment for steam-pressure canning, plus a saucepan or pot to heat the vegetables and another for boiling water.

2½ to 3½ pounds tomatoes = 1 quart
1½ to 2½ pounds celery = 1 quart

1. Choose fresh, firm, red-ripe, perfect tomatoes. Wash, peel, core, and chop them. Wash the celery thoroughly and chop it.
2. Organize and prepare equipment and work area.
3. Combine celery and tomatoes in a large saucepan or pot and heat to boiling. (You won't need to add any water, because the tomatoes will provide plenty of liquid.) Boil 5 minutes.
4. Pour or ladle into hot jars to within 1 inch of tops. Add ½ teaspoon salt to each pint or 1 teaspoon salt to each quart, if desired. Pour in boiling cooking liquid to within ½ inch of tops.
5. Run a slim non-metal tool down along the inside of each jar to release any air bubbles. Add more boiling liquid if needed to within ½ inch of tops of jars.
6. Wipe tops and threads of jars with damp cloth.
7. Put on lids and screw bands as manufacturer directs.
8. Process at 10 pounds pressure, 30 minutes for pints, 35 minutes for quarts. Follow manufacturer's directions for your canner.
9. Follow basic steps for steam-pressure canning, 10 through 24.

CHICK PEAS

Can your shelled chick peas for use in salads and casseroles. You'll need all the basic equipment.

3 to 5 pounds in pods = 1 quart
1 bushel (32 pounds) in pods = 6 to 10 quarts

1. Choose only young, tender chick peas.
2. Organize and prepare equipment and work area.
3. Wash, drain, and shell. Wash again.
4. **Cold pack:** Pack chick peas loosely into hot jars to within 1 inch of tops of pint jars, 1½ inches of tops of quarts. Don't press down or shake peas to pack more in the jars. They need space to expand as they cook. If desired, add ½ teaspoon salt to pint jars, 1 teaspoon to quarts. Pour in boiling water to within 1 inch of tops of jars. **Hot pack:** Cook chick peas in just enough boiling water to cover for three minutes. Pack into hot jars to within 1 inch of tops. Add ½ teaspoon salt to pints, 1 teaspoon to quarts, if desired. Pour in boiling water to within 1 inch of tops of jars.
5. Run as slim, non-metal tool down along the inside of each jar to release air bubbles. Add more boiling liquid to fill to within 1 inch of tops.
6. Wipe tops and threads of jars with damp cloth.
7. Put on lids and screw bands as manufacturer directs.
8. Process at 10 pounds pressure, 55 minutes for pints, 65 minutes for quarts. Follow manufacturer's directions for your canner.
9. Follow basic steps for steam-pressure canning, 10 through 24.

CORN, CREAM-STYLE

You don't add real cream to the kernels; the cream is juice from the cob that you scrape off with the back of a knife. You'll need all the basic equipment. Pick corn in small quantities (two to three dozen ears at a time) and rush it to the kitchen. This recipe calls for pint jars only.

3 to 6 pounds corn in husks = 2 pints
1 bushel (35 pounds) in husks = about 12 to 20 pints

1. Home-grown, very fresh corn is best. Work with small quantities, two to three dozen ears at a time.
2. Organize and prepare equipment and work area.
3. Husk corn and remove all silk. Wash corn well.
4. Cut corn from cob at about center of kernel.
5. Scrape cobs with back of knife to remove "cream." Mix cream with corn.
6. **Cold pack:** Pack corn and cream into hot jars to within 1½ inches of tops. Don't shake or press down; corn needs room to expand as it cooks. Add ½ teaspoon salt to each jar, if desired. Pour in boiling water to within ½ inch of tops of jars. **Hot pack:** Measure corn and cream into a large saucepan or pot and add 1 pint boiling water for each quart of cream corn. Heat to boiling. Pack corn and cooking liquid into hot pint jars to within ½ inch of tops. Add ½ teaspoon salt to each jar, if desired.
7. Run a slim, non-metal tool down along the inside of each jar to release air bubbles. Add more boiling liquid to within ½ inch of tops.
8. Wipe tops and threads of jars with damp cloth.
9. Put on lids and screw bands as manufacturer directs.
10. Process at 10 pounds pressure, 1 hour and 35 minutes for cold-packed pints, 1 hour and 25 minutes for hot-packed pints. Follow manufacturer's directions for your canner.
11. Follow basic steps for steam-pressure canning, 10 through 24.

CORN, WHOLE-KERNEL

For this kind of corn, you cut the kernel off closer to the cob than for cream-style corn. Use fresh corn and work with 2 or 3 dozen ears at a time. All the basic equipment is used.

3 to 6 pounds corn in husk = 1 quart
1 bushel (35 pounds) in husks = 6 to 10 quarts

1. Choose corn as fresh as possible, preferably freshly picked and rushed to your kitchen.
2. Organize and prepare equipment and work area.
3. Husk corn and remove all silk. Wash well.
4. Cut corn from cob at about ⅔ the depth of the kernel. Do not scrape cob.
5. **Cold pack:** Pack corn loosely into hot pint or quart jars to within 1 inch of tops. Don't shake or press down; corn needs room to expand as it cooks. Add ½ teaspoon salt to pints, 1 teaspoon to quarts, if desired. Pour in boiling water to within ½ inch of tops of jars. **Hot pack:** Measure corn into large saucepan or pot and add 1 pint boiling water for each quart of corn. Heat to boiling. Pack the corn and cooking liquid into hot pint or quart jars to within 1 inch of tops; make sure the corn is covered with liquid. If desired, add ½ teaspoon salt to pints, 1 teaspoon to quarts.
6. Run a slim, non-metal tool down along the inside of each jar to release air bubbles. Add more boiling liquid to within 1 inch of tops.
7. Wipe tops and threads of jars with damp cloth.
8. Put on lids and screw bands as manufacturer directs.
9. Process at 10 pounds pressure, 55 minutes for pints, 1 hour and 25 minutes for quarts. Follow manufacturer's directions for your canner.
10. Follow basic steps for steam-pressure canning, 10 through 24.

GREENS (beet, chard, collard, kale, mustard, and turnip)

You'll need all the basic equipment for steam-pressure canning, plus a large saucepan. This recipe is for the hot-pack method only.

2 to 6 pounds = 1 quart
1 bushel (12 pounds) = 2 to 6 quarts

1. Choose freshly picked, young, tender greens.
2. Organize and prepare equipment and work area.
3. Wash greens thoroughly in several changes of water and pick over carefully.
4. Cut out any tough stems and mid-ribs.
5. Put greens in large saucepan with just enough water to prevent sticking (usually the water that clings to the leaves is enough). Heat just until greens are wilted, (about ten minutes), turning

greens when steam begins to rise around the edges of pan. Before packing, cut through greens several times with a sharp knife or kitchen scissors.

6. Pack hot cooked greens very loosely into hot pint or quart jars to within 1 inch of tops. Add ½ teaspoon salt to each pint jar, if desired. Pour in boiling water to within ½ inch of tops of jars.

7. Run a slim, non-metal tool down along the inside of each jar to release air bubbles. Add more boiling liquid to within ½ inch of tops.

8. Wipe tops and threads of jars with damp cloth.

9. Put on lids and screw bands as manufacturer directs.

10. Process at 10 pounds pressure, 1 hour and 10 minutes for pints, 1 hour and 30 minutes for quarts. Follow manufacturer's directions for your canner.

11. Follow basic steps for steam-pressure canning, 10 through 24.

LENTILS

You'll need all the basic equipment for steam-pressure canning to can your lentils.

3 to 5 pounds in pods = 1 quart
1 bushel (32 pounds) in pods = 6 to 10 quarts

1. Choose only young, tender lentils.

2. Organize and prepare equipment and work area.

3. Wash, drain, and shell lentils. Wash again.

4. Cold pack: Pack lentils loosely into hot jars to within 1 inch of tops of pint jars, 1½ inches of tops of quarts. Don't press down or shake lentils to pack more in the jars. They need space to expand as they cook. If desired, add ½ teaspoon salt to pint jars, 1 teaspoon to quarts. Pour in boiling water to within 1 inch of tops of jars. **Hot pack:** Cook lentils in just enough boiling water to cover for three minutes. Pack lentils into hot jars to within 1 inch of tops. Add ½ teaspoon salt to pints, 1 teaspoon to quarts, if desired. Pour in boiling water to within 1 inch of tops of jars.

5. Run a slim, non-metal tool down along the inside of each jar to release air bubbles. Add more boiling liquid to within 1 inch of tops.

6. Wipe tops and threads of jars with damp cloth.

7. Put on lids and screw bands as manufacturer directs.

8. Process at 10 pounds pressure, 55 minutes for pints, 65 minutes for quarts. Follow

manufacturer's directions for your canner.

9. Follow basic steps for steam-pressure canning, 10 through 24.

MUSHROOMS

Can your extra mushrooms for use in sauces and casseroles. You'll need all the basic equipment, plus a large pot with a cover and a perforated insert for steaming. This recipe is for pint and half-pint jars only.

1½ pounds mushrooms = 2 pints
1½ pounds mushrooms = 4 half-pints

1. Choose firm, evenly sized, undamaged mushrooms.

2. Organize and prepare equipment and work area.

3. Trim mushrooms and cut off any damaged areas or discolored parts. Soak in water 10 minutes to remove soil. Wash mushrooms in clean water.

4. Cut large mushrooms in half or in quarters; leave small mushrooms whole.

5. Put mushrooms in perforated steamer insert and steam, covered, over boiling water for 4 minutes.

6. Pack hot mushrooms into hot jars to within ½ inch of tops. Add ½ teaspoon salt to each pint, ¼ teaspoon salt to each ½ pint if desired. Pour in boiling water to within ½ inch of tops of jars; make sure the mushrooms are covered.

7. For better color, add ascorbic acid—⅛ teaspoon (250 milligrams) for each pint.

8. Run a slim, non-metal tool down along the inside of each jar to release any air bubbles. Add more boiling water to within ½ inch of tops of jars if necessary.

9. Wipe tops and threads of jars with damp cloth.

10. Put on lids and screw bands as manufacturer directs.

11. Process at 10 pounds pressure for 30 minutes. Follow manufacturer's directions for your canner.

12. Follow basic steps for steam-pressure canning, 10 through 24.

OKRA

Okra has to be cooked briefly before processing, so have a saucepan or kettle ready in addition to all the basic equipment.

2 to 3 pounds okra = 1 quart
1 bushel (26 pounds) = 8 to 13 quarts

1. Choose small, young tender okra—freshly picked, if possible.
2. Organize and prepare equipment and work area.
3. Wash okra well and remove stem and blossom ends without cutting into pod.
4. Cook in boiling water for one minute.
5. Pack hot, cooked okra into hot pint or quart jars to within ½ inch of tops.
6. Add ½ teaspoon salt to pints, 1 teaspoon to quarts, if desired. Pour in boiling cooking water to within ½ inch of tops of jars. Use boiling water if you run out of cooking water.
7. Run a slim, non-metal tool down along the inside of each jar to release air bubbles. Add more boiling liquid to within ½ inch of tops.
8. Wipe tops and threads of jars with damp cloth.
9. Put on lids and screw bands as manufacturer directs.
10. Process at 10 pounds pressure, 25 minutes for pints, 40 minutes for quarts. Follow manufacturer's directions for your canner.
11. Follow basic steps for steam-pressure canning, 10 through 24.

PEAS, BLACK-EYED

You'll need all the basic equipment for steam-pressure canning. You'd probably also appreciate some help shelling the peas.

3 to 6 pounds in pods = 1 quart
1 bushel (about 30 pounds) in pods = 6 to 10 quarts

1. Select very fresh, young, tender peas.
2. Organize and prepare equipment and work area.
3. Wash, shell, then wash peas again.
4. **Cold pack:** Pack peas loosely into hot pint or quart jars to within 1 inch of tops. Don't shake or press down; they need room to expand as they cook. Add ½ teaspoon salt to pints, 1 teaspoon to quarts, if desired. Pour in boiling water to within 1 inch of tops of jars. **Hot pack:** Put peas in a large saucepan, cover with boiling water, and boil three minutes. Pack loosely into hot jars to within 1 inch of tops. Add ½ teaspoon salt to pints, 1 teaspoon to quarts, if desired. If needed, pour in boiling water or cooking water to within 1 inch of tops of jars.

5. Run a slim, non-metal tool down along the insides of each jar to release air bubbles. Add more boiling liquid to within 1 inch of tops, if necessary.
6. Wipe tops and threads of jars with damp cloth.
7. Put on lids and screw bands as manufacturer directs.
8. Process at 10 pounds pressure, 40 minutes for pints, 40 minutes for quarts. Follow manufacturer's directions for your canner.
9. Follow basic steps for steam-pressure canning, 10 through 24.

PEAS, SHELLING

Add a sugar-salt mixture to bring out the flavor in this recipe. Mix one part salt with two parts sugar and add two teaspoons of the salt-sugar mixture to each pint jar before sealing. You'll need all the basic equipment.

3 to 6 pounds in pods = 1 quart
1 bushel (30 pounds) in pods = 5 to 10 quarts

1. Choose young, tender, freshly gathered peas.
2. Organize and prepare equipment and work area.
3. Wash, shell, then wash peas again. Drain.
4. **Cold pack:** Pack the peas loosely into hot pint or quart jars to within 1 inch of tops. Don't shake or press down; peas need room to expand as they cook. Add ½ teaspoon salt to pints, 1 teaspoon to quarts, if desired. Pour in boiling water to within 1 inch of tops of jars. **Hot pack:** Put peas in a large saucepan, cover with boiling water, and heat to boiling. Boil small peas three minutes; larger ones five minutes. Drain, rinse in hot water, and drain again. Pack loosely into hot pint or quart jars to within 1 inch of tops. If desired, add ½ teaspoon salt to pints, 1 teaspoon to quarts. Pour in boiling water to within 1 inch of tops.
5. Run a slim, non-metal tool down along the inside of each jar to release air bubbles. Add more boiling liquid to within 1 inch of tops for hot pack, 1½ inches of tops for cold pack.
6. Wipe tops and threads of jars with damp cloth.
7. Put on lids and screw bands as manufacturer directs.
8. Process at 10 pounds pressure, 40 minutes for quarts and pints. Process extra-large peas for 10

minutes more. Follow manufacturer's directions for your canner.

9. Follow basic steps for steam-pressure canning, 10 through 24.

PEPPERS, SWEET

Use sweet peppers in this recipe, because they won't taste bitter when cooked. Pack only in 1/2-pint or pint jars. You'll need all the basic equipment.

1 to 1 1/2 pounds = 1 pint

1. Select perfect, well-colored sweet peppers.
2. Organize and prepare equipment and work area.
3. Remove the stems and seeds from the peppers.
4. In a large saucepan or pot, heat several inches of water to boiling. Add peppers and boil three minutes. Drain.
5. Pack drained, hot peppers into hot jars to within 1 inch of tops. Add 1 tablespoon vinegar and 1/2 teaspoon salt to each pint. Add boiling water to within 1/2 inch of tops of jars.
6. Run a slim, non-metal tool down along the inside of each jar to release air bubbles. Add more boiling water to within 1/2 inch of tops, if necessary.
7. Wipe tops and threads of jars with damp cloth.
8. Put on lids and screw bands as manufacturer directs.
9. Process at 10 pounds pressure, 35 minutes for 1/2 pints and pints. Follow manufacturer's directions for your canner.
10. Follow basic steps for steam-pressure canning, 10 through 24.

POTATOES

Potatoes have to be cooked before packing, so, in addition to the basic equipment for steam-pressure canning, you'll need a large saucepan or pot. You'll also need a vegetable peeler for the potatoes, unless you prefer to use a paring knife.

2 to 3 pounds = 1 quart
1 bushel (50 pounds) = 16 to 25 quarts

1. Select perfect, freshly dug potatoes.
2. Organize and prepare equipment and work area.
3. Wash potatoes well, using a vegetable brush. Pare and then wash them again. Dice potatoes into

1/2-inch cubes. To prevent potato cubes from darkening, dip them in brine (1 teaspoon salt to 1 quart water). Drain.
4. Cook potatoes in boiling water to cover for two minutes in a large saucepan or pot. Drain.
5. Pack hot potatoes into hot jars to within 1 1/2 inches of the tops. Add boiling water to within 1 inch of tops. Add 1/2 teaspoon salt to each pint, 1 teaspoon to each quart, if desired.
6. Run a slim, non-metal tool down along the insides of jars to release any air bubbles. Add more boiling water to within 1/2 inch of tops, if necessary.
7. Wipe tops and threads of jars with damp cloth.
8. Put on lids and screw bands as manufacturer directs.
9. Process at 10 pounds pressure, 35 minutes for pints, 40 minutes for quarts. Follow manufacturer's directions for your canner.
10. Follow basic steps for steam-pressure canning, 10 through 24.

SOYBEANS

You must really rush soybeans from field to jar—they start to lose flavor almost as soon as they're picked. Soybeans have to be briefly boiled before processing. All the basic equipment is used.

3 to 5 pounds in pods = 1 quart
1 bushel (32 pounds) in pods = 6 to 10 quarts

1. Choose only young, tender beans.
2. Organize and prepare equipment and work area.
3. Wash, drain, and shell beans. Wash again.
4. **Cold pack:** Pack beans loosely into hot jars to within 1 inch of tops of pint jars, 1 1/2 inches of tops of quarts. Don't press down or shake beans to pack more in the jar. They need space to expand as they cook. If desired, add 1/2 teaspoon salt to pint jars, 1 teaspoon to quarts. Pour in boiling water to within 1 inch of tops of jars. **Hot pack:** Cook beans in just enough boiling water to cover for three minutes. Pack beans into hot jars to within 1 inch of tops. Add 1/2 teaspoon salt to pints, 1 teaspoon to quarts, if desired. Pour boiling water to within 1 inch of tops of jars.
5. Run a slim, non-metal tool down along the inside of each jar to release air bubbles. Add more boiling liquid to within 1 inch of tops.
6. Wipe tops and threads of jars with damp cloth.

7. Put on lids and screw bands as manufacturer directs.

8. Process at 10 pounds pressure, 55 minutes for pints, 65 minutes for quarts. Follow manufacturer's directions for your canner.

9. Follow basic steps for steam-pressure canning, 10 through 24.

SPINACH, NEW ZEALAND SPINACH

You'll need all the basic equipment, plus a large saucepan. This recipe is for the hot-pack method only.

2 to 6 pounds = 1 quart
12 pounds (1 bushel) = 2 to 6 quarts

1. Choose freshly picked, young and tender spinach.

2. Organize and prepare equipment and work area.

3. Wash spinach thoroughly in several changes of water and pick over carefully.

4. Cut out any tough stems and mid-ribs.

5. Put spinach in large saucepan with just enough water to prevent sticking (usually the water that clings to the leaves is enough). Heat just until spinach is wilted, turning spinach when steam begins to rise around the edges of pan. Before packing, cut through spinach several times with a sharp knife or kitchen scissors.

6. Pack hot spinach very loosely into hot pint or quart jars to within 1 inch of tops. Add ½ teaspoon salt to each pint jar, if desired. Pour in boiling water to within 1 inch of tops of jars.

7. Run a slim, non-metal tool down along the inside of each jar to release air bubbles. Add more boiling liquid to within 1 inch of tops.

8. Wipe tops and threads of jars with damp cloth.

9. Put on lids and screw bands as manufacturer directs.

10. Process at 10 pounds pressure, 1 hour and 10 minutes for pints, 1 hour and 30 minutes for quarts. Follow manufacturer's directions for your canner.

11. Follow basic steps for steam-pressure canning, 10 through 24.

SQUASH, SUMMER

Summer squash is another home garden plant that sometimes overwhelms you with its production.

You'll need all the basic equipment to can summer squash.

2 to 4 pounds = 1 quart
1 bushel (40 pounds) = 10 to 20 quarts

1. Choose young, tender, thin-skinned squash.

2. Organize and prepare equipment and work area.

3. Wash well, but don't pare. Trim off ends.

4. Cut the squash into ½-inch slices or chunks (if large).

5. Put squash pieces in a large saucepan, add boiling water to cover, and heat to boiling. Pack squash loosely into hot pint or quart jars to within 1 inch of tops. Add ½ teaspoon salt to pints, 1 teaspoon to quarts, if desired. Pour in boiling cooking water to within ½ inch of tops. Add boiling water if there is not enough cooking water.

6. Run a slim, non-metal tool down along the inside of each jar to release air bubbles. Add more boiling liquid to within ½ inch of tops.

7. Wipe tops and threads of jars with damp cloth.

8. Put on lids and screw bands as manufacturer directs.

9. Process at 10 pounds of pressure, 30 minutes for pints, 40 minutes for quarts. Follow manufacturer's directions for your canner.

10. Follow basic steps for steam-pressure canning, 10 through 24.

SWEET POTATOES

Sweet potatoes have to be boiled or steamed before processing. All the basic equipment is used. Sweet potatoes can be dry packed with no extra water or wet packed with extra liquid — boiling water or a 40 percent syrup.*

2 to 3 pounds = 1 quart
1 bushel (50 pounds) = 16 to 25 quarts

1. Select plump, freshly dug, unshriveled sweet potatoes.

2. Organize and prepare equipment and work area.

3. Wash sweet potatoes well and sort according to size.

4. Boil or steam about 20 to 30 minutes, or until tender and skins slip off easily. (Don't pierce with fork.)

5. Peel and cut into slices or pieces.

6. **Dry pack:** Pack the slices or pieces tightly into hot pint or quart jars, pressing gently to fill the

spaces. Fill to within 1 inch of the tops. Don't add liquid. **Wet pack:** Pack the slices or pieces into hot jars to within 1 inch of the tops. Add ½ teaspoon salt to pints, 1 teaspoon to quarts, if desired. Pour in boiling water or 40 percent syrup to within 1 inch of the tops. Run a slim, non-metal tool down along the inside of each jar to release air bubbles. Do not add liquid or salt.

7. Wipe tops and threads of jars with damp cloth.

8. Put on lids and screw bands as the manufacturer directs.

9. Process at 10 pounds pressure. **Dry pack:** 65 minutes for pints, 1 hour and 35 minutes for quarts. **Wet pack:** 55 minutes for pints, 1½ hours for quarts. Follow the manufacturer's directions for your canner.

10. Follow basic steps for steam-pressure canning, 10 through 24.

*For 40 percent syrup, mix 3 cups sugar with 4 cups water until the sugar dissolves. Makes 5½ cups.

SUCCOTASH

Combine fresh corn with green beans or lima beans. Cut the corn from the cob as in whole-kernel corn and mix with an equal amount, or half as many beans. See the recipes for whole-kernel corn and green or lima beans for approximate yields. You'll need all the basic equipment for steam-pressure canning.

1. Choose the freshest corn possible. Select same-sized beans.

2. Organize and prepare equipment and work area.

3. Husk corn and remove silk. Wash well. Wash, drain, and shell lima beans and wash again. Wash the green beans, trim, string, and cut into 2-inch lengths.

4. Boil corn in a large saucepan for 5 minutes. Meanwhile, in another pan boil beans 3 minutes. Drain both vegetables. Cut corn from cob and mix with hot, drained beans.

5. Pack hot vegetables into hot jars to within 1 inch of tops. Add ½ teaspoon salt to each pint, if desired. Add boiling water to within 1 inch of tops of jars.

6. Run a slim, non-metal tool down along the inside of each jar to release air bubbles. Add more boiling water to within 1 inch of tops.

7. Wipe tops and threads of jars with damp cloth.

8. Put on lids and screw bands as manufacturer directs.

9. Process at 10 pounds pressure 1 hour for pints, 1 hour and 25 minutes for quarts. Follow manufacturer's directions for your canner.

10. Follow basic steps for steam-pressure canning, 10 through 24.

GREEN TOMATO MINCEMEAT

When the frost beats the ripening of some of your tomatoes, turn them into this terrific mincemeat. Because of low-acid ingredients, this recipe must be processed in a pressure canner. The yield is about 10 pints. You'll need all the basic equipment for steam-pressure canning, plus a grater and a large bowl.

2 quarts cored and chopped green tomatoes (about 20 small)	3½ cups firmly packed brown sugar
1 tablespoon salt	½ cup vinegar
1 orange (grate peel, chop pulp)	2 teaspoons ground cinnamon
2½ quarts chopped pared apples (about 12 medium)	1 teaspoon ground nutmeg
1 pound seedless raisins	1 teaspoon ground cloves
1½ cups (about 6 ounces) chopped suet	½ teaspoon ground ginger

1. Organize and prepare ingredients, equipment, and work area.

2. Sprinkle salt over tomatoes in a large bowl or container, and then let stand 1 hour. Drain.

3. Meanwhile heat water in large kettle to boiling. Add tomatoes and let stand 5 minutes. Drain well.

4. Combine all ingredients in large kettle and heat to boiling.

5. Pour or ladle hot mincemeat into hot jars to within 1 inch of tops of jars. Run a slim, non-metal tool down along the inside of each jar to release air bubbles. Add more hot liquid to within 1 inch of tops, if necessary.

6. Wipe tops and threads of jars with damp cloth.

7. Put on lids and screw bands as manufacturer directs.

8. Process at 10 pounds pressure for 25 minutes. Follow manufacturer's directions for your canner.

9. Follow basic steps for steam-pressure canning, 10 through 24.

STEWED TOMATOES

Even though you should store home-canned vegetables in a dark, cool place, you might like to leave a jar of your very own stewed tomatoes visible in your kitchen—just to show them off! This recipe makes about 7 pints and must be processed in a steam-pressure canner because of the low-acid ingredients. You'll use all the basic equipment.

4 quarts chopped, cored, peeled tomatoes (about 24 large)	¼ cup chopped green pepper
1 cup chopped celery	1 teaspoon sugar
½ cup chopped onion	2 teaspoons salt

1. Organize and prepare ingredients, equipment, and work area.

2. Combine all ingredients in a large kettle or saucepot, heat to boiling and simmer 10 minutes, stirring occasionally.

3. Ladle or pour hot tomatoes into hot jars to within ½ inch of tops. Run a slim, non-metal tool down along the inside of each jar to release air bubbles. Add additional hot liquid, if necessary, to within ½ inch of tops of jars.

4. Wipe tops and threads of jars with a damp cloth.

5. Put on lids and screw bands as manufacturer directs.

6. Process at 10 pounds pressure, 15 minutes. Follow manufacturer's directions for your canner.

7. Follow basic steps for steam-pressure canning, 10 through 24.

VEGETABLE SOUP

You can use any combination of vegetables you like for this easy soup. Chop or dice the vegetables so pieces are about the same size. Process for the time of the vegetable that needs the longest processing. The recipe makes about 7 quarts. You'll need all the basic equipment for steam-pressure canning.

2 quarts chopped, cored, peeled tomatoes (about 1 dozen large)	1 quart shelled lima beans
1½ quarts water	1 quart uncooked corn kernels (about 9 ears)
1½ quarts cubed peeled potatoes (about 6 medium)	2 cups sliced celery
	2 cups chopped onions
1½ quarts sliced pared carrots (about 1 dozen medium)	Salt

1. Organize and prepare ingredients, equipment, and work area.

2. Combine all the ingredients except the salt in a large kettle, heat to boiling, and boil 5 minutes.

3. Pour or ladle boiling soup into hot jars to within 1 inch of tops.

4. Add ¼ teaspoon salt to each pint or ½ teaspoon to each quart.

5. Run a slim, non-metal tool down along the inside of each jar to release any air bubbles. Add more boiling soup, if necessary, to bring to within 1 inch of the tops.

6. Wipe tops and threads of jars with damp cloth.

7. Put on lids and screw bands as manufacturer directs.

8. Process at 10 pounds pressure, 55 minutes for pints, 1 hour and 25 minutes for quarts. Follow manufacturer's directions for your canner.

9. Follow basic steps for steam-pressure canning, 10 through 24.

BOILING WATER BATH CANNING

Boiling water bath canning is the method used for home canning foods that are high in acid. Molds, yeasts, enzymes, and bacteria in high-acid foods are destroyed at a temperature of 212°F, which is the boiling point of water. Some pickles and relishes require a simmering water bath, or temperatures of 170° to 190°F. Always maintain the correct water temperature required for each recipe.

To process jars in a boiling water bath canner, place jars packed with hot food on a rack inside a water bath canner or deep pot. Cover the jars with 1 to 2 inches of boiling water and place lid on canner. Start processing according to your recipe instructions. The timing of most acid foods will begin when the water in the boiling water bath canner returns to a full boil. However, some pickled peppers simmer at 170°F, and fresh-pack pickles are timed from the moment the hot jars are placed in the boiling water; timing continues until the completion of the time specified in the recipe. For best results, always use up-to-date canning recipes.

Since foods high in acidity tend to resist the botulism bacteria, they are the easiest to can. Tomatoes are popular with home canners. Rhubarb, which is grown like a vegetable, but usually served in sweetened pies, is high enough in acidity to be processed as an acid food. Although prepared from cabbage fermented in salt, sauerkraut is so much higher in acidity than raw cabbage that it also becomes an "acid food." And, although often prepared from low-acid vegetables, pickles and relishes are also processed like high-acid foods because they are combined with acid-rich vinegar. All of these foods can be canned with the boiling water bath method.

If you live at high altitudes, you must remember to add additional processing time for every altitude above 1,000 feet above sea level. Make adjustments according to the chart below for high-altitude canning.

The boiling water bath canner

You'll need a water bath canner for processing acid foods such as tomatoes, kraut, pickles, and relishes. Several well-known pot and pan manufacturers

Altitude adjustment—boiling water bath canner		
Altitude (feet):	Increase processing time by:	
	(total time 20 minutes or less)	(total time more than 20 minutes)
1,000	1 minute	2 minutes
2,000	2 minutes	4 minutes
3,000	3 minutes	6 minutes
4,000	4 minutes	8 minutes
5,000	5 minutes	10 minutes
6,000	6 minutes	12 minutes
7,000	7 minutes	14 minutes
8,000	8 minutes	16 minutes
9,000	9 minutes	18 minutes
10,000	10 minutes	20 minutes

make water bath canners, usually of aluminum. The canner is a big pot (20- to 21-quart capacity) with a lid and a special rack that fits down inside the pot to hold the jars off the bottom and away from each other. Often this rack has handles and special ridges so that you can lift it out of the water and hold it in

place while putting in the jars. These pots are not very expensive and do make boiling water bath processing far more convenient than a makeshift canner. The pots are quite large, so plan your storage space accordingly. You can also use the pot for many other big cooking jobs — spaghetti and corn-on-the-cob, for example.

Make your own canner

If you already own a very large pot, you can probably turn it into a water bath canner by finding a rack that will fit down in the pot, covering the bottom. A rack or a cushion (made of a folded towel) is necessary to keep the jars from touching the hot bottom of the pot. If there is no cushion between the jars and the bottom of the pot, hot spots may be created and the jars may break before processing is complete.

The pot must be big enough to allow at least 4 inches of space above the jars as they sit on the rack or towel. (Check the depth of the pot before you start canning.) The jars must be covered by 1 to 2 inches of water, with another 1 to 2 inches allowed for boiling room. Of course, half-pint or pint jars can fit into a shallow pot. To help you estimate how big a pot you need, assume that pint jars need a pot that is at least 10 to 12 inches deep; quart jars need a pot at least 11 to 13 inches deep. If you plan to can regularly, it is worth investing in a commercial canner with a rack and a lid.

A rack inside the canner prevents jars from resting on the bottom and creating hot spots. A jar lifter is used to remove the jars from the canner.

How to Can Fruits and Vegetables

Maintaining proper heat levels

On old ranges, a big pot can sometimes cover a burner completely, shutting off the airflow to the pilot light or blocking the heat so that the enamel surface of the range overheats. Put the canner on the burner of your range to see whether it "seals off" the burner. If it does, get several blocks about 1/2-inch thick to raise the canner.

BASIC EQUIPMENT FOR
BOILING WATER BATH CANNING

The basic equipment needed for boiling water bath canning includes the following:

Boiling water bath canner	Wide-mouth funnel
Standard jars with 2-piece self-sealing lids	Ladle with a pouring lip
	Jar-lifter or tongs
Preserving kettle	Timer
Teakettle	Hot pads
Strainer	Plastic bubble-freer, narrow spatula, or other slim, non-metal tool
Spoons (wooden and slotted)	
Knives	
Measuring spoons	Wire cooling racks or folded dish towels
Measuring cups	

BASIC INGREDIENTS

Fresh, perfect, uniformly sized vegetables should be selected for canning. That means you'll have to spend time picking over the vegetables, discarding poor-quality produce, and sorting canning-quality vegetables by size. For many vegetables, uniform size is important for even, thorough processing.

Tomatoes should be red-ripe, firm, and free of blemishes. Some new tomato varieties are low in acid. Check with your Cooperative Extension Service if you are unsure about how to process your tomatoes.

Overripe tomatoes are low in acid and should not be canned. Overripe tomatoes are deep red, soft, and often have wrinkled skin.

Before canning tomatoes, cut out any dark spots on the surface, and wash the tomatoes well before peeling or cooking. You may add up to a total of 2 cups onions, celery, green peppers, or a combination of all three for every 12 cups of tomatoes. For instance, for 12 cups of sliced, ripe tomatoes, add 1 cup chopped onions, 1/2 cup

chopped celery, and 1/2 cup chopped green peppers for a total of 2 cups low-acid vegetables.

Water and salt, or a salt-sugar mix, are the only other ingredients used in the recipes in this book that aren't for sauces, pickles, or relishes. Since the salt called for in simple canning recipes is for flavoring only, you may omit it without affecting the canning process in any way. Some cooks like to add just a little sugar to tomatoes. Mix one part salt with two parts sugar and add two teaspoons of the salt-sugar mixture to each pint jar before sealing. Double the amount for quarts.

BASIC STEPS FOR
BOILING WATER BATH CANNING

1. Select foods that are perfect, just-mature, very fresh, and free from blemishes or decay. Sort by size and maturity.
2. Set out all the ingredients and equipment. Wash and dry all the equipment, counter tops, working surfaces, and your hands. Check jars for nicks and cracks. Wash and rinse the jars, lids, and screw bands, then keep them hot in a pan of hot water or in the dishwasher on the "dry" cycle. If the processing time given in the recipe is less than 15 minutes, sterilized jars and screw bands must be used. Sterilize jars and screw bands by boiling for 15 minutes and holding in hot water until you are ready to use them. Prepare the lids as the manufacturer directs (usually by simmering in water at about 180°F and keeping them in hot water until needed).
3. Wash vegetables very carefully, using several changes of washing and rinsing water and scrubbing them with a brush before breaking the skin. Remember that botulism bacteria are in the soil, and only thorough washing will eliminate them from the vegetables. Be sure that you lift the vegetables out of the rinse water to drain.
4. Prepare the produce as each recipe directs — cutting, paring, or precooking only enough for one canner-load of jars at a time.
5. Completing one jar at a time, pack food into jars as the recipe directs, leaving head space as the recipe specifies. (This varies from 1/4 or 1/2 to 1 inch, depending on the food and how much it expands during processing.) Stand the hot jar on wood or cloth while filling it.
6. Pour boiling water, cooking liquid, juice, brine, or pickling solution into the packed jars to the level given in the recipe.

7. Run a slim, non-metal tool or plastic bubble-freer down along the inside of each jar to release any air bubbles. If necessary, pour in additional boiling water to bring the liquid back up to the level specified in the recipe.
8. Wipe the tops and threads of each jar with a clean, damp cloth.
9. Put on lids and screw bands as the manufacturer directs. Tighten bands firmly by hand. Never use a jar wrench or any other device to tighten them.
10. As each jar is filled, place it in the canner. Arrange the jars on the rack so that they don't touch one another or bump against the side of the canner. Add hot water to cover the jars with one or two inches of water.
11. Cover the canner, and when water reaches a simmer or full boil (depending on the recipe) begin timing for processing. Adjust heat during processing so that the correct water temperature is maintained. Use a candy or meat thermometer to determine the temperature of the simmering water bath (170° to 190°F for some recipes). If the processing time is longer than 10 minutes you may need to add more boiling water, so keep a kettle of hot water on hand. Jars must be covered by 1 to 2 inches of water. If you live more than 1000 feet above sea level, adjust processing times according to the chart of page 398.
12. When the processing time is up, turn off the heat and carefully lift the jars out of the canner. Place the jars several inches apart on a folded towel or rack that is in an out-of-the-way, draft-free place. Don't tighten bands after processing.
13. Let the jars cool, undisturbed, for at least 12 hours. Don't cover the jars while they're cooling.
14. When the food in the jars is completely cool, remove the screw bands and check the seals. The lids should be depressed and, when the jar is tipped, there should be no leakage. If the center of the lid can be pushed down and comes back up, or if there are any leaks, use the food immediately (store it in the refrigerator). Or, pour it into another clean, hot jar, seal with a new lid, put the screw band on, and reprocess.
15. Wipe the jars with a clean, damp cloth, then label clearly with the contents, date, batch (if you do more than one a day), hot or cold pack method, seasoning, and/or special ingredients or information.
16. Be sure to remove the screw bands — if they're left on, they could rust in place. To remove stuck screw bands, wring out a cloth in hot water, then wrap it around the band for a minute or two to help loosen it. Clean and dry the bands and store them in a sealed plastic bag in a dry place.
17. Store the jars in a cool, dark, dry place where they won't freeze. You can put jars in the boxes they came in to protect them from light.
18. Before using, check for signs of spoilage. If you notice bulging or unsealed lids, spurting liquid, mold, off-odor, or slimy food, *do not use*. Discard the food where humans and animals can't get to it. (See page 402 for instructions on how to dispose of spoiled food.) You can salvage the jars, however. Wash them thoroughly, rinse, and then boil for 15 minutes.
19. As a further precaution, heat home-canned foods to boiling, cover, and boil acid foods 10 minutes and low-acid foods 20 minutes more. If the food foams, smells bad, or shows other signs of spoilage, dispose of it.

BOILING WATER BATH CANNING RECIPES

When choosing produce for these home-canning recipes, freshness is extremely important. Once vegetables are picked, they begin to lose flavor and can also start to spoil quite quickly. Rush produce from the garden to the kitchen and into the canning jars. Experts say two hours from harvest to jar is the best time span for capturing flavor. If you can't prepare foods right away, be sure to refrigerate them immediately — but don't let them remain in the refrigerator for too long.

Canning for special diets

In many of the recipes that follow, sugar and salt are included for flavoring. If there's a special dieter in your family, you may omit the sugar and/or salt. However, you may *not* omit the sugar or salt called for in recipes for pickles and preserves; it is crucial to the canning process in these recipes.

Processing times

The times in the recipes that follow are given for both pints and quarts. If you use ½-pint jars, follow the times for pints; if using 12-ounce or 1½-pint jars, process as for quarts. Never skimp on processing times. The correct times are given in each recipe.

PEANUT BUTTER

If you use shelled, salted nuts, omit the salt in the recipe. Makes about 6 pints. In addition to the basic equipment for boiling water bath canning, you'll need a food grinder or chopper or you can use a blender or food processor.

2 quarts skinned, shelled, roasted Spanish peanuts
2 tablespoons salt

4 quarts skinned, shelled, roasted Virginia peanuts

1. Organize and prepare equipment and work area.
2. Grind nuts in grinder, chopper, blender, or food processor. Add the salt and grind again until smooth and creamy.
3. Pack into hot jars to within 1 inch of top, trying to pack so that no air bubbles remain. (Remember to use a non-metal tool for packing.)
4. Wipe tops and threads of each jar with damp cloth.
5. Put on lids and screw bands as manufacturer directs.
6. Process in a boiling water bath, 1 hour for both ½ pints and pints. Check water bath about every 10 to 15 minutes and add additional boiling water, if necessary, to keep jars covered with 1 to 2 inches of water.
7. Follow basic steps for boiling water bath canning, 10 through 18.

RHUBARB

You'll need about ½ to 1 cup of sugar for each quart of rhubarb. The exact amount depends on the sweetness of the rhubarb and your taste. You'll need the basic equipment and a large bowl.

2 pounds = 1 quart
15 pounds = 7 to 8 quarts

1. Choose tender, nicely colored stalks. Discard the leaves.
2. Wash rhubarb well, trim off ends, but don't pare.
3. Cut stalks into 1-inch lengths.
4. In a large bowl, mix ½ to 1 cup sugar with each quart of cut rhubarb. Let stand 3 to 4 hours.
5. Organize and prepare equipment and work area.
6. Heat rhubarb and any juice left in bowl to boiling. Pack into hot jars to within ½ inch of tops. If you run out of syrup, use boiling water to fill the jars to within ½ inch of tops of jars.

7. Run a slim, non-metal tool down along the inside of each jar to release air bubbles.
8. Add additional syrup or boiling water, if necessary, to fill to within ½ inch of tops of jars.
9. Wipe tops and threads of jars with damp cloth.
10. Put on lids and screw bands as manufacturer directs.
11. Process in a boiling water bath 15 minutes for pints or quarts.
12. Follow basic steps for boiling water bath canning, 10 through 19.

TOMATOES

Tomatoes are preserved best when the hot pack method is used. You'll need a large pot as well as the basic equipment for boiling water bath canning.

2½ to 3½ pounds = 1 quart
1 lug (30 pounds) = 10 quarts
1 bushel (53 pounds) = 15 to 20 quarts

1. Choose fresh, firm, red-ripe, perfect tomatoes. Be sure they have no black spots, cracks, or soft spots. Imperfect tomatoes could harbor microorganisms that are harmful, so never select them for canning. Prepare only enough tomatoes for 1 canner-load.
2. Organize and prepare equipment and work area.
3. In a large saucepan heat several inches of water to boiling. Using a wire basket, colander, strainer, or a slotted spoon, dip the tomatoes into the boiling water for 1 minute to loosen the skins. Then dip into cold water. Slip off the skins.
4. Cut out the core and quarter the tomatoes.
5. Heat the tomatoes slowly to boiling point, stirring often. (The natural juice from the tomatoes should be sufficient. If not, add ¼ cup water to the pot.) Pack into hot pint or quart jars. Add ½ teaspoon salt for pints and 1 teaspoon for quarts if desired. Pack to within ½ inch of tops.
6. Run a slim, non-metal tool down the inside of each jar to release air bubbles. Add hot juice or hot water to fill to within ½ inch of the tops.
7. Wipe tops and threads of jars with damp cloth.
8. Put on lids and screw bands as manufacturer directs.
9. Process in a boiling water bath canner 35 minutes for pints and 45 minutes for quarts.

10. Follow basic steps for boiling water bath canning, 10 through 19.

TOMATO JUICE

You'll need all the basic equipment for boiling water bath canning, including a sieve or strainer.

3 to 3½ pounds = 1 quart
1 bushel (53 pounds) = 12 to 16 quarts

1. Choose perfect, firm, red-ripe tomatoes. Wash, drain, and remove core and blossom ends.
2. Organize and prepare equipment and work area.
3. Cut tomatoes into quarters or smaller pieces.
4. Put tomatoes into a large saucepan or kettle and simmer until soft, stirring often.
5. Press through a sieve, strainer, or food mill and return juice to the pan or kettle.
6. Heat juice just to boiling.
7. Pour hot juice into hot pint or quart jars to within ½ inch of tops.
8. Add 1 teaspoon salt or 2 teaspoons salt-sugar mixture (1 part salt to 2 parts sugar) to each quart, if desired.
9. Wipe tops and threads of jars with damp cloth.
10. Put lids and screw bands as manufacturer directs.
11. Process in a boiling water bath 35 minutes for pints or quarts.
12. Follow the basic steps for boiling water bath canning, 10 through 18.

TOMATO JUICE COCKTAIL

A zippy blend, this cocktail is great for appetizers or aspics. The recipe makes 2 quarts. You will need all the basic equipment for boiling water bath canning.

2 quarts tomato juice (prepare as
   directed in the
   recipe for tomato juice)
3 tablespoons bottled lemon juice
1 tablespoon salt
2 teaspoons grated celery
1 teaspoon prepared horseradish
1 teaspoon onion juice
Dash Worcestershire sauce

1. Organize and prepare ingredients, equipment, and work area.
2. Combine all ingredients and heat to boiling.

3. Pour juice into hot pint or quart jars to within ½ inch of tops.
4. Wipe tops and threads with damp cloth.
5. Put on lids and screw bands as manufacturer directs.
6. Process in a boiling water bath for 35 minutes for pints or quarts.
7. Follow basic steps for boiling water bath canning, 10 through 18.

PICKLES AND RELISHES

Pickles, relishes, and chutneys are vegetables prepared with brine (salt and water) or vinegar and some sugar and spices. The vinegar acts as a preservative, keeping any spoilage organisms from growing. Sealing pickled foods in jars and processing in a boiling water bath helps keep them fresh, crisp, and free from mold.

Whole, sliced, or chunked vegetables cooked in vinegar or a vinegar-sugar syrup, can become pickles. Chopped or ground combinations cooked with vinegar, sugar, and spices become relishes. Chutneys are highly spiced fruit and/or vegetable combinations.

The old-fashioned dill pickles and sauerkraut are actually fermented in brine, rather than cooked in vinegar. The brine, plus the sugar from the cucumber or cabbage, promote a special kind of bacterial action that, over several days or weeks, changes cucumbers to pickles and transforms cabbage to kraut.

Pickling pointers

Because certain ingredients are very important for proper pickling, you'll need to be aware of some of the following pointers:

1. Use produce that is as fresh as possible. Take it from the garden to your kitchen and into jars just

as rapidly as possible. If you can't process the produce immediately, be sure to keep it refrigerated. Vegetables should be just barely ripe; they'll keep their shape better than if they were fully ripe. Always select cucumber varieties that have been created for pickling. The large salad cucumbers were developed for salads, not for pickles. Use smaller, less-pretty cukes, with pale skins, plenty of bumps, and black spines. Never use waxed cucumbers. If in doubt about the variety, check with your local Cooperative Extension Service Office. Select evenly shaped and sized vegetables for even-cooking and better-looking pickles.

2. Water is an important pickle ingredient, especially for long-brined pickles. Soft water is best. Hard water can cloud the brine or discolor the pickles. If you don't have soft water, boil hard water for 15 minutes, then let it stand overnight. Skim off the scum, then carefully dip out what you need so you won't get any sediment from the bottom. Then add 1 tablespoon of salt for each gallon; or you can use distilled water if your water is hard.

3. Salt, too, makes a difference. Table salt contains special additives to prevent it from caking in your shaker, and these materials can cloud brine. Iodized salt can darken brine. Use only pure, granulated salt, also known as kosher salt, pickling salt, or dairy salt. Most supermarkets stock it with canning supplies.

4. Vinegar is a crucial ingredient for pickle recipes. Check the label when you shop, and be sure to get a good quality vinegar of from 4 percent to 6 percent acidity (sometimes listed as 40 to 60 grain). Weaker vinegar will not pickle foods. Use distilled white vinegar for light-colored pickles, cider vinegar for darker foods or more interesting flavor. Pickle recipes use a lot of vinegar, so buy a big bottle. Buy a fresh bottle every year; vinegar loses its acidity with age. Do not use imported or gourmet vinegars unless the label states that the product has 4 to 6 percent acidity. Some salad vinegars or aged vinegars are too low in acidity for use when pickling foods. Vinegar of unknown acidity should not be used.

5. Sugar can be brown or white granulated, depending on the lightness or darkness of food to be pickled. Or, if you wish, use half corn syrup or honey and half sugar. Don't use sugar substitutes unless you follow their manufacturers' directions.

6. Spices must be fresh. Old spices will make your pickles taste musty. Most of our recipes call for whole spices, which give stronger flavor and don't color the pickles as much. We suggest you tie the spices in a cheesecloth bag and add them to the kettle during cooking, then remove the bag before packing the pickles into jars. Some cooks like to leave whole spices in the jars for stronger flavor and just for appearance's sake, but loose spices may darken the pickles somewhat.

7. Alum, lime, and other ingredients added to crisp or color pickles are not necessary, and we don't recommend their use. These ingredients are often found in old-fashioned recipes. If you follow the recipes here, you won't need to use any of these additives.

8. Utensils used for heating pickling liquids should be unchipped enamelware, stainless steel, aluminum, or glass. Use a lead-free crock, glass, or plastic container for fermenting or brining. Do not use copper, brass, iron, or galvanized utensils. The acids and salt used in pickling may react with these metals and create undesirable color changes. Harmful compounds may also result if the wrong utensils are used.

How to prevent problems

There are so many factors involved in pickling — weather and growing conditions, type of salt, acidity of vinegar, storage temperature, time from gathering to pickling, processing — that sometimes things go wrong. Here are some common problems and causes.

● **Soft or slippery pickles** could result from not removing the scum from the surface of the brine; from not keeping the cukes submerged in the brine; from using too weak a brine or vinegar, using hard water, or not removing the blossom of a cucumber; from not sealing each jar as it is filled; from not heating long enough to destroy microorganisms; or from storing in too warm a spot. Check jars carefully for signs of spoilage.

● **Shriveled pickles** may be the result of too strong brine, vinegar, syrup, or pickling solution, or may mean cucumbers didn't travel from the field to the kitchen fast enough.

● **Hollow pickles** could result from too long a time between pickling and processing, from improper curing or too high a temperature during fermentation, or from bad growing conditions.

Don't use any cucumbers that float as you wash them.

- **Dark pickles** indicate iron in the water or cooking utensil, ground spices or whole spices left in jars, cooking too long with spices, or hard water.

- **Faded, dull pickles** result from poor growing conditions or too mature cucumbers.

- **White sediment in the bottom of jars** isn't harmful. It could come from not using pure granulated salt, or could be the result of fermentation. Check jars carefully for signs of spoilage.

- **Spoiled pickles** mean you didn't process them properly; that you used old ingredients, non-standard jars, or old lids; or that the pickling solution wasn't boiling hot, or you filled too many jars before sealing them. In other words, you didn't follow directions! The signs of spoilage are listed on page 397 .

Heat treatment to prevent spoilage

Spoilage organisms travel in the air. Molds, yeasts, and bacteria can cause spoilage in pickles that are not processed in a boiling water bath canner. This heat treatment is the final step in making pickles. Unfortunately, many veteran makers of pickles feel that heat treatment is not necessary because the product is so high in vinegar. However, research has proved that these spoilage organisms can grow in pickled products in they are not destroyed by heat.

Heat processing does not change the flavor of the pickles, but it does ensure a safe product. The heat treatment for pickles is always very short. The filled jars are heated just long enough to kill the bacteria and prevent spoilage.

Processing procedures for fermented cucumbers and fresh-pack dills are slightly different from the usual hot water bath procedures. To prevent the development of a cooked flavor, you start timing as soon as the jars are lowered into the actively boiling water.

CRISPY PICKLE OR ZUCCHINI SLICES

These are fresh-packed pickles and don't require curing or brining. You may know them as bread-and-butter pickles. This recipe makes 7 (1-pint jars). In addition to the basic equipment, you will need a large mixing bowl, clean plastic dishpan, or enamel kettle.

6 pounds medium pickling cucumbers or medium zucchini
1 pound small white onions
2 large garlic cloves, if desired
⅓ cup pure granulated salt

2 trays ice cubes
2 cups sugar
3 cups white vinegar
1½ tablespoons mustard seed
1½ teaspoons mixed pickling spice
1 teaspoon celery seed
½ teaspoon turmeric

1. Organize and prepare ingredients, equipment, and work area.
2. Select perfect, evenly sized cucumbers or zucchini. Don't use any that float. Wash the cucumbers or zucchini thoroughly and scrub them with a brush. Cut off both ends and discard. Slice the cucumber or zucchini about ⅛-inch thick into a large mixing bowl, dishpan, or kettle.
3. Pare the onions and slice them ½-inch thick; add them to the mixing bowl. Pare the garlic cloves, stick each on on a wooden pick (for easy spotting and removal) and add them to the vegetables along with the salt. Mix them well.
4. Cover the cucumber-onion mixture with ice cubes and set aside for 3 hours.
5. Drain the vegetables very well. Pick out garlic.
6. In a large kettle, combine all the remaining ingredients and heat to boiling. Add the sliced vegetables and heat over medium-high heat 5 minutes.
7. Ladle into hot jars to within ½ inch of tops.
8. Run a slim, non-metal tool down along the insides of jars to release any air bubbles. Spoon in additional brine from the kettle to fill jars to within ½ inch of the tops, if necessary.
9. Wipe tops and threads of jars with damp cloth.
10. Put on lids and screw bands as manufacturer directs.
11. Process in a boiling water bath for 5 minutes. Start counting processing time after water returns to a boil. Follow basic steps for boiling water bath canning, 10 through 18.

ARTICHOKE RELISH

You'll need a large, deep container in which to soak the artichokes and a food grinder or processor. The recipe makes 10 (½-pint) jars. In addition to the basic equipment you will need a large mixing bowl and a food grinder or mill.

2 pounds artichokes
1 cup salt
1 gallon water
6 to 8 sweet red or
    green peppers
6 to 8 large onions

1 pound sugar
1 quart vinegar
2 tablespoons mustard
    seed
1 tablespoon turmeric
½ teaspoon salt

1. Select fresh, tender artichokes. Wash well and trim, if necessary.

2. Dissolve 1 cup salt in water in a large pan. Add artichokes and let stand overnight. Drain well.

3. Organize ingredients, equipment, and work area.

4. Remove stems and seeds from peppers and peel onions. Grind peppers, onions, and artichokes, using coarse blade. Set aside.

5. In a large preserving kettle, combine vinegar, sugar, and spices and heat to boiling.

6. Add ground vegetables and heat to boiling.

7. Ladle boiling mixture into hot jars to within ¼ inch of the tops.

8. Run a slim, non-metal tool down along the insides of jars to release any air bubbles. Add additional relish, if necessary, to within ¼ inch of tops.

9. Wipe tops and threads of jars with damp cloth.

10. Put on lids and screw bands as manufacturer directs.

11. Process in boiling water bath 10 minutes. Follow the basic steps for boiling water bath canning, 10 through 18.

1. Wash tomatoes, cut out stem ends, and slice very thin. You should have about 4 quarts of thin slices.

2. Pare onions and slice thin. You should have about 2 cups of sliced onions.

3. Arrange a layer of tomatoes in a large mixing bowl, plastic dishpan, or enamel kettle, then top with a layer of onions and a layer of the salt. Repeat until all the tomatoes, onions, and salt are used.

4. Cover and let tomatoes and onions stand several hours or overnight.

5. Organize and prepare ingredients, equipment, and work area.

6. Drain the tomato-onion slices thoroughly and put them in preserving kettle along with the peppers, sugar, celery, and mustard seed.

7. Tie whole cloves, allspice, and cinnamon in a small cheesecloth bag and add it to the kettle.

8. Pour in enough vinegar to barely cover vegetables.

9. Heat vegetables to boiling over high heat, then reduce the heat and simmer 2 hours, adding more vinegar, if necessary, to keep them covered.

10. Ladle the hot pickles into hot jars to within ¼ inch of tops. Run a slim, non-metal tool down along the insides of jars to release any air bubbles.

11. Spoon in additional cooking liquid from the preserving kettle to fill jars to within ¼ inch of the tops, if necessary.

12. Wipe tops and threads of jars with damp cloth.

13. Put on lids and screw bands as manufacturer directs.

14. Process in a boiling water bath for 15 minutes. Follow the basic steps for boiling water bath canning, 10 through 18.

SPICY GREEN TOMATO PICKLES

The unique blend of spices sets this pickle recipe apart from other recipes. The recipe makes 5 (1-pint) jars. You will need the basic equipment for boiling water bath canning plus a large mixing bowl, clean plastic dishpan, or enamel kettle. Tie up your spices in a cheesecloth spice bag.

2 to 2¼ dozen medium
    to large green tomatoes
6 to 8 onions
½ cup pure granulated
    salt
2 green peppers,
    chopped
3 cups brown sugar
2½ tablespoons celery
    seed

2½ tablespoons
    mustard seed
2 tablespoons whole
    cloves
2 tablespoons whole
    allspice
3 sticks cinnamon
About 1 quart vinegar

UNCOMMONLY GOOD CANTALOUPE PICKLES

These are extraordinarily good pickles to serve at parties or company dinners. The recipe makes 4 (½-pint) jars. You will need all the basic equipment plus a large saucepan and mixing bowl and a cheesecloth spice bag.

1 medium not-quite-
    ripe cantaloupe
1 quart vinegar
2 cups water
2 sticks cinnamon

1 tablespoon whole
    cloves
1 teaspoon ground
    mace
4 cups brown sugar

1. Pare and seed the cantaloupe, cut it into 1-inch chunks and put in large mixing bowl.

2. In a saucepan, combine vinegar and water. Tie whole spices in a cheesecloth bag and add to the saucepan along with mace. Heat to boiling.

3. Pour boiling, spiced vinegar over cantaloupe in mixing bowl. Set the bowl aside and let it stand overnight.

4. Organize ingredients, equipment, and work space.

5. Drain vinegar into saucepan and heat to boiling. Add cantaloupe and sugar; heat to boiling, then reduce the heat and simmer about 1 hour, or until transparent.

6. Meanwhile, wash and rinse jars; keep them hot in a low oven or pan of hot water.

7. Pack hot cantaloupe into the hot jars to within ½ inch of tops.

8. Boil the vinegar-sugar mixture about 5 minutes or until syrupy.

9. Pour the syrup into hot jars to within ½ inch of tops. Run a slim, non-metal tool down along the insides of jars to release any air bubbles. Add additional syrup, if necessary, to within ½ inch of tops.

10. Wipe tops and threads of jars with damp cloth.

11. Put on lids and screw bands as manufacturer directs.

12. Process in a boiling water bath for 10 minutes. Follow the basic steps for boiling water bath canning, 10 through 18.

DOROTHY'S ONION AND PEPPER RELISH

This versatile relish is perfect on burgers, franks, or spread in a thin layer inside toasted cheese sandwiches. The recipe makes 5 (½-pint) jars. You will need the basic equipment plus a food grinder or mill.

6 to 8 large onions	1 cup sugar
4 to 5 medium sweet red peppers	1 quart vinegar
	4 teaspoons salt
4 to 5 medium green peppers	

1. Organize and prepare ingredients, equipment, and work area.

2. Pare and cut onions into quarters. Stem and seed peppers. Put them through the coarse blade of a food grinder, or chop coarsely.

3. Combine chopped vegetables in large preserving kettle with all remaining ingredients.

4. Heat to boiling, then reduce heat and boil slowly 45 minutes, or until slightly thickened, stirring

occasionally.

5. Ladle into hot jars to within ¼ inch of tops. Run a slim, non-metal tool down along the insides of jars to release any air bubbles. Add additional relish to within ¼ inch of tops, if necessary.

6. Wipe tops and threads of jars with damp cloth.

7. Put on lids and screw bands as the manufacturer directs.

8. Process in a boiling water bath 15 minutes. Follow the basic steps for boiling water bath canning, 10 through 18.

CONFETTI CUCUMBER RELISH

Bright with red and green peppers, this recipe is a good way to use cukes that grew too big to pickle. The recipe makes about 6 (1-pint) jars. You will need all the basic equipment plus a large mixing bowl and a cheesecloth spice bag.

4 to 6 medium to large cucumbers	2 sticks cinnamon
4 medium sweet red peppers	1 quart vinegar
	1½ cups firmly packed brown sugar
4 medium green peppers	
1 cup chopped onion	
2 teaspoons turmeric	
½ cup pure granulated salt	
1 tablespoon mustard seed	
2 teaspoons whole cloves	

1. Organize ingredients, equipment, and work space.

2. Scrub cucumbers and cut off stem and blossom end.

3. Chop cukes. Stem, seed, and chop peppers. You should have 2 quarts chopped cucumbers and 2 cups of each color of chopped pepper. Combine them with onion in a large mixing bowl; sprinkle the vegetables with turmeric.

4. Dissolve salt in 2 quarts cold water; pour over vegetables. Let stand for 3 to 4 hours.

5. Drain vegetables thoroughly. Cover them again with cold water and let stand another hour. Drain well.

6. Tie the spices in a cheesecloth bag and put in a large preserving kettle with the vinegar and sugar. Heat to boiling, then pour over the vegetables. Cover and set aside in a cool place for several hours or overnight.

7. Slowly heat the vegetables and syrup to boiling, then pack relish into hot jars to within ¼ inch of tops. Run a slim, non-metal tool down along insides of jars to release any air bubbles. Add additional relish, if necessary, to bring to within ¼ inch of tops.

8. Wipe tops and threads of the jars with damp cloth.

9. Put on lids and screw bands as manufacturer directs.

10. Process in a boiling water bath for 10 minutes. Follow basic steps for boiling water bath canning, 10 through 18.

PRIZE—WINNING PICCALILLI

The sweet and sour taste of this relish makes it a favorite for hot dogs or company roasts. The recipe makes 4 (1-pint) jars. You will use the basic equipment along with a food grinder or food processor, a large mixing bowl, a cheesecloth-lined colander or sieve, and a cheesecloth spice bag.

12 to 16 medium green tomatoes	2 tablespoons whole mixed pickling spice
3 medium sweet red peppers	2 sticks cinnamon
3 medium green peppers	1 tablespoon whole cloves
2 to 3 large onions	4 whole allspice
2 pounds cabbage	½ teaspoon ground ginger
⅓ cup salt	½ teaspoon ground nutmeg
3½ cups vinegar	
1½ cups brown sugar	

1. Stem tomatoes; stem and seed peppers. Pare and cut onions into quarters. Cut cabbage into chunks.

2. Put all vegetables through coarse blade of food grinder or chop coarsely.

3. In large mixing bowl, combine vegetables and salt. Set bowl aside and let stand several hours or overnight.

4. Line large sieve or colander with cheesecloth and pour in the vegetables. Drain well, then lift edges of the cheesecloth and squeeze to press out the liquid.

5. Organize ingredients, equipment, and work space.

6. Combine vinegar and sugar in large preserving kettle.

7. Tie whole spices in a cheesecloth bag and add to the kettle. Stir in ground spices. Heat to boiling.

8. Add drained vegetables and heat to boiling. Reduce heat and simmer about 30 minutes, or until vegetables begin to get juicy.

9. Remove the spice bag.

10. Ladle into hot jars to within ¼ inch of tops. Run a slim, non-metal tool down along the insides of jars to release any air bubbles. Add additional relish, if necessary, to within ¼ inch of tops.

11. Wipe tops and threads of jars with a damp cloth.

12. Put on lids and screw bands as manufacturer directs.

13. Process in a boiling water bath for 10 minutes. Follow basic steps for boiling water bath canning, 10 through 18.

ZUCCHINI—PEPPER RELISH

Sometimes zucchini grows to gargantuan proportions; you can use up those squash monsters in this snappy relish. The recipe makes 6 (1-pint) jars. You'll need a cheesecloth-lined colander or strainer and a food processor or grinder in addition to the basic equipment.

4 to 5 pounds zucchini	2 teaspoons celery or seasoned salt
6 to 8 large onions	1 teaspoon turmeric
⅓ cup pure granulated salt	1 sweet red pepper, chopped
3½ cups vinegar	1 green pepper, chopped
3 cups sugar	
1 tablespoons ground nutmeg	
1 tablespoon dry mustard	

1. Wash zucchini, pare if desired or if skin is very tough. Pare and cut onions into quarters.

2. Put vegetables through coarse blade of food grinder or chop coarsely.

3. In large mixing bowl, combine ground zucchini and onions with salt; mix well. Set aside and let stand overnight.

4. Next day, organize and prepare ingredients, equipment, and work space.

5. Drain vegetables into a cheesecloth-lined colander. Rinse with cold water and drain again.

6. In large kettle, combine all remaining ingredients and heat to boiling.

7. Stir in zucchini and onions and heat to boiling, then reduce heat and simmer 30 minutes, stirring occasionally.

8. Ladle relish into hot jars to within ¼ inch of tops. Run a slim, non-metal tool down along the

insides of jars to release any air bubbles. Add additional relish, if necessary, to within ¼ inch of tops.

9. Wipe tops and threads of jars with damp cloth.

10. Put on lids and screw bands as manufacturer directs.

11. Process in a boiling water bath for 20 minutes. Follow the basic steps for boiling water bath canning, 10 through 19.

CORN RELISH

Cabbage and red and green peppers add color and texture to the golden corn. The recipe makes about 6 (1-pint) jars. You will need all the basic equipment for boiling water bath canning.

18 medium to large ears just-ripe sweet corn	1 quart vinegar
	1 cup water
1 quart chopped cabbage	1 tablespoon celery seed
1 cup chopped sweet red peppers	1 tablespoon mustard seed
1 cup chopped green peppers	1 tablespoon salt
1 cup chopped onion	1 to 2 tablespoons dry mustard
1 to 2 cups sugar	2 teaspoons turmeric, if desired

1. Organize and prepare ingredients, equipment, and work space.

2. Husk corn and remove the silk. Cook ears in boiling water for 5 minutes. Cut the kernels from the cob and measure 2 quarts of kernels.

3. Combine the corn and all remaining ingredients in a large preserving kettle.

4. Heat the corn to boiling over high heat, then reduce heat and simmer 20 minutes, stirring frequently.

5. Ladle, while still boiling, into hot jars to within ¼ inch of tops. Run a slim, non-metal tool down along the insides of jars to release any air bubbles. Add additional relish, if necessary, to bring to within ¼ inch of tops.

6. Wipe tops and threads of jars with damp cloth.

7. Put on lids and screw bands as manufacturer directs.

8. Process in a boiling water bath for 15 minutes. Follow the basic steps for boiling water bath canning, 10 through 18.

GREEN TOMATO RELISH

Here is a great way to use those tomatoes that failed to ripen before the first frost. The recipe makes about 4 (½-pint) jars. In addition to the basic equipment, you will need a food grinder or mill and a cheesecloth spice bag.

2½ pounds green tomatoes	½ teaspoon white pepper
2 sweet red peppers	2 teaspoons mustard seed
1 to 2 large onions	
1½ cups cider vinegar	1 teaspoon whole allspice
¾ cup light corn syrup	
4 teaspoons salt	2 bay leaves

1. Organize and prepare ingredients, equipment, and work space.

2. Wash tomatoes, peppers, and onions. Stem tomatoes, stem and seed peppers, pare and cut onions into quarters.

3. Put vegetables through coarse blade of food grinder or chop coarsely.

4. Put chopped vegetables into large kettle along with vinegar, syrup, salt, and pepper.

5. Tie whole spices in cheesecloth bag and add to kettle.

6. Heat to boiling, then reduce heat to a simmer. Cook, stirring occasionally, about an hour, or until almost all the liquid has evaporated.

7. Ladle the hot relish into hot jars to within ¼ inch of tops. Run a slim, non-metal tool down along the insides of jars to release any air bubbles. Add additional relish, if necessary, to bring to within ¼ inch of tops.

8. Wipe tops and threads of jars with damp cloth.

9. Put on lids and screw bands as manufacturer directs.

10. Process in a boiling water bath for 10 minutes. Follow basic steps for boiling water bath canning, 10 through 18.

EAST INDIA RELISH

Stir a few tablespoons of this relish into mayonnaise when making a chicken salad, or try it with pot roast. The recipe makes 6 (1-pint) jars. You'll need a shredder or food processor in addition to the basic equipment for boiling water bath canning.

1½ quarts chopped onions (about 6 to 8 medium onions)
1 quart firmly packed shredded carrots (about 1 pound)
1 quart peeled, diced green tomatoes (about 8 medium)
1 quart chopped zucchini (about 2 pounds)

2 cups light corn syrup
4 cups white vinegar
2 tablespoons salt
1 tablespoon ground coriander
2 teaspoons ground ginger
1 teaspoon crushed red pepper
½ teaspoon ground cumin

1. Organize ingredients, equipment, and work space.
2. In a preserving kettle, combine the ingredients. Heat over medium-high heat to boiling. Reduce the heat and simmer 5 minutes.
3. Spoon the relish evenly into hot jars to within ¼ inch of tops.
4. Spoon hot liquid from the kettle to within ¼ inch of tops of jars. Run a slim, non-metal tool down along the insides of jars to release any air bubbles. Add additional relish, if necessary, to within ¼ inch of tops.
5. Wipe tops and threads of jars with damp cloth.
6. Put on lids and screw bands as manufacturer directs.
7. Process in a boiling water bath for 15 minutes. Follow basic steps for boiling water bath canning, 10 through 19.

PICKLED BEETS

When you have finished the beets, save the liquid in the jar. Drop in shelled hard-boiled eggs and refrigerate for a day or two, and you will have pickled eggs to serve as an appetizer or snack. The recipe makes 6 (1-pint) jars. You will need a small saucepan and a cheesecloth spice bag in addition to the basic equipment.

4 dozen small fresh beets
2 cups sugar
3½ cups vinegar
1½ cups water
1 tablespoon salt

2 sticks cinnamon
1 teaspoon whole cloves
1 teaspoon whole allspice
1 lemon, sliced thin

1. Cut tops off beets, leaving roots and about ½ inch of stem. Wash thoroughly. Cover with water in saucepan; boil and cook until tender.
2. Organize and prepare ingredients, equipment, and work space.
3. Cool beets slightly, slip off skins, and slice, cut in half, or leave the beets whole. Reserve.
4. Combine sugar, vinegar, water, and salt in a saucepan.
5. Tie spices and lemon slices in a cheesecloth bag and add to saucepan. Heat to boiling and boil 5 minutes.
6. Pack beets into hot jars to within ¼ inch of tops.
7. Pour boiling syrup over beets in jars to within ¼ inch of tops. Run a slim, non-metal tool down along the insides of jars to release any air bubbles. Add additional boiling liquid, if necessary, to within ¼ inch of tops.
8. Wipe tops and threads of jars with a damp cloth.
9. Put on lids and screw bands as manufacturer directs.
10. Process in a boiling water bath for 30 minutes. Follow basic steps for boiling water bath canning, 10 through 18.

DILLED BEANS

This recipe makes 6 or 7 (1-pint) jars. You'll need the basic equipment for boiling water bath canning.

4 pounds green beans
¾ to 1 cup dill seed
18 to 21 whole black peppercorns

3 cups vinegar
3 cups water
⅓ cup pure granulated salt

1. Organize and prepare ingredients, equipment, and work space.
2. Wash beans well; drain. Cut off ends and trim beans, if necessary, so they will stand upright in jars. (If beans are not the right length to fit in jars, just trim ends and cut them into 1- or 2-inch lengths.)
3. Pack beans into hot jars. Put 2 tablespoons dill seed and 3 peppercorns into each jar.
4. In a saucepan, combine all the remaining ingredients and heat to boiling.
5. Pour the boiling brine into jars to within ¼ inch of tops. Run a slim, non-metal tool down along the inside of each jar to release any air bubbles. Add additional boiling liquid, if necessary, to within ¼ inch of tops.
6. Wipe tops and threads of jars with a damp cloth.
7. Put on lids and screw bands as manufacturer directs.
8. Process in a boiling water bath for 10 minutes. Follow the basic steps for boiling water bath canning, 10 through 17.

PETITE SWEET PICKLES

These crisp, sweet pickles take a little bit of attention twice a day for 4 days, but they are well worth the effort. The recipe makes 7 to 8 (1-pint) jars. You'll need a vegetable brush, a large mixing bowl or clean dishpan, a fork, and a small saucepan in addition to the basic equipment.

7 pounds small cucumbers (1½ to 3 inches long)	2 teaspoons celery seed
½ cup pure granulated salt	2 teaspoons mixed pickling spice
8 cups sugar	½ teaspoon turmeric
1½ quarts vinegar	½ teaspoon fennel, if desired
4 sticks cinnamon	2 teaspoons vanilla

1. Day 1, morning: Wash cucumbers thoroughly, scrubbing with a brush. Be sure to remove any blossoms left on the ends, but leave a tiny bit of stem in place.

2. Drain, then put in a large mixing bowl or other container and cover with boiling water.

3. In the afternoon (or 6 to 8 hours later): Drain the cucumbers well. Cover them with fresh boiling water.

4. Day 2, morning: Drain the cucumbers. Cover them with fresh boiling water.

5. In the afternoon: Drain the cucumbers. Add salt and cover them with fresh boiling water.

6. Day 3, morning: Drain the cucumbers and poke each cuke in several places with a fork.

7. In a saucepan, combine 3 cups of the sugar, 3 cups of the vinegar, the whole spices, turmeric, and fennel. Heat to boiling and pour over the cucumbers. They will be only partially covered.

8. In the afternoon: Drain the cukes and save the syrup. Combine the syrup with 2 cups of the vinegar and 2 cups of the sugar in the saucepan. Heat to boiling and pour it over the cucumbers.

9. Day 4, morning: Drain and save syrup. Heat syrup with 2 cups of the sugar and 1 cup of the vinegar to boiling. Pour over cucumbers (now pickles).

10. In the afternoon, organize and prepare the work space. Drain and save syrup.

11. Combine syrup with the remaining 1 cup sugar and vanilla. Heat to boiling.

12. Pack pickles into hot jars and pour in the syrup to within ¼ inch of tops. Run a slim, non-metal tool down along the insides of jars to release any air bubbles. Add additional hot liquid, if necessary, to within ¼ inch of tops of jars.

13. Wipe tops and threads of jars with a damp cloth.

14. Put on lids and screw bands as manufacturer directs.

15. Process in a boiling water bath for 5 minutes. Follow basic steps for boiling water bath canning, 10 through 18.

CURRIED PICKLES

If your zucchini flourished, you can use them instead of cucumbers in this recipe. The recipe makes 9 (1-pint) jars. Use the basic equipment for boiling water bath canning.

5 pounds medium cucumbers	1 tablespoon celery seed
1 quart white vinegar	2 teaspoons curry powder
2 cups sugar	
¼ cup pure granulated salt	
¼ cup mustard seed (or ¼ cup mixed pickling spice)	

1. Organize and prepare ingredients, equipment, and work space.

2. Wash cucumbers well and cut them into 1-inch chunks.

3. In a large pot or kettle, combine all the remaining ingredients and heat to boiling.

4. Add cucumbers and heat to boiling, then reduce heat and simmer 10 minutes.

5. Ladle them into hot jars to within ¼ inch of tops. Run a slim, non-metal tool down along the insides of jars to release any air bubbles. Add additional boiling liquid, if necessary, to within ¼ inch of tops.

6. Wipe tops and threads of jars with a damp cloth.

7. Put on lids and screw bands as manufacturer directs.

8. Process in a boiling water bath for 15 minutes. Follow basic steps for boiling water bath canning, 10 through 18.

PETER PIPER'S PICKLED PUMPKIN

While the kids cut pumpkins for Jack O'Lanterns, you can cut one for these spicy, orange-flavored pickles. The recipe makes 8 to 9 (1-pint) jars. You will need the basic equipment for boiling water bath canning.

1 (5- to 6-pound)
  pumpkin
4 to 5 cups sugar (or 2 to
  3 cups sugar, 2 cups
  honey)
1 quart white or cider
  vinegar
3 cups water
2 sticks cinnamon
2 (½-inch) chunks fresh
  ginger root or ¼ cup
  chopped crystallized
  ginger

1 tablespoon whole
  allspice
1½ teaspoons whole
  cloves
1 can (6 ounces) frozen
  orange juice
  concentrate, thawed

1. Organize and prepare ingredients, equipment, and work space.

2. Wash the pumpkin, cut it in 1-inch chunks, and pare. You should have about 4 quarts of chunks.

3. In preserving kettle, combine sugar, vinegar, water, and spices. (Tie spices in cheesecloth, if desired.)

4. Heat over high heat until boiling, stirring constantly.

5. Continue to heat and stir until the sugar dissolves.

6. Stir in the pumpkin chunks and orange juice concentrate and heat to boiling.

7. Reduce heat to simmer and cook, stirring occasionally, until pumpkin is just barely tender, about 30 minutes.

8. Ladle into hot jars to within ¼ inch of tops, spooning in the hot liquid from kettle. Run a slim, non-metal tool down along the insides of jars to release any air bubbles. Add additional hot liquid to within ¼ inch of tops, if necessary.

9. Wipe tops and threads of jars with a damp cloth.

10. Put the lids and screw bands in place as manufacturer directs.

11. Process in boiling water bath for 10 minutes. Follow basic steps for boiling water bath canning, 10 through 18.

BRINED DILL PICKLES

You will need a 5-gallon crock to cure these pickles or 4 or 5 (1-gallon) mayonnaise jars could be used (if you happen to know a restaurant or delicatessen owner). In addition, you will need a cover or lid, and a weight to hold lid in place, as well as the basic equipment and a cheesecloth-lined strainer. For kosher dill pickles, add 1 bay leaf, 1 clove garlic (pared), 1 piece hot red pepper, and ½ teaspoon mustard seed to each jar.

20 pounds small
  pickling cucumbers,
  about 3 to 6 inches long
3 bunches fresh or
  dried dill
¾ cup mixed pickling
  spice

6 grape leaves
  (optional)
2½ gallons distilled
  water
2½ cups vinegar
1⅓ cups pure
  granulated salt

1. Wash cucumbers very well, scrubbing with a brush. Be sure to cut off any blossom that remains on ends.

2. Drain cukes thoroughly or dry them with paper towels.

3. Put half the dill in the bottom of the 5-gallon crock along with half the pickling spice. (Or, if using 1-gallon jars, distribute half of the dill, spice, and grape leaves among the jars).

4. Put in cucumbers to within 3 or 4 inches of the top of the crock. Scatter the remaining dill, spice, and grape leaves over top of the cucumbers.

5. Stir the water, vinegar, and salt together until the salt dissolves. Pour mixture over cucumbers.

6. Cover the cucumbers with a lid, plate, or other clean cover that just fits inside crock and can hold the cucumbers down under the brine. Put a closed jar of water, clean rock, or other weight on the cover to hold the cucumbers down under brine. Set the crock aside at room temperature (70°F) for about 2 to 3 weeks, checking every day and skimming off the foam that forms. The pickles should be olive-green, crisp, and flavorful with no white spots inside.

7. Organize and prepare ingredients, equipment, and the work space.

8. Pack pickles into jars to within ¼ inch of the tops, adding some dill to each jar.

9. Strain the brine into a saucepan; heat to boiling. The brine will probably be cloudy, due to fermentation. For sparkling clear brine, substitute new brine: Combine 1 gallon water, 4 cups vinegar, and ½ cup salt. Heat to boiling and pour over the pickles to within ¼ inch of tops of jars.

10. Run a slim, non-metal tool down along inside of jars to release any air bubbles. Add additional hot brine, if necessary, to within ¼ inch of tops.

11. Wipe off tops and threads of jars.

12. Put on lids and screw bands as manufacturer directs.

13. Process in a boiling water bath for 15 minutes. Start counting processing time as soon as filled jars are lowered into actively boiling water. Follow basic steps for boiling water bath canning, 10 through 18.

FRESH-PACK DILL PICKLES

These pickles are similar in flavor to the long-brined dill pickles, but less preparation time is involved. This recipe yields 9 quarts. Use the basic equipment for boiling water bath canning.

18 pounds small pickling cucumbers, 3 to 5 inches long
1½ cups pure granulated salt
2 gallons distilled water
1½ quarts vinegar
¾ cup pure granulated salt
¼ cup sugar
2¼ quarts distilled water
2 tablespoons whole mixed pickling spice
2 teaspoons per quart jar whole mustard seed
1 to 2 cloves garlic per quart jar (if desired)
3 heads dill or 1 tablespoon dill seed per quart jar

1. Wash cucumbers thoroughly. Scrub with vegetable brush. Drain, or dry with paper towels.
2. Combine 2 gallons water with 1½ cups salt. Stir until salt has dissolved.
3. Place cucumbers in a 5-gallon stone crock or plastic pail. Cover with salt and water mixture. Let stand overnight. Drain.
4. Combine vinegar, salt, sugar, water, and mixed pickling spices (tied in a clean, thin white cloth or cheesecloth). Heat to boiling.
5. Pack cucumbers into clean, hot quart jars. Add mustard seed, dill plant or seed, and garlic to each jar.
6. Cover each jar with boiling liquid to within ½ inch of tops of jars.
7. Wipe off tops and threads of jars.
8. Put on lids and screw bands according to manufacturer's directions.
9. Process jars in boiling water bath canner for 20 minutes. Start to count the processing time as soon as the hot jars are placed in the actively boiling water.
10. Follow basic steps for boiling water bath canning 10 through 18.

KATHY'S CATSUP

Tangy and fragrant, this catsup is easy to make if you use a blender to simplify the preparation. The recipe makes about 5 pints. In addition to the basic equipment, you will need a blender or food processor, a large mixing bowl, and a cheesecloth spice bag.

1 peck (8 quarts) ripe tomatoes
3 onions
2 dried red peppers, chopped or 1 teaspoon dried red peppers
1½ bay leaves
1 tablespoon whole allspice
1 clove garlic, pared
1 stick cinnamon
2 cups vinegar
½ cup sugar
1 tablespoon celery salt

1. Organize and prepare ingredients, equipment, and work space.
2. Wash, stem, and cut tomatoes into quarters. Pare and cut onions into quarters.
3. Fill blender container almost to top with the tomatoes and blend until smooth.
4. Set strainer over a large bowl and pour the blended tomatoes through it. Repeat the blending and straining for the remaining tomatoes, adding the onion quarters to the last blender batch of tomatoes.
5. Measure 4 quarts of puree into a large preserving kettle.
6. Tie the spices in a cheesecloth bag and add it to the kettle, along with all the remaining ingredients.
7. Heat to boiling over high heat, stirring constantly. Then reduce the heat slightly and boil until thick, about 1 hour, stirring frequently. Reduce the heat and stir more often during the end of cooking time to prevent sticking.
8. Skim foam with a slotted spoon, if necessary.
9. Ladle the hot catsup into hot jars to within ¼ inch of tops. Run a slim, non-metal tool down along the inside of each jar to release any air bubbles. Add additional catsup sauce, if necessary, to within ¼ inch of tops of jars.
10. Wipe tops and threads of jars with damp cloth.
11. Put on lids and screw bands as manufacturer directs.
12. Process in a boiling water bath for 10 minutes. Follow the basic steps for boiling water bath canning, 10 through 18.

CHILI SAUCE

Making this hearty chili sauce is a popular way to use up a surplus of tomato crop. The recipe makes about 8 (1-pint) jars. Use the basic equipment for boiling water bath canning.

3 quarts chopped,
stemmed, peeled
tomatoes
2 large green peppers,
stemmed, seeded, and
chopped
8 medium onions,
pared and chopped

1 cup chopped celery
1½ cups brown sugar
2 cups vinegar
1½ teaspoons ground
cinnamon
½ teaspoon cloves
½ teaspoon nutmeg

1. Organize and prepare ingredients, equipment, and work space.

2. Combine tomatoes, peppers, onions, and celery in preserving kettle. Heat to boiling, then reduce heat and simmer 1 hour, stirring occasionally.

3. Stir in all remaining ingredients and simmer 20 to 30 minutes longer, stirring frequently.

4. Ladle hot chili sauce into the hot jars to within ¼ inch of tops. Run a slim, non-metal tool down along the inside of each jar to release any air bubbles. Add additional chili sauce, if necessary, to within ¼ inch of tops of jars.

5. Wipe tops and threads of jars with damp cloth.

6. Put on lids and screw bands as manufacturer directs.

7. Process in boiling water bath for 15 minutes. Follow basic steps for boiling water bath canning, 10 through 19.

SAUERKRAUT

Creamy-white and tangy, kraut is fermented cabbage. You will need a 5-pound crock, a large heavy-duty plastic food bag, a kitchen scale, a large mixing bowl or other non-metallic container, and the basic equipment. Put the crock in a cool, out-of-the-way spot while the kraut ferments. The recipe makes 16 to 18 quarts.

40 pounds cabbage
1 pound (1½ cups)
pure granulated salt

1. Choose firm, mature heads of cabbage and remove outer leaves. Cut out any bad portions.

2. Wash cabbage well and drain.

3. Cut heads in half or in quarters and cut out cores.

4. Shred with a kraut shredder (or sharp knife) into shreds no thicker than a dime.

5. Weigh 5 pounds of shredded cabbage and put it into a large mixing bowl or other non-metallic container.

6. Sprinkle the cabbage with 3 tablespoons salt and mix well; let it stand several minutes until slightly wilted.

7. Firmly pack salted cabbage in even layers in a large, clean crock or other non-metallic container (such as a jar or a brand-new, clean plastic wastebasket or garbage can).

8. Repeat, weighing 5 pounds of cabbage and mixing it with 3 tablespoons salt, packing it into the crock until all the cabbage is used or until the cabbage is packed to within 3 or 4 inches of the top of the crock.

9. Press down firmly on the shredded cabbage in the crock until liquid comes to the surface.

10. Put a heavy-duty food bag on top of the kraut in crock and pour enough water into bag to completely cover surface of the kraut in the crock. Add enough additional water to provide sufficient weight to hold cabbage underneath brine. Tie bag with a twist tie, rubber band, or string.

11. Set the crock in a cool place (68° F to 72° F) for 5 to 6 weeks or until the mixture has stopped bubbling. The kraut should be creamy-white, mildly tart, and tangy.

12. When the kraut has stopped fermenting, transfer it — several quarts at a time — to a large kettle and heat just to simmering, but do not boil.

13. Organize equipment and prepare work space.

14. Pack the hot sauerkraut into hot quart jars to within ½ inch of tops.

15. Pour in the hot sauerkraut juice (from the kettle) to within ½ inch of tops. Run a slim, non-metal tool down along the insides of jars to release any air bubbles. Add additional hot juice, if necessary, to within ½ inch of tops.

16. Wipe tops and threads of jars with damp cloth.

17. Put on lids and screw bands as manufacturer directs.

18. Process in a boiling water bath, 15 minutes for pints, 20 minutes for quarts. Follow basic steps for boiling water bath canning, 10 through 19.

MUSTARD PICKLES

Unless you have an enormous cauldron, you may need to simmer the vegetables, vinegar, and spices in two batches, cooking about 3 quarts chopped vegetables and about 5 cups vinegar spice mixture for each batch. You will also need a large mixing bowl and the basic equipment for boiling water bath canning. Also known as Dutch salad, this recipe makes about 13 (1-pint) jars.

1 head (about 2 pounds) cauliflower, separated into small flowerets
1 head (about 2 pounds) cabbage, coarsely chopped
1 bunch celery, coarsely chopped
1 quart green tomatoes, coarsely chopped
1 quart cucumbers, coarsely chopped
1 quart onions, chopped
3 sweet red peppers, chopped
1 gallon water
1 cup pure granulated salt
3 cups sugar
1 cup flour
1 cup vinegar
3 pints (6 cups) white or cider vinegar
1 pint water
2 tablespoons celery seed
2 tablespoons mustard seed
1 tablespoon turmeric

1. Put all vegetables in large bowl or container. Combine the 1 gallon water and salt and stir until salt dissolves. Pour salt-water mixture over vegetables and let stand overnight.

2. The next morning, drain vegetables well.

3. Organize and prepare ingredients, equipment, and work space.

4. In preserving kettle, stir sugar and flour together, then mix in the 1 cup vinegar until smooth.

5. Stir in all remaining ingredients and heat to boiling.

6. Add drained vegetables. Heat to boiling, then lower the heat and simmer 20 minutes, stirring frequently.

7. Ladle relish into clean, hot, pint jars to within ¼ inch of tops. Run a slim, non-metal tool down along the insides of jars to release any air bubbles. Add additional relish, if necessary, to bring to within ¼ inch of tops.

8. Wipe off tops and threads of jars with damp cloth.

9. Put on lids and screw bands as manufacturer directs.

10. Process in a boiling water bath for 20 minutes. Follow basic steps for boiling water bath canning, 10 through 18.

PICKLED PEPPERS

Wear rubber gloves to protect your hands as you prepare the peppers—they can burn your skin. And never touch your face, or especially your eyes, while you are working with hot peppers. In addition to the basic equipment, you will need a large mixing bowl and a candy or meat thermometer. To keep peppers crisp, process in a simmering water bath of 170°F. This recipe makes about 8 pints.

4 quarts long red, green, or yellow peppers (Hungarian, banana, or other varieties)
1 gallon water
1½ cups salt
2½ quarts vinegar
2 cups water
¼ cup sugar
2 tablespoons prepared horseradish
2 cloves garlic, pared and stuck on wooden picks

1. Select fresh, tender, evenly sized peppers. Wash well. Wearing rubber gloves, cut two small slits in each pepper.

2. In large mixing bowl, dissolve the salt in the 1 gallon water. Add peppers and let stand in a cool place 12 to 18 hours.

3. Drain, rinse, and drain again. Organize remaining ingredients, the equipment, and work space.

4. In a large preserving kettle, combine all remaining ingredients. Heat to boiling, then reduce heat, and simmer 15 minutes. Remove garlic.

5. Pack peppers into hot jars to within ½ inch of the tops.

6. Heat simmering liquid to boiling and pour over peppers to within ¼ inch of tops of jars. Run a slim, non-metal tool down along the insides of jars to release any air bubbles. Add additional boiling liquid, if necessary, to within ¼ inch of tops of jars.

7. Wipe tops and threads of jars with damp cloth.

8. Put on lids and screw bands as manufacturer directs.

9. Process in a simmering water bath for 10 minutes. Use thermometer to determine simmering temperature (170°F). Start counting processing time as soon as water reaches 170°F. Adjust heat. Follow basic steps for boiling water bath canning 10 through 18.

PICKLED WATERMELON RIND

What a wonderful way to use up every bit of your home-grown watermelon! This recipe makes about 4 quarts. You will need a large mixing bowl or new, clean plastic dishpan or pail and a cheesecloth spice bag, in addition to the basic equipment for boiling water bath canning.

8 pounds watermelon rind
1 gallon cold water
1 tablespoon salt
6 cups sugar
6 cups light corn syrup
1 quart water
1 quart cider vinegar
8 sticks cinnamon
1 tablespoon whole cloves
1 lemon, sliced

1. Cut all green and pink portions off watermelon rind and cut in 1-inch chunks. Put in large mixing bowl or new, clean, plastic dishpan or pail.

2. Dissolve salt in water and pour over rind cubes. Add more water, if necessary, to cover cubes. Let stand 6 hours or overnight.

3. Organize and prepare ingredients, equipment, and work area.

4. Drain rind and rinse. Put in large preserving kettle or saucepot and add water to cover.

5. Simmer until rind is tender, about 20 minutes. Drain and set aside.

6. Measure sugar, corn syrup, water, and vinegar into preserving kettle and heat to boiling. Meanwhile tie spices in cheesecloth bag and add to kettle along with lemon. Boil 10 minutes.

7. Add rind to spice-syrup and simmer until rind is transparent. Remove spice bag.

8. Pack watermelon rind into hot jars to within ¼ inch of the tops. Pour hot syrup into jars to within ¼ inch of tops.

9. Run a slim, non-metal tool down along the insides of jars to release any air bubbles. Add additional hot syrup, if needed, to bring to within ¼ inch of tops.

10. Wipe tops and threads of jars with damp cloth.

11. Put on lids and screw bands as manufacturer directs.

12. Process in boiling water bath for 10 minutes. Follow basic steps for boiling water bath canning, 10 through 18.

PICKLED TINY ONIONS

If you make your own gift baskets at holiday times, include a jar of these zesty appetizers. The recipe makes 6 (1-pint) jars. You will need a large saucepan in addition to the basic equipment for boiling water bath canning.

4 quarts tiny white onions	3 tablespoons grated fresh or prepared horseradish
1 cup pure granulated salt	
2 quarts white vinegar	6 small red pepper pods
2 cups sugar	3 bay leaves, broken in half
3 tablespoons mustard seed	

1. Wash onions well; drain. Put onions in the sink or a large pan and pour boiling water over to cover. Let them stand 2 minutes, then drain.

2. Pour cold water over onions to cover. Let them stand just until cool. Drain and pare them.

3. Put the onions in a saucepan or a large mixing bowl, sprinkle with salt, and pour cold water over them to cover. Set the onions aside and let them stand overnight.

4. Organize remaining ingredients, the equipment, and work space.

5. Drain the onions, then rinse them well with cold water. Set them aside in a colander while preparing the syrup.

6. In a large kettle, combine the vinegar, sugar, mustard seed, peppercorns, and horseradish, and heat to boiling. Boil 2 minutes.

7. Add onions and heat to boiling.

8. Spoon the onions into hot jars, packing them gently to within ¼ inch of the tops.

9. Slip a red pepper pod and ½ bay leaf into each jar. Pour in the boiling hot syrup to within ¼ inch of the tops of jars. Run a slim, non-metal tool down along the insides of jars to release any air bubbles.

10. Wipe tops and threads of jars with damp cloth.

11. Put on lids and screw bands as manufacturer directs.

12. Process in a boiling water bath for 10 minutes. Follow basic steps for boiling water bath canning, 10 through 18.

RHUBARB CHUTNEY

Sweet-sour, spicy, and delicious. Try as a meat or poultry accompaniment. The recipe makes about 4 pints. You will need the basic equipment for boiling water bath canning.

2 quarts chopped
  rhubarb
3½ cups brown sugar
1½ cups chopped
  seedless raisins
½ cup vinegar
½ cup chopped onion
1 teaspoon ground
  allspice
1 teaspoon ground
  cinnamon
1 teaspoon ground
  ginger
1 teaspoon salt

1. Organize and prepare ingredients, equipment, and work area.

2. Combine rhubarb, sugar, raisins, vinegar, and onion in preserving kettle. Heat to boiling, then reduce heat to simmering. Simmer until thick, about 25 minutes, stirring occasionally.

3. Add spices and simmer 5 minutes longer.

4. Ladle into hot jars to within ¼ inch of tops.

5. Run a slim, non-metal tool down along the inside of each jar to release any air bubbles. Add additional chutney, if needed, to within ¼ inch of tops.

6. Wipe tops and threads of jars with damp cloth.

7. Put on lids and screw bands as manufacturer directs.

8. Process in boiling water bath 5 minutes. Follow the basic steps for boiling water bath canning, 10 through 18.

FRUIT RECIPES

Many fruits, among them apples, apricots, peaches, pears, and nectarines, tend to turn dark soon after air hits the cut surfaces. This darkening is caused by the natural enzymes found in all fruits and vegetables. The job of enzymes is to decay the produce. Oxygen in the air hastens this process on cut surfaces. In order to retard this browning or darkening process, light-colored fruits must be treated with crystalline ascorbic acid or a commercially prepared citric acid mixture. To use ascorbic acid crystals, combine 2 tablespoons crystalline ascorbic acid with one gallon water. Place peeled or cut fruit in the ascorbic acid mixture until you are ready to fill the canning jars. Fruits should not be held in this manner for more than 20 minutes before being transferred to the canning jars. Untreated fruits will continue to darken after they have been canned. When using a commercial product, follow the manufacturer's directions. Fruits may darken also if proper canning procedures are not followed. Darkening may be caused by one or more of the following:

- Fruit was not processed in boiling water bath long enough.
- Water did not reach a full rolling boil during processing.
- Water was not kept at a full rolling boil during processing.
- Processing time was inaccurate.
- Adjustments for altitude were not made.
- Boiling water was less than 1 inch above tops of jars.
- Pears, apples, or pineapples were packed raw. These fruits keep best if precooked before canning (that is, if they are canned by the hot pack method).

Before you begin preparing fruits for canning, read the entire recipe, and assemble all equipment and ingredients.

The boiling water bath canner used for processing jars of homemade jams and jellies must be large enough to accommodate the jars and leave adequate room for the action of the boiling water.

Syrups for canning fruit

	Sugar	Water	Yield
very light syrup	1 cup	1 quart	4½ cups
light	2 cups	1 quart	5 cups
medium	3 cups	1 quart	5½ cups
heavy	4¾ cups	1 quart	6½ cups

Combine desired amount of sugar with 1 quart water and bring to a boil, stirring often. Cover fruits with hot syrup.

APPLES (hot pack)

1 bushel = 16 to 20 quarts
2 to 3 pounds = 1 quart

1. Prepare light or medium syrup.
2. Wash the apples, peel, and cut into rings or slices.
3. Drop pieces into ascorbic acid water (2 tablespoons ascorbic acid dissolved in 1 gallon water) as you slice. Drain before precooking.
4. Simmer apples in sugar syrup 5 minutes.
5. Using a wide-mouth funnel, spoon apples into quart jars, leaving ½ inch head space.
6. Wipe jar rims with clean damp cloth.
7. Adjust lids and screw bands as manufacturer directs.
8. Process pints for 15 minutes and quarts for 20 minutes in a boiling water bath canner.
9. Remove jars, cool, label, date, and store.

↕ HEADSPACE

Some foods expand after being processed, and it's important to leave room, or head space, for this expansion. Always check your recipe to determine the head space required for the of produce you are preparing.

APPLESAUCE

2½ to 3½ pounds = 1 quart applesauce

1. Wash and quarter apples. Simmer, covered, in a small amount of water or apple cider until tender (15 minutes).
2. Press apples through a sieve or food mill.
3. If desired, add about ¼ cup sugar per 4 medium apples, or sweeten with honey to taste.
4. Fill jars leaving ½ inch head space.
5. Wipe jar rims with damp cloth.
6. Adjust lids according to manufacturer's directions.
7. Process pints or quarts 15 minutes in boiling water bath canner.
8. Remove jars, cool, label, date, and store.

APRICOTS

24 pounds = 10 to 12 quarts
2 to 2½ pounds = 1 quart

1. Wash apricots and blanch 30 seconds. Plunge into ice water for 30 seconds to arrest cooking action.
2. Slip skins off, cut each apricot in half, and remove pits.
3. To keep pieces from darkening, drop in ascorbic acid water (2 tablespoons ascorbic acid dissolved in 1 gallon water). Drain.
4. Pack in jars to within ½ inch of tops. Cover with syrup. Adjust lids.
5. Process in boiling water bath 25 minutes for pints and 30 minutes for quarts.
6. Remove jars, cool, label, date, and store.

BERRIES (soft)

Soft berries include blackberries, blueberries, and raspberries. Strawberries lose color and flavor when canned; they are best preserved by freezing.

4 to 8 pint-size baskets = 1 quart

1. Use fully ripe berries. Sort. Wash carefully by lifting from water. Drain. Cap and stem if necessary.
2. Pack raw berries into clean hot jars. Shake berries down to pack without crushing.
3. Cover with boiling medium syrup leaving ½ inch head space.
4. Wipe rims of jars with damp cloth.

5. Adjust lids and process in boiling water bath canner for 15 minutes for pints and quarts.

6. Remove jars, cool, label, date, and store.

BERRIES (firm)

Firm berries include currants and elderberries. See separate recipe for canning gooseberries and blueberries.

1 crate = 32 to 36 pints
1⅓ to 1½ pounds = 1 pint

1. Select fully ripened berries. Sort, wash carefully in cold water, and drain.

2. Add ½ cup sugar for each cup of berries. Place berries and sugar in large pan and bring to boil. Shake pan to prevent berries from sticking.

3. Pack hot berries into clean jars leaving ½ inch head space.

4. Wipe rims of jars with damp cloth.

5. Adjust lids and process in boiling water bath canner for 15 minutes.

6. Remove jars, cool, label, date, and store.

WHOLE CRANBERRY SAUCE

8 cups cranberries
4 cups sugar
4 cups water
zest of 1 lemon (optional)

Yield: 6 pints

1. Sort berries, removing any green or soft fruit.

2. Wash by lifting from water; remove any stems.

3. Combine sugar and water, bring to a boil, and boil for 5 minutes.

4. Add the cranberries and lemon zest (if desired).

5. Boil without stirring until skins burst, (about 10 minutes).

6. Ladle into hot jars to within ½ inch of tops of jars.

7. Wipe jar rims with damp cloth.

8. Adjust lids and process jars in boiling water bath canner for 15 minutes for pints and quarts.

9. Remove jars, cool, label, date, and store.

BLUEBERRIES

These firm berries are best preserved by freezing;

however, the method below can be successful for berries to be used in baking.

32 baskets = 16 pints

1. Select fully ripe berries. Wash, sort, and remove stems.

2. Place about 2 quarts berries in a large piece of cheesecloth or muslin. Holding cloth by the corners, dip blueberries into boiling water until spots appear on cloth.

3. Dip in ice water for 30 seconds to stop the cooking process.

4. Pack into clean hot jars leaving ½ inch head space. Do not add sugar or liquid to the blueberries.

5. Adjust lids and process in boiling water bath canner for 15 minutes.

6. Remove jars, cool, label, date, and store.

7. Repeat with next 2 quarts of berries.

CHERRIES (sweet or sour)

2 to 3 pounds = 1 quart
1 bushel = 22 to 23 quarts

1. Stem, wash, sort, remove stems; remove pits if desired.

2. If cherries are left whole, prick each one to prevent splitting (pie cherries should be pitted and may be canned in water).

3. Pack cherries into clean hot jars, shaking down to pack firmly. Cover sour cherries with boiling heavy syrup or water to within ½ inch of tops of jars. Use light syrup for sweet cherries.

4. Wipe jar rims with clean damp cloths.

5. Adjust lids and process jars in boiling water bath canner for 15 minutes.

6. Remove jars, cool, label, date, and store.

GOOSEBERRIES

4 to 8 ½-pint baskets = 1 quart

1. Sort, and remove stems. Wash and drain.

2. Pour ½ cup boiling medium syrup in each clean quart-size jar.

3. Add berries, shaking jar to pack berries firmly.

4. Fill jars to within ½ inch of top.

5. Wipe jar rims with clean damp cloth.

6. Adjust lids and process in boiling water bath canner for 15 minutes.

7. Remove jars, cool, label, date, and store.

FIGS

5 to 6 pounds = 2 to 3 quarts

1. Select fully ripe figs. Sort and wash.
2. Place figs in large pot and add small amount of water. Bring to a boil. Allow figs to sit in pot, covered, for 3 to 4 minutes. Drain.
3. Pack hot figs into clean pint or quart jars.
4. Add 2 teaspoons lemon juice to each pint or 4 teaspoons to each quart.
5. Fill jars to within ½ inch of tops of jars with hot medium or heavy syrup.
6. Wipe jar rims with clean damp cloth.
7. Adjust lids and process in boiling water bath canner for 1 hour. Add more boiling water if necessary during processing. Make sure there is 1 to 2 inches water above tops of jars at all times.
8. Remove jars, cool, label, date, and store.

PEACHES OR NECTARINES (raw pack)

1 bushel = 18 to 24 quarts
2 to 3 pounds = 1 quart

1. Use fully ripened (not hard) freestone peaches. Sort, wash, and peel. Cut each peach in half and remove pit.
2. Use a spoon to scrape out cavities to remove pink or red fibers (center will turn an ugly brown during storage if not scraped).
3. To keep from darkening, drop peach halves into ascorbic acid water (2 tablespoons crystalline ascorbic acid dissolved in 1 gallon water). Work quickly. Drain.
4. Pack peach halves cut side down in clean hot jars, leaving 1 inch head space.
5. Cover peaches with boiling light or medium syrup to within ½ inch of tops of jars.
6. Wipe jar rims with clean damp cloth.
7. Adjust lids and process in boiling water bath canner for 25 minutes for pints and 30 minutes for quarts.
8. Remove jars, cool, label, date, and store.

PEACHES OR NECTARINES (hot pack)

1 bushel = 18 to 24 quarts
2 to 3 pounds = 1 quart

1. Follow steps 1 to 3 for raw pack method (see previous recipe).
2. Heat peach halves in thin or medium syrup.
3. Pack with cut sides down into clean hot jars

to within 1 inch of tops of jars. Cover with hot cooking syrup to within ½ inch of tops of jars.
4. Wipe rims of jars with clean damp cloth.
5. Adjust lids and process in boiling water bath canner for 15 minutes for pints and 20 minutes for quarts.
6. Remove jars, cool, label, date, and store.

PEARS (hot pack only)

1 bushel = 18 to 24 quarts
2 to 2½ pounds = 1 quart

1. Use fully ripened pears that are firm and not soft. Sort, wash, and peel.
2. Cut pears in half and core with a small melon baller or paring knife (quarter if desired).
3. To prevent darkening, drop cut pears in ascorbic acid water (2 tablespoons ascorbic acid dissolved in 1 gallon water). If using a commercial preparation, follow manufacturer's instructions. Work quickly. Drain.
4. Boil pears for 3 to 5 minutes in light or medium syrup.
5. Pack hot pears into clean hot jars to within ½ inch of tops of jars.
6. Cover with hot cooking syrup to within ½ inch of tops of jars. If desired, and to further protect color, add 1 teaspoon lemon juice to each quart.
7. Wipe jar rims with clean damp cloth.
8. Adjust lids and process in boiling water bath canner for 20 minutes for pints and 25 minutes for quarts.
9. Remove jars, cool, label, date, and store.

PLUMS (raw pack)

This recipe includes fresh prune plums. Greenage plums are best for canning.

28 pound box = 12 to 15 quarts
2 to 2½ pounds = 1 quart

1. Select fully ripe plums that are just beginning to soften.
2. Wash and drain. Prick each plum if plums are to be left whole. This pricking will not prevent split skins but it does help prevent the plums from bursting.
3. If desired, cut each plum in half and remove pit.
4. Place plums in clean, hot jars to within ½ inch of tops of jars.

5. Cover with hot, light to medium syrup to within ½ inch of tops of jars.

6. Wipe rims with clean damp cloth.

7. Adjust lids and process in boiling water bath canner for 20 minutes for pints and 25 minutes for quarts.

8. Remove jars, cool, label, date, and store.

PLUMS (hot pack)

28 pounds = 12 to 15 quarts
2 to 2½ pounds = 1 quart

1. Follow steps 1 to 4 for raw pack (see previous recipe).

2. Heat plums in medium or light syrup.

3. Pack hot plums in clean, hot jars to within ½ inch of tops of jars.

4. Cover with hot cooking syrup leaving ½ inch head space.

5. Wipe jar rims with clean damp cloth.

6. Process in boiling water bath canner for 15 minutes for pints and 20 minutes for quarts.

7. Remove jars, cool, label, date, and store.

JELLIES
(Jams, preserves, conserves, and marmalades)

The perfect jelly is as marvelous a creation as any jewel. Jelly sparkles and has brilliance, clarity, and facets that reflect light and color. Jellies are the most pleasing of all preserves to make. Jelly is made from clear fruit juices (free of pulp), cooked with sugar and sometimes with pectin added. It should be firm and able to stand alone when emptied from a jar. When cut with a knife, jelly should maintain the angle of the cut.

BASIC EQUIPMENT

It's important to use the right equipment and techniques for making jelly. Skipping a step could result in syrupy jelly; using the wrong size pot could be extremely messy. The following list of equipment looks long, but probably includes only a few items that are not already in your kitchen. Items that you may need to buy are investments in future jelly-making.

- Kettle or saucepot. You will need a large 8- to 10-quart, nonreactive (stainless steel, aluminum, or enamel) kettle or saucepot. (If you are not sure how large your pot is, measure how much water it will hold.) Jelly needs space to boil high and wide, so this pot is essential to jelly-making. Never use cast iron or copper pots; these will discolor fruit juices and may give an off taste to the jelly.

- Jars (with two-piece lids). Jelly glasses are no longer accepted as adequate for safe jelly-making. Old peanut butter jars and other such containers are equally unsafe. Sealing jars with paraffin and the use of the open-kettle method have been ruled unsafe by the U.S. Department of Agriculture. Research has proven that paraffin sealing does not prevent the growth of harmful molds. Although this method was considered safe a few years ago, you will not find the open-kettle method used in any recipe in this book.

  Jars must be sterilized by boiling for 15 minutes and holding in hot water until ready to be filled. They are reusable if undamaged. Screw bands are sterilized in the same manner along with the jars. Do not boil flats (lids); the adhesive cannot stand the long boiling process. Do not use your oven or dishwasher to sterilize jelly jars. Check jars for nicks or cracks; use only perfect jars.

METAL SREW BAND

METAL LID WITH SEALING COMPOUND

SEALS HERE

Two-piece lids are the only closures considered safe for home canning.

- Two-piece lids. Two-piece lids consist of a metal screw band and a metal flat or lid with a sealing compound. Old zinc lids or those using a rubber gasket are no longer recommended for home canning. Use jars with these types of lids for storing dried foods, herbs, or leftovers in the refrigerator. Sterilize metal screw bands by boiling for 15 minutes along with jelly jars. Wash the screw bands and lids or flats in hot soapy water, then sterilize the screw bands by boiling. Screw bands must be in good condition and free of rust. Do not use warped bands. Flats or lids are not reusable and those you bought last year are not safe to use again. Purchase new lids each year. The sealing compound on old lids tends to dry out and may not seal. Sterilize lids by washing them in hot soapy water and holding them in hand-hot water until you are ready to use them.
- Large pot or water bath canner. You will need a large pot to sterilize the jars in. A large roasting pan with a lid works equally well. Add ½ cup vinegar to boiling water to prevent white chalky mineral deposits on the jars and the inside of the pot. You will also need this pot to process filled jelly jars. Jelly is processed for 5 minutes in a boiling water bath. Start counting the processing time as soon as the water in the canner returns to a boil. The 5-minute boiling process will not affect the jelly. The process sterilizes the **tops** of the jars and the jelly that has been exposed to air. It also creates a better vacuum in the head space of the jar to inhibit mold growth. Do not skip this process.
- Water bath canner. A water bath canner is needed to process the jelly. Make sure the canner is large enough to allow 1 to 2 inches of boiling water over the tops of the jars. Three additional inches of space is needed for the activity of the boiling water. Add ¼ to ½ cup vinegar to the water where hard water is a problem. Always cover the canner during processing.
- Jelly bag. A jelly bag is used to strain fruit for sparkling clear jelly. You can buy a ready-made

Among the equipment needed for jam and jelly making is a timer, measuring cups and spoons, a ladle, a wide-mouth funnel, a potato masher, sieves, and, of course, canning jars. You will also need a jar lifter for removing the jars from the canner. You can buy a lifter, or make one yourself from a wire coat hanger bent into a shape shown above.

A jelly bag is a bag made of muslin or cheesecloth through which fruit juices are strained for jelly-making. You can buy jelly bags anywhere canning equipment is sold, or you can make your own from muslin or cheesecloth.

- Measuring equipment. Measuring equipment, properly used, is important for successful jelly. A set of dry (metal) measuring cups (1/2, 1/3, 1/4, and 1 cup) and 1-quart liquid (glass) measures are needed.
- A lemon squeezer or juicer and grater should be at hand, unless you use bottled juice and rind.
- A household scale that can weigh from 4 ounces (1/4 pound) up to 10 or 25 pounds is handy. Many recipes in this book call for pounds of fruit or vegetables.
- A strainer, food mill, blender, food chopper, food processor, or grinder is helpful when preparing fruit. The recipe will tell you if one of these utensils is needed, so read the entire recipe before you begin preparation.
- Timer and/or clock with a second hand. Even half a minute of overcooking can scorch jellies, so watch the clock and stay right with the kettle.
- Wide-mouth funnel. This helps when pouring jelly into the jars, so you don't get it all over the counter. Some funnels have a measured base, to help you see head space at a glance.

bag, often with its own stand, wherever canning supplies are sold. Pour boiling water through the bag before using it for the first time. Always wash and rinse the bag thoroughly after each use. Instructions for making a jelly bag from cheesecloth or muslin are given later.
- Candy or jelly thermometer. A thermometer eliminates all guesswork when making jelly without added pectin. You will not need a thermometer if you use commercial pectin. Select a thermometer with a clamp so you can fasten it to the edge of the kettle. If you live high above sea level, boil some water and make a note of the boiling temperature. By adding 8°F to that figure you will know the proper temperature.
- Spoons. You will need several spoons. A large, long-handled wooden spoon is excellent for comfortable, silent stirring. A slotted spoon made of metal is best for skimming foam off jelly, since the foam stays on the spoon while the jelly slips back into the kettle. You will also need a full set of measuring spoons (1/4, 1/2, and 1 teaspoon, and 1 tablespoon).
- Knives. You will need a paring knife and a chopping knife or chef's knife.

Maintaining the correct temperature is very important in making jams and jellies. A candy thermometer clipped to the side of the pot will help you check that the temperature is correct.

- Ladle. A ladle, especially one with a little lip or spout, is invaluable for transferring hot jelly from the kettle to the jar. A liquid measuring cup can be used as a substitute.
- Jar lifters. These should be used for safe handling of hot jars.
- Hot pads, oven mitts, wire cooling racks, folded towels, and a cutting board on which to stand hot jars to cool are also necessary.
- Kettle of boiling water. You may need to add boiling water to the boiling water bath if the level above the jar tops is less than 1 inch.

How to make a jelly bag

Cut a 24-inch length of cheesecloth or muslin. Pour boiling water over the cloth. Cool. Wring dry. Place a colander in a large bowl and line the colander with the cheesecloth or muslin. Pour in the fruit. Gather the ends of the cloth and tie them in a large, loose knot. Hang the fruit over a bowl to catch the juice. A cupboard door handle, a faucet in the sink, or a broomstick across two chairs make good handles for hanging your homemade jelly bag. Or upend a stool or chair and hang the bag on the legs with a bowl underneath.

BASIC INGREDIENTS

It takes four ingredients to make jelly: pectin, fruit juice, sugar, and acid (from lemon juice or tart fruit). Combining these ingredients in the correct proportions and cooking them to the proper temperature makes jelly.

Pectin. Pectin is what makes jelly jell. Pectin is a natural substance found in many fruits. Apples, cranberries, blackberries, gooseberries, currants, citrus fruits, and Concord grapes all contain so much natural pectin that you do not need to add more to make them jell. Commercially made pectin is derived from apples and citrus fruits. The low-pectin fruits typically used in jelly making—strawberries, blueberries, peaches, apricots, cherries, and rhubarb—need added pectin to form a jell.

Commercial pectin is available in two forms: liquid pectin, which comes in 6-ounce foil pouches; and powdered pectin, which comes in 1¾-ounce packages.

Because powdered pectin is dehydrated, it must be added to the fruit juice before heating. The liquid pectin is added after the juice and sugar have boiled because it is a concentration of pectin in its natural form. *Liquid and powdered pectin cannot be used interchangeably.* Follow the recipe

A homemade jelly bag can be suspended over an upturned chair or stool, and a bowl placed on the stool to catch the juice.

and use the type each recipe specifies. Always check the date printed on powdered or liquid pectin boxes. Because pectin does not hold its strength from one year to the next, it must be discarded after the freshness date has expired. Liquid pectin must flow. Do not use if it has jelled in the package.

Fruit juice. Fresh fruits are an obvious choice for jelly-making, but frozen fruit concentrates or canned fruit juices can also be used. Fruits must be cooked in a small amount of water and strained for jelly making. Do not squeeze the jelly bag or scrape the outside of the bag to rush this process. Allow juices to drain overnight.

Sugar. Sugar is sugar, whether it comes from cane or beet. Use granulated sugar for jelly-making, not confectioner's or brown sugar.

Acid. Lemon juice is the acid most commonly used in jelly recipes. Use fresh, strained lemon juice, bottled lemon juice, or frozen lemon juice.

Testing jelly for proper jell

There are three ways to check to see if jelly without added pectin will jell: by temperature, by a sheet test, or by the refrigerator method.

Temperature. Clip a candy thermometer onto the side of the cooking kettle and adjust it so the tip is halfway down in the juice. The tip of the thermometer must be completely covered by the juice but not touching the bottom of the pan. The jelly is done when the thermometer reaches 8°F above the boiling point of water. If you live at sea level, this is 220°F. If you live above or below sea level, check the boiling temperature of water and add 8°F to determine the right temperature for jelly.

Sheet test. After the jelly has boiled for a few minutes, begin making this test. Dip a cool metal spoon into the boiling juice and fill it. Lift the spoon up above the kettle, high enough that it is

You can test the jellying point of jelly which does not include added pectin by using the sheet test. At first the jelly drops are light and syrupy, as shown in the top drawing, then they become heavier and, as the product jells, form a jelly that falls from the spoon in a sheet or flake.

out of the steam so you can see it. Tilt the spoon slowly (allow jelly to drip back into the kettle) so the jelly runs off the side. When jelly is cooked enough it will flow together and come off the spoon in a sheet or flake.

Refrigerator test. Always take the kettle off the heat while making this test. After the jelly has boiled for several minutes, spoon a tablespoon or so of juice onto a cool saucer or plate. Put the plate in a freezer section of your refrigerator for about 5 minutes. If the mixture jells, the jelly is done.

What can go wrong? Problems and their causes.

Nobody's perfect. There are so many factors involved in jelly- and jam-making—time, temperature, humidity, juiciness of fruits, proportion of ingredients—that sometimes things go wrong. Here are some common problems and causes.

Soft jelly. After the cooling period, the jelly is soft or syrupy. What went wrong?

- You may have used too much sugar or juice.
- You may have made too big a batch; never double the recipe.
- There may not have been enough acid in fruit, which is often the case with overripe fruit.

Soft jelly can be used to top ice cream, cheesecake, puddings, custards, or pound cake, or as a glaze for ham. Re-cooking is another answer to soft jelly. To re-cook jelly made with liquid pectin follow these steps:

1. Open the jars, measure the quantity of jelly.
2. For each quart (1 quart = 4 cups) of soft jelly measure ¼ cup sugar, ¼ cup water and 4 teaspoons powdered pectin.
3. Mix the pectin and water and bring to a boil, stirring constantly to prevent scorching.
4. Add jelly and sugar. Stir thoroughly.
5. Bring to a full rolling boil over high heat, stirring constantly.
6. Boil mixture hard for 30 seconds. (Use a timer.)
7. Remove jelly pan from heat after 30 seconds of hard boiling, skim, and pour into sterilized jars.
8. Adjust lids and process for 5 minutes in boiling water bath canner.
9. Remove jars to racks or folded towels. Cool about 8 to 10 hours.
10. Check seals, label, date, and store. (Open a jar to see if re-cooking solved the problem.)

To re-cook soft jelly made with powdered pectin, follow these steps:

1. Open the jars, measure the quantity of jelly.
2. For each quart (1 quart = 4 cups) of jelly measure ¾ cup sugar, 2 tablespoons lemon juice, and 2 tablespoons liquid pectin.
3. Pour soft jelly into large kettle and bring to a boil over high heat.
4. Quickly add sugar, lemon juice, and pectin, and bring to a full rolling boil, stirring constantly.
5. Boil mixture hard for 1 minute. (Use timer.)
6. Remove jelly from heat, skim, and pour into sterilized jars.
7. Adjust lids and process 5 minutes in boiling water bath canner.
8. Remove jars to racks or folded towels. Cool 8 to 10 hours.
9. Check seal, label, date, and store. (Open a jar to see if re-cooking has solved the problem.)

To re-cook soft jelly made without added pectin, follow these steps:

1. Open jars, pour jelly into large 8- to 10-quart kettle and boil for a few minutes.
2. Use one of the tests described earlier to determine how long to cook the jelly.
3. Remove jelly from heat; skim.
4. Ladle into sterilized jars.
5. Adjust lids and process for 5 minutes in a boiling water bath canner.
6. Remove jars to racks or folded towels. Cool 8 to 10 hours.
7. Check seal, label, date, and store. (Open a jar to see if re-cooking has solved the problem.)

Cloudy jelly. This usually results from improper straining of the juice or squeezing the jelly bag. Overly green fruit can also cause cloudy jelly.

Crystals. Crystals indicate too much sugar, or too little cooking. Follow recipe exactly next time. Crystals forming on top of an opened jar are caused by evaporation. Always cover and refrigerate opened jars of jelly.

Stiff jelly. Stiff jelly may be the result of too much pectin or overcooking.

Weeping jelly. Stored in a warm place, jelly will separate. Separation can also be caused by too much added acid. Measure lemon juice with standard measuring spoons—don't guess, and don't use regular kitchen spoons.

Moldy jelly. Mold is caused by too much head space or an improper seal. Jelly must be processed in a boiling water bath canner for 5 minutes before storing.

Jars did not seal. Inadequate sealing can result from the use of old canning lids or flats; leaving less than 1 to 2 inches of water over the tops of the jars during processing, or incorrect processing time. Use new lids and reprocess, or store unsealed jars in the refrigerator and use within a few weeks.

EXTRACTING FRUIT JUICE FOR JELLY-MAKING

To extract the juice from fruit to make jelly, follow these steps:

1. Select fully ripened fruit that is not green or overripe. Sort carefully.
2. Wash the fruit. If using berries, allow them to drain for a few minutes.
3. Peel, pit, crush, grind, or mash fruit as directed in recipe. The preparation required depends entirely on the type of fruits used in your recipe. When crushing berries, use a pestle or potato masher. Crush about one cup at a time in a bowl, then transfer crushed fruit to a nonreactive pot (stainless steel, aluminum, or unchipped enamel) large enough to allow fruit to boil.
4. Set the pot over medium-high heat and stir in a little water, ½ to 1 cup. The water will evaporate during cooking, but it is needed to get juices flowing and to keep the fruit from sticking during cooking. Stir occasionally, and bring mixture slowly to a boil.
5. Boil uncovered for 15 to 20 minutes or until fruit has rendered most of its juices. Stir occasionally.
6. Remove the pot from the heat and allow fruit to steep, covered, for 30 minutes to 1 hour.
7. Suspend a jelly bag over a large bowl. Fill the bag with cooked fruit and juice. Allow juices to drip, undisturbed, for 6 to 8 hours or overnight.
8. For grapes, cover the bowl of juices and refrigerate for at least 8 hours so that the sediment caused by the tartaric acid content of the grapes can settle. If you skip this step you will probably have grainy jelly.
9. Line a strainer with double layers of wet cheesecloth wrung out in cold water. Pour in juice carefully. You will see thick granular sediment in the bottom of the bowl. Discard the sediment.
10. Measure the juice and follow the recipe you have selected.

When making jams and jellies, wipe the tops and threads of each jar with a clean, damp cloth before putting on the tops and processing the jars in the boiling water bath canner.

Once the jam or jelly has cooled, check that the jar has sealed properly. The lid should be slightly depressed. Jars that have not sealed properly can be stored in the refrigerator and the contents used within a few weeks.

Terms used in recipes

Ladle into hot jars. Use a wide-mouth funnel and a ladle or cup to pour hot jelly into hot jars. Remove jars from hot water and fill one at a time. Work quickly.

Wipe rims of jars. Use a clean, damp cloth to thoroughly clean the top and threads of each jar before sealing. Jelly left on the rim may prevent the sealing compound from forming a seal.

Adjust lids. Remove lids from holding water one at a time. Place lid flat on jar rim, then place screw band on jar. Turn screw band until it is finger-tight but not too tight. Never use a jar wrench to tighten screw bands.

Check seals. After jars have cooled, the center of the lid or flat should be slightly concave, pulled down by the partial vacuum formed inside the jar during processing. You will hear a popping sound as jars vent and lids are snapped downward. Use unsealed jars within a few weeks.

Label. Always label each jar. Purchase decorative labels or use tape. Write on tape before removing from roll; it is easier. On the label, note contents, date of preparation, and your name.

CONCORD GRAPE JELLY

September 15, 1986

Mary Doe

Store. Remove screw bands (if desired). They can be re-used immediately (after thoroughly washing and sterilizing). If jars have sealed properly, storing them with screw bands is unnecessary. Store jars in a cool, dark place for up to one year.

PERFECT GRAPE JELLY

---

4 cups grape juice (from 3 1/2 pounds Concord grapes)
7 cups sugar
1 pouch liquid pectin

Yield: eight to nine 1/2 pints

1. Use fully ripe grapes. Sort and wash grapes. Remove from stems.

2. Crush grapes, 1 cup at a time. Add 1/2 cup water to crushed grapes and bring to boil on high heat. Reduce heat and simmer for 15 minutes.

3. Extract juice, according to directions on how

to extract grape juice in "Extracting fruit juice for jelly-making."

4. Measure 4 cups grape juice and pour into an 8- to 10-quart nonreactive kettle.

5. Stir in sugar. Place on high heat. Stirring constantly, bring quickly to a full rolling boil that cannot be stirred down.

6. Add liquid pectin and heat again to a full rolling boil. Boil hard for 1 minute.

7. Remove from heat. Skim foam with large metal spoon. Discard foam.

8. Ladle jelly immediately into hot, sterilized ½-pint jars leaving ¼ inch head space.

9. Wipe jar rims with clean, damp cloth.

10. Adjust lids, and process jars for 5 minutes in boiling water bath canner.

11. Remove jars to racks or folded towels. Cool 8 to 10 hours.

11. Check seals. Label, date, and store.

ROYAL RUBY JELLY

1 quart red currants
1½ quarts red raspberries
5½ cups sugar
1 package powdered fruit pectin

Yield: seven ½ pints

1. Pick over berries, removing green or damaged fruit. Wash. Remove any stems.

2. Crush berries 1 cup at a time according to instructions in "Extracting fruit juice for jelly-making."

3. Add ½ cup water to crushed fruit and cook over high heat for 15 minutes.

4. Place in a jelly bag and allow to drip overnight.

5. Next day, measure 4 cups juice into an 8- to 10-quart nonreactive kettle.

6. Stir in powdered pectin and bring mixture quickly to a full rolling boil.

7. Add sugar and return to a full rolling boil. Boil hard for 1 minute, using timer.

8. Remove from heat and quickly skim foam with large metal spoon. Discard foam.

9. Pour jelly into hot sterilized ½-pint jars leaving ¼ -inch head space.

10. Wipe jar rims with clean, damp cloth.

11. Adjust lids, and process in boiling water bath canner for 5 minutes.

12. Remove jars to racks or folded towels. Cool 8 to 10 hours.

13. Check seals. Label, date, and store.

BLACKBERRY JELLY

3 quarts fresh blackberries
7½ cups sugar
1 pouch liquid pectin

Yield: eight to nine ½ pints

1. Sort blackberries, then wash. Remove stems. Crush berries 1 cup at a time according to directions in "Extracting fruit juice for jelly-making." Place in an 8- to 10-quart nonreactive pot.

2. Add ½ cup water to berries and boil for 10 minutes. Place fruit and juice in jelly bag and allow to drip overnight.

3. Next day, measure 4 cups juice and place in an 8- to 10-quart nonreactive kettle. Stir in sugar.

4. Place on high heat. Stirring constantly, bring quickly to a full rolling boil that cannot be stirred down.

5. Add liquid pectin and return to a full rolling boil. Boil hard for 1 minute, using timer.

6. Remove from heat and quickly skim foam with a large metal spoon. Discard foam.

7. Pour jelly into hot, sterilized ½-pint jars, leaving ¼ inch head space.

8. Wipe jar rims with clean, damp cloth.

9. Adjust lids and process for 5 minutes in boiling water bath canner.

10. Remove jars to racks or folded towels. Cool 8 to 10 hours.

11. Check seals. Label, date, and store.

STRAWBERRY JELLY

3½ quarts fresh strawberries
7½ cups sugar
1 pouch liquid pectin

Yield: eight to nine ½ pints

1. Sort and wash strawberries. Hull and slice. Crush a cup at a time according to directions in "Extracting fruit and juice for jelly-making." Place in an 8- to 10-quart nonreactive pot.

2. Cook crushed berries 15 minutes in ½ cup water. Place fruit and juice in jelly bag and allow to drip overnight.

3. Next day, measure 4 cups juice into an 8- to 10-quart nonreactive kettle. Stir in sugar.

4. Place on high heat. Stirring constantly, bring to a full rolling boil that cannot be stirred down.

5. Add liquid pectin and heat again to a full rolling boil. Boil hard for 1 minute, using timer.

6. Remove from heat and quickly skim foam with large metal spoon. Discard foam.

7. Pour jelly into hot, sterilized ½-pint jars, leaving ¼ inch head space.

8. Wipe jar rims with clean, damp cloth.

9. Adjust lids and process for 5 minutes in boiling water bath canner.

10. Remove jars to racks or folded towels. Cool 8 to 10 hours.

11. Check seals. Label, date, and store.

PLUM-GOOD JELLY

5 pounds Damson plums
3 cups fresh basil leaves *or*
1½ cups dried basil
2-4 cups sugar (depending on juiciness of plums)
6 cups water

Yield: eight to nine ½ pints

1. Sort and wash plums. Cut each in half. Place in an 8- to 10-quart nonreactive kettle with water and 2 cups fresh basil leaves or 1 cup dried basil. Boil about 40 minutes.

2. Place in a jelly bag and drain overnight.

3. Next day, measure juice. For each 2½ cups juice add 2 cups sugar. Place in an 8- to 10-quart nonreactive pot.

4. Attach a candy thermometer to pot. Over medium heat, heat juice and sugar until dissolved. Turn heat to high and bring to full rolling boil. Boil until thermometer reads 220°F or 8°F above boiling point of water.

5. Skim foam with large metal spoon. Discard foam.

6. Chop remaining fresh basil finely and add to jelly. Stir.

7. Quickly ladle jelly into hot, sterilized ½-pint jars, leaving ¼ inch head space.

8. Wipe jar rims with clean, damp cloth.

9. Adjust lids, and process for 5 minutes in boiling water bath canner.

10. Remove jars to racks or folded towels. Cool 8 to 10 hours.

11. Check seals. Label, date, and store.

JAMS, PRESERVES, CONSERVES AND MARMALADES

Jams, preserves, conserves, and all kinds of marmalades are first cousins to jelly. They are the sweet and fruity-tasting additions to meals that we love. They are prepared in much the same way as jelly. Juice as well as pieces of fruit are made into a thick, semi-soft spread.

- **Jam.** Jam is softer than jelly and contains crushed or chopped fruit. It is often made with added pectin to give it a slight jell.
- **Preserves.** Whole fruits or pieces of fruit are simmered in syrup until plump and saturated. Longer cooking time (1 to 2 hours) is necessary.
- **Conserves.** Conserves are like jams but are usually made with more than one fruit, with raisins or nuts added.
- **Marmalade.** This is jelly with slices of fruit in it. Citrus fruits are traditionally made into marmalades, but other fruits may also be included.

Jams, preserves, conserves, and marmalades must be sealed in jars with two-piece lids and processed in a boiling water bath canner. This sealing process helps to prevent the growth of harmful molds and guarantees long-lasting quality.

When mold forms on the top of a product, too many people scrape off the layer of mold and serve the rest of the jar's contents. This is unsafe. Molds that grow in jars of home-canned foods can produce alfatoxins. Some alfatoxins have been found to be carcinogenic (cancer-causing), and all are highly toxic. The problem lies in discerning which molds are toxic and which are harmless, because there are no identifying characteristics that can be seen with the naked eye. Therefore, all molds should be regarded as harmful. Any product containing mold growth must be discarded.

Mold growing on a water-soluble product may appear to be restricted to the top layer. However, the entire jar is contaminated and the contents must be disposed of quickly. Wash and sterilize the jar by boiling it for 15 minutes to make reusable. Eating moldy products over a number of years can lead to serious health problems, or even death. Follow the recipes precisely to avoid mold growth.

Jams, preserves, conserves, and marmalades depend on the interaction of sugar with natural fruit acids and pectin to form a jell. It is essential to follow directions exactly when preparing these products. Never alter the proportions of sugar to fruit; a poor product may be the result.

The amount of sugar added to these products depends on the type of fruit and the amount of natural or added pectin present. Sugar is a preservative. Reducing the amount of sugar can result in mold growth or a soft syrupy jell. Follow the recipe to the letter and you should have no problems. Altering ingredients means changing the recipe. Read the section on basic jelly-making before proceeding with preparation of jams, preserves, conserves, or marmalades.

APRICOT AYANNA (JAM)

Hubbard, butternut, or acorn squash may be substituted for pumpkin in this recipe.

2 pounds chopped, dried apricots
6 pounds chopped pumpkin
1½ quarts water
11 ½ cups sugar
1¼ cups dried orange rind (optional)

Yield: 10 pints

1. Soak the chopped, dried apricots in water overnight (8 to 10 hours). Drain. Reserve the water.
2. Simmer the pumpkin in the water used for soaking the apricots until tender, about 30 minutes.
3. Put the pumpkin through a sieve or food mill.
4. Cook the pumpkin puree and sugar for about 30 minutes, stirring constantly to prevent sticking.
5. Add the chopped apricots and orange rind and cook for 30 minutes, until mixture is thick and apricots are soft.
6. Using a wide-mouth funnel, ladle hot mixture into hot, sterilized pint jars, leaving ¼ inch head space.
7. Wipe jar rims with clean, damp cloth.
8. Adjust lids, and process jars in boiling water bath canner for 15 minutes.
9. Remove jars and place on racks or folded towels. Cool 10 to 12 hours.
10. Check seals. Label, date, and store.

VERY EASY APRICOT JAM

Use Royal Anne apricots. Select rich yellow fruit with a bit of a blush. Avoid rock-hard fruit.

2½ pounds ripe apricots (3½ cups prepared fruit)
⅓ cups lemon juice
6½ cups sugar
1 pouch liquid fruit pectin

Yield: 6 ½ pints

1. Sort, wash, and pit apricots. Do not peel.
2. Grind or finely chop apricots. Add lemon juice to fruit immediately to prevent darkening.
3. Cut the top off pectin package and prop in a cup. Measure sugar and set aside.
4. Place measured fruit in an 8-quart saucepot.

5. Stir sugar into prepared fruit.
6. Bring to a full rolling boil over high heat. Stir constantly to prevent sticking.
7. After fruit mixture has reached a full rolling boil that cannot be stirred down, boil for 1 minute (use timer). Stir constantly.
8. Remove from heat.
9. Add liquid pectin. Stir well.
10. Skim foam with large metal spoon. Discard foam.
11. Stir jam about 2 minutes. This helps to prevent fruit pieces from floating.
12. Immediately ladle jam into hot, sterilized pint and ½-pint jars, leaving ¼ inch head space.
13. Adjust lids, and process in boiling water bath canner for 15 minutes.
14. Remove jars and place on racks or folded towels. Cool about 8 to 10 hours.
15. Check seals. Label, date, and store.

GINGERED BLUEBERRY JAM

Candied ginger can be found in gourmet food stores. Or you may substitute crystalline ginger which can be found in most supermarkets. Crush crystals with a mallet and measure ¼ cup.

4 cups crushed blueberries
1 package powdered pectin
5 cups sugar
¼ cups finely slivered candied ginger (or crushed crystalline ginger)
1 teaspoon lemon juice

Yield: 6 to 7 pints

1. Sort and wash blueberries. Drain.
2. Crush blueberries in a single layer with a potato masher, or chop them finely. Chopped or crushed fruit should measure 4 cups.
3. Place blueberries in an 8-quart pan. Add powdered pectin and stir well.
4. Place on high heat, stirring constantly to bring to a full rolling boil.
5. Add sugar, continue stirring, and heat again to a full rolling boil. Boil hard for 1 minute (use timer), stirring constantly.
6. Remove from heat. Skim foam with a large metal spoon. Discard foam.
7. Ladle jam into hot, sterilized pint jars, leaving ¼ inch head space.
8. Wipe jar rims with clean, damp cloth.
9. Adjust lids, and process 5 minutes in a boiling water bath canner.

10. Remove jars to racks or folded towels. Cool 8 to 10 hours.

11. Check seals. Label, date, and store.

BAR LE DUC (FRENCH CURRANT JAM)

Bar le Duc is an elegant topping for ice cream or cheesecake. It is also excellent as an accompaniment to game or pork, or as a glaze for ham.

3 pounds currants
2³/₄ to 3 cups sugar
¹/₃ cup honey

Yield: 6 pints

1. Wash and sort currants. Remove stems.

2. Measure half the currants into an 8-quart kettle or pot and heat over low heat, pressing with potato masher or spoon to release juice. When juicy, stir in remaining currants.

3. Heat to boiling, stirring constantly.

4. Stir in sugar. Heat again to boiling, stirring constantly, then reduce heat and simmer for 5 minutes.

5. Stir in the honey and simmer 5 minutes longer. Remove from heat and ladle into hot, sterilized pint jars, leaving ¹/₄ inch head space.

6. Wipe jar rims with clean, damp cloth.

7. Adjust lids, and process in boiling water bath canner for 15 minutes.

8. Remove jars and place on racks or folded towels. Cool 8 to 10 hours.

9. Check seals. Label, date, and store.

STRAWBERRY-RHUBARB JAM

1 quart strawberries
1 pound rhubarb
6¹/₂ cups sugar
¹/₄ cup water
1 pouch liquid pectin

Yield: 6¹/₂ pints

1. Sort and wash strawberries. Remove caps.

2. Crush strawberries, crushing a single layer at a time. Set aside.

3. Wash rhubarb stalks. Do not peel. Slice thinly.

4. Place rhubarb in an 8-quart saucepot. Add water and cook, covered, for 5 minutes. Add cooked rhubarb to crushed strawberries. Prepared rhubarb and strawberries should measure 3¹/₂ cups.

5. Measure sugar. Set aside. Open pectin pouch. Set aside.

6. Return rhubarb and strawberry mixture to 8-quart saucepot.

7. Stir in sugar and bring mixture to a boil over high heat, stirring constantly.

8. Bring fruit back to a full rolling boil that cannot be stirred down. Using timer, boil 1 minute, stirring constantly.

9. Remove from heat. At once add liquid fruit pectin. Stir well.

10. Skim foam with large metal spoon. Discard foam.

11. Continue stirring for 2 minutes; this helps to prevent floating fruit pieces.

12. Immediately ladle jam into hot, sterilized pint and ¹/₂-pint jars, leaving ¹/₄ inch head space.

13. Adjust lids, and process jars for 5 minutes in boiling water bath canner.

14. Remove jars and set on racks or folded towels. Cool 8 to 10 hours.

15. Check seals. Label, date, and store.

GREEN AND WHITE GRAPE JAM

This is a delightful change from grape jelly.

2 pounds seedless green grapes
3 cups white grape juice or one 24-ounce bottle of white grape juice
1 stick cinnamon
7 cups sugar
1 pouch liquid pectin

Yield: 10   ¹/₂-pints

1. Wash grapes, stem, and cut in halves. Put grapes into a large saucepot along with 1 cup grape juice and the cinnamon stick.

2. Heat to a boil, then reduce heat to a simmer. Cover and simmer 15 minutes.

3. Stir in remaining grape juice and sugar. Heat to full rolling boil, then boil hard for 1 minute (use timer), stirring constantly.

4. Immediately remove jam from the heat and stir in liquid pectin.

5. Skim foam with large metal spoon. Discard foam.

6. Stir jam for 5 minutes to prevent fruit from floating. Remove cinnamon stick.

7. Ladle jam into hot, sterilized pint jars,

leaving ¼ inch head space.

8. Wipe jar rims with clean, damp cloth.

9. Adjust lids, and process in boiling water bath canner for 15 minutes.

10. Remove jars to racks or folded towels. Cool 8 to 10 hours.

11. Check seals. Label, date, and store.

NECTARINE RUM JAM

You can vary this simple recipe in several ways: use peaches or apricots (unpeeled) in place of nectarines; omit the rum completely; or replace the rum with orange liqueur, peach or apricot brandy, or 2 tablespoons vanilla.

4 cups chopped peeled ripe nectarines
1 package powdered fruit pectin
5 cups sugar
¼ cup rum

Yield: 6 pints

1. Combine chopped fruit and pectin in an 8-quart pot and heat to boiling over high heat, stirring constantly.

2. Add sugar. Cook and stir until sugar dissolves.

3. Heat to a full rolling boil, then boil hard for 1 minute (use timer), stirring constantly.

4. Immediately remove pot from heat. Skim foam with large metal spoon. Discard foam.

5. Stir jam for 5 minutes to prevent the fruit from floating.

6. Stir in the rum.

7. Ladle jam into hot, sterilized jars, leaving ¼ inch head space.

8. Wipe jar rims with clean, damp cloth.

9. Adjust lids, and process in boiling water bath canner for 15 minutes.

9. Remove jars and place on racks or folded towels. Cool 8 to 10 hours.

10. Check seals. Label, date, and store.

PEARS PAMELA

Served over plain pound cake with a swirl of whipped cream, simple ingredients become an elegant gourmet dessert. Use green underripe pears for this recipe. Chill before serving. Use Bartlett, Comice, or Kieffer pears. Half or quarter the pears, or leave small pears whole. Peaches can be substituted for pears in this recipe.

16 green, underripe pears
8 cups full-bodied red wine
3 cups sugar

Yield: 4 quarts

1. Wash and peel pears. Cut in half and scoop out core with a teaspoon or melon baller. (Quarter pears if desired.) To prevent darkening, immediately drop pears into acidulated water. (1 quart water and ¼ cup lemon juice.)

2. Combine wine with sugar in an 8-quart pot and bring to a boil over high heat. Boil for 1 minute (use timer).

3. Drain pears and add to wine syrup.

4. Simmer for 3 minutes.

5. Pack pears into clean, hot, quart-size jars. Add syrup to cover pears, leaving ½ inch head space.

6. Stir gently with a rubber spatula to release air bubbles.

7. Wipe jar rims with clean, damp cloth.

8. Adjust lids, and process in boiling water bath canner for 1 hour. Do not adjust time. The wine must cook in order to avoid fermentation. Keep a kettle of boiling water on hand. Add more boiling water if necessary. Water must cover jars by 1 to 2 inches throughout the 1 hour processing time.

9. Remove jars to racks or folded towels. Cool.

10. Check seals. Label, date, and store.

Note: If using peaches, omit the simmering process in step 4.

BERRY-CHERRY PRESERVES

Use dark sweet cherries (Royal Anne or Bing) or tart red ones (Morello) or a combination of the two. These preserves are delicious with hot buttered bran muffins or toast.

1 quart strawberries
2 pints raspberries
1½ pounds tart red cherries or sweet dark cherries
1 cup lemon juice
1 box powdered fruit pectin
4 to 5 cups sugar (use 4 cups for sweet cherries)

Yield: eight ½ pints

1. Sort, wash, then stem cherries. Remove pits.

2. Wash berries, hull, and drain.

3. Place fruit in 8-quart pot, and mash with a potato masher. Stir in lemon juice and powdered fruit pectin.

4. Heat to full rolling boil that cannot be stirred down. Boil for 1 minute, using timer.

5. Immediately remove preserves from heat. Skim foam with a large metal spoon. Discard foam.

6. Ladle preserves into hot, sterilized jars, leaving ¼ inch head space.

7. Wipe jar rims with clean, damp cloth.

8. Adjust lids, and process in boiling water bath canner for 15 minutes.

9. Remove jars to racks or folded towels. Cool 8 to 10 hours.

10. Check seals. Label, date, and store.

NUTTY ORANGE-PLUM PRESERVES

2 oranges
3 pounds plums
4 cups sugar
1 cup blanched, chopped walnuts

Yield: six ½ pints

1. Wash the unpeeled oranges and mince them finely, reserving juice. (The food processor works well here.)

2. Pit the plums. Put pits in a cheesecloth bag and crush with hammer or mallet.

3. Put plums, minced oranges, juice, pits (in cheesecloth bag), and sugar into a large 8-quart kettle and heat slowly to boiling point, stirring to dissolve sugar.

4. Simmer over low heat about 1 hour.

5. Add walnuts and simmer 30 minutes longer. Remove cheesecloth bag.

6. Ladle preserves into hot, sterilized pint jars, leaving ¼ head space.

7. Wipe jar rims with clean, damp cloth.

8. Adjust lids, and process in boiling water bath canner for 15 minutes.

9. Remove jars to racks or folded towels. Cool 8 to 10 hours.

10. Check seals. Label, date, and store.

WILD GRAPE CONSERVE

If wild grapes are unavailable, use Concord grapes. Skinning grapes may seem difficult (and tedious) but the end product makes the extra effort well worth it. You will need a food mill.

3 pounds wild grapes or Concord grapes
2 cups raisins
zest of one orange (use vegetable peeler)

½ cup fresh orange juice
2½ cups sugar
1 cup finely chopped hickory nuts or pecans

Yield: 8 ½-pints

1. Pick over grapes, removing damaged fruit. Wash, drain, then remove from stems over a bowl.

2. Slip skins off grapes, working over a bowl to catch juice. Reserve skins.

3. Cook pulp with seeds for about 5 minutes, simmering slowly.

4. Put hot pulp through a sieve to remove seeds. Discard seeds.

5. Grind the raw skins in food mill with raisins and orange peel.

6. Mix pulp and skin mixture in large, 8-quart pot. Add sugar and orange juice.

7. Cook over low heat about 1 hour, stirring often to prevent sticking.

8. Add chopped nuts, stir well, and cook slowly 2 minutes longer.

9. Ladle hot conserves into hot, sterilized pint jars, leaving ¼ inch head space.

10. Wipe jar rims with clean, damp cloth.

11. Adjust lids, and process in boiling water bath canner for 15 minutes.

12. Remove jars to racks or folded towels. Cool 8 to 10 hours.

13. Check seals. Label, date, and store.

DAMSON CONSERVE

This is excellent with pork, duck, or wild game.

3½ cups finely chopped Damson plums (about 1½ pounds)
1 cup finely chopped orange pulp
zest of ½ orange
2 cups water
½ cup raisins
1 package powdered pectin
7 cups sugar
½ cup chopped black walnuts

Yield: eight ½ pints

1. Sort and wash plums. Cut in half over a bowl and remove pits. Chop plums finely.

2. Wash, peel, and chop orange carefully so that no seeds get into pulp.

3. Use a grater to remove orange zest, avoiding bitter white pith. Measure sugar; set aside.

4. Place orange pulp, orange zest, and water in

a large 8-quart pot. Cover and simmer about 20 minutes.

5. Measure chopped plums into pot with orange mixture. Add raisins and pectin, stir well.

6. Place over high heat and bring to a boil, stirring constantly.

7. Add sugar and continue to stir. Heat to a full rolling boil that cannot be stirred down. Boil hard for 1 minute (use timer), stirring constantly.

8. Add nuts and stir well.

9. Remove from heat and skim foam with a large metal spoon. Discard foam.

10. Ladle conserve into hot, sterilized ½-pint jars and process for 5 minutes in boiling water bath canner.

11. Remove jars to racks or folded towels. Cool 8 to 10 hours.

12. Check seals. Label, date, and store.

ROSY ROCHELLE MARMALADE

Use Jonathan, Red Delicious, or Winesap apples. This marmalade is excellent on hot buttered biscuits.

8 cups crisp, tart, red apples, thinly sliced
1 large orange (1 cup), unpeeled
1½ cups water
5 cups sugar
2 tablespoons lemon juice

Yield: seven ½ pints

1. Select firm red apples, free of bruises. Wash, quarter, and core apples. Do not peel. Sprinkle with lemon juice.

2. Wash orange and slice thinly. Remove seeds.

3. Combine water and sugar. Heat until sugar is dissolved. Add apples.

4. Boil rapidly, stirring constantly, until mixture thickens, about 30 minutes. Marmalade should reach 220°F on a jelly thermometer or 8°F above the boiling point of water.

5. Remove from heat and skim foam with large metal spoon. Discard foam.

6. Fill hot, sterilized half-pint jars, leaving ¼ inch head space.

7. Wipe rims with clean, damp cloth.

8. Adjust lids, and process in boiling water bath canner for 5 minutes.

9. Remove jars to racks or folded towels. Cool 8 to 10 hours.

10. Check seals. Label, date, and store.

BLUSHING FIG MARMALADE

Select red stalks of rhubarb; the redder the stalk, the deeper the flavor. Rhubarb leaves are poisonous and should never be eaten.

1 pound rhubarb, diced
¼ cup dried figs, diced
2 cups sugar
juice of ½ lemon

Yield: five ½ pints

1. Wash rhubarb stalks and dice finely. Dice dried figs.

2. Place rhubarb, figs, sugar, and lemon juice in saucepan. Cover and let stand 24 hours.

3. Next day, cook marmalade over medium-high heat, stirring frequently. Boil for about 45 minutes until thickened. Marmalade should reach 220°F on a jelly thermometer or 8°F above the boiling point of water.

4. Ladle marmalade into hot, sterilized ½-pint jars, leaving ¼ inch head space.

5. Wipe jar rims with clean, damp cloth.

6. Adjust lids, and process in boiling water bath canner for 5 minutes.

7. Remove jars to racks or folded towels. Cool 8 to 10 hours.

8. Check seals. Label, date, and store.

How to Dry Fruits and Vegetables

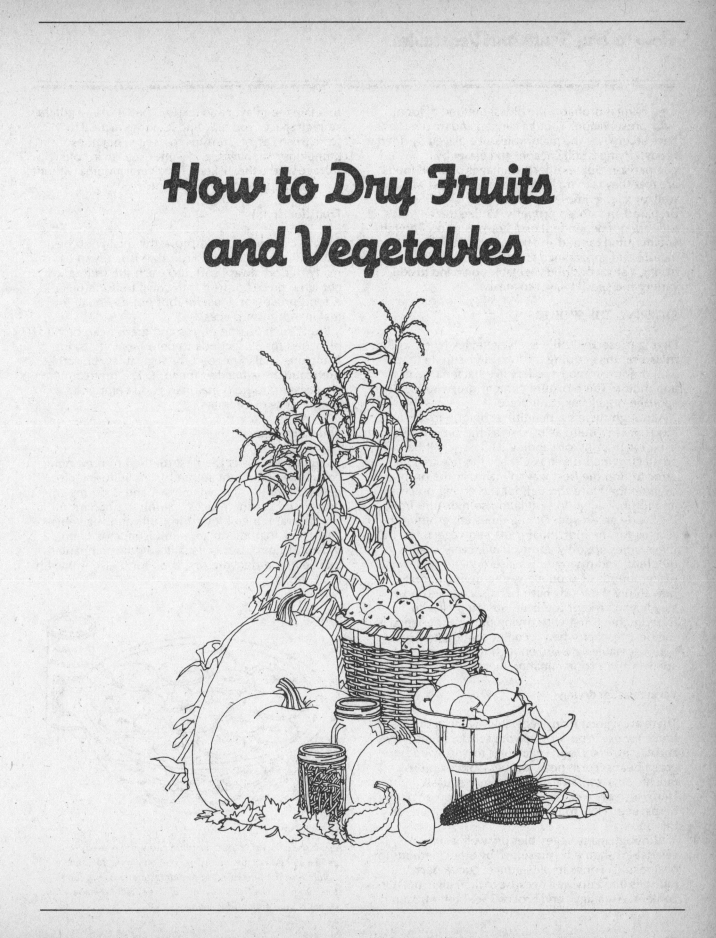

How to Dry Fruits and Vegetables

Drying is probably the oldest method of food preservation. Though canned and frozen foods have taken over the major role once played by dried foods, drying is still cheaper and easier by comparison. Some other advantages of dried foods are that they take up less storage space and will keep well for a long time — up to 12 months — if prepared and stored properly. Unlike frozen foods, they are not dependent on a power source. Though you may find canned and frozen vegetables are closer in taste and appearance to fresh food, you'll like having a stock of dried vegetables on hand to add variety and special flavor to meals.

STOPPING THE SPOILERS

Drying preserves fruits and vegetables by removing moisture, thus cutting off the water supply that would nourish food spoilers like bacteria, yeasts, and molds. The moisture content drops so low that spoilage organisms can't grow.

Although there's a definite technique to drying foods, it isn't quite as precise as the procedures used for freezing or canning. Unless you'll be using an electric food dryer, you'll have to use trial and error to find the best way to maintain the proper oven temperature throughout the drying process and to provide good ventilation so moisture from the food can escape. Drying times are given in the recipes for the individual fruits and vegetables, but these times are only approximate. Every oven is different, and drying times also depend on how many pounds of produce you're drying at once, how thinly the foods have been sliced, and how steady you've kept the heat. So you'll have to experiment at first with drying times. Experience is the best teacher when it comes to judging when your vegetables are dry enough to keep the spoilers from contaminating them.

Vegetables for drying

There are a great many vegetables you can dry at home for use in perking up your salads, soups, stews, and casseroles. Good vegetables to dry include green beans, corn, peas, peppers, okra, onions, mushrooms, tomatoes, and summer squash. Herbs also dry well. For more information on drying herbs, see "How to Store and Use Herbs," later in this book.

Although many vegetables dry well, some vegetables should be preserved by other methods for best results. For example, lettuce, cucumbers, and radishes don't dry well because of their high moisture content. Asparagus and broccoli are better frozen

to retain their flavor and texture. And if you've got the storage space, you may find it more practical to store fresh carrots, turnips, parsnips, potatoes, pumpkins, rutabagas, and winter squash in cold storage where they'll keep for several months without any special preserving treatment.

Fruits for drying

Drying fruit does not improve the quality, so begin with fully ripened fruit. Fruit that is ready to eat is ready to dry. Always sort and wash the fruit, and cut large pieces of fruit into small uniform pieces. A food processor is useful (but not essential) for making uniform pieces.

Fruits such as ripe plums and grapes can be blanched for 30 seconds to help break the skins. Blanching is also needed for vegetables, but other pretreatment is needed for fruit. The pretreatment is necessary to help maintain good color and prevent loss of vitamins.

Pretreatment methods

1. **Sulfuring.** This is the best method of preventing color change in light-colored fruit. Sulfuring also helps prevent loss of vitamins A and C during the drying and storing process. Sulfur is not harmful; it is a natural mineral found in fruits and vegetables. The active ingredient, sodium bisulfite, is often difficult to find, but is usually sold by companies that sell food dehydrators. Look for it also in health food stores.

A sulfur solution of sodium bisulfite and water is used to pretreat some fruits before drying. Use only pure, food-grade sodium bisulfite purchased from a drugstore or health food store. Do not use garden-dusting sulfur or practical-grade sulfur; neither is pure enough for eating.

To make the solution, add 1 to 2 tablespoons sodium bisulfite to a gallon of water. Mix thoroughly. Soak the fruit pieces for 5 to 10 minutes. Drain the fruit and dry on paper towels. Do not rinse fruit before drying. Proceed with the drying method immediately.

When purchasing sodium bisulfite for home use, buy only a pure, food-grade product from a drugstore or health food store. Neither garden-dusting sulfur nor practical-grade sulfur should be used on food. They are not pure enough for consumption.

2. **Ascorbic acid.** Mix 2½ teaspoons ascorbic acid with one cup water. Sprinkle over light-colored fruit as you cut the fruit. Stir lightly to coat the fruit with the ascorbic acid mixture. The quantity given will coat about 5 quarts of fruit. Ascorbic acid crystals can be purchased at the drugstore. Commercial antioxidants (anti-darkening agents) may be used instead of ascorbic acid. If you use a commercial product, follow the label directions.

3. **Natural pretreatments.** Pineapple juice or lemon juice may be used as a natural pretreatment to reduce browning or darkening of light-colored fruits. Drop pieces of fruit directly into the juice for 2 to 5 minutes, drain, and blot with paper towels to absorb excess moisture.

FOOD DRYING METHODS

The sun, of course, is the food dryer our ancestors used. If you live where Old Sol shines long, you too can dry fruits and vegetables outdoors. But those in less sunny regions will want a little help from a kitchen oven (gas, electric, convection, or microwave) or one of the new electric dryers or dehydrators. You can also make your own box dryer.

Oven drying is faster than using an electric dryer or dehydrator, but the electric dryers can handle much larger food loads than any of the ovens. Oven drying is best for small-scale preserving, since the ordinary kitchen model will hold no more than four to six pounds of food at one time. If you've got an extra-big vegetable garden and expect to dry food in quantity, you may want to investigate the new electric dryers or dehydrators, available in some stores and through seed catalogs. Several of the small convection ovens now on the market also have special racks available for drying vegetables. When using an electric dryer or a convection or microwave oven for drying vegetables, always read and follow the manufacturer's directions.

Oven drying

Oven drying may be the easiest way for you to dry food, because it eliminates the need for special equipment. If you've never tried dried fruits and vegetables before, why not prepare a small batch and sample the taste and texture?

Gas and electric ovens. Preheat your gas or electric oven to 140°F for drying fruits and vegetables; you'll need an oven thermometer that registers as low as 100°F in order to keep this temperature constant throughout the many hours of the drying process. Since ovens will vary, you'll probably have to experiment until you learn what works best with yours. For example, the pilot light on some gas stoves may provide just enough heat, or the light bulb in the oven may keep it warm enough for drying foods. Some electric ovens have a "low" or "warm" setting that may provide the right temperature for drying.

You must keep the oven door open slightly during drying, so moist air can escape. Use a rolled newspaper, wood block, hot pad, or other similar item to prop open the oven door about one inch for an electric oven and four to six inches for a gas oven. Sometimes it also helps to place an electric fan set on "low" in front of the oven door to keep air circulating. Don't use a fan for a gas oven with a pilot light, though; it can blow out the pilot.

You'll be able to read the oven thermometer easily if you put it in the middle of the top tray of vegetables. Take a reading after the first 10 minutes, and, if necessary, make adjustments in the door opening or the temperature control. After that, check the oven temperature every 30 minutes during the drying process to be sure it remains constant at 140°F.

To keep air circulating around the food, your drying trays should be one to two inches smaller all around than the interior of your oven. If you want to add more trays, place blocks of wood at the corners of the oven racks and stack the trays at least one-and-a-half inches apart. You can dry up to four trays at once in a conventional oven, but remember that a big load takes longer to dry than a smaller one. Don't use the top position of the oven rack in an electric oven for drying, because food on the top tray will dry too quickly.

Since the temperature varies inside the oven, it's important to shift your vegetable drying trays every half-hour. Rotate the trays from front to back, and shift them from top to bottom. Numbering the trays will help you keep track of the rotation order. You'll also need to stir the vegetables every 30 minutes, to be sure the pieces are drying evenly.

Convection ovens. To dry fruits or vegetables in a convection oven, arrange them on the dehydrating racks provided, and place the racks in a cold oven. Set the temperature at 150°F for fruits and vegetables, 100°F for herbs. The air should feel warm, not hot. Keep an oven thermometer inside the oven, so you can keep track of the temperature. Prop the oven door open one to one-and-a-half inches to allow moisture to evaporate. Set the oven timer to the "stay on" option, set it for maximum time possible, then reset it during drying if necessary. Drying times in a convection oven are usually shorter, so check foods for doneness at the lower range of times given in the recipes. Rotate the racks and stir the fruits or vegetables as you would using a conventional oven.

Microwave ovens. To dry foods in a microwave oven, follow the directions that come with your appliance. Usually, you arrange the prepared produce in a single, even layer on paper towels, cover them with more paper towels, and then dry the food at a reduced power setting. If you have a microwave roasting rack, arrange the fruits or vegetables on it before drying. Stir the food and replace the paper towels with fresh ones periodically. Exact drying times can vary widely, depending on the wattage and efficiency of your oven, the food itself, and the humidity, so you'll need to check frequently *and* keep a record of best drying times for reference.

Food dryers

Both commercial and homemade food dryers provide automatically controlled heat and ventilation. You can buy the new electric dryers or dehydrators in many hardware, housewares, farm supply, and health food stores. Prices depend on the size of the appliance and other special features.

Electric dryers or dehydrators. These are lightweight metal boxes with drawer racks for drying foods, which will hold up to 14 pounds of fresh vegetables. If you'll be doing a great deal of home drying, look into an electric dryer, because drying large quantities of vegetables could tie up your kitchen oven for days at a time. Although electric dryers use less electricity for drying than would an electric oven for the same amount of vegetables, electric dryers run at lower temperatures and drying times are a bit longer.

When using an electric dryer or dehydrator, always follow the manufacturer's directions for drying foods.

Electric food dehydrators are available commercially in rectangular or circular designs. The rectangular type is more readily available, but the circular format does a better job of evenly drying and does not require that the trays be rotated during drying. Electric dehydrators range in price from about $35 to $125, and can be a wise buy if you dry large quantities of fruits and vegetables at home.

When drying food in the oven on trays or racks, make sure to leave 2 inches of space all around the rack to allow free air circulation. Use an oven thermometer that can register as low as 100°F to maintain correct oven temperature.

How to make drying trays for the oven

An easy-to-make oven drying tray can be constructed from wooden slats and nylon netting or cheesecloth. (You may have alternatives, too. Your radiator may send out enough heat to dry foods in winter. Or your attic may get hot enough in summer to act as a natural dehydrator. Never use a space heater for drying foods, though, because space heaters stir up dust and dirt which will contaminate the food.)

Frames for drying trays can be constructed from narrow slats stapled or nailed together. Measure your oven rack and build the tray 2 inches smaller in all directions than the oven rack (the extra space is needed to allow air to circulate around the food). Place the food to be dried on the trays and place the trays in the oven.

An even simpler way to use the oven rack for drying is to cover it with nylon netting. You can also make a cheesecloth cover (use two thicknesses of cheesecloth) to fit over the rack. Again, there should be 2 inches of space between the food and

An electric dryer, or dehydrator, is a wise buy if you're drying large quantities of vegetables at home; it takes a little longer than your electric oven, but uses less energy.

the sides of the oven. (If you want to dry foods in the sun, the tray you use must have a cover to protect the food from dust and insects.)

Baking sheets or cookie trays should not be used as drying trays. These metal trays do not allow free airflow around the produce and the top of the food will dry out while the underside remains wet.

When drying foods in the oven, follow these instructions:

1. Arrange the trays in the oven, and set the temperature. Use an oven thermometer that will read as low as 100°F for maintaining the proper temperature.
2. Leave the oven door ajar to allow moist air to escape.
3. Place an electric fan on a stool or to one side of the open oven door.
4. If you are drying more than one tray of food at a time, make sure there is 2 inches of space between the drying trays. Don't prepare more food than you can dry in one oven-load.
5. Do not use baking sheets or cookie sheets as drying trays.

Making your own dehydrator

If you are handy with tools, or know someone who is, you can construct a homemade dehydrator for less than it costs to buy a commercial one. Information on how to do it is available from your local Cooperative Extension Service.

When buying the necessary materials, do not buy aluminum screening for trays. Aluminum discolors and corrodes easily. Do not use copper because copper destroys vitamin C. Cheesecloth, nylon netting, or muslin can be used to cover galvanized screening. Stay away from fiberglass mesh because the fibers can get into the food and become dangerous.

If you use cheesecloth on which to dry herbs, use a double thickness to prevent the seeds or crumbled pieces from falling through the mesh—the pieces will shrink even smaller as they dry.

Air-drying chili peppers

Hot chili peppers can be air-dried in your kitchen without using an oven drying method or an electric dehydrator. Use small chili peppers. Do not use the large green or yellow varieties. To make a string of chilis, follow these steps:

1. Select small hot chilis that are uniform in size. Wash and dry on paper towels.

Chili peppers can be air-dried without the use of either your oven or an electric dryer. The chilis are threaded on a sturdy string and hung up to dry. When you want to use them, just pick them from the string.

2. Thread a trussing needle with sturdy string and tie a bow at the end. Wear rubber gloves if necessary to protect your fingertips.
3. Insert needle through green stem of each pepper. Work on a flat surface and string peppers in an alternate left and right arrangement.
4. Tie a loop in the other end of the thread and clip excess thread.
5. Hang the strung peppers in a warm area for about 2 weeks. Cover with cheesecloth if necessary to protect from dust.
6. For use, break the chilis from the stem as needed.
7. Wash your hands carefully after handling fresh or dried chilis; the oils may cause burning.
8. Dried chilis retain their flavor for about a year to 18 months.

BASIC DRYING EQUIPMENT

Unless you decide to buy an electric dryer or dehydrator, you've probably already got everything necessary for home drying vegetables. In addition to an oven you'll need:

- A scale to weigh food before and after drying.
- An oven thermometer that will read as low as 100°F for maintaining proper oven temperature.
- Sharp stainless steel knives that won't discolor the vegetables, for thin-slicing, paring, or cutting.
- A cutting board for chopping and slicing. Be sure to scrub the board thoroughly before and after use.
- Drying trays made of muslin or double layers of cheesecloth attached to a wooden frame. Or cover your oven rack with clean muslin or cheesecloth. Do not use baking sheets or cookie trays unless you are making fruit leathers.
- A blancher for pretreatment of most vegetables. Use a ready-made blancher; or make one using a deep pot with a cover, and a colander or basket that will fit down inside the pot.
- A long, flexible spatula for stirring the vegetable pieces to insure even drying.
- Airtight storage containers, with tight-fitting lids, that are also moisture/vaporproof. Use glass canning or other jars, coffee cans lined with plastic bags, freezer containers, or refrigerator-ware. You can also use double plastic bags; close them tightly with string, rubber bands, or twist ties.
- An electric fan to circulate the air in front of your oven, if necessary.
- Sodium bisulfite or ascorbic acid for pretreating light-colored fruit.

BASIC INGREDIENTS

Choose perfect, full-ripened produce that is tender, mature (but not woody), and very, very fresh. Fruits and vegetables are best if dried immediately after harvesting, or they will begin to lose flavor and quality. Vegetables and berries are especially delicate. Every minute from harvesting to the drying tray counts—so hurry. Never use produce with bad spots, and harvest only the amount of fruit or vegetables you can dry at one session.

Since vegetables must be chilled quickly after blanching, you'll need ice at hand to keep the cooling water really cold. Keep a reserve of ice in the freezer so you won't run short. One way is to start filling heavy-duty plastic bags with ice cubes a few days before you'll be home drying; or rinse out empty milk cartons, then fill them with water and freeze.

The kitchen sink is a favorite spot for holding ice water to chill vegetables, but if you want to keep it free for other uses, a plastic dishpan or other large, clean container also works very well.

BASIC DRYING TECHNIQUES

Although the techniques for drying foods aren't as precise as those for freezing or canning, there's definitely a right way to go about it. As with all preserving methods, you must always begin with the freshest and highest-quality produce to insure good results. Cleanliness and sanitation when handling and preparing the food are also crucial. And though drying produce isn't difficult to do, it demands plenty of careful attention. The pieces of produce must be stirred, the temperature checked, and tray positions changed about every half hour. That means you must be at home during the whole time it takes to dry your fruits and vegetables.

Fruits must be fully ripened but not overripe. Overripe fruit contains too much juice and will suffer flavor loss. Pretreat apples, peaches, nectarines, and strawberries. Berries with tough skins must be blanched or slashed so that the inside of the fruit can dry.

Speed is of the essence when preparing foods to dry. For best results, vegetables should be blanched, cooled, and blotted dry within a very short time of harvesting. And you must never interrupt the drying process once it's begun. You can't cool partly dried food and then start it up again later, because there's a chance bacteria, molds, and yeasts will find a home in it. Always schedule your home drying for a day when your work is not likely to be interrupted.

Cleaning and cutting

Harvest only as much food as you can dry at one time. Using a kitchen oven, that's about four to six pounds; an electric dryer or dehydrator can handle up to 14 pounds of fresh produce. Wash and drain the vegetables, then cut and prepare as the recipe directs. Depending on the size of the fruits and vegetables and the drying method, that could mean slicing, grating, cutting, or simply breaking the food into pieces so it will dry evenly on all sides. Remember that thin pieces dry faster than thick ones. If you have a choice between French-cutting and crosscutting green beans, remember that the French-cut beans will dry faster.

How to Dry Fruits and Vegetables

Blanching

Nearly all vegetables must be blanched before drying. Blanching—a brief heat treatment—stops the action of enzymes, the catalysts for chemical change that are present in all foods. If certain enzymes aren't deactivated before vegetables are dried, the flavor and color of the food will be destroyed. The drying process alone isn't enough to stop enzyme activity.

Always follow the blanching times given in the recipes exactly. Over-blanching will result in the loss of vitamins and minerals; under-blanching won't do the job of stopping enzyme action. Either way, you'll end up with an inferior product.

Boiling water blanching. Heat one gallon of water to boiling in a blancher. Put no more than one pound or four cups of prepared vegetables at a time into the blancher's insert, colander, or strainer, and carefully lower it into boiling water for the time given in the recipe.

Chilling

You must always chill blanched vegetables before drying them, to be certain the cooking process has stopped. After removing the vegetables from the blancher, immerse the colander or steamer rack full of vegetables in a sinkful of ice water or a dishpan full of ice water. The vegetables should be chilled for the same amount of time the recipe gives for blanching in boiling water. Drain well, then blot with paper towels.

Preparing to dry

Spread the blanched vegetable pieces or pretreated fruit pieces in a single, even layer on the drying tray. (You can dry more than one vegetable at the same time, but strong-smelling vegetables such as onions, cabbage, and carrots should be dried separately.) Put the trays in the oven or electric dryer, leaving at least one to two inches between the trays for air circulation.

Do not try to dry strong-flavored vegetables with fruit. Dried fruits are best when prepared with other fruits; stick to batches of berries or batches of cut fruits, but don't mix the two.

Maintaining proper drying temperature

Produce must be dried at low, even temperatures—just enough heat to dry the pieces without cooking them. The proper temperature for drying in a conventional oven is 140°F, 150°F for convection ovens. Follow the manufacturer's directions for microwave ovens and all other appliances. Maintaining the right temperature steadily, with some air circulation, is the essential to successful drying. Electric dryers and dehydrators automatically maintain the right temperature. For oven drying or when using a homemade box dryer, check your oven thermometer every half hour. To insure even drying, you must also stir the produce every 30 minutes or so, shift the trays from top to bottom, and rotate the trays from front to back.

Although rapid drying is important, too rapid drying in an oven will result in the outer surface of the food hardening before the moisture inside has evaporated (case hardening). You can prevent case hardening by keeping a constant watch on the oven temperature and doing whatever is needed to maintain the heat at 140°F.

Scorching. Each fruit and vegetable has its own critical temperature beyond which a scorched taste will develop. Although there's not much danger of scorching at the start of the drying process, vegetables can scorch easily during the last couple of hours. Even slight scorching will ruin the flavor and affect the nutritive value of dried foods, so be extra vigilant about maintaining the proper temperature toward the end of the drying process.

Ventilation. When foods are drying, the moisture they contain escapes by evaporating into the surrounding air. If the air around the food is trapped, it will quickly reach a saturation point. Trapped, saturated air won't be able to hold any additional moisture—and drying won't take place. For this reason, ventilation in and around your oven is as important as keeping the temperature constant.

Electric dryers or dehydrators automatically provide proper ventilation. With oven drying or when using a homemade box dryer, you'll need to leave the oven door slightly ajar—and possibly use an electric fan to insure good air circulation.

In addition, homemade drying trays you use for oven drying should be at least one to two inches smaller than the oven rack all around so air can circulate around the front, sides, and back of the trays. There should also be at least three inches of air space at the top and bottom of the oven.

Testing for doneness

In most forms of food preserving, processing times are exact. You know just how long it takes before the food is done. However, the times for drying vary considerably—from four hours to more than 12—depending on the kind of produce, how thinly it's sliced, how much food is on each tray, and how much is being dried in the oven or dryer at one time. The recipes that follow give you the drying time range for each type of produce, but the only way you can be sure the food is sufficiently dry is to test sample pieces.

When you think the vegetables are dry, remove a few pieces from the tray, then return the tray to the oven. Let the sample pieces cool before testing—even food that's perfectly dry will feel soft and moist while still warm. When the pieces are cool, follow the test for doneness given for the vegetable in each recipe. A rule of thumb is that properly dried vegetables are hard and brittle to the touch. Exceptions to the rule are mushrooms, sweet peppers, and squash, which will feel pliable and leathery when dry. Some food experts recommend the hammer test: if sufficiently dry, the vegetable pieces will shatter when struck with a hammer.

Conditioning

Foods don't always dry evenly, nor does each piece or slice dry at exactly the same rate as all the others. To be sure all the food in a single batch is evenly dried, you'll have to condition it. Put the cooled, dried pieces into a large, deep crock, dishpan, jar, or coffee can; then store it in a warm, dry room for a week to 10 days. Cover the jar or can lightly with cheesecloth to keep out insects, and stir the dried pieces at least once a day so that the moisture from any under-dried pieces will be absorbed by the overdried pieces.

After conditioning, give the food one final treatment to get rid of any insects or insect eggs. Either put the dried vegetables in the freezer for a few hours, or heat them on a cookie sheet in a closed oven at 175°F for 15 minutes. Be sure to let the food cool completely again before packaging.

HOW TO STORE DRIED FOODS

Keeping out air and moisture is the secret to good dried foods. To maintain the quality and safety of your dried food items, you'll need to take special care when packaging and storing them.

Even when you're using an oven or an electric dehydrator, you'll have to watch out for the effects of humidity on drying foods. Choose a bright, sunny day for your home drying—that way you'll keep the dried foods from picking up moisture

from the surrounding air after they leave the oven or dryer.

Packaging

Dried foods are vulnerable to contamination by insects as soon as they're removed from the oven or electric dryer. To protect them, you must package dried produce in airtight, moisture/vaporproof containers just as soon as it is completely dry. Canning jars that have been rinsed out with boiling water and dried make good containers, as do coffee cans and plastic freezer bags. When using a coffee can, first wrap the food in a plastic bag to keep the metal of the can from affecting the flavor of the food.

Pint-size containers or small plastic bags are best for packaging dried foods. Try to pack the food tightly but without crushing it. If you're using plastic bags, force out as much air as possible before closing them. By using small bags, several may be packed into a larger jar or coffee can—that way you can use small portions as needed, without exposing the whole container to possible contamination each time it's opened.

Storing dried foods safely

Store your packaged, dried fruits and vegetables in a cool, dark, dry place. The cooler the temperature of the storage area, the longer foods will retain their high quality. However, dried foods can't be stored indefinitely, since they do lose vitamins, flavor, color, and aroma during storage. Your pantry or kitchen cupboards may provide good storage, if the area remains cool. A dry basement can also be a good spot. Dried produce can be stored in the freezer, too—but why take up valuable freezer space with foods that will keep at cool room temperature?

Dried foods are favorites with campers because they are very light in weight and can be stored in small spaces. Thus they are well-suited for trail food and outdoor cooking.

Many dried fruits and vegetables will keep up to 12 months, if properly stored. Carrots, onions, and cabbage will spoil more quickly, so use them up within six months.

To be on the safe side, check the packages of dried vegetables from time to time. If you find mold, the food is no longer safe and should be discarded immediately. If you find a little moisture, but no spoilage, heat the dried vegetables for 15 minutes in a 175°F oven; then cool and repackage. If you find much moisture, the vegetables must be put through the entire drying process again. Remember, you must always cool dried foods thoroughly before packaging; if packaged while still warm, they'll sweat and may mold.

HOW TO USE DRIED FRUITS AND VEGETABLES

To used dried fruits or vegetables, you have to reverse the drying or dehydration process to rehydrate them, that is, replace the water that was removed. This is accomplished in water or other liquid. If you soak dried vegetables before using them, they will require less cooking time.

To rehydrate vegetables, add two cups hot water for each cup dried vegetables and allow vegetables to soak for an hour. Dried fruits are soaked in the same manner (you may substitute fruit juice for the water). Do not add sugar to fruits until after they have been rehydrated; sugar will toughen the product. After soaking, the dried food should regain nearly the same size as when fresh.

Rehydrated or refreshed vegetables require less cooking time than fresh vegetables. Simply simmer them to the desired degree of firmness. Taste can be improved by the addition of butter and other seasonings. Rehydrated vegetables are best used in soups, stews, salads, casseroles, and other combination dishes. See the recipes given later in this chapter for some serving suggestions.

To use dried fruits, rehydrate and simmer (if desired) until tender. The same spices and flavorings that are appropriate for fresh fruits are also suitable for dried fruits. Add such flavorings as cinnamon, ginger, or nutmeg after the fruits are plump again. Dried fruits are excellent in cobblers, breads, puddings, and pies.

THE NUTRITIONAL VALUE OF DRIED FOODS

Some changes can be expected in the nutritional value of foods that have been dried. The calorie content, of course, remains the same as for the fresh foods, although fruits taste sweeter without the addition of extra sugar. The calorie content per unit of weight, however, is higher because the nutrients and natural sugars are concentrated due to the removal of water content. A cup of dried grapes (raisins) contains more calories than a cup of fresh grapes simply because of the size difference, which means you can get a lot more raisins than fresh grapes into the cup.

The mineral and fiber content of foods remains the same after drying, and research indicates little change in the amount of vitamins A and C retained in dried foods. Sulfur (sodium bisulfite) used during the drying process does, however, affect the B vitamins retained in dried fruits. The fruits with which the use of sodium bisulfite is suggested in this book are very low in B vitamins, thus the loss of these vitamins is only slight.

BASIC DRYING STEPS

The recipes that follow give you specific directions for drying each fruit and vegetable. To prevent problems, keep these basic steps in mind when home drying foods. Remember that only the highest quality fruits and vegetables are suitable for drying.

1. Select fruits and vegetables that are freshly picked, tender, and just mature enough to eat.
2. Set out all ingredients and equipment. Wash and dry all utensils, countertops, working surfaces, and your hands.
3. Preheat your conventional oven to 140°F, or follow the manufacturer's directions for your electric dryer or dehydrator, or for a convection or microwave oven.
4. Wash the produce thoroughly, scrubbing with a brush if necessary, but handling gently to avoid bruising.
5. Cut, slice, or grate the food according to the recipe directions.
6. Blanch vegetables in small amounts at a time, according to recipe directions. Fill the blancher about half full, then begin heating. After blanching, chill the vegetable pieces in ice water for the same amount of time the recipe gives for blanching.
7. Drain the produce well, blot dry, then spread in a single, even layer on the racks of an electric dryer. Don't crowd the pieces on the tray, and don't prepare more produce than you can dry at one time.
8. For conventional oven drying, put an oven thermometer toward the back of the tray. Put the tray on the top shelf in a preheated oven, and maintain an oven temperature of 140°F.
9. For convection oven drying, place the racks full of food into a cold oven. Set the temperature at 150°F. Open the oven door 1 to 1¼ inches. Set the oven timer to the "stay on" position, or for as long as it will run, resetting as needed.
10. For drying in an electric dryer or dehydrator, or a microwave or convection oven, follow the manufacturer's directions.

11. Check the trays often (every hour or so), and stir the pieces on the trays, moving the outside pieces to the center. For oven drying, turn the tray from front to back and—if drying more than one tray—change the trays from shelf to shelf for even drying. Check the trays more frequently during the last few hours of drying to prevent scorching. For microwave oven drying, follow the manufacturer's directions. Use the lower end of drying times given in the recipes as a guide for doneness when you're using a conventional, microwave, or convection oven. The upper range of drying times is a guide to doneness when you're using an electric dryer or dehydrator.

12. To test for doneness, remove sample pieces, cool, and then follow the recipe directions for testing for doneness. When the produce is completely dry, as described in each recipe, remove from the oven or dehydrator and let stand until cooled. Test the pieces again after cooling. If the food still shows some moisture, return it to the oven or dryer until completely dried.

13. Turn the dried foods into a deep container, cover lightly with cheesecloth, and condition, stirring once a day for a week to 10 days.

14. Pack into vapor/moistureproof, airtight containers or double plastic bags and store in a cool, dark, dry place for up to 12 months.

15. To rehydrate, put the pieces in a pan or bowl, and add just enough boiling water to cover—usually 2 cups of water per cup of dried produce—anywhere from ½ hour to several hours, depending on the type of produce.

16. Cook fruits or vegetables in their soaking water until tender, or drain and add to recipes just as you would fresh fruits and vegetables.

RECIPES FOR DRYING FRUITS AND VEGETABLES

Remember that a certain amount of trial and error is needed when drying foods. Although a range of drying times is provided for each item, it sometimes happens that the produce will need even longer to dry than the recipe has indicated. When you think the food is ready, follow the test for doneness given in each recipe. You'll soon develop the knack for judging proper dryness.

BEANS, GREEN

6 pounds (1-inch pieces) = ½ pound or 2½ pints

1. Choose fresh, just-mature green beans.

2. Wash beans, then drain. Trim off ends and cut beans into 1- to 2-inch pieces.

3. Blanch in boiling water 2 minutes. Drain well, chill, and pat dry with paper towels.

4. Arrange in a single, even layer on racks.

5. Dry until brittle, 3 to 14 hours.

6. Condition and store according to basic drying steps 13 and 14.

7. Rehydrate in 2½ cups of boiling water for each cup of beans, about 1 hour.

BEANS, SHELLING (broad, dry, or lima)

If you're planning to sprout shelling beans, do not use this recipe, but use the recipe below for slow air-drying.

7 pounds = 1¼ pounds or 2 pints

1. Choose fresh, just-mature beans.

2. Shell the beans; then wash and drain.

3. Blanch in boiling water 15 minutes. Drain well, chill, and pat dry with paper towels.

4. Arrange the beans in a single, even layer on racks.

5. Dry until brittle, 4 to 12 hours.

6. Condition and store according to basic drying steps 13 and 14.

7. Rehydrate in 2½ cups of boiling water for each cup of beans, about 1½ hours.

BEANS, SPROUTING (dry or mung)

Beans to be sprouted must be dried slowly, without the blanching or heating used in the method above, because processing kills the seed. Only live seed can be sprouted.

7 pounds = 1¼ pounds or 2 pints

1. Leave dry beans on the plants until the pods have matured and the leaves have turned brown. The seeds should be dry and hard.

2. Harvest the beans by pulling up the entire plant. Shake loose dirt from the roots.

3. Tie the plants in bundles and hang them to dry in a warm, dark, dry place; or spread them on clean newspaper on the floor in a dark, warm, dry room.

4. Let dry 1 to 3 weeks, until beans are completely dry and hard. To test, shell a bean and bite it; you should hardly be able to dent the seed with your teeth.

5. When beans are completely dry, shell them.

Discard the pods.

6. Store according to basic drying step 14.

7. Use for sprouting or for planting the following year.

BEETS

15 pounds = 1½ pounds or 3 to 5 pints

1. Choose firm, undamaged beets.

2. Remove tops and roots from beets.

3. Blanch in boiling water about 45 minutes, or until tender. Drain well, chill, and pat dry with paper towels. Slip off skins and cut into ⅛- to ¼-inch slices or strips.

4. Arrange in a single, even layer on racks.

5. Dry until brittle, 3 to 12 hours.

6. Condition and store according to basic drying steps 13 and 14.

7. Rehydrate in 2¾ cups of boiling water for each cup of beets, about 1½ hours.

BRUSSELS SPROUTS

Yield varies widely depending on size and moisture content of sprouts.

1. Choose perfect, evenly sized sprouts. Remove any discolored leaves.

2. Wash sprouts well; drain. Slice lengthwise, ½-inch thick.

3. Blanch 4½ to 5 minutes in boiling water. Drain very well, chill, and pat dry with paper towels.

4. Arrange slices in a single, even layer on racks.

5. Dry until brittle, 4 to 12 hours.

6. Condition and store according to basic drying steps 13 and 14.

7. Rehydrate in 3 cups of boiling water for each cup of Brussels sprouts, about 1 hour.

CABBAGE

Yield varies widely depending on moisture content of the cabbage.

1. Choose firm, compact heads with unblemished leaves.

2. Wash, remove the outer leaves, then cut in quarters and core the cabbage. Cut cabbage into slices, ¼-inch thick or less.

3. Blanch 2 minutes in water, until leaves are wilted. Drain very well, chill, and pat dry with paper towels.

4. Arrange in a single, even layer on racks.

5. Dry until brittle, 1 to 12 hours.

6. Condition and store according to basic drying steps 13 and 14.

7. Rehydrate in 3 cups of boiling water for each cup of cabbage, about 1 hour.

CARROTS

15 pounds = 1¼ pounds or 2 to 4 pints

1. Choose crisp, young, tender carrots.

2. Wash well, pare, and cut off tops and ends.

3. Slice very thin, crosswise or lengthwise. Or shred and put shreds into a cheesecloth bag.

4. Blanch in boiling water. If using carrot shreds, blanch about 1½ to 2 minutes. Drain well, chill, and pat dry with paper towels.

5. Arrange the slices in a single, even layer on racks.

6. Dry until very tough and leathery, 4 to 12 hours. If using carrot shreds, dry until shreds are brittle.

7. Condition and store accordingly to basic drying steps 13 and 14.

8. Rehydrate in 2¼ cups of boiling water for each cup of carrots, about 1 hour.

CAULIFLOWER

Yield varies widely depending on the size and moisture content of flowerets.

1. Choose perfect, firm heads. Break into small flowerets.

2. Blanch in boiling water until just tender. Drain well, chill, and pat dry with paper towels.

3. Cut into slices, if you wish.

4. Arrange slices or flowerets in a single, even layer on racks.

5. Dry until crisp, 4 to 12 hours.

6. Condition and store according to basic drying steps 13 and 14.

7. Rehydrate in 3 cups of boiling water for each cup of flowerets, about 1 hour.

CELERY

12 pounds = ¾ pound or 3½ to 4 pints

1. Choose young, tender stalks with tender, green leaves.

2. Wash the stalks and leaves well; shake dry. Trim the ends.

3. Slice the stalks thinly.

4. Blanch in boiling water about 2 minutes. Drain well, chill, and pat dry with paper towels.

5. Spread the slices in a single, even layer on racks. Spread leaves in a single, even layer.

6. Dry until brittle, 3 to 12 hours.

7. Condition and store according to basic drying steps 13 and 14.

8. Rehydrate in 2 cups boiling water for each cup of celery, about 1 hour.

CHICK PEAS

If you plan to sprout chick peas, don't use this procedure; follow the instructions in this section under Beans, sprouting.

7 pounds = 1¼ pounds or 2 pints

1. Choose fresh, just-mature chick peas.

2. Shell the peas; then wash and drain.

3. Blanch in boiling water about 15 minutes. Drain well, chill, and pat dry with paper towels.

4. Arrange the peas in a single, even layer on racks.

5. Dry until brittle, 4 to 12 hours.

6. Condition and store according to basic drying steps 13 and 14.

7. Rehydrate in 2½ cups of boiling water for each cup of peas, about 1½ hours.

CHINESE CABBAGE

3 pounds = ¼ pound or 5½ pints

1. Choose very fresh, perfect leaves.

2. Wash the leaves well; shake dry. Remove any large, tough stalks.

3. Blanch in boiling water about 1½ minutes until completely wilted. Drain very well, chill, and pat leaves dry with paper towels.

4. Arrange leaves in a single layer on racks.

5. Dry until brittle, 2½ to 8 hours or more.

6. Condition and store according to basic drying steps 13 and 14.

7. Rehydrate in 1 cup of boiling water for each cup of Chinese cabbage, about ½ hour.

CORN

If you plan to sprout corn kernels, don't use this procedure; let the corn slowly air-dry on the cob according to the directions in this section under Beans, sprouting.

18 pounds = 2½ pounds or 4 to 4½ pints

1. Choose young, tender ears of very fresh corn.

2. Husk the ears, remove the silk, and then wash the corn.

3. Blanch in boiling water about 1½ minutes or until milk doesn't come out of the cut kernels. Drain, chill, and pat dry with paper towels.

4. Cut the kernels from ears and spread them in a single, even layer on racks.

5. Dry until very brittle, 2 to 10 hours. Tap a single kernel with a hammer; if done, it will shatter easily.

6. Condition and store according to basic drying steps 13 and 14.

7. Rehydrate in 2¼ cups boiling water for each cup of corn, about ½ hour.

EGGPLANT

Yield varies widely according to size and moisture content of eggplant.

1. Select perfect, plump, well-colored eggplant.

2. Wash, trim, and cut into ¼-inch-thick slices.

3. Blanch 3 minutes in boiling water. Drain well, chill, and pat dry with paper towels.

4. Spread slices in a single, even layer on racks.

5. Dry until leathery, 3½ to 12 hours.

6. Condition and store according to basic drying steps 13 and 14.

7. Rehydrate in 2½ to 3 cups of boiling water for each cup of dried eggplant, about 1 hour.

GREENS (beet, chard, collard, kale, mustard, and turnip)

3 pounds = ¼ pound or 5½ pints

1. Choose very fresh, perfect leaves.

2. Wash leaves well; shake dry. Remove any large, tough stalks.

3. Blanch in boiling water about 1½ minutes until completely wilted. Drain very well, chill, and pat leaves dry with paper towels.

4. Arrange leaves in a single layer on racks.

5. Dry until brittle, 2½ to 8 hours or more.

6. Condition and store according to basic drying steps 13 and 14.

7. Rehydrate in 1 cup of boiling water for each cup of greens, about ½ hour.

HORSERADISH

Horseradish doesn't require blanching. Add dried shreds as desired when cooking. Yield varies widely depending on size and moisture content of roots.

1. Select firm, unblemished roots.

2. Wash well and remove small roots and stubs; then pare and grate.

3. Spread grated horseradish in a single, even layer on racks.

4. Dry until brittle, 3 to 10 hours.

5. Condition and store according to basic drying steps 13 and 14.

LENTILS

If you plan to sprout lentils, don't use this procedure; follow the instructions under Beans, sprouting.

7 pounds = 1¼ pounds or 2 pints

1. Choose fresh, just-mature lentils.

2. Shell the lentils; then wash and drain.

3. Blanch in boiling water 15 minutes. Drain well, chill, and pat dry with paper towels.

4. Arrange the lentils in a single, even layer on racks.

5. Dry until brittle, 4 to 12 hours.

6. Condition and store according to basic drying steps 13 and 14.

7. Rehydrate in 2½ cups of boiling water for each cup of lentils, about 1½ hours.

MUSHROOMS

Mushrooms don't require blanching.

1 pound = 1½ to 2 cups

1. Choose young, fresh, evenly sized, tender mushrooms with tightly closed heads.

2. Wash them very well, scrubbing with a brush. Remove and discard any stalks that are tough or woody, and trim off the ends of any

remaining stalks.

3. Slice, or leave medium and small mushrooms whole, as you wish. Slice large mushrooms.

4. Arrange the slices or whole mushrooms in a single, even layer on racks.

5. Dry until leathery and hard, usually 3 to 12 hours. Small pieces may be brittle.

6. Condition and store according to basic drying steps 13 and 14.

7. Rehydrate in 2 cups boiling water for each cup of dried mushrooms, about 1 hour.

OKRA

Okra doesn't require blanching. Yield varies widely depending on the size and moisture content of the pod.

1. Select fresh, perfect pods.

2. Wash well, then trim off the tops and tips. Cut crosswise into ⅛- to ¼-inch-thick slices.

3. Arrange slices in a single, even layer on racks.

4. Dry until very brittle, 4 to 10 hours.

5. Condition and store according to basic drying steps 13 and 14.

6. Rehydrate in 3 cups boiling water for each cup of okra, about ½ hour.

ONIONS

Onions require neither blanching nor rehydrating as long as the pieces are small and you're adding them to other foods that have some moisture.

12 pounds = 1½ pounds or 11½ pints

1. Choose large, flavorful, perfect onions.

2. Cut off the stems and bottoms, and remove the peels.

3. Slice the onions very thin or chop finely. Separate the slices into rings.

4. Arrange the pieces or rings in a single, even layer on racks.

5. Dry until very crisp and brittle, 3 to 12 hours.

6. Condition and store according to basic drying steps 13 and 14.

7. If desired, rehydrate in 2 cups boiling water for each cup of dried onions.

PEANUTS

Peanuts should be air-dried slowly, without the blanching and heating used for other foods. Use raw, dried peanuts for sprouting or baking; roast the dried nuts for snacks and peanut butter.

7 pounds = 1¼ pounds or 2 pints

1. Leave peanuts in the soil until the leaves have turned yellow.
2. Harvest peanuts by digging up the entire plant, before the first killing frost. Shake loose dirt from the roots.
3. Tie the plants in bundles and hang them to dry in a warm, dark, dry place; or stack them on the floor in a warm, dark, dry room.
4. Let dry for 1 week, until the plants are dry and brittle. Shake off any remaining soil.
5. Pull the peanuts off the plants and spread them on clean newspaper on the floor in a warm, dry room. Let dry 1 to 2 weeks, until the peanuts are completely dry.
6. When peanuts are completely dry, shell them and discard the pods.
7. Store according to basic drying step 14.
8. Use for sprouting or for planting the following year.
9. To roast shelled nuts, spread in a shallow pan. Roast in a conventional oven at 350°F, 20 minutes.

PEAS, BLACK-EYED

If you plan to sprout black-eyed peas, don't use this procedure; use the procedure in this section for Beans, sprouting.

7 pounds = 1¼ pounds or 2 pints

1. Choose fresh, just-matured peas.
2. Shell the peas; then wash and drain.
3. Blanch in boiling water 15 minutes. Drain well, chill, and pat dry with paper towels.
4. Arrange peas in a single, even layer on racks.
5. Dry until brittle, 4 to 12 hours.
6. Condition and store according to basic drying steps 13 and 14.
7. Rehydrate in 2½ cups of boiling water for each cup of black-eyed peas, about 1½ hours.

PEAS, SHELLING

If you plan to sprout shelling peas, don't use this procedure; use the procedure in this section for Beans, sprouting.

8 pounds = ¾ pound or 1 pint

1. Choose young, tender peas.
2. Shell peas; then wash and drain.
3. Blanch in boiling water about 2 minutes. Drain well, chill, and pat dry with paper towels.
4. Arrange peas in a single, even layer on racks.
5. Dry until very crisp, 3 to 12 hours or more. Tap a single pea with a hammer. When done, it will shatter easily.
6. Condition and store according to basic drying steps 13 and 14.
7. Rehydrate in 2½ cups water for each cup of peas, about ½ hour.

PEPPERS, SWEET OR HOT

Peppers don't need to be blanched or rehydrated. Dried sweet peppers are handy to toss into soups, stews, and casseroles. Yield varies widely depending on the size and moisture content of the peppers.

1. Choose tender, ready-to-eat, sweet or hot peppers.
2. Cut out the stems and seeds.
3. Chop in ¼-inch pieces.
4. Arrange pieces in a single, even layer on racks.
5. Dry until brittle, 3 to 12 hours.
6. Condition and store according to basic drying steps 13 and 14.
7. If desired, rehydrate in 2 cups boiling water for each cup dried peppers, about 1 hour.

POTATOES

Yield varies widely depending on the size and moisture content of the potatoes.

1. Select freshly dug, perfect potatoes.
2. Scrub well and then pare. Cut into julienne or shoestring strips about ¼-inch thick, or slice ⅛-inch thick.
3. Blanch in boiling water 5 to 6 minutes. Drain well, chill, and pat dry with paper towels.
4. Spread in a single, even layer on racks.
5. Dry until brittle, about 4 to 12 hours.
6. Condition and store according to basic drying steps 13 and 14.
7. Rehydrate in 1½ to 2 cups of boiling water for each cup of potatoes, about ½ hour.

PUMPKINS

11 pounds = ¾ pound or 3½ pints

1. Choose mature, firm pumpkins.
2. Cut into chunks, scrape out the seeds and string. Cut in 1-inch wide slices. Pare.
3. Slice 1-inch strips crosswise into thin slices.
4. Blanch in boiling water about 1 minute. Drain well, chill, and pat dry with paper towels.
5. Arrange in a single, even layer on racks.
6. Dry until tough, 4 to 12 hours or longer. Thinner slices may be brittle.
7. Condition and store according to basic drying steps 13 and 14.
8. Rehydrate in 3 cups of boiling water for each cup of pumpkin, about 1 hour.

PUMPKIN SEEDS

Use this procedure for drying winter squash seeds. Yields about the same bulk of seeds.

1. Wash seeds thoroughly in cold water to remove all pulp and strings; be careful not to damage the seed coating.
2. Rinse well, drain thoroughly, and pat dry with towels.
3. Spread seeds in a single, even layer on paper towels resting on racks.
4. Let dry in a warm, dry place until completely dry, 12 to 24 hours.
5. Store according to basic drying step 14.
6. Use for sprouting or for planting the next year.
7. To roast for snacks, dry completely as above, or oven roast after washing. Spread in a shallow pan and roast at 350°F, 20 minutes, or until crisp and light brown.

RHUBARB

12 pounds = ³/₄ pound or 3¹/₂ to 4 pints

1. Choose young, tender, perfect rhubarb. Trim off leaves and root ends; wash well.
2. Slice about ¹/₄-inch-thick.
3. Blanch in boiling water 2 minutes. Drain well, chill, and pat dry.
4. Spread the slices in a single, even layer on racks.
5. Dry until hard, about 8 to 16 hours.
6. Condition and store according to basic drying steps 13 and 14.
7. Rehydrate rhubarb in 1¹/₄ cups of boiling water for each cup of rhubarb, 2 to 3 hours or overnight.

SOYBEANS

If you plan to sprout soybeans, don't use this procedure; follow the instructions in this section for Beans, sprouting.

7 pounds = 1¹/₄ pounds or 2 pints

1. Choose very fresh, evenly sized beans.
2. Wash soybeans, but don't shell.
3. Blanch in boiling water 10 minutes. Drain, chill, pat dry with paper towels, and shell.
4. Arrange in a single, even layer on racks.
5. Dry until brittle, usually more than 12 hours. Tap a single bean with a hammer; if done, it will shatter easily.
6. Condition and store according to basic drying steps 13 and 14.
7. Rehydrate in 2¹/₂ cups of boiling water for each cup of beans, about 1¹/₂ hours.

SPINACH, NEW ZEALAND SPINACH

3 pounds = ¹/₄ pound or 5¹/₂ pints

1. Choose very fresh, perfect leaves.
2. Wash leaves well; shake dry. Remove any large tough stalks.
3. Blanch in boiling water about 1¹/₂ minutes or until completely wilted. Drain very well, chill, and pat dry with paper towels.
4. Arrange leaves in a single, even layer on racks.
5. Dry until brittle, 2¹/₂ to 8 hours or more.
6. Condition and store according to basic drying steps 13 and 14.
7. Rehydrate in 1 cup of boiling water for each cup of spinach, about ¹/₂ hour.

SQUASH, SUMMER

10 pounds = ³/₄ pounds or 5 pints

1. Choose young, tender squash with tender skins.
2. Wash well, cut off the ends, and slice about ¹/₄-inch-thick.
3. Blanch in boiling water about 1¹/₂ minutes. Drain well, chill, and pat dry with paper towels.
4. Arrange in a single, even layer on racks.
5. Dry until brittle, 4 to 12 hours.
6. Condition and store according to basic drying steps 13 and 14.

7. Rehydrate in 1¾ cups of boiling water for each cup of squash, about 1 hour.

SQUASH, WINTER

Paring winter squash is not the easiest job in the world, but the storage space you save by drying squash may make it worthwhile.

11 pounds = ¾ pound or 3½ pints

1. Choose mature, well-shaped squash.

2. Cut the squash into chunks, scrape out the seeds and string. Cut in 1-inch-wide slices. Pare.

3. Slice 1-inch strips crosswise into thin slices.

4. Blanch in boiling water about 1 minute. Drain well, chill, and pat dry with paper towels.

5. Arrange in a single, even layer on racks.

6. Dry until tough, 4 to 12 hours or longer. Thinner slices may be brittle.

7. Condition and store according to basic drying steps 13 and 14.

8. Rehydrate in 3 cups of boiling water for each cup of squash, about 1 hour.

TOMATOES

14 pounds = ½ pound or 2½ to 3 pints

1. Choose perfect, red-ripe tomatoes.

2. Wash tomatoes. Drop into boiling water for 1 to 2 minutes to loosen the skins. Pat dry with paper towels. Peel, core, and slice ¼- to ½-inch-thick. Cut small plum, pear, or cherry tomatoes in half. Tomatoes don't require blanching.

3. Arrange in a single, even layer on racks.

4. Dry until leathery, 6 to 12 hours.

5. Condition and store according to basic drying steps 13 and 14.

6. Rehydrate in 2 cups of boiling water for each cup of tomatoes, about 1 hour.

TOMATO LEATHER

This is great just as is for a snack, added to soups or stews, or rehydrated to make tomato sauce. Use fleshy cherry tomatoes or large tomatoes. Add ingredients of your choice: green peppers, garlic, onion, lemon juice, even honey. Yield varies widely depending on the size and moisture content of the tomatoes, and on the additional ingredients you select.

1. Select perfect, well-fleshed tomatoes.

2. Wash well and remove stems.

3. Puree in a blender with any added ingredients and blend until smooth.

4. Cover a tray with plastic wrap, wetting the edges of the wrap to hold it in place on the tray, or taping it in place.

5. Spread the blended tomato mixture evenly on the sheet to ⅛- to ¼-inch thickness.

6. Dry until leathery, 6 to 24 hours.

7. Peel off the plastic wrap, and let the tomato leather cool. Then roll it up in a fresh piece of plastic wrap. Seal in bags or foil. Do not rehydrate.

TOMATO PASTE

Yield and drying time varies widely depending on the moisture content and size of the tomatoes.

1. Choose perfect, red-ripe tomatoes. Wash and cut them into quarters into a large saucepan.

2. Simmer until thick, about 1 to 2 hours; stir occasionally while the tomatoes simmer.

3. Put the tomato mixture through a food mill to remove skin and seeds.

4. Pour the mixture into a cheesecloth-lined strainer to remove the juice.

5. Spread the pulp (from the cheesecloth in the strainer) in a thin, even layer on trays.

6. Dry until leathery.

7. Cut into squares and store according to basic drying step 14. Add to liquid mixtures without rehydrating in place of canned tomato paste.

APPLES

Apple varieties best suited for drying include Winesap, Jonathan, Greening, Rome Beauty, and Red and Golden Delicious.

12 pounds = 1¼ pounds or 3 pints

1. Peel and core the apples and cut into very thin (⅛-inch) slices or rings.

2. Drop slices into a sulfur solution of 2 tablespoons sodium bisulfite to a gallon of water, or dissolve 2½ teaspoons ascorbic acid in 1 cup water and sprinkle over apple pieces.

3. Soak in sulfur solution (if used) 2 minutes.

4. Drain, and blot well with paper towels.

5. Arrange in single layers on racks.

6. Dry until pliable (no moisture beads will

appear when a piece is cut), about 6 to 12 hours.

7. Condition and store according to basic drying steps 13 and 14.

8. Rehydrate 1½ cups apples in 1 cup hot water 30 minutes to 1 hour.

APRICOTS

12 pounds = 2 pounds or 4 pints

1. Pit and slice apricots.
2. Drop slices into sulfur solution of 2 tablespoons sodium bisulfite to 1 gallon water; or dissolve 2½ teaspoons ascorbic acid in 1 cup water and sprinkle over slices.
3. Soak in sulfur solution (if used) 2 minutes.
4. Drain, and blot with paper towels.
5. Arrange in single layers on racks or trays.
6. Dry until pliable (no moisture beads will appear when a slice is cut), about 16 to 36 hours.
7. Condition and store according to basic drying steps 13 and 14.
8. Rehydrate 1 cup apricots in 2 cups hot water for 1 hour.

BERRIES (firm)

This category includes berries that are firm and have a natural waxy coating, like blueberries, cranberries, currants, or gooseberries.

8 pounds = ¾ pound or 1 pint

1. Sort, wash, and drain berries.
2. Plunge into boiling water bath for 15 to 20 seconds.
3. Stop cooking action by placing fruit in ice water for 1 minute.
4. Drain on paper towels.
5. Arrange in single layers on racks or trays.
6. Dry until leathery or crisp, 24 to 36 hours.
7. Condition and store according to basic drying steps 13 and 14.
8. Rehydrate 1 cup berries in 2 cups warm water for 1 hour.

BERRIES (soft)

Soft berries often have so many seeds that the finished dried product isn't consistently very good. If you want to try, follow these instructions.

8 pounds = ¾ pound or 1 pint

1. Sort and wash fruit carefully. (Slice strawberries.) Drain on paper towels.
2. Arrange in single layers on trays or racks.
3. Dry until crisp, 24 to 36 hours.
4. Condition and store according to basic drying steps 13 and 14.
5. Rehydrate 1 cup berries in 2 cups warm water for 1 hour.

CHERRIES

Royal Anne or black cherries are the best choices for drying.

25 pounds = 5 pounds or 3½ pints

1. Sort, wash, and remove stems and pits. Cut each cherry in half.
2. Arrange cherry halves in single layers on trays or racks.
3. Dry until shriveled, leathery, and dry with no moisture pockets. Check by cutting a piece, and checking for moisture beads after 5 minutes. Cherries will take 24 to 36 hours to dry.
4. Condition and store according to basic drying steps 13 and 14.
5. Rehydrate 1 cup fruit in 2 cups hot water for 1 hour.

CITRUS PEEL

The peel from grapefruits, limes, lemons, and thick-skinned navel oranges (not Valencias) is excellent when dried. Use it in baked foods and desserts.

1. Scrub fruit with stiff vegetable brush.
2. Carefully remove outer 1/16 to 1/8 inch of peel; do not peel down to the bitter white pith.
3. Arrange in single layers on trays or racks.
4. Dry 8 to 12 hours until crisp.
5. Crush if desired.
6. Store according to basic drying step 14.

GRAPES

Muscat or Thompson red or green seedless grapes make excellent raisins. Green Thompson grapes make golden raisins. Red or black Thompson seedless grapes make large sweet raisins.

12 pounds = 1½ pounds or 3 to 4 pints

1. Remove grapes from stems. Sort, wash, and drain on paper towels, *or*

2. Blanch for 30 seconds and then place in ice water bath for 1 minute to stop cooking process. Drain. (Blanching is optional.)

3. Dry 15 to 36 hours until centers are completely dry. The fruit should be raisin-like in texture.

4. Condition and store according to basic drying steps 13 and 14.

NECTARINES

12 pounds = 1 to 1½ pounds or 3 pints (quartered)

1. Wash fruit, pit, and cut into quarters. (It is not necessary to peel nectarines for drying.)

2. Pretreat in pineapple juice or sprinkle with lemon juice or ascorbic acid water.

3. Drain, and pat dry with paper towels.

4. Arrange pieces with the skin side down on racks or trays.

5. Dry 36 to 48 hours or until soft and pliable, with no moisture beads forming in center when piece is cut.

6. Condition and store according to basic drying steps 13 and 14.

7. Rehydrate 1 cup nectarines in 2 cups hot water for 1 hour.

PEARS

Pears are prepared in the same way as apples.

12 pounds = 1¼ pounds or 3 pints

1. Peel and core the pears and cut into very thin (⅛-inch) slices or rings.

2. Drop slices into a sulfur solution of 2 tablespoons sodium bisulfite to a gallon of water, or dissolve 2½ teaspoons ascorbic acid in 1 cup water and sprinkle over pear pieces.

3. Soak in sulfur solution (if used) for 2 minutes.

4. Drain, and blot well with paper towels.

5. Arrange in single layers on racks or trays.

6. Dry until pliable (no moisture beads will appear when a piece is cut), about 6 to 12 hours.

7. Condition and store according to basic drying steps 13 and 14.

8. Rehydrate 1½ cups pears in 1 cup hot water 30 minutes to 1 hour.

PLUMS

Dried plums are known as prunes.

25 pounds = 8 pounds or 12 pints

1. Wash plums, cut in half, remove pits. Slice into ⅜-inch slices, or leave whole.

2. Arrange in single layers on trays or racks.

3. Dry until leathery. If plum is left whole, pit should not move when dried plum is squeezed.

4. Condition and store according to basic drying steps 13 and 14.

5. Rehydrate 1 cup dried plums (prunes) in 2 cups hot water for 1 hour.

How to Sprout Vegetables

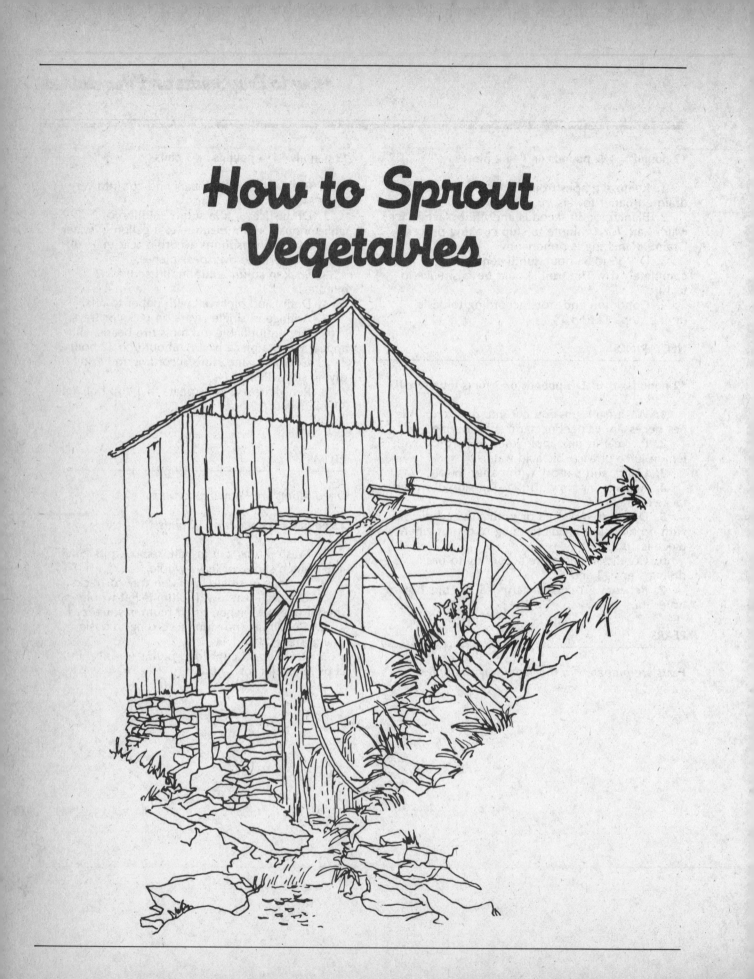

Sprouting is one of the easiest ways to grow fresh vegetables for eating — both in and out of season. While mung bean sprouts have long been familiar in Chinese cooking, alfalfa and other sprouts have become equally well-known in recent years. More and more ingenious and health-conscious cooks are adding a variety of sprouts to salads, sandwiches, soups, and other dishes — for both the crunch and the nutrition. Sprouts are bursting with nutrients, and certain vitamins even increase when seeds are sprouted — up to 600 percent.

And sprouts are economical, too — from a single pound of seeds, you can produce from six to eight pounds of sprouts. All you have to do is add a little moisture and a little warmth to the seeds, set them in a dark place, then sit back and watch your garden grow in just a few day's time.

It's fun to have several jars of sprouts going at once, so you'll always have variety as well as a good supply. For example, put a couple of tablespoons of alfalfa seeds in one jar, a cup of wheat or rye berries in another, and a half cup or so of lentils in a third jar. Alfalfa takes about five days to reach just the right stage for eating, but your wheat sprouts will be ready by the end of the second day. It's a fast, easy, and very rewarding way to enjoy vegetables — both the ones you grow yourself and the ones you don't.

BASIC SPROUTING EQUIPMENT

All you need to sprout seeds is a jar, some cheesecloth, plastic mesh, or plastic screen to cover the jar, and a rubber band to hold it in place. But you can also sprout seeds on a tray, on damp towels, in a clay flowerpot saucer, or in a thin layer of soil. You may also want to try the ready-made sprouters that are available in large department stores and health food stores. For example, you can buy mesh trays or sprouting lids made of plastic mesh that fit on standard one-quart canning jars. It's a good idea to try various methods to find ones that are most convenient and work best for you.

BASIC INGREDIENTS

You can sprout all kinds of seeds, legumes, and grains. Try wheat, rye, alfalfa, mung beans, chick peas, soybeans, pumpkin seeds, sesame seeds, or any of the other sprouting seeds, grains, and vegetables suggested in "Directions for Sprouting," later in this chapter. Only one thing is essential — when buying seeds for sprouting, *always* check to be sure you're getting live, untreated seed. Seeds that are intended to grow crops are specially treated to make them resistant to insects and plant

diseases — and you shouldn't eat sprouts started from these chemically treated seeds.

You also can't sprout seeds that have been heat-treated, because even relatively low temperatures kill the seeds, leaving them edible but no longer capable of growth. For this reason, if you're growing beans, peas, or other vegetables for sprouting, be sure to use the drying method recommended for this purpose. Seeds dried by blanching, chilling, and heating will not sprout.

The only other ingredient you'll need for sprouting is water. Some experts recommend that you let city water (which may be high in chlorine) sit for a day or two before you use it, in order to let the chlorine dissipate into the air. When sprouting seeds, use lukewarm or room-temperature water, rather than cold or hot.

BASIC SPROUTING TECHNIQUES

Sprouting can be done in a jar, in a tray, on a towel, in a clay saucer, or in a thin layer of soil. Each method works best for certain kinds of seeds, as you'll see from the following descriptions.

Although the basic steps are quite similar from one method to the next, the times and temperatures for sprouting will vary due to temperature and humidity variations in your home. That means you've got to check sprouts frequently. After your first couple of batches, you'll have a good idea how long it takes to produce the flavor you prefer in sprouts. Many sprouters also like to save the water drained from sprouts for use in soups or sauces, or for watering houseplants.

Jar sprouting

This method works best for small seeds, such as alfalfa, clover or radish.

1. Rinse the seeds in lukewarm water.
2. Put the seeds in a jar, then add 3 times as much water as you have sprouts. Cover with a plastic mesh lid, cheesecloth, or nylon net, then fasten with a rubber band or canning jar screw band. (You won't need to remove the mesh covering until the sprouts are ready to harvest.) Set aside and soak for the time given in the recipe.
3. At the end of the soaking time, drain off the water (through the mesh covering).
4. Rinse the seeds with lukewarm water and drain.
5. Set the jar in a warm (60°F), dark place, at an angle so that the sprouts can drain.

6. Rinse and drain the sprouts twice a day, or as the recipe directs. (In hot, dry weather, rinse them 3 to 4 times a day.) Turn the jar gently as you rinse and drain so that the sprouts won't break off. If the weather or your kitchen is very humid, move the sprouts to a dry place, such as near the stove or wrapped in a towel (to keep out light) near a sunny window. Too much humidity will prevent sprouting. Temperatures above 80°F can also prevent sprouting.

7. On about the fourth day, move the jar of sprouts into the sunlight so that chlorophyll can develop and turn the leaves green. Continue to rinse and drain.

8. Move the sprouts from the jar to a strainer, and rinse well to remove the hulls, if desired. Hulls can shorten storage life of sprouts, but they also add flavor.

9. Use sprouts immediately in salads, sandwiches, or as the recipe suggests. To store, put in plastic bags and refrigerate.

10. Wash and dry all equipment and put away for next use.

Tray sprouting

This method works best for seeds such as mung bean, chia, and lettuce.

1. Rinse the seeds in lukewarm water.
2. Put the seeds in a jar, then add 3 times as much water as you have sprouts. Cover with a plastic mesh lid, cheesecloth or nylon net, then fasten with a rubber band or canning jar screw band. Set aside and soak for the time given in the recipe.
3. At the end of the soaking time, rinse the seeds and spread in a tray. (The tray can be a wooden box with a plastic, nylon, or wire mesh bottom, or a perforated plastic tray.)
4. Cover the tray with plastic wrap and then with newspaper or another light-blocking cover. Keep one end of the tray bottom propped up so the sprouts can drain. Set the tray in warm (70°F), dark place.
5. Rinse and drain sprouts twice a day. (In hot, dry weather, rinse them 3 or 4 times a day.) Rinse gently (so the sprouts won't break) under a faucet (not full-force), the sprinkler attachment of your sink, or by lowering the tray slightly into a sink of lukewarm water. Cover the tray again after each rinsing.
6. On about the fourth day, move the tray of sprouts into sunlight so chlorophyll can develop and turn the leaves green. Continue to rinse and drain.
7. Move the sprouts from the tray to a strainer, and rinse well to remove the hulls, if desired.

Tray sprouting gives you sprouts from seeds in four days; it's the best method to use for sprouting seeds like mung bean, chia, and lettuce.

Hulls can shorten storage life of sprouts, but they also add flavor.

8. Use sprouts immediately in salads, sandwiches, or as the recipe suggests. To store, put in plastic bags and refrigerate.
9. Wash and dry all equipment and put away for next use.

Towel sprouting

This method works best for larger grains and seeds.

1. Soak the seeds in a jar in 3 times as much water as you have seeds for time given in recipe, then rinse and arrange on a damp towel.
2. Cover with another damp towel, and wrap in plastic wrap or place inside a plastic bag.
3. Set the bag of towels aside, in a warm (70°F), dark place.
4. Dampen the towels daily by misting them with water.
5. If the seeds haven't sprouted after 2 days, change the towels to prevent spoilage.
6. On about the fourth day, remove the top towel and move the sprouts into the sunlight so that chlorophyll can develop and turn the leaves green. Mist as needed.
7. Move the sprouts from the towel to a strainer, and rinse well to remove the hulls, if desired. Hulls can shorten the storage life of sprouts, but they also add flavor.
8. Use sprouts immediately in salads, sandwiches, or as the recipe suggests. To store, put in plastic bags and refrigerate.
9. Wash and dry all equipment and put away for next use.

Clay saucer sprouting

This method works best for gelatinous seeds that are difficult to rinse in jars.

1. Use a clean, unglazed clay flowerpot saucer.
2. Put equal amounts of seeds and water into the saucer.
3. Set the saucer in a larger pan and pour water into the pan to within ½ inch of top of saucer.
4. Cover with a plate and set aside in warm (70°F), dark place.
5. Check the seeds daily, misting them if they become dry, or removing the plate cover for a day if they're too wet.
6. On about the fourth day, move the sprouts into the sunlight so the leaves turn green. Mist as needed.

7. Move the sprouts from the saucer to a strainer, and rinse well to remove the hulls, if desired. Hulls can shorten storage life of sprouts, but they also add flavor.
8. Use sprouts immediately in salads, sandwiches, or as the recipe suggests. To store, put in plastic bags and refrigerate.
9. Wash and dry all equipment and put away for next use.

Soil sprouting

This method works best for sprouting tiny greens for salads or for wheat, rye, or triticale grasses.

1. Spread a 1-inch layer of equal parts of moist peat moss and top soil over the bottom of a box.
2. Soak the seeds in 3 times as much water as you have seeds and soak for the time given in the recipe; rinse and jar sprout for 16 to 24 hours.
3. Spread the seeds over the soil in the box.
4. Cover with plastic wrap and then newspaper or black plastic (to keep out light).
5. When the sprouts are 1 inch tall, remove the cover and move them into sunlight so that chlorophyll can develop and turn the leaves green. Water as needed.
6. When greens are the desired height — about 2 to 3 inches — pull or cut them, wash them well, and use them in salads. To store, put in plastic bag and refrigerate.
7. Wash and dry all equipment and put away for next use.

DIRECTIONS FOR SPROUTING VEGETABLES

Try sprouting just about any seed, grain, or legume for some of the most delicious, nutritious, and economical foods to be found anywhere. Sprouts can be added to many dishes besides salads, soups, and sandwiches. They're delicious baked into whole-grain breads or muffins, blended into juices, or added to granola or yogurt. You can sprinkle them on casseroles and on meat, fish, or fowl dishes of all kinds. You can even top sprouts with tomato sauce and eat them like spaghetti.

The instructions below will give you some idea of the yield you can expect from sprouting various seeds and grains, but yields can vary considerably, depending on the size of the seeds, the temperature, and the length of the sprouts when you harvest them. Generally, small seeds — like chia — yield about eight times their original bulk in sprouts; large seeds — like corn — yield about three times their original bulk. Experiment with these wonder foods — you'll create some family favorites of your own.

Aduki (azuki) or pichi beans

Use about ½ cup seeds in a 1-quart jar, which will yield about 2 cups of sprouts. Soak for 12 hours. Rinse 3 to 4 times daily for 3 to 4 days. Harvest when the sprouts are ½ to 1½ inches long. Good in salads or casseroles, or stir-fried.

Alfalfa

Use about 2½ tablespoons seeds in a quart jar, or sprout on trays. This will yield about 1 quart of sprouts. The yield will be 1½ cups for each ¼ cup sprouted, and the sprouts will be very short — only about ⅛ inch long. Soak for 8 hours. Rinse 2 to 3 times daily for 4 to 6 days. Move into sunlight to green, then harvest when the sprouts are 1½ to 2 inches long. Use in salads, sandwiches, omelets, or as garnish. To use in baked goods, harvest sprouts after just 2 days.

Barley

Use 1 to 1½ cups seeds in a 1-quart jar, which will yield about 1 quart of sprouts. Soak for 12 hours. Rinse 2 to 3 times daily for 2 to 3 days. The sprouts will be the length of the seed. Use in salads, casseroles, and breads.

Beans, dry

Use ¾ cup mature beans in a 1-quart jar, which will yield about 1 quart of sprouts. Soak for 14 hours. Rinse 3 or 4 times daily for 3 or 4 days. Harvest when sprouts are 1 to 1½ inches long. Use in casseroles, soups, or dips, or steam them.

Beans, mung

Use ⅓ cup in a 1-quart jar, or tray sprout, which will yield about 1 cup of sprouts. Soak for 16 hours. Rinse 3 to 4 times daily for 3 to 5 days. Harvest when the sprouts are 1 to 3 inches long. Use in oriental dishes, salads, sandwiches, omelets, or stir-fry.

Cabbage

Use 3 tablespoons seeds in a 1-quart jar, which will yield about 1 quart of sprouts. Soak for 10 hours. Rinse 2 to 3 times daily for 3 to 5 days. Move into sunlight to green, then harvest when the sprouts are 1 to 1½ inches long. Use in salads and sandwiches.

Chia

Use ¼ cup seeds in a clay saucer or tray, which will yield about 2 cups of sprouts. There's no need to soak or rinse and drain; just mist the seeds regularly to keep them moist. After 3 to 5 days, move into sunlight to green. Harvest when the sprouts are 1 to 1½ inches long. Use in salads, sandwiches, casseroles, and as a garnish.

Chick peas

Use 1 cup in a jar, or tray sprout, which will yield about 3 cups of sprouts. Soak for 14 hours. Rinse 3 to 4 times daily for 3 to 4 days. Harvest when sprouts are ½ inch long. Use in casseroles, soups, salads, steamed, or as a base for dips.

Chinese cabbage

Use 1 tablespoon seeds in a 1-quart jar, or tray sprout, which will yield about 2 cups of sprouts. Soak for 8 hours. Rinse 2 to 3 times daily for 4 to 5 days. Move into sunlight to green, then harvest when the sprouts are 1 to 1½ inches long. Use in salads, sandwiches, and juices.

Corn

Use 1 cup kernels in a 1-quart jar, or tray sprout, which will yield about 3 cups of sprouts. Soak for 20 hours. Rinse 3 times daily for 2 to 4 days. Harvest when the sprouts are ½ inch long. Use in casseroles, soups, and tortillas, or bake, steam, or stir-fry.

Clover

Use 1 tablespoon seeds in a 1-quart jar, or tray sprout, which will yield about 2 cups of sprouts. Soak for 8 hours. Rinse 2 to 3 times daily for 4 to 6 days. Move the jar into sunlight to green, then harvest the sprouts when they're 1½ to 2 inches long. Use in salads, sandwiches, and juices. To use in baked goods, harvest the sprouts after just 2 days.

Cress

Use 1 tablespoon of seeds in a clay saucer or tray, which will yield about 1½ cups of sprouts. There's no need to soak or rinse and drain; just mist with water 3 times daily for 3 to 5 days. Move into sunlight to green, then harvest when the sprouts are 1 to 1½ inches long. Use as a spice (very peppery flavor), in salads, sandwiches, or baked goods.

Dill

Use ¼ cup in a 1-quart jar, or tray sprout, which will yield about 2 cups of sprouts. Soak for 8 hours. Rinse 3 times daily for 3 to 5 days. Move into sunlight to green, then harvest when the sprouts are 1 to 1½ inches long. Use in salads, sandwiches, and juices.

Fenugreek

Use ¼ cup in a 1-quart jar, or tray sprout, which will yield about 1 quart of sprouts. Soak for 10 hours. Rinse 2 to 3 times daily for 3 to 5 days. Mist with water if tray sprouting, to keep damp. Harvest when ½ to 2 inches long. Use in salads and sandwiches.

Flax

Use ¼ cup in a clay saucer, or tray sprout, which will yield about 1 cup of sprouts. Without soaking or rinsing the seeds, mist with water 3 times daily for 3 to 5 days. Move into sunlight to green, then harvest when the sprouts are 1 to 1½ inches long. Use in salads or juices.

Lentils

Use ¾ cup in a 1-quart jar, or tray sprout, which will yield about 6 cups of sprouts. Soak for 8 to 10 hours. Rinse 2 to 3 times daily for 2 to 3 days. Harvest when the sprouts are ¼ to ½ inch long. Use in salads, sauces, dips, juices, soups, or casseroles.

Lettuce

Use 3 tablespoons in a 1-quart jar, or tray sprout, which will yield about 2 cups of sprouts. Soak for 8 hours. Rinse 2 to 3 times daily for 4 to 5 days. Move into sunlight to green. Harvest when the sprouts are 1 to 1½ inches long. Use as a garnish (flavor is strong).

Millet

Use 1½ cups in a 1-quart jar, or tray sprout, which will yield about 2 cups of sprouts. Soak seeds for 8 hours. Rinse 3 times daily for 4 to 5 days. Harvest when sprouts are ¼ inch long. Use in salads, soups, baked goods, casseroles, and juices.

Mustard

Use 3 tablespoons in a 1-quart jar, or tray sprout, which will yield about 1 quart of sprouts. Do not soak.

Rinse 2 to 3 times daily for 4 to 5 days. Move into sunlight to green, then harvest when the sprouts are 1 to 1½ inches long. Use in salads, juices, or as garnish.

Oats

Use 1½ cups in a 1-quart jar or sprout on towels, which will yield about 2 to 3 cups of sprouts. Soak for 1 hour. Rinse once or twice daily for 3 days. The sprouts will be the length of the seed. Use in salads, granola, and baked goods.

Peas

Use ½ cup black-eyed or shelling in a 1-quart jar, or tray sprout, which will yield about 1 cup of sprouts. Soak for 12 hours. Rinse 2 to 3 times daily for 3 days. Harvest when sprouts are ¼ to ½ inch long. Use in salads, soups, omelets, and casseroles.

Peanuts

Use 1½ cups in a 1-quart jar, or tray sprout, which will yield about 1 quart of sprouts. Soak for 14 hours. Rinse 2 to 3 times daily for 3 to 4 days. Harvest when sprouts are ¼ to 1 inch long. Use in soups, steam, or stir-fry.

Pumpkin

Use 1½ cups in a 1-quart jar, or tray sprout, which will yield about 3 cups of sprouts. Soak for 10 hours. Rinse twice daily for 2 to 3 days. Harvest when the sprouts are 1 to 1½ inches long; pick off hulls and rinse. Use in sauces, dips, and baked goods.

Radish

Use 3 tablespoons in a 1-quart jar, or tray sprout, which will yield about 1 quart of sprouts. Soak for 8 hours. Rinse 2 to 3 times daily for 4 to 5 days. Move into sunlight to green, then harvest when the sprouts are 1 to 2 inches long. Use in salads, sandwiches, and juices.

Rye

Use 1 cup in a 1-quart jar, or tray sprout, which will yield about 2 to 3 cups of sprouts. Soak for 12 hours. Rinse twice daily for 2 to 3 days. Sprouts will be the length of the seeds. Use in granola, salads, baked goods.

How to Sprout Vegetables

Sesame

Use 1 cup in a 1-quart jar, or tray sprout, which will yield about 2 cups of sprouts. Soak for 8 to 10 hours. Rinse 3 to 4 times daily for 3 days. The sprouts will be the length of the seed. Use in granola, baked goods.

Soybeans

Use ¾ cup in a 1-quart jar, or tray sprout, which will yield about 1 quart of sprouts. Soak for 12 to 24 hours, changing the soaking water once. Rinse 3 to 4 times daily for 3 to 4 days. Harvest when sprouts are ½ to 2 inches long. Use in oriental dishes, salads, casseroles, baked goods, or steam.

Squash

Use 1 cup in a 1-quart jar, or tray sprout, which will yield about 3 cups of sprouts. Soak for 10 hours. Rinse twice daily for 2 or 3 days. Harvest when the sprouts are 1 to 1½ inches long; pick off hulls and rinse. Use in sauces, dips, and baked goods.

Sunflower, hulled

Use 1 cup in a 1-quart jar, which will yield about 3 cups of sprouts. Soak for 10 hours. Rinse 2 to 3 times daily for 2 to 5 days. Harvest when the sprouts are 1 to 1½ inches long. Use in salads, sauces, and dips.

Triticale

Use 1 cup in a 1-quart jar, which will yield about 2 to 3 cups of sprouts. Soak for 12 hours. Rinse twice daily for 2 to 3 days. The sprouts will be the length of the seed. Use in granola, salads, soups, and baked goods.

Turnip

Use 3 tablespoons in a 1-quart jar, which will yield about 1 quart of sprouts. Soak for 12 hours. Rinse twice daily for 3 to 4 days. Move into sunlight to green, then harvest when the sprouts are 1 to 1½ inches long. Use in salads and sandwiches.

Wheat

Use 1 cup in a 1-quart jar, or tray sprout, which will yield about 4 cups of sprouts. Soak for 12 hours. Rinse twice daily for 2 to 3 days. The sprouts will be the length of the seed. Use in granola, salads, soups, baked goods.

How to Store and Use Herbs

How to Store and Use Herbs

Herbs are the secret ingredient in many a fine recipe — from the most delicate gourmet dish to the heartiest of folk fare. Yet herbs are also among the easiest vegetables to grow, to use fresh, or to store for the winter. If you live in a mild climate, you can grow herbs year-round in your garden, in window pots, along walkways, or near doorways or patios. And if you live where winters get too cold for outdoor gardening, you can grow little pots of basil or chives indoors, and freeze, dry, or salt the rest of your herb crop. Dried herbs will keep for up to a year; frozen herbs will keep fresh for several months if properly wrapped and stored.

Herbs are popular in cooking not only for the way they enhance the flavor of many foods, but for the fact that they add no calories. If you're on a special diet, herbs can add zest to those low-cal or no-salt recipes. For example, when cooking potatoes or rice, add a pinch of rosemary instead of salt to the cooking water to add a special flavor.

GROWING HERBS: ROBUST AND FINE

Some herbs are used only in food preparation (robust herbs); and others can be eaten raw as well (fine herbs). Among the most popular herbs are basil, chives, dill, garlic, marjoram, oregano, parsley, rosemary, sage, sweet marjoram, and thyme. Grow them where you can enjoy their beauty and fragrance, as well as harvest the leaves at just the peak moment for use in your favorite foods. Detailed information on growing these and other herbs is given in Parts 1 and 2.

USING FRESH HERBS

You can use fresh herbs throughout the growing season. First, gently remove a few leaves at a time, or pinch or cut off sprigs to be chopped and added to your soups, salads, and sauces. For immediate use, rinse the herbs, pat them dry, and then chop finely. If you can't use fresh herbs at once, wrap them in a damp paper towel, then in plastic wrap or a plastic bag, and refrigerate. Fresh herbs can be kept refrigerated for a few hours or up to a day or two — but no longer than that.

Fresh herbs are wonderful in any recipe that calls for herbs. However, if your recipe specifies a dried herb, you can substitute fresh by using three to four times more finely chopped fresh leaves — one teaspoon of fresh herbs is equal to ¼ teaspoon of dried. Fresh herbs also make beautiful garnishes. Save a perfect sprig to give the finishing touch to vegetables, salads, drinks, fish, meats, casseroles, and sandwiches.

HARVESTING HERBS FOR STORAGE

Herbs can be frozen, dried, or salted for use during the fall, winter, and spring. Depending on the method you'll be using, you can cut whole stalks, remove just the leaves, or pinch off sprigs for your herbs. The dried seeds of some herbs — anise, caraway, coriander, dill, fennel, and sesame — are also used for flavorings, but most herbs are grown for their leaves.

You should harvest herbs to be stored when the flowers of the plant are just beginning to open; this is the moment when flavor is at its peak. Cut the plants on a dry, sunny morning—after the dew has dried, but before the sun gets too hot. The leaves you want are the young, tender, pungent ones growing at the top six inches of the plant. Strip off the tough, lower leaves and remove the flower clusters. Rinse the herbs with cold water to remove dirt and dust, then blot them dry with paper towels.

If you're growing herbs for their seeds, harvest the seeds as soon as the heads turn brown, but before they ripen completely and begin to fall off. Harvest the seeds on a warm, dry day, and then dry them, as detailed below. Seeds are dried in their pods, husks, or coverings. You remove these coverings by winnowing — rubbing a few seeds at a time between your palms to loosen the pod or husk, which will then fall away. Herb seeds should not be frozen or salted.

HOW TO FREEZE HERBS

Freezing is a quick way to preserve herbs that will be used in cooked dishes. Since herbs become dark and limp during freezing, they can't be used as garnishes — but their flavor remains just as good as fresh. You can chop herbs before freezing, or freeze sprigs and then just snip them, right from the freezer, into the food you're cooking.

Frozen herbs will keep for several months. If you want to store herbs for longer periods, dry them instead.

To freeze herbs, follow these step-by-step procedures:

1. Have ready a knife or scissors, paper towels, plastic bags, freezer wrap or boilable pouches, cardboard, freezer container or envelope, and labels.
2. Pick fresh, perfect herb sprigs or leaves. Wash them well, then drain and pat them dry with paper towels.
3. Pack recipe-size amounts in small plastic bags or packets made from plastic wrap, freezer

Freeze small amounts of herbs in individual plastic packets and staple them to a piece of cardboard. Label the packets and seal well.

paper or foil, or pack in boilable pouches. Seal well.

4. Staple these individual packets to a piece of cardboard, label the cardboard, and then freeze. Or pack several packets in a freezer container, large envelope, or plastic bag. Seal, label, and freeze.

5. For bouquet garni: Tie together several sprigs of different herbs — parsley, bay leaf, and thyme, for example — and pack as above. When you're ready to use it, add the whole bouquet to the recipe.

HOW TO DRY HERBS

Herbs need no pretreatment before drying, just careful selection and gentle harvesting. Always choose the tender, aromatic leaves growing on the upper six inches of the plant. Herbs may be air-dried in paper bags or dried in your kitchen oven. Herbs should *never* be dried in the sun because direct sunlight destroys their natural aroma.

For perfect dried herbs, follow these step-by-step procedures:

1. Have ready paper towels, a knife or scissors, string, plastic wrap, cookie sheets, racks or trays and wire mesh or cloth, or brown paper bags.

2. For herb leaves, choose herbs that are just about to blossom. Make sure the herbs are tender and well-colored, with perfect leaves and no bugs. Cut off the top two-thirds of the plant. Pick early in the morning, if possible. For herb seeds, choose seeds that are fully developed and mature.

3. Wash off any dust or dirt from the leaves. Shake them gently and pat dry with paper towels.

4. Dry in bags; on trays; or in a conventional, microwave, or convection oven, as explained below.

Bag-drying herbs

1. Cut mature stalks that have just started to flower, and cut lengths of about 6 to 8 inches. Use the tender tops. Trim off all brown leaves and lower leaves.

2. Rinse stalks in cold water. Blot dry with paper towels.

3. Tie 6 to 8 stalks together with string or a rubber band.

4. Tie a large brown paper bag around the bunch of stalks. The bag should be large enough for the herbs not to touch the bottom or sides.

5. Make 8 to 10 small holes all around the bag.
6. Hang in a warm, dry, airy room or attic for 1 to 2 weeks.
7. Remove leaves, crush or store whole in glass jars or airtight containers. Label and date.
8. Store away from heat. Herbs dried in this manner will keep for about 2 years.

Tray drying herbs

1. Remove the leaves from the stems of the plant and place them on a cloth-covered rack or mesh screen.
2. Place the racks in a warm, dry, well-ventilated room away from direct sun.
3. Stir the leaves from time to time to be sure they dry evenly.
4. When the leaves crumble easily, they're dry.
5. Store the dried whole leaves in labeled, airtight containers, in a dark, cool, dry, place.

Drying herbs in a conventional oven

1. Remove the leaves from the stalks of the plant, and arrange them in a single, even layer on cookie sheets, racks, or trays. Use drying trays 1½ to 2 inches smaller all around than the inside of your oven, so air can circulate freely around them.

2. Set the trays in the oven, with at least 1½ inches between the layers of drying trays.
3. Dry the leaves in a 120°F oven or in a drying box until the leaves will crumble easily between your fingers. Prop the oven door open slightly for ventilation and to keep the oven temperature from rising too high. The herbs will dry in 2 to 4 hours.
4. Store the dried leaves whole in labeled, airtight containers, in a dark, cool, dry, place.

Drying herbs in a microwave oven

1. Place 3 or 4 stalks between several thicknesses of paper towels on a drying rack or cookie sheet.
2. Set the sheet in the oven.
3. Dry at medium power for 2 or 3 minutes, or until the leaves crumble easily. If the herbs still aren't dry, return the leaves to the oven at the same heat for an additional 30 seconds.
4. Store the dried whole leaves in labeled, airtight containers, in a dark, cool, dry place.

Drying herbs in a convection oven

1. Remove the leaves from the stalks, and arrange them in a single, even layer on cookie

Hang bunches of herbs in a warm, dry place to dry; tie a paper bag over the bunch of seed herbs like dill or caraway to catch the ripening seeds.

sheets, racks, or trays.
2. Set the racks in a cold convection oven.
3. Set the oven temperature setting below the "warm" or 150°F setting. Use an oven thermometer to be sure the temperature inside the oven doesn't exceed 100°F.
4. Dry the leaves until they are brittle.
5. Store the whole leaves in labeled, airtight containers, in a dark, cool, dry place.

HOW TO DRY HERB SEEDS

Herb seeds can be dried by the same method used to dry leaves. After drying, remove the outer covering from dried seeds. Just rub a few seeds at a time between the palms of your hands, and then shake them gently to let the outer seed covering fall away. Store seeds in labeled, airtight containers in a dark, cool, dry place.

STORING DRIED HERBS

As soon as the leaves are dry, store herbs whole in labeled, airtight containers in a dark, cool, dry place. Coffee cans lined with a plastic bag or tinted glass containers are best, since they keep out light. Don't crush the leaves until you're ready to use them, because whole herbs hold their flavor the longest. During the first week after drying, check the herbs to be sure they're completely dry. If you notice any moisture at all, dry the leaves a little longer.

You can keep dried herbs up to a year, if they're stored properly in a dark, cool, dry place. If your storage area is too warm, the leaves will begin to lose flavor. If the area is too moist, the herbs may cake, change color, or spoil. Always remember to close the containers tightly after each use to prevent the loss of the volatile oils which are what make herbs so flavorful.

If you want to verify the freshness of herbs you've been storing for some time, rub a leaf between your palms. If the herb is still potent, strong aroma will be released. If there's little or no fragrance released, the flavor has faded, and you'll need to put up a fresh supply.

COOKING WITH DRIED HERBS

When using dried herbs, first crush or chop the leaves to release the flavor and aroma. Use herbs singly or combine one particularly strong herb with several other milder ones. You can also make a bouquet garni by tying together or placing in a cheesecloth bag bunches of herbs such as celery leaves, parsley, onion, and thyme. Or, mix three or more herbs to make fine herbs. The most familiar combinations for fine herbs are chervil, chives, and parsley; and basil, sage, and savory.

You'll get the most from herbs in cooking if you add them at the right time. For example, when preparing stews or soups that must cook for several hours, add herbs during the last half hour of cooking time. The flavor and aroma of herbs can be lost if they cook too long. In foods that cook quickly, add the herbs immediately.

You'll get best results if you add herbs to the liquid portion of your recipe before mixing it with the rest of the ingredients. Moistening the herbs first with a little water, oil, or other suitable liquid and allowing them to stand for 10 minutes will bring out the flavor even more.

When substituting dried herbs for fresh in a recipe, use ¼ amount specified. One teaspoon fresh herbs equals ¼ teaspoon dried.

SALTING HERBS FOR STORAGE

You can salt away some herbs to preserve them for future use. Use pure granulated or pickling salt, not iodized table salt. This method is most popular for basil, but it can be used for other herb leaves too.

To salt herbs down, follow these step-by-step procedures:

1. Have ready pickling salt, paper towels, and jars or other containers with tight-fitting lids, and labels.
2. Choose perfect, fresh basil or other herb leaves. Wash and drain, then pat them completely dry with paper towels.
3. Pour a layer of salt into the container and arrange a layer of leaves on top.
4. Pour in another layer of salt, then add a layer of leaves. Repeat until the container is full, ending with a layer of salt. Press down firmly.
5. Cover the container tightly, label, and store it in a dark, cool, dry place. Use salted herbs just as you would fresh herbs, but be sure to rinse thoroughly to remove the salt before adding them to food.

SPECIAL TREATS WITH HERBS

A little herb goes a long way in cooking, so you'll want to find other uses for the bounty of your herb garden. Herb vinegars, herb teas, herb butters, and herb jellies are easy to make and delicious to use.

How to Store and Use Herbs

Herb vinegars

Adding sprigs of fresh herbs to vinegar provides wonderful flavor. Pretty bottles of your own herb vinegars make wonderful gifts, too. You can use any herb you like, or any combination you prefer. Tarragon in white wine vinegar, basil and garlic in red wine vinegar, and mint or savory in white or cider vinegar are just a few examples.

1. Have ready measuring cups, glass mixing bowl, saucepan, strainer, jars or bottles, and labels.
2. Select perfect, fresh herb leaves. (You'll also want perfect sprigs to go in the bottles, but don't harvest these until after you've let the leaves steep in vinegar for a few days.)
3. For each pint of herb vinegar, lightly crush about ½ cup of fresh herb leaves in large glass mixing bowl. Add 1 pint white, cider, or wine vinegar. Cover and set aside for 3 to 5 days.
4. Now gather as many perfect herb sprigs as you'll have bottles of vinegar. Wash them.
5. Wash the bottles well, rinse, and then sterilize them by simmering in water to cover for about 5 minutes.
6. Strain the vinegar and discard the herbs. Heat the vinegar to boiling.
7. Pour the hot vinegar into hot bottles or jars. Add a sprig of fresh herb to each bottle or jar.
8. Close the bottles with corks, lids, or other airtight seals. Label and store in a dark, cool, dry place.

Herb teas

Fresh herbs have long been favorites for use in infusions, or teas. You can use almost any dried herb you like, but you'll have to test and taste to determine how strong you like it. Mint, rosemary, marjoram, and thyme are favorites for tea, but why not experiment with some others, too? Use about one teaspoon of dried herb (or a combination of herbs) for each teacup (six ounces) of boiling water. Put the herbs directly into the teapot and add the boiling water, or put the herbs in a tea ball. Let steep for five to 10 minutes. Don't add milk or cream. Sweeten, if desired, with honey or sugar.

Herb butters

Herb-flavored butters make marvelous toppings for bread, vegetables, meats, and seafoods. Use anise or oregano butter on your own sweet corn; basil butter on broiled tomato slices; tarragon butter on broiled fish filets; garlic and oregano butter on French bread slices; and marjoram butter on fresh green peas.

You can chop or crush fresh or dried herb leaves to cream with softened butter, or mix the leaves and butter together in a blender or food processor. Use about two tablespoons dried or ½ cup fresh herbs for each stick (½ cup) of butter. Store herb butters tightly covered in the refrigerator. Use in a few days.

Herb jellies

Delicately flavored jellies are a wonderful accompaniment to meats. Jelly is easy to make, but requires the same attention to cleanliness and detail as canning. For general directions and hints on canning, see "How to Can Vegetables."

REAL MINT JELLY

Fresh mint steeped in apple juice provides the mint flavor. A delicious accompaniment to lamb, this jelly is also tasty dabbed on a broiled peach or grapefruit half. The recipe makes 5 to 6 (½-pint) glasses or jars.

Ingredients	Equipment
2 cups fresh mint leaves	5 to 6 (½-pint) jelly glasses with metal lids or canning jars with 2-piece self-sealing lids
2½ cups apple juice (Use canned or bottled juice or cook 1½ to 2 pounds apples with 1½ cups water, about 25 minutes or until soft. Drain through a jelly bag until you measure 2½ cups.)	Paraffin Large saucepan Masher Wooden spoon Strainer Measuring cups Preserving kettle
2 tablespoons lemon juice	Ladle Wide-mouth funnel
A few drops green food coloring, if desired	Clean, damp cloth Labels
3 to 3½ cups sugar	
½ bottle liquid pectin	

1. Sterilize the glasses or wash and rinse the jars; keep them hot. If using jars, prepare the lids as the manufacturer directs. If using glasses, melt the paraffin and reserve.
2. Wash the mint leaves well; drain and put them in a large saucepan. Mash with a masher or wooden spoon.

3. Add the apple juice and heat to boiling. Remove from the heat, cover, and let it steep for 10 minutes. Strain and discard the mint leaves.

4. Stir the lemon juice and a few drops of green food coloring into the mint-apple juice, then measure 1 ¾ cups of juice into a preserving kettle.

5. Stir in the sugar and heat to a full, rolling boil, stirring constantly. Stir in the pectin, return to a boil, and boil hard for 1 minute, stirring constantly.

6. Immediately remove it from the heat. Skim the foam.

7. Ladle through the funnel into hot glasses or jars. Fill glasses to within ½ inch of tops. Fill jars to within ⅛ inch of tops.

8. Wipe the tops of the glasses or jars, inside edge of glasses, and threads of jars with damp cloth.

9. Seal glasses with a ⅛-inch layer of paraffin. If using canning jars, put on the lids and screw bands as the manufacturer directs, and process jars in boiling water bath for 5 minutes. (See "How to Can Vegetables" for boiling water bath basic steps.) *Caution: Do not process glasses sealed with paraffin.*

10. Set the sealed glasses or jars out of the way in a draft-free place and let stand overnight.

11. Check the seal on paraffin by looking for leaks. On jars, test the seal by pushing the center of the lid with your forefinger. If the lid doesn't give, the jar is sealed.

12. Cover paraffin-sealed glasses with metal covers, waxed paper, or plastic wrap. Remove screw bands from canning jars so they won't rust in place.

13. Wipe outside of glasses or jars with a clean, damp cloth.

14. Label with type of jelly and date.

15. Store in cool, dark, dry place.

HERB JELLY

Pick your favorite herb or combination of herbs for this jelly. Herb jelly is delicious with meat. This recipe makes 4 (½-pint) glasses or jars.

Ingredients

¼ cup dried herbs (sage, thyme, marjoram, rosemary, tarragon, or combination)
2½ cups boiling water
4 to 4½ cups sugar
¼ cup cider or wine vinegar
A few drops green food coloring
½ bottle liquid pectin

Equipment

4 (½-pint) jelly glasses with metal lids or canning jars with 2-piece self-sealing lids
Paraffin
Large glass mixing bowl
Strainer
Large saucepan
Measuring cups
Measuring spoons
Wooden spoon
Ladle
Wide-mouth funnel
Clean damp cloth
Labels

1. Sterilize glasses or prepare jars by washing and rinsing; keep them hot. If using glasses, melt the paraffin and reserve. If using jars, prepare the lids as the manufacturer directs.

2. Pour boiling water over herbs in a large glass mixing bowl; cover and let steep for 15 minutes. Strain and measure 2 cups of the herb "tea" into a large saucepan.

3. Stir in the sugar, vinegar, and food coloring. Heat to a full rolling boil, stirring constantly.

4. Stir in the pectin, return to a boil, and boil hard for 1 minute, stirring constantly.

5. Immediately remove from the heat. Skim off the foam.

6. Ladle through the funnel into hot glasses or jars. Fill glasses to within ½ inch of tops; fill jars to within ⅛ inch of tops.

7. Wipe tops of glasses or jars, inside edges of glasses, and the threads of jars with damp cloth.

8. Seal glasses with a ⅛-inch layer of paraffin. If using canning jars, put on the lids and screw bands as the manufacturer directs and process the jars in a boiling water bath for 5 minutes. (See "How to Can Vegetables" for boiling water bath basic steps.) *Caution: Do not process glasses sealed with paraffin.*

9. Set the sealed glasses or jars out of the way in a draft-free place and let them stand overnight.

10. Check the seal on the paraffin by looking for leaks. On jars, test the seal by pushing the center of the lid with your forefinger. If the lid doesn't give, the jar is sealed.

11. Cover paraffin-sealed glasses with metal covers, waxed paper, or plastic wrap. Remove screw bands from canning jars so they won't rust in place.

12. Wipe the outside of glasses or jars with a clean, damp cloth.

13. Label with type of jelly and date.

14. Store in a cool, dark, dry place.

Part 5
References

The next best thing to knowing all the answers is knowing where to go to find out. Here's where to buy your seeds, plants, and trees, and how to locate the experts who can answer your gardening questions.

State Cooperative Extension Service Offices

Experienced and inexperienced gardeners alike sometimes run into problems they can't solve by themselves, even with the help of the local garden center and friendly neighbors. At these times one of the most valuable bits of information any gardener can have on hand is how to get in touch with the local Cooperative Extension Service.

The Cooperative Extension Service was created by the Smith-Lever Act (1914) as an organizational entity of the United States Department of Agriculture and the state land-grant colleges and universities. Its purpose is to disseminate information from experts in various areas to the public through publications, correspondence, and other educational activities of an informal, nonresident, problem-oriented nature. These activities are carried out primarily by the extension staffs at the county and state levels.

Extension people can supply the specialized information you need to make planning and planting decisions like which plants to grow, which varieties of plants and seeds to choose, when to plant, and what improvements you might need to make in your soil. And they can help you with other problems you may encounter.

Although the Cooperative Extension Service is a bountiful source of information, there's a catch: You have to find them. This isn't so hard at the state level. You simply write to the Cooperative Extension Service at your state land-grant institution's College of Agriculture (you'll find the address at the end of this chapter). But at the local level, this service goes by different names in different places, or may be listed differently in local phone books. A good place to start tracking down your local extension service is under the name of your land-grant educational institution and then under Cooperative Extension Service or College of Agriculture. Or you can look under the name of your county and then for titles, such as extension agent, extension adviser, county

agent, or farm adviser. If you can't find these people—they are not lost, they know where they are—write your state land-grant institution.

Once you've found where to write for extension service information, knowing who to write to will speed the response to your written requests. For information about cultural problems in general and recommended varieties of plants, consult your *extension horticulturist*. The *extension entomologist* is the person to write about bugs and other undesirable garden livestock. Questions about plant diseases should be directed to the *extension plant pathologist*. These experts are often available at both the county and state levels.

Sometimes getting a satisfactory answer to your questions will require sending a specimen of your plant or pest to an extension expert. Popping the material naked into an envelope usually results in the specimen being squashed beyond recognition when it goes through the postal system. So here are some suggestions that will make consultation by mail worth the effort and the postage.

First, write a letter to send with the specimen. This letter should include all of the following information (if it applies) plus any other information you think might be pertinent:

- Date specimen was collected.
- Kind of plant, if you know.
- Description of problem and severity.
- Description of recent watering and fertilizing schedules, including what kind of fertilizer you used, how much you used, and when you applied it.
- Description of recent pest or disease control measures you have used.
- Your name and address (people who fail to include this information don't get a reply).

Next, gather together the mailing materials you will need. These will consist of a dry paper towel, waxed paper, aluminum foil, or a plastic bag in which to wrap the specimen and a crushproof box or mailing tube large enough to hold the wrapped specimen.

After all this is done, collect the specimen. How much of a specimen you enclose depends on your question. If it concerns plant identification, send at least one whole leaf and part of a stem. If the question is about a pest or disease, the specimen should show the entire range of symptoms. Wrap your specimen and seal it tightly. DO NOT ADD MOISTURE. Place the sealed specimen in the mailing container and send it off at once. The freshness of the specimen is extremely important. Try to make sure it arrives at the extension early in the week, rather than late Friday afternoon.

State extension service addresses

Listed here are the names and addresses of the land-grant colleges and universities that serve as state headquarters for the Cooperative Extension Service. For general information regarding the overall services available in your state or to find out the address of your local extension service, direct your correspondence to the Extension Director of your state's land-grant institution. For more specific questions, write to the extension expert in the appropriate field: Extension Horticulturist (cultural problems, recommended plant varieties, availability); Extension Entomologist (bugs and insects); or Extension Plant Pathologist (diseases).

        Example: Appropriate Title
                  College of Agriculture
                  State Land-Grant Institution
                  City, State, Zip

Alabama: Auburn University, Box 95151, Auburn, AL 36830

Alaska: University of Alaska, Fairbanks, AK 99701

Arizona: University of Arizona, Tucson, AZ 85721

Arkansas: University of Arkansas, Fayetteville, AR 72701

California: University of California, Berkeley, CA 94720

Colorado: Colorado State University, Fort Collins, CO 80521

Connecticut: University of Connecticut, Storrs, CT 06268

Delaware: University of Delaware, Newark, DE 19711

District of Columbia: Federal City College, Washington, DC 20001

Florida: University of Florida, Gainesville, FL 32601

Georgia: University of Georgia, Athens, GA 30601

Hawaii: University of Hawaii, Honolulu, HI 96822

Idaho: University of Idaho, Moscow, ID 83843

Illinois: University of Illinois, Urbana, IL 61801

Indiana: Purdue University, W. Lafayette, IN 47907

Iowa: Iowa State University, Ames, IA 50010

Kansas: Kansas State University, Manhattan, KS 66502

Kentucky: University of Kentucky, Lexington, KY 40506

Louisiana: Louisiana State University, Baton Rouge, LA 70803

Maine: University of Maine, Orono, ME 04473

Maryland: University of Maryland, College Park, MD 20742

Massachusetts: University of Massachusetts, Amherst, MA 01002

Michigan: Michigan State University, East Lansing, MI 48823

Minnesota: University of Minnesota, St. Paul, MN 55101

Mississippi: Mississippi State University, Mississippi State, MS 39762

Missouri: University of Missouri, Columbia, MO 65201

Montana: Montana State University, Bozeman, MT 59715

Nebraska: University of Nebraska, Lincoln, NE 68503

Nevada: University of Nevada, Reno, NV 89507

New Hampshire: University of New Hampshire, Durham, NH 03824

New Jersey: Rutgers, The State University, New Brunswick, NJ 08903

New Mexico: New Mexico State University, Las Cruces, NM 88003

New York: Cornell University, Ithaca, NY 14850

North Carolina: North Carolina State University, Raleigh, NC 27607

North Dakota: North Dakota State University, Fargo, ND 58103

Ohio: The Ohio State University, Columbus, OH 43210

Oklahoma: Oklahoma State University, Stillwater, OK 74074

Oregon: Oregon State University, Corvallis, OR 97331

Pennsylvania: Pennsylvania State University, University Park, PA 16802

Puerto Rico: University of Puerto Rico, Rio Piedras, PR 00927

Rhode Island: University of Rhode Island, Kingston, RI 02881

South Carolina: Clemson University, Clemson, SC 29631

South Dakota: South Dakota State University, Brookings, SD 57007

Tennessee: University of Tennessee, P.O. Box 1071, Knoxville, TN 37901

Texas: Texas A & M University, College Station, TX 77843

Utah: Utah State University, Logan, UT 84321

Vermont: University of Vermont, Burlington, VT 05401

Virgin Islands: Virgin Islands Agriculture Project, Kingshill, St. Croix, VI 00801

Virginia: Virginia Polytechnic Institute and State University, Blacksburg, VA 24061

Washington: Washington State University, Pullman, WA 99163

West Virginia: West Virginia University, Morgantown, WV 26506

Wisconsin: University of Wisconsin, Madison, WI 53706

Wyoming: University of Wyoming, Laramie, WY 82070

Major Seed Companies

The following are recommended suppliers of vegetable seeds and plants. Those marked with a * have a good selection of herb seeds and plants. Since it's not as easy to find suppliers of herbs as it is to find suppliers of vegetables, contact your local Cooperative Extension Service for any information they may have on suppliers in your area. Good sources of herbs are often available locally—the trick is to find them. The seed company listings are followed by two reliable sources for fruit trees and bushes.

*W. Atlee Burpee
(3 locations)
Riverside, CA 92502 or
Warminster, PA 18974 or
Clinton, IA 52732

Burgess Seed & Plant Co.
P.O. Box 3000
Galesburg, MI 49053

D. V. Burrell Seed Growers Co.
Box 150
Rocky Ford, CO 81067

Comstock, Ferre & Co.
Wethersfield, CT 06109

Farmer Seed & Nursery
Division of Planting, Inc.
Faribault, MN 55021

Henry Field Seed & Nursery Co.
407 Sycamore St.
Shenandoah, IA 51601

Gurney Seed & Nursery Co.
1448 Page St.
Yankton, SD 57078

Joseph Harris Co., Inc.
Moreton Farm
Rochester, NY 14624

Chas. C. Hart Seed Co.
Main & Hart Streets
Wethersfield, CT 06109

H. C. Hastings
P.O. Box 4088
Atlanta, GA 30302

J. L. Hudson
P.O. Box 1058
Redwood City, CA 94604

J. W. Jung Seeds & Nursery
Randolph, WI 53956

L. L. Olds Seed Co.
Box 1069
Madison, WI 53701

*Geo. W. Park Seed Co., Inc.
Greenwood, SC 29646

Seedway
Hall, NY 14463

R. H. Shumway Seedsman
628 Cedar St.
Rockford, IL 61101

Stokes Seeds, Inc.
Box 548 Main Post Office
Buffalo, NY 14240

*Thompson & Morgan, Inc.
Box 24
Somerdale, NJ 08083

Otis S. Twilley Seed Co.
Salisbury, MD 21801

Organic seed source:

Johnny's Selected Seeds
Albion, ME 04910

Fruit trees and bushes:

Miller Nurseries
J. E. Miller
Canandaigua, NY 14424

Stark Bros. Nurseries
Louisiana, MO 63353

Glossary

Acid foods. Foods that normally contain from 0.36 to 2.35 percent or more natural acid. Foods that may contain very little natural acid, but that are preserved in vinegar, are treated as acid foods in canning. Acid foods can safely be processed in a boiling water bath canner at 212° F. Acid foods include fruits, rhubarb, tomatoes, sauerkraut, pickles, and relishes.

Annual. A plant that grows only one season, producing its flowers and seeds, then dying within one year.

Antioxidant. An agent that helps keep the cut surfaces of some fruits from darkening when exposed to air. Used in preparation of fruits for freezing.

Ascorbic acid. Vitamin C. Used as an antioxidant, or anti-darkening agent, in the preparation of light-colored fruits for freezing.

Bacteria. Microorganisms found in the soil, water, and air. In food that is to be preserved, certain bacteria produce harmful toxins that must be destroyed by processing. Some bacteria thrive in conditions common in low-acid canned food, and can be conveniently neutralized only by superheating to 240° F. For this reason, low-acid foods must be processed in a steam-pressure canner.

Balanced fertilizer. A fertilizer that contains equal or near-equal percentages of nitrogen, phosphorus and potassium, e.g., 10% N-10%P-10%K or 12-12-12 or 12-10-8.

Barrel storage. A method of storing vegetables without processing or refrigeration. The vegetables are packed into a barrel laid on its side and nested into the ground outdoors. A heavy covering of organic material is mounded over the barrel to keep the vegetables from freezing. *See also* Mound storage, Frame storage.

Biennial. A plant that usually grows one season and then produces flowers and fruits the second. If conditions are right, it can do this in one season.

Blanch. The process of bleaching plants or parts of plants by excluding light, in order to improve the flavor or color of the edible parts of the plant. Also, the technique of loosening the skins of fruits and vegetables by scalding with boiling water. Blanching vegetables in boiling water also slows the actions of enzymes as a preparation for freezing.

Boil. To heat water or food to 212° F. Boiling water, when referring to the boiling water bath canner, means a full rolling boil for the entire processing time.

Boiling water bath canner. A kettle large enough to allow complete immersion of canning jars for processing of food. The boiling water bath canner is used for sterilizing acid foods and their containers.

Bolt, bolting. The term used when a vegetable, such as lettuce or spinach, goes to seed and sends up a flower stalk, thus ending its use as a vegetable.

Botulism. A poisoning caused by a toxin produced by the growth of spores of *Clostridium botulinum*. The spores are usually present in dust and wind, and in soil clinging to raw foods. Home canners who use the correct methods of selecting, packing, and processing foods have no reason to worry about botulism.

Brining. *See* Pickling.

Bulb. A modified underground stem and shoot surrounded by modified leaves in which food is stored.

Caging. A method of supporting a plant and confining its growth within a square or round container of wire or wide mesh. Usually employed with tomato plants.

Candy thermometer. A special thermometer that can be used to measure the temperature of candy, jelly, and other products during the cooking process.

Can-or-freeze jar. *See* Jar.

Cap. Any of various closure devices for sealing

Glossary

Mason canning jars. Of the most popular today are the metal screw bands that are used to hold vacuum lids in place during processing.

Clay. A soil made up mostly of particles that are less than $\frac{1}{31750}$ inch in diameter; clay holds more water and packs more closely than other soils.

Cold frame. An outdoor, enclosed structure, usually covered with glass, that employs solar heat and is used to harden off young plants. Also used to extend the natural growing season by providing a warm environment for starting cold-sensitive plants.

Cold pack. Filling jars with raw, rather than hot, food prior to processing. Sometimes called *raw pack*. Preferred where foods are delicate or hard to handle after cooking.

Cold storage. Storing fresh, whole vegetables without processing or refrigeration; the vegetables are held at temperatures and humidity levels at which they will neither freeze nor decompose. *See also* Root cellar.

Cole family. The cabbage family of vegetables, including broccoli, Brussels sprouts, cabbage, cauliflower, collards, kale, kohlrabi, rutabagas, and turnips.

Companion planting. Planting together two or more crops, each requiring a different length of time to mature.

Complete fertilizer. A fertilizer containing nitrogen, phosphorus, and potassium.

Compost. Decomposing organic matter.

Cool. To chill quickly in ice water after blanching in order to stop the cooking process in foods being prepared for freezing.

Cool crop. Crops, like cabbage, lettuce, and peas, that need cool weather to produce a satisfactory crop.

Cool place. Used when referring to storage of canned jars of food. Ideally, a cool place should be around 50° F.

Cotyledon. The first leaf or leaves that appear when a seed germinates.

Crop rotation. The practice of alternating the crops grown in a given planting area to reduce disease problems.

Cross-pollination. Fertilization by transfer of pollen from one flower to another by wind, insects, or people.

Cucurbits family. The family of vegetables that includes cucumbers, gourds, muskmelons, pumpkins, squash, and watermelons.

Cultivation. Scratching the soil to frustrate weeds and to facilitate the penetration of water.

Curing. Holding vegetables at a warm temperature (70° F to 85° F) for one to two weeks to harden the skins and rinds and help heal surface cuts. This helps reduce mold and rot and is usually done to prepare vegetables for cold storage.

Dehydration. The process of drying foods for storage. Drying removes enough water from foods to prevent spoilage organisms from growing and multiplying during storage. Dehydration can also occur in improperly packed frozen foods, resulting in freezer burn.

Dial gauge. *See* Pressure gauge.

Direct seeding. Sowing seed directly in the soil where the crop is to mature.

Drainage. The movement of water through soil. Also, the ability of soil to retain moisture. Drainage varies according to soil type.

Drip line. Outer canopy of a tree or shrub.

Dry shed. A cool or cold dry place where vegetables can be stored without processing or refrigeration. The vegetables are held at temperatures and humidity levels at which they will neither freeze nor decompose. *See also* Root cellar.

Early. A plant variety that matures faster (earlier) than others of its kind.

Enzyme. A protein that functions as a catalyst in organisms. In food, enzymes start the process of decomposition, changing the flavor, texture, and color. Freezing and canning neutralize the action of enzymes.

Extension service. A cooperative federal, state, and county service whose purpose is to disseminate expert agricultural and home management information to the public through publications, correspondence, and other educational activities.

Fermentation. A physical change caused by yeasts that have not been destroyed during processing of canned food, or yeasts that enter the food before it is sealed. With the exception of some pickles, fermented canned food should not be used.

Fertilizer. Organic or inorganic materials usually added to soil to provide plants with increased usable amounts of nutrients.

Flat. A shallow rectangular container used for starting seeds or cuttings.

Forcing. Bringing a plant to maturity out of season; or speeding up the growth process by providing ideal conditions for growth.

Forking. The dividing of a root, such as a parsnip, when it meets an obstruction in the soil. Also used for turning over soil with a gardening fork.

Frame storage. A method of storing celery and celerylike vegetables without processing or refrigeration. The vegetables are packed upright, with their roots in moist sand or soil, and protected with a framework of boards covered with a layer of organic material. A frame can be used either outdoors or in a root cellar or basement storage room. *See also* Barrel storage, Mound storage.

Freezer burn. Dehydration of improperly packed frozen food leading to loss of flavor, texture, and color.

Frost. The temperature that causes freezing. Also, a covering of minute ice crystals on a cold surface. A killing frost is a frost that causes moisture in plants to freeze; this kills some plants.

Fungicide. A material used to prevent, slow down, or kill fungi.

Germination. The beginning of seed growth; the sprouting of seeds; the starting of plants from seeds.

Grafting. The process of creating a new plant by combining two existing varieties. The root system (rootstock) of a hardier variety is combined with the flower or fruit-producing portion (scion) of a more productive variety of the same type of plant. Many modern fruit trees are grafted.

Growing season. The period between the last killing frost in spring and the first frost in fall.

Half-hardy. Refers to plants unreliably resistant to cold.

Harden, hardening off. The process of gradually moving plants from a sheltered or indoor environment to an open or outdoor location. This helps the plants adjust to new growing conditions and improves the chances of their survival.

Hardiness. A term used to describe a plant's ability to tolerate cold.

Harvest. A crop; the picking or gathering of a crop; the season for gathering a crop.

Head space. An area left unfilled between the top of the food in a jar and the inside bottom of the lid.

Herbicide. A weed killer. Some are selective and kill only certain types of plants. For example, only narrow-leaved plants like grasses; or only broad-leaved plants like some weeds and vegetables. Some destroy germinating seeds; some kill plants only above ground level.

Hilling. Mounding soil around the lower parts of a plant to support a weak stem, to provide winter protection, or to deprive the plant part of sunlight to whiten or "blanch" it.

Hot frame. An outdoor, enclosed structure, usually covered with glass, and heated either naturally by means of fermenting compost or by artificial means, such as electric cables. Used for growing cold-sensitive plants. Also used to extend the natural growing season by providing a warm environment for starting cold-sensitive plants.

Hot pack. Filling jars with precooked hot food prior to processing for canning. The preferred method when food is firm enough to hold its shape after processing.

Humus. Decayed or partially decayed organic matter added to soil to improve water retention and to supply nutrients.

Hybrid. A plant produced by crossing two pureline parent plants, each with some desirable characteristics. These characteristics are then inherited uniformly by the offspring (hybrid).

Inoculant. Material dusted on pea and bean seeds to provide or increase numbers of nitrogen-fixing bacteria in the soil.

Insecticide. An insect killer. The most common insecticides kill either by external contact with the insect's body or by attacking internal organs when the insect eats a treated plant.

Inverted hill. A planting area made by removing an inch of topsoil from a small area (about 12 inches in diameter) and using this soil to form a rim around the circle wherein seeds are planted.

Irrigation. Watering by artificial means to provide soil moisture at a level sufficient for maximum plant growth.

Jar. A glass container that is specially heat-treated for use in home canning and, if desired, in freezing. Also known as a Mason jar.

Jelly bag. A commercially made or homemade bag of cheesecloth or muslin through which fruit juices are strained for jelly-making.

Glossary

Late. A plant variety that matures more slowly (later) than others of its kind.

Lid. A flat metal disc with a flanged edge and a sealing compound on its underside, used in combination with metal screw bands for sealing jars.

Loam. Good growing soil consisting of clay, silt, and sand particles spiked with a good supply of humus.

Long-season crop. A crop that requires a long frost-free period to produce a harvest.

Low-acid foods. Foods that contain less than 0.36 percent natural acid. All vegetables except tomatoes are in the low-acid group.

Macronutrients. The nitrogen, phosphorus, and potassium in the soil.

Manure. Excretion from animals. When well-rotted, used as fertilizer or mulch.

Metal band. A threaded screw band that is used to hold a metal vacuum lid in place on a canning jar during processing.

Micronutrients. Elements such as zinc, iron, magnesium and manganese found in the soil.

Mircoorganism. A living plant or animal of microscopic size, including molds, yeasts, and bacteria, that can cause spoilage in canned or frozen food.

Moisture/vaporproof. Impermeable by moisture or water vapor; refers to containers or materials treated to prevent dehydration or absorption in frozen foods.

Mold. Microscopic fungi that grow as threads, appear as fuzz on food, and can produce toxins. They are easily destroyed by processing at temperatures between 140° F and 190° F.

Mound storage. A method of storing vegetables without refrigeration or processing. The vegetables are stored outdoors, with a heavy covering of organic material mounded over them to hold them at temperatures and humidity levels at which they will neither freeze nor decompose. *See also* Barrel storage, Frame storage.

Mulch. Material placed around plants to cut down soil erosion, to conserve soil moisture, to insulate the soil, and to help control weeds.

Nitrogen. A macronutrient essential for the deep-green color of a plant's foliage. The percentage of nitrogen, chemically expressed as N, is always listed first on a commercial fertilizer package.

Nonreactive. Used in the context of cookware to mean a finish that will not react with cooked foods and cause color and flavor changes. Aluminum, stainless steel, and enamel cookware are nonreactive. Iron or copper cookware will affect the color and flavor of certain foods.

Organic fertilizer. Complex fertilizer of plant or animal origin, usually insoluble in water. Since it has to be broken down by microorganisms before nutrients are available to plants, an organic fertilizer releases nutrients slowly over a long period of time.

Overnight. About 12 hours.

Oxidation. A chemical change in improperly packed frozen food brought on by contact with oxygen, leading to loss of flavor, texture, and color.

Peat moss. Shredded or milled spaghnum moss.

Pectin. A substance that occurs naturally in some fruits and causes them to form a jell when cooked. Pectin is also available commercially in powdered or liquid form, and is added to fruits that do not contain sufficient natural pectin to form a jell when used in jelly- or jam-making.

Perennial. A plant that can grow more than one season, and is capable of producing flowers and seeds each year.

Perlite. Volcanic ash used in growing mixes that holds no water or plant nutrients but helps provide aeration and drainage.

Pesticide. A pest killer. General term for those materials used to control diseases (fungicides), insects (insecticides), weeds (herbicides), and other pests.

pH, potential of hydrogen. A measuring system in chemistry for determining the acidity or alkalinity of a solution or substance. In gardening, soil pH affects plant growth; in canning, different processing techniques are used for acid and low-acid foods.

Phosphorus. A macronutrient needed by plants for good root growth and fruit production. The percentage of phosphorus, chemically expressed as P, is always listed second on commercial fertilizer packages.

Pickling. Preserving foods in a solution of brine or vinegar, often with spices added.

Pollen. Dustlike material, usually yellow or white, produced on the male sexual organs of flowering plants.

Pollination. Fertilization by transfer of pollen from the male flower or flower part to the female flower or flower part by wind, insects, or artificial means.

Potassium. A macronutrient needed by plants for root development and disease resistance. The percentage of potassium, chemically expressed as K, is always listed third on chemical fertilizer packages.

Pressure gauge. A device with a dial or weight that measures the steam pressure inside a steam-pressure canner.

Pretreatment. Treatment with an anti-darkening agent to prevent color changes in light-colored fruits when the cut surfaces are exposed to air. Ascorbic acid (vitamin C), sodium bisulfite (sulfur), lemon or pineapple juice, or commercial products can be used to pretreat fruits.

Processing. Sterilizing jars and the foods they contain in a steam-pressure canner or boiling water bath canner to destroy harmful molds, yeasts, and bacteria.

Propagation. Growing of plants from seeds, divisions, or cuttings. Starting new plants.

Pruning. The science of removing unwanted plant growth to increase productivity and control the size and shape of the mature plant.

Raw pack. *See* Cold pack.

Ripe. Refers to mature vegetables that are ready to harvest.

Root cellar. A cold, usually moist place where vegetables can be stored without processing or refrigeration. The vegetables are held at temperatures and humidity levels at which they will neither freeze nor decompose. *See also* Cold storage.

Rootstock. The root system which is grafted onto the flower- or fruit-producing top of another plant of the same type to produce a new variety.

Rototiller. A gasoline-powered machine used to prepare garden soil for planting.

Rubber. A flat rubber ring used as a gasket between a zinc cap or glass lid and a canning jar.

Sand. A soil made of particles over $\frac{1}{3175}$ inch in diameter. Sandy soil does not hold water as well as soil made up of smaller particles.

Scion. The productive upper half of the plant, which is grafted onto the root system of another variety to produce a new plant with the best characteristics of both.

Seed. Embryo that forms a new plant.

Self-fertile. Refers to plants whose flowers can be fertilized by their own pollen.

Self-fruitful. The ability of a plant to bear fruit without requiring another plant or another variety of the same type of plant for cross-pollination.

Self-unfruitful. The inability of a plant to fruit without another plant or another variety of the same type of plant for cross-pollination.

Set. To plant, to "set out;" also a term used when a plant develops, or "sets." Also used to describe one-year-old onion bulbs that are planted in the early spring to produce large bulbs the same season.

Shoot. A sprout; new growth from seed or plant.

Side-dressing. The application of fertilizer just beyond the roots of young plants, on either side of a row, or in a circle around individual plants.

Silt. A soil whose particles range in size from those of clay to those of sand, and that may act like either sand or clay, depending on the size of the particles.

Simmer. To cook gently just below the boiling point between 180° F and 200° F. At these temperatures, bubbles rise gently from the bottom of the pot and the surface is slightly disturbed.

Sodium bisulfite. Sulfur, used as an antioxidant (anti-darkening agent) to prevent the cut surfaces of light-colored fruits from changing color when exposed to air.

Soil. The top layer of the earth's surface that contains minerals, organic material, moisture, and air. Also refers to a soilless mix — an artificial mix of organic products in which plants can be grown.

"Soil-less" soil. A growing medium that does not include typical garden soil.

Solanaceous family. The family of vegetables that includes eggplant, potatoes, peppers, and tomatoes.

Spaghnum moss. A swamp-growing plant that eventually creates a peat bog.

Spoilage. Deterioration of stored or preserved foods, caused by improper selection, handling, or processing. Signs of spoilage include bulging lids, broken seals, leakage, foaming, moldiness, gassiness, spurting liquid when the container is opened, unusual softness or slipperiness, cloudiness, off-odors, and changes in color, texture, and taste.

Sprouting. Encouraging germination of seeds of vegetables or grains in order to produce young sprouts for use as a vegetable.

Staking. Inserting a stake or pole in the ground next to a plant to which the plant will be attached for support as it grows.

Stalk. A plant stem, usually the main stem.

Starter solution. Liquid solution of fertilizer, preferably with a high phosphorous content, that is applied to the soil around freshly transplanted plants to reduce shock and to speed development.

Steam-pressure canner. A heavy kettle with a lid that can be clamped on to make a steam-tight fit. The lid is fitted with a safety valve, a petcock (vent), and a pressure gauge. The steam-pressure canner is used for processing low-acid foods, since the steam under pressure reaches 240° F, adequate to destroy harmful bacteria that thrive in these foods.

Succession planting. Replacing crops with the same or different crops at intervals to increase the harvest.

Suckers. Fast-growing vertical twigs arising from the root system of trees or bushes. Suckers should be pruned out because if they are allowed to grow they will overtake the productive portion of the plant.

Synthetic fertilizer. Fertilizer manufactured from organic and inorganic substances. Generally, synthetic fertilizers are water soluble and provide nutrients instantly to plants.

Tender. Refers to a plant that has limited tolerance to extreme temperatures. Not tough.

Tendril. A modified stem that will hold or cling to an upright support. Found on such plants as grapes, cucumbers, melons, vining squash, and peas.

Till. To prepare soil for growing crops.

Trace elements. Elements such as copper, iron, and manganese that are needed in minute amounts for plant growth and are usually supplied by the soil.

Trickle irrigation. An irrigation system that attaches to the main garden hose and uses permeable or perforated tubes to direct water into the soil surrounding plants. Also known as drip irrigation.

True leaves. The real leaves; the leaves that appear after the first leaves.

Tuber. A swollen storage root or stem, usually growing underground.

Vacuum seal. The absence of normal air pressure in airtight jars, achieved by processing in a steam-pressure canner or boiling water bath canner.

Variety. A type of plant that has characteristics different in some degree from others of the same species. A variation from the basic species.

Venting. Forcing air to escape from a jar by applying heat, or permitting air to escape from steam-pressure canner. Also called *exhausting*.

Vermiculite. Sterile expanded baked clay used in growing mixes that holds 100 times its own weight in water.

Viable. Capable of living and growing.

Watersprouts. Fast-growing, typically nonproductive, vertical twigs rising from horizontal branches. Watersprouts should be pruned if the tree is to be fully productive.

Weighted gauge. *See* Pressure gauge.

Yeast. Microscopic fungi grown from spores that cause fermentation in food. Yeasts are inactive in food that is frozen and are easily destroyed by processing at temperatures from 140°F to 190°F.

Index

A

Acorn squash. *See* Squash, winter

Acidity, 389
  acid and low acid foods, 389, 390, 391

Aduki, 472

Alfalfa, 472

All-America selection, the, 19

Altitude
  adjustment chart, boiling water bath canner, 413
  adjustment chart, steam pressure canner, 398
  high, and canning, 397

Aluminum sulfate, 287

American plum. *See* Plum

Animal pest, 93, 346
  See also individual vegetables, fruits, and herbs

Anise *(Pimpinella anisum)*, 248–49

Anthracnose, 92

Ants, 88

Aphids, 27, 90

Apple *(Malus pumila)*, 288–91, 378–79, 432, 448, 465
  cold storage of, 354
  preparing for refrigerator storage, 340
  preserving, 337
  pruning, 286
  storage conditions, recommended, 344
  wrapping, 347
  yield, 286
  See also Vegetables, how to dry fruits and

Apple maggots, 285

Apricot *(Prunus armenica)*, 291–93, 379, 385, 432, 444, 466
  preparing, for refrigerator storage, 340
  preserving, 337
  pruning, 286
  yield, 286

Artichoke, globe *(Cynara scolymus)*, 111–113, 367, 402, 419–20
  cold storage of, 350
  preparing for refrigerator storage, 337
  preserving, 335

Artichoke, Jerusalem. *See* Jerusalem artichoke

Asparagus *(Asparagus officinalis)*, 113–115, 367, 403
  preparing for refrigerator storage, 337
  preserving, 335

Attic storage, 348–49

Aubergine. *See* Eggplant

Varieties, 18–19

Vegetables. *See* individual listings, 111–244
  hardy, 13, 18
  tender, 13, 18
  very hardy, 13
  very tender, 13

Vegetables, freezing. *See* Freeze, fruits and vegetables, how to. *See also* individual listings
  basic steps for, 366–67
  basic techniques, 361–65
  equipment, 358
  freezer, 359
  ingredients, 361
  recipes for, 367–75

Vegetables, how to can fruits and, 388–448
  boiling water bath, 412–448
  choosing method, 390
  equipment, 390–94
  hot and cold pack, 396–97
  jars and lids, 390–91
  problems, how to prevent, 397
  safe food handling, rules for, 395–96
  sealing, jars, 392
  spoiled food, how to dispose of, 402
  steam pressure, 398–412
  techniques, 391, 394–95
  timing, 391
  types of, 389

Vegetables, how to dry fruits and, 449–67
  equipment, 455
  ingredients, 455
  methods, 450–54
  recipes for drying, 459–67
  steps, 458–59
  store, how to, 457–58
  techniques, 455–57
  use, how to, 458

Vegetables, how to store, 334–55
  refrigerator storage, 336
  preserving methods (chart), 335–36

Vegetable pear. *See* Chayote

Vegetable puree, 375

Vegetable rating guide, 32–34

Ventilation, for cold storage, 347–48

Violet *(Viola species)*, 75

Viruses, 92

Water bath canning. *See* Canning, boiling water bath

Watercress. *See* Cress

Watering, 78–81. *See also* individual listings for vegetables, fruits, and herbs
  container-grown plants, 102

Watermelon *(Citrullus vulgaris)*, 240–42, 375, 429–30
  cold storage of, 354
  preparing for refrigerator storage, 340
  preserving, 336
  storage conditions, recommended, 343

Wax bean. *See* Bean, green or snap

Wax pepper, *See* Pepper

Weeding, 70–75

Wheat, 474

White cabbage. *See* Chinese cabbage

White potato. *See* Potato

Whiteflies, 91

Wild marjoram. *See* Oregano

Index

Planting Notes

SPRING   **Crop/Date Planted**   **Notes**

FALL   **Crop/Date Planted**   **Notes**

Harvesting Notes

Crop   **Yield/Dates**   **Notes**